LEISURE AND THE ENVIRONMENT
ESSAYS IN HONOUR OF *PROFESSOR J. A. PATMORE*

This volume is published on the occasion of the retirement of Professor J. Allan Patmore, to celebrate his career and his lifelong concern for issues of leisure and the environment in both the academic and practitioner spheres. All of the contributors have worked closely with Allan. We thank him for his unstinting encouragement, advice and fellowship, and we wish Allan and Barbara a long and happy retirement—and more than a little leisure!

LEISURE AND THE ENVIRONMENT
ESSAYS IN HONOUR OF
PROFESSOR J. A. PATMORE

EDITED BY
SUE GLYPTIS

BELHAVEN PRESS
LONDON AND NEW YORK

CO-PUBLISHED IN THE AMERICAS BY HALSTED PRESS AN IMPRINT OF
JOHN WILEY & SONS INC.

Belhaven Press
(a division of Pinter Publishers)
25 Floral Street, Covent Garden, London, WC2E 9DS, United Kingdom

First published in Great Britain 1993

Co-published in the Americas by Halsted Press, an imprint of John Wiley & Sons, Inc., 605 Third Avenue, New York, NY 10158-0012

British Library Cataloguing in Publication Data
A CIP catalogue record for this book is available from the British Library

ISBN 1 85293 258 9

Library of Congress Cataloging-in-Publication Data
Leisure and the environment: essays in honour of Professor J. A. Patmore/edited by Sue Glyptis.
     p.   cm.
   Includes bibliographical references and index.
   ISBN 1-85293-258-9 (U.K.).—ISBN 0-470-22001-5 (U.S.)
     1. Outdoor recreation—Environmental aspects—Great Britain.
2. Outdoor recreation—Environment aspects.   3. Leisure—Great
Britain—Planning.   4. Leisure—Planning.   5. Leisure—Social
aspects—Great Britain.   6. Leisure—Social aspects.   I. Patmore,
J. Allan (John Allan)   II. Glyptis, Sue.
GV191.48.G7L45   1993
790'.0941—dc20

ISBN 0-470-22001-5 (in the Americas only)   93-10002
                                                                  CIP

Typeset by BookEns Ltd.
Printed and bound in Great Britain by Biddles Ltd of Guildford and King's Lynn

CONTENTS

LIST OF PLATES

LIST OF FIGURES

LIST OF TABLES

FOREWORD: J.A. PATMORE

ROBERT W STEEL

I should have been embarrassed had I been asked by the Editor of this volume to contribute a chapter to a volume on *Leisure and the Environment*; but I am honoured to be invited to write a Foreword to this collection of essays that is a tribute to the work and influence of Emeritus Professor J. Allan Patmore.

Allan and I have known one another for more than a third of a century—in fact for thirty-six years. Allan, indeed, has been aware of my existence for even longer, since he attended (so he tells me) some of my lectures in the School of Geography in the University of Oxford where I was a Lecturer when he was reading the Honours School of Geography as an undergraduate at Pembroke College between 1949 and 1952.

When I left Oxford to become the John Rankin Professor of Geography in the University of Liverpool in 1957, I found Allan as one of the youngest members of the staff in the Department of Geography, and we were friends and colleagues until he left to become Professor of Geography in the University of Hull in 1973. He was, characteristically, enthusiastic, willing and innovative, and as always very hard-working. He was devoted to the teaching of his subject and outstanding in his relationships with our students. He and I shared, in particular, a strong belief in human geography and in its application to the problems of society. In the fifties and sixties, the specialism that marks geography today had not yet developed, and most geographers understood what their colleagues were doing and teaching. We worked particularly closely in the running of residential week-end field courses for first-year students, generally in North Wales or in the Yorkshire Dales where Allan drew on his considerable knowledge of that area from his home life in Wetherby and his school days at the Grammar School, Harrogate. From those experiences in Allan's life there emerged both his Oxford B.Litt. thesis on Harrogate and Knaresborough (1959) and *An Atlas of Harrogate*, published by the Corporation of Harrogate in 1963.

It may seem strange to write in 1992 that, three decades ago, human geography was having to fight for recognition as a social science. The Heyworth Report on Social Studies, published in 1965, had been mainly concerned with the traditional social sciences—economics, political science, sociology, social psychology and social anthropology—and it did very little for human geography; and the Social Science Research Council came into existence in the same year with no geographical representative. Fortunately, the spirited case that five of us put to the Council's Chairman, Dr Michael Young (later Lord Young of Dartington), changed that and led to the creation of a Committee for Human Geography and Planning under the chairmanship of Michael Chisholm in 1967.

Thus, in 1966 geography, now so well established as a discipline that it is the background, indeed the backbone, of most of the essays in *Leisure and the Environment*, was still marginal to the thinking of many with a concern for the problems of society. It was in that year that The British Academy advertised for the first time the award of a Fellowship financed by the 'Thank-Offering to Britain Fund'. This endowment had been generously given by a group of refugees from Nazi oppression. It was their way of expressing appreciation for the welcome that Britain had given them and the opportunities provided for them to settle and work in the country. The holder had to study a subject that had 'some bearing on the well-being of the people of the British Isles'. Allan recalls that I first mentioned the Fellowship to him as we walked up Mount Pleasant from Liverpool Central Station to what is now the Roxby Building in the University precinct. I suggested that this provided us with an opportunity to stress that some of us at least saw human geography as a respectable social science with a very positive contribution to make to society. I also felt that here was a chance for Allan to show his abilities to the world outside academic circles. He needed some convincing, perhaps a little gentle persuasion, but in the event he submitted an application and was in due course shortlisted, interviewed and then awarded the Fellowship.

In retrospect, that award proved to be a turning point in Allan Patmore's career. For two years he turned his attention away from the problems of urban settlement and from the teaching of students to consider in depth the problems of leisure and the environment that constitute the content of this volume. Out of his research came his book, *Land and Leisure*, published in 1970, and eventually there emerged from it a whole set of new interests that led to his involvement in a range of committees and councils at both regional and national levels. Allan was not a colleague with whom I normally discussed events at Anfield or Goodison Park on Monday mornings when we were colleagues in Liverpool, and after his departure to Humberside (mine a year later to South Wales) I never recall talking to him about what was happening at Boothferry Park or to Hull Kingston Rovers. Yet there was a logic in his appointment in 1978 to the Sports Council, of which he has been a member continuously since then. More recently, he has become a member of the Countryside Commission, to whose work he clearly has a major contribution to make.

This Foreword is designed to introduce a particular, and rather special, volume of essays, a tribute to Allan Patmore from more than a score of his associates in several different walks of life for his great contribution to our appreciation of the impact of leisure upon the environment. But there must be some brief mention of all that he has done for geography everywhere, and particularly in the two British universities which he served, as well as in universities in New Zealand and in the United States of America. He worked in Liverpool from 1954 to 1973 and in Hull from 1973 until his retirement as an Emeritus Professor of Geography in 1991. He was Head of Department in Hull for two periods, and he served the whole university for two years as Dean of the Faculty of Social Sciences and for three years as a very active and highly respected Pro-Vice-Chancellor.

His prowess as an educationalist has also shown itself in the Institute of British Geographers, on whose Council he served for several years including membership of its Editorial Board and a spell as Assistant Editor of the Institute's *Transactions*. Even more noteworthy is his work with the Geographical Association, of which he was President in 1979–80. When in 1991 he was made an Honorary Member of the Association, the citation admirably summarized his career as a geographer: 'in recognition of outstanding contributions to geographical education'. He has been a member of committees of the Economic and Social Research Council and of the Schools Council, and he was President of Section E of the British Association for the Advancement of Science in 1987–8. Worthy of note, too, is his long stint as an awarder in Advanced Level of Geography for the Oxford Delegacy of Local Examinations, sharing the work with me from 1961 to 1966 and then as senior awarder until his retirement from the appointment in 1980.

Outside academic life Allan has been very active. His recreations, as recorded in *Who's Who*, are 'pursuing railway history, and enjoying the countryside'. His love of railways has been life-long and his zeal for Methodism every bit as great. He has been a fully accredited Local Preacher—very effective and much appreciated, as I know from personal experience—and a member of several important Methodist national committees. He has been a Governor of Schools—Chairman of the Governors of Hunmanby School in Yorkshire and a Life Governor of Hymers College in Hull; and since 1975 he has been a Justice of the Peace in the County of Humberside.

In this Foreword there should be special mention of his tremendous activity in the planning and leisure fields and his great contribution in the public service, particularly in the matters that are discussed in *Leisure and the Environment*. Even before his recent appointment as a Countryside Commissioner, he had been very closely associated with the work of the Commission, the Council for National Parks, the North York Moors National Park Committee, and the Yorkshire and Humberside Regional Council for Sport and Recreation. The appreciation of his work for the Sports Council ever since he first joined it in 1978 is shown by his re-appointment to the Council on four subsequent occasions and his election in 1988 as Vice-Chairman. He was a member of the Minister of Sport's Review of Sport and Recreation in Inner Cities between 1988 and 1990 and many years before, in 1972–3, he was specialist adviser to the Select Committee of the House of Lords on Sport and Leisure.

Despite all these commitments, Allan remains at heart a family man, and no tribute to him would be complete without a reference to his family—his parents, his wife, and his children. Significantly *Land and Leisure* is dedicated 'To my mother and father who first taught me to love and to explore the land of Britain'. Barbara has been his devoted wife for more than thirty-six years, and she has always been encouraging and supportive of all his endeavours, and tolerant and understanding about his frequent absences from home. Their three children, and now their spouses, and their grand-children, also share Barbara's pride in Allan's achievements, just as he derives great pleasure and satisfaction from all that his family does and means to him.

My personal tribute to Allan is for his friendship and companionship over many years, but I know that I speak for many others when I refer to the influence and inspiration, along with encouragement, that he has freely given to us all. Perhaps this is especially true of those who have collaborated with Professor Sue Glyptis in the production of this volume. It is presented to Allan, and to the public generally, as a measure of our affection and respect for a very special geographer.

Robert W Steel
Principal, University College of Swansea, 1974–82
Vice-Chancellor, University of Wales, 1979–81
November 1992

CONTRIBUTOR BIOGRAPHIES

John Bale is a senior lecturer in the School of Human Development at Keele University. He has published widely on the place of sport in contemporary society and has pioneered the geographical study of sports. His books include *Sports Geography* and *Sport, Space and the City*. He is currently preparing a study of the landscape of sports.

Mark Blacksell is Reader in Human Geography at the University of Exeter, and a former member of the Dartmoor National Park Committee and Council for National Parks. His publications include *The Countryside: Planning and Change* written jointly with Andrew Gilg, and *Justice outside the City: access to local services in rural Britain* written jointly with K. Economides & C. Watkins.

Sally Bucknall was born in 1948 in Harrow, North London. Early memories of the then beautiful woods and hedge lined lanes of Hertfordshire gave her an interest in the landscape and wildlife which led to an honours degree in Agriculture and subsequently an MSc and PhD in Ecology and Land use. Her thesis involved the effects of the waste products of whisky distillation on the vegetation of heather moorlands in North East Scotland. After graduating from Aberdeen University she was appointed, in 1974, to the Countryside Commission in Cheltenham as Agricultural Policy Adviser. Subsequently she moved to the Commission's Leeds Office when it was established in 1977 and after a secondment as the first woman Assistant National Park Officer in the North York Moors, she became the Regional Officer for Yorkshire and Humberside where she now leads a Commission's team of 18 staff.

Gordon Cherry is Emeritus Professor at the University of Birmingham. He read Geography at Queen Mary College, University of London, and subsequently qualified as a town planner and a chartered surveyor. Between 1956 and 1968 he worked with local planning authorities, latterly as Research Officer in Newcastle upon Tyne. He was then appointed to the University of

Birmingham as Deputy Director of the Centre for Urban and Regional Studies. In 1976 he was elected to the Chair of Urban and Regional Planning. Between 1981 and 1986 he served as Dean of the Faculty of Commerce and Social Science and in 1987 he assumed the Headship of the School of Geography. He took retirement in 1991. He has published widely on planning matters including recreation planning, but particularly planning history, and is a joint editor of *Planning Perspectives*. He was President of the Royal Town Planning Institute in 1978–9. He is President of the International Planning History Society, and Chairman of the Bournville Village Trust.

Paul Cloke is Reader in Geography at the University of Bristol, having previously been Professor of Human Geography at St. David's University College, Lampeter. He is founder and editor of the *Journal of Rural Studies*, and has published a series of books on the human geography and planning of rural areas, including *The Rural State* (Oxford University Press, with Jo Little) *Policies and Plans for Rural People* (Unwin Hyman), *Rural Land Use Planning in Developed Nations* (Unwin Hyman) and *Rural Planning: Policy into Action* (Harper and Row). He has also published more general books on human geography and planning including *Approaching Human Geography* (Paul Chapman Publishing, with Chris Philo and David Sadler) and *Policy and Change in Thatcher's Britain* (Pergamon Press). He has recently completed a research programme on Rural Lifestyles in England and Wales, and is currently pursuing research interests in the commodification of leisure and recreation attractions in rural areas.

Michael Collins was trained in urban and historical geography and town planning. He worked as a planner on housing, traffic and town centre schemes in London, then was manager of the Greater London Group at LSE where he produced with Tim Pharaoh *Transport Organisation in a Great City* (Allen & Unwin 1974). For seventeen years he was Head of Research and Strategic Planning at the Sports Council where he authored *Sport in the Community: The Next 10 Years* (1982) and oversaw its review *Into the Nineties* (1987). He is now Director of the Institute of Sport and Recreation Planning and Management at Loughborough University where he is researching on urban recreation, sport in the countryside and children's play.

Terry Coppock is Professor Emeritus of Geography at the University of Edinburgh and Honorary Director of the Tourism and Recreation Research Unit. He is also a Fellow of the Tourism Society and a member of the advisory boards of *Tourism Management* and *Leisure Studies*. His life-long interest has been in the use of rural resources and it was this that first attracted his interest in outdoor recreation and rural tourism and led to the establishment of the Tourism and Recreation Research Unit at Edinburgh in 1972. He served for twelve years on the Scottish Sports Council and was chairman of its Facilities Planning Committee; he also has an interest in conservation and was a member of the England Committee of the Nature Conservancy for six years and chairman of its land-use panel. He is a frequent visitor to Australia. He is the co-author with Brian Duffield of *Outdoor Recreation: a Spatial Perspective*, and edited most of the forty nine reports published by the Unit.

Neil Cossons has been Director of the Science Museum—the National Museum of Science & Industry—since 1986. The museum includes the National Railway Museum, York and the National Museum of Photography, Film and Television in Bradford. For twelve years until he was appointed Director of the National Maritime Museum, he was the first Director of the Ironbridge Gorge Museum in Shropshire. He is a Fellow and Past President of the Museums Association, an English Heritage Commissioner and member of the Design Council. Neil Cossons graduated in Geography from Liverpool University, where he holds a Honorary LittD. Allan Patmore was tutor for his MA and he is now a member of the National Railway Museum Advisory Committee and Chairman of the Museum's Friends organization.

Michael Dower, a chartered surveyor and town planner, is Director General of the Countryside Commission. He was in the Civic Trust team which produced in 1964 the proposals for the Lea Valley Regional Park. He then wrote *Fourth Wave: the Challenge of Leisure*, published by the Civic Trust in 1965. In that year, he joined the United Nations Special Fund team in the Republic of Ireland; and also became a founder member of the United Kingdom Sports Council. He served on that Sports Council till 1972; and as a member of the English Tourist Board from 1969 to 1976. From 1967 to 1985, he was Director of the Dartington Amenity Research Trust, based in Devon. In this capacity, he led a research team focusing on leisure studies, conservation and rural development; and pursued many initiatives, including creation of the open air museum at Morwellham. From 1985 to 1992, he was Director of the Peak District National Park.

Martin Elson is Professor in Planning at Oxford Brookes University. Over the past twenty years he has carried out a wide range of research on sport and recreation topics, the environment and land use planning. His particular interests are in green belt policy and the management of conflicts between sport and environmental interests in the countryside. He has recently completed studies on *Planning Obligations* for the Sports Council, and the *Effectiveness of Green Belts* for the Department of the Environment.

Mike Fitzjohn graduated in Town and Country Planning from the University of Manchester. In a career spanning 20 years with the Greater London Council, the North West Council for Sport and Recreation and the Sports Council he has been involved in a wide range of sports research, planning and policy development. He currently works as a Senior Research Officer for the Sports Council, for which he has written the Council's five year strategy, *Into the 90s (1988)* and *The Playing Pitch Strategy (1991)*. At present he is responsible for the development of a National Register of Recreational Land.

John Gittins has been a teacher, researcher and practitioner in the countryside recreation, conservation and outdoor education fields for more years than he would like to remember. A Churchill Fellow and Fellow of the Royal Geographical Society, he is currently Director of the Cheshire Landscape Trust where his work is based on local community environmental action.

Sue Glyptis is Professor of Recreation Management at Loughborough University. A geographer by training, she took an honours degree at the University College of Wales, Aberystwyth, followed by a PhD, under Allan Patmore's supervision, at the University of Hull. She worked for five years as Research Officer to the Sports Council, based in London, and was involved in commissioning a wide ranging research programme on countryside and water sports, leisure participation patterns, and facility management. She moved to Loughborough in 1981 to join the Department of Physical Education, Sports Science and Recreation Management as Lecturer in Recreation Management. Subsequently appointed to Senior Lecturer in 1987 and to the newly established Chair in Recreation Management in 1990, she lectures and researches mainly in the fields of countryside recreation, leisure and lifestyle, and recreation in urban and rural settings. She has produced over 70 publications in these fields, including, most recently, *Countryside Recreation* (1991, Longman).

Timothy O'Riordan is Professor of Environmental Science at the University of East Anglia and Associate Director in the Economic and Social Research Council funded Centre for Social and Economic Research on the Global Environment. He has taught in Canada, the United States and New Zealand, as well as in England. His special research interests cover environmental policy analysis, environmental impact assessment, international environmental governance and the interconnections between the natural and social sciences as they relate to applied environmental problem solving. Professor O'Riordan chairs the Environmental Science and Society Programme of the European Science Foundation and also the Environmental Research Working Group of the UK Economic and Social Research Council. He is a Member of the Broads Authority, a National Park organisation in England, and chairs its Environment Committee. He has written over one hundred articles and authored or co-authored over a dozen books. He is currently directing an international research project into the response of various European nations to the requirements imposed by the United Nations Framework Convention on Climate Change.

Adrian Phillips, a geographer and planner, has had two spells at the Countryside Commission, interspersed with seven years abroad on the international environmental scene. On returning to the UK in 1981, he became Director General of the Commission. Under his leadership, the Commission launched its Recreation 2000 programme, the Countryside Stewardship initiative and the programme of Community Forests and the National Forest—and generally underwent a significant expansion in budget, staffing and influence. He was the Commission's assessor to the Edwards Panel that reviewed national parks, and reported in 1991. In 1992, he left the Commission to become part time Professor of Countryside and Environmental Planning at the University of Wales, Cardiff, and a freelance consultant. He remains closely involved in conservation and environmental issues, in Wales, the UK and internationally. In particular, he is Deputy Chair of the World Conservation Union's international Commission on National Parks and Protected Areas.

Brian Rodgers, after war service as an RAF pilot, graduated in geography at the University of Manchester in 1948 (MA 1951). He lectured at Manchester, then in 1963 moved to the University of Keele, where he later became Professor. From 1972 to 1989 he was Professor of Geography at the University of Manchester, also serving as Senior Pro Vice Chancellor from 1984 to 1989. He was a member of the Sports Council during the 1970s, and Adviser to the House of Lords Select Committee on Sport and Leisure. He is author of the *Pilot National Recreation Survey* (PNRS) and many other published works in the fields of leisure, planning and regional development.

Roger Sidaway worked for the Forestry Commission in the North York Moors and the Forest of Dean before joining the Countryside Commission where he became Head of its Recreation and Access Branch. During that time he chaired the Countryside Recreation Research Advisory Group and the joint Sports Council/Social Science Research Council Panel on leisure and recreation research. He later directed the Centre for Leisure Research in Edinburgh before becoming an independent Research and Policy Consultant specialising in policy evaluation and strategic planning. Two studies, *Sport, Recreation and Nature Conservation*, and *Good Conservation Practice for Sport and Recreation*, both published by Sports Council, led to his current research on environmental conflicts. He has been studying conflicts in the UK, the USA, and The Netherlands, funded by the Economic and Social Research Council, while based at the Institute of Ecology and Resource Management at Edinburgh University where he is a Research Fellow. He once had the awesome task of briefly deputising for Allan Patmore giving lectures on recreation at Hull University. That experience he has put to good use in his current teaching on conflicts and methods of conflict resolution to Resource Management and Human Ecology students in the Institute.

Derek Statham is the National Park Officer for the North York Moors, a post he has held since 1974. He has a background of training in geography and planning and has worked in Yorkshire, Cumbria and East Anglia. He has researched and published articles on rural land use and has pioneered a number of land management projects in the North York Moors and the Pennines. He is a Fellow of the Royal Town Planning Institute and has held the offices of Chairman of the Association of National Park Officers and Research Fellow of the Centre for Environmental Studies.

Robert W Steel, Emeritus Professor of the University of Wales, taught in the Universities of Oxford and Liverpool (where Allan Patmore and he were colleagues in the Department of Geography). He was Principal of the University College of Swansea from 1974 to 1982 and Vice-Chancellor of the University of Wales from 1979 to 1981. His research interests extending over more than half a century have centred on problems of land use and population in Africa. He was a member of the Economic and Social Research Council from 1983 to 1986. He has been President of the Institute of British Geographers and of the African Studies Association of the United Kingdom and—like Allan Patmore—President of the Geographical Association and of Section E (Geography) of the British Association for the Advancement of Science. He has honorary degrees from the Universities of Salford, Liverpool and Wales and from the Open University, and is an Honorary Fellow of the University College of Swansea and of Jesus College, Oxford. He was awarded the CBE in 1983.

Jean Tallantire qualified as a physical educationist at Nonington College of PE in Kent in 1957. After a short period teaching in Nottinghamshire and then lecturing in Further Education in Derbyshire, she joined the Central Council for Physical Recreation in Yorkshire and Humberside in 1963. She was subsequently appointed as a Senior Regional Officer with the Sports Council in 1975 where she holds special responsibility for countryside and water recreation. Her lifelong interest in the countryside was initially fostered through school geography camps in the Lake District. Since then she has travelled extensively. Following her trip to the Himalaya in 1988, she was a member of the 1991 US/UK Countryside Stewardship Exchange to the Northern Forest Lands of New Hampshire. In 1992 she visited The Netherlands and Germany to study provision for open air recreation in urban areas. Her favourite pastime is fell walking in the Yorkshire Moors and Dales.

Michael Tanner worked at the London School of Economics and Liverpool University before becoming Lecturer in Geography at the University of Birmingham. He was also Research Officer to the Water Space Amenity Commission 1974–6 and Visiting Professor at Oklahoma State University in 1981–2. His main research interests are in the recreational and amenity uses of water resources in Britain and North America. This has led to a series of reports on different aspects of such uses for various statutory bodies, including the Countryside Commission, National Rivers Authority, Sports Council and Water Space Amenity Commission.

Malcolm Tungatt graduated as a geographer at the University of Hull before undertaking research into the recreational patterns of non-car owners for a Masters degree. He joined a Sports Council research team at Durham University in 1976, investigating a range of participation and facility planning issues. In 1979, Malcolm joined the Sports Council's Research Unit, based in Manchester, and he has been involved in a wide variety of strategic planning research studies and research into participation issues. Since 1984, the team has been responsible for the monitoring and evaluation of pioneering sports development projects, including the Sports Council's National Demonstration Projects programme and Malcolm has led this team since 1987.

Tony Veal is Associate Professor in the School of Leisure and Tourism Studies, University of Technology, Sydney. Before moving to Australia in 1986 he worked at the Polytechnic of North London and the University of Birmingham. He is a member of the Board of Directors of the World Leisure and Recreation Association, a past chair of the UK Leisure Studies Association and a member of the Editorial Board of *Leisure Studies*. He is author of numerous publications on leisure, including *Leisure and the Future*, (Allen and Unwin, 1987) and *Research Methods for Leisure and Tourism* (Longman, 1992).

Roger Vickerman is Professor of Regional and Transport Economics and Director of the Channel Tunnel Research Unit at the University of Kent at Canterbury. Educated at the Universities of Cambridge and Sussex, his research interests are in transport economics, the economics of urban and regional development, the economics of integration in the European Community and the economics of leisure and recreation. He is the author or editor of seven books on these subjects and numerous academic articles. In 1986 he founded the Channel Tunnel Research Unit at the University of Kent, set up to provide a focus for academic research on the tunnel and its effects, including collaborative work with colleagues at the University of Lille in France. Professor Vickerman has also been consultant to Kent County Council, the Kent Impact Study Team, and the European Commission and acted as specialist adviser to a House of Commons Committee. He is currently working on the evaluation of transport infrastructure in Europe.

Geoff Wall is Professor of Geography at the University of Waterloo, Canada, where he is also cross-appointed with the Department of Recreation and Leisure Studies. He is a member of the International Academy for the Study of Tourism and is the author (with E. Heath) of *Marketing Tourism Destinations: A Strategic Planning Approach* (Wiley, 1992); (with A. Mathieson) *Tourism: Economic, Physical and Social Impacts* (Longman, 1982); (with C. Wright) *The Environmental Impact of Outdoor Recreation* (University of Waterloo, 1977); and editor of *Outdoor Recreation in Canada* (Wiley, 1989); (with J. Marsh) *Recreational Land Use: Perspectives on its Evolution in Canada* (Carleton Library Series 1982); and *Recreational Land Use in Southern Ontario* (University of Waterloo, 1978); and numerous papers on tourism and recreation in academic journals. Dr. Wall was awarded the Roy Wolfe Award of the Association of American Geographers in 1991 for his contributions to the understanding of the geography of tourism and recreation.

PART I
INTRODUCTION

PERSPECTIVES ON LEISURE AND THE ENVIRONMENT

SUE GLYPTIS

Both leisure and the environment are multi-faceted and of major contemporary significance. The interplay between them is a fascinating and vital concern of academic and practitioner alike. The environment, in its many different forms, poses both opportunities and constraints for leisure. Leisure, in turn, exerts its own impacts, whether in the enjoyment or consumption of resources, the fostering of individual and community development, the generation of financial costs and benefits, or sheer pressure of demand which beckons a policy or planning response.

This chapter has two basic purposes. First, it outlines the growth and contemporary importance of leisure and some related issues. Second, it outlines the aims, structure and scope of the book, highlighting its embrace of issues ranging from local to global, its international relevance and its perspectives on continuity and change.

The terms 'leisure' and 'environment' have a familiar ring in everyday parlance, concept and concern, yet their full ramifications and the complex interrelationships between them are rarely embraced. Leisure typically becomes structured and segmented into discrete activities or events and addressed by academics, policy-makers and participants as sport, tourism, a day in the countryside, a night at the theatre, and so on. Yet leisure is more than the sum of such pieces. It has been defined in three broad ways. The first measures leisure as time, 'the time available to the individual when the disciplines of work, sleep and other basic needs have been met' (Countryside Recreation Research Advisory Group, 1970, p.5). Defining leisure as a mere left-over, however, fails fundamentally to ascribe to it any positive character or value. Leisure is not simply time free from other things; as many unemployed and retired people would testify, free time can be far from leisurely: in large measure or enforced incidence it can be more a burden than a blessing.

The second approach sees leisure more positively, as particular types of activity, lending palpable reward, be it enjoyment, rest and recuperation, diversion, excitement, companionship, escape, or physical or mental re-creation. The third approach adds a crucial perceptual dimension, recognising that leisure, essentially, is in the mind of the participant; that any tidy cataloguing of pursuits as 'work' or 'leisure' denies the simple truth that one person's pleasure may be another's penance, gardening and DIY being obvious examples. Leisure is, above all, subjective; no satisfactory definition could go beyond saying that leisure is activity (or inactivity) freely chosen and enjoyed.

By any measure, leisure is a significant domain of life, typically occupying, in the developed world, one-third or more of our existence. Its importance, though, derives not from quantity alone but from its intimate interconnection with the quality of people's lives. That link has long been recognized in the policy deliberations and prescriptions of central and local government. In the UK the House of Lords Select Committee on Sport and Leisure (1973), to which Allan Patmore and Brian Rodgers were specialist advisers, averred that 'Leisure is as much a part of life as work and it plays an equally impor-tant part in man's development and . . . quality of . . . life'. Soon after the White Paper *Sport and Recreation* (Department of the Environment, 1975) endorsed that view: 'The Government's concern with recreation stems basically from their recognition of its importance for the general welfare of the community. In a society which enjoys substantial leisure time the Gov-ernment have a responsibility to examine the contribution which recreation can make to a full life.'

In fact leisure was seen not only as enhancing the positive aspects of qual-ity of life but also as avoiding the negative: 'By reducing boredom and urban frustration, participation in active recreation contributes to the reduction of hooliganism and delinquency among young people' (ibid.). More recently, both facets were reinforced by the Minister for Sport's Review Group on Sport in the Inner City (Department of the Environment, 1989): 'An indi-vidual's quality of life and sense of well-being can be greatly enhanced through the sheer fun and enjoyment which can be gained from participation. Also activity through involvement in sport and recreation can assist in the reduction of tension and stress within communities'.

Leisure in the 1990s

Heady optimism in the 1960s and early 1970s held that we were fast creating an age of leisure. Indeed, with time, money and mobility as key facilitators of leisure, there is no shortage of evidence to show that we have indeed become a more leisured society. The working week has reduced a little: in Britain since 1961 the normal basic working hours of employees in manual occupations have fallen by nearly four hours a week. Holiday entitlement has grown dramatically. In 1961 only 3 per cent of manual workers were entitled to more than two weeks' holiday; now all but 1 per cent have four weeks or more. Reduced retirement ages and longer life expectancy lend the likelihood of a substantial block of largely free time at the end of a typical working life. At the start of the 1990s, men reaching the age of sixty can expect to live a further seventeen years and women a further twenty-one years; those reaching seventy can expect a further eleven and fourteen years respectively (*Social Trends*).

For most, the benefits of additional time have been more than matched by the bonus of increased wealth. In Britain, real household disposable income has risen by over 40 per cent since the mid-1970s, an increase from which leisure spending has benefited disproportionately. Over the same period, spending on television and video grew by 142 per cent and that on vehicle purchase by 109 per cent. Indeed, the increase in leisure spending has far outstripped the increase in leisure time. Martin and Mason (1991) estimate that in the 1980s leisure time increased by only 2 per cent, but that leisure spending increased by 150 per cent, and even more markedly in the spheres of home entertainment and overseas holidays. Over the decade video ownership increased from 3 per cent of households to nearly 70 per cent. In 1990, 25 million overseas holidays were purchased, compared with only 14 million ten years earlier. Furthermore, greater mobility is manifest not only in annual holiday taking but also in everyday lifestyles. Twice as many households as in 1961 now have cars (64 per cent compared with 31 per cent), and one in five households have two or more. We also spend money to save, to structure and to 'shift' time and place, with the 1980s heralding the era of the mobile telephone, the video recorder, the filofax, the fax machine and the microwave oven. On the face of it, the age of leisure has arrived.

So, too, would imply our leisure participation statistics, at least at aggregate level. Periodic *General Household Surveys* since 1977 show the trends for sport. Adult participation has risen steadily. Over the decade from 1977 men's participation in outdoor sport (including walking) rose from 35 per cent to 40 per cent and women's participation from 21 per cent to 24 per cent. In indoor sport the corresponding increases were from 31 per cent to 35 per cent of men and from 13 per cent to 21 per cent of women. In individual as opposed to team-based sports, in activities linked with exercise and health, and in the more adventurous and glamorous pursuits, growth has been quite dramatic, especially in sports which make use of countryside and water resources. Indeed, that range of sports is fast diversifying, with the emergence of new sports such as clay-pigeon shooting, jet-skiing and microlighting. There is pressure for access from those seeking greater challenge. The challenge in turn for planners is to find ways of accommodating the pace and transformation of growth, within a finite and sensitive resource and alongside other established uses.

None the less, despite its unquestionable scale and significance in social and economic terms, sport remains a minority activity. The leisure activities with mass appeal are still the more informal, social and passive. Surveys for the Countryside Commission (1991) show that in 1990 76 per cent of the population had visited the countryside for purposes of recreation, generating over 1,600 million trips and £12,400 million of expenditure. Most visits (four-fifths) were taken from home, but a substantial minority while on holiday. Countryside visiting attracts not only a large number of people but also a high frequency of participation. In 1990, as many as 19 per cent of the population had visited the countryside within the past week, and nearly half had done so within the past month. At the other extreme, however, two per cent had never been to the countryside.

In leisure, as in other realms of life, there are social inequalities. They are lessening with time but remain clearly etched. In Britain and in most West European countries, leisure participation generally, and sports participation particularly, is dominated by men, young people, white people, car owners and those in white-collar occupations. The participation rates of women, older people, ethnic minorities, and those in blue-collar occupations are generally lower.

Access to leisure can be constrained for many reasons. For the retired, there may be an abundance of free time, but perhaps declining health, wealth or mobility—or the simple fact that many elderly people have not been accustomed to having time on their hands, nor introduced to satisfying leisure opportunities in their younger years; as Rodgers (1977) put it, they may be 'illiterate' as far as leisure activities are concerned. Women may be constrained by domestic responsibilities, a shortage of free time, the unpredictability and fragmented incidence of their free time, and gender stereotypes and expectations which stifle the expression of personal out-of-home leisure interests. Unemployed people have time in large measure but limited means to enjoy it, and have the problem of finding a real sense of purpose outside the world of work, cast suddenly adrift into unstructured days and weeks from the familiar time structure imposed by work. Ethnic minorities are over-represented among the poor, the poorly housed and unemployed, their disadvantage often compounded by barriers of language or custom, and often torn between upholding their own cultural identities and traditions and assimilating into the way of life of their host communities. Young people are eager to establish their independence and individuality, but usually with only low incomes, low mobility, and cut off from the ready-made recreation provisions and peer-group networks available in school.

Perhaps unexpectedly, children, too, can be disadvantaged in terms of access to leisure opportunities. Stephens (1990, p.594) describes opportunities for play in a relatively wealthy district in south-east England:

. . . children's lives were becoming more and more restricted. The increase in traffic limited the distance they can safely travel from home; poor housing design meant that there was little easily accessible play space; they weren't allowed to go to the park alone . . . there was virtually no provision of safe, supervised activities for children . . . changing patterns in parents' lives meant that there was little shared play between adults and children during the working week; and . . . parents' anxieties for their children's personal safety meant that even 9 and 10 year olds were not allowed out after school.

For most children the play environment meant the confines of their bedroom, and their play companions were the television and the computer. How long, I wonder, before we produce the totally plug-in child with only second hand experiences to draw on and to signpost their way towards adulthood?

Demand may be constrained not only by barriers linked with age, gender, class and income, but also by lack of facilities and opportunities. Studies in

Belfast (Roberts, Dench *et al.*, 1989) have shown how levels of participation can be lifted and social inequalities overcome by increased facility provision. Between 1977 and 1984 fourteen new municipal leisure centres were built in Belfast, making it the United Kingdom's best provided city in terms of indoor sports facilities per head of population. In the late 1980s 58 per cent of Belfast's adults were taking part in at least one sport, compared with only 25 per cent nationally. Furthermore, conventional class contrasts were greatly diminished: overall participation rates were 60 per cent among those in white-collar occupations, 68 per cent among skilled manual workers and 55 per cent among those in unskilled manual jobs.

This brief review has sought to set the scene by considering some of the catalysts and constraints to leisure, charting its recent growth, and acknowledging its social importance and inequities. Its centrality to the quality of life was recognized at the outset by Allan Patmore in *Land and Leisure* (p.264): 'Much of this book has been concerned, explicitly or implicitly, with pressure, the pressure of an escalating demand for outdoor recreation on finite resources of land and water. In the long run other pressures may be more critical, but few are as intimately involved with the potential quality of life in town and country.' So, too, were the resource challenges signalled (p.1): 'For the planner, these pressures present an urgent and varied challenge, a challenge bedevilled by the inherent paradox of the need not only to conserve the scarce resources of land and amenity, but also to provide for their fuller use and enjoyment.' We turn now to explore the interrelationships of leisure with the environments in which it takes place which are treated in more detail throughout the rest of the book.

Aims and purpose of the book

The book aims to provide a broad-ranging review of the ways in which leisure makes use of, places impacts upon, and is affected by the various environments in which it takes place. The emphasis is on the physical environment and those forms of leisure which make use of the natural resource base or purpose-built provision, though there is strong reference throughout to the impact of social and economic environments.

The themes addressed

We start by examining leisure as a product and promoter of social change. How leisure is perceived, experienced and valued by populace or policy-maker depends on prevailing social attitudes and priorities. The book therefore begins with the theme Leisure, Perception and Social Change. Michael Dower begins (Chapter 2) with a retrospective critique of his seminal work, *Fourth Wave: the challenge of leisure*, published in 1965, and that of J. Allan Patmore, *Land and Leisure*, published in 1970. The chapter compares the reality of leisure in the 1990s with the assumptions and expectations prevailing in the expansionist 1960s.

Taking a century-long perspective, Gordon Cherry (Chapter 3) charts the changing use of the countryside in the context of changing social attitudes and national circumstances. The start of the century saw a yearning for pastoralism, impelled not least by the growth of squalid urban conditions and the impersonal nature of the city, resulting in a view of rural Britain as a respository of rural traditions and virtues. The inter-war period saw the origins of the mass user, the spread of urban influence on the countryside, and concerns for the preservation of scenic quality. The national parks movement, and later the reality of mass use, prompted official concern, with a phase of planning for the mass user and meeting the needs of a motorized society occupying the period from 1945 until recently. Now, with the growth of environmentalism, a concern to protect the landscape is once again paramount.

Shifting concerns and priorities also fashioned the evolution of attitudes towards industrial landscapes, and these are examined by Neil Cossons (Chapter 4). The chapter contrasts the artist's view of the picturesque and sublime in the late-eighteenth century, through the disillusionment and anti-industrialism which developed in the nineteenth century, to present day perspectives in which industrial monuments are valued as relics of our culture, yet with the danger that we romanticize what was once degrading work and turn cultural heritage into a spectator sport.

This latter concern has echoes in the contemporary countryside. How countryside is commodified and rural life exploited as a spectacle are themes developed in Chapter 5 by Paul Cloke. Cloke argues that rural leisure is increasingly packaged and offered in the form of a pay-as-you-enter countryside, a trend fuelled by the economic and social restructuring of rural areas and the emergence of new consumption norms. Case studies in Devon and Dyfed illustrate the opportunities offered, and the images of the rural portrayed by such attractions as waterfowl centres, rare-breeds farms, 'rides and slides' theme parks, country sports parks, shire-horse centres, and the like. Such developments may bring positive economic return and positive public enjoyment, but they represent an increasing orientation towards entertainment within, rather than enjoyment of, a countryside environment, and perhaps create potential tensions with the emerging environmentalist mood charted by Cherry.

Both in urban and rural environments the growth and diversification of leisure demand and its integration with other resource uses have prompted a policy and planning response. Seven chapters therefore concern Planning for Leisure, focusing on post-war, and mainly post-1960s developments. First is a comparative overview of planning for conservation, recreation and tourism in Britain and Australia by J. T. Coppock (Chapter 6), examining the structure and functioning of central government in these fields in countries of vastly differing area, population pressure and governmental structures. In Chapter 7, A. J. Veal charts the development of planning for leisure in Britain, linking its various phases with the prevailing social, economic and political environments of the time. Three broad stages are identified since 1960: a 'demand' phase, a 'needs' phase and an 'enterprise' phase. The characteristics of each phase and their related planning rationales are discussed.

In Chapter 8, Michael Tanner traces the complex and ever-changing approaches to the planning and management of water resources in England and Wales, from the early effects of urbanization through to the privatization of the water industry in 1989. The chapter explains why recreation and amenity interests were slow to be recognized at national level, but how, on privatization, they came to be lodged with both the private water companies and the newly established regulatory body, the National Rivers Authority.

More comprehensive and more integrated planning for leisure in England has been undertaken at regional rather than national level, principally by the Regional Councils for Sport and Recreation. H. B. Rodgers (Chapter 9) charts the emergence and development of the regional planning strategies, their relationship to national strategy making, and their emphasis on partnership working among the Regional Councils, local authorities, statutory bodies, commercial interests and voluntary organizations. Taking the specific case of north-west England, the chapter underlines the importance of undertaking systematic appraisals of local leisure markets as an input to regional strategy formulation, and proffers a method of doing so based on selected demographic and social indicators.

The next three chapters focus on the planning of specific types of leisure resources. Martin Elson (Chapter 10) traces changing government attitudes to the sport and recreational use of green belts, as evidenced in successive planning circulars and guidance notes and in newly emerging developments such as the creation of Community Forests. Elson concludes that the leisure potential of green belts is as yet unfulfilled and proposes action to enhance it. Mike Fitzjohn and Malcolm Tungatt (Chapter 11) examine the changing nature of sports provision and urban land use, tracing developments in swimming provision, indoor sports facilities, playing fields and golf courses. John Bale (Chapter 12) focuses on changes in the form and functioning of a single facility type, the British football stadium, developing a four-stage evolutionary model. Bale shows how, in just over a century, the sites at which football is played have changed from being open, informal environments to enclosed and highly territorialized spaces, subjected to strong surveillance, and with rigidly enforced segregation of spectators from players, and of rival spectator groups from each other.

Leisure, especially in the rural environment, is only rarely the sole or prime user of land. More often than not it coexists—and sometimes conflicts—with conservation value, and with other uses. There are convincing and disturbing catalogues of habitat loss: nearly a quarter of our area of upland heather lost in the last fifty years; 85,000 kilometres of hedgerows lost in only six years from 1984 to 1990; species-rich grasslands covering only 3 per cent of their area fifty years ago; and certain bird species depleted or virtually destroyed (Department of the Environment, 1992). Three chapters therefore address aspects of Management for Recreation and Conservation. Roger Sidaway (Chapter 13) reviews evidence about the impact of sport and recreation on nature conservation, concluding that they are not major environmental threats, but can cause significant local damage. Such damage can often be overcome or prevented, however, by good management practice, and the chapter outlines several possible solutions. The 'limits of acceptable change' planning system is advocated as a valuable approach, not least for its participatory decision-making, involving scientific experts, managers and users. Often the management need is not just to bring recreation and conservation into balance but to ensure the healthy development of agriculture and enhancement of landscape too. Most of our fine landscapes depend directly on established systems of farming. Sally Bucknall (Chapter 14) therefore traces the changing environment of countryside management with particular reference to the role of the farming community. Economically and environmentally it is essential that most of our countryside continues to be farmed, but with food in surplus rather than in shortage the need is for farmers to be supported as—and to see themselves as—stewards of a multipurpose countryside. The recent establishment of Environmentally Sensitive Areas and Countryside Stewardship schemes is discussed and evaluated. John Gittins (Chapter 15) recognizes a role for the whole community in caring for the environment, and demonstrates the value of voluntary environmental action in improving the countryside, fostering a sense of ownership and empowerment, and providing an enjoyable leisure time pursuit in its own right.

Attention then turns to Leisure and Economic Change. Michael Collins (Chapter 16) examines the impact of the single European market on sport in Europe. Comparisons and contrasts between the constituent states are drawn in terms of present participation and spending levels. The implications for sport of the enhanced freedom of movement for people, goods and services are debated, as are the effects of possible future additions to the twelve existing member states. Roger Vickerman (Chapter 17) explores the implications for tourism of the Channel Tunnel. These are of two broad types: first, the pure transport effect, in generating or diverting traffic, second, the regional development effect and the role that tourism might play in the adjacent regions.

The penultimate part of the book examines Leisure in Special Environments and discusses the role and management of national parks and wilderness areas. Adrian Phillips (Chapter 18) traces the changing attitudes towards balancing conservation and public enjoyment in the national parks of England and Wales. The chapter examines the concerns underlying the 1949 National Parks and Access to the Countryside Act (and its precursor reports by John Dower and Hobhouse), the Sandford Report of 1974, and the Edwards Report of 1991, and the solutions proposed. Derek Statham (Chapter 19) outlines the interplay between conservation, recreation, farming and land ownership in the specific case of the North York Moors National Park in northern England. Attention is drawn to factors which have dominated the debate on the management of the wilder areas and to the management approaches adopted. Timothy O'Riordan (Chapter 20) examines the environmental politics of managing the Broads and proposes the Broads Authority as the model upon which future national park administrations should be structured. Mark Blacksell (Chapter 21) discusses wilderness in the very different physical and cultural context of the United States, examining the nature of the American wilderness, the measures taken for its protection and the lessons for the future and for other countries.

The final section of the book glimpses broader horizons still, in relation to Leisure and the Global Environment. Jean Tallantire (Chapter 22) traces the origins and growth of adventure tourism and its incursions into hitherto remote places. Its impact on the environment, people and economy of remote areas is examined through case studies of three areas in the Himalaya. Measures are proposed for minimizing future adverse impacts. In the final chapter of the book, Geoffrey Wall assesses the likely impacts on tourist activity in different areas of the world of predicted global warming. The chapter demonstrates the vulnerability of tourism given a modified natural resource base and changed lengths of seasons and highlights the importance and urgency of strategic policy action to anticipate and adjust to the predicted changes.

Any book on a theme of such broad embrace inevitably leaves aspects uncovered and depths unexplored. Indeed, it is hoped that the 'stock-taking' which this volume represents will stimulate further enquiry and fuller academic and policy concern. The chapters range widely across different environments, contrasting forms of leisure, and varied policy and management concerns. As well as the strength and breadth of the leisure–environment relationship, three particular threads run through. The first is the matter of scale. The chapters demonstrate that leisure–environment links pervade all levels of analysis from local-site level through to city, regional, national, international and global concerns. The second facet is international applicability. The majority of themes are addressed in a British context, although experience is also drawn directly from Australia, North America, the European Community, India and Nepal. The issues addressed, however, are of international significance throughout, whatever local variations in political and economic systems, physical resource bases, planning mechanisms, land ownership and leisure demand might do to modify policy priorities and management approaches. The third facet is a perennial interplay of continuity and change, in recognition that both leisure and its many environments are dynamic entities. Every chapter addresses enduring concerns, but encounters ever-changing relationships.

Fittingly, in a volume to celebrate the career of J. Allan Patmore, one further hallmark of the chapters is relevance. The combination of scholarship, relevance and concern shines through every aspect of Allan's work, and that combination has inspired every contributor. What he himself said of geography strikes a receptive chord with all who write here of Leisure and the Environment:

It is a subject, above all, of both head and heart. With rigour and precision of technique and concept we seek to measure, to describe and understand the mechanisms which dictate the shifting patterns of the occupance of the earth. But earth is home, shot through with beauty and with squalor, opportunity and despair. We cannot be detached from home: our attempted understanding of its face is quickened by our wonder in its delights and our concern for its condition: in wonder and in concern, as much as in understanding, is the mark of relevance in geography. (Patmore, 1980, p.283)

All who contribute here, from their varied disciplinary perspectives, would readily concur.

References

Central Statistical Office, annual, *Social Trends*, HMSO, London.

Countryside Commission, 1991, *Visitors to the countryside*, Cheltenham, Countryside Commission, CCP341.

Countryside Recreation Research Advisory Group, 1970, *Countryside Recreation Glossary*, London, Countryside Commission.

Department of the Environment, 1975, *Sport and Recreation*, Cmnd. 6200, London, HMSO.

Department of the Environment, 1989, *Sport and active recreation provision in the inner cities. Report of the Minister for Sport's Review Group 1988–89*, London, DOE.

Department of the Environment, 1992, *Action for the countryside*, London, DOE.

Dower, M., 1965, 'Fourth wave: the challenge of leisure', a Civic Trust survey reprinted from the *Architects Journal*, London, Civic Trust.

Martin, W. and Mason, S., 1991, 'The Thatcher years', *Leisure Management*, **11**, 7: 40–2.

Office of Population Censuses and Surveys, annual (but leisure data included only in 1973, 1977, 1980, 1983, 1986, 1989, 1990), *General Household Survey*, London, HMSO.

Patmore, J. A., 1970, *Land and leisure*, Newton Abbot, David and Charles.

Patmore, J. A., 1980, 'Geography and relevance', *Geography*, **65**, 4: 265–83.

Roberts, K., Dench, S., Minten, J. and York, C., 1989, *Community response to leisure centre provision in Belfast*, London, Sports Council Study 34.

Rodgers, H. B., 1977, *Rationalising sports policies. Sport in its social context*, Strasbourg, Council of Europe.

Stephens, K., 1990, 'Central issues in children's play' in Williams, T., Almond L. and Sparkes, A., *Sport and physical activity. Moving towards excellence*, London, Spon: 591–6.

PART II
LEISURE, PERCEPTION AND SOCIAL CHANGE

2

'FOURTH WAVE' REVISITED

MICHAEL DOWER

At the beginning of his seminal book *Land and Leisure*, published in 1970, Allan Patmore quoted the opening words from my own work of five years earlier, *Fourth Wave: the Challenge of Leisure*:

Three great waves have broken across the face of Britain since 1800. First, the sudden growth of dark industrial towns. Second, the thrusting movement along far-flung railways. Third, the sprawl of car-based suburbs. Now we see, under the guise of a modest word, the surge of a fourth wave which could be more powerful than all the others. The modest word is *leisure*. (Dower, 1965, p.123)

Patmore and I were writing in a period of unbroken economic growth, the post-war boom; and we both anticipated continuation of that growth. We observed the rapid rise of demand for leisure activity, caused by that economic growth and related factors. We believed that the nation was moving rapidly towards 'leisure for all': I predicted, indeed, that demand for active leisure might well treble within this century.

He a geographer, and I a planner, focused on the impact which that demand would have upon the land; and we called on government to put in hand effective planning so that, in my words, leisure could 'enhance the lives of our people without ruining the island they live upon' (p.123). Patmore's conclusion was that

Pressures of leisure on land are now such that there can be no laissez faire alternative to some measure at least of public direction. That direction should be not only balanced but bold, so that the quality of living as well as the quality of both rural and urban landscapes may be enhanced . . . With a rich heritage to conserve, in a compact island with a large and growing population, the challenge of leisure is immediate and insistent, demanding effective and inspiring solutions. [Patmore, 1970, p.290]

Modified growth

Looking back, how should one judge these predictions and that call for action? Patmore and I could not predict the Israeli/Arab conflict of 1973, the use of oil as an economic weapon, the surge of inflation and the recession that followed. We could not foresee the further recessions of the early 1980s and the early 1990s; nor the sharp impact of Thatcherite policies over the last thirteen years; nor the growing pessimism about the world and the rapid rise in environmental concerns.

These factors have had a major impact upon the trends that we foresaw. They contributed to a slowing-down, then a halt, in the rise of population in Britain; to slower than predicted growths in personal incomes; to stabilizing, rather than the predicted sharp fall, in the length of the working week— these being three of the key factors which cause growth in leisure demand.

Another key result of these changes in the last twenty years has been the rise in unemployment, a form of leisure enforced upon those affected but seldom accompanied by the financial means or the morale to permit the full enjoyment of that leisure. The effect of these changes upon the demand for leisure activity was summarized in 1982 in *Leisure Policy for the Future*, which stated that 'Spending on leisure grew rapidly in the period up to 1973, has grown more slowly since then, and is expected to show moderate and fluctuating increase over the next decade' (Chairmen's Policy Group, 1983, p.4). That prediction has been broadly accurate in that leisure spending has grown in real terms during the past decade, with the rise in personal incomes, but fell back during the recession of the early 1990s.

Leisure not for all

So, the dramatic and continuous growth in leisure demand that we predicted in 1965 and 1970 has not been realized. More significant in human terms, this country is very far from achieving 'leisure for all'. The report *Leisure Policy for the Future* recorded that:

There are still large numbers of people who are short of money or of other resources, or who are affected by ill-health or other disability, so that their leisure is severely constrained. They include the low-paid, many of the growing millions of pensioners, the disabled and the handicapped, and those who are unemployed . . . (p.3).

The fall in real personal incomes and the rise in unemployment draw attention strongly to those who—through poverty or personal constraints—are unable to take a full part in a leisured society . . . (p.4).

Many people have health problems: these may inhibit their leisure activity, or may be a reason for such activity. Nearly one million people are registered as disabled: their needs pose a challenge for leisure provision. Many others are affected by personal constraints of other kinds. (p.4) (Chairmen's Policy Group, 1983).

This disenfranchisement of perhaps a quarter of our population from the 'leisure society' is for me a bitter disappointment, a human offence. When writing *Fourth Wave*, I had seen leisure as a human boon, offering 'that widening of life, of human pleasure and achievement, which the Greeks understood and which generous-hearted men have dreamed of for long generations' (p.123). Working as consultant for the Countryside Commission and others in the early 1970s, I had addressed the impact which this leisure was beginning to place upon the land, but always with pleasure that people had the opportunity for leisure. Then I teamed up with Rhona and Robert Rapoport and their colleagues for the major research project, with fieldwork in a middle London borough, which culminated in the report *Leisure Provision and People's Needs* (Dower, Rapoport *et al.*, 1981).

This research gave me a salutary, and sobering, insight into the meaning of leisure to people, its contribution to their quality of life, and how their needs and preoccupations change at different points in their life-cycle. I was able to admire the resourcefulness that people bring to their lives and to understand the ways in which people (individually, and in their local communities) can be and are their own leisure providers. But I was struck by the severe constraints which very many people experience—lack of money, lack of personal transport, poor housing, personal disability, the need to care for children or elderly people or sick relatives, and (most unexpected to a man like me, living in the countryside) the deep fear which many, particularly women, have of venturing on to urban streets at night. These constraints force people inwards into themselves: they make more blessed the boon of television, but they rob millions of our fellow-citizens of the chance for varied leisure activity.

Leisure provision

This reflection on those who cannot take part tempers my pleasure in the generous progress that has been made in many of the areas of leisure provision that I called for in *Fourth Wave*. I wrote it in late 1964, prompted by the knowledge I had gained as one of the small Civic Trust team which, under Leslie Lane's direction, prepared the proposals for 'A Lea Valley Regional Park'. Leslie Lane had remembered, from his time as chief planner of London County Council, the proposal made by Patrick Abercrombie in the Greater London Plan of 1944. Abercrombie wrote that 'The Lee Valley gives the opportunity for a great piece of constructive, preservative and regenerative planning . . . a great recreational and open-air lung to a crowded East End' (Abercrombie, 1945, p.105).

Twenty years after Abercrombie, we were able to do the detailed survey of that remarkable twenty-mile valley and to give shape to the great park that he had envisaged. In the process, I met many of those who were involved in the fields of sport, tourism, and outdoor recreation . . . and this was *before* we had any government agencies concerned with these things.

The timing proved to be right. The local authorities agreed to set up the Lea Valley Regional Park, and *Fourth Wave* appeared just as the first of the leisure quangos was about to be set up. These 'quasi-autonomous non-government organizations' are, in fact, agencies of central government (outside the official structure of departments) who are given responsibility for particular sectors of initiative by government. Within four years were created the Sports Council, the Countryside Commissions, and the Tourist Boards; and new briefs related to leisure provision were given to the Forestry

Commission, the British Waterways Board, and the local authorities. When Allan Patmore wrote *Land and Leisure* in 1970 he was able to record the early stages of action by these bodies.

The last twenty years have seen massive spending by leisure providers, in both the public and private sectors. In 1991–2, in England and Wales alone, local authorities expected to spend about £2.4 billion gross (or £1.7 billion net of income) on provision for leisure and recreation, this being a 60 per cent increase in real terms on their spending ten years earlier (Chartered Institute of Public Finance and Accountancy, 1991).

Achievements and gaps

Spending of this order means that substantial progress has been made in some of the areas of leisure provision considered in *Fourth Wave*. In the cities, we are now vastly better equipped than we were in 1965 with sports halls, stadiums, swimming-pools, athletics tracks and some other built facilities. Some of these have been constructed to high standards of sophistication, with 'tropical' leisure pools and diverse cultural facilities. Some cities have been able to extend and improve their playing fields and park systems, with imaginative use of river valleys, disused railway lines and derelict lands such as those redeemed by the sequence of Garden Festivals. Some have also been able to sustain and improve their network of neighbourhood-level facilities—libraries, halls, leisure centres, all-weather surfaces.

But may gaps remain or have appeared. Too many playing fields are still poorly equipped or inadequate in area. Too many branch libraries have had to close. Too few schools have been put to effective dual use for the community. Too many towns and cities have no system of cycleways, no safe places for children to play. Far too much of our housing is still unfit for leisure use—damp and cramped, with little privacy, small gardens or no gardens at all, no garages, no workshops, only an occasional community room—and opening on to streets into which many residents fear to venture.

A wry reflection on the 'city' section of *Fourth Wave* is that in 1965 I described how the disused Round House at Camden Town was to be converted into the multi-purpose arts Centre 42; and I featured the plan prepared by Cedric Price for Joan Littlewood for a Fun Palace, commenting that 'it may never be built, but it deserves a place as a superb idea' (p.147). Nearly thirty years later, the Round House is again disused and may find new life as an Earth Centre; and while the Fun Palace has not been built in this country, the French have built its twin in the Pompidou Centre. Comparing also the French *'foyers ruraux'* (which are run by communes, usually with active cultural programmes) with our village halls, one wonders whether we British have quite the panache that is needed in that aspect of leisure provision.

Turning to the countryside, there has been a spectacular increase in formal provision of many kinds, encouraged by the Countryside Commissions, the Tourist Boards and other government agencies and undertaken by a very wide variety of actors in the public and private sectors. A large part of this provision has been aimed at car-borne day visitors. Public bodies have offered country parks, picnic sites, forest lay-bys, car parks on the coast or lakeside reservoirs, with space to picnic or walk, play ball or pursue other activities. Private landowners, and voluntary bodies such as the National Trusts or the Wildlife Trusts, have sought to attract visitors off the road to enjoy themselves and spend money.

Much of this provision has been done to a high standard, with supporting facilities and good or adequate management of the land or facilities which the public uses. The shortcomings tend to relate to what happens before or after the visitor reaches the car park or to those who cannot (or do not wish to) travel by car.

Thus, a growing number of places are facing severe traffic congestion at peak visiting times which diminishes the leisure experience and irritates local residents. The volume of use by visitors, once they are on their feet, is in many other places causing erosion of land surfaces, for example on the moorlands and mountain flanks of northern England and parts of the Welsh coast. In many parts of England and Wales, the poor condition of footpaths prevents people from making effective use of our remarkable system of rights of way. Meanwhile many millions of car-less or house-bound people cannot take part in countryside recreation because it is too far away from them.

More effort is needed to address these problems: to initiate traffic management schemes; to curb, and prevent further, erosion; to put right the widespread faults in our system of rights of way; and to 'bring the countryside to the people' rather than assuming that people can only enjoy the countryside if they come some distance from their homes by car. This idea of giving townspeople direct access to the countryside underlies the ambitious programme of Community Forests sponsored by the Countryside Commission and the Forestry Commission. It is also among the objectives of the National Forest being created north of Birmingham; and of the growing family of Groundwork Trusts, which are local partnerships of local authorities, private firms and voluntary bodies whose purpose is to enhance the landscape of many of our industrial towns and their surroundings.

After the cities and the countryside, the third major theme I pursued in *Fourth Wave* was tourism, 'coping with the holiday boom'. My focus then was mainly on the British holiday-makers; the growing pressure which their demands were placing on the coasts, National Parks and elsewhere; and the opportunities which resources still largely untapped—our forests, inland waters and estuaries—might provide for them.

In the event, the growth in holiday-making by British people has not been as great as I predicted; moreover, the advent of mass package-deal holidays abroad has sucked much of that growth out of the country. More formidable in its impact on our resources has been the growth in tourists coming from overseas, encouraged by massive advertising by our Tourist Boards. Fortunately the same Tourist Boards did much in the 1970s to boost the capacity of hotels and other facilities to cater for these visitors; and the tourist industry has made a major effort to raise standards in face of the competition from other countries.

Of recent years, decline in other sectors of the economy has prompted local authorities, tourist boards and government agencies such as the Rural Development Commission and the Ministry of Agriculture to promote tourism in areas where it was not previously significant. In some such areas, tourism is generating significant income and jobs. But it is a volatile trade, in which different areas compete with each other for shares in a limited market and in which it is very difficult to gain the right amount of business. Some places, such as the more remote and 'down-market' of the long-established coastal resorts, are too reliant on tourism and yet gain too little to be viable. Others, such as some of the historic towns most popular among overseas tourists, can readily feel over-run.

This was one of the themes addressed by the Task Force on 'Tourism and the Environment' which reported in 1991. The Task Force concluded:

Tourism undoubtedly brings great benefits . . .

However, there is also a negative side to tourism. It imposes extra costs on local authorities in terms of maintenance and on local communities in terms of congestion; the sheer weight of visitors can damage buildings and landscapes and affect their special character; and the needs of visitors can generate unsuitable development.

Tourism carries the inherent danger that it can destroy the thing that generated it in the first place.

The key to ensuring that this does not happen—and that the benefits outweigh the costs—is to recognize that tourism and the environment are mutually dependent. [Task Force, 1991, pp.46–7]

The Task Force went on to outline measures which must be taken to address the problems, using language which echoed directly that which Allan Patmore and I had used twenty and twenty-five years earlier. They advocated assessing the capacity of places to take visitors; the management of traffic; strong control of development; and better coordination at a policy level between the various agencies concerned with tourism and environment.

I should own up to being a member of the Task Force, with a fairly strong hand in the drafting. Perhaps it is not surprising that the same ideas come through after a quarter-century. Nor is it surprising that Allan Patmore's own signature appears, as Vice-Chairman of the Sports Council, on the (March 1992) policy report on sport and recreation in the countryside. His life-long concerns shine through his Foreword to this report:

The English countryside is a precious heritage. Sport is one of the many uses which it sustains and resulting pressures mean that wise and responsible use must be the keynote. The countryside should be a place of great enjoyment for sport and for other recreation activities. However, it is a finite resource and it is essential that it is fully respected as such if its use for sport is to be healthily sustained. [Sports Council, 1992, p.1]

I salute Allan Patmore, and I thank him for this excuse to revisit *Fourth Wave*.

References

Abercrombie, P., 1945, *Greater London Plan 1944*, London, HMSO.

Chairmen's Policy Group, 1983, *Leisure Policy for the Future*, London, Sports Council.

CIPFA (Chartered Institute for Public Finance and Accountancy), 1991, *Leisure and Recreation Statistics 1991–92 Estimates*, London, CIPFA.

Dower, M., 1965, 'Fourth Wave: the Challenge of Leisure', A Civic Trust Survey reprinted from the *Architects' Journal*, London, Civic Trust.

Dower, M., Rapoport, R., Strelitz, Z. and Kew, S., 1981, *Leisure Provision and People's Needs*, London, HMSO.

Patmore, J. Allan, 1970, *Land and Leisure*, Newton Abbot, David and Charles (also in Pelican Books, 1972).

Sports Council, 1992, *A Countryside for Sport*, London, Sports Council.

Task Force on Tourism and the Environment, 1991, *Maintaining the Balance*, London, English Tourist Board.

3

CHANGING SOCIAL ATTITUDES TOWARDS LEISURE AND THE COUNTRYSIDE IN BRITAIN, 1890–1990

GORDON E. CHERRY

Historical perspectives on countryside recreation in Britain during the twentieth century have been accorded only fleetingly in a burgeoning literature inspired more from geography, sociology and planning. Definitive histories on particular topics such as National Parks (Cherry, 1975) and green belts (Thomas, 1970) have been undertaken, and there are flashes of the past in the social history of holiday making (Walton, 1983), studies in confrontation such as organized trespassing (Lowerson, 1980) and in certain environmental reviews (Sheail, 1975), but there has been little recognition of the need for a century-long framework within which leisure needs and aspirations might be charted against changing circumstances. This chapter seeks to redress that omission, albeit briefly and obviously very much in the form of an interim statement.

In selecting four periods—the 1890s, the 1930s, the 1960s and the 1990s—I sketch the main features of the time from the point of view of social attitudes towards the countryside and the community's enjoyment of it. Of course the periods are not watertight, and while they have distinctive features separate from the rest, continuities between them and indeed throughout the century are readily apparent. However, the four separate decades are useful markers in an intriguing story. Recreation geographers and planners of today cannot afford to ignore how their subject matter has both changed and remained constant throughout the century.

1890s

In the economic transformations of the nineteenth century Britain was the first country in the Western world both to industrialize and to urbanize. By the end of the Victorian period London was internationally pre-eminent, with a population of 4.5 million. Britain possessed eight other cities of more than 250,000 people, and the country was the workshop of the world. There was a mixed reaction to these achievements: pride at scientific progress, a glow at urban power and splendour but alarm at the hardships and squalid environments which suggested that great cities somehow impoverished human life for too many people. London and the manufacturing towns had become targets of concern as much as objects of satisfaction. They were unhealthy and centres of crime and vice; the ugliness of their housing conditions for the overcrowded poor militated against the population developing any sensitivity to beauty.

The antidote was to seek refreshment in the countryside, and the years around the turn of the century marked a period when Britain (but typically urban England) found a new interest in its rural areas (Cherry and Sheail, 1993). A return to pastoralism in various guises marked a new departure in social attitudes. Jan Marsh (1982) has suggested that 'the pastoral impulse' from 1880 to 1914 constituted a major influence on the countryside. A back-to-the-land philsophy rejected the impersonal cities; it favoured rural village life, welcomed a return to craft workshops and opened up opportunities for people to experience again the virtues of a rural environment.

A return to the countryside's natural beauty was to escape from the insensate cities. The philosophy was direct and appealing and was taken up on many fronts. John Ruskin envisioned a quasi-feudal agrarian society; William Morris encouraged craft design and founded the Society for the Protection of Ancient Buildings in 1877; and Edward Carpenter advocated the simple lifestyle in harmony with natural surroundings. Writers and artists reflected a love of the countryside; painters sought out the Surrey Hills and unspoilt country around London, Hardy found inspiration in Wessex, Housman in Shropshire, and in music the English folksong was popularized and folk dancing rediscovered.

One associated feature of this deepening interest in the countryside was that the urbanite gave increasing support to the furtherance of a rural conservation movement. The protection of old rural landscapes attracted the attention of many protest groups, particularly centred on the open commons around London where urban encroachment and dispossession for private development provided the scene for furious confrontation. The Commons Preservation Society, founded in 1865, was successful in opposing building on Hampstead Heath and in saving a number of London Commons, notably Wimbledon, Plumstead, Coulsdon, Banstead and Petersham. Beyond London, it was necessary to resort to 'direct action' to safeguard Berkhamstead Common and Epping Forest. By the end of the century (1899) the Society had merged with the Footpaths Preservation Society (founded in 1884); the addition of 'Open Spaces' to the title followed in 1910. A complementary development was the launching of the National Trust for Places of Historic Interest or Natural Beauty by the Reverend Hardwicke Rawnsley, Canon of Carlisle, in 1895.

The conservation ethic went hand in hand with an enthusiasm for natural history. Fieldwork undertaken by a widening group of amateurs, often including the country parson, sustained the many local naturalist societies founded at this time. Geological explorations led to an interest in landforms and coastline formations. Birds, lepidoptera, flora and fauna all provided raw material for the late Victorian obsession with collection and classification. The scope was wider still as the field naturalist was joined by the field archaeologist in countryside investigation and analysis.

Anti-urbanism and anti-industrialism fed on these sentiments. The contrast between the country and the factory was self-evident. As the journalist Robert Blatchford in his book *Merrie England* (1894) observed: 'The value of beauty is not a matter of sentiment: it is a fact. You would rather see a squirrel than a sewer rat. You would rather bathe in the Avon than in the Irwell. You would prefer the fragrance of a rose-garden to the stench of a sewage works. You would prefer Bolton Woods to Ancoats slums' (p.23). This was the context in which increasing numbers of people were attracted to the countryside for its enjoyment and instruction. An agenda was set which would last with recurrent themes for a century and more. Increasing interference with footpaths led to moves for footpath protection; enclosure of land led to demands for access. James Bryce's campaign against the enclosure of Scottish deer forests fostered his introduction of the Access to Mountains (Scotland) Bill in 1884, a Bill applying to England and Wales introduced four years later. The value of open space was strongly emphasized, and around the turn of the century the first suggestions for a green girdle around London were put forward.

A yearning for rurality influenced many aspects of life: for example, country locations for a revival of handicrafts which formed the basis of the Arts and Crafts movement, and house design, which emphasized the cottage and the manor house. In matters of dress the Rational Dress Society (founded 1881) advocated simpler apparel than the prevailing Victorian clothing; Gustav Jaeger of Stuttgart made wool fashionable on account of its alleged 'healthiness'; and sandals became popular. With regard to food, vegetarianism was promoted on grounds of health and hygiene; a Dr J.H. Kellogg attracted attention as a supervisor of a vegetarian sanatorium in Michigan.

The virtue of country air underpinned new outdoor pursuits. Camping under canvas became popular and the Boys' Brigade, the Church Lads' Brigade and the Scouts all embraced the camping tradition. Commercial tenting began with Joseph Cunningham who developed his first site at Llandudno before moving on to the Isle of Man. The hop pickers of East London enjoyed their working holidays in open air, accommodated in a variety of sheds, barns, tents and chalets. Rural living, as an escape from the cities was increasingly sought out, by the well-to-do as well as by those at the other end of the scale who built their shacks on 'plot lands' in their own arcadia (Hardy and Ward, 1984). Meanwhile, ubiquitously, the introduction of the modern safety bicycle in the early 1890s permitted regular countryside excursions for the urbanite.

1930s

Forty years on, circumstances, attitudes and responses had changed—in certain cases appreciably. Urban influences on the countryside had been extended considerably. For example, four million dwellings were built in Britain between the wars, the vast majority of them on urban peripheries in forms of low-density suburban development. Nowhere was this territorial expansion better seen than in outer London and particularly in north-west London where a new property company, created to manage and develop the Metropolitan Railway Company's estates, built a series of new estates from Neasden out through Wembley and Ruislip to Amersham.

Beyond the physical continuity of the suburbs, a pervading urban impact was readily discernible. H.J. Massingham, an observer of rural life in the tradition of William Cobbett and W.H. Hudson, maintained in 1939 that

. . . many a retired corner of genuine country England is being transformed from a village into a suburb. New roads appear for the Monday morning exodus; garages spring up and the tide of townish wants creeps in. The sons of husbandry also are magnetized into the towns, but they do not return for the weekend. In twenty years, a new culture has taken the place of the old in the village. But a village culture it is no more. [Abelson, 1988]

The form of urban sprawl was distinctive and jarred against the natural beauty of the countryside. The likes of Jaywick Sands, Canvey Island and Peacehaven were perhaps exceptional in their desecration of landscape, but there were countless other, lesser examples of building form and settlement that attracted the hostility of contemporary observers. The architect Clough Williams-Ellis (1928) likened urbanization to an octopus, with tentacles of growth over the countryside.

Ribbon development and formless sprawl were derided. The town planner Thomas Sharp (1932) pleaded for a clear separation of town from country. But by 1939 one-third of all the houses in England and Wales had been built since 1918, and the countryside was being absorbed by an urban environment. A rural way of life was pressured by an alien culture. Part of the problem was the continued contraction of British agriculture (Creasey and Ward 1984). In the 1920s Britain became a dumping group for the world's agricultural surpluses. The rural economic base was shattered: the older rural industries had already gone and further decline came with the reduction of the agricultural workforce by about one-third between the wars, as a quarter of a million men left the land. Farming expenditure fell, resulting in a lowering of cultivation standards, poor drainage, overgrown hedgerows and countless buildings in disrepair.

It was against this background that the inter-war years threw up two prevailing sentiments (perhaps irreconcilably) with regard to the countryside: to protect the natural heritage and to seek access to it for enjoyment. The release of the pastoral impulse at the end of the last century had already presaged the former and a regard for the scenic beauty of Britain was easily sustained. The magazine *The Countryman* was founded in 1927, and from the Batsford press came a stream of illustrated regional books on the British landscape. The geographer Vaughan Cornish sought to provide a scientific basis for the study of scenic amenity, regarding scenery as the stage on which Nature plays the drama of the senses. 'Thus, not only the form and colour of the landscape, but the song of birds, the sounds of running water, the fragrance of the field, and the mere breath of pure, fresh air are scenic amenities. Discordant noises are an offence . . . smoke doubly offensive, since it disfigures buildings and contaminates the air' (1937).

The landscape geography of Britain, compact, small scale and of infinite variety, lent itself well to a national nostalgia about the past. It was right to take steps to protect it, and the Council for the Preservation of Rural England, founded in 1926, took a lead in this regard. Planning powers were weak and slow to be strengthened. The word 'country' was included in planning legislation for the first time in 1932 (Town and Country Planning Act, having first appeared as a Rural Amenities Bill), but the prevailing obligation to pay compensation in the event of a refusal of planning permission fatally weakened the effectiveness of local control. Agitation for National Parks came to nothing, but London County Council support for the London Green Belt estates helped to establish the outer rim for the metropolis. Certain enterprising County Councils were innovative in seeking to protect areas of scenic quality, for example, West Sussex for the South Downs, and Surrey for its many beauty spots (Sheail, 1981).

Against these defensive, protective measures was pitted the advancing tide of urban recreation pressures. Health and fitness were major issues, and enjoyment of the countryside became a recreational imperative of the period. It took many forms: cycling, independently and in organized clubs; informal walking and more formal hiking and rambling (the Ramblers Association was founded in 1935); scenic tours by motor cycle, car and coach; railway excursions, not just to the coast but to inland centres such as Windermere and the Lake District; and holiday-making in informal settings such as those popularized by the newly founded Youth Hostels Association (1930) and the new generation of holiday camps, beginning with Butlins at Skegness, opening in 1936.

Today we can only absorb ourselves in the literature of the day to catch the full flavour of the social attitudes that underpinned the countryside revolution of the 1930s. But it is easy to see two things: the disgust at the despoilation of rural England and the enthusiasm for sharing a mass enjoyment of scenic beauty. The philosopher C.E.M. Joad (1945) described a long winding valley running up from Marlow into the Chilterns, and this relates equally well to the previous decade. He found 'a muddy road running through an avenue of shacks, caravans, villas, bungalows, mock castles, pigsties, disused railway carriages and derelict buses . . . each dingy little abode . . . distinguished by some dreadful appellation as, for example, Eretiz, The Nest, The Splendide, Kosy-Kot, Mon Absi, Linga-Longa, or U-an-I' (p.37). Against this cultural shabbiness, he described the ramblers 'at the Central Station at Manchester early on a Sunday morning, complete with rucksacks, shorts and hobnailed boots, waiting for the early trains to Edale, Hope and the Derbyshire moors . . . In our day hiking has replaced beer as the shortest cut out of Manchester' (p.17). No wonder, years earlier, in 1932, there had been the celebrated organized trespass on Kinder Scout, quite apart from the rash of smaller gatherings elsewhere in the Peak, such was the interest in unrestrained open air activity.

1960s

The issues of post-war reconstruction affected virtually every aspect of public policy, and concern about rural problems extracted government commitments on a range of questions to an unprecedented extent. By the time of the 1960s a very different situation obtained in countryside affairs from that prior to the outbreak of war.

Three things in particular had changed, and they combined to influence important attitudes towards the protection of scenic quality and opportunities for outdoor recreation. The first concerned the role of agriculture in landscape management, where the judgement and recommendations of the *Report of the Committee on Land Utilisation in Rural Areas* (1942), proved crucial. It was chaired by veteran countryside campaigner Lord Justice Scott; equally significant, the geographer Dudley Stamp, renowned for his work on land-use mapping, was vice-chairman and Thomas Sharp, the planner, was a joint secretary. The committee established the view that post-war rural policy should be based on the maintenance of a healthy and well-balanced agriculture—in other words a revival of the traditional mixed character of British farming. A sound economic base would resuscitate village and country life and underpin the preservation of landscape amenities. They made the point that the essence of the British countryside was that it was farmed, and the best way to maintain its well-loved features was to keep it farmed in a traditional way. 'In addition to their function of producing food and timber from the land, farmers and foresters are unconsciously the nation's landscape gardeners, a privilege which they share with the landowners' (p.47). The Agriculture Act 1947 introduced the principle of guaranteed farm prices and on this subsidy basis the post-war prosperity of British agriculture was assured. The belief was that in part at least the agriculturalist would play a major role in landscape preservation.

A supplementary role was provided by a strengthened land-use planning system. The Town and Country Planning Act 1947 provided for the obligatory preparation of Development Plans covering the whole country, as well as arrangements for the control of virtually all building operations by local councils. Compensation was not payable on refusal of planning permission, so cost to the public purse did not get in the way of judgement as to the 'right use of land'. There was professional and political commitment to restrain building severely in the countryside and to contain cities within fairly tight and well-defined boundaries. Pre-war criticism about the urban despoilation of the countryside had been met, and an urban containment policy was strengthened further with, first, confirmation of the London Green Belt and then the Ministerial Circular 42/55, which called for green belts elsewhere in the country—an invitation to which the County Councils responded with enthusiasm. Powers of landscape protection had never been so strong.

Meanwhile the twin objectives of scenic protection and countryside recreation had been pursued through the National Parks movement (Cherry, 1975). A Report by John Dower (1945) and the work of a committee chaired by Sir Arthur Hobhouse (1947) for England and Wales and reports in respect of Scotland by Sir Douglas Ramsay (1945, 1947) had set the scene, vociferous support given by the influential Standing Committee for National Parks chaired by Lord Birkett. In 1949 the National Parks and Access to the Countryside Act set up the National Parks Commission, charged with overseeing the designation of National Parks; between 1950 and 1957 ten were designated in England and Wales, their total area amounting to 9 per cent of the total surface area of the country. The Act did not relate to Scotland, where there has been reliance on other forms of scenic protection.

On the face of it, by the end of the 1950s, the countryside situation ought to have reassured sceptics that post-war initiatives in public policy were capable of addressing the needs and problems of the 1930s. Building in the countryside was now rigorously controlled; agriculture had been restored to prosperity and employment on the land had remained constant; National Parks had been designated in areas of finest landscape and the Commission had embarked on a programme of giving special protection to a reserve list—Areas of Outstanding Natural Beauty. Furthermore, the Nature Conservancy, set up in 1949, was acquiring National Nature Reserves and was designating large numbers of Sites of Special Scientific Interest. Local authorities, albeit somewhat laboriously, were preparing definitive maps of footpath networks, and the National Parks Commission had embarked on new footpath construction.

But situations do not stand still, nor do public attitudes to changing situations remain constant. In spite of all the public-sector achievements, the protection of scenic quality remained high on the countryside agenda. Post-war Britain had assumed that the state could be relied upon to be the guardian of amenity, but a number of high-profile, disquieting events suggested that no such reliance could be enjoyed. In the late 1950s, in the Pembroke National Park, an oil terminal was approved at Milford Haven to take advantage of deep-water harbour facilities. In Snowdonia approval was given to a nuclear power station at Trawsfynydd, complete with new balancing reservoir and striding pylons. In North York Moors, at Fylingdales, a ballistic missile early-warning station punctuated the open skyline. Elsewhere scenic amenity issues were mounting: conflict from potash mining, limestone quarrying, road improvements and holiday homes, all in areas supposedly of protection.

This anxiety continued, but during the 1960s the question of demand for outdoor recreation facilities assumed priority. From the mid-1950s, the last remnants of wartime austerity shed, Britain experienced growing affluence and increased leisure time (particularly in the form of the weekend). Additional disposal income supported significant rises in standards of living, the most remarkable advances perhaps being made in car ownership. In 1949 the number of cars on British roads had recovered to the 1939 figure—two million. By 1959 this figure had doubled to four million and by 1961 had trebled to six million. One and a quarter million new vehicles were being registered every year; the motor age with its potential for personal mobility had arrived.

There was a rapid increase in informal recreation in the countryside, based on the family, car-borne excursion; demand multiplied for picnic sites, lay-bys, car parks, access to beauty spots, and the opening up of water space. These changes prompted fears of a 'leisure revolution' about to break across the face of Britain, potentially more powerful than earlier incursions created by urbanization, the development of railways and the growth of suburbs (Dower 1965). The problem now was to absorb mass recreation into the countryside as a whole but particularly around the urban fringes; in the 1930s the problem had been much more confined to the right to roam in selected areas. The focus on National Parks was supplanted by the need for country parks, and the creation of 'honey pots' of activity seemed more important than measures for scenic protection.

1990s

Countryside concerns have reverted to protection of landscape and matters of scenic quality with a vengeance during the last twenty years. Questions of outdoor recreation certainly remain important. Participation rates in virtually every outdoor activity have increased: visits to stately homes, National Trust properties and sites of historic interest; also angling, field sports and boating, hiking, camping, caravanning and of course informal walking and the family outing by car. There is evidence in plenty that the recreation boom of the 1960s was no short-lived affair (Coppock and Duffield 1975; Patmore 1983). Today certain sites of visitor attraction may remain overcrowded, but by and large providers have coped well in meeting demands. Numbers have been absorbed remarkably satisfactorily and the problem no longer appears to be lack of facilities or range of choice (though the current demand for golf courses causes certain difficulties).

Instead, attention has switched markedly once more to landscape protection. The environmental debate is not new, but it has certainly taken a more popular embrace in recent decades. This cannot be the occasion to trace the world-wide steps in the growth of environmentalism as a late-twentieth-century ethic, but the movement in Britain is set in that international context. Three early books proved particularly influential both in professional circles and with voluntary interest groups: Robert Arvill's *Man and Environment* (1967), Max Nicholson's *The Environmental Revolution* (1970) and Barbara Ward and Rene Dubos' *Only One Earth* (1972). All emphasized the unity of the planet and Man's capacity to misuse or fail to control technology.

In respect of the British countryside attention soon centred on the performance of scientific agriculture. The Scott Report, we may recall, envisaged no conflict between a healthy and efficient agriculture and the conservation of agriculture and wildlife; indeed the country's traditional landscape pattern was seen to be derived from established (and broadly unchanging) farming practices. But this security proved to be ill-founded. British agriculture, far from being the guardian of inherited landscape, proved to be an unwelcome enemy.

New farm technology and the widespread application of chemical fertilizers made farming more productive than ever before and with less labour. But there was a cost, seen in the alien scale of agribusinesses, the rationalization of field boundaries which not only destroyed intimacy but was adverse to wildlife interests, the associated removal of hedgerows, ploughing up of marginal moorland, the drainage of wetlands and disruption of fragile habitats. Changed farming methods were proving capable of transforming traditional landscape, both upland and lowland. An early example was highlighted on Exmoor—a National Park designated to protect its open moorland skyline, but where reclamation by ploughing (action which did not require planning permission and could not be controlled by the National Park Authority without the special Moorland Conservation Orders then being proposed) was destroying the very qualities for which it had been acclaimed.

The perceived destruction of the English landscape by scientific farming practices provided a new cutting edge to powerful countryside lobbies. Marion Shoard (1980), one influential polemicist, wrote of 'the theft of the countryside'. Eulogizing a landscape of a 'patchwork quilt of fields, downs and woods, separated by thick hedgerows, mossy banks, sunken lanes and sparkling streams', she alleged that it was under sentence of death. 'The executioner is not the industrialist or the property speculator, whose activities have touched only the fringes of our countryside. Instead it is the figure traditionally viewed as the custodian of the rural scene—the farmer' (p.9).

In a dramatically changed situation, the countryside question was once again about the reconciliation of conflict. But whereas sixty years previously the issue had been about public access to private land for the purposes of mass recreation, in the last quarter of the century it has been about the farmers' rights to take advantage of technological change and pit them against a value stance which prizes the conservation of landscape heritage.

By the 1990s some of this fire had been drawn. Public policy has been redefined towards the farming industry and is no longer geared towards maximizing output or achieving greater efficiency. Diversified farm incomes are supported, land has been withdrawn from conventional production, land may be 'set aside' to resist adverse environmental impact and new farm woodlands may be created. Environmentally Sensitive Areas have been designated to protect particularly vulnerable areas such as grassland (as on the South Downs or in the Pennine Dales), grazing marsh (as in the Somerset Levels), or small-scale field systems (as in west Cornwall). Extra protection has been given to the Broads and the New Forest. Encouragement to woodland has been given through Community Forests and particularly the National Forest, proposed for Middle England between Charnwood and Needwood.

But the broad countryside sentiment remains, with the current pendulum of fashion strongly in favour of landscape and scenic protection and against any form of building development outside the urban envelope. Green belts are sacrosanct, even though they do not accord with the reality of the dispersed metropolitan city. Every mile of motorway or country bypass is bitterly fought. Urban spread is anathema; new village communities are simply trojan horses. Almost any form of development is seen as alien and intrusive. The guardians of amenity are now the special interest groups, lobbies for privilege, declared in the public interest. Sometimes the recreationists themselves fall victim to their objectives as with the demand for new golf courses and activities generally which intrude and impact adversely. We may well wonder what changes of attitude will take place in the next thirty years.

A final word

Four brief snapshots in time do not make a comprehensive canvas. But the markers are instructive for what is in fact a unified story—the urbanites' approach to and utilization of the countryside. One hundred years ago, when the mass invasion of the countryside was only just beginning, an elitist view favoured rural Britain (rural England in particular) as a retreat for the rediscovery of rural traditions, insulated from the philistinism of manufacturing industry and city life. Sixty years ago the preservation of scenic quality was all important, again middle-class led, but strongly influenced by the demands and aspirations of active recreationists. Thirty years ago landscape protection seemed less of an issue; more important was to meet the needs of a motorized, leisured society, still interested in the National Parks and the coast but seeking out facilities on a much broader geographical scale. Today, impelled by a dominant environmentalist ethic, landscape protection and resistance to forms of urban-inspired development are once again priority concerns. *Plus ça change, plus c'est la même chose.*

References

Abelson, E. (ed), 1939, *A Mirror of England: an Anthology of the Writings of H.J. Massingham (1888–1952)*, Bideford, Green Books, 1988. Extract: *A Countryman's Journal*, London, Chapman and Hall: 41–4.

Arvill, R., 1967, *Man and Environment*, Harmondsworth, Penguin.

Blatchford, R., 1894, *Merrie England*, London, Clarion.

Cherry, G. E., 1975, *Environmental Planning, Vol II, National Parks and Recreation in the Countryside*, London, HMSO.

Cherry, G. E. and Sheail J., 1993 forthcoming, *The Urban Impact on the Countryside*, Cambridge, Cambridge University Press.

Coppock, J.T. and Duffield, B.S., 1975, *Recreation in the Countryside*, London, Macmillan.

Cornish, V., 1937, *The Preservation of our Scenery*, Cambridge, Cambridge University Press.

Creasey, J. S. and Ward, Sadie B., 1984, *The Countryside between the Wars 1918–1940*, London, B.T. Batsford.

Dower J., 1945, *National Parks in England and Wales*, Ministry of Town and Country Planning, Cmd 6628, London, HMSO.

Dower, M., 1965, 'The Fourth Wave, the challenge of leisure', A Civic Trust Survey reprinted from the *Architects' Journal*, London, Civic Trust.

Hardy, D., and Ward, C., 1984, *Arcadia for All: the Legacy of a Makeshift Landscape*, London, Mansell.

Hobhouse, Sir Arthur, 1947, *Report of the National Parks Committee (England and Wales)*, Cmd 7121, London, HMSO.

Joad, C.E.M., 1945, *The Untutored Townsman's Invasion of the Country*, London, Faber and Faber.

Lowerson, J., 1980, 'Battles for the Countryside' in F. Gloversmith (ed.), *Class, Culture and Social Change*, Brighton, Harvester: 258–77.

Marsh, J., 1982, *Back to the Land: the Pastoral Impulse in Victorian England, from 1880 to 1914*, London, Quartet Books.

Nicholson, M., 1970, *The Environmental Revolution*, London, Hodder and Stoughton.

Patmore, J.A., 1983, *Recreation and Resources: Leisure Patterns and Leisure Places*, Oxford, Blackwell.

Ramsay, Sir Douglas J., 1945, *National Parks*, Cmd 6631, London, HMSO.

Ramsay, Sir Douglas J., 1947, *National Parks*, Cmd 7235, London, HMSO.

Report of the Committee on Land Utilisation in Rural Areas, 1942, Ministry of Works and Planning, Cmd 6378, London, HMSO.

Sharp, T., 1932, *Town and Countryside*, Oxford, Oxford University Press.

Sheail, J., 1975, 'The concept of National Parks in Great Britain 1900–1950', *Institute of British Geographers Transactions*, 66: 41–56.

Sheail, J., 1981, *Rural Conservation in Inter-war Britain*, Oxford, Clarendon Press.

Shoard, M., 1980, *The Theft of the Countryside*, London, Temple Smith.

Thomas, D., 1970, *London's Green Belt*, London, Faber and Faber.

Walton, J.K., 1983, *The English Seaside Resort*, Leicester, Leicester University Press.

Ward, B. and Dubos, R., 1972, *Only One Earth*, London, Andre Deutch.

Williams-Ellis, C., 1928, *England and the Octopus*, Penrhyndeudraeth, Portmeirion.

4

LANDSCAPES OF THE INDUSTRIAL REVOLUTION: MYTHS AND REALITIES

NEIL COSSONS

Britain emerged in the eighteenth century as the first industrial nation, in the nineteenth as 'workshop of the world'. This extraordinary period that we call the Industrial Revolution has left us with a landscape rich in the remains of early industrialization. It has also created in us an ambivalence that not only overwhelms our view of the past but colours contemporary attitudes to science, engineering and manufacture. The myth of an Arcadian, pre-industrial England pervades our culture; we value the past at the expense of the present, the countryside above the city. In contemplating a future for the historic landscapes of industrialization we have to penetrate the mythology and find a new and appropriate formula to secure their proper care and protection.

The cultural conventions that guide what the eye of the beholder accepts or reacts against are as important in determining our view of landscape as they are of painting or sculpture and never more so than in the value we place upon the landscapes of the Industrial Revolution. The moral crusade against industry and new concepts of amenity at the end of the nineteenth century and latterly the limitations of established aesthetic values and traditional scholarship, the sheer weight of historical determinism, have profoundly influenced the views most of us share of the material evidence of the first industrial society.

But while painters and sculptors have freed themselves from almost every constraint of convention, and achieved increasing public recognition and appreciation, the liberating forces of what the late Sir James Richards (1907–92) defined so eloquently as the functional tradition (Richards, 1958) and which reached their apogee in the industrial age before 1850, seem condemned, at least for the time being, to the shadows. At one social level the historical values of the National Trust prevail, at another the derivative recidivism of the Prince of Wales, Quinlan Terry or Robert Venturi, while for a mass audience there is always the neo-Georgian front door, with built-in fanlight, available off the peg; all emblems of the prosperity generated by industrial capitalism fossilized in an age of uncertainty.

But above all it was certainty that characterized the industrialization of eighteenth-century Britain. That certainty conspired with topography and technology to create extraordinary new landscapes that accorded with, and in part inspired, the newly emerging aesthetic discourse on the sublime and the picturesque. These scenes had a compelling attraction for artists, especially those influenced by the views of Burke, Gilpin and Price. Edmund Burke (1727–97) published his philosophies on the sublime first in 1757. In the 1790s Sir Uvedale Price (1747–1829) developed in detail the theories on the picturesque promoted initially by the Reverend William Gilpin (1724–1804), whose illustrated tours of Britain had been published in 1781. The new industrial landscapes provided ready-made raw material for their adherents.

Water power for the bellows of blast furnaces or the hammers of forges and, after 1770, for driving machinery in the new textile mills, brought industry to steep-sided and steeply graded stream and river valleys. These were essentially rural locations, providing settings at once dramatic and picturesque. Joseph Wright's (1734–97) painting of Arkwright's great cotton mill at Cromford catches the spirit of this early industrial period; so too does the George Robertson (1742–88) *View of the Iron Bridge* of 1788, one of a series of six, this one now extant only in the engraving by James Fittler (1758–1835) (Smith, 1979, p.29). But the single image that more than any other has become the archetypal descriptive of the rise of industrial Britain is Phillippe de Loutherbourg's (1740–1812) *Coalbrookdale by Night* of 1801 (Smith, 1979, p.46, see Plate 4.1), exploiting the topography of the Severn Gorge in Shropshire and combining the moonlit chiaroscuro effects of Joseph Wright and the brothers Pether with the dramatic intensity of the flames and molten metal of the pig bed. De Loutherbourg's skill as a theatre-scene painter, his understanding of the illusions of projected light—developed most notably for his *Eidophusikon*, a form of theatrical moving-picture show (Hyde, 1988)—qualified him uniquely to capture in Coalbrookdale the vivid exhilaration that was already attracting a growing tide of travellers and diarists —the first generation of industrial tourists.

Coalbrookdale was inevitably the target for their attention for here were being pioneered new technologies for making and using iron. In 1709 the Quaker ironmaster Abraham Darby (1668–1717) (Trinder, 1973) had successfully smelted iron using coke as a fuel. In the succeeding century the Coalbrookdale area became the scene of new applications for both cast and wrought iron; in the 1720s the first iron wheels, the first iron rails in 1767, and the first iron bridge in 1779 (Cossons and Trinder, 1979). The first iron boat was launched into the Severn here in 1788, and it was to the Coalbrookdale Company that Richard Trevithick (1771–1833) came in 1802 seeking their skills to assist with a steam railway locomotive, a concept he was to demonstrate successfully at Penydarren, south Wales in 1804.

But the optimism did not last. 'There was a palpable change in the mood of British intellectuals after 1798 . . .' (Klingender/Elton, 1968, p.109) coinciding with the rising debate around Malthus's *Essay on the Principle of Population*, published in that year, and reflecting a growing despondency, partly the result of political disillusionment, fuelled by the tyrannies of post-

Plate 4.1 Coalbrookdale by Night

Revolution France, but also 'a dissonance between the knowledge existing in society and the *economic* changes of the time . . .' (ibid., p.110). The self-confidence of the age of reason, the synergy between art and science of the eighteenth century, was wearing thin. This was not so much a reflection on the conduct of science or scientists as a growing belief that science was part of—perhaps even the engine of—a process of economic and social change, the evils of which were now becoming evident. Economic depression after the Napoleonic wars, the rise of Luddism and the machine-wrecking that went with it, the beginnings of a revolution in the use of child labour and, at least as important as all of these, a belief that the English countryside was being destroyed, created the feelings that led Wordsworth to lament:

Here a huge town, continuous and compact
Hiding the face of earth for leagues—and there,
Where not a habitation stood before,
Abodes of men irregularly massed
Like trees in forests—spread through spacious tracts,
O'er which the smoke of unremitting fires
Hangs permanent, and plentiful as wreathes
Of vapour glittering in the morning sun.

This pessimism, a despairing eulogy of the rural in the face of advancing industrialization and urbanization and the 'utilitarian and materialistic habit of mind these conditions represented' (Wiener, 1981, p.29) was at the heart of the literary confrontation between Southey and Macauley in the late 1820s. In denouncing the modern age the Poet Laureate was to be joined by whole generations of articulate advocates hostile to progress and, in particular, to industrial capitalism. Macaulay's was a lone voice in extolling the inevitability of material advance and against what he saw as nostalgic fantasy. Even the populist views of Samuel Smiles (1812–1904) in his *Lives of the Engineers*, portraying the Industrial Revolution as a great achievement of English history and lionizing engineers as 'the men above all . . . who made . . . the country what it is . . .' appeared increasingly anachronistic as the prevailing intellectual mood became unequivocally anti-capitalist. The disillusionment with the scientist of the early nineteenth century was to spread to the engineer before the beginning of the twentieth, both victims of attitudes that were essentially anti-industrial.

Moreover, the hardening of this view was taking place before the most visible and all-embracing period of the Industrial Revolution had ever begun. Southey's expression of anguish had been published in the *Edinburgh Review* in 1830, the year of the opening of the Liverpool & Manchester Railway, and as good a date as any to pinpoint as the beginning of the railway age. The railway was to cement all the disparate achievements of industrialization so far. It brought together town and country into mutual interdependence. Its arrival was invariably greeted with rejoicing. Among the great advances of nineteenth-century industrialization, it was to be readily assimilated into rural society and the landscape of the countryside. (See Plate 4.2). Although aesthetes abhorred its arrival, as they did the motorway a century later, once the scars of its construction had healed, the railway

Plate 4.2 Ribblehead Viaduct

became an integral part of the rural scene. The stationmaster, after the squire and the vicar, found a worthy place in the social hierarchy of the English village, and the country parson was to provide the metaphor for the gentleman railway enthusiast. A century later the demise of the railway was equally lamented.

Although most artists had by now turned their backs on industry—Turner's *Rain, Steam, Speed*, first exhibited in 1844, is the exception that proves the rule—the railway commanded at a less-esteemed level the meticulous documentary attention of John Cooke Bourne (1814–96), whose perceptive and intelligent views of the construction of the London & Birmingham Railway of 1839 and *The History and Description of the Great Western Railway* (1846), both published as folios of lithographs, 'reflect the jubilant self-confidence of the early railway age' (Klingender/Elton, 1968, p.152). Half a century later the Leicester photographer S.W.A. Newton (1875–1960) was to record with even greater diligence, and similar lack of contemporary recognition, the construction of the Great Central Railway's 'London Extension' from Nottinghamshire to Marylebone (Cossons 1963, Rolt 1971, Hartley 1992).

But the early railway period was also the age of political reform, of tough new Poor Laws and the revelations about public health and water supply of Edwin Chadwick. Soon Disraeli was to write of the two nations, Mrs Gaskell to contrast the south and the north—the landed gentry and the *nouveau riche*—and to stress the nobility of poverty and the plight of the labouring classes. Good housing and the creation of an '. . . ideological theme of intervention by authority in matters of private liberty for reasons of public good . . .' (Tarn, 1971, p.3) were progressively to dominate the nation's thinking.

And the uniting of Britain physically, which the railway had brought about, furthered those trends already recognized by Richard Guest in *A Compendious History of the Cotton Manufacture*, published in 1823. Guest drew a clear distinction between the scattered nature of domestic textile manufacture and its new factory-based industrial scale which he noted had '. . . introduced great changes into the manners and habits of the people. The operative workmen being thrown together in great numbers, had their faculties sharpened . . . and from being only a few degrees above their cattle in the scale of intellect, they became Political Citizens . . .'

Political awareness and progressive reform coupled with the growth of responsible local government were inevitable responses to the urbanization that was itself a consequence of industrialization. But these forces were not in themselves against industry. That was the province of the new professional classes which W.D. Rubinstein had described as 'profoundly anti-capitalist . . .'. of an educational establishment modelling itself on traditional public schools and in which there was a 'virtual absence of science of any sort in their curricula' (Wiener, 1981, pp.16–17) and a new and increasingly powerful intellectual elite who were to dominate the Civil Service and eventually subvert, by a process of gentrification, the entrepreneur class itself. What Walter Bagehot was to call 'the rough and vulgar structure of English commerce . . . the secret of its life' was to succumb to a 'counter revolution of values' (Weiner, 1981, p.27).

It took a German prince to see the crisis Britain was creating for herself by turning her back on industry. But the Great Exhibition of 1851, Albert's vision of at once celebrating industrial enterprise and stimulating a cultural and educational investment in it, represented an end rather than a beginning. It may have marked the zenith of the 'workshop of the world' but it was also something of a valediction. Before the decade was out John Ruskin's nightmare of the twentieth century, published in *The Two Paths* in 1859, presented a view to which the new establishment of the bourgeoisie was to subscribe in increasing numbers:

The whole of the island . . . set as thick with chimneys as the masts stand in the docks of Liverpool; that there shall be no meadows in it, no trees; no gardens; only a little corn grown upon the house tops, reaped and thrashed by steam; that you do not even have room for roads, but travel either over the roofs of your mills, on viaducts; or under their floors, in tunnels; that, the smoke having rendered the light of the sun unserviceable, you work always by the light of your own gas; that no acre of English ground shall be without its shaft and its engine . . .

As the nineteenth century progressed English cultural life and intellectual attitudes came to be dominated by a belief in the perfection and tranquillity of a rural, medieval and essentially gothic tradition. The past and the countryside became synonymous, invested with a romantic aura of the rosy-cheeked peasants of Merrie England, hollyhocks at the doors of their thatched cottages, on the one hand, and on the other the lord of the manor secure in his timeless position of benign power and patronage. It was easy to create a new mythology of the countryside in a nation that had undergone such radical economic and social change. England, uniquely in Europe, had lost much of her rural way of life. The prevailing folk culture was of the new industrial working class. Memories of squalor and poverty in the pre-enclosure countryside had been lost, leaving the way open to play out an elegy to a rural nation that had never existed. A century later Robert Hewison and other critics of the heritage movement were to make similar observations on the nostalgia that pervaded much of our view of vanished nineteenth-century industry (Hewison, 1987; Fowler, 1992).

From their various standpoints, John Ruskin and William Morris, Thomas Hardy and Richard Jeffries, Norman Shaw and C.F.A. Voysey defined 'Englishness'. Industrialization had no place in their vision. In *News from Nowhere*, published in 1890, William Morris 'dreams of a future golden age in which a medieval society has returned to England and where human sensibilities . . . are allowed free play in a communist society liberated from the restrictions of urban capitalist living' (Rich, 1990, p.216). His vision of an England based on small towns and villages where 'the difference between town and country grew less and less' comes almost exactly a century before the Prince of Wales was to express similar views.

And yet whole tracts of the countryside 'where time stands still' were themselves quite new, a product of the forces of economic change that had led to enclosures and the revolution in agriculture. The Midlands village might trace its origins back to the Saxons, but its surrounding patchwork of fields and hedgerows was less than fifty years old when the first railways came through. By the same token the museums of rural life that scatter the country today are full of the products of Birmingham and Black Country industry, rarely the results of the thousand-year tradition of rural craftsmanship. Even Tess of the d'Urbervilles had been reduced to serving the 'red tyrant'—the steam powered threshing machine—before her symbolic sacrifice at Stonehenge.

The creators of this mythic image of Arcadian England also laid the foundations for its preservation. The Society for the Protection of Ancient Buildings (SPAB), founded in 1877, set the tone, pillorying the new and those who over-restored the old. Material prosperity was itself a menace as it allowed greater opportunity to tear down old buildings. For the first time the values of the past were to be elevated over those of the present. The National Trust, set up almost twenty years later, had more progressive aspirations, reflecting in part the ideals of the newly emergent amenity movement. It began by preserving open spaces by ownership, only later taking on historic buildings and the numerous 'stately homes' by which it is today best known. Its current portfolio of properties vividly encapsulates, and its policies still perpetuate, the convergence of socialist anti-materialism and patrician Tory beliefs in rural values that have been the hallmark of countryside preservation for over a century.

Attitudes in cities changed more rapidly. In the last two decades of the nineteenth century the agricultural labour force declined by 30 per cent, continuing a trend that had begun over a century earlier. The proportion of the population living in towns and cities rose from 60 to 77 per cent. Britain had become an urban nation, its popular culture stemming more from the city terrace or street corner pub than from farm or village. The Health Acts of 1848 and 1875 and the first housing legislation (the Artisans' and Labourers' Dwellings Act, 1868 and the Labourers' Dwellings Improvement Act, 1875) set the scene for improvements of a more radical and interventionist nature, the 'spatial separation of the good and bad in the urban environment' (Smith, 1974, p.16) leading to the 'bold assumption that the clue to the salvation of the city lay in the proper development of sylvan and genteel suburbs within which town and country benefits were to be evenly mixed, where there would be neither "the noise and dirt of the crowded metropolis; nor the rustic feudalism" of rural life. This view seemed to accept that beauty could not be achieved in the city but that where rural charms could be intermixed with urban necessities, some enhancement of the man-made environment was obtainable' (Smith, 1974, p.17). Urban transport in the form of the suburban railway, and more importantly outside London the street tram, made this new form of city living possible. Arguably it accentuated still further the feelings of alienation that the population at large felt towards industry, which was increasingly seen as inherently distasteful and standing discrete from the progressively improving quality of living space.

Paradoxically, it has been the ultimate manifestation of that planning dream, of white towers in green parks, that has become the focus for contemporary discontent with urban environments. We demolish these towers; the houses that replace them bear striking visual similarities to their Victorian predecessors. Some even attempt to recreate in their brick-built terraces a sort of latter day Coronation Street sub-culture, evoking nostalgic views of a recently disappeared community spirit. Historical precedent suggests we may assume that the tower blocks of the 1960s will eventually command affection too for in 1839 the *Penny Magazine* stated: 'There is still . . . a woeful perversion of what is called taste exhibited in the villas or cottages which surround the metropolis and fill its suburbs . . . the vicinities of Bayswater, Maida Hill, Hampstead, Islington, Hackney, Camberwell and other suburban districts are like so many multiplying glasses, in which, wheresoever we direct our attention, we discover objects similar in form, size, colour and unornamental plainness.' And in 1901 *Darlington's Handbook of London* noted that: 'Respectable or middle class London . . . represents a relatively enormous section of the community—comprising long, dreary, semi-suburban streets . . . rows and rows of dull little houses and shops, all equally depressing and exactly like each other.'

But changes in attitude towards Industrial Revolution landscapes have been slower and more complex. Over a period of a century or so they have seen sequentially the first moves towards the museum preservation of important engineering artifacts, the recognition that the Industrial Revolution had an archaeology, and the beginnings of efforts to record and preserve its material evidence, the development of a new sub-species of open-air museum within which to preserve not only buildings and objects but also processes, *in situ* preservation and interpretation, and a realization that surviving industrial buildings and landscapes offered opportunities for adaptive re-use—that they had asset value because of their aesthetic qualities.

The first serious and systematic attempt to immortalize the engineering heroes of the Industrial Revolution, by preserving examples of their work, was through the establishment of the Patent Museum by Bennet Woodcroft (1803–79), appointed Assistant to the Commissioners of Patents in 1852. Without any official mandate this relentless collector was able to secure such seminal objects as William Hedley's *Puffing Billy* of 1813, the oldest surviving steam railway locomotive, the Stephenson's *Rocket* of 1829 and Timothy Hackworth's *Sans Pareil*, one of its rivals at the Rainhill trials on the Liverpool & Manchester Railway. Woodcroft also traced and saved Symington's marine engine and in 1864 arranged for James Watt's home workshop to be collected (Hewish, 1979).

These objects were to be transferred in 1884 to the South Kensington Museum which had opened in 1857 on land purchased with profits from the Great Exhibition. The museum was to divide at the end of the nineteenth century into the Victoria & Albert and Science Museums, a further example of contemporary attitudes to art and science, and a stinging denial of Albert's vision of art and industry united. Half a century later C.P. Snow (1905–80) was to define what he regarded as a widespread and debilitating cultural phenomenon—'the two cultures'. Meanwhile Woodcroft's collection has become the core of the Science Museum's outstanding holdings in the fields of science, technology and medicine, the largest and most comprehensive of their kind in the world. These collections transcend the national context. They represent the material evidence of the emergence of modern scientific and industrial Man, the birth of the first industrial nation.

Other museums of industry, notably in Newcastle-upon-Tyne and Birmingham, and later in Manchester, also built up collections, pursuing traditional policies of acquisition and presentation pioneered in pre-existing museums of archaeology and history. But after the Second World War there was growing recognition that something should be done to record and preserve the outstanding landscape remains of industrialization. Legislation existed under the Ancient Monuments and Planning Acts respectively to Schedule and List important structures and buildings. It had already been used on occasion for industrial structures—the celebrated Iron Bridge in Shropshire, for example, had been scheduled as early as 1934.

But it was not until the 1960s that industrial archaeology was to emerge (Rix, 1955) in response to the accelerating pace of industrial and urban renewal. It was initially very much a popular movement, outside the mainstream of conventional and well-established archaeology and without an academic infrastructure. It had some support from economic historians and historians of technology, and from museums (the then Director of the Science Museum for example, Sir David Follett (1907–82), was a staunch advocate of the need to preserve evidence of industrialization), but much of the activity derived, as it had in the late nineteenth century, through the work of local antiquarian and archaeological societies, from amateurs grouped broadly into those engaged in survey and recording, and others—there is little overlap—primarily concerned with preservation. Regional studies were published (Green, 1963; Buchanan and Cossons, 1969; McCutcheon, 1980), but there has never been a systematic national survey of the industrial archaeology of the British Isles nor is there any agency dedicated specifically to this work to match the achievements of the Historic American Engineering Record in the United States. On the other hand, the respective Royal Commissions on historical monuments, in England, Wales and especially Scotland, have accumulated and occasionally published (Hay and Stell, 1986) significant photographic and survey archives.

The foundations for the wider-spread interest in industrial archaeology had already been laid in numerous unconnected initiatives. The Wind and Watermills Section of the Society for the Protection of Ancient Buildings, for example, extended the interests of the Society into this specialist but predominantly rural and pre-industrial area of preservation. The Newcomen Society for the Study of the History of Engineering and Technology, founded in 1919 as a result of the James Watt centenary celebrations, has also built up a significant record of research and publication, mostly devoted to the Industrial Revolution period. A further and significant influence was the work of Francis Klingender (1906–55) who in 1947 published *Art and the Industrial Revolution*, the first comprehensive perspective on how artists perceived the processes of industrialization taking place around them. But it was the editing and substantial rewriting of Klingender's work by Sir Arthur Elton (1906–73), including new illustrations from Elton's own outstanding collection (now in the Ironbridge Gorge Museum) that was to reveal its full contribution to Industrial Revolution studies (Klingender/Elton, 1968). And the engineering biographies of L.T.C. Rolt (1910–74) were to bring names like Telford, the Stephensons and Brunel into the informed popular consciousness.

New types of museums were set up, too, designed to meet the intractable problems of preserving not just the moveable plant of industrialization but the buildings that housed it and its social and economic context. Open-air museums were and still are rare in Britain. Largely because industrialization had become established so early, the study of folk culture—of pre-industrial rural societies and in particular the material evidence of their history—had not developed to anything like the extent in the rest of northern Europe. Consequently the open-air folk museum model established at Skansen near Stockholm by Artur Hazelius (1833–1901) and widely repeated across Europe from Scandinavia to the Black Sea in response to the profound changes resulting from industrialization, urbanization and associated rural depopulation and mass emigration was unknown in England. Only in Wales did a rural tradition, reinforced by the powerful stimulus of a language under threat, lead to the setting up of an open air museum on the Scandinavian model; the Welsh Folk Museum at St Fagans inspired by Iorwerth Peate (1901–82) and opened in 1948 remains the only fully developed example in Britain. The Ulster Folk Museum in Northern Ireland is another.

The industrial open-air museum in Britain, however, owes as much to North American influences as it does to the European folk tradition, attempting not simply to preserve individual buildings but also to recreate, through the juxtaposition of their reconstruction, some sense of the disappearing industrial community from which they had been drawn. It is a persuasive formula, and although widely scorned in the 1970s by the advocates of building conservation, as a *genre* it seems to have found its place as a legitimate means of making industrial history and archaeology popular and accessible. The Black Country Museum and the North of England Open Air Museum at Beamish in County Durham are the most notable examples, together with Blists Hill Open Air Museum at Ironbridge.

But Blists Hill is only one component of a different type of preservation project. The Ironbridge Gorge Museum was set up in 1967 to preserve *in situ* the remains of industrialization in the three-mile section of the Severn Gorge in Shropshire, including the pioneer industrial communities of Coalbrookdale, Ironbridge and Coalport as well as the Iron Bridge itself. Only buildings that cannot be preserved where they stand—most of them from the area of the old East Shropshire Coalfield to the north—are dismantled and reconstructed at Blists Hill. But the primary purpose of the open-air museum is to preserve in operation industrial processes of which the most ambitious are a foundry and an ironworks where wrought-iron is made using puddling furnaces, a steam hammer and steam-powered rolling mill.

The preservation of industrial sites and buildings, and their contents, *in situ*, and on occasion in some form of operation, has expanded rapidly since the 1960s, initially in response to the threat posed by post-war modernization, more recently in the face of large-scale de-industrialization and the virtual elimination of many traditional coal, iron and steam-based industries.

In the absence of initiatives by public authorities charged with protecting and managing sites and monuments, industrial archaeological preservation has in the main been taken up by preservation societies, based on dedicated groups of amateurs raising capital by appeal and who maintain and operate by voluntary methods what in other circumstances would be seen as the natural responsibility of the state. Neither the National Trust nor the Historic Buildings and Monuments Commission (English Heritage) manage—through ownership or guardianship like Listing and Scheduling—more than a handful of industrial sites, although there has been an increasing willingness to see government capital grants go towards the preservation by others of industrial monuments and buildings. As a result the largest part of the archaeology of the Industrial Revolution period—the material evidence of the first industrial nation—is held in the non-statutory sector, in contrast to the remains of all previous cultures. This is unlikely to change. Only in exceptional circumstances is Guardianship now regarded as an option, and as English Heritage is unlikely to shed existing commitments—in order to balance its property portfolio, so to speak—other mechanisms must be found to afford industrial sites the equivalent quality of protection. The recent move to preserve Queen Street Mill, Burnley, the last steam-powered textile mill in Britain, is therefore encouraging. Capital funds from English Heritage, the National Heritage Memorial Fund and the Science Museum's Fund for the Preservation of Industrial and Scientific Material have encouraged Lancashire County Council and Burnley Borough Council to come together in order to manage the mill and present it to the public. Whether some form of manufacturing can be continued in order to demonstrate the machinery and generate revenue from the sale of cloth is still open to question.

But, in the main, industrial sites and monuments do not enjoy the guarantees of inalienability that public-sector funding and management have traditionally afforded. Although the monuments of the Ironbridge Gorge now have the benefit of a capital endowment from the Department of the Environment, the longer-term future of Cromford or New Lanark remains less certain. The pumping stations at Crofton and Claverton on the Kennet and Avon Canal; the 1787 Elsecar engine near Barnsley—the oldest steam engine in the world still *in situ*; Temple Meads station, Bristol; the Ditherington flax mill, Shrewsbury—the world's first iron-framed building; the great mill complexes of Saltaire and Manningham are industrial sites of more than national significance. The obligation to ensure their future survival and well-being is immutable.

Only in the sense that many industrial buildings often afford opportunities for re-use are there more imaginative, and fundable, opportunities for conservation. The adaptive re-use of redundant buildings for new purposes, which on a small scale has always been part of the normal process of urban renewal, has since the 1960s become a major force in conservation, generating its own architectural styles and clichés. Old industrial buildings in particular have benefited and on occasion suffered at the hands of conservation architects. This movement—for such it has become—has its origins in the United States where between 1964 and 1968 some $12 million was spent on the purchase and conversion of the Ghirardelli chocolate factory in San Francisco into a retail complex (Diamonstein, 1978). Nearby waterfront ice houses were re-developed as showrooms and offices. San Francisco was to provide the inspiration for innumerable developments of a similar kind, re-cycling old

Plate 4.3 Ditherington Flax Mill

industrial buildings as attractive alternatives to new construction, revitaliz-
ing decaying downtown areas and restoring confidence in the future of
urban living. The formerly most unattractive quarters of many nineteenth-
century industrial cities took on a new and glamorous style. 'Warehouse culture' is now a worldwide fashion, as visible in London's docklands as in
Boston or Minneapolis. In Massachusetts the future of the great decaying
textile town of Lowell has been predicated on the rehabilitation of mills for
new commercial and even manufacturing uses. In the United States too
there was positive encouragement, through the 1976 Tax Reform Act, for
example, to make the rehabilitation of historic buildings competitive with
new construction and to discourage their demolition (Thomas, 1978).

Waterfronts too are now sought after, although not all owe their success to
the recycling of old buildings. The Inner Harbour in Baltimore has converted a
decayed waterfront into new retail and leisure developments. Its offspring
can be seen throughout the world. Its green roofs have been translated to
Darling Harbour, Sydney and Meadowhall, Sheffield. But in Bristol, with
Bush's 1837 tea bond—now a gallery and offices—and in Liverpool with the
Albert Dock warehouse complex, the newly perceived aesthetic qualities of
nineteenth-century warehouses, their proximity to reasonably wholesome
water, and the opportunity to have historic ships coming and going, have
provided an immensely attractive formula for rehabilitation. Albert Dock,
described in 1875 by J.A. Picton in his *Memorials of Liverpool* as 'a hideous
pile of naked brickwork' is now seen as a model for a new kind of future
based on recycling the old (see Plate 4.4). Indeed, the eye has been so
deflected by the elegant and simple rhythm of old brick buildings newly
cleaned, their minimalist interiors and seductive adaptability, that a new
architectural style has been created. Today perhaps one of the greatest
threats to the rehabilitation of nineteenth-century warehouses arises from
the fact that it is now easier to build a new one from scratch which can have
all the qualities of the old but none of its problems (see Plate 4.5).

All this has taken place in a period when attitudes not only to the past but,
at least as important, opportunities for access to it have been revolutionized.
In the 1960s the word 'Victorian' changed, almost overnight, from being a
pejorative to the descriptive of a golden age characterized by quality, craftsmanship, confidence and certainty. 'By the 1980s Victorian values were
being heralded as the historical justification for an enterprise culture
designed to replace the collapse of confidence in many aspects of post-war
society. This use or misuse of history for political polemic, the replacement
of guilt about the past with a recognition of its virtues' (Cossons, 1991, p.22)
flies in the face of the long-established propaganda of the intelligentsia that
from the second half of the nineteenth century had despised and demeaned
industrial capitalism. The 'declinist' views of Wiener and, more recently,
Correlli Barnett (Barnett, 1986) have been challenged too (Edgerton, 1991).

At the same time a new, mobile and relatively affluent audience for the
past was growing up. Untainted by old hostilities towards industrialization,
and unfamiliar with traditional antiquarian values, this new public 'pays
eagerly at the gate to see the working lives of their grandparents brought to
life. And the great-grandchildren of those elitists who so skilfully castrated

Plate 4.4 Albert Dock

Plate 4.5 Green Park Station

industry in the late nineteenth century are now turning their attention to the new ogre of commerce—tourism—fearful that its economic success may swamp their cultural enclaves with hordes of customers' (Cossons, 1991, p.23). Only in its death throes has the Industrial Revolution come to gain popular acceptability. But the very popularity of what has come to be called heritage tourism is seen by a new generation of intellectuals to be culturally threatening. It has become fashionable to denigrate 'heritage', to condemn tourism and the pressures that the new leisured classes place upon the landscape.

Heritage itself and in particular its place in the new leisure revolution, and its perceived qualities of populist values and commercial management are now the subject of cultural comment (Lowenthal, 1985). Some of this is overtly critical but fails to offer a constructive alternative view on how preservation can be reconciled with the almost insatiable demands for public access (Wright, 1985; Hewison, 1987; Fowler, 1992). There are startling similarities in tone, if not in elegance of expression, between those who today confound heritage and the critics of industrialization a century and a half ago.

It is a paradox that industrial sites, the preserved remains of what a previous generation despised, should now, in the hour of their salvation, attract the opprobrium of those who see them as the source of a new commercial plague—symbols of a new form of invasive commercialism. And for those whose business is the preservation and interpretation of industrial sites there are real dilemmas. The essential archaeological and historical imperative is that the nation's most important remains of the Industrial Revolution should be protected and interpreted in a responsible manner, based on sound scholarship, and to intellectual and technical standards already widely accepted elsewhere. These remains must also be free from undue market pressures that leave them vulnerable to short-term fluctuations in demand and income and have led some of the less well run to dilute their conservation and interpretative standards in the interest of attracting large numbers of visitors. This implies some form of proper regulation backed by funds—which need not be large—sufficient to make the difference between the standards of the best and those of the indifferent.

Only English Heritage has the authority to wield both stick and carrot in pursuit of a responsible national policy. A useful partner could be the Science Museum, whose Fund for the Preservation of Industrial and Scientific Material, which in the past has been primarily devoted to acquisition, is now increasingly directed towards the conservation needs of historic machinery. To develop that policy and, in particular, to follow through its implications in conservation and management terms requires a solid academic and scholarly infrastructure. A free-standing university department of industrial archaeology, with undergraduate courses and postgraduate programmes—some of them vocational—would help to achieve this. The demand for people is undoubtedly there.

And any policy must be based on a full archaeological analysis of need to ensure a seamless response embracing recording, preservation (in the monument or museum sense), and proper control of the adaptive re-use process. New uses must enhance rather than degrade the historical qualities of

Plate 4.6 Coppull. Lancashire

redundant industrial buildings (see Plate 4.6). Inevitably much of the operation and management will continue to rest in the non-statutory, non-profit sector where some form of wider national co-ordination—outside English Heritage itself—may be necessary. Perhaps a National Trust for Industrial Archaeology is needed.

The utmost care and sensitivity will be required if public, and therefore political, opinion—which is currently supportive—can be maintained. Places of work converted into places of education or pleasure evoke uncomfortable feelings of guilt. The Industrial Revolution has left us not only with an outstanding physical legacy in terms of the remains themselves but also a persistent cultural ambivalence which shows little sign of ebbing away. What is essential, however, is that our successors in a thousand years' time will have the opportunity to see and understand the origins of world industrialization and to appreciate through the surviving evidence around them the extraordinary achievements, the economic benefits, and the social consequences of the birth of the first industrial nation.

References

Barnett, C., 1986, *The Audit of War: the Illusion and Reality of Britain as a Great Nation*, London, Macmillan.

Buchanan, R.A., and Cossons, N., 1969, *Industrial Archaeology of the Bristol region*, Newton Abbot, David and Charles.

Cossons, N., 1963, *Contractors Locomotives GCR*, Leicester, Leicester City Museums.

Cossons, N., 1991, 'Class, Culture and Collections' in G. Kavanagh, (ed.), *The Museums Profession: Internal and External Relations*, Ch. 2, Leicester, Leicester University Press, pp. 13–24.

Cossons, N. and Trinder, B.S., 1979, *The Iron Bridge: Symbol of the Industrial Revolution*, Bath, Moonraker.

Diamonstein, B., 1978, *Buildings Reborn: New Uses, Old Places*, New York, Harper & Row.

Edgerton, D., 1991, 'The prophet militant and industrial: the peculiarities of Correlli Barnett', *Twentieth Century British History*, **2**, 3: 360–79.

Fowler, P.J., 1992, *The Past in Contemporary Society: Then, Now*, London, Routledge.

Green, E.R.R., 1963, *The Industrial Archaeology of County Down*, Belfast, HMSO.

Hartley, R.F., 1992, 'S.W.A. Newton and the Building of the Great Central Railway', *Forward, the Journal of the Great Central Railway Society*, **85**, January 1992: 8–13 and **86**, March 1992,: 7–14 (this journal is available in the library of the National Railway Museum, York).

Hay, G. and Stell, G.P., 1986, *Monuments of Industry: an Illustrated Historical Record*, Edinburgh, Royal Commission on the Archaeology and Historic Monuments of Scotland.

Hewish, J., 1979, *The Indefatigable Mr. Woodcroft: the Legacy of Invention*, London, British Library/Science Reference Library.

Hewison, R., 1987, *The Heritage Industry: Britain in a Climate of Decline*, London, Methuen.

Hyde, R., 1988, *Panoramania!*, London, Trefoil, in association with the Barbican Art Gallery.

Klingender, F. (edited and revised by Elton, A.), 1968, *Art and the Industrial Revolution*, Bath, Evelyn, Adams & Mackay.

Lowenthal, D., 1985, *The Past is a Foreign Country*, London, Cambridge University Press.

McCutcheon, W.A., 1980, *The Industrial Archaeology of Northern Ireland*, Belfast, HMSO.

Rich, P., 1990, 'The Quest for Englishness', in G. Marsden (ed.), *Victorian Values*, Ch. 17, pp.211–25, London, Longman.

Richards, J.M., 1958, *The Functional Tradition in Early Industrial Buildings*, London, Architectural Press.

Rix, M.M., 1955, 'Industrial Archaeology', *The Amateur Historian*, **2**, 8: 225–9.

Rolt, L.T.C., 1971, *The Making of a Railway*, London, Hugh Evelyn.

Smith, D.L., 1974, *Amenity and Urban Planning*, London, Granada.

Smith, S.B., 1979, *A View from the Iron Bridge*, Ironbridge, Ironbridge Gorge Museum Trust.

Tarn, J.N., 1971, *Working Class Housing in 19th Century Britain*, Lund Humphries for the Architectural Association (Paper No. 7), London.

Thomas, S., 1978, *Rehabilitation: an Alternative for Historical Industrial Buildings*, Historic American Engineering Record, Washington DC, US Department of the Interior.

Trinder, B.S., 1973, (2nd edition 1981), *The Industrial Revolution in Shropshire*, London, Phillimore.

Wiener, M.J., 1981, *English Culture and the Decline of the Industrial Spirit, 1850–1980*, London, Cambridge University Press.

Wright, P., 1985, *On living in a Foreign Country: the National Past in Contemporary Britain*, London, Vero.

5

THE COUNTRYSIDE AS COMMODITY: NEW RURAL SPACES FOR LEISURE

PAUL CLOKE

Introduction

This chapter outlines some ideas about the changing nature of 'rural' space and stresses the importance of understanding the social and cultural constructs of rurality which are attached to recognizing, valuing and using that space. Although the illustrations used relate to the production, consumption and reproduction of specific rural spaces for people engaged in tourism, recreation and leisure, the underlying arguments and issues are equally applicable, I believe, to people wishing to 'buy into' a rural lifestyle either in terms of residential status or the display of specific commodities in their homes via their clothes, furnishings, and many other symbolic ways. My starting point is that our understanding of rural change may be as dependent on recognizing symbolic constructions and reconstructions of rural spaces as on the more material construction or reconstruction of sites, facilities and opportunities.

Such an acknowledgement, of course, is not novel. The heightened awareness of the importance of *cultural* arenas in the countryside is drawn both from the changing relations between society and space in contemporary times and from the recently changing nature of social scientific study. Definitions of the 'rural' have shifted accordingly. Traditionally, rural spaces have been defined in terms of specific rural functions. Rurality was thus closely associated with extensive, usually agricultural, landscapes and sparsely populated settlement patterns, and rural space could be defined in relation to remoteness, peripherality and dependence upon 'rural' economic functions. As pointed out elsewhere (Cloke and Park, 1985), such definitions are still held to be applicable in many nations where rural spaces so defined have been less subject to the economic restructuring and social recomposition associated with urbanization, suburbanization and counterurbanization. Others, however, began to challenge the notion of functional discreteness for rural areas (see Hoggart, 1990). Adopting concepts from political economy approaches in urban and regional social science, the changes occurring in rural space were seen by many researchers as being inextricably linked to the wider dynamics of the national and international political economy. In this context the definition of rural space is rather more problematic, as 'rural' people are recognized to be culturally urban, and changes in the countryside are seen to respond to political and economic decisions and signals which often emanate from well outside the area concerned. With these political economy approaches, 'rural' has sometimes been conflated with 'agricultural' (suggesting that this is still 'safe' rural territory) and the wider label of rural space has been used in a rather pragmatic manner (Cloke, 1989a).

Alongside these changes of approach to the study of rural space, the nature of the relationship between society and space outside of cities has also changed. Mormont (1990) identified five aspects of such change:

(i) increased mobility of people, goods and messages has eroded the autonomy of local communities;
(ii) delocalization of economic activity makes it impossible to define homogeneous economic regions;
(iii) new specialized uses of rural spaces (as tourist sites, parks, development zones etc.) have created new specialized networks of relationships in the areas concerned, many of which are no longer localized;
(iv) people who 'inhabit' a given rural area include a diversity of temporary visitors as well as residents;
(v) rural spaces increasingly perform functions for non-rural users and in these cases can be 'characterized by the fact that they exist independently of the action of rural populations' (p.31).

Mormont concludes that we should no longer think of a single type of rural space but rather recognize a multiplicity of social spaces overlapping in geographical area. Each social space has 'its own logic, its own institutions, as well as its own network of actors—users, administrators etc.—which are specific and not local' (p.34).

The question of defining rurality, therefore, becomes one of ascertaining how occupants (permanent or temporary) of rural spaces construct themselves as 'rural'. This partly represents a recirculation of ideas from the 1970s suggesting that a place is what it is perceived to be. Thus Moss (1978) suggested that 'the village can be described as a place where the countryside meets the town and where distinction between rural and urban lies very much in the eye of the beholder' (p.101), and Thorburn (1971) defined a village as 'any place which most residents think of as a village' (p.2).

Mormont's discussion, though, points to more than perception. Rurality is viewed as a social construct, and 'rural' thereby becomes a world of social, moral and cultural values in which the occupiers of rural space participate. Behaviours and decisions will thus be influenced by the social constructs which indicate that a place or space is rural, and these constructs in turn will be closely linked with the *cultural* arena, which, as Jackson (1989) claims, is best approached 'in terms of the processes through which meanings are constructed, negotiated and experienced' (p.180).

Our understanding, then, of the changing nature and use of rural space, for leisure as for other uses, will greatly be enhanced by examining processes by which the meaning of 'rural' is constructed, negotiated and experienced.

Commodification and rural spaces

In a recent review of countryside change during the Thatcher era (Cloke, 1992), I have outlined a significant shift in the nature and pace of commodification in rural Britain giving rise to a series of new markets for countryside commodities:

the countryside as an exclusive place to be lived in; rural communities as a context to be bought and sold; rural lifestyles which can be colonized; icons of rural culture which can be crafted, packed and marketed; rural landscapes with a new range of potential from 'pay-as-you-enter' national parks, to sites for the theme park explosion; rural production ranging from newly commodified food to the output of industrial plants whose potential or actual pollutive externalities have driven them from more urban localities. [p.293]

Some characteristics of production and consumption associated with the commodification of rural spaces are discussed below. First, however, it is appropriate to examine the concept of commodification itself, for here too there are changes to be recognized in the material exploitation of resources available in rural areas and also important differences in the ways in which the study of commodification has sought to balance the understanding of the material and imagined worlds of political economy and culture.

An excellent review of these differences is that of Best (1989) who traces the conceptualization of commodification through the work of Karl Marx, Guy Debord and Jean Baudrillard. For Marx (1978), commodification represented an inversion of exchange value over use value. An object thus becomes a commodity when it assumes an exchange value over and above its use value; the exchange value both allows that object to be traded and allows a quantitative value to be placed on the object even though it may be qualitatively unique. In this way commodification denotes an abstraction of the object from its use value and therefore from social references about the need for the object and the quality of it. In Best's words:

Once object exchange has been abstracted from sensuous needs and qualities, from any social referent (the referent has become uprooted, privatized, fragmented among competing private interests), once it extends beyond the factories to penetrate all cultural and interpersonal relations, it has a profound corruptive and distorting effect. The inversion that occurs in the economy, and which affects the whole of social life, is then directly transferred to the cultural and personal realm *where commodity fantasy begins.* [p.27]

Here then is a directly relevant link between commodity and culture, in what Marx saw as the exploitative corrupting and distorting effects of the social and cultural constructions of the value of commodity (Best terms this *the society of the commodity*).

The same idea is translated into the situation of late capitalist economy and society by (among others) Debord (1983), who saw social control as being based on consensus rather than force. Such consensus was achieved through a cultural hegemony realized through the transformation of the society of the commodity into the *society of the spectacle*. Here, people are led to consume a world which is constructed by others and not themselves and which consists of a series of spectacles designed to pacify and depoliticize. Such a society still deals in commodities, but production is seen as being reorganized at a higher and more abstract level with the object of maintaining non-evolutionary consensus: 'The spectacular society spreads its narcotics through the cultural mechanisms of leisure and consumption, services and entertainment, within a culture that has grown (relatively) autonomous from the social totality' (Best, 1989, p.29).

Such a view suggests that contemporary society is mainly geared towards the production of spectacle, and social and cultural constructs of commodity (including the 'rural' or the countryside) should be seen in that light; it suggests that commodification has been extended into previously uncommodified areas of social life; and perhaps most importantly, it suggests that commodification for spectacle is explicitly concerned with the production of illusive and artificial counterfeits of real objects and relations. Best then proceeds to use the work of Baudrillard (1983a; 1983b) to suggest a third stage in understanding how reality is commodified.

With Baudrillard, we move to a whole new era of social development . . . We leave behind the society of the commodity and its stable supports; transcend the society of the spectacle and its dissembling masks; and enter the society of the simulacrum, an abstract non-society devoid of cohesive relations, social meaning, and collective representations, an imploded socius of signs. [p.33]

This *society of the simulacrum* forms part of Baudrillard's description of post-modernity in which he theorizes a cybernetic society based on consumption and information technology. In such a society, exchange is carried out at the level of signs, images and information, and commodification is not just the selling of an object in terms of its image and spectacle, it is in an abstract sense the absorption of the object into the image so as to allow exchange to take place in semiotic form. Society is thus full of 'sign-exchange values', and the development of commodities is principally to do with the structural logic of the signs concerned, with the production and consumption of the commodities centering on the conspicuous nature of their social meanings. Production and consumption are thereby converted into a system of abstract signifiers which are not constrained by any necessary relationship with objects and can therefore float into other meanings via processes of manipulation (for example by advertising) which code associations and differences in semiotic chains. Thus, for Baudrillard, the commodity is eclipsed by the sign which can be unrelated to reality altogether.

This brief and oversimplified summary of these vast literatures serves at least to demonstrate that recognition of newly commodified rural spaces for leisure, or other uses, should be sensitive to wider debates relating to the imagery of spectacle and the shadowy signifiers of the simulacrum. Such sensitivity is only currently emerging in the literature on leisure and recreation in rural areas (see, for example, Urry, 1991). Here there is scope only for a brief review of the structural and spectacular characteristics of production and consumption associated with newly commodified rural spaces and of the importance of iconography in conveying social and cultural constructions of meaning about these places.

Producing rural spaces

The 1980s have witnessed the implementation of a series of political programmes designed to transfer the focus of development and decision-making increasingly into the private sector. Much has been written on this (see, for example, Gamble, 1988; Green, 1987; Jessop et al. 1988; King, 1987; Veljanovski, 1987), but the resulting transformations of the underlying conditions for change in rural areas have received less attention (though see Bell and Cloke, 1989; Blowers, 1987; O'Riordan, 1992; and Potter and Adams, 1989). I argue that Britain in the 1980s and early 1990s has experienced a political climate which has encouraged both the establishment of new rural spaces for leisure and recreation and the refurbishment of existing attractions, often to include entertainments which appear to be closely associated with the notion of spectacle, as discussed above. The political climate has been fuelled by privatization and deregulation. Privatization has been pursued in all economic sectors and in rural areas has served to open up opportunities for new commodified uses of rural land. The denationalization of previously public-sector utility companies is an important example. Newly privatized gas, electricity and water enterprises have quickly sought to maximize all of the assets included in their privatization portfolio. In the case of the water and electricity companies in particular, these include tracts of rural land, ranging from very valuable peri-urban riverside sites to more remote upland catchments and electricity generation establishments.

One result of utility privatization, therefore, has been the disposal of, or more usually the increased commodification of, rural land for leisure. This is not to suggest that such land uses were not available under previous public-sector regimes but rather that much more effort is now given to presenting these spaces to consumers as attractions worth paying to visit. For example, in west Wales, Powergen have restyled and heavily promoted the opportunity to buy a day's fishing at reservoirs such as Dinas and Nant-y-Moch ('the best variety of freshwater angling in West Wales', day permit £7.00). Their publicity suggests: 'Dinas covers 38 acres in pleasant rural surroundings and has gained an enviable reputation as a well stocked put and take fishery, offering excellent value for money . . . Whoever takes the largest fish each year wins a handsome trophy . . . so have a go!' Equally, their Rheidol hydro-electric scheme is being increasingly promoted as a 'great day out' (family ticket £3.50) during which you can

— *visit* Rheidol Power Station Information Centre with its exhibition, video room, souvenir shop and refreshments
— *tour* the power station and its fascinating fish farm
— *picnic* at the lakeside picnic area
— *drive* around the scenic upland reservoirs
— *fish* for trout in one of the lakes
— *enjoy* a romantic view of the floodlit Felin Newydd Weir.

Welsh Water are engaged in the same kind of exercise. For example, Llysyfran reservoir was opened in the 1970s, but only in 1990 was its visitor centre with restaurant, shop and exhibition centre built to become a focus for visitor spending. The publicity now boasts 'there's so much to see and do' at Llysyfran—'fishing, sailing, canoeing, boardsailing, shop, restaurant, picnic areas, nature trail . . . AND a 100 ft. high dam'.

Such examples are very familiar, yet when networked across the British countryside they represent an important component in the production of an increasingly pay-as-you-enter countryside experience. The informal and free forms of outdoor recreation in the countryside are gradually being replaced for many by a more formal, attraction-based, day out in which the countryside experience is packaged and paid for. Public-sector management of rural land is being pushed strongly in the same direction, as illustrated by the various debates over charging for use of national parks and nature reserves.

However, it is not just privatization which presents the opportunity for new and repackaged rural spaces. Deregulation, too, is feeding this process of change for plots of land in two main ways. First, the gradual and often camouflaged deregulation (or at least redirection) of state support for agriculture has served to fuel the process of agricultural diversification. A new perception of the land budget required for agriculture has attained common currency, with some commentators suggesting that up to one-third of land currently used for farming could be surplus to requirements for producing food within twenty-five years. Suggestions as to how this 'surplus' land might be used have ranged from more extensive forms of 'environment friendly' farming to fears of a period of free-for-all development in rural areas.

One of the most practicable things a farmer can do to cope with the new political economy of agricultural support is, however, to diversify into some form of tourist accommodation or recreational attraction, often with the aid of government grants. Evidence of such diversification is increasingly apparent, especially in terms of advertising material available at tourist information centres. Visitors are bombarded with opportunities to pay for a day out on a farm, lured by the idea of a 'rides and slides' theme park, visiting a working farm, waterfowl centres, rare breeds farms, farm museums, country sports parks, woodland parks, butterfly farms, shire horse centres and so on. Each contributes to a new era of commodifying rural space, characterized by a speed and scale of development which far outstrip farm-based tourism and recreation of previous eras.

The second way in which deregulation has aided the availability of new rural spaces for commodification concerns the way in which town and country planning has itself been gradually deregulated during the 1980s. I have argued elsewhere (Cloke, 1989b) that a culture of 'anti-planning' arose in the 1980s as part of the Thatcherite project of setting about the creation of a political economic environment for new rounds of economic restructuring. The authority and scope of development planning has been reduced, and a series of deregulatory devices has resulted in what Thornley (1991) recognized as effectively three different planning systems:

(i)   areas of elite landscape, such as national parks, where planning restrictions have been maintained or even strengthened;
(ii) enterprise zones, simplified planning zones and urban development corporation zones where responsibility for the shape of development has been handed over to the private sector;
(iii) the rest of the country where the previous system remains in place but has become more market-driven.

Although as yet category (ii) has not been applicable to the countryside, the distinction between categories (i) and (iii) is important. In the non-elite countryside, planners have been encouraged by central advice to be sympathetic to the needs of farm diversification, particularly where a country location is necessary for the new enterprise (thereby *including* all farming- or animal-based attractions) and where redundant farm buildings can be converted. In the elite countryside such as green belt and national park areas, it has not been so easy for farmers to take advantage of a deregulated planning regime, although diversification has still occurred in these areas.

Consuming rural spaces

This era in which the production of new rural spaces has been encouraged as part of a wider programme of privatization and deregulation has also been associated with new forms of consumption of leisure and recreation. Featherstone (1991), for example, has pointed to the increasing salience of leisure in the form of consuming experiences and pleasure such as at theme parks, and tourist and recreation centres, and there is a burgeoning literature on the interconnectivities between consumption and culture (see, for instance, Adorno, 1991; Billington *et al.*, 1991; Miller 1987). The interesting yet almost unanswerable question is to identify to what extent new consumption practices are driven by contemporary social change, by the vigorous promotion of the products (the new rural spaces) concerned or by some complex ensemble of relations in which production and consumption meld together in a form of what has been called 'structured coherence' (Cloke and Goodwin, 1992).

Urry's (1988; 1991) work on socio-cultural change and leisure suggested that the rise of a 'service class' in the 1980s provides an example of social change influencing consumption practices associated with leisure and recreation in the countryside. He argues that the distinctions of taste exhibited by the service class 'have become highly significant for other classes and social groups' (Urry, 1988, p.41) and suggests certain attributes of taste which have become widely adopted by consumers of rural spaces including:

— a reverence for the pastoral idyll;
— an acceptance of certain cultural symbols such as old houses, antiques, health foods and real ale;
— an enjoyment of outdoor pursuits such as jogging, cycling, fly-fishing, windsurfing and mountaineering.

He stresses, however, that such traits of consumption represent a *subversion of*, rather than support for, the established social order and that service classes have been ready to transgress the cultural norms of age, class, gender, or ethnic groups. Harrison (1991) picks up this theme and describes how the willingness of service classes to 'decentre' their identity has impinged more widely on the culture of leisure in contemporary Britain:

This 'decentering' of identity has many expressions, for example, in the transgression of boundaries through play, the casting on and off of identities and the opportunities to engage vicariously in other people's lives. Theme parks, medieval fayres and feasts, pop festivals and 'living' museums provide the opportunities to temporarily adopt identities which have new meanings for their participants. As part of post modernism this dismemberment of group norms allows people to lead eclectic lives, unshackled by the legacy of tradition or collective expectation, and to respond freely to the market place. [p.59]

In terms of the countryside, however, this kind of account can be both chaotic and confusing because the 'new' forms of consumption of leisure tend to mirror many of the traditional themes. The novelty of contemporary consumption lies in different motives for consumption rather than in the manifestation of new products *per se*. Thus the conventional concerns with pastoral idyll, histories and traditions, and outdoor pursuits are still evident in the consumption of the countryside, but such experiences increasingly seem to be served up and received so as to provide identity-giving spectacle or interpretation without a reinforcement of cultural norms; infusing the attraction with 'tradition' without appearing to be shackled by the legacy of tradition; promoting high visitor levels without conforming to collective expectation; offering 'new' meanings to participants while reproducing historical signs, symbols and displays.

Such dualisms inevitably provoke conflicting levels of satisfaction from consumers with regard to particular rural spaces and the events and attractions hosted therein. Just as there are conflicts over the consumption of the 'open' countryside within and between such groups as, say, the residents of Castlemorton Common and the travellers and 'ravers' who used this rural space as a festival site in May 1992, so the 'closed' commodified countryside has become a site of cultural conflict and compromise in the respective buying and selling of cast-off identities. In part, such conflict can be overcome by the provision of elite 'niche market' products, for example the production of spaces for individual or small-group participation in country sports and pursuits. In the more mass-market places which have been the result of most diversification, however, there remains something of a common currency of signs and meanings which presents the countryside as a package for consumers. In this sense much consumption is market-led but only if the market excludes attractive and desirable symbols of the countryside. Even then, it seems likely that the visitor's reading of rural symbols may sometimes be very different from that intended by the producer, resulting in either a subversion of social constructs by the consumer or a reproduction of that space and its symbols by the producer, or both.

Producing imagined rural spaces: representation and iconography

This discussion of the consumption of countryside attractions brings us almost full circle to the idea that the countryside is a repository of socially constructed meanings. If the new rural spaces for leisure and recreation discussed above do represent the guiding of, and response to, contemporary cultures of consumption then the signs, symbols and meanings attached to these spaces and attractions will reflect some of the social constructs of rurality which are currently being represented. Substantiation of such a claim would involve lengthy and detailed research, but as a brief introduction to the interesting and significant nature of the iconography of rural 'attractions' it is possible to make use of the advertising brochures for such attractions which are readily available from tourist information centres.

It is impossible to do justice to the richness of texts which can be found in a sample of merely twenty-five such brochures from Devon and Dyfed (see Appendix). Nevertheless, generalizations can be made which support the suggestion that although each brochure seeks to outbid competitors and is therefore in a very real sense individual, there are some very clear *common* meanings relating to the countryside portrayed within them. For example, the overwhelming colour choices for backwash and lettering are green and brown, although a seemingly deliberate attempt to be 'different' may be seen in the Shire Horse Centre's choice of red and yellow. Pastel shades, sepias and watercolour effects are also used frequently. The use of photographs and less often, artists' impressions, means that the brochures are often showing a representation of a representation of the reality of the attraction. Scenes represented photographically typically mix shots of people of all ages enjoying themselves at the attraction with views of the deeper visual field of surrounding landscape—thus bringing together the enclosed commodified space with the wider countryside as if one definitely belonged to the other. Symbols and logos used in the brochures reflect an extremely strong set of images of farm animals—cattle, sheep, bees, horses and so on—often (although sometimes identification is impossible!) masculine.

The text in the brochures repeatedly represents common signals and meanings about the rural spaces concerned. Five common themes are identified below, but they are neither mutually exclusive nor exhaustive:

(i)   *Landscape*—the importance of a 'rural' landscape setting is stressed by almost all attractions, especially those which are disconnected from an agricultural focus. Oakwood theme park, for example, stresses that its mix of adventure and fun on rides and slides is 'set in 80 acres of beautiful Pembrokeshire Countryside'. Thus outdoor fun is equated with a countryside setting. In many cases, the 'agricultural' landscape is stressed pictorially. Signals of the great outdoors portrayed by photographs, however, have to be constrained by reference to some manufactured immunity from the weather. Folly Farm in Pembrokeshire, for example, advertises itself as 'the all-weather entertainment: come rain or sunshine the whole family will enjoy it'. The visitor experience of the working countryside is thus sanitized so as to exclude experience of the open landscape in the rain!

(ii) *Nature*—reference to animals, plants or insects is almost ubiquitous apart from the 'rides' theme parks. The natural idyll is reflected in several descriptions, for example, 'a truly fantastic display of the world's most beautiful and rarest orchids—see them in our Paradise Garden' (Orchid Paradise). The importance of conservation and educational interpretation is also stressed: 'pause to learn about the animals from our "Secrets of the Woodland" feature' (Gorse Blossom Miniature Railway & Woodland Park); 'learn about how they [bees] communicate, make wax, and collect pollen and nectar' (Quince Honey Farm); 'Lands as diverse as ancient woodland and marshland, rich in rare wildlife, are conserved and managed, along with important historical sites' (Morwellham Quay). Most brochures highlight the ability to achieve close contact—even participation—with nature in the rural space concerned: 'a fun, hands-on farming experience. Milk a cow! Bottle feed and cuddle the baby animals! Climb aboard a vintage tractor!' (The Milky Way and N. Devon Bird of Prey Centre). Note, though, how hands-on-contact is in fact carefully controlled in these spaces—no driving of a vintage tractor or cuddling of birds of prey here!

(iii) *History*—history seems to be as important as nature to the social constructions of the countryside represented in these cases. Some attractions make this their focal theme. Morwellham Quay, for example, is represented as 'the Greatest Copper Port in Queen Victoria's Empire ... researched and restored ... and vividly brought to life'; Tuckers Maltings offers 'an unforgettable journey into the past' and Parke Rare Breeds Farm stresses that 'some of these breeds were tended by farmers in the Middle Ages and many can be traced back to prehistoric times'. Even attractions based on a 'natural' landmark signal for themselves an historical heritage. Thus Becky Falls, Dartmoor is represented as 'much loved since Victorian Times'. This allows the suggestion that the countryside not only contains the palimpsest of different histories but has also been cherished through history. The invitation is not only to step back in time but also to continue to cherish by visiting and learning about particular rural spaces. Some entrepreneurs themselves attempt to integrate family history with the legitimacy of the historic dimension of the attraction: 'The Museum comprises mostly of equipment owned and used by the Luke family throughout the last nine decades. As a family we have been farming in Pembrokeshire since the early 1970s' (Selvedge Farm Museum). Others stress that tradition equates with the 'best': 'enjoy the very best of Wales, a special blend of place and people, rich in history, rooted in tradition' (Melin Tregwynt).

(iv) *Family orientation*—rurality is for all the family, according to the brochures. This seems to reflect not only an obvious wish to attract groups of visitors but also to suggest strongly that the rural space of the attraction is *safe*. Thus at The Miniature Pony Centre, Dartmoor, 'the children's playground is . . . fenced all round providing a safe area for children to play', and at Gorse Blossom Park parents are invited to 'relax' because cars are safely segregated from the main grounds. More generally, the emphasis appears to be on 'conventional' household structures and the ability of the countryside experience to satisfy all age groups. This might even be interpreted as an attempt to represent the feel of an imagined rural 'community' at the attraction.

(v) *Craft and country fayre*—in almost all cases the commodification of the countryside as represented in the brochures creates the impression that certain craft items, and types of refreshment (both of course, available on site) are somehow part of the total packaging of a countryside experience. Thus the St. David's Farm Park, for example, offers 'a range of gifts and crafts for sale, with wildlife and countryside themes, to remind you of your enjoyable day out', and Brimstone Wildlife Centre similarly offers 'a range of quality gifts reflecting the countryside'. The claims regarding 'country' food vary considerably. For example, at Dairyway at Folly Farm we are told that 'parents can enjoy a Pembrokeshire Cream Tea . . . where all the 'goodies' are made on the premises from traditional recipes', while Selvedge Farm Museum invites visitors to 'savour the homemade dishes of Wales'—which include wholemeal lasagne! Obviously the 'health food' image of wholemeal rather than the ethnicity of lasagne is held to be representative of rural Wales here.

This rather superficial summary of advertising materials suggests that there is considerable scope for interpreting the representation of countryside meanings, signs and symbols from these sources. Socially constructed rurality, as applied to these new produced spaces reflects the perhaps predictable themes of nature, outdoor fun and history; and also the slightly less predictable themes of family safety, 'hands-on' or 'up-close' experiences of nature; and the specific commodity links with souvenir craft and particular foods and drinks which form integral components of the packaged day out in the countryside.

Conclusions

Leisure and recreation in the countryside have conventionally been viewed as seeking out the natural in a 'get away from it all' or even wilderness experience. For such an experience to be 'free as nature', it was important that access to nature should be free. Therefore, although the provision of 'facilities' for recreation has become an increasingly important part of planning for recreation, there has until recently been societal acceptance of the role of the public sector as provider of necessary facilities. Rural recreation and leisure were therefore almost part of the welfare state, providing a lung for the cities and a social service to the urban masses. Although in traditional tourist areas there has been a steadily growing private-sector involvement with the provision of basic facilities, it seems that for the wider countryside the onset of commodification associated with leisure and recreation has come rather later than in urban areas.

This chapter suggests that the *society of the commodity* has taken root in the countryside at least partly in response to wider political economic processes of privatization and deregulation, which have opened up the opportunity for countryside sites to be developed as pay-as-you-enter or pay-as-you-use attractions. Interpretations as to whether this is just the expected outcome of increasingly market-orientated politics and economics, or whether it is indicative of more Marxian ideas of the exploitative, corrupting and distorting effects of the socio-cultural constructions of commodity value, will differ. It certainly appears that this commodification of the countryside can be linked *both* to a state response to the farm crisis *and* to a response to growing environmental pressures by facilitating the serving up of an environmental experience of the countryside in such a way as to be part of a more general defusing of any revolutionary interest in environmental change and conflict.

Similarly, a closer look at some of the new rural spaces given over to commodified 'attractions' supports the suggestion that a *society of the spectacle* is also emerging in the contemporary countryside. Evidence that the social and cultural constructs of a commodified countryside are fashioned in terms of the production of spectacle is available from the advertising brochures discussed above. Many attractions offer specific spectacle. For example, Morwellham Quay offers an outdoor *theatre* of a rural history:

the quay workers, cooper, blacksmith, assayer and servant girls dressed in period costume, recreate the bustling boom years of the 1860's . . . Chat with the people of the past. Sample for yourself the life of the port where a bygone age is captured in the crafts and costumes of the 1860's . . . Try on costumes from our 1860's wardrobe.

The invitation is to spectate and participate in the history which is 'captured' by the attraction and presented for today's visitors in the form of spectacle.

Most attractions offer spectacle of varying degrees. The National Shire Horse Centre, for instance, enhances the more expected displays of shire horses with 'special events': western weekends ('You will see Cowboys, Indians, Outlaws . . . with an authentic shoot-out display'), Teddy Bears' Picnics and Dollies' Tea Parties, steam and vintage rallies and classic car shows. Perhaps the most striking example of the move towards spectacle is the way in which historic sites are commodified using 'events'. Cadw in Wales, for example, has a programme of theatrical, musical and other performance events at their Castles, Abbeys and Palaces. Witness living history with displays of archery, armour, combat and dancing at Raglan Castle; marvel at huge and spectacular kites representing the red and white dragons from Celtic mythology at Beaumaris Castle; Tretower Court is the 'perfect backdrop' for a celebration involving 'theatre, romance, music, crafts . . . and even medieval alchemy'; listen to the Llannig Silver Band among the museum workshops and quarries of the Welsh Slate Centre at Llanberis.

The message in these and other cases is that attractions in the countryside are being commodified in such a way as to go well beyond the real objects and relations of the sites and buildings concerned. Some spectacle makes claim to authenticity, particularly in the attempts to recreate history. Elsewhere, however, the conspicuous consumption of the symbols on offer—western shoot-outs, vintage cars, teddy-bears' and dollies tea parties, craft, alchemy etc.—suggests that some new rural attractions are emphasizing signs which are unrelated to the specific reality of a place, its landscape and its history. It seems timely, therefore, to investigate far more thoroughly the importance of sign-exchange values and the conspicuous nature of social meanings that are now being represented in new rural places.

References

Adorno, R., 1991, *The Culture Industry*, London, Routledge.

Baudrillard, J., 1983a, *Simulations*, New York, Semiotext.

Baudrillard, J., 1983b, *In the Shadow of the Silent Majority*, New York, Semiotext.

Bell, P., and Cloke P., 1989, 'The changing relationship between the private and public sectors: privatization and rural Britain', *Journal of Rural Studies*, **5**: 1–15.

Best, S., 1989, 'The commodification of reality and the reality of commodification: Jean Baudrillard and post-modernism', *Current Perspectives In Social Theory*, **19**, 23–51.

Billington, R., Strawbridge, S., Greensides, L. and Fitzsimmons, A., 1991, *Culture and Society*, London, Macmillan.

Blowers, A., 1987, 'Transition or transformation?—environmental policy under Thatcher', *Public Administration*, **65**: 277–94.

Cloke, P., 1989a, 'Rural geography and political economy', in R. Peet, N. Thrift, (eds), *New models in Geography*, London, Unwin Hyman.

Cloke, P., 1989b, 'Land use planning in rural Britain' in P. Cloke (ed.), *Rural Land Use Planning in Developed Nations*, London, Unwin Hyman.

Cloke, P., 1992, 'The countryside: development, conservation and an increasingly marketable commodity' in P. Cloke (ed.), *Policy and Change in Thatcher's Britain*, Oxford, Pergamon.

Cloke, P. and Goodwin, M., 1992, 'Conceptualizing countryside change: from post-fordism to rural structured coherence', *IBG Transactions*, **17**.

Cloke, P. and Park, C., 1985, *Rural Resource Management*, London, Croom Helm.

Debord, G., 1983, *Society of the Spectacle*, Detroit, Red and Black.

Featherstone, M., 1991, *Consumer Culture and Postmodernism*, London, Sage.

Gamble, A., 1988, *The Free Economy and the Strong State: the Politics of Thatcherism*, London, Macmillan.

Green, D., 1987, *The New Right: the Counter Revolution in Political Economic and Social Thought*, Brighton, Wheatsheaf.

Harrison, C., 1991, *Countryside Recreation in a Changing Society*, London, TMS Partnership.

Hoggart, K., 1990, 'Let's do away with rural', *Journal of Rural Studies*, **6**, 245–57.

Jackson, P., 1989, *Maps of Meaning*, London, Unwin Hyman.

Jessop, B., Bonnet, K., Bromley, S. and Ling, T., 1988, *Thatcherism*, Oxford, Polity Press.

King, D., 1987, *The New Right: Politics, Markets and Citizenship*, London, Macmillan.

Marx, K., 1978, *The Marx-Engels Reader* (2nd edn), R. Tucker (ed.), New York, Norton.

Miller, D., 1987, *Material Culture and Mass Consumption*, Oxford, Blackwell.

Mormont, M., 1990, 'Who is rural? or how to be rural: towards a sociology of the rural' in T. Marsden, P. Lowe, S. Whatmore (eds), *Rural Restructuring*, London, David Fulton.

Moss, G., 1978, 'Rural settlements', *Architects Journal*, **18**, January: 101.

O'Riordan, T., 1992, 'The Environment' in P. Cloke (ed.), *Policy and Change in Thatcher's Britain*, Oxford, Pergamon Press.

Potter, C. and Adams, B., 1989, 'Thatcher's countryside: planning for survival', *Ecos*, **10**, 4: 1–3.

Thorburn, A., 1971, *Planning Villages*, London, Estates Gazette.

Thornley, A., 1991, *Urban Planning under Thatcherism*, London, Routledge.

Urry, J., 1988, 'Cultural change and contemporary holiday-making', *Theory, Culture and Society*, **5**: 35–55.

Urry, J., 1991, *The Tourist Gaze*, London, Sage.

Veljanovski, C., 1987, *Selling the State: Privatization in Britain*, London, Weidenfeld & Nicolson.

Appendix: The sample of brochures for rural attractions in Devon and Dyfed

Becky Falls, Dartmoor
Brimstone Wildlife Centre, Penuwch
Buckfast Butterfly Farm and Dartmoor Otter Sanctuary
CADW: Events 92 at Historic Sites
Devonshires Centre, Bickleigh
Folly Farm, Pembrokeshire
Gorse Blossom Miniature Railway and Woodland Park, Bickington
Heatherton County Sports Park, St. Florence
Herons Brook, Narbeth
Llangloffan Farmhouse Cheese Centre, Castle Morris
Melin Tregwynt, Letterston
Milky Way and North Devon Bird of Prey Centre, Clovelly
Miniature Pony Centre, Dartmoor
Morwellham Quay, Tavistock
National Shire Horse Centre, Yealmpton
Oakwood, Canaston Bridge
Orchid Paradise, Newton Abbot
Parke Rare Breeds Farm, Bovey Tracey
Pennywell, The South Devon Farm Centre, Buckfastleigh
Quince Honey Farm, South Molton

River Dart Country Park, Ashburton
Selvedge Farm Museum, Clarbeston Road
St. David's Farm Park, St. David's
Tuckers Maltings, Newton Abbot
World of Country Life, Exmouth

PART III
PLANNING FOR LEISURE

GOVERNMENT, CONSERVATION, OUTDOOR RECREATION AND TOURISM: A BRITISH–AUSTRALIAN PERSPECTIVE

J. T. COPPOCK

The relationship between conservation and leisure, particularly its subsets of recreation, sport and tourism, and central government are complex and have presented problems for politicians and administrators in all developed countries. Neither conservation nor leisure fits happily into governmental structures and policy-making, especially where these are sectorally-based, as is generally the case. Conservation represents an ethic which should influence the activities of all governmental departments and agencies, and while leisure concerns a large number of them, it is rarely, if ever, central to any. As a consequence, conservation and leisure tend to be either marginalized where they are deemed politically unimportant, or the subject of interdepartmental conflict or rivalry where each seeks to assert its primacy, as the recent struggle between the Department of the Environment and the Ministry of Agriculture, Fisheries and Food over responsibility for conservation in the English countryside has demonstrated.

In the post-war period, particularly over the past decade, the political importance of conservation has been rising, assisted by well-organized lobbies and by growing concern over damage to the global environment, so that at least lip service has to be paid to policies intended to promote conservation. Leisure has not achieved the same political significance, in part because of its great diversity, the absence of strong lobbies to attract political attention and a feeling in some quarters that it is not a proper topic for government intervention; nevertheless, the growth of leisure time, the rise in disposable income and the increasing mobility of the population have created problems that cannot be ignored. Tourism is, to some extent, the exception, being perceived as a good thing because of its effect on jobs and on balances of payments, but in practice it is not easy to separate the roles of citizens as tourists and as recreationists.

This chapter is concerned with these issues in the context of conserving the rural environment and catering for outdoor recreation. The discussion is primarily concerned with structures and functions of central government in these fields in two contrasting environments, the United Kingdom, a small unitary state with considerable pressure of population on resources, and Australia, a federal state of continental extent, with an area some thirty times as large but with less than a third of the population. Because of limitations of space, the discussion is necessarily selective and focuses primarily on England and Scotland within the United Kingdom and on Victoria and Western Australia within Australia. It also ignores the important roles (particularly in the UK) of local government and its partner, the voluntary sector.

The United Kingdom

In theory, the United Kingdom is a unitary state, with a single legislature and government and a strong tendency towards centralization. In practice, there is considerable administrative devolution to the four constituent countries of England, Northern Ireland, Scotland and Wales, particularly in respect of conservation and recreation. Although their economies operate under the same rules, and broad political objectives and policies are the same in all four countries, the governmental structures are often somewhat different. The contrast with England, the dominant country by size and population, is most marked in Northern Ireland, which had a separate parliament until 1973 and where local government is weak; it is least marked in Wales, which has long been integrated for political purposes with England and where administrative devolution is comparatively recent. Scotland, with its own legal and educational system, has enjoyed considerable administrative devolution since 1888 and with an area two-thirds that of England but a population little more than a tenth as large, has a much lower pressure of population on resources (only sixty-four persons per square kilometre compared with 349 in England). Moreover, whereas some two-thirds of Scotland is uncultivated moorland, which has a special significance for both conservation and recreation, the proportion in England is only a tenth.

Official involvement in rural conservation and the environment in the United Kingdom dates effectively from 1949, when the *Nature Conservancy* was created by Royal Charter and the *National Parks Commission* was established under the National Parks and Access to the Countryside Act, with responsibilities for scenic conservation and informal recreation in the countryside, although the Conservancy's remit was limited to Great Britain and the Commission's to England and Wales. This creation of agencies outside departments, with a primarily advisory function and generally with a sponsoring ministry through which a junior minister exercises broad political control, was to be repeated, with variations, for sport and tourism. No government minister had overall responsibility for either conservation or leisure throughout the United Kingdom, nor, as far as is known has there been a cabinet committee or committee of senior officials in either field. With the creation of agencies for sport and for tourism, there has emerged a degree of informal liaison through the *Chairmen's Policy Group*, a periodical meeting of the heads of agencies, which did in fact take the lead in 1983 in sponsoring a conference on leisure policy for the future. More recently, a *Ministry of National Heritage* was created in 1992, with responsibilities, among other matters, for conservation, recreation, sport and tourism, although many of these functions in Northern Ireland, Scotland and Wales will continue to be exercised by their respective Secretaries of State.

Great Britain

Before examining structures in England and Scotland, mention should first be made of three bodies that operate within Great Britain (England, Scotland, Wales), although one of these, the *Nature Conservancy Council*, ceased to exist in 1991. The other two are resource-owning bodies in which conservation and recreation have a minor part to play.

The *Forestry Commission* was created in 1919 and is responsible in policy terms to the Minister of Agriculture and the Secretaries of State for Scotland and Wales. It has the status of a government department and is the largest public owner of land, with an estate of some 900,000 hectares. It has a dual role as Forest Enterprise, managing that estate, primarily for timber production, and as Forest Authority, administering government policy in relation to private woodlands. It has a part-time chairman and ten commissioners (four full-time) and is charged with striking a balance between its forestry functions and conservation. The Commission has also become increasingly sensitive to the scenic aspects of its new plantations and has a duty to develop the recreational potential of its woodlands. It has designated large areas of more limited value for forestry as forest parks, allows access on foot to its forests and, since 1970, has provided specific recreational opportunities such as forest walks and drives and facilities for camping and car parking. As well as encouraging informal recreation in its forests, it allows active sports such as shooting and orienteering, as well as commercially sponsored car rallies on its forest roads. In its capacity as Forest Authority, it has a conservation role through the issue of Tree Preservation Orders, and conservation and public access are among its considerations in making grants for forest operations to owners of private forests. It has also been working with the Countryside Commissions to develop community forests near urban areas.

British Waterways is a statutory body responsible for navigation on canals and waterways, and comprises a chairman and five members, all part-time and appointed by the Secretary of State for the Environment. It is responsible for operating canals, feeder reservoirs and navigable waterways in Great Britain and has a statutory role in providing for recreation. Three-fifths of the waterways it controls are cruising waterways available for sailing, boating, canoeing, angling and other appropriate activities, and it can acquire adjacent land on which to provide services and facilities for recreationists. It also licenses pleasure boats. The towpaths along its waterways, one-third of which are rights of way, are also an important recreational resource. The

Board is advised on amenity and recreation matters by an Inland Waterways
Amenity Advisory Council.

The *Nature Conservancy Council*, the successor in 1973 to the Nature Conservancy, was itself replaced in 1991 by separate bodies for England, Scotland
and Wales. However, from 1949 to 1991, it was the principal body with
responsibility for wildlife conservation, acting both as an advisory body to
government and as a manager of National Nature Reserves, which preserve
representative examples of natural habitats. These, occupying a little over
160,000 hectares, were originally envisaged as being in public ownership,
but such status was achieved by only a minority of Reserves, most being
leased private land or managed under a Nature Reserve Agreement with the
owners of such land. The Council was also able to notify areas of private
land as Sites of Special Scientific Interest on account of their importance for
conservation, and since 1981, their owners have been required to consult the
Council over proposals to undertake potentially damaging operations that
might adversely affect the conservation interest. The Council also advised
on conservation aspects of proposed developments, including those for recreation, and opposed several projects. Since 1973, the Council has been sympathetic to public access to Reserves where this is compatible with conservation
objectives, but its recreational involvement has been minor, and it has
expressed concern that conservation of wildlife has not been adequately
considered in National Parks. Its character changed somewhat over the
forty years as its membership was widened from predominantly scientific,
and appointments became more 'political', reflecting in part sensitivities
over its role in relation to developments on privately owned land.

England

Since 1991, the Council has been replaced by *English Nature*, essentially the
remainder of the Council after its loss of responsibility for Scotland and
Wales. It remains a body whose members are appointed by the Secretary of
State for the Environment and with the functions outlined above. Unlike
Scotland and Wales, where nature and scenic conservation have been amalgamated, their separation has been maintained in England, although no
explanation for the different approach has been offered. Possible factors
may be the much larger size of the organizations in England and the existence
of more powerful lobbies opposed to change.

The Countryside Commission was established in 1968 as the successor body
to the National Parks Commission, with greater resources and a wider remit
relating to the countryside as a whole, but retaining its dual functions of promoting the conservation of scenery and encouraging the provision of
facilities for public enjoyment of the countryside, functions that are always
potentially in conflict but with priority in disputes given to the former. Its
members are appointed by the Secretary of State for the Environment and
cover a wide range of interests. The Commission is primarily an advisory
and promotional body with powers to designate National Parks, Areas of
Outstanding Natural Beauty and National Trails, and to give grant aid to

local authorities, land owners and others in order to further its objectives. Its conservation objectives are achieved primarily by designation and by advice to public bodies, landowners and others, and in the 1980s it became increasingly pro-active in creating new and beautiful landscapes. It fulfils its recreation role through its powers to promote access and by grant aid, limiting its attention to quiet informal recreation; it is not itself a provider but approves and grant-aids proposals by local authorities and others for the creation of country parks, areas of countryside set aside primarily for recreation, and picnic sites. It is not concerned with competitive sport or noisy activities, although it negotiates with other bodies to minimize conflicts. Since 1991 it has lost its responsibilities for Wales, for which it had a separate Committee, to a new Countryside Council for Wales, which also has responsibility for nature conservation. In England, the Countryside Commission, within its narrower territorial base, has retained its separate identity and continues its existing functions.

The Sports Council was created by Royal Charter in 1972 as an independent agency, with its members appointed by the Secretary of State for the Environment. It succeeded a voluntary Council and has strong links with a voluntary body, the Central Council of Physical Recreation. It also acts in some matters as a Sports Council for the whole of the United Kingdom, although the distinction between its British and English roles has not always been very clearly recognized. It, too, is primarily an advisory and promotional body, although it owns and runs a number of national centres for particular sports. It aims to promote both excellence in performance and wide participation in sport and physical recreation and does so chiefly through grant aid to local authorities and voluntary bodies, advice and special programmes. Its main emphasis is urban, but some sports are space demanding or require access to particular natural resources and so are primarily rural. It has established a Countryside and Water Recreation Policy Group to deal with such issues.

The English Tourist Board was established as a government agency in 1969 and also succeeded a voluntary body. It is an independent statutory body, with members appointed by the Secretary of State for Trade and Industry. Its role is essentially promotional, to encourage both visitors and residents of the United Kingdom to take holidays in England, and it does so by marketing and by grant aid to assist the development of tourist facilities. During the 1980s it became increasingly involved with tourism in rural areas, developing a strategy to strengthen rural economies, conserve the countryside and provide for visitors' enjoyment, and has agreed a list of principles with the Countryside Commission towards these ends.

The National Rivers Authority was established in 1989 by the legislation that privatized the water industry; previously there had been a National Water Council, assisted by a Water Space Amenity Commission and ten Regional Water Authorities. Its members are appointed by the Secretary of State for the Environment, but it is largely self-financing, any deficit being met by government grant. It is responsible for monitoring water quality, controlling pollution and maintaining and developing fish stocks. It also has a duty to conserve the water environment, protect its amenity and promote recreation.

Much of its income comes from managing and letting fishing rights, and it seeks to minimize conflict through discussion and agreement.

Scotland

The Countryside Commission for Scotland was established by legislation in 1967 as a reaction to growing pressure on the countryside by both residents and tourists. It had similar functions to the Countryside Commission, but its members, under a part-time chairman, were appointed by the Secretary of State for Scotland and its parent ministry was the Scottish Office Environment Department. Unlike its counterpart in England and Wales, the Scottish Commission had no powers to designate National Parks, whose establishment had been strongly opposed by civil servants, local authorities and landowners when mooted in the 1940s. Instead of National Parks and Areas of Outstanding Natural Beauty, it designated National Scenic Areas where developments require consultation with the Commission, and was given powers to designate Regional Parks, embracing a number of Country Parks linked by footpaths.

The Commission has recently been amalgamated with the Nature Conservancy Council, Scotland, to form a new body, *Scottish Natural Heritage*, which took over in 1992. The Nature Conservancy had earlier had a Scottish Committee, with a chairman approved by the Secretary of State, but on the formation of the Nature Conservancy Council, this Committee was downgraded to an advisory role. It was reconstituted in 1991 as a separate *Nature Conservancy Council, Scotland*, a move which facilitated its fusion with the Commission shortly afterwards. It is too soon to know how effective this amalgamation of functions will be; but there is a widespread feeling that, had conservation bodies been created for the first time in 1991, an agency covering both functions would have been formed.

The Scottish Sports Council and the *Scottish Tourist Board*, which were likewise preceded by voluntary bodies, were created at the same time as their English counterparts and fulfil similar functions. Liaison with other conservation and recreation bodies is achieved through regular meetings of chairmen and chief executives. No analagous body to the National Rivers Authority exists in Scotland where water supply and sewerage are a local authority responsibility and control over pollution is exercised by river purification boards.

Conclusion on the United Kingdom

For reasons of space, only the more important agencies have been mentioned in this brief review. The typical official agency in Great Britain is an appointed body rather than a government department, operating under a statute or Royal Charter, which determines its own objectives within broad policy directives from government ministers. Detailed policy is determined by the appointed board or commission, whose members have other occupations, and generally represent a wide range of interests, although the chairman is frequently part-time. Apart from broad policy directions, governments can also exert influence through the appointment of members and through negotiations over the level of funding, usually by grant in aid. With the exception of the Forestry Commission and British Waterways, their role is primarily advisory and is not generally concerned with public land; instead, they seek to influence the actions of local authorities, voluntary bodies and private individuals by advice, discussion and financial aid. Liaison with other agencies is primarily informal, although there is some evidence that the fact that most agencies are responsible to the Secretary of State for Scotland makes for greater coherence.

Australia

Structures for conservation and recreation in Australia are not strictly comparable owing to its federal constitution. The constituent states preceded the formation of the Commonwealth in 1901 and all powers not specifically surrendered then remain with them, although with the development of a modern economy and through its powers over taxation, the Commonwealth government has been able to exercise increasing influence, a tendency strengthened by the growing number of international agreements and the precedence given to Commonwealth laws where there is a conflict with state laws. The states, however, retain responsibility for land and natural resources, both key elements in conservation and outdoor recreation, and the Commonwealth government plays a largely coordinating role, chairing committees of ministers or officials from the states and territories. Only in the territories does the Commonwealth have direct responsibility, and this is disappearing with the adoption of self government. The relative roles of the Commonwealth and the states are well illustrated by their responsibilities for national parks. All the states had extensive systems of protected areas in place before the Commonwealth expressed an interest in 1975 through the creation of the Australian National Parks and Wildlife Service. Only two of Australia's many national parks, Uluru and Kakadu, both in the Northern Territory, have been designated by the Commonwealth. The Commonwealth has also designated the Great Barrier Reef Marine Park, which lies beyond the three-mile coastal limit, the boundary of state jurisdiction. The roles of the *Australian National Parks and Wildlife Service* are primarily in the provision of expertise and advice and in links with external bodies. The *Australian Tourism Commission* is similarly responsible for promoting Australia as a tourist destination for overseas visitors. Commonwealth policy in these fields is primarily the responsibility of the *Department of the Arts, Sport, the Environment, Tourism and Territories*, which brings together many aspects of conservation and leisure, although other Departments, such as Primary Resources, Energy and Transport, have remits that impinge on these fields and, since the Australian government has adopted the World Conservation Strategy, all departments can be said to have a concern for conservation.

Western Australia and Victoria are respectively the largest and smallest of the mainland Australian states. The former occupies more than 2.5 million square kilometres, more than three times the area of the United Kingdom, but with a population of only 1.6 million (two-thirds in the Perth Metropolitan Region). Victoria, with only 227,000 square kilometres, is less than a tenth of the size, yet has a population of 4.3 million, mostly in and around the state capital, Melbourne. Recreation in both states is primarily domestic, with the greatest pressures around the state capitals; but much more of Victoria is accessible to day recreationists, and it shares with New South Wales and the Capital Territory the Australian Alps, a major recreational resource for both winter and summer visitors. It is also the least arid of the states, whereas large parts of Western Australia are desert or semi-desert.

Western Australia

As in the other states, the emphasis in governmental involvement in both conservation and recreation is on the use of Crown land. Western Australia has adopted a State Conservation Strategy, which helps to give some coherence in respect of conservation. The most important department in this context is *Conservation and Land Management* (CALM), formed in 1987 on the recommendation of a Committee of Inquiry into Land Use Management that responsibility for forests, national parks and wildlife should be brought together in a single agency. The public lands for which it is responsible, totalling more than 170,000 square kilometres, or 8 per cent of the state, are vested in two statutory bodies, the *National Parks and Nature Conservation Authority* and the *Lands and Forest Commission*, and its origins are reflected in its organization, with directors responsible for each of the three main fields. They constitute a small policy directorate, which seems to function effectively, although the forestry component is by far the largest. The department has clear objectives for both conservation and recreation, set out in its corporate plan and requiring the establishment of a system of reserves and of areas suitable for recreation. CALM seeks to develop opportunities for recreational use of the land and water resources which it controls that are consistent with the purpose for which the land is held, sustainable, provide a return, and are equitable among different groups of recreationists. There are now fifty-eight national parks, a number that increased greatly in the 1970s and 1980s, within all of which recreation is an objective of management. National reserves, numbering over 1,110 and occupying twice the area under national parks, exist primarily to conserve flora and fauna, and recreation is not generally encouraged. State forests, which occupy only a tenth of CALM lands, are managed for multiple use, and conservation and recreation can both be given priority within Management Priority Areas. The department's responsibilities for the conservation of flora and fauna are not confined to CALM lands but extend throughout the state.

Responsibility for water resources is shared between the *Water Authority of Western Australia*, which is responsible for water, sewerage and drainage, and the *Waterways Commission*, established in 1977 and responsible for preserving or enhancing the quality of the waterways environment, primarily in respect of the three major coastal inlets. Domestic water supply comes mainly from the Darling Ranges in the hinterland of Perth, where recreation is excluded from supply reservoirs and their environs, although access on foot is allowed to most parts of the catchments. A *Water Resources Council* advises ministers and has supported a number of major studies.

Monitoring the State Conservation Strategy and coordinating compliance with it is the responsibility of the *Environmental Protection Authority*, a long-established body which took the lead in securing the expansion of the area of protected land noted above. It has responsibility for the control of pollution and for environmental assessments of proposed developments on both state and private land. The agency has no specific policy on recreation, although several of its actions have implications for recreation.

Another supervisory and regulating agency, the *State Planning Commission*, established in 1985, is responsible for coordinating and producing urban, regional and land-use plans. The Commission prepares regional plans and strategies, many of them with recreational and tourist components and has policies on open space and regional parks and for the conservation and development of the coast, a major recreational and tourist resource. Recreation is not seen as a major concern, although the Commission has played an important part in securing land for outdoor recreation and safeguarding recreational/tourist resources.

The remaining two agencies with responsibilities for aspects of leisure are the *Department of Sport and Recreation*, and the *Western Australia Tourist Commission*, both of which are essentially advisory and promotional bodies. The former has had a primarily urban orientation but now aims to make outdoor recreation a priority area. It is not, however, a provider but rather a source of advice to other departments and to local authorities. The Commission's role is to market Western Australia as a tourist destination, both within Australia and overseas, and to encourage residents of the State to travel within it. It can assist both private developers and local authorities in developing tourist facilities and infrastructure. It has also sought to minimize tourist impacts on sensitive environments. It has commissioned, in collaboration with the Environmental Protection Authority, Environmental Guidelines for Tourism, and is strongly supportive of the development of tourism based on natural attractions.

Although the formation of CALM and the State Planning Commission have ensured that governmental structures and policies for conservation and recreation and tourism are better coordinated than formerly, there is still considerable fragmentation of responsibility, especially for recreation. While the State Conservation Strategy and the Environmental Protection Agency's role in monitoring it do give policy for conservation greater coherence, recreation is handicapped by the paucity of qualified staff in this field and by lack of finance. Thus, although management plans are required on all CALM lands, preparing them will take a long time. The creation of a strong State Premier's Department does, however, appear to have led to better integration of policies, in part through the creation of an integrated management group.

Victoria

Victoria has probably gone further than any other state in developing a coherent approach towards conservation and in coordinating responsibilities. This is helped both by the adoption of a State Conservation Strategy and by the acceptance by the state government of conservation as a major objective of state policy.

The Department of Conservation, Forests and Lands (CFL) was until recently the principal department with responsibility for conservation and outdoor recreation. It was formed in 1987 and brought together the national parks, fisheries, and wildlife parts of the former Ministry of Conservation, the Lands Department, the Victoria Forestry Commission and the Soil Conservation Authority. It has responsibility for the planning and management of national parks and reserves, of state forests and of other Crown land, fishing and the conservation of flora, fauna and soil (although, as in Western Australia, the last functions are state-wide and not confined to Crown land). CFL has three main activities—productive resource use, recreation and conservation, and resource protection—and is assisted in these by advisory panels.

In respect of conservation and recreation, its aims are to conserve, develop and facilitate the use of the national, state and regional parks for conservation and recreation and to ensure that other Crown land is managed to provide for public recreation and enjoyment. The national parks occupy more than 80 per cent of land under parks of all kinds, an area that has quadrupled since 1970 and is still growing. Here the emphasis is on informal recreation and quiet enjoyment. State and regional parks are generally smaller and place greater emphasis on outdoor recreation, while fauna and flora reserves have little recreational significance. Much of the recreational land is forest land, 30 per cent of which is designated as parks and reserves. The Lands Division is responsible for the management of reserves, often through delegated powers. Like CALM in Western Australia, the department has been developing a set of comprehensive policies covering all aspects of conservation and recreation, an approach made necessary by the adoption of a policy of devolvement to regions. Coordination, particularly at state level, is a problem, especially given the different disciplines and backgrounds of staff. A corporate management team here appears to have been unsuccessful and has been abandoned; the emphasis has increasingly been on delegation to regional teams. CFL has since absorbed the Department of Water Resources to acquire an even wider remit, and has been renamed the *Department of Conservation and Environment*.

The second major department is the *Ministry of Planning and Environment*, created in 1988. It is concerned with planning and regulation of development in the private sector; it is also the parent department of two important statutory authorities, the Land Conservation Council and the Environmental Protection Agency. The Ministry is the lead agency for the State Conservation Strategy and coordinates the efforts of other agencies and departments to give effect to it. It is currently developing a strategy for the provision of open space throughout the state.

The Environmental Protection Authority has a mandate to protect the air, land and water environments, in practice concentrating on air and water, with land the responsibility of the Lands Division of CFL. Its chairman chairs the Advisory Environment Council.

The Land Conservation Council was created in 1970 to investigate and make recommendations on the use of public land in the state. It operates primarily through staff seconded from relevant agencies. After public scrutiny and discussion, its recommendations go to the government for approval, which is nearly always forthcoming. It attempts to strike a balance between protection of the environment and the provision of goods and services needed by the community, including recreation. Although its main emphasis is on Crown land, it also has some responsibilities for private land, making recommendations on land use in catchments. The chairman of the LCC is also the Commissioner for the Environment and is required to produce an annual State of the Environment Report.

In addition to the Crown land, the Crown has the right of use and control of water resources in the state. and the *Department of Water Resources* was until recently responsible for their planning and management, although the latter is primarily a function of the Metropolitan Board of Works and the Rural Water Commission. During the 1980s the department adopted an integrated view of water management. A ministerial standing committee for catchment and watershed management and planning was established, and a state-wide plan for water management was in preparation. The Metropolitan Board of Works, founded in 1890, has extended its remit from water supply, drainage and sewerage to meeting community needs for open space by establishing a system of parks in river valleys on land of little value for other purposes. *The Rural Water Commission*, formed only in 1984, is responsible for water supply in the rest of Victoria, where storages for irrigation in the dry north west make a major contribution to outdoor recreation.

The Victorian Tourism Commission, which is responsible to the Department of Industry, Technology and Resources, was established in 1982 to provide leadership to the tourism industry. Its main functions are the marketing and stimulation of tourism, and it encourages the creation of necessary infrastructure and public facilities. The government has approved a State Tourism Strategy which aims to improve and manage the recreation and tourism industries to maximize benefits to the community within the tolerance of ecosystems. *An Alpine Resorts Commission* manages and develops resorts in the Australian Alps. *The Department of Sport and Recreation* is also primarily a promotional and advisory body. Its aim is to oversee the development and management of sport and recreation, to promote participation and to ensure an equitable distribution of recreational opportunities. Although its emphasis is on competitive sport, it recognizes the importance of outdoor recreation. It is not primarily a provider but is concerned to promote greater access to land and water resources.

Victoria is a compact state, with a wide range of environments and recreational resources. Because of the recentness of changes, it is difficult to evaluate how far the concentration of government responsibilities for conservation and outdoor recreation in the Department of Conservation, Forests and Lands, and subsequently in the Department of Conservation and Environment, has provided better coordination. It appears to work best at the sub-state level to which administration and decision-making have been increasingly delegated. Whatever the answers, achievement of consistent policies seems to have been helped by the adoption of the State Conservation Strategy and the recognition of conservation as a major policy objective. There also seems little doubt that the Land Conservation Council has played a major role in securing the wise use (including that for recreation) of the public lands, which occupy a third of the state.

Conclusions on Australia

The emphasis in Australia, where both conservation and recreation are primarily state responsibilities, has been on the management of the Crown lands. It seems to have been easier to establish a coherent approach for conservation, particularly where states have adopted conservation strategies, following the lead of the Commonwealth government; and while it has not been possible to establish how effective this has been in influencing the policies of departments, at least a mechanism is in place. An integrated approach to outdoor recreation seems much less evident, and a large number of agencies, only partially represented in this summary account, has responsibility for provision, in none of which it is central. It is also unclear how far the plans and strategies that have been and are being prepared are likely to help achieve a greater coherence. What is clear is a trend towards increasing concentration of functions, although it is too soon to know whether this is leading to better coordination. This concentration is generally within government departments, often absorbing previously semi-independent agencies, and much of the power seems to rest in the hands of public servants, in part because of the common practice in state governments for ministers to hold multiple and often unrelated portfolios, leading to a degree of detachment from their departments.

Conclusions

There are obvious differences between the governmental structures adopted for conservation and recreation in Australia and in the United Kingdom. In large measure these reflect the differences between sources of power in a unitary and a federal state, and between one in which there is little public land and one in which it is extensive. Differences in scale are also a factor, although, despite the vast areas involved, Australia is essentially a commonwealth of city states, most of them with populations comparable in size to those of a large English county or Scottish region. In general, local government outside the cities is weak in Australia and much provision is by the state on Crown land. In the United Kingdom, local government is much stronger and is a major provider of recreational facilities. What seems to have happened in both countries is first an *ad hoc* reaction to problems as they occur, with some modification of functions as the nature and scale of problems have changed, and then some attempt to integrate a number of functions in a single agency, a tendency which has been more marked in Australia. In 1971–2 *The Select Committee on Scottish Affairs*, examining governmental responsibilities for land use, including conservation and recreation, debated the merits of consolidating functions within a single agency—in that context a Department of Rural Affairs—versus a number of independent agencies and came down in favour of the latter, preferring public debate between agencies rather than resolution behind departmental doors. Although the Commonwealth Department of the Arts, Sport, Environment, Tourism and Territories is now well established, it is unclear whether benefits have come from bringing these functions together; the British government's creation of a Ministry of National Heritage is too recent for any judgement to be possible. Similar trends are observable at state and country level, although the trend is more marked in Australia, where changes are also too recent to evaluate. What is certainly true in both countries is that it has been easier to achieve a more integrated approach to conservation than it is to recreation; whether it is more effective is a matter of debate.

References

This chapter is based largely on two sources, an investigation of the structures and policies of the Australian States and Territories for conservation, outdoor recreation and tourism, undertaken in the 1980s in collaboration with Dr G. Yapp, then of the Land and Water Resources Division of the Commonwealth Scientific and Industrial Research Organization, and the author's personal experience over twenty-seven years of the conservation, recreation and tourism fields in the United Kingdom, including as a member of the England Committee of the Nature Conservancy (1965–71) and of the Scottish Sports Council (1976–87). The former study was based largely on interviews with officials in the various departments and agencies, together with perusal of a great many published and unpublished official documents, many of them only marginally concerned with the topics under investigation. Owing to illness and industrial action the study extended over several years, during which there were numerous changes in structure. For these reasons, in many cases it is not possible to cite sources for statements made. The author possesses only his notes. It would be invidious to cite an extensive bibliography for the United Kingdom, for which there is much more published material; only a limited bibliography is therefore given.

United Kingdom

Chairmen's Policy Group, 1983, *Leisure policy for the future*, London, Sports Council.
Cherry, G.E., 1975, *Environmental Planning Vol. 2, National Parks and Recreation in the Countryside*, London, HMSO.
Council for National Parks, 1986, *50 years for National Parks*, London, CNP.

English Tourist Board, Countryside Commission, 1989, *Principles for Tourism in the Countryside*, Cheltenham, Countryside Commission.

Glyptis, S., 1991, *Countryside Recreation*, Harlow, Longman.

House of Lords Select Committee on Sport and Leisure, 1973, *Second report*, London, HMSO.

MacEwen, A. and MacEwen, M., 1982, *National Parks: Conservation or Cosmetics?*, London, Allen & Unwin.

National Parks Policies Review Committee, 1974, *Report*, London, HMSO.

Patmore, J.A., 1983, *Recreation and Resources*, Oxford, Blackwell.

Poore, D. and Poore, J., 1987, *Protected Landscapes: the United Kingdom Experience*, Gland, International Union for the Conservation of Nature.

Australia

Anon., 1984, *The Tourism Strategy: Victoria, the Next Decade*, Melbourne, Government Printer.

Anon., 1987, *Protecting the Environment: a Conservation Strategy for Victoria*, Melbourne, Government Printer.

Department of Conservation and Land Management, 1987, *Strategies for Conservation and Recreation on CALM lands in Western Australia*, Perth, CALM.

Mercer, D., 1977, *Leisure and Recreation in Australia*, Melbourne, Sorrett.

Mercer, D. (ed.), 1981, *Outdoor Recreation: Australian Perspectives*, Melbourne, Sorrett.

National Parks Authority (Western Australia), 1981, *National Park Management Policies*.

State Conservation Strategy Western Australia Working Group, CALM, 1987, *A State Conservation Strategy for Western Australia: a Sense of Direction*, Bulletin 270, Perth, CALM.

7

PLANNING FOR LEISURE: PAST, PRESENT AND FUTURE

A. J. VEAL

Planning for leisure in a comprehensive, systematic way is a relatively new form of human endeavour. In many countries, during the latter half of the twentieth century, attempts have been made to determine appropriate roles for planning in relation to leisure and to devise suitable planning techniques and approaches. This chapter seeks to summarize the history of these efforts in one country—Great Britain—and to consider prospects for the future.

The environment of planning for leisure in Britain over the last thirty years can be characterized by three distinct phases: these might be termed the *demand* phase, the *need* phase and the *enterprise* phase. In each the basic premises upon which public leisure provision was based were different.

The 'demand' phase: 1960–72

In the 1960s, when leisure, in various forms, was 'discovered' as a public planning issue, the central focus was on *demand*. In a period of rapid technological change and increasing population, incomes, and car-ownership, *leisure* and its consequences in the form of such phenomena as mass-recreation-demand pressures in the countryside, or the potential for unrest occasioned by the lack of 'constructive' leisure outlets for 'idle youth', threatened to overwhelm society unless something was done about it. The aim of planning was to measure and forecast the totality of leisure demand and then put in place policies to provide for that demand.

While elements of the demand approach were evident in the 1960 report of the Wolfenden Committee, *Sport and the Community* (1960), and in the Arts Council's 1959 report on *Housing the Arts* (ACGB, 1959 p.5), the era was most clearly epitomized by Michael Dower's influential paper, *Fourth Wave—the Challenge of Leisure*, in which he stated:

Throughout the nation people have more leisure than ever before: the opportunity and desire to use it are being profoundly influenced by the growth of income, of mobility and of education. The result is a fast growing and changing demand for leisure activities. Our towns and countryside do not match this demand. We need more spacious and adaptable homes, more sophisticated leisure buildings, more coherent open space, more accessible countryside, a better deal for tourists . . . This presents a planning challenge no less urgent than those of housing or traffic, and one which must be built into the whole range of land use planning and environmental design. [Dower, 1965, p.189]

There was no doubt in Dower's mind as to where the responsibility for meeting this challenge lay:

The Government should initiate . . . an assessment of national demand for leisure facilities, and should formulate broad principles for satisfying this demand . . . the Government should also initiate research into standards of provision for buildings and other facilities for leisure in urban areas. Regional planning boards should treat leisure as a major factor in preparing regional plans . . . Local planning authorities, in undertaking the review of leisure facilities requested by the Government, should then take into account the national principles, the regional proposals and the recommended standards of provision. Grant aid from Government to local authorities and leisure organizations should be made conditional upon the satisfaction of these principles and standards and should be used to encourage a more generous provision for leisure by local authorities themselves. [p.189]

And so it came to pass. With the change to a Labour government in the mid-1960s, the Sports Council, the Countryside Commission, and later tourism agencies came into being and, together with local government, sprang into action, at a time when growth in the public sector was the norm. Many of the Wolfenden Committee's recommendations were implemented and Dower's approach was followed almost to the letter—particularly in the work of the Sports Council. In the late 1960s the first serious national surveys of leisure participation added quantification to the Wolfenden and Dower scenarios by demonstrating, on the one hand, the high level of demand for outdoor recreation, indicating the need for facilities to meet growing pressures, and on the other hand, the relatively low levels of participation in sport and the arts, indicating the need for increased provision to facilitate and stimulate demand (Rodgers, 1967; Sillitoe, 1969).

It was the thinking in the late 1960s and early 1970s which set in train the mechanisms that created the public-sector leisure industry to be seen in Britain today, in the form of 2,000 indoor leisure centres, a vastly increased number of swimming pools, scores of arts centres and dozens of new municipal theatres, Country Parks, Long Distance Footpaths (now National Trails) and the network of local government departments and national and regional QUANGOs. The demand phase established a wide range of public leisure facilities as accepted parts of the range of basic services to be provided or supported by various levels of government. The facilities were provided for all, with the intention of meeting the demands of all sections of the community. Planning for leisure, while paying some attention to the efforts of the voluntary sector, was primarily focused on public provision. Little attention was paid by public-sector planners and policy-makers to those sectors of leisure serviced by the private sector.

The 'need' phase: 1973–85

Despite the fact that the 'demand' phase enjoyed its heyday under the auspices of a Labour government, the overall approach did not involve a 'welfare' perspective. There was little or no reference to particular priority groups; the aim was provision for all. During the 1970s the mood changed, and instead of attempting to measure, forecast and provide for leisure demand in its entirety, the rhetoric suggested that policy priorities were now to be focused on those in need, whether this was specifically recreational need or more general social need.

In 1973 a House of Lords committee, under the chairmanship of Lord Cobham and serviced by Allan Patmore and Brian Rodgers, produced a report, Sport and Leisure, which asserted that leisure services were now accepted as 'part of the fabric of the social services' (Cobham, 1973) and this was later supported in the 1975 White Paper, Sport and Recreation (DOE, 1975). This view was reflected in the approach of several studies at the time, including Rhona and Robert Rapoports' Leisure and the Family Life Cycle (Rapoport and Rapoport, 1975), and the Department of the Environment study Recreation and Deprivation in Urban Areas (DOE, 1977). Ralph Glasser (1975) attacked what he called the 'demand and supply school of thought', and the Rapoports attacked the 'palpable demand' approach to leisure provision for failing to consider people's underlying needs. They were able to pursue that concern in the late 1970s, when their Institute of Family and Environmental Research collaborated with Michael Dower's Dartington Amenity Research Trust on the Department of the Environment sponsored Leisure Provision and People's Needs project, (Dower, et al., 1981), at that time the most expensive leisure research project ever mounted in Britain. Based on case studies of groups with poor quality of life, the study called for a 'new culture of leisure provision' (p.2), reflecting the idea that different people had different needs and that needs could be met in a variety of ways, involving a 'pluralist view of leisure provision' (p.142).

The 'need' emphasis lasted through into the 1980s, as indicated by the 1982 Chairmen's Policy Group report (drafted by Dower), which declared: 'Leisure provision has become accepted as a major element of social policy, aiming at the enhancement of the quality of life of all citizens. This calls for a change in emphasis, away from catering simply for leisure demands, to the understanding and meeting of needs' (Chairmen's Policy Group, 1982, p.62).

In fact the Chairmen's Policy Group did not make clear the difference between need and demand. It was implied, however, that in the past leisure provision had been thought of as catering only to 'demand'—an economist's term which gave no indication of the importance of leisure for people's quality of life. But leisure provision should, it was now believed, be thought of as a 'need', as important and as vital as the 'need' for other essentials of life such as housing or health services. Leisure 'needs' were much more important than leisure 'demands' and therefore justified, and indeed required, public-sector action.

The need approach arose partly as an opportunistic response by the public leisure industry to changing political and economic circumstances, particularly the efforts of both Labour and Conservative governments to reduce public expenditure; public leisure services would, it was hoped, be safe from financial cuts if they were seen as meeting essential needs. But it arose also from research-based analyses of the effects of the universal 'demand' approach, which established that the prime beneficiaries of public provision were often not the poorer sections of the community but the middle classes (Young and Willmott, 1973, p.214; Built Environment Research Group, 1977; Hillman and Whalley, 1977). This, of course, should not have come as a surprise, since those sections of the community in which sports participation and the arts were already part of the culture and who enjoyed higher levels of car-ownership and mobility were more likely to want and be able to take advantage of the facilities available. Public leisure services had not been organized on the same basis as public housing, for example, as provision for those who could not afford the private sector; they had been established as a universal service for all. The middle classes more readily availed themselves of the service than did the more deprived groups. Some evidence suggested that, when facilities were provided on a sufficient scale and with appropriate management styles, a full cross-section of the community could effectively be catered for (Whalley, 1980), but rather than pursuing a strategy of 'saturation provision' to reach the needy, the tendency was for planners and policy-makers to adopt a strategy of 'targeting' the deprived.

The 'enterprise' phase: 1983–present

The enterprise phase reflects the philsophy of the Conservative government, that the private sector is a more effective mechanism for delivering a wide range of services hitherto provided by the public sector and that market processes are better at discovering and meeting people's needs than public planners and agencies. The Thatcher government came to power in 1979 but took some time to turn its attention to leisure. The turning point was probably an interview in *The Director* in 1983, when, in commenting on the proposal to build a theme park near the former steel town of Corby, Mrs Thatcher declared that 'There is much industry to be had from people's pleasures' (Thatcher, 1983). Reflecting this terminology, the Conservative Central Office published the report *New Jobs from Pleasure* (Banks, 1985) which recommended deregulation of large sections of the commercial leisure industries such as pubs, restaurants and gambling. The government report *Pleasure, Leisure and Jobs: The Business of Tourism* (Young, 1985), which followed later the same year, adopted the same approach, focusing on the private sector and the need to lift barriers to competition and government regulation, stating that 'private enterprise is the backbone of the industry and it has never looked to Government for handouts . . . The success story of the leisure and tourism industry is essentially a flowering of private enterprise' (Young, 1985).

The message that leisure was to be seen as an industry producing jobs and not as a social service dependent on taxes stimulated at least two of the major QUANGOs to produce studies to demonstrate the economic value of their particular sector of the industry (Myerscough, 1988; Henley Centre for Forecasting, 1986).

The culmination of the enterprise approach was the introduction of 'Compulsory Competitive Tendering' (CCT) through the 1988 Local Government Act, requiring that the management of most of the leisure services provided by local government must be put out to tender, so that both the traditional local government departments and private companies might compete for the contracts to operate them. This reflects the belief that such services might be run more cheaply, if not profitably, by, or in conjunction with, private enterprise management.

CCT has had wider ramifications than the narrowly economic or financial. The drawing up of terms of contracts for tender documents and consideration of ways in which private-sector operators' performance might be monitored have caused local councils to think through the aims and objectives of their various services in more detail than hitherto and to consider more closely the purposes, incidence and costs of subsidy.

Planning approaches in the demand phase

Until the 1960s virtually the only guidance available to leisure planners was the National Playing Fields Association's (NPFA) 'standard' of six acres of open space for every 1,000 people. This standard, though periodically reviewed, originated in 1925 and was based on an assessment of the requirements of the estimated 200 adults in every 1,000 who would be active in sport (NPFA, 1971).

The techniques used in planning for leisure in the 1960s and early 1970s developed the standards approach into a demand-based approach appropriate to the policy preoccupations of the time. The *Planning for Sport* report (Sports Council, 1968) sought to quantify total demand for sport based on participation rates derived from social surveys and, on the basis of these assessments, to produce targets for provision of sports facilities. Local councils developed plans and proposals within regional and national frameworks and attracted modest grant aid for their projects as a result. In countryside recreation more was left to planning at County Council level, but much research was conducted to find ways to quantify, predict and model outdoor recreation demand (as summarized by Coppock and Duffield, 1975).

In urban areas the aim was to quantify total community demand, convert this into facility requirements and then to prepare a plan to provide that quantity of facilities, whether they were playing fields, sports centres, swimming pools, golf courses or community centres. In rural outdoor recreation planning, despite some efforts at modelling, the relationships between demand and facility needs were more informally delineated, as was the case with the arts.

Planning approaches in the needs phase

The 'needs' phase produced its own approaches to planning. The 'new culture of leisure provision' advocated in *Leisure Provision and People's Needs* (Dower *et al.*, 1981) has already been referred to. While this exhorted planners to be more human, more concerned with variations in needs and with alternative ways of meeting needs, and to involve the community more in decision-making, it did not go so far as to provide planners with practical guidelines to follow: while the report may well have had a qualitative effect on the 'culture' of planning, it is difficult to identify any concrete effects in real planning situations.

The 1975 White Paper had recommended the designation of 'Recreational Priority Areas' along the lines of other spatially targeted public-service programmes of the time. While this recommendation was not fully adopted (although the Sports Council earmarked funds for inner-city areas), research was carried out by the Greater London Council (Nicholls, 1975) in London and the Tourism and Recreation Research Unit (TRRU, 1982) in Scotland to explore the possibilities of identifying recreationally deprived, and therefore needy, areas using computer-mapping technology—a technique followed up in modern approaches such as the ACORN (A Classification of Residential Neighbourhoods) lifestyle mapping system (Shaw, 1984). However, few planning agencies appeared to have the resources to adopt this approach in their own areas, even if they had the inclination.

There was, in retrospect, a certain lack of consistency in the needs approach, in that it assumed, but did not explicitly state, that while the needs of the deprived were to be met by the targeted public programmes, the requirements of everyone else could be met in some other, unspecified, way. Suddenly a service which had hitherto been 'for all' was to be focused on certain sectors of the community only: public leisure provision was no longer to be viewed as a universal service. In other areas of the public service, such as health and education, moves from universal to targeted—'means tested'— delivery attract widespread criticism because of the 'second-class citizen' implications of the policies and the belief that they are primarily motivated by a desire to save money. Such criticisms were not, however, heard in the case of leisure services: those involved in public leisure services seemed content to trade off universalism in exchange for the mantle of 'social service' and the accompanying warm glow from the feeling that provision was being directed towards the deprived.

The logical inconsistency of this position can be demonstrated by examining arguments in favour of publicly provided leisure facilities. As Gratton and Taylor (1991, p.55) point out, government provision in an otherwise market-based economic system is justified on equity and efficiency grounds; the equity argument is the justification for the needs approach, while the efficiency argument, concerned as it is with the delivery of 'public good' and externality benefits, justifies a universal, totally demand-based service.

Sport in the Community—the Next Ten Years, the Sports Council's 1982 plan, was published towards the end of the 'needs' era and shows evidence of continuation and reaffirmation of the 'demand' approach as well as taking on board aspects of the 'needs' approach. Thus a 'shopping list' of facilities is presented as before, but participation targets are also produced, with higher increases proposed for women than for men because of the lower existing participation rates of women and the desire to achieve more equality. Setting targets was a new development in the demand approach, acknowledging that demand is not a fixed phenomenon but may be promoted and stimulated by public policy actions. The approach has not, however, been generally taken up by local authorities. In addition to its continuing commitment to the demand approach, the 1982 report also reflected the concerns of the needs era in stating that 'resources will need to be selectively concentrated on promotional programmes for certain target groups and selected sports; certain geographical areas' (Sports Council, 1982, p.2).

The net effect of the 'needs' era was therefore that the old demand-based planning continued, but with an increase in public consultation, and priority for funding given to facilities located in generally deprived areas.

Planning approaches in the enterprise phase

What planning methods have emerged to reflect the requirements of the enterprise approach to provision? Henry and Spink (1990, p.63) refer to the growing significance of 'market-led' approaches to planning, involving such features as planning gain (where private developers undertake to provide public leisure facilities as part of a commercial development), design briefs, private tenders and management contracts. Such phenomena are, however, not planning methods or approaches in the sense discussed here but alternative means of implementing plans. This is, however, the essence of the enterprise era: that services should be *delivered* by the private sector even if they continue to be planned, paid for and underpinned by the public sector. This in turn reflects an ideological commitment to reducing the role of the state and extending the role of private enterprise and also a belief that savings can be made through reduction of 'X' inefficiency—the supposed tendency for state organizations to be less efficient than equivalent private-sector organizations (Gratton and Taylor, 1991, p.96).

The enterprise era may, however, mean more than a change in the type of organization which operates the facilities. It also implies that net public expenditure on leisure provision should be reduced, not just through cost savings, but by requiring the user to pay more. However, accepting that the user should pay the *full* economic cost of provision would imply a rejection of virtually all of the arguments for public provision: the service may as well be provided by the private sector. If there is a major move towards 'user pays', involving substantial price increases, then demand estimates will need to be re-assessed since they are based on certain assumptions about the availability of subsidized prices for various leisure services. If these relative prices are changed substantially then, until their effects can be monitored, it will be impossible to estimate demand. It could be, of course, that the traditional economists'—and politicians'—belief in the importance of price levels has been misplaced all along and that demand will quickly recover from the imposition of price increases, especially if the high-price regime results in a higher quality of service. Alternatively there could be a once-for-all reduction in participation in some activities—possibly negating the achievements of decades of public-sector effort in increasing participation (Campbell, 1992; Coalter, 1992).

It might be thought that planning with private-sector operation in mind would cause public authorities to adopt new planning approaches. However, in so far as the expectation is simply that private companies may operate public facilities under contract there is no reason why the approach to planning should be affected. If a universal demand approach is adopted then total demand must be assessed in order to determine the required level of provision of facilities, whether they are to be managed by the public or the private sector. Similarly, if a targeted-needs approach is adopted, priority groups and areas must be determined regardless of the type of organization which is to manage the provision.

If, on the other hand, it is expected that private-sector involvement will entail the raising of prices and reductions in subsidies, then clearly the 'needs' approach to planning becomes less relevant, but the traditional 'demand' approach is still valid, albeit with overall demand levels reduced by the effects of higher prices. Both public and private-sector planning depends on assessment of levels of likely demand. In the case of the public sector the tendency is to assume that all of the assessed demand (or, in the 'needs' approach, that part of it emanating from deprived groups) is to be catered for. Single private-sector organizations tend not to consider meeting the whole of demand but to achieve a reasonable 'market share' on the assumption that other competing providers will also be involved. However, the basis of the approach for both sectors is an assessment of current and future demand.

Planning methods

How then does the practice of thirty years of planning for leisure in Britain relate to the theory? A review of available planning methods published in 1982 listed eight different approaches to planning for leisure (Veal, 1982). These are reviewed below and their continued relevance in the light of the above discussion is assessed.

1. *Standards*—planning based on per-capita specifications of levels of provision laid down by some authoritative body. Soundly based standards are generally based on demand estimates. Despite their limitations standards continue to have their uses, provided they are periodically reviewed and updated and emanate from a disinterested source.
2. *Gross demand*—estimation of broad demand levels based on existing

national or regional participation surveys. This is the most basic of demand estimation approaches, which can be applied with varying levels of sophistication to take account of variations in local socio-demographic conditions.

3. *Spatial approaches*—localized demand estimation incorporating consideration of facility catchment areas. This is a necessary development of the 'gross demand' approach when considering the question of facility location.

4. *Hierarchies of facilities*—an approach which recognizes that different types and scales of facilities have different catchment areas. This method is particularly appropriate when planning for new communities which, though hardly relevant in contemporary Britain, is a consideration in many other parts of the world. The approach is also relevant when considering facilities involving spectator audiences.

5. *Grid or matrix approach*—a method involving examination of the impact of all of an authority's leisure services on all social groups. This is less a demand estimation process than an impact evaluation/effectiveness approach. As such it has a potential role to play in the corporate management process, in which public bodies are increasingly being called upon to evaluate the outcomes of their policies.

6. *Organic approach*—strategy development based on assessment of existing service provision and spatial gaps in demand. This is an incremental rather than comprehensive approach and is similar to the way in which many private-sector organizations operate.

7. *Community development approach*—planning and policy development based on community consultation. This is very much a product of the 'needs' era and is out of tune with the rhetoric of the enterprise era. However, public participation is now part of the local political scene and so continues to play its part in public planning.

8. *Issues approach*—plans based on initial identification of 'key issues' rather than comprehensive needs/demand assessment. This approach is particularly in tune with the ideas of the enterprise era and corresponds to the fashionable private-sector SWOT (Strengths, Weaknesses, Opportunities, Threats) analysis. It is the approach which is most likely to justify *ad-hoc*, one-off 'hallmark' projects.

With the possible exception of the hierarchies approach, which is particularly applicable to 'green field' situations, and the grid/matrix approach, which few authorities have the data or resources to implement, each of the above approaches continues to play its part in planning for leisure.

The future

From this discussion of the British experience of planning for leisure in the 'demand', 'needs' and 'enterprise' environments, one clear conclusion emerges: namely, that regardless of the particular political or economic conditions of the time, and regardless of the rhetoric of politicians, the task of the leisure planner is to estimate demand. Whether the aim is to provide a universal service, a needs-based targeted service or a user-pays service, and whether the strategy is to meet existing demand or to promote and stimulate new demand, the challenge of planning for leisure remains to find ways of more accurately matching supply with demand.

The future is, of course, uncertain: governments of different complexions will come and go; economic fortunes will continue to fluctuate; there will no doubt be variations in the importance people attach to leisure time as opposed to work and the desire for more material possessions; the level of concern for the environment will vary; the future may be characterized by a 'self-service economy' (Gershuny, 1978) or an 'information economy' (Stonier, 1983). But in the long run leisure is likely to continue to increase in economic and social significance and so public, private and voluntary organizations will be increasingly involved in providing facilities and services for leisure (Veal, 1987).

People engage in leisure activities for the satisfaction and fun which they offer: and, as Isaac Asimov (1976, p.109) put it: 'Fun is . . . always to be found in feasting and laughing and loving and roughhousing and gambling and hiking and noisemaking and yelling and moving chessmen and chasing rubber balls and sleeping in the sun and dancing and swimming and watching entertainers and risking one's neck for foolish reasons.'

The role of the leisure planner in the future will be to make some contribution to ensuring that, in an increasingly complex society, time and space for the enjoyment of these activities are not only preserved but extended.

References

Arts Council of Great Britain, 1959, *Housing the Arts in Great Britain: Part I; London, Scotland, Wales*, London, ACGB.

Asimov, I., 1976, 'Future fun', in *Today and Tomorrow and . . .*, London, Scientific Book Club.

Banks, R., 1985, *New Jobs from Pleasure: a Strategy for Producing Jobs in the Tourist Industry*, London, Conservative Central Office.

Built Environment Research Group, 1977, *The Changing Indoor Sports Centre*, Study 13 London, Sports Council.

Campbell, H., 1992, 'Local authority pricing: incentive or constraint?', paper for European Leisure and Recreation Association Congress, *Leisure and the New Citizenship*, Universidad de Deusto, Bilbao, Spain.

Chairmen's Policy Group, 1982, *Leisure Policy for the Future*, London, Sports Council.

Coalter, F., 1992, 'Participation: price or priorities?', paper for the European Leisure and Recreation Association Congress, *Leisure and the New Citizenship*, Universidad de Deusto, Bilbao, Spain.

Cobham, Lord, 1973, *Sport and Leisure*, Reports of the House of Lords Select Committee on Sport and Leisure, London, HMSO.

Coppock, J.T. and Duffield, B.S., 1975, *Recreation in the Countryside: a Spatial Analysis*. London, Macmillan.

Department of the Environment, 1975, *Sport and Recreation*, Cmnd 6200 London, HMSO.
Department of the Environment, 1977, *Recreation and Deprivation in Urban Areas*, London, HMSO.
Dower, M., 1965, *Fourth Wave: The Challenge of Leisure*, London, Civic Trust.
Dower, M., Rapoport, R., Strelitz, Z. and Kew, S., 1981, *Leisure Provision and People's Needs*, London, HMSO.
Gershuny, J.I., 1978, *After Industrial Society? The Emerging Self-Service Economy*, London, Macmillan.
Glasser, R., 1975, 'Leisure policy, identity and work' in J.T. Haworth and M.A. Smith, (eds), *Work and Leisure*, London, Lepus.
Gratton, C. and Taylor, P., 1991, *Government and the Economics of Sport*, Harlow, Longman.
Henley Centre for Forecasting, 1986, *The Economic Impact and Importance of Sport in the UK*, London, Sports Council.
Henry, I. and Spink, J., 1990, 'Planning for leisure: the commercial and public sectors' in I. Henry (ed.), *Management and Planning in the Leisure Industries*, London, Macmillan.
Hillman, M. and Whalley, A., 1977, *Fair Play for All: A study of Access to Sport and Informal Recreation*, Broadsheet 571, London, PEP.
Myerscough, J., 1988 *The Economic Importance of the Arts in Britain*, London, Policy Studies Institute.
National Playing Fields Association, 1971, *Outdoor Play Space Requirements*, London NPFA.
Nicholls, M., 1975, *Recreationally Disadvantaged Areas in Greater London*, Research Memorandum 467, London, Greater London Council, Policy Studies Unit.
Rapoport, R. and Rapoport R.N., 1975, *Leisure and the Family Life Cycle*, London, Routledge and Kegan Paul.
Rodgers, B., 1967, *Pilot National Recreation Survey*, Keele, Staffs., British Travel Association/University of Keele.
Sillitoe, K.K., 1969, *Planning for Leisure*, London, HMSO.
Shaw, M., 1984, *Sport and Leisure Participation and Life-styles in Different Residential Neighbourhoods: An Exploration of the ACORN Classification*, London, Sports Council/SSRC.
Sports Council, 1968, *Planning for Sport*, London, Central Council of Physical Recreation.
Sports Council, 1982, *Sport in the Community: The Next Ten Years*, London, Sports Council.
Stonier, T., 1983, *The wealth of Information: a Profile of the Post-industrial Economy*, London, Thames Methuen.
Thatcher, M., 1983, interview in *The Director*, September.
Tourism and Recreation Research Unit, 1982, *Priority Groups and Access to Leisure Opportunity*, Edinburgh, Lothian Regional Council, Dept. of Leisure Services.
Veal, A.J., 1982, *Planning for Leisure: Alternative Approaches*, Papers in Leisure Studies No. 5, London, Polytechnic of North London.
Veal, A.J., 1987, *Leisure and the future*, London, Allen and Unwin.
Whalley, B., 1980, *Sports Centre Planning and Provision in England and Wales*, M.Phil. thesis, Centre for Urban and Regional Studies, University of Birmingham.
Wolfenden, Lord, 1960, *Sport and the Community*, London, Central Council of Physical Recreation.
Young, Lord, 1985, *Pleasure, Leisure and Jobs: The Business of Tourism*, Cabinet Enterprise Unit, London, HMSO.
Young, M. and Willmott, P., 1973, *The Symmetrical Family—a Study of Work and Leisure in the London Region*, London, Routledge and Kegan Paul.

8

RECREATION, CONSERVATION AND THE CHANGING MANAGEMENT OF WATER RESOURCES IN ENGLAND AND WALES

MICHAEL F. TANNER

Introduction

The privatization of the water industry in 1989 brought to an end a process of integrating water management in England and Wales that began in late-Victorian times. It was argued that transferring the industry to the private sector would free it from restrictive government intervention and exposure to market forces would lead to greater efficiency. Initially the government proposed to privatize the ten water authorities as they stood, thereby preserving the integrity of the catchment-based multi-purpose management system that had existed only since 1974. It became clear, though, that the regulatory and environmental functions of the water authorities made this impracticable and, in the event, only the utility functions of water supply and sewage disposal were transferred into private ownership. The remaining functions of the water authorities were retained in the public domain by transferring them to a newly established government agency, the National Rivers Authority.

As with other privatized public utility monopolies, the government set in place a regulatory framework to protect the interests of consumers, but the new private water companies were also given clear duties relating to conservation, the enhancement of natural beauty and the recreational use of their land and water resources. In addition, they may only dispose of such resources with the consent of the Secretary of State, who may impose special conditions where the resource concerned lies within national parks or other areas of recognized amenity or scientific importance. Such limitations on the freedom of private companies seems somewhat anachronistic in the context of a measure ostensibly intended to expose the water industry to market forces. This chapter examines how this situation has come about.

Background

The character of the water industry in England and Wales can only be fully understood in the context of the rapid urbanization during the nineteenth century. Previously, the only well-established water management functions were land drainage and navigation. Land drainage had already transformed the landscape of extensive lowland areas, while the inland waterway system, at its peak, extended to more than 7,000 kilometres of canals and river navigations. Associated with the 4,400 kilometres of canal were over 100 canal feeder reservoirs amounting to 1,600 hectares, most still in existence. Water supply needs, in contrast, were mainly satisfied at the local community level from wells or by abstraction from nearby rivers and streams, although cisterns and small storage reservoirs were also frequently used. Only rarely did the larger communities draw their water from more distant sources, usually as a result of municipal enterprise or the activities of private companies (Tanner, 1976).

Development of upland reservoirs

Urbanization and industrialization brought dramatic changes. Rapidly increasing demands for water quickly outstripped the capacity of local sources, while rivers and streams became polluted by sewage and industrial wastes. Many communities, therefore, had to seek cleaner and more productive sources, ideally by damming a valley in nearby upland so that the water could be transported and distributed by the use of gravity. During the first half of the nineteenth century, over forty such reservoirs larger than 2.4 hectares were built, mainly in the southern Pennines to supply water to the new industrial towns of Lancashire and Yorkshire.

Initially, the reservoirs were relatively small and isolated, but a new phase of development began in 1847 when the City of Manchester obtained parliamentary approval to exploit the water resources of the Longdendale Valley, 25 kilometres to the east of the city. This involved constructing a chain of seven reservoirs and acquiring a catchment area of 7,800 hectares. During the next fifty years Manchester's example was followed by several other northern and midland cities, including Liverpool, with its Lake Vyrnwy catchment (8,900 hectares) in north Wales, Manchester itself, which developed its Thirlmere catchment (4,000 hectares) in the Lake District, 154 kilometres from the city in the 1880s, and Birmingham, which began to draw water from its Elan Valley catchment (17,800 hectares), 120 kilometres away in mid-Wales, towards the end of the century (Tanner 1977).

The justification for this approach depended partly upon the need to satisfy rapidly growing demand but also upon concern about the relationship between polluted water supplies and the incidence of disease. Before the

development of modern treatment methods the only way the water undertaking could protect the purity of supply was by acquiring both the water
source itself and the surrounding catchment so that it could control land use
and public access. Most of the Private Bills authorizing the purchase of such
areas included provision for the water undertaking to make bye-laws to prevent
or restrict access.

As a result, the second half of the nineteenth century saw the completion of
another 250 reservoirs, still mainly concentrated in the southern Pennines, but
also in the Lake District, upland Wales and parts of lowland England. Most
were developed by urban authorities, although a few private companies sur-
vived the general trend towards the municipalization of water supplies. At
the turn of the century parliamentary pressure also led to the establishment
of Joint Boards which enabled authorities to share the development of
resources in the interests of water conservation, most notably in the Derwent
Valley in the heart of the Peak District.

The pollution problem

The deteriorating state of many watercourses as a result of urban and industrial effluents also led to legislation to enable public action in relation to two
other water management functions. Concern over the decline of salmon
fisheries, caused both by pollution and the creation of obstructions, led to
the appointment of a Royal Commission and the passing of the *Salmon
Fisheries Act 1861*. This placed general responsibility for salmon fisheries
under the control of the Home Office and permitted the appointment of two
Salmon Fisheries Inspectors who began a series of annual reports that continued until shortly before the Second World War. An attempt to deal with
the problem at source was made by the *Rivers Pollution Prevention Act 1876*,
which gave local authorities limited powers to control pollution, although
these remained ineffective until local authorities in northern England began
to take joint action in the 1890s. In all these arrangements water management
functions were administered separately, and this remained a dominant feature
of the water industry until the mid-twentieth century.

The emergence of amenity and recreation interests

To an extent this fragmentation obscured the gradual emergency of amenity
and recreational interests as influences on water resource management, a
process that began surprisingly early. First in the field were the anglers. By
the 1850s several angling clubs had been established, mainly representing
landed interests and concerned with the preservation of salmon and latterly
trout fisheries. From the 1860s a new form emerged from the urban working
classes whose concern was the protection of the coarse fish populations of
lowland rivers from poachers and pollution. These developed into remarkably
effective pressure groups, both at local level, where they petitioned local
authorities and others against the discharge of sewage and other noxious

substances, and at national level, where it was mainly the activities of the London and Sheffield anglers that led to the introduction of a close season for coarse fish by the *Freshwater Fisheries Act, 1878* (Calcut, 1924). Consultation with recreational fishing interests thus became widely accepted as part of the water management process.

Impact on amenity

Recognition of the impact of water development projects on amenity came a little later. Most urban water supply schemes were subject to scrutiny by the parliamentary Private Bill procedure, but the main subjects for debate were the rights of landowners and the determination of appropriate compensation flows (Sheail, 1984). This changed when the City of Manchester made its first incursion into the Lake District during the late 1870s, when it sought permission to exploit the water resources of the Thirlmere catchment. There was already a nascent conservation movement in the Lake District, originally stimulated by the closure of footpaths and opposition to the coming of the railways, and from this sprang the Thirlmere Defence Association, with influential support. Its campaign was organized by two of the founder-members of the National Trust, Octavia Hill and Canon Rawnsley, and led to the insertion of 'environmental clauses' into Manchester's Bill during its parliamentary passage (Berry and Beard, 1980).

In particular, the *Manchester Corporation Water Act, 1879* requires the Corporation to have 'all reasonable regard' for 'the preservation, as well for the public as for private owners, of the beauty of the scenery of the said Lake District' (42 VICT, Ch XXXVI, sec 13). The significance of this victory lay in the recognition that environmental as well as engineering considerations might need to be taken into account in meeting urban water supply needs. Similar debate about the conflict between amenity and efficiency, measured in both engineering and economic terms, has attended many subsequent reservoir proposals, most notably in Manchester's three later attempts to develop the water resources of the Lake District.

The access question

Manchester's 1879 Act was also significant in that it included a clause protecting existing rights of access to the mountains and fells surrounding Thirlmere (sec 62). The nineteenth-century access movement was a response to the loss of public rights to the use of commons and footpaths, initially caused by agricultural enclosure and later by urban development. The acquisition by urban authorities of upland catchments and the adoption of protective measures had the effect of enclosing extensive areas of open moorland to which there had traditionally been unrestricted access. At the same time grouse shooting was gaining popularity among the landed classes and leading to the exclusion of the public from similar areas elsewhere. Indeed, many of the owners of upland catchments retained the sporting rights when they sold the land, while water undertakers who acquired such rights frequently leased them to others.

In spite of this protective clause, Thirlmere was regarded for almost a century as the classic example of the water industry's restrictive attitude towards the recreational use of its land, primarily because of the afforestation of the catchment and the prevention of public access to the lake. The real breakthrough for such access came in 1892 when Birmingham's Bill to develop the Elan Valley catchment was, like Manchester's Thirlmere Bill, opposed in Parliament by the Commons, Open Spaces and Footpaths Preservation Society (Eversley, 1910). As a result, more extensive public rights of access were inserted into the Act ensuring that 'The public shall be entitled to a privilege at all times of enjoying air exercise and recreation on common and unenclosed land acquired by the Corporation' (55 & 56 VICT Ch clxxii, sec 53). These 'Birmingham Clauses' became regarded as the model for protecting public access and were incorporated into several subsequent Acts providing for the purchase of upland catchments.

Water resource management before the Second World War

By the beginning of the twentieth century amenity and recreational interests were firmly embedded in the water management system in the sense that their representatives expected to be consulted, or were at least active in opposition, and that measures for their protection were normally built into legislation. Yet they had not emerged as policy issues in the political sense and this was to remain so until well after the Second World War because of the limited attention given to the management of water resources at national level and its continued fragmentation in institutional terms. Whereas different aspects of water resources had been investigated by eight Royal Commissions and numerous other enquiries during the nineteenth century, the only equivalent initiative during the first forty years of the twentieth century was the appointment of the Water Power Resources Committee in 1918.

This Committee was given a broader remit than its title suggests and it recognized the importance of taking account of 'public and private amenities' in planning to meet future demands for water (Board of Trade, 1920), but its wide-ranging recommendations had little policy impact. Instead, the Ministry of Health, which had become the responsible department, focused largely on public water supply, the development of which had become a routine operation governed by well-established procedures (Sheail, 1983). It therefore adopted an essentially administrative approach, seeking progressively to introduce greater efficiency by encouraging the amalgamation of water undertakings. It achieved some success, for the number of undertakings fell from over 2,000 in 1914 to fewer than 950 in 1950 (Institution of Water Engineers, 1950), but the lack of major policy initiatives gave amenity and recreational interests little chance to extend their influence.

Amenity and recreation interests

They were not dormant during the inter-war period, although there was surprisingly limited opposition from the amenity lobby to Manchester's second attempt to develop the resources of the Lake District, probably because it offered more remote and less visited valleys than the Thirlmere scheme (Rollinson, 1967). The enabling Act for the Haweswater scheme, given Royal Assent in 1919, provided for the raising of the water level in Haweswater by ninety-five feet and the construction of two other reservoirs. Work did not begin until ten years later and was completed in 1941, while the remaining stages were implemented between 1956 and 1974 (Manchester Corporation, 1974).

Angling interests were more active in seeking to offset the low priority given to water pollution questions during the inter-war period. Recognition of the growing importance of angling was reflected in the establishment of fisheries boards, whose membership included anglers, by the *Salmon and Freshwater Fisheries Act 1923*, but there was little other legislative action on pollution. Although the establishment of the Water Pollution Research Board in 1929 began to provide a scientific basis for pollution control, the main concern of the Ministry of Health was to remind local authorities of their powers under the 1876 Act. In practice, most took little action, and it has been suggested that the enterprise of angling clubs in taking legal action against polluters was often more effective than the use of these powers (Rhodes, 1981, p.133).

The inter-war access movement

Such activity attracted little attention, unlike the access movement, which became a major force. Its strength lay in the federations of rambling clubs which emerged in the industrial cities of the Midlands and North during the 1920s, and its primary concern was to secure rights of access to open moorland. Attention was particularly focused on the Peak District, a key location between the two major rambling centres of Sheffield and Manchester which was largely closed to the public (Stephenson, 1989, p.46).

The main target was the property of the large landowners, not specifically the gathering grounds of the water undertakings, although the participants in the famous Kinder Scout Mass Trespass made contact with Stockport Water Board officials during their march (Rothman, 1982, p.24). This changed somewhat during the 1930s as increasing attention was paid to the restrictive policies of the water industry, which controlled extensive areas of open moorland, including much in the Peak District. In 1935, the Council for the Preservation of Rural England initiated discussions with the British Waterworks Association, together with the Camping Club, the Commons Society, the Ramblers' Association and the Youth Hostels Association, but these proved abortive. Nevertheless, continued pressure led to the passing of the *Access to Mountains Act 1939*, more than half a century after the first such measure was introduced into Parliament, although this was rendered ineffective by the opposition of the landowning interests, including the British Waterworks Association (Stephenson, 1989).

Towards a national water policy

The move towards a national policy for water that would integrate its various functions began during the Second World War. This was to be guided for over thirty years by the Central Advisory Water Committee, first appointed in 1937 as a standing committee and made statutory in 1945. Unlike previous committees which had advised government on water questions, it comprised representatives of a wide range of interests, including fisheries and navigation but not amenity and recreation. The Committee produced several influential reports, the third of which advocated River Boards to perform a number of river management functions and also noted the growing demand for 'bathing, boating and similar forms of recreation' on rivers and canals (Ministry of Health, 1943, p.16). Its recommendations were accepted in a White Paper on *A National Policy for Water* (Ministry of Health *et al.*, 1944) and implemented by the *River Boards Act 1948*, which initiated a process of restructuring the water industry that was probably not completed by privatization in 1989. The responsibilities of the new River Boards included fisheries as well as land drainage and pollution control but did not extend to public water supply, which remained largely the province of local authorities.

Access to gathering grounds

This continued separation of water management functions meant that questions of amenity and public access to catchment areas became bound up with the broader political movement towards the establishment of national parks and the provision of public access to the countryside. In 1939 the Ministry of Health had issued its advisory Memorandum 221, widely interpreted as meaning that there should be no public access to reservoirs and gathering grounds in the interest of preserving the purity of supply (Ministry of Health, 1939). Nevertheless, when John Dower produced his report on national parks, he noted wide variation in the degree of public access to gathering grounds and suggested that restrictive policies were often the result of prejudice and irrelevance (Ministry of Town and Country Planning, 1945). Such variation was similarly reported by the Hobhouse Committee on *Footpaths and Access to the Countryside*, which recommended that public access to catchment areas for the purposes of air and recreation should normally be permitted, except where special restrictions were necessary (Ministry of Town and Country Planning, 1947). The Heneage Committee on *Gathering Grounds*, a sub-committee of the Central Advisory Water Committee, also concluded that there was no reason to exclude the public from gathering grounds, subject to adequate safeguards (Ministry of Health, 1948).

Recreational use of reservoirs

The Heneage Committee's report also formally recognized the existence of a new recreational force that had emerged largely unnoticed but which was to become highly significant over the next twenty years. This was the demand for recreational use of the reservoirs themselves. The Committee found that angling was already permitted at many reservoirs and sailing had recently been introduced by the Bristol Waterworks Company at its Cheddar Reservoir. In fact, the use of reservoirs for fishing had begun during the nineteenth century and was widespread before the Second World War, although it was usually carefully regulated by issuing day tickets or leasing rights to clubs. What was new was the demand for activities that might involve bodily contact with the water, which was regarded as undesirable on public health and aesthetic grounds. The Committee therefore concluded that the public should generally be excluded from the banks of reservoirs and that bathing should not be permitted, although fishing and boating might be allowed where subject to rigorous control.

In spite of the committee's reservations, pressure for such uses gradually built up, particularly in the late 1950s. As a result, the use of reservoirs for fishing continued to expand, while sailing was introduced by several other water undertakings towards the end of the decade. This led the Institution of Water Engineers to examine the whole question of recreational use in a report published in 1963 which still adopted a rather cautious approach and paid particular attention to how activities should be organized. While fishing was generally regarded as acceptable, sailing should only be introduced where it could be strictly controlled by delegating management to a club. Rowing might also be permitted in certain cases, but severe doubts were expressed about canoeing. Other activities, especially swimming and water skiing, should be excluded (Institution of Water Engineers, 1963).

Changes in water resource management practice

Two changes in the way in which water resources were being developed resulted in questioning existing attitudes towards the recreational use of reservoirs and catchments. The first was a trend away from traditional impounding reservoirs, from which water is normally transported by pipeline, towards regulating reservoirs. These are used to control flow in rivers, which can then be used as natural aqueducts to supply areas downstream. There is a long history of river regulation in England and Wales (Sheail, 1988), but its expansion during the 1950s meant that new reservoirs were being constructed where it was difficult to justify the restriction of public access to water that would be discharged into rivers where it could not be protected from the risk of pollution. This was recognized by the Institution of Water Engineers, which recommended that such reservoirs might be used for all activities for which they were suitable.

It was also significant that these regulating reservoirs might be constructed by river boards as well as by water supply undertakings. When the next restructuring was carried out by the *Water Resources Act 1963*, replacing the thirty-two River Boards by twenty-nine River Authorities, the new bodies were expressly authorized to permit the recreational use of their reservoirs and were given powers to provide the necessary facilities.

The second change was the trend away from the use of impounding reservoirs in the uplands, most of which were small and inaccessible, to larger reservoirs in the lowlands. Various factors contributed. Most of the best upland sites had already been exploited, but a significant element was the growing strength of the amenity lobby in resisting the development of reservoirs in national parks and similar areas. Its most notable victory came in 1962 when Manchester's plans to develop Ullswater as a source of supply and to build a new reservoir in Bannisdale were rejected by the House of Lords. The Ministry of Housing and Local Government, then the responsible department, set up a conference under Lord Jellicoe, including representatives of the National Parks Commission, to investigate water supply in the north west. The report, published in 1963, though inconclusive in some respects, led to the dropping of the reservoir scheme on amenity grounds and the adoption of a short-term solution to Manchester's problems by abstracting water from Ullswater and Windermere without any works to raise their levels (Dolbey, 1974).

This episode, in which amenity organizations proved to be powerful and influential opponents, was a salutary experience, not only for Manchester Corporation but also for the water industry as a whole. It led to much greater attention to environmental considerations in the planning of reservoir schemes and careful consultation with the amenity lobby. It also encouraged proposals for the development of reservoirs in the lowlands where opposition on amenity grounds was likely to be less effective. Because such reservoirs normally drew their water from nearby rivers where purity could not be ensured, it was considered essential to give it full treatment before it was taken into supply. There were, therefore, no public health reasons for preventing the reservoirs' use for the wide range of recreational activities for which their location and physical characteristics made them suitable. Providing facilities for such activities might also be regarded as a form of compensation for the loss of agricultural land and other amenities, thereby lessening local opposition.

As a result, most of the major new reservoirs planned or constructed in the mid-1960s were in the lowlands and made extensive provision for recreation, including Grafham Water (635 hectares) near Huntingdon, and Draycote Water (243 hectares) near Rugby. Both provided high-quality club sailing and day-ticket game fishing based on the artificial stocking of the reservoirs with trout, a pattern that was to be repeated at many other new reservoirs over the next twenty years. Opportunities to use reservoir surrounds for informal recreation were more limited, but most schemes provided quite extensive car parks, picnic sites and similar facilities enabling people to reach the water's edge. Such reservoirs represented an important addition to inland opportunities in areas of shortage for water-based recreation at a time when participation was growing rapidly as well as providing a model for the way in which recreation could be accommodated at water supply reservoirs without interfering with their primary function.

Changing attitudes in the 1960s

The need for such reservoirs stemmed from rapidly escalating demand for water which had been examined by the Central Advisory Water Committee (1962) and had been motivating factors in the 1963 restructuring. Demand seemed set to rise by almost a quarter between 1955 and 1965 (Ministry of Housing and Local Government, 1962). This growth seemed likely to continue for much of the rest of the century, so that more new reservoirs would be required, with the expectation that these would provide new opportunities for recreation. This was not considered sufficient by supporters of the main water sports, now better organized as they had grown in popularity, who remained highly critical of the water industry's cautious attitude, both in terms of the number of reservoirs opened up and the range of activities permitted. In this, they were influenced by the success of large lowland schemes, like Grafham Water, which heightened the contrast with older reservoirs where the public were still excluded, often from both the water itself and the catchment area. They therefore pressed for the opening up of reservoirs, especially those in accessible locations.

This campaign met with some sympathy from the new government elected in 1964, which had decided to give priority to the management of national resources, creating a new (if short-lived) department, the Ministry of Land and Natural Resources. The establishment of the Sports Council in 1965 also provided a mechanism by which the needs of sport and recreation could be articulated within the central government system, while the creation of Regional Sports Councils enabled similar pressures to be exerted more locally. As a result, the government itself took the initiative in trying to persuade the water industry to adopt a more liberal approach to recreation. This was done in several ways, beginning in February 1966 when the White Paper *Leisure in the Countryside* included a statement that access to reservoirs was in many cases restricted or prohibited without sufficient reason (Ministry of Land and Natural Resources, 1966a). In the same year, a joint circular on the *Use of Reservoirs and Gathering Grounds for Recreation* was issued by the Ministry of Land and Natural Resources and the Department of Education and Science, which had become responsible for sport (Ministry of Land and Natural Resources, 1966b). In 1967 the Ministry of Housing and Local Government issued a report on the management of waterworks, paying particular attention to the needs of recreation but adopting a more cautious approach than the earlier statements. While recognizing that there was no reason why regulating resources should not be used for all forms of recreation, it also pointed out that access to reservoirs where water was taken direct into supply must involve a risk of pollution. Any recreational use should be carefully controlled (Ministry of Housing and Local Government, 1967).

These statements clearly reflected growing government recognition of the recreational potential of the resources owned by the water industry. Whether they had significant influence on the realization of this potential is more difficult to judge, partly because of the surprising lack of data. Two attempts to rectify this deficiency were made in the late 1960s, both within the water industry and both suggesting that the recreational use of reservoirs was more extensive than had previously been thought. The first was an unpublished survey carried out by the Clerk of the Trent River Authority in 1968 which found that angling was permitted at over half of the 492 reservoirs covered and boating at fifty. The second, carried out by the British Waterworks Association, covered only 420 reservoirs and was based on incomplete returns. This suggested that a high proportion of reservoirs were used for angling, bird watching, walking and similar activities, but only thirty-nine for sailing. It also found that there were eighty-two reservoirs of more than forty hectares not used for any form of boating activity, although only two of these were regulating reservoirs (British Waterworks Association, 1969; for a summary of those two surveys see Tanner, 1973). The new attitude of the water industry towards amenity and recreation was also reflected in the establishment in 1969 of a Committee on the Recreational Use of Reservoirs by the British Waterworks Association, which also decided to send two of its senior members to the United States to examine experience there (Johnstone and Brown, 1971).

The 1973 reorganization

The *Water Resources Act 1963* was intended to create a lasting structure, but serious problems soon emerged. In particular, projections by the Water Resources Board suggested a doubling of demand for water by the end of the century, requiring a massive programme of reservoir building. It was felt that the existing division of responsibilities between the River Authorities and the water undertakings would make this difficult to achieve efficiently. There was also concern over the lack of progress in improving the water quality of rivers which was partly attributed to the fact that sewage disposal remained the responsibility of individual local authorities. The solution adopted was to bring together these and other water managemement functions into a single system of catchment-based authorities. This was implemented by the *Water Act 1973*. In 1974 ten new Regional Water Authorities took over the responsibilities of twenty-nine River Authorities, 157 statutory water undertakings and 1,393 sewage disposal and sewage departments of local authorities (Department of the Environment, 1973). Originally it had been proposed to include also the canals and river navigations of the British Waterworks Board (Department of the Environment, 1971a), but this was strongly resisted by the inland waterways lobby, mainly representing recreational and amenity interests and was abandoned.

This major reorganization was decided upon in the late 1960s following lengthy preparation and consultation. Particular attention was paid to the need to devise suitable management structures to ensure the effective integration of the various water management functions, including for the first time some recognition of recreation, amenity and conservation. The general issues were investigated by the Central Advisory Water Committee (Department of the Environment, 1971b), while a special committee appointed by the Department of the Environment considered appropriate management structures for individual Water Authorities. This recognized that demand for recreation was likely to increase faster than that for water, so that in time it would develop as a water management function in its own right. It therefore included proposals for integrating recreational responsibilities into its recommended management structures for large and small Water Authorities (Department of the Environment, 1973).

The *Water Act 1973* imposed on Water Authorities clear responsibilities relating to all amenity, recreational and environmental concerns. Section 20 of the Act required both them and the private water companies to take such steps as were reasonably practicable to put their rights to the use of water and associated land to best use for recreational purposes. Similarly, section 22 set out the Water Authorities' duties relating to nature conservation and amenity, including a requirement for them to 'have regard to the desirability of preserving natural beauty, of conserving flora, fauna and geological and physiographical features of special interest, and of protecting buildings and other objects of architectural, archaeological or historical interest', as well as 'of preserving public rights of access to areas of mountains, moor, heath, down, cliff or foreshore and other places of natural beauty'.

Water Space Amenity Commission

To assist the Water Authorities in carrying out these responsibilities, the Act established the Water Space Amenity Commission as a central advisory body in parallel with a new National Water Council whose remit extended to all other water management functions. The Commission was given no executive powers, but its membership was carefully constructed to foster a spirit of cooperation and understanding between the newly integrated water industry and the various recreational and amenity interests. It comprised the chairmen of the ten Water Authorities and ten other members appointed in consultation with other statutory bodies with recreation and amenity responsibilities, including the Countryside Commission, the Sports Council, the English Tourist Board and the local authority associations, as well as representatives of the different recreational and amenity interests. Among them was Francis Ritchie who had been active in the access movement in the inter-war period and was a member of the first National Parks Commission.

It is difficult to assess the effectiveness of the Water Space Amenity Commission because much of its work was advisory or promotional, but one achievement was compilation of a database that could be used in judging the performance of the Water Authorities in developing the recreational and amenity uses of their resources. Information was collected about 537 reservoirs of two hectares or more owned or managed by the Water Authorities and Water Companies, amounting to a total surface area of 22,885 hectares. Associated with them were gathering grounds and other land totalling

131,925 hectares, of which 48,305 hectares were in the North West Water Authority area and 26,127 hectares in Wales. The survey showed that recreational use was already widespread, 344 reservoirs supporting some form of active recreation, either on the water surface or on surrounding land, including 327 used for fishing and eighty-four for sailing. There were extensive facilities for informal recreation, including five country parks, forty-five picnic areas, nineteen viewing points and ninety-six car parks, while 286 reservoirs were reported as being used for birdwatching. The survey also revealed that there were often good reasons why particular reservoirs had not been opened up to recreation, including inaccessibility, altitude, the limited land surrounding the reservoir in ownership of the authority, and the fact that sporting rights had been retained by original landowners or their successors which was the case at fifty-six reservoirs (Tanner, 1977).

Another initiative of the Commission related to the impact of land drainage on conservation which had been largely ignored at national level in spite of the emergence of local problems. Here a conference (Water Space Amenity Commission, 1975) led to the establishment of a working party which spent nearly five years investigating current practice and consulting with the various interests leading to a report and guidelines (Water Space Amenity Commission, 1980a, 1980b), the latter subsequently revised to take account of changes introduced by the *Wildlife and Countryside Act 1981* (Water Space Amenity Commission, 1983). Subsequently, similar advisory reports were issued by the Nature Conservancy Council (Newbold *et al.*, 1983), the Royal Society for the Protection of Birds (Lewis and Williams, 1984) and the Countryside Commission (Travers Morgan, 1987), each urging the water industry to take account of amenity and conservation in its engineering activities.

Expansion in the use of water supply reservoirs for recreation had also caused growing concern about its impact on the wildfowl they support, especially during the winter months, and the Commission investigated this. In many areas the construction of reservoirs had served to compensate wildfowl for the loss of their natural wetland habitats, so that they had come to make an important contribution to wildfowl conservation. It also quickly became clear that the new large lowland reservoirs, which provide such good facilities for water-based recreation, were equally attractive to wildfowl, whose populations built up rapidly. While recreational activity was largely confined to angling, serious problems seldom occurred, but it was felt that the introduction of sailing and other active sports might cause unacceptable disturbance. Analysis of the relationship between wildfowl populations and the distribution of recreational activities showed that the major concentrations of wildfowl were on relatively few large lowland reservoirs, many of them built in the previous thirty years and heavily used for recreation. Although the relationship between wildfowl and the habitat provided by reservoirs was clearly complex, it was concluded that many of the adverse effects of recreational use could be alleviated by careful planning and management. (Tanner, 1979).

Amenity and recreation as water management functions

After the 1974 reorganization came gradual acceptance by the water industry of amenity and recreation as valid water management functions, though not without resistance, for attitudes within the industry were strongly influenced by its long engineering tradition. The imposition of clear statutory duties, however, made this difficult to sustain. The Water Authorities also found that provision for amenity and recreation was important in public relations terms. Whether the Water Space Amenity Commission contributed to this change in attitude is more difficult to assess, but when it was abolished in 1983, together with the National Water Council, a reason given was that its job was done. By the mid-1980s all Water Authorities were actively providing recreational opportunities and were conscious of their environmental responsibilities. In this, they were encouraged by various legislative measures at both national and European Community level.

These changing attitudes were not reflected in a dramatic opening up of existing reservoirs, although there was some widening in the range of activities permitted, to include new sports such as sailboarding and even, in a few places, waterskiing. Gradual introduction of full water treatment made it possible to open up some of the upland catchments to which access had traditionally been restricted and to permit recreation at some of the more accessible reservoirs close to urban areas, like Bartley Green Reservoir on the edge of Birmingham. There was also extensive recreation provision at all the major reservoirs constructed in this period, most of which dated back to proposals by the Water Resources Board in the late 1960s or earlier. Some were very large, like Rutland Water (1,255 hectares) in the East Midlands and Kielder Water (1086 hectares) in Northumberland, and not only provided for a full range of water-based activities but also were carefully landscaped to make them attractive for informal recreation.

In planning such schemes, the Water Authorities were also careful to be seen to take full account of their likely environmental impact, like the North West Water Authority's environmental appraisals by independent consultants for possible alternative schemes (Land Use Consultants, 1978). This did not stop the Authority being rebuffed in the early 1980s when, like Manchester Corporation, one of its predecessor bodies, it sought to develop new water resources in the western part of the Lake District which would have had a serious impact on two of the most attractive lakes (Berry, 1982). Similar care was being taken to ensure that the impact of their river engineering activities on the environment and ecology of rivers and streams was minimized. Some Water Authorities employed landscape architects and ecologists to provide professional advice comparable to that already being received from their land drainage engineers and fisheries officers as well as issuing their own guidelines to demonstrate that it was possible to combine engineering efficiency with wildlife conservation.

Privatization of the water industry

By the time the government's plans to privatize the water industry were announced in early 1985, amenity and recreation functions were firmly embedded not only in the legislative framework but also in the management structures and working practices of the Water Authorities. The importance of their recreational and environmental role was also widely recognized outside the industry. This, coupled with the Water Authorities' vital regulatory functions, was to make privatization much more complex than originally anticipated. The government's first thoughts were that the principles of integrated river basin management could be retained by transferring all water functions into private ownership (Department of the Environment et al., 1986). At the same time, it was clearly aware of the sensitivity surrounding the Water Authorities' environmental responsibilities and issued a separate consultation paper on 'the water environment' (Department of the Environment and Welsh Office, 1986). The response was so hostile that the government announced only a few months later that its privatization plans were to be postponed.

A very different structure was proposed in a new Consultation Paper a year later. Only the utility functions of water supply and sewage treatment were to be privatized, leaving the Water Authorities' environmental and regulatory responsibilities in the public sector. These were to be administered by a new body, the National Rivers Authority, which would carry out most of its functions through a regional management structure, including fisheries, conservation and recreation (Department of the Environment et al., 1987). There was mixed reaction within the industry, concerned about the risk of fragmentation. Interests outside generally welcomed the establishment of the National Rivers Authority, so long as it was given sufficient power and resources, but there was concern about the future of the Water Authorities' recreation and conservation functions. This focused on the environmental implications of privatization and on the future of the Water Authorities' extensive land holdings, including both the question of public access to upland catchment areas and the recreational use of lowland reservoirs (Bowers et al., 1988). Given this intense interest, it is surprising how little information about this land was presented in the prospectus when the Water Authorities came to be offered for sale, especially when compared with the detailed financial data provided (Shroders, 1989). According to the prospectus, the water industry's estate amounted to some 171,184 hectares, about two-thirds of which was described as catchment. Analysis by the *Daily Telegraph* suggested a figure of over 200,000 hectares and quoted a Countryside Commission report as showing that 135,576 hectares (68 per cent) of this was of conservation or recreational value (Clover, 1989).

The Water Act 1989

These concerns continued to be pressed during the passage of the privatization Bill through Parliament which emerged with a number of safeguards for amenity, conservation and recreational interests. This was done by imposing on both the National Rivers Authority and the new privatized water companies general duties relating to conservation, public access and recreation, broadly similar to those introduced by the 1973 Act. The Act also made provision for the preparation of an approved *Code of Practice on Conservation, Access and Recreation*, to guide these bodies in the exercise of these duties (Department of the Environment *et al.*, 1989). This Code was subsequently adopted by all of the new water utility companies, which also make an annual 'Environmental Activity Report' to the Department of the Environment describing their work in the conservation, access and recreation fields.

The water industry since privatization

It is too early to assess the long-term impact of privatization on the recreational and environmental work of the water industry. The indications are that this has not been disrupted to any significant extent and that in some areas the new management regime may have had beneficial effects. The companies appear to be very conscious of the need to reassure the public of their intentions in these areas now that they have moved into the private sector. In particular, they emphasize their commitment towards public access and to protecting and improving the environment. They have also often invested heavily in publicizing the recreational opportunities which continue to be available on their land and water.

Overall it seems likely that there has been some increase in opportunities since privatization. Most companies report the planning or implementation of schemes to extend public access and provide new recreational opportunities. In some cases, recreation and amenity budgets have increased, although they remain small in relation to overall expenditure. North West Water, the largest landowner in the industry, has also established a Conservation, Access and Recreation Advisory Committee to assist in its work. There is unlikely to be a significant increase in recreation and conservation opportunities as a result of new reservoir development. Severn Trent's new Carsington Reservoir on the southern fringe of the Peak District, opened by the Queen in 1992, is described as 'almost certainly the last major reservoir to be built in the UK this century' (Severn Trent Plc, 1992). This offers a visitor centre and a full range of land and water-based activities and is likely to become a regional recreation site of some significance. Unless there is a major change of policy, such a development is unlikely to be repeated in the foreseeable future, so any increase in recreational opportunities will need to come from the use of the industry's existing land and water resources.

The recreational and environmental work of the National Rivers Authority, with its slogan 'Guardians of the Water Environment', has also continued much as under the former water authorities. Apart from its long-standing duties relating to fisheries, it proposes to develop and implement a strategy for conservation, covering both the general conservation of the aquatic environment and the need to take account of conservation in carrying out its other functions. Its *Corporate Plan* also recognizes the significance of its recreational role and the close links which exist between recreation and its other functions. It has therefore also adopted the promotion of recreation as an objective and plans to increase its expenditure in this area (National Rivers Authority, 1991).

Conclusions

This story raises questions both about the way in which issues get on to the political agenda and about the way in which solutions are found. Three separate issues relating to the development and management of water resources had emerged well before the end of the nineteenth century. Each was promoted by a particular interest group which sought to influence the way in which water was managed and achieved some success at local level, mainly by exerting political pressure during the passage of Private Bills through Parliament. They failed, however, to get amenity and recreation questions on to the political agenda in relation to national policy for the development of water resources, in so far as such a policy existed. It is true that anglers were granted representation on the new fisheries boards created after 1923, but amenity and recreation were not given full recognition for another fifty years, with the passage of the *Water Act 1973*, in spite of at least intermittent pressure extending over nearly a century and specific flare-ups, like the 1932 mass trespass and the conflicts over Manchester's incursions into the Lake District.

One way of interpreting this delay is to use the ideas of John Kingdon (1984). He envisages the public-policy process as a system in which the two key elements are agenda setting and the specification of alternative courses for action. The 'agenda' is defined as the list of issues or problems to which government officials are giving serious attention at any one time, while 'alternatives' are the possible courses of government action that are being seriously considered by those same officials. Flowing through this system are three 'process streams': a 'problem stream' in which problems are recognized, a 'policy stream' in which policy proposals are generated, and a 'political stream' in which the various actors in the political process promote their ideas. From time to time, these three streams come together to create a 'policy window' which provides an opportunity for political actors to draw attention to problems and advocate their chosen solutions. The most obvious window of opportunity in the public-policy system is when changes in administration are being considered.

In these terms, the failure of environmental and recreational interests successfully to press their case may be attributed to the policy vacuum in which water management largely existed between the public health legislation of the second quarter of the nineteenth century and the post-war restructuring of the industry. Although questions of amenity and public access clearly existed in the problem stream throughout much of this period, and solutions were advocated from time to time in the policy stream, it was not until the need for reform was recognized in the political stream that progress was made. It is also clear from the experience of the 1989 privatization that once a problem has been recognized as being on the political agenda and appropriate solutions adopted, it is remarkably difficult to remove.

References

Berry, G., 1982, *A Tale of Two Lakes: the Fight to save Ennerdale Water and Wastwater*, Keswick, Friends of the Lake District.

Berry, G. and Beard, G., 1980, *The Lake District: a Century of Conservation*, Edinburgh, Bartholomew.

Board of Trade, 1920, *Second Interim Report of the Water Power Resources Committee*, Cmd. 776, London, HMSO.

Bowers, J., O'Donnell, K. and Whatmore, S., 1988, *Liquid Assets: the Likely Effects of Privatisation of the Water Authorities on Wildlife Habitats and Landscape*, London, Council for the Protection of Rural England.

British Waterworks Association, 1969, *Amenity Use of Reservoirs: Analysis of Returns*, London, The Association.

Calcut, W.G., 1924, *The History of the London Anglers' Association*, London, W.G. Calcut.

Central Advisory Water Committee, 1962, *Sub-Committee on the Growing Demand for Water: Final Report*, London, HMSO.

Clover, C., 1989, 'Land, land everywhere', *Telegraph Weekend Magazine*, 14 January: 14–24.

Department of the Environment, 1971a, *Reorganisation of Water and Sewage Services: Government Proposals and Arrangements for Consultation*, Circular 92/71, London, HMSO.

Department of the Environment, 1971b, *The Future Management of Water in England and Wales: a Report by the Central Advisory Water Committee*, London, HMSO.

Department of the Environment, 1973, *The New Water Industry: Management and Structure*, London, HMSO.

Department of the Environment and Welsh Office, 1986, *The Water Environment: the Next Steps. The Government's Consultative Proposals for Environmental Protection under a Privatised Water Industry*, London, Department of the Environment.

Department of the Environment, Ministry of Agriculture, Fisheries and Food, Welsh Office, 1986, *Privatisation of the Water Authorities in England and Wales*, Cmnd. 9734, London, HMSO.

Department of the Environment, Ministry of Agriculture, Fisheries and Food, Welsh Office, 1987, *National Rivers Authority: the Government's Proposals for a Public Regulatory Body in a Privatised Water Industry*, London, Department of the Environment.

Department of the Environment, Ministry of Agriculture, Fisheries and Food, Welsh Office, 1989, *Water Act 1989: Code of Practice on Conservation, Access and Recreation*, London, Department of the Environment.

Dolbey, S.J., 1974, 'The Politics of Manchester's water supply, 1961-7', in R. Kimber and J.J. Richardson (eds), *Campaigning for the Environment*, London, Routledge and Kegan Paul.

Eversley, Lord, 1910, *Commons, Forests and Footpaths: the Story of the Battle During the Last Forty-Five Years for Public Rights over the Commons, Forests and Footpaths of England and Wales*, Revised Edition, London, Cassell.

Institution of Water Engineers, 1950, *Manual of British Water Supply Practice*, Cambridge, W. Heffer.

Institution of Water Engineers, 1963, *Final report of the Council on the Recreational Use of Waterworks*, London, The Institution.

Johnstone, D. and Brown, K.S., 1971, *Amenity Use of Reservoirs: Study Tour of the USA, Report*, London, British Waterworks Association.

Kingdon, J.W., 1984, *Agendas, Alternatives and Public Policies*, Boston, Mass., Little Brown.

Land Use Consultants, 1978, *Environmental Appraisal of Four Alternative Water Resource Schemes: Haweswater, Borrowbeck, Morecambe Bay*, Warrington, North West Water Authority.

Lewis, G., and Williams G., 1984, *Rivers and Wildlife Handbook: a Guide to Practices which Further the Conservation of Wildlife on Rivers*, Sandy, Royal Society for the Protection of Birds.

Manchester Corporation, 1974, *Water for the Millions: Manchester Corporation Waterworks 1947-1974*, Manchester, The Corporation.

Ministry of Health, 1939, *Memorandum on the Safeguards to be Adopted in the Day to Day Administration of Water Undertakings*, Memorandum 221, London, The Ministry.

Ministry of Health, 1943, *Third Report of the Central Advisory Water Committee: River Boards*, Cm. 6465, London, HMSO.

Ministry of Health, Ministry of Agriculture and Fisheries, Department of Health for Scotland, 1944, *A National Water Policy*, Cmd 6515, London, HMSO.

Ministry of Health, 1948, *Gathering Grounds: Report of the Gathering Grounds Subcommittee of the Central Advisory Water Committee*, London, HMSO.

Ministry of Housing and Local Government, Ministry of Agriculture, Fisheries and Food, 1962, *Water Conservation: England and Wales*, Cmnd 1693 London, HMSO.

Ministry of Housing and Local Government, 1967, *Report on Safeguards to be Adopted in the Operation and Management of Waterworks*, London, The Ministry.

Ministry of Land and Natural Resources, 1966a, *Leisure in the Countryside: England and Wales*, Cmnd. 2928, London, HMSO.

Ministry of Land and Natural Resources, Department of Education and Science, 1966b, *Use of Reservoirs and Gathering Grounds for Recreation*, MLNR circular 3/66 and DES circular 19/66 London, HMSO.

Ministry of Town and Country Planning, 1945, *National Parks in England and Wales: Report by John Dower*, Cmd 6628, London, HMSO.

Ministry of Town and Country Planning, 1947, *Footpaths and Access to the Countryside: Report of the Special Committee (England and Wales)* Cmd 7207, London, HMSO.

National Rivers Authority, 1991, *Corporate Plan, 1991/92* London, The Authority.

Newbold, C., Purseglove, J. and Holmes, N., 1983, *Nature Conservation and River Engineering*, London, Nature Conservancy Council.

Rhodes, G., 1981, *Inspectorates in British Government: Law Enforcement and Standards of Efficiency*, London, George Allen and Unwin.

Rollinson, W., 1967, *A History of Man in the Lake District*, London, J.M. Dent.

Rothman, B., 1982, *The 1932 Kinder Trespass: a Personal View of the Kinder Scout Mass Trespass*, Altrincham, Willow Publishing.

Schroders, 1989, *The Water Shares Offers: Prospectus*, London, Schroders.

Severn Trent Plc, 1992, *Report and Accounts 1991-92*, Birmingham, Severn Trent.

Sheail, J., 1983, 'Planning. Water supplies and ministerial power in inter-war Britain', *Public Administration*, **61**, (Summer): 386–95.

Sheail, J., 1984, 'Constraints on water-resource development in England and Wales: the concept and management of compensation flows'. *Journal of Environmental Management*, **19**: 351–61.

Sheail, J., 1988, 'River regulation in the United Kingdom: an historical perspective',

Regulated Rivers: research and management, **2**, 3: 221–32.

Stephenson, T., 1989, *Forbidden Land: the Struggle for Access to Mountain and Moorland*, edited by Ann Holt, Manchester, Manchester University Press.

Tanner, M.F., 1973, *Water Resources and Recreation*, London, Sports Council.

Tanner, M.F., 1976, 'Water resources and wetlands in England and Wales' in Royal Society of Arts, *Recreation and Conservation in Water Areas*, Report of a Conference held in London, 23 November, 1976: 5–13.

Tanner, M.F., 1977, *The Recreational Use of Water Supply Reservoirs in England and Wales*, WSAC Research Report 3, London, Water Space Amenity Commission.

Tanner, M.F., 1979, *Wildfowl, Reservoirs and Recreation*, WSAC Research Report 5, London, Water Space Amenity Commission.

Travers Morgan, 1987, *Changing River Landscapes: a Study of River Valley Landscapes Undertaken for the Countryside Commission*, CCP 238, Cheltenham, Countryside Commission.

Water Space Amenity Commission, 1975, *Conservation and Land Drainage Conference, Thursday 29 May 1975* London, The Commission.

Water Space Amenity Commission, 1980a, *Conservation and Land Drainage: Working Party Report*, London, The Commission.

Water Space Amenity Commission, 1980b, *Conservation and Land Drainage Guidelines*, London, The Commission.

Water Space Amenity Commission, 1983, *Conservation and Land Drainage Guidelines*, second edition, London, The Commission.

9

ESTIMATING LOCAL LEISURE DEMAND IN THE CONTEXT OF A REGIONAL PLANNING STRATEGY

H. B. RODGERS

The construction of regional recreation strategies is a harmless and diverting pastime: any number of committees consisting of a limitless number of members may play. Special skill or previous experience is considered unnecessary, for this is essentially an amateur pursuit: professional expertise, for example in the form of a serious research base, introduces a suspect element of precision into what is otherwise an agreeable, free-wheeling exercise. Few sports (except rugby) have a known inventor, but this one has. Denis Howell, late in his long and fruitful incumbency as Minister for Sport decreed: 'let there be regional recreation strategies'—a cry that launched a thousand working papers. This at least imposed a specific task on England's Regional Councils for Sport and Recreation (RCSRs, previously set up by the Minister) and helped to justify their otherwise rather precarious existence as advisory bodies without a funding base or executive powers.

Mr Howell was a very unusual Minister for Sport. He actually believed in his job and was prepared to confront Cabinet and especially Treasury colleagues to try to get more funding for it. Successors in the office mostly sat quietly hoping for better things, most reluctant to offend their betters by causing a fuss, until promotion or oblivion overtook them. Mr Howell was much more combative. His approach, reduced to basics, built a national case for resources from regional enquiries. Stocktakings of regional demand for new facilities set against the existing system of supply were to be made; summed nationally these would present an argued statement of total deficit which could be costed and a case for funds developed. (Ignore the difficulty that no acceptable measures of standards of provision existed, then or now, to put these calculations on a firm footing.) In effect the achievement of these intentions involved the development of a strategy by each of the Councils. All duly did, but with a wondrous variety of specification and method, and to a timescale that bit deeply into the next decade. But Mr Howell had gone from office in 1979, and later ministers had little idea what to do with these diverse documents from the regions (of which an example is North West Council for Sport and Recreation, 1980). They were in general ignored after brief and formal treatment as Sports Council agenda items.

Strategies reborn

Given the mute, inglorious fate of the first strategies it might seem surprising that the idea was revived, almost exactly a decade after the first round, in a second cycle of strategy-making. But now the context was different: regional strategies were spawned by a national overview. The Sports Council published, in 1988, its own forward look at prospects and problems as *Sport in the Community: into the 90's*, a thoughtful and well-researched analysis which was virtually a national strategy. It was to service as a model for a set of regional analyses that would be derived from it and so would be directly comparable with each other. Fed back as regional contributions to national-level discussion, these would impact upon the next (1992–3) revision of a national strategy. Thus a centre–periphery dialogue would be built up on a far more systematic basis than previously. So far, so logical; but is it all so simple? A regional recreation strategy is, in effect, as the forward plan of the Regional Council, a corporate document that must reflect all the many roles and functions of the Council. It is the one clear opportunity to suspend *ad hocism* (the common mode of operation of the Councils) and to look more broadly at a definition of goals and priorities and the ways to achieve them. This must mean persuasive dialogue with all those agencies and interests in the region involved in recreation development, public and private, statutory and voluntary, great and small. Indeed the Councils exist to make such interaction possible.

It follows, therefore, that regional strategies must look two ways: they look upwards and outwards to the national level on the one hand but inwards and downwards on the other hand to a wide diversity of regional and community interests. Indeed, the second of these has much more influence than the first in guiding the general policy and practice of the Council, year by year. However, the broad pattern and design of the strategy, closely specified from above, mirrors the need to impose a common structure on all the strategies so that they 'fit' easily to generate national statements. But this conformity rather militates against what is arguably their more important role, for it limits fluency and flexibility in the debate with regional interests.

That debate is crucial to the purpose of the Councils. They are talk-shops, with no resources except a real potential to persuade spending agencies to integrate their policies and coordinate their investment. Each is a forum that brings together in regular contact a most diverse assembly: the local authorities (both levels, members and officers), the relevant statutory agencies (like The Countryside Commission), some commercial interests (notably the water companies), and the whole range of voluntary associations with a sport or leisure concern. Lacking either executive powers or a funding base (except for an advisory role in the spending of the very limited Sports Council regional grants), the Councils work by persuasion and promotion, within a system of partnerships, to achieve their goals. They are among those few organizations fuelled more by enthusiasm than by funding; as a lobby for recreation they have had an influence far beyond their tiny resources. Their constant tactic has been to apply just enough leverage by grant, or loan, combined with moral pressure, to secure favourable investment decisions by providers and managers. In some very important areas the argument is much less about spend than about broad policy: an example is the continued pressure to unlock school facilities for community use. All in all the RCSRs work by debate and exhortation. In this the regular shaping and up-dating of a strategic overview is a very significant task, not least because the results may flow into the corporate planning of partners with substantial budgets potentially available for recreational development. The title of the North West region's review, *Progress through Partnership* (1989) encapsulates the point.

Local communities as leisure managers

By the late 1980s there was a clear need for a radical review of the policies of the Regional Councils: the entire political environment in which they operated had changed fundamentally at the hands of a government of the radical right, determined to roll back the frontiers of the state and particularly in relation to social policy. Thus there has come about a sea change in social philosophy, from an almost universal agreement that active and creative leisure pursuits deserved to be promoted as widely as possible, with the support of public funding and subsidy, to an increasing emphasis on the concept that the provision of recreation is simply another service industry best left to the operation of the market for most efficient delivery at least cost. This progressive shift in view, from a conviction that leisure is a significant welfare service, delivered to all free or at supported prices as a factor in quality of life and part-payment of a social wage, to a simple reliance on the market-place must clearly have a major impact on regional strategies for policies of recreation provision. It implies a much less central role for local authorities (themselves caught up in a cash crisis) and a less varied menu of provision by them coupled with a more commercial discipline in their approach to leisure management. There is an obvious assumption that the private sector will be a more general provider and to this the new regional strategies must adapt by making more effective approaches to the commercial entrepreneur. Certainly the old primary alliance between the local authorities and the national agencies seems likely to broaden to a much more intricate network of partnerships crossing the public–private divide.

One issue arises at once from this shift of emphasis from public provision to a market context. Local communities vary enormously as leisure-markets. Some are blighted by unemployment and depression, with low population growth and strong symptoms of social stress; clearly these offer little commercial opportunity and would fare badly in any system of market-led provision. Others are prosperous and secure with high disposable incomes and little sign of economic and social stress. The former may have real leisure needs—as a palliative to unemployment for example—but reveal little demand that can pay its own way; in contrast in the latter cases the market may well provide perfectly adequately left to itself, whether the entrepreneurs are fully commercial or local authorities acting the part as providers/managers minimizing subsidy. Some assessment of these district-by-district contrasts is clearly a necessary input in formulating a regional strategy. If public funds have to be spread much more thinly and selectively, then this sort of analysis would show which areas in a region have the best case for a probably limited continuation of support.

This was attempted for the North West of England, (figure 9.1) a region with a particularly sharp mosaic of socio-economic contrasts ranging from declining and deeply depressed inner-city communities to county districts that rival those of the south east in indices of prosperity and growth. Two principles are explored in this classification of local leisure markets:

(i)   Much leisure demand (both in terms of total volume and structure) is age-related: thus a study of age patterns and their trends of change over a forecast period will provide pointers to future change in leisure demand.
(ii) Socio-economic well-being is another powerful determinant of the volume and pattern of leisure demand, current and future.

Having examined these two aspects of community prosperity separately it is possible to combine both in a single statement of the varying strength of districts as potential markets for leisure provision. A clear typology of districts emerges, revealing profound differences in the ability of different communities to support market-based systems of provision.

Age-related market sectors

Attempts to analyse local age structures by measuring the trend of change in specific and critical age groups over a predictive time span are beset by difficulty. No effective and common data sets exist, and so statements as in Tables 9.1 and 9.2 have to be pieced together from varying sources with inconstant specifications. For the county districts it is possible to assemble age-trend data for the decade 1983–93 (the ideal for a strategy with a currency until 1993), but for the metropolitan districts only a 1981–91 analysis is possible. For both types of district it is possible to identify four age groups that represent the significant elements in the leisure market:

(i)   The teenage–young adult range, much the most active in terms of general recreational demand and especially for the most active pursuits. It is an age group in almost universal decline across the region.
(ii) The age range that broadly reflects the family phase in life (25–44) associated with a distinctive set of leisure interests.

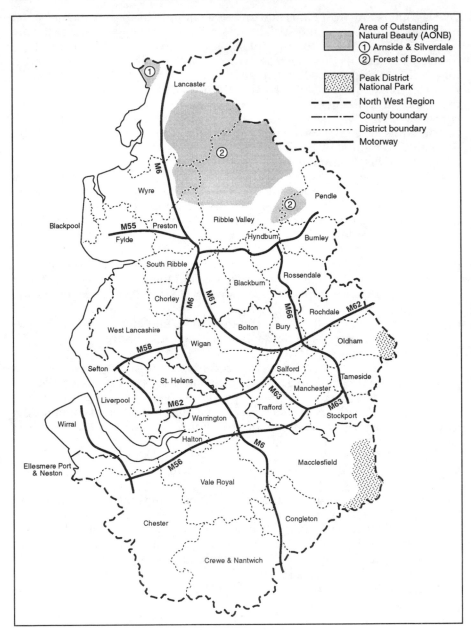

Figure 9.1 The North West Region

(iii) A post-family phase (45–*c*.60) in which interest in active recreations may decline but a range of general leisure activities may continue quite strongly.

(iv) The elderly, with a generally passive range of interests.

As the tables show, it is not possible to assemble data for these various age groups, with their predicted trend, to exactly similar specifications. All the urban areas share exactly similar age limits for the four groups, but the counties have conducted their age-structure predictions with group limits that differ not only between Lancashire and Cheshire but also with the metropolitan districts. Some looseness in the comparisons that may be drawn is therefore inevitable, but the problems are not serious. Certainly the data differences are complex enough to make two tables necessary, one for metropolitan and the other for county districts.

To take the former first (Table 9.1), the general trend is one of overall population decline during the period, coupled with an ageing process; both suggest weakness in leisure demand. The strongest cases are those in Group A: here there is at least some sectoral growth in particular age groups, notably in the family and post-family phases. Rochdale and Wigan show a very positive trend, promising some real if selective growth in leisure demand and market opportunity. But the young-adult group—so important a generator of recreational demand—shows a decline throughout these areas in Group A. Group B consists of inner-city districts with catastrophic rates of population loss and no sign of any change except steep decline in any of the age-related leisure market sectors. To let the market provide for the needs of these disadvantaged communities would be to place a false faith in it. The Group C cases are intermediate. The most serious feature is that their rates of loss of the young-adult sector almost rival the rates of the inner-city areas of Group B. Thus this most active market sector is in steep decline in all these districts. But all of them show some selective growth in leisure demand, a modest rise in a single age group, either the family or the post-family phase.

Extending this analysis to the county districts (Table 9.2) is possible only with approximate comparability. Most seriously, neither for Lancashire nor for Cheshire can a 13–24 age group be identified: for the former a 16–24 group must suffice and for the latter a 15–24 group. This tends to minimize the population loss in this lowest age range, so that some of the lowest increases in this group (of 4 per cent or less) would become decreases if a 13–24 group could be identified and its trend projected. Other discrepancies for the post-family and elderly groups are less significant. Given these caveats the county data reveal some points of real interest. Uniquely within the region there is a group of districts that show overall and rapid population growth shared by all age bands (Group A+). Chorley and Congleton show particular strength, with real growth even at the young-adult level, which is in such serious decline elsewhere. Three of these areas (Warrington, Halton and, to some extent, Chorley) reflect New Town development. All four districts in this strongest group will experience a far faster and more general growth in leisure demand than any of the urban areas of the two conurbations; here the market tempts the entrepreneur. At the opposite pole only one county district can be placed in Group B, together with the weakest of the metropolitan areas: this is Burnley, a remote ex-textile community long bled by out-migration, with an adverse trend across all the age ranges.

The other county districts fit neatly enough into the two main Groups (A and C) identified in Table 9.1. Nine of them—in Cheshire and West and North Lancashire—fall into Group A and show real strength in the leisure markets with a less than average decline in the youth sector. Macclesfield and Fylde are typical cases, with strong growth after age twenty-four. Crewe and Vale Royal (neighbours in mid-Cheshire) are odd in their weakness in the middle age ranges (25–64). But in all these cases there are elements of growth, some new demand to be met, some encouragement to market provision, though the patterns vary. The Group C cases suggest growth only in a single market sector, against a background of general demographic decline. As in the metropolitan districts in the same group, this sector of growth is

Table 9.1 Trends in age-related leisure market sectors: metropolitan districts

Group A Growth in 'family' and 'post-family' markets: below average decline 13–24 market

% change 83–93	Rochdale (+2)	Stockport (+2)	Bolton (+1)	Wigan (−1)	Oldham (−2)	St Helens (−1)	Tameside (−1)
13–24	−12	−16	−15	−17	−17	−18	−19
25–44	10	7	8	2	3	5	5
45–59	7	8	9	16	9	6	5
60–74	0	0	−8	−7	−11	0	−10

Group B Overall decline in age-related leisure markets: extreme decline 13–24

	Liverpool (−11)	Knowsley (−12)	Salford (−28)
13–24	−30	−35	−28
25–44	−3	0	0
45–59	−9	−15	0
60–74	−10	+12	−11

Group C General decline: some growth in a single market sector

	Bury (−3)	Wirral (−2)	Trafford (−3)	Sefton (−4)	Manchester (−5)
13–24	−17	−21	−27	−24	−29
25–44	−2	+8	+10	+7	+14
45–59	+11	0	−2	−2	−9
60–74	−9	−8	−7	−4	−16

Note: (x) = overall projected population trend (%) 1983–93

Table 9.2 Trends in age-related leisure market sectors: county districts

Group A+ Overall growth with some increase in 'youth' market

	Chorley (+9)	Congleton (+6)	Warrington (+18)	Halton (+5)
15/16–24	+21	+18	+3*	+4*
25–44	+14	+7	+29	+17
45–59/64	+15	+14	+10	+5
65+/60–74	−6	+12	+11	+17

* these would be decreases in a 13–24 age range.

Group A Growth in at least 2 sectors below average decline in 'youth market'

	Fylde (+8)	W. Lancs. (0)	Macclesfield (+3)	Vale Royal (+12)	Ellesmere Port (−3)	Crewe (0)	Ribble Valley (−3)	Lancaster (+7)	Hyndburn (+1)
15/16–24	−2	−2	−3	−2	−17	−4	−9	−3	+2*
25–44	+28	+13	+12	−2	+5	+8	+6	+27	+15
45–59/64	+5	+13	+4	+11	+6	0	+4	+2	−7
65+/60–74	−5	0	+7	+12	+16	+5	−10	−10	−11

Group B

	Burnley (−9)
15/16–24	−16
25–44	0
45–59/64	−11
65+/60–74	−14

Group C General decline: growth in a single market

	Preston	Chester	Blackpool	Wyre	Blackburn	Pendle	South Ribble	Rossendale
	(+1)	(+1)	(−3)	(+1)	(−3)	(−3)	(0)	(−1)
15/16–24	−9	−4	−14	−4	−6	−14	+2*	0
25–44	+28	+14	+16	+16	+11	+9	−2	+8
45–59/64	−15	0	−9	−3	−10	−9	+8	−5
65+/60–74	−4	−6	−17	−7	−14	−12	+1	−10

Cheshire age ranges are 16–24, 45–64, 65 and over
Lancashire age ranges are 15–24, 45–59, 60–74

Note: Data show trend (as %) 1981–91 (x) = overall trend

commonly the family phase from 25 to 44, an age band that generates high levels of demand for a specific group of interests. A decline in the young-adult sector is a constant factor in the Group. There are many oddities not easy to interpret: for example, the very strong increase in the 25–44 group in every district in Lancashire north of the River Ribble. Chester shows the same trend. So Group C offers genuine market opportunities, though selective in nature.

Some general conclusions of relevance to the planning of leisure futures may be derived from this analysis:

(i)   A common feature of districts within the region (it is true of fourteen out of thirty-seven cases) is that there is no growth in any market except the family phase. In this there is real growth in leisure demand despite an adverse general population trend and at rates much above the national average for the 25–44 band, of plus 4 per cent. Here is real market opportunity for a range of recreations: fitness training, outdoor pursuits in the countryside, some water-based sports, swimming, ten-pin bowling, and badminton, among others.

(ii) Conversely, there is less than national average growth in the post-family phase, and what there is tends to be localized: the industrial towns of Greater Manchester, West Lancashire and parts of north Cheshire are the main cases (but distinctly not Merseyside). Bowls, fishing, dance, keep fit, and walking are among the recreations most common in this group, not on the whole activities likely to excite the commercial provider.

(iii) Except in or near areas of planned growth, decline in the youth market is universal. It is far above the national average rate on Merseyside (where there has been a huge fertility loss over the last twenty years) and more selective in inner Manchester. Elsewhere it runs rather consistently at 13 per cent to 17 per cent but is much lower in Cheshire and western Lancashire. There are obvious implications, not least for the team games that are dominated by the dwindling group (though it may later recover).

(iv) Of the over-sixties' market little can or need be said: trends vary complexly. Oddly, there is no consistent growth in traditional retirement areas. Leisure demand is in any case low and dwindles with age.

(v)   There are sub-regional extremes in the trend of leisure demand. Merseyside is an area of extreme weakness—far beyond national or regional norms—and by no means confined to the inner city. There is virtually no growth in any sector. Against this the Mid-Mersey area, driven by New Town projects, shows universal cross-sector growth; while east Cheshire (with Congleton as the extreme case) shows almost a 'southern' profile. Maybe here the market may be left largely to provide, steered lightly by whatever pressure the planning system can apply.

Prosperity contrasts and the market mosaic

Age structure, and its trends of change, is a strong influence on the size and nature of recreation demand; so too, even more directly, is the pattern of socio-economic contrast. Social well-being in the most general sense is a strong influence on both the volume and structure of leisure demand and on the relative roles of public and commercial provision in meeting it. The search for such an indicator raises a whole complex of technical problems not pursued here. In fact, a single ready-made negative index of social well-being exists but in a form far from ideal for the present purpose, not least because like all such indices it lacks income data on a local scale. This is the Department of Environment (DOE) Social Deprivation Index, a composite measure at district level derived from data on unemployment, overcrowding, single-parent and pensioner households, housing quality and ethnic origin. To give it an income proxy, districts in the region were ranked not only on this measure of social stress but also in terms of car ownership. Mean rank on the DOE scale and on car-ownership ratio was taken as a simple but effective socio-economic indicator for purposes of examining intra-regional contrasts.

These are extreme. Seven North West districts are among the 10 per cent most deprived nationally, as stressed as the inner London boroughs: twenty-three districts in the region fall into the lowest three deciles in the national data. Most of these weakest areas fall within the inner cities—or on Merseyside more generally—and in the old textile-weaving towns of East Lancashire. Only nine districts are in the upper half of the national scale, but some of these are so high as to resemble southern rather than northern communities: Macclesfield, Chester and the Fylde are outstanding; most areas of north Cheshire and north west Lancashire are not far behind. A message for recreation planning flows from these patterns. Areas with low ranks on these indices (about twenty-four of the thirty-eight regional districts) have high levels of stress coupled with low prosperity; here effective recreational provision should continue to be seen as a form of welfare service directed towards the betterment of quality of life. Commercial provision is unlikely to reach large sections of their communities. Conversely there are areas, much fewer in number and confined to the prosperous parts of Lancashire and Cheshire, where a more commercial approach to provision and management would be more acceptable. Perversely enough some of these most prosperous areas—the Cheshire districts for example—have a strong tradition of vigorous and successful public provision of leisure activities, while some of the poorest and most stressed areas have a very poor record of public initiative.

In this study and as an aid to regional recreation planning, the North West is viewed as a mosaic of local leisure markets, strong or weak both in relation to level of demand and capacity to pay for activity in a market place. But the analysis is bi-focal: it uses separate age-related and prosperity-related approaches to these issues. Finally an attempt is made to fuse these distinct approaches into a single overview. This is done in the simplest possible way by creating a two-dimensional matrix to which the districts are assigned.

The dimensions are:

(i) the general level of social well-being, derived from the Department of the Environment deprivation scale modified by car-ownership data: this is the horizontal dimension;
(ii) the general trend of growth or decline and age-related sectoral change in the nature of the leisure market at district level: this is the vertical axis.

A typology of markets

Within this matrix the districts arrange themselves neatly enough into coherent and consistent groups, and the contrasts between them have a clear relevance for the policies and priorities of the Regional Council for Sport and Recreation. Some central issues are given a sharper focus, especially the crucial question of whether a shift from a welfare approach to a market principle is likely to meet local leisure needs effectively. Four groups are identifiable (see Figure 9.2):

(i)   About a dozen districts are placed in the top-left quadrant of the matrix, high on both indices. These are areas of prosperity, with little unemployment, high levels of car ownership, few social problems and (doubtless) high average income levels for the region. They also show some strength in terms of the growth of demand for recreational services. They have fairly marginal decline in the 13–24 age group (even in two cases a genuine growth) coupled with substantial increase in the family and post-family sectors of leisure demand. These are areas inherently attractive to the commercial provider: for large sections of the community and for many recreations a blend of private-sector and voluntary body provision, with local authorities acting largely with a 'market' philosophy, might offer an effective formula. The case for massive direct subsidy is relatively weak, against the stronger conflicting claims of less fortunate areas. On the other hand there are concentrations of 'target groups' in these areas—the young, housewives, the 'active elderly'. It is to these, perhaps, that support and subsidy should be selectively directed. Some of these areas have (for the North West) a strongly rural element in their population, with particular problems of access.

(ii) Another group of about nine cases (with several others marginal to the group) occupies the bottom-right corner of the matrix. These score low on 'prosperity', and the age-related leisure markets show steep decline, relieved in a few districts by minor growth in a single sector. Inner-city districts, Merseyside areas and some textile towns of rapid population loss are the typical cases. Here general levels of prosperity hardly support the hypothesis that the market will provide, left to itself. Indeed the market is both declining numerically and weak in spending power. The case for social provision of recreational opportunities is a clear one, yet the need is (at least numerically) shrinking. In areas like these the most disadvantaged of the target groups are concentrated: the unemployed,

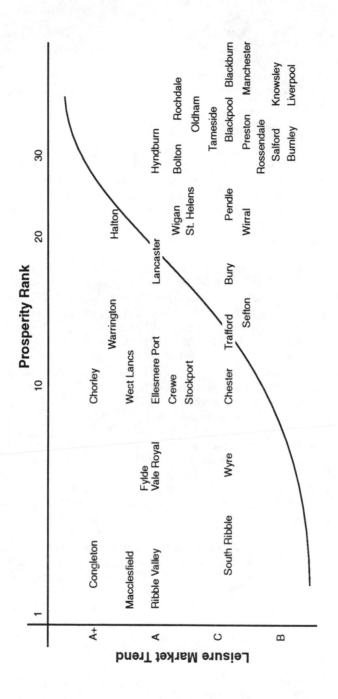

Figure 9.2   A typology of markets

one-parent families, the poor and elderly and the ethnic minorities. The classic case for subsidized public provision continues. Perhaps, however, new partners need to become closely associated with the Council's work such as the health authorities and the urban aid agencies: the latter direct central government funds into areas of great stress and have been a significant source of support for recreation projects. The old arguments for targeted provision to offer a palliative to misfortune and an enhancement of quality of life still apply.

(iii) To another group of about half-a-dozen districts (of which Hyndburn and Rochdale are typical) these same arguments apply with even greater force, since here low 'prosperity' indices are linked to significant selective growth of leisure markets (especially in the family and post-family stages, and with an ethnically distinctive element). Here, too, target groups are concentrated but with greater growth potential than in group (ii). Here funding via urban aid and redevelopment programmes is absent or limited. These areas present the Regional Council with a particular challenge in that the 'welfare' aspect of recreation provision persists as a need.

(iv) In the last group of only two or three districts the converse circumstances apply; very reasonable prosperity but little prospect of significant leisure-market growth. Since the group is so limited, comment is perhaps superfluous. Districts like these clearly have a doubly weak case for substantial external public funding for recreational provision.

There are difficult and sensitive policy issues in these contrasts, unlikely to be settled without controversy. In essence, should the Regional Council's policy, in the allocation of scarce support funding, be different in the four cases identified above?

(i)   In the areas of relative prosperity, with enough growth impetus in the leisure market to attract the private investor, should funds be allocated sparingly and essentially to support voluntary-sector initiatives or in collaboration with the commercial developer?

(ii)   Should substantial funding be reserved for areas of low prosperity and social stress, deployed in a traditional way to support recreational provision as a welfare service strongly targeted at disadvantaged groups? Or should the priority be to influence the pattern of spending of the much larger flows of urban-aid funding?

(iii)   Have areas of rather low prosperity but having some real growth of recreation demand a special claim on Council resources?

(iv)   Do areas that combine reasonable prosperity with a low growth potential have a weak claim on resources, which might here be available only to support exceptional projects?

It is not of course the purpose of applied research to supply instant answers to questions such as these: its function, rather, is to permit sequences of policy questions to be posed more precisely for debate and resolution. This done, a study such as this reaches its own natural termination.

References

Department of the Environment, 1983, *Urban Deprivation*, Information note no. 2, London, DOE.

North West Council for Sport and Recreation, 1980, *Regional Recreation Strategy*, published as a sequence of reports and specialist studies, Manchester, The Council.

North West Council for Sport and Recreation, 1989, *Progress through Partnership: A Strategy for the Development of Sport and Recreation in the North West, 1989–1993*, Manchester, The Council.

Sports Council, 1988, *Sport in the Community: Into the 90s*, London, The Council.

10

SPORT AND RECREATION IN THE GREEN BELT COUNTRYSIDE

MARTIN J. ELSON

Green belts are broad areas of countryside adjoining towns and cities where, through the strict application of development control, the open rural appearance is retained. Their main purposes are to check urban sprawl, avoid the coalescence of towns, and safeguard the countryside from further encroachment (Department of the Environment, 1988a). Approved green belts now cover some 3,824,000 acres, about 12 per cent of England. Their extent is expected to grow in the next few years. Proposals for new green belts around Norwich in East Anglia and Portsmouth–Southampton on the south coast are currently under consideration, as is the possibility of introducing green belts into Wales (Welsh Office, 1991; Elson, 1992a).

Sport and recreation have been associated with green belts from their inception. Public opinion surveys suggest that provision for recreation, and protection of the landscape, have greater credibility to lay persons than more esoteric notions of urban growth management (Consumers Association, 1989). In the inter-war period Sir Raymond Unwin, adviser to the Greater London Regional Plan Committee, saw green belts as providing open recreation land on the edges of large urban areas to compensate for the lack of space within city boundaries. His subsequent 'green girdle' proposal for London would have amounted to a green belt around the city defined in terms of open space and recreation needs. As sport and recreation demands on the urban fringe rose in the 1960s and 1970s, more *defensive* attitudes prevailed, often supported by farming and other landowning interests keen to insulate themselves from what were regarded as intrusive activities. The designation of country parks, with their promise of 'containing' visitors in purpose-designed areas, thereby protecting wider areas of farmland, suited this imperative well (Elson, 1986; Harrison, 1991).

Government recognition of the mutuality between green belt policy and recreation objectives has a distinguished pedigree. As long ago as 1973 the House of Lords Select Committee on *Sport and Leisure* asserted:

recreation facilities are a proper use of the existing green belt and can help to pre-serve it against other demands . . . a positive approach in recreational terms, making the green belt into a lung for the town, rather than a negative approach which . . . threatens to convert the green belt into a demilitarized zone, should secure that the urban fringe is properly exploited. [House of Lords 1973]

The Countryside Review Committee, a grouping of civil servants from various ministries, suggested later in the decade that provision for recreation should be made a positive objective of green belt policy (Countryside Review Committee, 1977). This proposal was taken up more recently by the Countryside Commission in its study *Planning for a Greener Countryside* (Countryside Commission, 1989). The Review Committee thus presaged by fourteen years the 1991 announcement by Michael Heseltine that he was considering extension of the formal purposes of green belt to include those of increasing opportunities for quiet enjoyment of the countryside and the enhancement of natural beauty.

Importance of urban fringe

The countryside near towns has considerable potential to cater for sport and recreation demands. It is recognized as:

1. a supply area—with high accessibility to population centres, and rela-tively good public transport links; one in five informal recreation day trips to the countryside have a round trip distance of ten miles or less (Countryside Commission, 1992);
2. a safety valve or overflow area—acting to accommodate uses such as playing fields, golf courses or football stadiums displaced from urban areas;
3. an interceptor area—where new provisions for sport may reduce pressures in more 'fragile' countryside areas; and
4. an opportunity area—where environmental improvement and landscape regeneration can lead to new forms of sport and recreation provision.

A number of factors re-enforce these propositions. Active sport in the countryside is the fastest growing sector of countryside recreation. There has been rapid growth in activities such as horse riding, golf, and the newer, more adventurous countryside sports. Waterskiing, for example has waiting lists at one-third of clubs nationally, and demands for activities as diverse as hang-gliding, boardsailing and paragliding continue to grow (Elson, 1989). A transport policy based on precepts of minimizing recreation travel, in the interests of reducing pollution, would also elaborate the importance of the urban fringe locale. The willingness of farmers to diversify their activities into sport and recreation, in response to problems of indebtedness and pres-sures from Europe, is also relevant. The recent designation of twelve Com-munity Forests, areas of 8,000–20,000 hectares (30–80 square miles) each, will create new patterns of land use in the countryside. They will combine forestry and tree planting, sport and recreation provision, environmental improvements, and provision for craft industries. This new impetus for positive landscape design has the potential to create new environments for leisure in the fringe (Countryside Commission, 1989; Bishop, 1991; Thames Chase Community Forest, 1992; Pitt, 1991).

The green belt concept

The particular green belt concept, however, put in place nearly forty years ago, stresses certain attributes. These may be increasingly out of step with the trends and pressures outlined above. Development control in the green belt, for example, is aimed towards:

1. retention of the *open character* of the area, implying virtually no new building;
2. the creation and retention of a *clear cut boundary* between urban and rural land; and
3. retention of the *rural appearance* of the area, by maintaining agriculture and landscape features.

The policy for England states 'approval should not be given, except in special circumstances for the construction of new buildings or for the change of use of existing buildings for purposes other than agriculture, outdoor sport, cemeteries, institutions standing in extensive grounds, or other uses appropriate to a rural area' (DOE, 1988b, p.2).

In 1988 the Government substituted the words 'outdoor sport' for 'sport', in order to make it clear that sports development which involved significant new buildings would not normally be seen as appropriate. The issue of new buildings is an important one for many sports, whether to form a club house, social meeting venue, or a covered court or a pitch. It is for the applicant to argue that particular buildings are a necessary ancillary to the sports use, are unlikely to be successfully located elsewhere, and will do little damage to the rural appearance of the land. Pressures for diversification on agricultural land, and for the re-use of redundant buildings have led to the following minor relaxation of policy in new guidance issued in 1991: 'the suitable conversion of redundant buildings may be needed to facilitate outdoor sport in the Green Belts. In very special circumstances such sport may require the construction of small ancillary buildings, unobtrusive spectator accommodation, or other essential facilities' (p.6). Also, in more general terms, the Guidance states: 'outdoor sport may offer a means of improving the environmental quality of Green Belt land, and there may be opportunities for new outdoor sport provision in connection with the redevelopment of redundant hospital sites' (DOE, 1991, p.6).

Case Study Evidence

The detailed interpretation of the phrase 'outdoor sport' in green belts has proved difficult for a number of reasons.

1. The intensity of use of land for sport, and therefore its potential impact on the environment, is difficult to judge. There is concern that if agreement is given to a change of use, the scheme could grow almost uncontrollably thereafter, adversely affecting local residents and environments.
2. Many sports clubs combine open air and covered provision (for example tennis or rugby clubs). Some require ancillary buildings. How this ancillary development should be defined, justified and controlled has proved problematic.
3. It may be argued by applicants for a sports development, for example a golf course, that a hotel, restaurant or even housing may be needed to make the scheme viable.
4. It may be argued that to fund the improvement of degraded and despoiled areas of green belt, some form of built development should be contemplated. David Hares has recently described an 'enabling development' on green belt land at Bedfont in West London. The construction of some office buildings will fund, among other facilities, a motorcycle training area on restored mineral land (Hares, 1992). The London Planning Advisory Committee has also investigated the problems of twenty sites on the inner edge of the Metropolitan Green Belt in terms of costs and methods of environmental improvement (Land Capability Consultants, 1991).

In order to illuminate these issues, an analysis of fifty green belt planning appeal cases involving sport was carried out. They comprised a selection of decisions made by inspectors and the Secretary of State over the period July 1989 to March 1991. A basic pattern emerged from the analysis. At appeal inspectors assessed:

1. whether the proposal was an appropriate outdoor sport or recreation activity in the green belt. There is no definitive list of what is appropriate. (The cases investigated covered a very wide range of activities such as microlighting, motor sports, horse riding, golf and water sports);
2. whether any other activities and proposed buildings applied for could be regarded as ancillary to the main sports use. Simple changing rooms and pavilions would be reasonable but a large fitness club might not be. Other commercial additions, such as shops, were also likely to fall foul of the policy;
3. whether the impact on nearby residents and wildlife was considered to be annoying or intrusive or was likely to unacceptably alter the character of the area; and
4. whether the traffic generated would be difficult to accommodate on the local road network.

Thus a sports scheme which is, in principle, an acceptable category of use, can be refused on grounds of general impact on the environment. If the sport is not a normally acceptable green belt outdoor activity, the inspector has to assess whether there are 'very special circumstances' which would allow the permission to be granted. These might include the unique suitability of the topography of the site, the lack of any alternative sites, or an overriding national need.

The appeal evidence also suggests that sports schemes which are small scale are more likely to succeed. This involves paying close attention to the level of activity and the potential for growth. Schemes involving little or no new building are preferred. Thus the re-use of an existing barn for an indoor riding school, or a farm building for a gymnasium or fitness centre are seen as more desirable than new building. If building is to be justified, extensions to existing buildings are far more likely to succeed than new building. The conversion of farm buildings with intrinsic character is also more likely to be approved. New hotels are normally refused in green belts, as are new indoor sports centres, squash courts or tennis centres involving covered courts. In addition, proposed football stadiums on the edges of Oxford, Southend and Bristol have been refused in green belt. A non-league club ground has been approved in green belt on the edge of High Wycombe. The need for the local hospital to use part of the club's urban site for a hospital extension weighed heavily in the inspector's assessment of the decision.

It is clear that these cases involve the wide use of discretion by planners, inspectors and ministry officials. The detailed application of development controls may vary across the country, being more strict around London, and less severe in areas such as the North West, and Yorkshire and Humberside, where job creation issues assume wider importance. In Cheshire, for example, the expansion of existing businesses in green belt locations is allowed for in policy.

Sustainability, sport and the green belt

Many countryside policies are in flux. However, indicators suggest that in the future we should provide for a multi-activity countryside near to towns (Newby, 1991). Policies for sport should be seen as part of a strategy for green belt land use guaranteeing:

- greater access for leisure;
- the safeguarding of valued landscape and wildlife resources; and
- an effective system of management to resolve any conflicts between sports and other activities and users (Elson, 1992b).

Sports provisions in green belts can be sustainable. Active sports participation is not the major numerical pressure in green belts, as pointed out by the Countryside Commission in its paper, *Visitors to the Countryside* (Countryside Commission, 1991). Sport in the countryside is not a major polluter of the environment; and it rarely has serious impacts on landscape and vegetation. Agricultural activity has created more pollution and destroyed immeasurably more habitat in the last forty years than 'marginal impact' activities such as sport and recreation. In the interests of equity and sustainability, new sports provisions should be located:

- near to public transport corridors to minimize private car travel; and
- away from the most fragile environments; for example ancient woodlands and sites of high wildlife value.

Management should aim to reduce the level of 'travel for its own sake' by getting people out of cars and on to well-defined and maintained footpath and bridleway networks. Contact with the countryside itself must become the 'utility' for the visitor, not the act of driving even further around the general countryside.

In terms of encouraging sport in green belts, the following actions would have most effect:

1. a reconsideration of the definition of acceptable development for outdoor sport, allowing the replacement of visually undistinguished farm buildings with well-designed sport and recreation buildings of similar or lower floor area;
2. allowing buildings for indoor sport on non-prominent parts of sites which have predominantly outdoor recreation use;
3. promoting county and district countryside strategies for sport which would then provide the key to major funding of sports provisions;
4. encouraging the zoning of areas within green belts where sport and recreation facilities will have extra priority for natural grant aid; and
5. allowing a wider range of sports facilities in defined circumstances in Community Forests.

In these ways a reasonable compromise may be struck between positive provision and the traditional notion of a green belt as a broad rural zone near to towns.

References

Bishop, K., 1991, 'Community forests—implementing the concept', *The Planner*, 77, 18: 6–10.

Consumers Association, 1989, 'The Green Belt', *Which Magazine*, August, 338–41.

Countryside Commission, 1989, *Planning for a Greener Countryside*, CCP 264, Cheltenham, Countryside Commission.

Countryside Commission, 1991, *Visitors to the Countryside*, CCP 341, Cheltenham, Countryside Commission.

Countryside Commission, 1992, *Enjoying the Countryside—Policies for People*, CCP 371 Cheltenham, Countryside Commission.

Countryside Review Committee, 1977, *Leisure and the Countryside: A discussion Paper*, London, HMSO.

Department of the Environment, 1988a, *The Green Belts*, London, HMSO.

Department of the Environment, 1988b, *Green Belts*, PPG 2, London, HMSO.

Department of the Environment, 1991, *Sport and Recreation*, PPG 17, London, HMSO.

Elson, M.J., 1986, *Green Belts—Conflict Mediation in the Urban Fringe*, London, William Heinemann.

Elson, M.J., 1989, *Motorized water sports*, London, Sports Council.

Elson, M.J., 1992a, 'Green Belts for Wales: Political Priorities and Policy Responses', *The Planner*, **78**, 9: 10–11.

Elson, M.J., 1992b, 'Green Belts—A Symbol of Green Planning?', *Landscape Design*, February: 11–13.

Hares, D., 1992, 'Lakes from Wasteland', *Landscape Design*, February: 24–6.

Harrison, C., 1991, *Countryside Recreation in a Changing Society*, London, TMS Partnership.

House of Lords Select Committee on Sport and Leisure, 1973, *Second Report*, 193–1, London, HMSO.

Land Capability Consultants, 1991, *Damaged Land in the Urban Fringe*, Romford, LPAC.

Newby, H., 1991, 'The Future of Rural Society—Strategic Planning or Muddling Through', paper to Dartington Conference, November.

Pitt, J., 1991, 'Community forest cities of tomorrow', *Town and Country Planning*, **60**, 6: 188–90.

Thames Chase Community Forest, 1992, *Thames Chase Plan: Draft for Consultation*, Brentwood, TCCF.

Welsh Office, 1991, *Green Belts for Wales*, Cardiff, Welsh Office.

THE CHANGING NATURE OF SPORTS PROVISION AND URBAN LAND USE

MIKE FITZJOHN AND MALCOLM TUNGATT

Introduction

Provision of new sports facilities has been explosive in the past twenty-five years. Leisure pools, floodlit golf centres, artificial turf pitches and 'mega everything' are now common features of most of our towns and cities. They have been in the vanguard of the leisure revolution, are well documented, and virtually everyone will know of local examples. But there have also been other changes—the closure of older facilities, changes in location and changes in use—which are more subtle and less understood outside the world of the leisure professional. In aggregate, however, all these changes have had a significant impact on the distribution of facilities and on urban land use.

In this chapter we trace such developments and changes in four types of sports provision: swimming pools, indoor sports facilities, playing fields and golf courses. There have also been changes in provision for informal recreation such as the growth of country parks and linear routes; we omit them here simply because they are dealt with in other chapters. We examine provision, and its impact on urban land use, at three points in time—1964, 1978 and 1992—and assess the intervening changes. We conclude with a look to the future.

The first date, although approximate for our purposes, marks a significant watershed between the old and the new. By and large the pattern of provision which then existed had changed little in the previous twenty-five years, principally because of the Second World War and post-war capital controls on public expenditure. The year 1964 witnessed a change in government which perhaps provided a focal point for a growing political, professional and public interest in sport and leisure. The appointment of Denis Howell, whose personal contribution can never be underestimated, as Minister for

Sport was to be followed by the establishment of the Sports Council in 1965 and the Countryside Commission in 1968. As controls on local authority expenditure eased, the first post-war swimming pools appeared in the early 1960s, to be followed by the earliest indoor sports centres in the late 1960s.

The year 1978 was chosen as the mid-point between 1964 and the present but is again approximate. It was not a watershed like 1964, nor was it without significance. The late 1960s and early 1970s had seen a rapid growth of sports provision, culminating in the opening of large leisure centres in many towns when the local government structure was reorganized in 1974. However, by 1978 the rate of development was starting to slacken as the national economy again turned downwards. Political and policy questions were being asked about whether sport, and other public expenditure, was reaching the most disadvantaged members of society, especially those living in inner cities. Many older sports facilities, especially swimming pools, were reaching the end of their economic lives. And within a year there was to be a change in government which, in very general terms, would usher in a period of public-sector constraint and the growth of the commercial sports and leisure sector.

Changes in provision were not simply fuelled by these political and economic trends. Running in parallel were significant social trends—changing demography, increasing mobility, changing leisure fashions, and a rise in health consciousness.

In the analysis which follows we use the stylized 'Midtown' to illustrate significant changes. We have in mind a local authority district of about 150,000 population, with a large town, Midtown, at the core, and a rural hinterland. Midtown itself is sited on a river and has a traditional, but declining, manufacturing base. Originally a small market town, it expanded in the second half of the nineteenth century, and peripheral growth continued, particularly in the 1950s. In 1974, at local government reorganization, Midtown Municipal Borough joined with Midtown Rural District to form Midtown District, and the new Council created a Recreation Department to manage the town's public sports facilities. Midshires is the County Council and Education Authority.

Swimming

Although swimming baths were originally introduced into Britain by the Romans, it was the cholera outbreaks of the 1830s which prompted a new interest in public health. Initially individual baths were provided, but during the final three decades of the nineteenth century large pools were added. There were less costly to run and became an attraction for children (Laing and Laing, 1982, p.16). In Midtown the Corporation opened a twenty-five yard pool in the town centre in 1890 which, although still operating in 1964, was nearing the end of its useful life.

The growth of provision continued into the early twentieth century, and over 500 baths were open to the public by 1914. However, after the First World War, and the universal introduction of piped water into people's homes, there was a change of emphasis, and swimming baths became centres

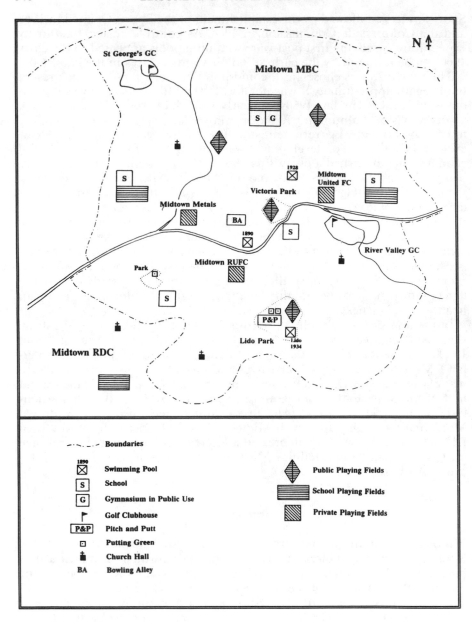

Figure 11.1 Midtown 1964

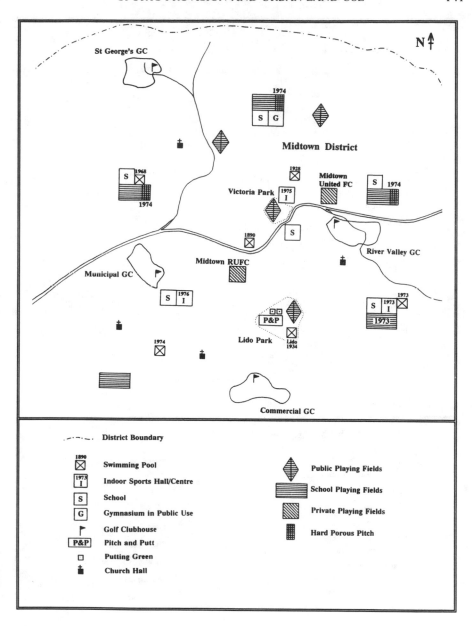

Figure 11.2 Midtown 1978

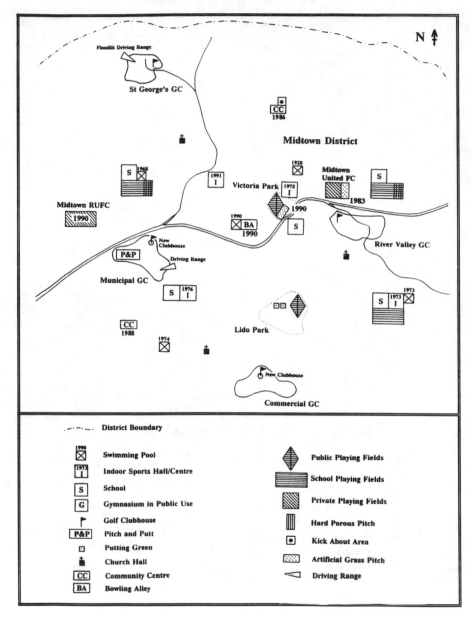

Figure 11.3   Midtown 1992

of sport, amusement and healthy recreation (Cross, 1938, p.7). New indoor pools were built in the developing suburbs, and Midtown was no exception. A spacious and architecturally grand twenty-five yard pool, which also included a small refreshments area, was opened in the northern suburbs in 1928.

The 1930s' emphasis on the virtues of sun and fresh air brought about a new phenomenon, the outdoor pool or lido, and over 100 were built in England in the inter-war years. Midtown provided a 600-square-yard lido, complete with poolside grassed banks for sunbathing and an open air cafeteria area, in the large park, renamed Lido Park, in the south of the town.

And there provision stopped. The austerity years of the 1940s and 1950s saw little public money available for new sport or leisure buildings. By 1964, pool provision remained only the heritage of previous generations; Midtown had its three pools, two indoor and one outdoor.

Swimming was a popular activity in Midtown during the late 1960s and early 1970s. As school rolls increased two new pools were provided in conjunction with Midshire County Council. One was added to an existing secondary school in 1968 and the second jointly provided as part of a new Community School in 1973. Both were fairly basic twenty-five-metre pools, but they provided access for the public in the evenings and, at the Community School, at weekends.

In common with many other towns (Sports Council, 1982a, p.17), the biggest boom to swimming in the district came with local government reorganization in 1974. The rate surplus of Midtown Rural District was invested in a thirty-three-metre pool built on the edge of a large 1950s' housing estate. The pool had a separate diving area and a small learner pool alongside.

So, in 1978, Midtown considered itself more than adequately provided, with one indoor pool per 30,000 people and a lido. But there were problems. The old town-centre pool was dilapidated and had only a few users; it was becoming structurally dangerous, but a strong lobby, led by Midtown Swimming Club, had kept it open. There were plans to replace it, but the Council was in financial difficulties. The 1928 suburban pool was becoming increasingly costly to maintain, although it was very popular with regular swimmers. Most worrying was the lido. There had been plans to close it in 1974, following the opening of the two new indoor pools in the south of the town, as it was regularly losing money. However, the hot summers of 1975–7 brought large numbers of users, and the plans were deferred.

Since 1978 Midtown has seen these problems multiply, but at the same time demand has increased, especially from the adult market, particularly women. The 1890 town-centre pool has finally closed, lost under an inner ring road. The lido was simply filled in during the late 1980s, and few people now miss it. However, in 1990, the growth of 'leisure' swimming in other towns led Midtown to provide a large new swimming complex in the town centre, in conjunction with a commercial developer and management company, reversing the trend for decentralized, easy access pools. The new Octopus centre has a large leisure pool, complete with flumes and a wave machine and a twenty-five metre square short-course pool for serious swimming and competition. Built alongside a thirty-six lane ten-pin bowling rink and cinema, the complex is now a central focus for the town's leisure, and families flock to the pool by car at weekends.

The facility has had an impact on the other pools. The public pool built in 1974 is now seen as inadequate and is proving expensive to maintain and refurbish to modern standards. The future of the two school pools is in doubt as the new legislation for the local management of schools introduced under the Education Reform Act has its impact on school budgeting arrangements (HMSO, 1988b). And the future of the 1928 pool, its architecture still seen as part of the town's heritage, remains in doubt. Contemporary developments may yet return Midtown to the era when the town-centre pool was the only opportunity for swimming, albeit in a modern complex hugely popular with the general public and prized by local swimming clubs.

Indoor sports facilities

In 1964 large indoor sports halls (capable of accommodating three or more badminton courts) were few and far between. Some had been purpose-built in universities in the 1920s and 1930s, and some were to be found on military bases, often in converted aircraft hangars. Public access was rare. Many schools had much smaller gymnasia, but their use outside school hours was severely restricted, perhaps to an Adult Education class, and even this was often no more than a 'front' for recreational use by a few close sporting friends of a PE teacher at the school. Such limited access was available at one secondary school in the north of Midtown.

Indoor sports participation, such as it was, largely took place under the aegis of a closed group (for example, a sports club, youth club) in a wide variety of non-purpose-built premises. Youth organizations played table tennis in youth centres, snooker was to be found in social clubs, but perhaps the archetype was the badminton club playing in the church hall, with only one court and a roof beam to restrict high shots. The only other indoor facility in Midtown was a twelve-lane ten-pin bowling rink, opened in a former cinema in 1955. By 1964, however, the sport was in decline, and there were constant rumours in the local press that it was to close.

The first purpose-built indoor sports halls and centres appeared in the mid-1960s at Crystal Palace, Harlow and Stockton, their design influenced by similar indoor halls at Lilleshall National Sports Centre and the Queen's Club in London. All were provided by visionary local authorities, supported by the Central Council of Physical Recreation and the embryonic Sports Council, willing to lead the United Kingdom into a trend already established on the Continent. Other local authorities followed, slowly at first, but increasingly quickly in the early 1970s. As with swimming pool provision, it was a trend fuelled by local government reorganization (Sports Council, 1982b, p.19). In Midtown a major indoor centre was opened close to the town centre in 1975. As well as a main hall accommodating four badminton courts, it had two smaller practice halls and four squash courts. However, unlike many centres built elsewhere at the time, it did not have a swimming pool, since the town centre pool was still operating. In order to save cost and time in land acquisition, it was built on part of Victoria Park, half a mile from the pool.

The late 1960s and early 1970s also witnessed an expansion in school building as rolls increased. The government and the Sports Council gave considerable emphasis to joint provision between Education Authorities and local authorities, although the local response varied across the country. Even where joint provision was not possible, Education Authorities were encouraged to make facilities available for community use. When the new Community School was built in Midtown in 1973, it included not only the jointly provided swimming pool but also a four-badminton-court indoor sports hall, martial arts room, squash courts and refreshments facilities. In 1976 the County Council also built a new sports hall at an existing secondary school south of the river, since the school had no playing fields, but there was little community use. Despite this volume of new building, however, the previous use of church halls and other non purpose-built facilities continued largely unabated. The ten-pin bowling rink, however, had closed by 1978.

In the 1980s capital expenditure by local authorities became even more tightly controlled, and the rate of provision of major new public indoor centres slowed. At the same time questions were raised about the accessibility of large town-centre facilities to many sections of the population (Sports Council, 1982b, pp. 28–30). The result of these trends, and others, was a greater diversification in the pattern of provision through the decade. By 1992 the major indoor centre in Midtown town centre was now seventeen years old, and some of the fabric decidedly worn out, both from age and lack of reinvestment. Under the compulsory competitive tendering regulations of the Local Government Act 1988 (HMSO, 1988a) its management was contracted out to a private operator.

But further new opportunities have been created in Midtown. Secondary school reorganization in the mid-1980s, consequent upon falling school rolls, led to the closure of the school in the north of the town. The large funds received by the County Council from the sale of the playing fields for housing development allowed Midtown to take over the school gym and associated facilities for a peppercorn rent in order to provide a small community centre, which opened to the public in 1986. The local management of schools legislation passed schools management to the governors (HMSO, 1988b, pp. 29–47), and those at the school with the sports hall built in 1976 opened it up for community use, both to develop the school's role in the community and to raise money.

One of the old churches in the town has been demolished, and half the site developed for sheltered housing; the hall attached to the new church has been designed with community uses, including sport, in mind. Ten-pin bowling has re-emerged as part of the new town-centre complex, and a commercial developer has provided an indoor cricket centre on an industrial estate just to the west of the town centre.

Playing fields

As with swimming pools and indoor facilities, the pattern of playing field provision in Midtown in 1964 had changed little since the Second World War. The only exception was that the County Council had provided a playing field in Midtown Rural District in 1955 close to a new housing estate. This was a 'detached' field, to which pupils were bussed from the secondary schools in the town centre and in the south west of the town. The other schools had playing fields on site.

There were concentrations of public pitches in Victoria Park and Lido Park, and a few pitches in each of two smaller parks in the north of the town. Midtown United Football Club, which played in the Football League's Third Division, had its ground on the fringe of the town centre, and Midtown Rugby Club owned its own pitches just south of the river. Midtown Metals had a 'works' sports ground to the west of the town centre. All of these private grounds had remained largely unchanged since they were first laid out towards the end of the nineteenth century.

As school rolls rose in the the early 1970s the new Community School was built in the east of the town with its own playing fields attached. However, school pitches were becoming increasingly costly to maintain, and so the County Council built a hard porous pitch at each of its school sites. The attentions of the local authority were focused on local government reorganization, and public pitches continued largely unnoticed. However, as capital resources were deployed on indoor provision, there was little investment in playing fields which, coupled with poor maintenance, led to a general deterioration.

As the economy went into recession at the end of the 1970s Midtown Metals came close to bankruptcy and, following a rigorous asset-stripping exercise, was able to obtain planning permission for a mixed housing and industrial development on its sports ground. Thus, between 1964 and 1978 Midtown had gained new school playing fields on the edge of town but lost a private ground close to the town centre.

This relatively stable position changed dramatically, however, in the 1980s. As already noted, the Council sold the school in the north of the town as part of its reorganization of schools in the middle of the decade. However, pressure from local parents led to the creation of an enclosed kick-about area as part of the former hard porous pitch alongside the indoor community facilities now managed by Midtown Council. The school rolls had also fallen substantially in the south west of the town, as the population of the 1950s' estate had aged, and the detached playing field was sold for an out-of-town shopping complex. Pupils who previously used the site now travel to the Community School, which is operating at under-capacity.

In the early 1980s Midtown United were relegated to the Football League's Fourth Division and gates fell dramatically. In order to generate additional income the club entered into a partnership with Midtown Council and the Sports Council to provide community facilities. Although there was not enough land available for a full-size pitch, an artificial training pitch suitable for six-a-side soccer was developed in 1983 on part of the club's car park.

In 1986 Midtown Rugby Club was approached by a supermarket chain with a view to purchasing its site on the southern fringes of the town centre. After much heart searching by the club, considerable local opposition and a Public Inquiry, the Secretary of State for the Environment eventually gave permission in 1989 for the development to go ahead. With the proceeds, the club was able to re-establish itself on surplus agricultural land near the District boundary. The site has twice as many pitches as the previous site and a splendid clubhouse.

As the 1980s finished, Midtown Council came under increasing pressure from the town hockey club, which hitherto had played in Lido Park, to provide a floodlit artificial grass pitch comparable with that enjoyed by hockey clubs elsewhere. With the assistance of a Sports Council grant, the Council was able to provide such a pitch alongside the indoor sports centre in Victoria Park. There were no land acquisition costs, and changing accommodation was already available in the sports centre.

In 1991 the Council's revenue budget was under continuing pressure, and demand for soccer pitches had levelled as the number of young adults in the population fell. Controversially, the Council decided to cease maintaining the public pitches in the north of the town, though the sites remain as informal parkland, and to concentrate all soccer on the public pitches at Victoria Park and Lido Park.

Golf courses

Many eighteen-hole golf courses, owned or leased by the club members who used them, were developed on the fringes of towns during the early years of the twentieth century (Royal and Ancient Golf Club, 1990, p.1). In addition, many large urban parks developed pitch and putt courses—now more commonly known as 'par 3' courses—and putting greens during the 1930s.

It was this legacy which provided opportunities for golf in Midtown in 1964. The St. George's Club, and its associated club, the Midtown Ladies Club, had developed their course in the Edwardian years on the sandy heathlands to the north west of the town. It formed the focus of the expansion of the town in the 1920s and 1930s, and its pleasant, well-maintained character contrasted with the working agricultural land and became a sought after outlook for new property owners.

A second club, River Valley Golf Club, had been established in the late 1920s by a breakaway group who wanted to have more access to the course. They were essentially golfers rather than socializers. Facilities were limited, and lady golfers were not allowed, but the course was longer and more challenging than St. George's, although its river valley location caused some flood problems.

Lido Park had a small but well-maintained pitch and putt course and two putting greens, the latter alongside bowling greens. A full-time greenkeeper was employed to maintain both facilities and also to look after the putting green in the small park on the south western edge of the town centre.

In common with the rest of England (Sports Council, 1988, p.32), the late

1960s and early 1970s saw Midtown's golfing population expand dramatically until, by 1975, both existing clubs were effectively full. Although almost half of the players were from the professional and managerial groups, the game had become popular with growing numbers of self-employed skilled manual workers and shift workers. As a result of this growth in demand, by 1978 two new courses had opened in Midtown. An entrepreneurial farmer had submitted proposals for a nine-hole course on poor agricultural land in the former Rural District in 1975. However, he was approached by a group of existing players, who suggested a partnership to develop a full-size course, which a new club would manage on his behalf. In addition, the growing public demand for open public access prompted Midtown Council to develop a municipal course and practice ground, partly on the site of a small park and partly on land reclaimed from the riverside meadows. Membership was encouraged, but the Council was determined to keep access open to all.

The intervening period since 1978 has seen a slackening in the growth of golf but a growth nevertheless, particularly among women. Commercial interest has also expanded. In the late 1980s proprietary 'pay-as-you-play' courses, managed as business ventures, and frequently associated with hotels or other leisure developments, have become the vogue. While Midtown had no additional courses by 1992, it had experienced some of the commercial expansion typical of the country as a whole. The commercial course now has a new clubhouse and there are plans to expand this into a hotel.

The municipal course was voluntarily put out to competitive tender by the Council in 1988, and is now managed by a Golf Development Company, which has expanded from its original interests in managing timeshare courses in Spain. A new clubhouse, social facilities and gymnasium have been opened, together with a driving range and a new pitch and putt course. The Council has ensured that the 'pay-as-you-play' ethos remains, although the members now operate as a semi-private club and have negotiated exclusive use on a programmed basis.

The old pitch and putt course in Lido Park has now been closed, partly for financial reasons and partly because the new course has taken its market. The two putting greens and bowling greens at Lido Park are now maintained by private contractors.

For the private clubs there have been two major changes. In cooperation with a commercial operator, St. George's has developed a floodlit driving range, despite opposition from some local property owners. River Valley, under pressure to bring in more money to finance drainage improvements, has opened the course to women on weekdays.

Future provision

For several years '1992' and '1993' have been on the horizon: a general election; the single European market; the Channel Tunnel. All point to a new era. But is it a new era for sport in urban areas? In concluding, we try to gaze into the crystal ball for the next decade.

For swimming pools, the trend in public demand of the late 1980s and early 1990s towards 'indoor water adventure centres', rather than conventional swimming opportunities, will probably be confirmed. The scale of resources required for such provision will dictate continuing public–commercial partnerships, probably on town-centre sites. However, this type of provision is increasingly geared to the car owner, and there are already signs in some areas of provision following retailing to the urban fringe. Indoor pools in hotels and private leisure complexes may provide further opportunities for those willing to pay more for their swim. But the great wave of 1960s and 1970s provision by the public sector faces an uncertain future as the main services of those pools reach the end of their useful lives. Some have already closed and been demolished; others will follow. The rest are likely to limp along, being patched up as limited resources permit, in an attempt to serve the needs of local communities and the aim of the new National Curriculum that all pupils should be able to swim at least twenty-five metres by the age of eleven (Department of Education and Science, 1991, p.19).

A similar, if less severe, fate awaits the municipally provided indoor sports facilities of the 1970s. The refurbishment of such town-centre sports facilities may depend on whether commercial funds can be injected, perhaps in conjunction with the development of newer, more lucrative facilities alongside. The shift towards more specialist commercial provision for indoor cricket, ten-pin bowling, roller skating, etc, is likely to continue. Whether these facilities survive into the twenty-first century, however, will depend almost exclusively on market forces. Opinions remain divided on whether the local management of schools' legislation will produce more or less community access to school halls and other indoor facilities, and only time will tell. For many sections of society, however, they may provide the only opportunities which are physically and financially accessible.

In the last few years, 'green issues' generally, and urban open space and playing fields in particular, have risen on the political and policy agenda. As this chapter has shown, there have been economic and demographic influences on the provision of pitches, and these are likely to continue. However, with a levelling in demand over the next ten to fifteen years for demographic reasons on the one hand, and a greater concern for protecting existing resources on the other, it seems likely that the rate of change will slacken considerably. The growth in provision of artificial grass pitches, especially for hockey, is likely to continue.

Golf will almost certainly maintain its growth in popularity, and much of the new demand will probably be met by commercial leisure providers developing courses in rural areas on former agricultural land (Royal and Ancient Golf Club, 1990, pp. 28–33). These new courses may become more open to public access as the 'pay-as-you-play' ethos spreads. For private clubs, the 1990s will probably see increases in maintenance costs and, perhaps, a slow decline in membership as other opportunities emerge. But we believe there will also be an increasingly active commercial sector within the private clubs to attract new finance through driving ranges and 'par-3' golf. 'Electronic golf', imported from Japan, may flourish.

In summary, our stylized Midtown is undoubtedly better off in overall provision than ever before. Its population has responded to sports promotional campaigns and the health and fitness boom of the 1980s and is seeking an active lifestyle. Its younger people, growing up with the new National Curriculum, have greater sporting expectations across a much wider range of sports than previous generations. All of this means that across the country as a whole there is considerable scope for the commercial sector to thrive in a wide range of sporting markets; almost by definition, many of these markets are mobile. Town-centre sites, suburban sites and out-of-town sites are all viable options. But there is also a need for a continuing, and strong, public sector to retain, refurbish and improve the sporting infrastructure which has developed in our towns over the last hundred years, especially the last twenty-five years, if society is genuinely to subscribe to 'Sport for All'.

References

Cross, K.M.B., 1938, *Modern Public Baths*, London, Amateur Swimming Association.

Department of Education and Science, 1970, *Circular No. 2/70—The chance to share*, London, DES.

Department of Education and Science, Welsh Office, 1991, *Physical Education for Ages 5 to 16*, London, HMSO.

Laing, H. and Laing, A., 1982, 'The history of baths provision', in *Taking the Plunge*, London, Save Britain's Heritage.

HMSO, 1988a, *Local Government Act 1988*, London, HMSO.

HMSO, 1988b, *Education Reform Act 1988*, London, HMSO.

Royal and Ancient Golf Glub, 1990, *The Demand for Golf*, St. Andrews, Royal and Ancient Golf Club.

Sports Council, 1982a, *National Swimming Pools Study, Report 1*, London, Sports Council.

Sports Council, 1982b, *Sport in the Community, the Next Ten Years*, London, Sports Council.

Sports Council, 1983, *Digest of Sports Statistics*, London, Sports Council.

12

TERRITORIALITY AND THE ENVIRONMENT OF BRITISH FOOTBALL

JOHN BALE

Introduction

A *Punch* cartoon included in Allan Patmore's classic study, *Recreation and Resources*, summarized in a light-hearted way a basic change in the configuration of the sports landscape. Two countryside visitors are shown looking over a rural idyll. One says to the other, 'Let's enjoy it while we can—this is where they're going to build the new Leisure Centre' (Patmore, 1983, p.238). It is this kind of spatial confinement of leisure space which forms the central focus of this chapter, illustrated in the topical context of the British football stadium. Over the last two centuries such confinement has resulted in an activity initially played in a rough and tumble manner in 'open' environments, traditionally having weak rules of exclusion and relatively permeable boundaries, becoming one which is highly organized and regimented, with strong exclusionary rules and impermeable barriers.

Such developments can be interpreted as part of the broader tendency towards territoriality. As interpreted by Robert Sack, territoriality means that people have been removed from, or possess restricted access to, one kind of place and that specifically prescribed spaces have been allocated for particular activities. Territoriality creates the idea of a space to be filled and emptied at particular times; it is viewed as a process—'the attempt by an individual or group to affect, influence or control, phenomena and relationships, by delimiting and asserting control over a geographic area' (Sack, 1986 p.19). In other words, it is a 'primary geographical expression of social power' (p.5), a definition close to Michel Foucault's view that the notion of territory is 'first of all a juridico-political one: the area controlled by a certain kind of power' (Foucault, 1980, p.68).

Foucault's (1979) work on the micro-spaces of various 'institutions' of internment (that is hospitals, prisons, asylums) can also be applied to the leisure environment of the sports stadium. Indeed, many leisure environments might be described as focal points for the application of Foucault's 'great confinement', consisting of the application of numerous small but significant forms of 'bio-power' and rendering, as they do, a form of docility and individualization in the population. The relative neglect of Foucault's work in sports studies is somewhat paradoxical in view of his central concern with the human body, which, in Harvey's (1989, p.45) words, is 'the "site" at which all forms of repression are ultimately registered'. One of the purposes of this chapter, therefore, is to extend the analogy (but it is only an analogy) between the prison and the stadium, already noted in passing, for example, by Brohm (1978) and Eichberg (1988).

According to Foucault, power over the body is developed around two poles. The first consists of various forms of control such as spatial confinement and surveillance which seek to regulate the population. The second pole is made up of various 'disciplines' which provide procedures for training bodies. For example, physical education, sport and football can each be regarded as a discipline, inculcating as they do certain desired bodily practices—or discipline. Such disciplines may be regarded as 'internalized norms, a secular version of the pastoral system of power and strategies of the government of individuals seen previously with the Church' (Harvey and Sparks, 1991, p.170). Having all too briefly reviewed some ideas of Sack and Foucault, I now contextualize them within the changing milieu of British football.

I will do this by viewing the British football stadium as a four-stage model spanning a period of about two hundred years. The stages are (i) an antecedent stage of unenclosed folk-football; (ii) rule boundedness; (iii) commodification and segregation; and (iv) containment and panopticism. These stages describe the enclosure and territorialization of football space which, as a result, provides an example of a locality of resistance in a leisure setting. Each stage, and the nature of such resistance, can now be outlined.

The enclosure and territorialization of football space

A major feature of pre-industrial football was its lack of spatial regulation and an absence of geographic confinement. The antecedent of the modern stadium was therefore the multi-functional landscape of pre-industrial Britain. In folk-games no standardized rules of play existed, and games took place between villages and towns—not simply in the sense that these places competed against each other but also literally, between each other—in a spatial sense (Dunning and Sheard, 1978). Pre-modern football took place on existing landscapes—roads, commons, fields, public spaces holding spectacular events analogous to the outdoor 'spectacle' of punishment prior to its removal from public space and the development of prisons. There were few places specially set aside solely for 'sports' for the masses, and in many ways football played in the medieval streets and on the eighteenth-century common was similar to the carnival where the weak rules of exclusion meant that there was a tendency to 'not acknowledge any distinction between actors and spectators' (Bakhtin, 1968, p.5).

The second stage in the geographical evolution of the modern football landscape started during the late eighteenth and nineteenth centuries with the increasing division of labour in society, accompanied by an increasing division of space and time. There was a time for work and a time for play; there were to be specific places where various activities, formerly undertaken on streets, squares and commons, could be accommodated. Activities became codified; various forms of 'movement culture' like folk-football became 'sportified'.

In all sports, spatial parameters define the limits within which the activity can take place and Wagner (1981, p.89) has noted the way in which sport stands out clearly 'from all other recreational activity, and even from work, by virtue of an essentially geographic attribute, its time–space specificity'. During the nineteenth century progressive refinements of the rules meant that football space was becoming delimited by the application of arithmetic and geometry to the field of 'play'. The unspecified spaces in which folk-football was played were replaced by straight lines defining where play could, and could not, take place. Such development was incremental. For the best part of twenty years following the formulation of the 1863 rules, the boundaries between players and spectators remained relatively permeable. With the absence of touchlines players mingled with spectators, the latter often encroaching on to the pitch so that only about thirty metres of playing space were left. This inexact division of space, a residual of the folk-game tradition, was formally brought to an end in 1882 when the demarcation of the touchline was introduced. Such exact partitioning of space, resulting from the formalization of the game's rules, facilitated inter-regional competition, but it also had the effect of making the game more achievement-orientated by isolating the experts (that is players) from the spectators, reflecting the rationalizing tendencies present in broader aspects of nineteenth-century society.

It has been argued that a major characteristic of the development of capitalism was the increased commodification of space (Lefebvre, 1991) or the idea that space should be made to pay. Football space was no exception in this respect, and following its enclosure, someone, somewhere felt that it would be worth charging for admission to watch games. The sport became 'paying consumption rather than participating recreation and could be more easily confined in particular locations and particular time slots' (Thrift, 1981, p.66). Charging for admission seems to have developed rapidly from the mid-1870s (Mason, 1980).

Initially a roped or fenced-off field sufficed, but soon clubs began to segregate their spectators, already segregated from the players by the white chalk line, by providing superior forms of accommodation. Pavilions, often leased from cricket clubs, could be used by those who wanted additional comfort or space to entertain business acquaintances (Inglis, 1989). As the popularity of the sport increased, other forms of segregation could be adopted; grandstands with sections to accommodate directors were built, and standing on the terraces was supplemented by seats. The social geographies of the new stadiums came to mirror those of the cities in which they were found.

In the mid-twentieth century segregation was based on economic criteria rather than on team affiliation, and movement between terraces was widely practiced as supporters changed 'ends' at half time. Boundaries between particular parts of the terraces were still permeable into the late 1950s, and the pitch itself, long separated from spectators by the straight white lines, was far from impermeable; crowds often spilled on to the pitch after the game to congratulate players or to remonstrate with the referee. But the term 'pitch invasion' would carry all the wrong connotations.

The fourth stage of the model is one characterized by further containment and the addition of sophisticated forms of surveillance, and starts in the early 1960s with the development of segregation on the basis of team affiliation. Such segregation arose, first, from the increased need to 'control' the perceived problem of crowd misbehaviour and, second, from the worsening economic situation in British football which was believed to be, in part at least, to result from the 'hooligan problem'. As a result, the parallelization of stadium space assumed a number of dimensions, including the spatial demarcation by team allegiance, the sub-division of terrace space on grounds of safety, the hardening of the boundary between players and spectators by the erection of perimeter fences, the accommodation of more exclusive accommodation for an economic elite and the move towards all-seater stadiums.

I noted earlier the tendency during the 1950s for fans to change ends at half time. In the mid-1960s crowds became more assertive, and the popular press identified gangs who staked out territorial claims behind each goal. Home gangs increasingly watched matches from fixed locations, but the absence of any barriers to movement meant that some gangs were able to 'take' the opposing 'end'. Such inter-territorial rivalries and their associated exchange did undoubtedly take place but tended to be over-reported in the mass media, with a resulting 'moral panic'. The result was a new phase of spatial control.

The 'thin blue line' of the police increasingly gave way to much stronger exclusionary measures with the enforced segregation of home and away supporters by the erection of physical barriers and 'pens'. In the mid-1980s an electrified fence was installed at one London ground, but following protests this was never actually used. Segregation by economic class also continued to intensify, and while the more lumpen of football's fandom was being herded into insanitary pens, the more socially and economically acceptable were increasingly distanced from grass-root support by more expensive forms of segregated accommodation—the special, glass-fronted 'executive boxes'. Such developments were often accompanied by the destruction of the more popular parts of the ground.

There were two important implications of such physical changes in the stadium's environment:

First, the image of the spectator as someone who can only be tempted to watch a game if it offers standards of physical comfort which he [sic] would expect to find elsewhere. Second, it implies a particular way of watching the game. Seated, dispassionately critical, the new spectator waits to be entertained. The show is something out there, not something of which he is part. In the gaps in the entertainment, he expects to be provided with food and drink, music and spectacular demonstrations [Clarke, 1978, p.47]

The luxury boxes identified a new kind of spectator; 'no impassioned trouble maker he—no physical involvement, chanting or swearing in these new stands'. With 'whisky in hand' he is the recipient of 'instant entertainment' (Critcher, 1979, p.178). Meanwhile, the community of local fans was relegated to insanitary, alcohol-free pens.

With such territorialization, people come to, literally, know their place, encouraging a status quo view of the world (Sibley, 1981, p.45). But despite these measures considerable concern about the behaviour of fans inside stadiums continued into the 1980s. The response was for all clubs to install closed-circuit television in order to identify trouble-makers. This modern form of panopticism encourages comparison with Foucault's description of the prison; the spectator, like 'the inmate must never know whether he is being looked at at any moment; but he must be sure that he may always be so' (Foucault, 1979, p.201). Where people had to be contained, efficient surveillance was a necessity; surveillance provided knowledge, while knowledge provided power.

A further tendency in the British stadium was to increase the proportion of spectators in seated accommodation. Seating was a response, not simply to the view (which is contestable) that it would provide greater comfort but also to the view (which is also contestable) that seats would restrain the violent tendencies of the 1970s and lead to safer stadiums. With seats, however, the stadium would approximate to an 'enclosed, segmented space . . . in which the individuals are inserted in a fixed place' (Foucault, 1979). Following the Taylor report (Taylor, 1990) into the Hillsborough disaster, it was recommended that British football should be watched in all-seater stadiums. 'Anchorage in a space is an economic–political form', noted Foucault (1980, p.68), and a numbered seat meant that 'each individual has his own place; and each place its own individual' (Foucault, 1979, p.143). The all-seater stadium therefore represents 'a compact model of the disciplinary mechanism' (Foucault, 1979, p.197). With computerized ticketing, the physical evidence of spatial separation (that is barriers and 'pens') might be reduced, as electronic means of surveillance would extend beyond the video camera to data banks derived from computerized information. Accompanying this would be a common characteristic of modernity—that people would be treated less like people and more like things (or numbers).

Some British clubs experimented with 'family sections', but this move can also be viewed as an analogy of Foucault's description of the growth of the prison. As with the hierarchical 'family' of supervisors in progressive nineteenth-century prisons, the nuclear family, seated together as 'docile bodies' replaces the fear of continual visual inspection with the anti-institutional and natural weapon of the family—perhaps the ultimate in the art of power relations (Foucault, 1979).

Reaction

The British stadium, whose security system is likened by some foreign observers as being 'more suitable to a prison' (Arens, 1980, p.80)—reinforcing the Foucaultian analogy used earlier—reflects the view that 'the rationalization of spectator sports has had counter-productive effects in relation to audience satisfaction' (Hargreaves, 1987, p.157). The Taylor Report noted that 'the spectacle of these cage-like fences is inconsistent with a sports ground being for pleasure and recreation . . . Having to stand in a cage for your Saturday afternoon recreation inevitably causes resentment' (Taylor, 1990, p.31). The stadium is therefore all too often the antithesis of play and freedom and more often a symbol of control and restraint.

But dissatisfaction and resentment to such changes has been accompanied by forms of resistance. This is nothing new and has been associated with the increasing spatial confinement of football since its folk-game days.

The enclosure of common land and the appropriation of streets had great implications for people's leisure as well as for their work. The fact that folk-football was often banned does not mean that resistance was inevitably useless. It is recorded, for example, that a football riot was associated with the successful defiance of an attempt to enclose Holland Fen in Lincolnshire (Malcolmson, 1979), though law and order did eventually prevail. Over two hundred years later Coventry City fans resisted the introduction of seats to their Highfield Road stadium by simply tearing them out. Articulation of opposition to more recent developments can be found in the literature of the somewhat anarchic fanzine movement (made up of several hundred 'unofficial' football magazines produced by fans themselves) which has been a feature of the British football scene in recent decades. Such publications, totalling around 400 and read by more than one million people, are fugitive and ephemeral but almost certainly reflect the 'insider's' view of football better than any other printed source. They therefore constitute a valuable research resource.

In one such fanzine, *Off the Ball*, it was noted that embourgeoisified football 'is reduced to ritzy-glitzy hype, heavily commercialized with forced and ordered excitement. This sanitized soccer becomes, to the hamburger culture society, just another thing to do—last week the cinema, this week football, next week the theme park' (Beauchampe, 1986, p.6). Such qualitative statements as this can be supplemented with the results of a number of attitude surveys into fans' reactions to the recommendations of the Taylor Report (Taylor, 1991) that all supporters in British football grounds should be seated. Such surveys reveal that the percentages of respondents who prefer to stand to watch a match range from 44 per cent (Canter *et al*, 1989) to 80 per cent. Of respondents to a survey undertaken by Millwall Football Club, 93 per cent believed that they should have the 'right to stand', while a survey of members of the Football Supporters' Association showed that 69.3 per cent would oppose seating in their own clubs' grounds while 15.6 per cent stated that they would not watch their club in an all-seater ground (Sir Norman Chester Centre for Football Research, 1989). In the case of one club which installed seats (Coventry City) negative attitudes were converted to actions and fans reacted by tearing the seats out.

In the early 1990s several events have suggested that resistance was not entirely useless. The Football League is reconsidering its views on all-seater stadiums; the perimeter fences around many grounds have come down; observers are talking about 'celebration' rather than 'aggravation' among football fans (Taylor, 1991) and zany dress styles, face paints and a music–football nexus are bringing fun back to the terraces (Redhead, 1991). The Football Supporters' Association and the fanzines have become mouthpieces through which the voices of many of the sport's supporters can be heard, combining to create a form of cultural resistance. In the case of the British football stadium, however, the confounding tendencies which I have described above have been resisted—with varying degrees of success—at both the start and at the current stage of the 'great confinement'.

Although it is difficult to talk about 'post-modern' tendencies in British football space—simply because the sport has barely started being modernized—the softening of the boundaries and the weakening of the rules of exclusion within grounds invite analogies with post-modern movements in other spheres. In architecture it is widely regarded that the symbolic end of modernism was in 1972 when the Pruitt-Igoe apartment blocks in St. Louis (constructed in the mid-1950s) were dynamited and demolished; they had become uninhabitable. In British football, 1990 might be identified as the beginning of the post-modern stadium when the metal fences surrounding many grounds were taken down and scrapped. As Hillsborough had demonstrated, the terraces (like Pruitt-Igoe) had become uninhabitable. The old suddenly seemed to be new again. And the ambiguity of modernization itself was revealed in the short-lived presence in English League football of the plastic pitches (subsequently replaced by grass) in a small number of grounds. While disliked by players and fans, plastic pitches temporarily signalled a return to the multifunctional use of space—a return to mixed land use where football could take place alongside a range of other activities, many of which were less 'serious' and involved greater community use than was possible on the monocultural 'sacred turf' of sportscape. Whether technology produces further innovations in playing surfaces, satisfactory to all participants in football, remains to be seen.

Conclusion

In this chapter I have tried to show not simply how the environment in which sport is played has changed over time but also how some of these changes might be interpreted. I have attempted to illustrate the fact that since the eighteenth century, football, the game itself and later, those who watched it, have regularly been subjected to various forms of territorialization or spatial confinement. The game has moved from being a form of corporal, to one of carceral, participation. Initially, a limitation on playing space, then an exact spatial definition of the pitch, and today enforced segregation of spectators both from players and other spectators, the story of the stadium has indeed been one of 'great confinement'. Whereas the intra-stadium space of the early twentieth century included a number of 'permeable boundaries', in the modern stadium the boundaries between various groups (players/spectators, home/away fans, rich/poor fans) tend to be 'impermeable'. In this sense, the stadium is an archetype of modernity (Archetti, 1992). I have also illustrated how surveillance is central to a major leisure activity. The chapter has also shown how the sites of football have assumed some of the characteristics of spaces of resistance in which 'marginalized' groups (in this case, football fans) have shown themselves to be far from passive. Finally, the chapter has indicated the centrality of the spatial dimension in the leisure environment and how a politics of territory remains crucial to an understanding of that environment.

References

Archetti, E., 1992, 'Il calcio: un rituale della violenza?' in P. Lanfranchi (ed.), *Il Calcio e iluo Pubblico*, Naples, Edizione Scientifiche Italiane.

Arens, W., 1980, 'Playing with aggression' in J. Cherfas and R. Lewin (eds), *Not work Alone*, London, Temple Smith.

Bakhtin, M., 1968, *Rabelais and his World*, Cambridge, Mass, MIT Press.

Beauchampe, S., 1986, 'Family fodder', *Off the Ball*, November.

Brohm, J.-M., 1978, *Sport: a Prison of Measured Time*, London, Ink Links.

Canter, D., Comber, M., and Uzzell, D., 1989, *Football in its Place*, London, Routledge.

Clarke, J., 1978, 'Football and working class fans; tradition and change' in R. Ingham *et al.* (eds), *Football Hooliganism: the Wider Context*, London, Inter-Action Inprint.

Critcher, C., 1979, 'Football since the war' in J. Clarke, C. Critcher and R. Johnson (eds), *Working Class Culture*, London, Hutchinson.

Dunning, E. and Sheard K., 1978, *Gentlemen, Barbarians and Players*, Oxford, Martin Robertson.

Eichberg, H., 1988, *Leistungsraume: Sport als Umweltproblem*, Munster, Lit Verlag.

Foucault, M., 1979, *Discipline and Punish*, Harmondsworth, Penguin.

Foucault, M., 1980, *Power/Knowledge: Selected Interviews and Other Writings*, Brighton, Harvester.

Hargreaves, J., 1987, 'The body, sport and power relations' in J. Horne, D. Jary and A. Tomlinson (eds), *Sport, Leisure and Social Relations*, Sociological Review Monograph, 33, London, Routledge.

Harvey, D., 1989, *The Condition of Postmodernity*, Oxford, Blackwell.

Harvey, J. and Sparks, R., 1991, 'The politics of the body in the context of modernity', *Quest*, **43**: 164–89.

Inglis, S., 1989, *The Football Grounds of Great Britain*, London, Collins.

Lefebvre, H., 1991, *The Production of Space*, Oxford, Blackwell.

Malcolmson, R.W., 1979, *Popular Recreations in English society, 1700–1850*, Cambridge, Cambridge University Press.

Mason, T., 1980, *Association Football and English society, 1863–1915*, Brighton, Harvester Press.

Patmore, J.A., 1983, *Recreation and Resources: Leisure Patterns and Leisure Places*, Oxford, Blackwell.

Redhead, S., 1991, *Football with Attitude*, Manchester, Wordsmith.
Sack, R., 1986, *Human Territoriality*, Cambridge, Cambridge University Press.
Sibley, D., 1981, *Outsiders in Urban Societies*, Oxford, Blackwell.
Sir Norman Chester Centre for Football Research, 1989, *Football and Football Spectators after Hillsborough: a National Survey of Members of the Football Supporters Association*, Leicester, Department of Sociology, Leicester University.
Taylor, I., 1991, 'From aggravation to celebration', *The Independent*, April 21: 31.
Taylor, Lord Justice, 1990, *The Hillsborough Stadium disaster: Final Report*, London, HMSO.
Thrift, N., 1981, 'Owners' time and own time', in A. Pred (ed.), *Space and Time in Geography*, Lund, Gleerup.
Wagner, P., 1981, 'Sport: culture and geography', in A. Pred (ed.), *Space and Time in Geography*, Lund, Gleerup.

PART IV
MANAGEMENT FOR CONSERVATION AND RECREATION

SPORT, RECREATION AND NATURE CONSERVATION: DEVELOPING GOOD CONSERVATION PRACTICE

ROGER SIDAWAY

Introduction

This chapter takes a retrospective look at a series of reports and articles on sport in the countryside and its effects on wildlife which were initiated by the Sports Council in 1986 (Sidaway, 1988, 1990, 1991; Sidaway and Thompson, 1991). The reports synthesized much of the relevant research published in English, and although the management issues and suggested solutions covered in this chapter are specific to Britain, the approach to decision-making is of far wider relevance.

The general thesis advanced in the initial report, *Sport, Recreation and Nature Conservation*, remains largely unchanged. That is, in a context of major environmental threats, the impacts of sport and outdoor recreation are not of major significance but can cause local damage, which in most circumstances can be ameliorated by good conservation practice.

There are three important qualifications to this statement:

—first, when sport and recreation are coupled with economic development (that is usually labelled tourism), then the associated developments can result in significant loss of habitats, for example development of tourist resorts;
—second, recreational impacts can be particularly acute in habitats that lack resilience. In these cases the biological system has a low dynamic and recovery cycles are very long, for example alpine and certain coastal ecosystems; and,
—third, increasing mobility and affluence, particularly among younger sections of the population, coupled with the introduction of new technology, provide a fertile market for new recreation activities, for example, jet skiing and mountain biking. At best, these effects are only temporary, and only last until management measures are developed to ameliorate them.

As suggested in an article on the uplands (Sidaway and Thompson, 1991), the inability to devise effective management systems which ensure that development is sustainable is at least as critical as the lack of technical information on biological impacts although that in itself is scarce.

When do recreational impacts matter?

Damage to vegetation

An earlier overview (Speight, 1973) provided an exhaustive list of possible impacts that recreational activities might have on habitats and geological systems. A more recent checklist (Sidaway, 1988) suggests three major categories—damage to vegetation, disturbance to fauna, and damage to geological features. Given that the early focus of 'recreation ecology' was botanical, it is hardly surprising that much of the work in this field in the 1970s concentrated on damage to vegetation. The effects are immediately obvious, although a matter of perception—one person's linear erosion may be another person's path.

Seen from a broader perspective, trampling of vegetation or damage by recreational vehicles can occasionally be locally devastating but does not threaten the survival of plant species or habitats. Thompson and Horsfield (1990) demonstrate that the conservation significance of recreational activities in the uplands is outranked by afforestation, overgrazing, agricultural reclamation and, depending on the conservation criteria used, acidic deposition. In their estimation, recreation affects approximately 12 per cent of plant communities unique to the British uplands and about 8 per cent of all upland plant communities.

A review of Scottish mountain footpaths considered that:

> while ecological effects may be locally severe on the path, and may extend beyond it, sometimes for considerable distances, as a result of vegetation burial by gravel wash and by walkers straying from rough path surfaces . . . mountain paths do not as a rule present any very significant threat to ecological resources . . . they may even on balance help to reduce wider disturbance to flora and fauna by concentrating most walkers on a restricted line. [Aitken, 1984, p.18]

Nevertheless, on major upland routes, the Pennine Way, the West Highland Way, many mountain peaks in the Lake District, and the increasingly popular Scottish 'munros' (over 3,000 feet), the effects of trampling feet are particularly serious. There is a growing problem of path maintenance, particularly on peaty ground. Most pathways have followed desire lines and been worn rather than purposefully constructed, so that the combination of poor surface drainage, abrasion from repeated use and harsh winter conditions leads to gullying and erosion and prevents the recovery of vegetation. Walkers seek to find parallel routes as the surface deteriorates and the path can widen dramatically in a few years. The widening of paths can create barriers to the movement of certain species, notably invertebrates. But in the countryside more generally, these problems are exceptional and on most of the rights of way in England and Wales the impact of recreational walking is so minimal that paths are often difficult to find.

Access to the wider countryside in vehicles, either on motor or mountain cycles or in four-wheel drive vehicles, provokes an emotional response from regular walkers and local communities. It is a difficult, and possibly meaningless, task to isolate the separate effects of wheels, feet and horses' hooves. Often the debate is more concerned with who has legitimate rights of passage and which use is 'appropriate' in the countryside than with who causes the most damage. In the worst cases, one use compounds the other. There is little concrete evidence of significant physical damage being caused to vegetation by trail riding (motor cycles), particularly when compared to agriculture or forestry vehicles (Dartington Amenity Research Trust, 1979) or the tracks constructed to higher altitudes by agriculture, forestry, shooting or even telecommunication interests. The use of unmetalled highways by four-wheel drive vehicles attracts controversy, but again the perception of the problem may be far greater than the reality.

Lack of provision for youngsters for motorbike scrambling, preferably close to home, presents a particular problem when the 'waste ground' they use may well be a high-quality wildlife site or even a Site of Special Scientific Interest (SSSI). A survey by the Royal Society for Nature Conservation instanced damage or disturbance by motor vehicles at sixty-eight SSSIs and forty-four County Wildlife Trust Reserves (RSNC, 1987). This and other evidence of damage to SSSIs has led to planning permission being required if these protected sites are to be used by motor sports (DOE, 1991).

Disturbance to birds

There is a similar need to take a cool look at the disturbing effects of recreation on birds and mammals, and in recent years the limited research on this topic has focused on breeding and over-wintering birds. The most comprehensive research on breeding birds and recreation has been undertaken in the Netherlands, where researchers have been keen to distinguish between immediate behavioural responses and longer-lasting effects of significance to the survival of the local population (Van der Zande, 1984). The range of potentially disturbing effects is categorized in Table 13.1. For example, disruption to feeding may only be significant if it is prolonged during a particularly critical period in the winter when food supplies are restricted and feeding times reduced by short days or tidal conditions for migratory waders. In other conditions, the birds' response of moving to undisturbed territory is usually sufficient. Even during breeding periods it is important to distinguish between responses which are intended to distract predators away from nests and young (and are part of a highly evolved survival technique) and more serious long-term effects. Ground-nesting birds in the uplands are generally considered to be more vulnerable although individual species have developed techniques such as 'sitting tight' on the nest to avoid detection.

Concern has been expressed about the effects on breeding populations of characteristic species of moorland areas caused by disturbance from walkers using the most popular routes. Research has been undertaken on very few species. A recent study on one of the species considered most sensitive (Golden Plover) compared breeding on heavily and lightly used areas in the Peak District. It found that breeding was less successful when the birds were frequently disturbed during a cold spring which delayed their settling into nesting territories. In these years breeding success may be affected, but the population is likely to recover as other plovers move into vacant territories to breed in subsequent years. More frequent problems arise when walkers' dogs run uncontrolled through nesting areas or where there are multiple paths so that few areas are left undisturbed (Yalden and Yalden, 1989). The problem appears to be a local one with the overall population level unaffected as long as there are undisturbed areas providing a 'reservoir' of breeding birds. This research has led to some reassessment of the assumptions previously made about disturbance. The prospecting period when birds establish territories is now considered more critical than later periods of the breeding season.

Several other vulnerable habitats receive much higher levels of recreational use which could present potential problems for the breeding success of their characteristic birds. In particular, water margins are inherently attractive for recreation so that both the incidence and duration of disturbance at any one popular spot is likely to be high. Picnickers or anglers who spend several hours in an area are more likely seriously to disturb breeding birds than passing walkers. For example, there is evidence of a decline in waders breeding on the beaches of Loch Morlich in Glen More Forest Park, where car parks have been provided at the water's edge (Watson et al., 1988) and of bankside angling affecting a range of common species nesting around gravel pits in the Thames Valley (Tydeman, 1977). Yalden (1992) has observed an apparent reduction in the breeding population of common sandpipers along parts of the shoreline of Ladybower Reservoir, Derbyshire, which are subject to regular disturbance from anglers and other visitors. Unrestricted access to inter-tidal and coastal areas may also cause disturbance to flocks of feeding or roosting waders (Mitchell et al., 1988).

Consideration of individual activities

The recent round of research reviews instigated by the Sports Council shows, perhaps somewhat surprisingly, that there were as many if not more examples where recreational effects on wildlife could be mitigated than vice versa (Sidaway, 1988). The principal case studies conducted showed that:

—the impacts of caving on underground geological features and hibernating bats were ameliorated by conservation-minded caving clubs strictly regulating access and enforcing a code of conduct;
—the potentially disturbing effects of climbing on cliff-nesting protected birds (such as the peregrine falcon) were virtually removed by nationally

Table 13.1 Summary of potentially disturbing effects on birds which can be caused by recreation

Effects	Possible consequences
(a) Temporary disruption to feeding or resting—less critical in late summer post-breeding season.	bird takes cover or flies to undisturbed area
—more critical when food supply restricted and daylight hours/ feeding time reduced, eg over-wintering or winter migratory species	high energy loss compared to food supply; repeated disturbance leads to exhaustion and vulnerability to predators
(b) Effects on breeding adult— (i) disturbance when prospecting for suitable nesting sites[1]	delay in breeding; loss of suitable site to others of same species
(ii) disturbance during incubation period	exposure of eggs, heat loss; non-incubation; increased risk of predation
(c) Effects on young (i) if adult flushed from nest and/ or delayed return	exposure of chick; heat loss; loss of food; increased risk of predation
(ii) if taking cover in response to alarm calls of parent bird[2]	interruption to feeding; interruption to brooding (heat loss), predators attracted by alarm calls
(d) Effects on habitat from accidental fire	Loss of breeding cover, loss of food supply

[1] Feature of particular importance for raptors and upland waders
[2] Features of certain ground-nesting species breeding in open country, eg common sandpiper, golden plover

Effects b (i) and d may affect size of breeding population;
b (ii), c (i) and c (ii) may affect breeding success

Source: after Sidaway, 1990

agreed voluntary seasonal restrictions on specific climbs where there were known nesting sites;
—in the case of orienteering event planning, local negotiations with land owners and conservationists and competition rules minimized trampling and disturbing effects;
—winter sailing and angling, out of the traditional closed seasons, appeared to affect over-wintering wildfowl populations, but in some cases, at least, disturbance could be reduced by zoning or seasonal restrictions.

A further classification of activities, impacts and possible solutions is set out in Table 13.2.

Table 13.2 Classification of recreational impacts

Activity	Possible problems	Some solutions
Impact low and local, but widespread		
Motor sports	Damage to vegetation	Public rights of way (PROW) management
		Provision near towns
Off-road cycling	Damage to vegetation	Code of practice
Riding	Damage to vegetation	PROW management
Walking	Damage to upland vegetation	PROW management Repair/construction of mountain paths
	Disturbance by dogs	Restrictions in nesting season
Fishing	Disturbance of nesting birds	Restrictions in nesting season
Impact specific and locally acute		
Shooting	Size of cull	Bag restriction
	Disturbance	Controlled access
	Track construction	
Caving	Damage to features	Controlled access
Rock climbing	Disturbance of nesting birds	Voluntary restrictions
Orienteering	Disturbance of nesting birds	Scheduling of events
Birdwatching/ photography	Disturbance of migratory, and nesting birds	Code of practice
All Activities	Moorland fires	Controlled access in high-risk periods

Source: Sidaway and Thompson, 1991

Ameliorating impacts

Concentration or dispersal?

If as the Yaldens' research illustrates, the potentially harmful effects of sport or recreational activity may not be as they first appeared, the objective of recreation management must be to identify harmful effects with some precision. If this is not done, then not only will management be ineffective but the wrong message may be given to the wrong people making future cooperation difficult to achieve. Site management needs to focus down from strategic to tactical decisions considering, in the first instance, whether there are greater benefits to be achieved by concentrating or dispersing recreational activities, according to the characteristic species of the ecosystem that are of concern. There is a natural tendency of recreational users to congregate at points of particular attraction. This leads to the familiar symptoms of over-use—localized damage to vegetation and surface erosion, especially when exacerbated by poor drainage conditions.

If use is to continue, the land manager is faced with certain options: either to accept a certain level of localized damage, or to provide a resilient load-bearing surface, or to develop a counter-attraction elsewhere. There has been a desire to retain the 'natural' character of the site, often coupled with a reluctance to change its appearance, by providing hard wearing surfaces to accommodate high levels of use. The reasons for resisting change are often concerns about aesthetics and appearance, when the effects on wildlife are usually localized and rarely threaten the long-term survival of species. Trying to disperse people more widely may do more harm than good; indeed it may increase disturbance.

The choices are often complex. For example, vegetation is more likely to be damaged on poorly drained soil or where surface water collects, while birds or animals may be affected by the positioning of a path if it affords them greater visibility of recreational users. Thus the siting of a ridge path could be attractive to recreational users; it may be relatively well drained and therefore do little damage to vegetation. However, its frequent use may lead to an increase in disturbance to fauna over a wider area than an alternative route sited through a poorly drained valley bottom, where the vegetation may be less resistant to wear and tear. Concentration may make economic sense. It is usually cheaper to repair one small intensively damaged area than a very wide area of lesser damage.

Zoning and seasonal restriction

Thus concentration of use, zoning to separate sports and keep them apart from wildlife, time sharing of seasonal restrictions, and self-regulation by users are the principal weapons in the recreation manager's armoury. Zoning enables recreational uses to be graded across the ideal site from noisy to quiet activities which least disturb other users and wildlife. But there are limits on what a small site can accommodate, and it may be more realistic to allocate water bodies to different uses than expect them to co-exist in a confined space which usually means that wildlife is seriously affected. Time-sharing arrangements have usually been applied to water bodies and depend on the observance of closed seasons or programming activities on a strict timetable. Management problems may arise from activities which are used to having exclusive use of an area but ought to be persuaded to restrict and share that use so that other areas can remain undisturbed.

Self-regulation

Ideally users manage themselves. Acceptance of responsibility for conserving wildlife in a sport or recreation participant is one of the most effective conservation measures, but it has to be used in conjunction with other devices. Self-regulation is most effective when there is a common interest in seeing wildlife protected between participants who want access, conservation organizations, and landowners. Usually this is more easily achieved when most participants belong to a club which can negotiate access with a landowner and can impose codes of conduct or rules on their members. The limitations of self-regulation are all too evident when it is the sole mechanism in operation, particularly if there are large numbers of casual participants in an activity who are not members of a club. Many generalized codes of practice issued by sports organizations or equipment manufacturers have little effect when they are the sole mechanism. In the best instances—climbers and cavers— the reasons for conservation are well understood; the messages are understandable and specific; and peer-group pressure within the sport is far more effective than 'interfering wardens'.

The role of governing bodies

In Britain, many governing bodies of sport have led the way in developing and implementing good conservation practice. Governing bodies are the national voluntary organizations, often initially federations of local clubs, which coordinate the sport and are recognized as its representatives by the Sports Council. In ideal circumstances the governing body allocates responsibility for conservation policy to a major committee with a nominated volunteer or professional conservation officer. A general code of practice is issued to participants in the sport and, as in the case of coarse angling, detailed codes apply to a range of practices. Voluntary restrictions may be negotiated at a national level relating to specific sites or close seasons, and clubs are encouraged to become involved in managing controlled access. Competitive events are planned well in advance and venues negotiated with landowners and conservation bodies. Disciplinary procedures against infringement of competition rules are enforced and the organization is well informed by monitoring or conducting its own research. Few governing bodies meet all of these conditions, but many more are being encouraged to develop on these lines by the Sports Councils and by countryside and conservation agencies.

The principles of good practice

The principles of good conservation practice have been set out in a publication jointly sponsored by these bodies (Sidaway, 1991) which advocates sensitive management.

Multiple use and creative conservation—Given the scarce resources of the countryside, there are few areas in Britain which can be devoted to an exclusive use. Wherever possible, recreation areas should be managed to increase their conservation value, while public access should be normally permitted to areas of nature conservation interest. In practice, this may mean that on sensitive habitats only certain recreational activities are permitted or possibly none at all, while parts of recreation areas or nature reserves remain undisturbed.

Clarity of purpose—Management should operate with clear objectives, stated in a published management plan, which takes both recreation and nature conservation considerations into account.

Participatory management—Such plans should be devised in consultation with all user and interest groups.

Impact assessment—Management should be based on a sound knowledge of the habitat, its characteristic species and their sensitivity or resilience to recreational use and economic considerations. The levels and patterns of recreational use need to be known. The impacts of new activities or facilities should be assessed prior to development to ensure that in the long term, they will not affect the conservation of the site. Where development is permitted, standards need to be set as a basis for maintaining quality, for both the visitor and wildlife, and for assessing change.

Monitoring and review—There is no finite threshold or plateau of excellence to be reached which enables managers to rest comfortably on their laurels. Good practice is a continuous process that has to be flexible and sensitive to developing events such as the colonization of new habitats or the development of new sports. There is a need for periodic adjustment and for phasing in activities and assessing their impact. Monitoring and the review of a management plan are the key methods to ensure that good practice is continuously developed and quality maintained.

The limits of acceptable change

The planning system which appears to incorporate all of these principles to best effect is managing to the *limits of acceptable change* (LAC). The approach was developed by the US Forest Service (Stankey *et al.*, 1985) and has the merit of not only assessing the likely impact on wildlife of a new recreational facility or new activity but also of agreeing in advance what environmental changes are to be tolerated and what action will be taken if these 'quality standards' are exceeded. The technique was developed as an alternative to assessing the carrying capacity of wilderness areas. Apart from its conceptual problems, there is no accepted method of assessing carrying capacity.

LAC assumes that there are limits to use which should not be exceeded, but instead of these being determined by scientific experts and imposed by managers on unsuspecting users, the decision is taken collectively by the managers and users, advised by the experts. The exercise has to go through all the classic stages of planning:

— setting the *objectives* of management;
— describing how different uses will affect both the biological and social characteristics of the area—the *likely impacts* on wildlife and the experience of the visitor;
— having identified the dimensions which may change, judgements have to be made about *which changes are acceptable*, whether these are crowding, noise, loss of vegetation or disturbance to breeding birds;
— setting *standards*—the limits to acceptable change, and these have to be quantified, so that it can be agreed in advance what *level of change* will trigger a specified response, the action to be taken by managers to remedy the situation;
— *monitoring* the situation. Regular measurements have to be taken so that the extent of any change is known;
— the whole *process is a continuing one* so that as new factors arise management can respond to them.

In Britain, the method has recently been applied by the Institute of Terrestrial Ecology (ITE) to the Aonach Mor ski development near Fort William and the Three Peaks footpaths in Yorkshire (Bayfield *et al.*, 1988). It is too early to assess its long-term effectiveness, but it is a promising collaborative approach.

It is the emphasis on collective decision-making by a working party or task force which is the most positive and encouraging aspect of LAC. It recognizes that users have a stake in the area and that they will act responsibly to conserve it, and that conservation is as much in their interests as it is in anyone else's.

References

Aitken, R., 1984, *Scottish Mountain Footpaths: a Reconnaissance Review of their Condition*, Perth, Countryside Commission for Scotland.
Bayfield, N.G., Watson, A. and Miller, G.R., 1988, 'Assessing and Managing the effects of recreational use on British hills' in M.B. Usher and D.B.A. Thompson (eds), *Ecological Change: the Uplands*, Oxford, Blackwell.
Dartington Amenity Research Trust, 1979, *Green Lanes: a Report to the Countryside Commission*, Dartington, DART.
Department of the Environment, 1991, 'Sir George Young announces additional safeguards for Sites of Special Scientific Interest', *Department of the Environment News Release*, 24 September 1991, London, DOE.
Mitchell, J.R., Moser, M.E. and Kirby, J.S., 1988, 'Declines in midwinter counts of waders roosting in the Dee estuary', *Bird Study*, **35**: 191–8.
Royal Society for Nature Conservation, 1987, *Damage to Wildlife Sites by Off-road Motor Vehicles*, London, RSNC.
Sidaway, R., 1988, *Sport, Recreation and Nature Conservation*, Research Study 32, London, Sports Council.
Sidaway, R., 1990, *Birds and Walkers: a Review of Existing Research on Access to the Countryside and Disturbance to Birds*, London, Ramblers' Association.
Sidaway, R., 1991, *Good Conservation Practice for Sport and Recreation*, London, Sports

Council, Countryside Commission, Nature Conservancy Council and World Wide Fund for Nature.

Sidaway, R. and Thompson, D., 1991, 'Upland recreation: the limits of acceptable change', *Ecos*, **12**: 31–9.

Speight, M.C.D., 1973, *Outdoor Recreation and its Ecological Effects: a Bibliography and Review*, Discussion Papers in Conservation, No. 4, London, University College.

Stankey, G.H., Cole, D.N., Lucas, R.C., Peterson, M.E. and Frissell, S.J., 1985, *The Limits of Acceptable Change (LAC) of Wilderness Planning*, Forest Service General Technical Report, Int–176, Ogden, Utah, USDA.

Thompson, D.B.A. and Horsfield, D.H., 1990, 'Towards an assessment of nature conservation criteria in the British uplands', in D.B.A. Thompson and K. J. Kirby (eds), *Grazing Research and Nature Conservation*, R & S Report, No. 31, Peterborough, NCC.

Tydeman, C.F., 1977, 'The importance of the close fishing season to breeding bird communities', *Journal of Environmental Management*, **5**: 289–96.

Van der Zande, A.N., 1984, *Outdoor Recreation and Birds: Conflict or Symbiosis*, Alblasserdam, Offsetdrukkerij Kanters.

Watson, A., Nethersole-Thompson, D., Duncan, K., Galbraith, H., Rae, S., Smith, R. and Thomas, C., 1988, 'Decline of shore waders at Loch Morlich', *Scottish Birds*, **15**: 91–2.

Yalden, D.W., 1992, 'The influence of recreational disturbance on common sandpipers, *Actitis hypoleucos*, breeding by an upland reservoir in England', *Biological Conservation*, **61**: 41–9.

Yalden, D.W., Yalden, P.E., 1989, *Golden Plovers and recreational disturbance*, NCC Contract Research Report, NCC, Edinburgh.

14

MANAGING THE COUNTRYSIDE— CONCEPT AND OPPORTUNITY IN A CHANGING ENVIRONMENT

SALLY BUCKNALL

As the twentieth century draws to a close and we are witnessing an unprecedented increase in environmental awareness, it is easy to assume that the manipulation of the planet by mankind is a relatively new concept. Certainly it has only been in this century that we have begun to recognize that our activities could be moving towards the domination and destruction of those resources that sustain not just our own species but also most other life forms. Yet the seeds of the process which have brought us to this situation were sown when humans first started to move towards domesticating and harvesting animals and plants, as long as 20,000 years ago.

The action of any living thing has an effect upon its surroundings. Man's technical abilities have enabled us not only to bring about significant and lasting effects on the resources of the planet but also to defend ourselves in ways that limit the number of organisms that can harm us, thus ensuring our breeding success and survival.

But a basic biological rule for survival is that a species must live in balance with the resources it needs for existence. In other words, there is little merit in using up the entire food source available and risking starvation unless the species concerned has the flexibility to adapt to another food source. A number of species including man have this flexibility enabling them to colonize new areas and spread. Thus we are not dependent on a small range of resources. Perhaps because of this we have been lulled into believing that there is always another source of food, energy or water around the corner, and we have become careless of these resources and thoughtless in relation to the way in which we manage and harvest them.

It is clear from archaeological and anthropological studies that for thousands of years our ancestors managed the land to provide food in ways that while technologically limited still altered the countryside significantly. Settled populations involved in early forms of farming in Europe cleared the vast forests which had grown luxuriantly on the rich alluvial soils left behind after the retreat of the last glaciers.

It is estimated that by 3,500 years ago the greater part of Europe had been deforested. Even in the uplands where the soils were poorer, tree cover had been removed and repeated ploughing had caused severe erosion and soil loss. It is hard for us to imagine how such feats as massive forest clearance were achieved with tools made without metal, and certainly the discovery of copper about 8,000 years ago and later iron must have accelerated the speed at which resources could be managed, exploited and damaged.

In the intervening centuries there are diverse theories as to why civilizations rose and fell. Many of them were dependent on the success or otherwise of their utilization of natural resources and their control over the environment. There are a number of factors which explain why, by the twentieth century, this swinging pendulum began to swing out of control. Perhaps the most significant are the development of energy which purely in economic terms is relatively cheap; the invention of methods of storage for the majority of our food crops and exponential population growth.

The most significant changes have been since the Second World War, although in the later part of the last century a sense of unease was developing in relation to the absence of protective mechanisms for the countryside. More especially, there was grave concern that because of the land ownership patterns which have developed in England and Wales there were few opportunities for access to the countryside for those people newly shackled to the cities and factories of the industrial revolution and thus deprived of the fresh air and open spaces enjoyed by their rural forebears. In the early campaigning days the driving force of the movement was to create and maintain access for such recreation. It naturally followed that it was important to preserve and enhance the natural beauty of these areas while at the same time safeguarding the needs of wild species.

The 1949 National Parks and Access to the Countryside Act was a manifestation of the activity of the first part of the twentieth century and would have been enacted much earlier but for the delays caused by the Second World War. Yet even then, the post-fifties' threats to the countryside were undreamed of. In those days the influence of agriculture on the landscape was one of protection and stewardship. The importance of much of Britain's basic food requirements at low prices and the resultant agricultural depression meant that there was no incentive for increased production and capitalization, and many areas of previously farmed land became abandoned or were farmed in traditional, low-input ways resulting in the maintenance of woodlands, wet areas and herb-rich meadows.

All this was to change as a result of the food shortages caused by the war blockade, and the Ministry of Agriculture, Fisheries and Food saw the need to re-vitalize farming in Britain. Part of this reform was encapsulated in the 1947 Agriculture Act which, among other things, introduced a system of price guarantees for many agricultural products and encouraged high standards of production by a scheme in which free professional advice was available to any farmer who wanted it.

This advice was backed up by attractive government grants to carry out programmes of 'improvement' work to bring more land into cultivation and raise its fertility and productivity. This posed a threat to many of the landscapes and habitats that gave depth and diversity to the rural heritage, and as a result and using tax-payers money, hedges were removed, woodlands felled, wet areas drained and uplands and other marginal areas ploughed. The horrific figures of losses during the sixties and seventies are etched on the minds of conservationists, and the frustration caused by the passage of three decades of imbalance when there were no mechanisms to counteract this loss is still strongly felt.

The increased zeal with which farmers applied themselves to the need for home-produced food was paralleled by a revolution in agricultural technology. In the first three decades of the twentieth century it was still common to see horses used to power agricultural machinery. After the war of 1939–45 thousands of them were slaughtered, displaced by powerful and time-saving tractors. Inevitably, larger machinery leads to larger fields and the loss of boundaries and field corners.

Over the seventies and eighties farming became big business, especially arable farming. Incentives for higher production levels led to increased capitalization and to fund this farmers were driven to borrow more and more money. This approach was fully supported by the government of the day, through advice and funds from the Ministry of Agriculture and the guidance given by White Papers like *Food from Our Own Resources* in 1975 and *Farming and the Nation in 1979.*

Developing in parallel with concern about the impact of intensive farming on wildlife habitats and landscape features were fears about the changes occurring in the more marginal farming areas of the uplands of the United Kingdom. The cause of these changes was basically economic. After generations of living in balance with the countryside, farmers in these areas, like the population as a whole, were seeking higher standards of living and better prospects for their children. The effects of rural depopulation were resulting in an insidious but noticeable decline in the way in which the countryside was managed.

The crucial factor here was the supply of labour. As young people left the land for better-paid jobs, farmers tried to manage with less; it became increasingly difficult for them to maintain in good repair the stone walls, gates, footpaths, hedges and copses that contribute so much to the sense of place and scene enjoyed by visitors. In many cases the skills which were needed for these tasks were being lost, and it became easier to fill in a wall with an old bedstead or a corrugated iron sheet than replace the stones in the traditional way.

If, as we thought, the problem was in essence economic, one solution would be to inject small sums of money to purchase, for the public, a product other than food and forestry, namely landscape beauty and access. This public acceptance of the fact that farmers were more than just producers of food marked a fundamental change in countryside management, one that was to lay the foundation for a range of new concepts.

The first experiments were set up in parts of Snowdonia and the Lake District as a result of a partnership between the Countryside Commission, the Ministry of Agriculture, Fisheries and Food, the National Farmers Union, the Country Landowners' Association and the Treasury. Two formal objectives were set:

—to test a method of reconciling the interests of farmers and visitors in the uplands by offering financial encouragement to farmers to carry out small schemes which improve the appearance of the landscape and enhance the recreational opportunities of the area;
—to assess what effect, if any, the methods will have on farmers' attitudes towards recreation.

The projects commenced in 1969 and ran initially for three years. They were the first to use the philosophy that today has become known formally as Countryside Management. The concept relies upon the employment of a project officer who is independent of the farming and landowning community, yet who has sufficient understanding of the needs and aspirations of both the farmer and the visitor to identify conflicts and problems and resolve them to everyone's satisfaction by a mixture of financial support, negotiation, local help in kind and good common sense.

After a few years it was clear that the first of the two objectives was being met with a great deal of success. The second may have been too ambitious given the scale of the projects, although it is hard to measure changes in attitude which may require many years to manifest themselves.

The philosophy established in these pilot projects has been developed subsequently by the Countryside Commission usually in partnership with Local Authorities. The methodology is applicable to a wide range of situations and to problems much more complex than found in the uplands, such as in the urban fringe areas of our towns and cities and our Heritage Coasts.

The approach has its critics, those who say that it is small scale and cosmetic, tackling the tip of an iceberg of problems that needs radical reform and a changed attitude to land management that has far deeper roots. New attitudes must be developed on a much less parochial basis, taking into account the views of a far wider constituency including not only those with a direct interest in the land but also those who make decisions about agricultural policy at national, European and international level and those whom these politicians represent.

Farming is not the only form of management which can lead to a reduction in the diversity of our rural landscapes. Much more insidious and permanently disfiguring is the steady spread of concrete and tarmac. During the last forty years we have seen an era of increased affluence, improved standards of living and population growth that has required a massive land-take to provide services to support a larger, wealthier, more demanding population. The urbanization of large areas of previously attractive countryside has, in many people's eyes, been far more damaging than anything that farmers and landowners have done.

Housing, industrial and commercial development, roads, motorways, shopping complexes, recreation sites and car parks have eaten up vast areas, most especially in the home counties, where much of the economic boom of the eighties was felt. Increased wealth and development puts greater pressure on the countryside for the generation of power, the storage and distribution of water and the winning of coal and hard rock. Advances in telecommunications and electronics have led to the need for more aerials and masts and plagues of satellite dishes springing out of the roofs and walls of buildings. In addition to this the demands of this expanding, more leisured society bring their own forms of damage; over-use and erosion of footpaths, traffic congestion on country roads, vandalism, disturbance to stock and the inevitable infra-structure of the tourist industry.

The resources of our countryside are threatened and shrinking; they are suffering from the conflicting interests of different and various demands put upon them. Unless we are able to use the skills and experience of a sophisticated, concerned society to bring about environmental sustainability, we will lose them.

From the historical background it is clear that our ability to influence our environment has accelerated this century, most significantly over the last two decades. Since the forties we have built up a formidable array of fundamentally passive mechanisms to protect our countryside. More than 10 per cent of the land surface of England and Wales is covered by some form of landscape designation—National Parks, Areas of Outstanding Natural Beauty and Heritage Coast forming the most important. Geologically and ecologically rich areas are protected by National Nature Reserves and Sites of Special Scientific Interest and a democratic planning system has, for almost fifty years, maintained some degree of control over the development of the built environment. However, the protective strength of these systems lies basically in negative control rather than positive management, and the philosophies which brought them into existence were developed in a very different political and environmental climate than that of present times.

During the years when countryside management policies were driven by the single goal of maximizing food production, environmental issues were very low down on the political agenda. Despite the dire warning of the prophets of the ecological revolution, there were few legislative steps taken to provide a strong framework for a more balanced and sustainable way to manage the resources of the countryside between 1949 and 1980. However in the last years of the seventies and in 1980 work was in hand to produce a piece of legislation which was to change the basis upon which the previous protective processes had been based and which would lay the foundation for much of what has followed.

This was the highly contentious Wildlife and Countryside Act of 1981. Its critics said that it was a jumble of ill-thought-out reactions to newly recognized problems laced together with bits of previously enacted legislation. Its supporters welcomed it with enthusiasm as at least the first step towards recognizing that positive action was needed to protect the rich diversity of the landscape and wildlife of Britain that is enjoyed and treasured by many people. Some important provisions did not get through the parliamentary procedure, but on balance, it represents a milestone in furthering the protection of wildlife habitats, individual rare and threatened species, cherished landscapes and the rights of the public to enjoy access to the countryside. It was a turning point in the nation's attitude to environmental care and management.

During the eighties there has been another kind of revolution, the reasons for which are complex. It was a revolution in the way in which ordinary people view their environment. Perhaps it has been partly a result of the improved communication systems that have enabled us to see how we are damaging the resources of the planet in many different places. Our televisions show us pictures which bring home to us a realization of our own dependence upon natural resources and our vulnerability to the effects of their abuse.

It is sufficient to say that the people of the United Kingdom, in common with many of the developed nations, have taken note of the seminal views of some outspoken and highly respected world authorities on environmental matters. This has led an unprecedented increase in public awareness of these issues which has been nurtured by the media and taken up by politicians who believe that there are serious problems to be solved and votes to be gained by the promotion of green policies.

Erstwhile purely scientific debate about the Greenhouse Effect, the real or perceived threat of Global Warming and desertification has entered the homes of the British people. As a result there are indications that the public, the government and those who use the resources of our countryside to produce the goods that support twentieth-century civilization, have come, finally, to the realization that many resources are not renewable in the short or medium term, and some are not renewable at all under the present global pressures. The message that we are all dependent on the health of the environment and that economic development can only flourish if practised in a sustainable way may be getting through.

Closer to home there is also public uneasiness in relation to the current problems inherent in the Common Agriculture Policy (CAP). Over the past thirty years the CAP has provided a stable basis for the development of farming and support for farm incomes. The result has been massive increases in food production at a price that is too high, both in terms of taxpayers' money, and, by default, in the damage that it has caused to our countryside. The public are confused and concerned that the EC CAP expenditure appears to be running out of control. They see large amounts of money being spent to produce food that the Community does not need, followed by more funds to store or dispose of the surplus. That this situation seems to be getting progressively worse, despite a diverse array of schemes designed to bring it back into balance, is also of grave concern to many people.

The problem of agricultural surpluses within the EC has exercised the minds of the Community governments since the early 1980s and continues to do so in the nineties through protracted and complex discussions about CAP reform and its relationship with international trade agreements. Various means of reducing the cost of subsidies have been tried. Some of the earliest involved the introduction of milk quotas and changes to the beef, oilseed and cereals regimes which limited access to intervention. In 1988 a substantial package of reforms was agreed. It included the opportunity for producers to put some of their arable land into set-aside; in other words they were paid to leave the land fallow for up to five years.

The concept of set-aside was heavily criticized by some conservationists as a missed opportunity for the positive management of land for an environmental premium. Apart from the financial gain, it was unpopular with many farmers who felt uncomfortable with a system in which they were paid not to produce.

One more positive step came in the guise of EEC Regulation 797/85 Article 19 which allowed and provided funds for the establishment of Environmentally Sensitive Areas or ESAs. This provision was brought into British law by means of the 1986 Agriculture Act, and by 1987 five ESAs were established. The scheme allows for owners and occupiers of land within ESAs to make voluntary agreements with the Ministry of Agriculture, Fisheries and Food (MAFF) whereby they undertake to follow prescribed farming practices to maintain traditional farming methods and discourage the draining and ploughing of land for arable cultivation.

The contribution that such a scheme can make to reducing production is limited, but it has considerable potential for increasing the wildlife diversity and the richness of our landscapes, while also supporting marginal farming and preserving old farming and countryside management skills. The original five schemes were carefully monitored by MAFF; as a result a programme of extensions and new ESAs was announced in 1992. Perhaps one of the greatest achievements of the ESA scheme is the philosophy that it has established in relation to the changed roles of farmers and the general acceptance that conservation is a bona fide agricultural product.

However MAFF and the ESA scheme cannot be given total credit for this progressive achievement. The Countryside Commission, the government's advisers on landscape matters, has also been developing ideas in the wake of its earlier countryside management policies. One of the Commission's concerns has been that while the EC has recognized the need to introduce mechanisms which both control production and take environmental and social issues into account, in practice this has resulted in a plethora of schemes which are both confusing to the farmer and complex and expensive to administer and monitor.

In 1989 the Commission produced *Incentives for a New Direction in Farming*, a report which suggested that farm support systems were in need of a thorough re-think with the aim of producing a simple scheme of incentives in which producers could select those which were most appropriate to their farming enterprise. It was suggested that this selection could be made from a comprehensive menu of annual and capital grants, covering everything from exclusively agricultural activities to payments for conservation or recreation projects. There would be a higher rate of grant for those who were willing to adopt pre-determined management prescriptions to conserve certain nationally important landscape types or who were willing to adopt an overall farm plan with strong conservation or recreation benefits.

This report stimulated a great deal of discussion, both within farming organizations and more significantly between MAFF and the Department of the Environment (DOE). Eventually it emerged in 1992 as a DOE initiative to be run by the Countryside Commission called Countryside Stewardship. It differs from the ESA scheme in a number of important ways. It is a pilot project, testing a method which could form a basis for the future management of farmed countryside. It is not dependent upon designated areas but instead targets specific landscape or habitat types such as chalk and limestone grassland and coastal farmland. Most significantly it aims to integrate ways of managing all the demands placed upon the countryside including the demand for access and informal recreation.

In 1992 and 1993 the number of targeted landscape types was expanded, and detailed monitoring is taking place to establish the credibility of the approach in terms of countryside management and to assess the extent to which it can open up opportunities for the public to enjoy both new experiences of the countryside and an improved understanding of the farming community. Countryside Stewardship does not meet all the objectives of *Incentives for a New Direction in Farming*. Because of its different parentage, it is not integrated into the farm support scheme. It is this division of effort that is now of great concern to countryside conservationists.

The government has set out a framework for the countryside policies of the nineties in its Environmental White Paper, *This Common Inheritance*. It recognizes that in the past the beauty of our countryside has developed as a by-product of economic, social and environmental processes. Now we find ourselves in a rapidly changing world and in situations which bring both fearsome prospects and the possibility of great opportunities if we can be far-sighted and are able to think strategically enough to develop them.

International trade agreeements and CAP reform will lead to considerable changes in our countryside. At present, estimates suggest that we need to reduce arable land in Britain by at least 15 per cent. This amount of land offers exciting opportunities for conservation and recreation; new multipurpose forests and extensive woodlands, wild areas where low-intensity grazing might be the only management carried out or even the withdrawal of all forms of countryside management in an attempt to reverse the impact of man's interference which might also mean restrictions on access. With care we may be able to exercise damage limitation and creative control over the countryside of the twenty-first century.

In the beginning of our history we may not have been much concerned with the consequences of our actions. Now we have learned many things about cause and effect and the cost of what we do. What we may not be able to learn is how to work in cooperation nationally and internationally in time to build mechanisms which will ensure the sustainability of the planet's natural resources and thus ourselves.

References

Agriculture Act 1986, Chapter 49, London, HMSO.

Andrews, M., 1991, *The Birth of Europe*, London, BCA.

Blunden, J. and Curry, N., (eds), 1985, *The Changing Countryside*, London, Croom Helm.

Countryside Commission, 1974, *Upland Management Experiment*, Cheltenham, The Commission.

Countryside Commission, 1976, *The Lake District Upland Management Experiment*, Cheltenham, The Commission.

Countryside Commission, 1981, *Countryside Management in the Urban Fringe*, Cheltenham, The Commission.

Countryside Commission, 1989, *Incentives for a New Direction for Farming*, Cheltenham, The Commission.

Countryside Commission, 1989, *Planning for a Greener Countryside*, Cheltenham, The Commission.

Countryside Commission, 1991, *Caring for the Countryside*, Cheltenham, The Commission.

Department of the Environment, 1990, *This Common Inheritance*, Cm 1200, London, HMSO.

Food from our own resources, 1975, Cmnd. 6020, HMSO, London.

Farming and the nation, 1979, Cmnd. 7458, HMSO, London.

Garner, J.F., and Jones, B.L., 1987, *Countryside Law*, London, Shaw and Sons Ltd.

Ministry of Agriculture, Fisheries and Food, 1991, *Our Farming Future*, London, MAFF Publications.

Wildlife and Countryside Act, 1981, Chapter 69, London, HMSO.

COMMUNITY INVOLVEMENT IN ENVIRONMENT AND RECREATION

JOHN GITTINS

Introduction

Allan Patmore's classic work, *Land and Leisure* (1970) influenced a generation of people studying and working in the fields of geography, planning, environmental studies, conservation, countryside management and formal and informal recreation. *Land and Leisure* links four key words: Land, Leisure, People and Place. Three further words also come to mind to express the complex interaction between the first four: Partnership, Participation and Community. Listed in Raphael and McLeish's (1981) *The List of Books—A Library of Over 3000 Books* as a key text, *Land and Leisure* has the hallmarks of relevance, readability and practicality. Interestingly, though, it contains no reference to practical work in the environmental conservation field undertaken by volunteers as a form of recreational activity. In this, it is not alone. The other influential text of the time, Michael Dower's *The Challenge of Leisure* (1965), makes no reference to this growing phenomenon either. Nor does the pioneering *Pilot National Recreation Survey* undertaken by the British Travel Association and the University of Keele (1967).

Such activity was readily identifiable. For example, the Conservation Corps, founded in 1959, was by the late sixties well established at both national and local levels. Recreational organizations, for example the Ramblers Association and conservation bodies such as the Society for the Promotion of Nature Reserves (now The Royal Society for Nature Conservation) and the Royal Society for the Protection of Birds were active in promoting the cause of access to the countryside and nature conservation through parliamentary lobbying and practical action on the ground.

People's concern increased during the 1980s. Eighty per cent of us now admit to worries about the environment. Millions of people spend time enjoying the countryside and its villages as visitors and residents. Yet, only a tiny minority—three per cent—have engaged in environmental action for the countryside (Countryside Commission, 1990).

By the early 1990s global environmental problems and the need for local action were both topical and enjoying political favour. H.M. Government, in *This Common Inheritance—Britain's Environmental Strategy* (1990), expressed the position clearly *vis-à-vis* practical environmental work, stating (p. 17) that 'voluntary action plays a vital part in maintaining and improving the countryside'. It recognized also that this applies equally in the urban context, referring to Groundwork Trusts which, since the establishment of the first in 1981 'have shown that they can mobilize effort and funds and deliver significant environmental benefits at the local level for relatively small public cost' (p. 123). Community participation in practical conservation action and lobbying is thus highly valued both as a 'means' of recreation, and for its 'end', in the form of environmental improvements.

Setting the scene

Nineteen fifty-nine is a significant date in the history of voluntary practical conservation action. It is the year in which the Council for Nature appointed Brigadier Armstrong to form the Conservation Corps (precursor to the British Trust for Conservation Volunteers—BTCV) to involve volunteers in practical conservation work. The first project was held in February 1959 at Box Hill in Surrey; forty-two volunteers took part, including 'Conservation Action Man' David Bellamy. Working at weekends and in vacation time, on National Nature Reserves and Sites of Special Scientific Interest, these groups consisting mainly of young, articulate students started a movement which swiftly gathered pace. In 1964 the Conservation Corps extended its work to include education and practical tasks in the wider countryside. One of the by-products of the residential Conservation Corps activities was that volunteers were drawn from all over the country and many returned home fired with the enthusiasm to continue the work in their local home areas.

By 1963 the Council for Nature, together with partner organizations, had established National Nature Week, and with the Duke of Edinburgh's enthusiastic backing, set up a series of conferences on the theme 'The Countryside in 1970'. This initiative culminated in the Council of Europe designating 1970 as European Conservation Year, in many ways a watershed. The year was marked across Britain by an upsurge in community-based conservation projects. In Wales alone, there were over 500 different initiatives (Countryside in 1970 Committee for Wales, 1970). Throughout England and Wales, the Women's Institute movement provided a lead through grass-roots action. Schools played a key role, with Shell UK Ltd. funding a scheme to encourage school children to participate in the improvement of their natural environment. In the same year the Conservation Corps, operating under its new name, The British Trust for Conservation Volunteers (BTCV), became an independent organization.

Among the other early players in the environmental action game were County Wildlife Trusts, the Inland Waterways Recovery Group (canals), the Ramblers Association, the Association of Voluntary National Parks and Countryside Wardens, the National Trust, local authorities, and county-based

Rural Community Councils who provided a lead in parish-based initiatives through their annual 'Best Kept Village' competitions.

The movement grew by building on a very British idea, that of 'getting involved', a deeply held commitment to voluntary work, incorporating the desire to serve one's community. This is often about meeting a need, having fun, gaining knowledge of skills, with the additional satisfactions of doing a job well and achieving a sense of 'ownership' of one's environment.

By the start of the eighties, community involvement in environmental conservation and recreation had taken off. Global environmental problems had begun to capture media attention. Television producers were making environmental programmes which attracted large audiences. Bookshops, particularly the large national chains, were giving increasing shelf space to works on natural history and environmental topics. Magazines on environmental topics proliferated. As more and more people were getting out into the countryside, or wished to know more about their local area, sales of Ordnance Survey maps increased: data from Ordnance Survey show sales of 2.1 million copies of the 1:50000 maps in 1990 compared with 480,000 copies of the equivalent maps (1:63360) in 1970; corresponding figures for the 1:25000 series were 1.12 million copies in 1990 compared with 381,000 in 1970. Indeed publishers David and Charles achieved commercial success with their reproductions of early editions of Ordnance Survey maps.

As the profile of environmental action increased, so too did the need for funding, in which Shell UK again played a leading role. At the start of the eighties Shell, together with the Nature Conservancy Council (now English Nature) and the Civic Trust, redefined the 'Shell Better Britain Competition' into one which sought to encourage and support local action by any group of volunteers involved in practical schemes to improve the environment. Renamed the 'Shell Better Britain Campaign', the partnership was enlarged to include the BTCV, who contributed their considerable knowledge and skills in practical conservation work. Since 1970 the Shell initiative has issued over 100,000 information packs to local groups, with an estimated 1,250,000 people benefiting directly or indirectly from the ideas and support available. In addition, over 6,000 projects have received grants. The campaign also received additional funding through the Countryside Commission's 'Community Action Programme' described below. Today, many other private-sector companies actively support community-based environmental action through national initiatives including British Gas, Sainsburys, ICI and Marks and Spencer. The scale of company support for environmental initiatives at local level is substantial but impossible to quantify.

Community-based environmental action projects attract people of all ages, backgrounds and abilities. The particular contribution of unemployed people merits special mention. Workplaces range from the inner city, through the urban fringe, across farmland to the wildscapes of our National Parks. Volunteers can be seen in action every day of the week throughout the year, working both in their home areas and through, for example, the BTCV 'Natural Break' programme of working holidays, throughout Britain and Europe. Work includes tree planting and after-care; habitat creation, protection and management; restoring derelict land; creating wildflower meadows; enhancing ponds and other wetland features; woodland and hedgerow management; and improving access to the countryside through the footpath and bridleways network.

The move away from a top-down to a bottom-up approach involving partnerships, networks and cooperation has been a key feature of recent years. In this the Countryside Commission, through its seventeen Community Action Demonstration Projects (BDOR, 1992) from 1985 to 1992 has given the lead. Initiatives funded include Common Ground's 'Parish Map/Village Appraisal Project'. Common Ground is a small charitable organization which encourages people to value and enjoy their own familiar surroundings regardless of whether they are rare or unusual. They believe that conservation should begin with the commonplace things surrounding our daily lives. One of their strategies for change is to forge links between practice and enjoyment of the arts and conservation of landscapes and nature. Through publications and projects involving the arts, they hope to inspire people and strengthen the resolve of those willing to speak out about the value of the world about them.

Other projects funded include the Taf and Cleddau Rural Initiative in south west Wales, aimed at promoting social and economic development especially through tourism; the Cheshire Landscape Trust's Parish Landscape Strategy and Action Plan Project and Northamptonshire County Council's Pocket Parks scheme. The concept of pocket parks goes back to 1920s' New York when the term 'vest pocket parks' was coined to describe community areas. A pocket park is an area of land of any size, serving any purpose, having any content—in fact, whatever the community determines. They can be in urban, urban fringe and rural areas. A pocket park can be on land owned or leased by a community group, or simply managed on behalf of another owner. Fundamentally, the local community runs a pocket park, but it can enlist other resources, for example, successful groups negotiate partnerships such as persuading a developer to provide financial support for running a community event or giving money to a local community group to develop a park.

Pocket parks were first developed in England in Northamptonshire where, despite good intentions and the planning process, open spaces and access to the wider countryside were declining. Local people took up the cudgels and, with small amounts of grant aid through parish councils and other groups, acquired small pieces of land. This process grew into the Pocket Park Project which developed the process, running from 1987 to 1989, jointly funded by the Countryside Commission and Northamptonshire County Council. As with other community environmental action initiatives it linked both product (tangibles) and process (intangibles) elements.

The initiative demonstrated that if people care about an area, vandalism drops dramatically. Recreational, educational and wildlife habitat benefits accrue with local people gaining the feeling of empowerment and ownership. A major strength of the Countryside Commission's initiative has been the monitoring and evaluation of projects by independent consultants. The wisdom of this approach has set new standards for planning and implementing such environmental projects and has forged long-lasting partnerships between the organizations involved.

Table 15.1 Achievements

Products (tangibles)
12,500 trees and shrubs have been planted (75 per cent by local people)
£8,500 raised in grant-aid
500 miles of hedgerow replanted
3 parish and 6 junior tree wardens enrolled
2 school-based parish tree nurseries established
3 children's activity days organized
Regular press coverage, including radio and television interviews
Public exhibitions, talks and guided walks organized
New landscape project begun

Processes (intangibles)
Greater cooperation between individuals and groups
Sense of achievement, and growing confidence
New skills acquired, for example, fund raising, tree planting, landscape design,
    lobbying, negotiating, staging exhibitions, working with the media
Previously unused resources tapped
Greater awareness and understanding of local and global issues

---

Selected case studies

(i)   The Burtonwood Community Action Project
      Burtonwood is a former coal mining village of 10,000 inhabitants in
      north west Cheshire. In 1850 there were 250 miles of hedgerows; in 1980
      there were twelve miles. Situated within the boundary of Warrington
      New Town, much of the land is of high quality and is given over to
      intensive arable production.
          Until October 1990, none of the residents had been involved in any
      form of community-based environmental action. Since that time, they
      have invested some 2,000 volunteer days in such activity. Under the
      banner of the Cheshire Landscape Trust's Community Landscape Pro-
      ject (jointly funded by the Countryside Commission and Cheshire
      County Council) a Parish Landscape Strategy and Action Plan has
      been produced and implemented. A Community Woodland and
      Nature Park has been established and is managed by a community-led
      Advisory Group. Local farmers have become supportive. The Project
      has involved parish, borough and local councils, schools, voluntary
      groups and the University of Manchester's School of Landscape.
          Notable achievements have been made (see Table 15.1), and there are
      ambitious plans for the future. The tree wardens are a key in promoting
      regular environmental action projects. In Burtonwood, the parish
      council, the parish tree wardens, the two primary schools, the
      Burtonwood Environmental Action Group and the Cheshire Landscape
      Trust are the key to promoting and sustaining environmental action
      projects. The initial phase has been achieved in little more than a year.

Burtonwood people are also helping others both within the county and beyond to set up their own community environmental projects. Their efforts were recognized in April 1992 when they won the Cheshire County Council's Environment Year Community Action Award.

(ii) Another excellent example of partnership and networking is the nationwide Parish Tree Warden Scheme. This movement started twenty-one years ago in Leicestershire, led by the county branch of the Council for the Protection of Rural England and strongly backed up by the County Council. Since 1989 the Tree Council, founded in 1974 with the aim of promoting the improvement of the environment by planting and conserving trees and woods in town and country throughout the United Kingdom, has been the national coordinator of the Scheme, with sponsorship from British Gas. Tree Wardens are appointed by Parish Councils (Community Councils in Wales) or local community groups to gather information, give advice and encourage practical projects relating to trees in the community. They are not expected to be experts. What is important is that they should genuinely care for trees and for the environment.

(iii) Another example is the approach which Common Ground has taken to community-based environmental action. They have been particularly innovative in engaging people at grass-roots level and in linking the arts and artists to sustainable environmental action through projects such as their Local Distinctiveness Programme, Tree Dressing Initiative and Orchards Scheme.

Encouraging and supporting volunteers

Training is vital to help volunteers make the best of their time and experience. Since 1968 BTCV has played a leading role in this respect through training courses and their outstanding series of practical handbooks. Others have followed and developed new directions. For example, the Mersey Basin Trust, with help from IBM Ltd., have organized workshops for voluntary environmental groups in north west England, on topics such as marketing, personal skills and project management.

Over the years competitions and award schemes have been seen as a way of stimulating voluntary environmental action. While some might question their value, particularly in terms of project sustainability, they have helped to engender awareness, understanding and, above all, action. They include the county-based Rural Community Councils' Best Kept Village Competition which covers most counties in England and Wales, the Prince of Wales Awards (in Wales only) and, more recently, the Esso Footpath Awards.

For a growing number of people, taking part in community-based environmental action has led them into first or second careers in country-side and environmental management. There is now a substantial body of evidence to show that the experience and training which volunteers gain stands them in good stead for future careers in the environmental field. For example, many countryside rangers have come into full-time employment having first worked in a voluntary capacity with Countryside Management Services, the Groundwork Trust, the British Trust for Conservation Volunteers or County Wildlife Trusts. Twenty of Cheshire County Council Countryside Management Services' thirty-four full-time rangers started in this way. In a similar vein, six of the current staff of the Bollin Valley Countryside Management Project's total staff of eight came via having worked in a voluntary capacity for the Project.

In another direction, the growth of Green or Eco Tourism has seen community groups playing leading roles in developing, promoting and supporting environmentally friendly projects. Indeed, community involvement is the hallmark of sustainable tourism. Examples include the 'Mid Wales Festival of the Countryside' and the Herefordshire 'Big Apple Festival'.

At UK level, two national campaigns run on an annual basis have acted as valuable catalysts for increasing public awareness. Each May, the Civic Trust, with sponsorship from British Telecom, organizes National Environment Week, and in late November/early December, the Tree Council promotes National Tree Week.

Currently one of the most exciting initiatives is the national programme to create community forests on the outskirts of major towns and cities in England and Wales. A joint initiative of the Countryside Commission and Forestry Commission, this bold and imaginative move will help to transform derelict and unkept parts of the urban fringe into places that people will want to cherish, visit and enjoy. Community forests will provide opportunities for recreation, wildlife habitats, landscape enhancement, timber, jobs, space for arts events including sculpture parks and concerts and outdoor classrooms for school children and other groups. The real challenge facing the lead agencies is how to involve people in the planning and management of these areas, thereby avoiding being accused of mere tokenism.

Conclusion

In the review of their first thirty years, the BTCV in stressing the importance of local action stated that 'you don't have to go to the Amazon to help the environment' (Boyle, 1989), an expression of which is the fact that by late 1991 the BTCV campaign to plant a million trees had achieved its target and was going on to the next million. In the spring 1991 issue of their *Local Groups Newsletter*, the BTCV quote HRH the Prince of Wales: 'It is, in my experience, at the community level that most is being done to protect the environment. We can all too easily get caught up in global negotiations, whilst forgetting that people need to be free to pursue sustainable development for themselves'.

The signposts of such action are many and various. The number of volunteer days spent in community environmental action is increasing annually as is the number of groups operating throughout Britain. People are at the heart of community-based environmental and recreation action. While they may bring skills, knowledge and experience, they often, initially at least, lack confidence, know-how and the contacts to get things going.

Community involvement concerns people where they live and work. Priorities arise from their everyday experiences but can also be extended to areas further afield. The way in which a project is carried out and the quality of people's experience in doing it (the process) are as important as the quantity of what is achieved (the product)—indeed, some would argue, more so. The challenge is to achieve a sustainable balance between the intangible process and the tangible product. A product-orientated approach alone is likely to yield less sustainable community involvement in the long term.

Community-based environmental action is concerned with change. It often results in changed attitudes, physical environments, uses of the environment, personal and organizational relationships and much more. It involves shifts in control and power. Indeed, one of the objectives of such action is to empower people who previously may have felt powerless. Professionals and their organizations which get involved in this work need to take risks and provide resources in ways which recognize the importance of process as well as product. Community-action enablers do not need to be environmental experts, but they do, however, need human resource management skills, particularly in networking, motivating and facilitating. They should know where to get advice, help and funding and feel that they have achieved success when they are no longer required.

Community involvement in the environment and recreation has the advantage of being: (a) appropriate—local people bring their knowledge to bear on their problems; (b) good value—labour, skills and materials are given free or at reduced rates; (c) sustainable—when people have been involved in planning, creating or improving something, they have a vested interest in ensuring that it is protected and properly maintained (such facilities may be less likely to be vandalized); (d) effective—practical involvement in real enterprises creates an awareness and understanding of the environment; for example clearing a stream or pond can lead to an appreciation of the broader issues of waste and pollution (Shell Better Britain Campaign, 1988).

Community involvement is an approach based on certain beliefs and values. For instance, our rich and diverse countryside and urban areas in England and Wales have been fashioned by people who saw that a continuing positive interaction with the environment needs to be fostered and developed. A sustainable and environmentally sound future will only be achieved if individuals change their behaviour and work together to create their own improvements and then persuade others to emulate them. So long as environmental issues remain the sole preserve of the professional there will be no incentive for people in general to become involved in their own back yard, and they will remain sceptical about the chances of improving the quality of their lives and cynical about the contribution they can make to larger environmental problems. The benefits of community involvement come from *how* something is achieved as well as *what* is achieved. Community action is concerned with belonging, that is the nature of human relationships with place, the sense of place. Environment and recreation are, however, only two elements in the whole spectrum of socio-economic activity which constitutes community action.

It is important to appreciate the limits of the community as well as its strengths. For example, a sense of scale is important. Community action is not going to solve all local environmental problems. For some major schemes large-scale public investment and special teams are needed. Equally, it will not solve problems everywhere; some communities are more ready to respond to the challenge of action than others. The need is for public agencies and specialists to offer the community real opportunities to participate in decision-making in their area, thus sowing the seeds for possible future action.

Having considered some of the signposts for the way ahead, what about resourcing? People are keen to get involved. Volunteering is not just a British phenomenon; across Europe, Africa, India, Japan, Australia and America imaginative schemes are under way. In Britain projects are attracting support from central and local government, the private sector and charitable trusts. Indeed, the imaginative ways in which individual projects go about securing funding is a constant source of amazement.

In isolation, community action is less effective; its wheels need to be oiled occasionally by other organizations (public, private and voluntary). The need to work in partnership is vital. Certainly the experience of the Mersey Basin Campaign Voluntary Sector Network (now the Mersey Basin Trust) has demonstrated in north west England over the past six years the value of this approach. In similar vein, the County Networks, currently being established under the government-funded Rural Action for the Environment programme, aim to help people make their own decisions about the countryside—both remote countryside and that close to towns—by encouraging and supporting direct action by people to create a sustainable environment in the places where they live and work.

While community action is not the miracle cure for all ills, it is a valuable part of a complex jigsaw, which when pieced together can make a positive impression on the local environment. Neither is it a cheap option. It requires organizational commitment, skilled motivators working on the ground, and money to pump-prime projects.

Community involvement in the environment as a recreational activity is about awareness, knowledge, understanding, enabling, empowerment, partnership, cooperation, networking and sustainable action. It is also about enjoyment and satisfaction. It is indeed 're-creation' for individuals, communities and the environment, brought about by acting locally and thinking globally.

As we move into the twenty-first century, Michael Dower's *The Challenge of Leisure* will surely include community involvement in environment and recreation as a significant leisure-time activity. It is in fact an additional dimension to the 'people' and 'places' base of Allan Patmore's classic work, *Land and Leisure*.

References

Boyle, A. (ed.), 1989, *BTCV Protecting the Environment—1959–1989*, Wallingford, British Trust for Conservation Volunteers.

BDOR Bristol, 1992, *Countryside Community Action—an Appraisal*, Cheltenham, Countryside Commission.

British Travel Association/University of Keele, 1967, *Pilot National Recreation Survey*, report number 1, British Travel Association/University of Keele.

British Trust for Conservation Volunteers, 1991, *Local action*, Wallingford Local Groups Unit of the British Trust for Conservation Volunteers.

Countryside Commission, 1990, *Annual Survey of People's Countryside Behaviour*, Cheltenham, Countryside Commission.

Countryside in 1970 Committee for Wales, 1970, *European Conservation Year 1970, The Welsh Contribution*, Bangor, Gwynedd.

Dower, M. 1965, *The Challenge of Leisure*, London, Civic Trust.

H.M. Government, 1990, *This Common Inheritance—Britain's Environmental Strategy*, Cm. 1200, London, HMSO.

Patmore, J.A., 1970, *Land and Leisure*, Newton Abbot, David and Charles.

Raphael, F. and McLeish, K., 1981, *The list of Books—a Library of over 3000 Books*, New York, Harmony Books.

Shell Better Britain Campaign, 1988, *Making Community Action Work in the Environment*, Birmingham, Shell.

PART V
LEISURE AND ECONOMIC CHANGE

SPORT IN EUROPE AND THE SINGLE EUROPEAN MARKET

MICHAEL F. COLLINS

Introduction

Sport is a major interest in modern society with more people taking part than ever before, most purely for enjoyment, some for fitness, and a few to attain international excellence or to earn a living as professionals. Sport is not only a major social movement organized by volunteers for mutual production and consumption, or part of communal welfare provided by public service, but also a major service industry with commercial trading and associated functions like sponsorship.

Participation structures and the economic importance of sport in Europe

Rodgers (1977) attempted to make comparisons between different countries for the Council of Europe in 1977, using indices of *penetration* (the proportion of the population who have ever participated), *fidelity* (the ratio of those who still participate occasionally or regularly to those who have ever done so) and *intensity* (the ratio of those who participate regularly to those who participate at all).

The problems of comparability were that different countries counted different activities as sport and used different measures of 'ever' or 'regularly' participating. Thus, because of these data problems, detailed comparisons could only be made for Flanders, France and Britain. Even today, with more surveys carried out periodically in more states, comparisons are no easier because each country and survey client continues to use its own measures. To unravel these differences and conduct contemporary versions of the Rodgers analysis would be worthwhile and informative. Meantime, only broad generalizations and individual examples can be cited.

Overall, the developed long-standing sports systems in northern and western Europe support participation rates of 50–70 per cent, and any rates of increase on such a large base are slow. There is an upper limit formed partly physiologically (a minority of people are too old, too disabled or too sick to participate) and partly psychologically: a sizeable proportion of the population do not see themselves as 'sporty'. In England in 1991 this was 24 per cent of men and 38 per cent of women, with respectively 34 per cent and 46 per cent among people over fifty-five (Sports Council/Health Education Authority, 1992). Some people in this 'non-sporty' group are susceptible to involvement by marketing campaigns, increasingly linked to health, and to feeling and looking better, but some are not. Participation rates in southern and eastern Europe, with lower per capita incomes and less-developed provision systems tend to be 20–40 per cent and continue to show more rapid growth.

'Frequent and regular participation' attracts a subset of this population: in Britain 45 per cent take part once a month or more often; in Sweden 44 per cent; in Switzerland it is claimed that 50 per cent play once a week. Many of the frequent participants take part through clubs, especially in countries where a strong club sector has developed through workers' movements (Germany, Denmark, Finland and the former 'Eastern Bloc') or where clubs have been seen as a major agent for managing public sports facilities (Germany, The Netherlands and Sweden). Interestingly, participation is spread over a varying range of sports; in the United Kingdom and in Germany it is over 100 different activities; in Scandinavia, for climatic and historic reasons, less than half that number is available widely.

The growth of interest in sport for competition, and sport as a means of fitness, demands regular participation: it is also in the interests of clubs and suppliers of equipment to foster this group, the former as a source of membership income and a pool for recruiting competitors, the latter as a market for repeat sales. In addition, sports federations have become better organized and for competitive sport, especially in countries where licences are needed to play (for example France), recruitment has become more efficient. Club membership varies greatly throughout Europe from as much as 43 per cent of the population in Finland and West Germany to 13 per cent in the United Kingdom (see Table 16.1). In the West, only in Finland is it stable, but membership of the club system that was state supported is falling in Poland, Hungary, Bulgaria and other former 'Eastern Bloc' countries as they seek to reorganize their finances on a market basis.

At the top of the sporting pyramid are the elite squads and teams of performers in national and international competition. Numbers never exceed a few thousand, but the unit cost of support and success is high. Growth here tends to be in the range of sports in which a country is represented, and in the number of events in the calendar, together with their associated opportunities for sponsorship.

This massive sporting interest is very differently organized throughout Europe. In the West a group of countries have always seen sport as an activity that should be led by the voluntary sector, which then acts as a channel for government grant aid: here are found three of the Scandinavian countries and Italy, where sport is organized through the Olympic Committee (see

Table 16.1 Sports sectors and expenditure in selected European countries

	(A) Expenditures per head $US equivalent 1985				*(B) Club Sport*		
	consumers	state	gambling	sponsors	no. of clubs ('000s)	av. no. of members per club	% popu- lation in clubs
BELGIUM	106	37	1	2	25	81	26
DENMARK	85*	35	n.a.	2	13	166	43
FINLAND	106	36	n.a.	7	7	382	43
HOLLAND	151	38	1	8	34	115	25
UK	100	25	36	5	150	43	12
WEST GERMANY (pre- unification)	125*	n.a.	n.a.	3	65	32	34
PORTUGAL	31*	2	n.a.	n.a.	5		
ITALY					62	72	8
FRANCE	125	n.a.	n.a.	4	156	71	22
ICELAND	121	n.a.	56	10	313	276	41

* including gambling

Sources: Jones 1989; Collins, 1990

Table 16.2 Sports leadership structures (EC members in capitals)

Government Ministries	— Education (Austria, BELGIUM, IRELAND, Iceland, PORTUGAL) — Youth and Sport (FRANCE, Turkey, Finland) — Arts/Sport/Culture (Flemish BELGIUM, GREECE) — Physical Education and Sport (LUXEMBOURG) — Sport (Malta) — Sport and Tourism (French BELGIUM) — Interior (Switzerland)
Government Agencies	— Sports Councils (UK, Scotland, Wales, Northern Ireland) — Sports Commissions (New Zealand, Australia, Hong Kong) — Sports Board (Cyprus)
National Olympic Committee	— ITALY, United States
Sports Federations/Councils	— DENMARK, Norway, Switzerland, Sweden, SPAIN
Hybrid government/ non-governmental organization	— NETHERLANDS (Health and Culture—Sports Federation) — GERMANY (Interior—Sports Federation) — Finland (Sport and Youth—Sports Council)

Table 16.2). In other countries the state takes a lead, most often through a ministry concerned with education, sometimes culture, home affairs, tourism or health. Such links aid particular types of programmes to do with young people, preventative health, or environment and planning. In other states, government adopts an arm's-length approach by creating an agency or bureau, as in the United Kingdom.

The independence of agencies is often constrained by government influence, or by the approval of appointees to the body and substantial dependence on government grant, as in the United Kingdom. The hybrid arrangement or partnership exists where there is strong support for sport from both government and the organized volunteers, typified by Germany, the Netherlands and Finland.

This varied sporting structure is reflected in the differing contributions of the state (notably least in the United Kingdom), the consumer (including club members), the gambler, and the sponsor in supporting the large economic nexus which is sport (see Table 16.1). Many European governments, while maintaining a rhetoric of goodwill for sport, have been trying to ring-fence and hold down public subsidies for capital and revenue which have grown to a stage where voluntary bodies can be grant-dependent upon central or local government, or sponsors (Riskjaer, 1990). The state provides some two-fifths of expenditure in several advanced economies (notably less in the United Kingdom) while gambling contributes more than the much publicized role of sponsorship.

Some see that there might be a transfer of activity back to the voluntary sector, but whether it could support the scale of activity that has developed, especially of infrastructure or its management, must be doubted; certainly if state support is limited it is difficult to see access for the underprivileged being maintained (Wicklin, 1992). Yet the health and vitality of the voluntary self-help sector in sport is crucial to the organizing and regulation of competition and is often seen as an index of healthy citizenship.

What do the two main institutions for the Council of Europe do in support? The Council of Europe is a cultural rather than an economic organization and influences sport through two of its organs. The Standing Conference of Regional and Local Authorities in Europe (CRLAE) is concerned with all local government issues; it has recently recognized the importance of sport and leisure to the quality of life in towns through the European Urban Charter. A more specialized body has been the Committee for the Development of Sport which is also looking to revise the Sport for All Charter drawn up in 1966 in the light of the dramatic changes in Europe. It has listed its current initiatives as (Davies, 1991):

Ethical values   — promoting fair play
                        — encouraging positive attitudes between sport and by the media
                        — encouraging positive attitudes between sport and commercial interests
                        — against doping in sport (run by a group monitoring a convention)

Sport for All   — testing physical fitness (in adults, following an
                         earlier programme for children)
                       — sport and young people (previous programmes con-
                         cerned older people, women, school leavers)
                       — traditional games
Safety   — promoting safe play (avoiding injuries)
                       — promoting safe facilities (notably monitoring a con-
                         vention on spectator violence, focused upon
                         Sport for All)
Long-term planning   — planning future sports policies
                       — sports management training
                       — the Urban Charter

Eight members are associated with the Committee and more of the Baltic and Eastern European states are seeking to be so; this can be seen as a way of getting into a European network prior to considering membership of the EC.

The Commission is concerned with implementing the 'Single European Act' 1986; much of its concern will be expressed through ensuring freedom of goods and services and its concomitant emphasis on safety, standards and public purchasing, freedom of movement and associated issues of equivalence of qualifications and training. These are dealt with below. It has also been concerned to communicate and promote the concept of the community as a coherent unit which it has done by sponsoring events, often specially created, for example, the Round Europe Yacht Race from Hamburg to Toulon in 1989. It proposes to continue this policy, to set up a new consultative body involving not only the Council of Europe but also National Olympic Committees and non-governmental organizations and to pursue specific programmes like events for disabled people and exchanges of people involved in sport (CEC, 1991). It has recently commissioned a major study of the impact of EC legislation on sport in eleven different areas of action.

What of trends in sports participation in Europe? Roberts and Kamphorst (1989) suggested that participation was static to declining. Such data as their European contributors provide, and that available through the Council of Europe, suggest that this is an exaggeration (see Table 16.3). Most countries show continued if reduced growth in overall participation in the 1980s: for example, people in Flanders taking part once a year grew from 53 per cent to 69 per cent to 72 per cent between 1969, 1979 and 1989. The growth of the membership core and its volume of frequent participation and consumption was even more marked.

Sport and the single market

The primary purpose of the Single European Act was to create a single market of 320 million people in which capital, goods, services, and people can freely move: the Single Market therefore will have impacts on sport but often indirectly. These are reviewed briefly.

Table 16.3 Sports participation

	Increasing		% Change Per Annum Stable		Decreasing	
Overall participation (once a year or more often)	Belg(Fl.) Bulgaria Czech. France Italy Holland	79–89+ 0.3 76–85+21.4 75–85+11.4 73–81+14.9 82–85+11.4 79–87+0.75				
Regular participation (once a month or more often)	France Italy UK	73–81+16.4 85–88+ 0.3 77–86+ 0.5				
Frequency	UK	77–86+ 3.4				
Club membership	Czech. Denmark Germany Italy Holland Portugal	73–85+12.0 75–84+ 2.0 77–87+ 3.6 74–81+21.2 84–86+ 0.6 74–84+ 9.3	Finland 	72–85+0 	Poland Hungary	82–85−0.2 87–89−9.6
Licensed competitors	France Luxem.	75–85+ 6.3 75–86+ 4.8	Finland	72–85+0		

Sources: Roberts & Kamphorst. 1989; Remans and Delforge. 1987 Council of Europe Clearing
House Bulletins. various dates; General Household Surveys. 1977. 80. 83. 86.

Free movement of finance

Individual sports investments are mainly modest but can reach billions of
dollars for world championships and the Olympic Games; in the EC these
may increasingly be funded from overseas rather than domestic banks. The
sports facilities are often seen as short-term 'loss-leaders' in return for the
visibility given to a state or city by the event as a place to invest in or trade
with: for example the football World Cup in Argentina in 1978 and the
Olympics in Barcelona in 1992 (Collins, 1991b). It can be used to accelerate
infrastructure in roads and transport, hotels, stadiums and telecommunications, as in Albertville for the 1992 Winter Olympics, or to give impetus to
urban and economic regeneration as at the Sheffield World Student Games
1991 (Wilkinson, 1990) and in Barcelona.

Europe's states and cities still host a high proportion of the world's sports
events every year, and its legacies of domestic venues and organizations are
often used as fall-back locations if Second or Third World states cannot

organize events. Competition for such events throughout the world grows as the number of places with high-quality modern venues increases, and skilled marketing teams hunt for events to fill their large facilities up to a decade in advance. The lessons seem to be to cement a close and committed partnership between government, municipalities, voluntary sports bodies, sponsors, television and commerce to ensure that the sports facilities can be economically used for domestic programmes or international events and that accommodation and organization venues can be re-used commercially (Collins, 1991a).

Harmonization of the varying value-added and excise tax rates will also affect sports people as performers, spectators or holidaymakers (for example for skiing, fishing, golf, sailing). It could affect the prices of:

Travel: making petrol dearer in Germany and the United Kingdom and raising the general costs of air fares (which may be offset if the move to more competition reduces intra-European fares);

Accommodation: making France cheaper and Spain and Greece more expensive;

Alcohol: an accompaniment to much sport, making it cheaper in the United Kingdom but more expensive in France and Germany.

Free movement of goods and services

Apart from sharing the citizens' general benefits of easier foreign travel with fewer border formalities, two matters regarding the movement of goods are exercising EC officials: how to distinguish sporting guns from arms for terrorism; and the all-too-flourishing trade in banned drugs for enhancing sports performance. Rather less visible, but of greater importance, are the technical issues of attempting to harmonize standards of sporting goods and services. European committees are currently trying to produce standards for:

- avalanche beacons and mountaineering equipment
- paragliding equipment
- waterslides
- underwater diving equipment
- stationary fitness training equipment
- children's play
- gymnastic equipment

Other standards (for pistols, rifles, skis, parachutes and lifejackets) already exist, and many others will surely follow.

The general effect of such work is slowly to increase the standards of safety and performance, though there is much backstage infighting as national producers lobby for tests and standards which suit them best. Standards for service provision are as yet more of a novelty, though the Commission has adopted as CEN 2900 the British Standard BS 5750 for Quality Assurance in goods and services. The British Quality Assurance

Association, the British Leisure Contractors' Association and the Sports Council are still in the early stages of articulating what this means for recreation management; managers of British multipurpose leisure centres are often regarded as a model of how to cope with conflicting demands from sophisticated consumers, both organized and casual. The other effect of quality control is a modest but steady upwards pressure on cost of purchase and use.

The growth in scale of the new market will help those who have the organization or the consumer 'niches' for specialized products to exploit its potential; most West European countries are net importers of sports goods, and Table 16.4 shows the growth in trade in the 1980s. As Boulter (1990) points out, however, they will no longer be able to exploit certain national markets by wholesaling the same goods at different prices.

Table 16.4   Value of sports trade in the EC

	goods		footwear	
	1980	1989	1980	1989
Exports	46.5	99.3	26.8	118.2
Imports	69.5	168.0	49.3	125.7
Internal	62.5	125.0	32.7	89.6

Index: base year 1985 = 100

Source: EC, 1992

Free movement of people

The EC law gives workers the right to earn a living in any member state. One small but contentious issue has been the limitation by some international sports federations on the number of professionals who can play in domestic teams; it may not matter so much for cricket but has become contentious for the universal game, football; the Union of European Football Associations (UEFA) has proposed that first division clubs should be allowed three non-nationals and two more with five years' experience in that division.

The larger question is of ensuring the general mobility of labour. The EC has been working for many years to achieve mutual recognition of qualifications: directives in 1988 compelled member states to recognize those obtained by three or more years' higher education and training, and in 1990 a directive for two-year courses was introduced, though host states can require examinations or demonstrations of competence if there are major differences from courses in the worker's home nation.

New courses are emerging, not only in sports management but in conjunction with leisure studies, physical education, human movement studies, tourism and arts management. There are few professional institutes with the scope of the United Kingdom's Institute of Leisure and Amenity Management with its 6,000 members. A Europe-wide qualification in sport and recreation management has not yet appeared but its precursors may be seen in

- MA in European Leisure Studies shared by Katholieke Universiteit Brabant, Vrije Universiteit Brussel, Universidad de Deusto Bilbao, and Loughborough University (1991)
- MA in Leisure and Tourism Studies coordinated by the University of Ghent with partners in six EC and four other countries (1992)
- MSc in Adapted Physical Activity shared by Universities in seven EC and two other countries (1992).

These issues will become increasingly important. A private organization in France seeking to cover sport management internationally suggested founding a European Institute.

Beyond the twelve

The Common Market was an economic project with a political end. It has succeeded to the point of 1992 because the more prosperous nations needed the economic solidarity of the 320 million (now with the former East Germany 340 million) market, and the smaller nations shared that need, but also the benefits of agricultural protection and regional and social aid. But they were underpinned by two other major shared beliefs: in democratic, usually social democratic government; and in the state as an enabler to companies, voluntary bodies and citizens.

As this is written there is confusion about how the twelve will go forward after a Danish referendum rejected the treaty negotiated in Maastricht in 1991. The United Kingdom has deep suspicion of loss of sovereignty, of delegating decisions to member states ('subsidiarity') being more a token than a reality, and of an already substantial net input from a few countries needing to grow considerably if smaller and weaker economies join.

Yet countries are queueing up to join: three of the European Free Trade Association States have applied (Austria, Sweden and Finland) and Switzerland and Norway may do so. Economic association status has been negotiated with Poland, Hungary and the former Czechoslovakia and is likely to be pursued with Romania, Bulgaria and the Baltic states. All of these, with Russia, are members of the Council of Europe. This process could mean by 2000 AD a market of twenty-four members with a population of 450 million and an active sporting market exceeding two hundred million. Eventually Turkey and the six European republics of the former Soviet Union may also fulfil the membership requirements of democracy and a developed economy.

For sport in this growing market, apart from the issues of nationalism and representation, there are trends overreaching national boundaries: old and young populations, rich and poor, and the activity of multinational companies.

Old Europe and young Europe

There is a strong trend throughout northern and western Europe towards an ageing population; in 1980, 31 per cent of the EC population was aged under 20. In 1988 this was down to 25 per cent and by 2020 it is forecast to shrink to 21 per cent; conversely those aged 60 and over grew from under 18 per cent in 1980 to over 19 per cent in 1988, and are forecast to reach over 26 per cent by 2020.

The implications for sport are substantial. First, there will be fewer people to sustain team games, and interest in individual medium-energy-expenditure activities, some linked to health, will continue to grow: for example badminton, bowls, swimming, cycling and keep fit. In countries with younger populations, notably Ireland, Portugal and Spain, all sports can be expected to grow.

Second, the costs of pension schemes will rise dramatically and the cost of private insurance will rise unless preventative medicine can become more effective. Sport and recreation have a role here: the growth of obesity, the continued high levels of heart disease, back pain, and osteoporosis in older women could all be helped by exercise—consuming more of the growing calorie input in increasingly inactive societies while strengthening bones, joints, muscles and heart-lung systems, and maintaining mobility in older age. Sport and active recreation now provide 70 per cent of the occasions of exercise vigorous enough to protect against heart disease in England (Sports Council/HEA, 1992). Sport is institutionally linked with health only in the Netherlands, but health benefits are substantially recognized in the policies of Finland and Germany. In many other countries these benefits have yet to be fully accepted and set alongside nutrition, anti-smoking and cholesterol-lowering programmes: the implementation of national strategies for Health for All to the year 2000 and local strategies for Healthy Cities in many European states should help this process.

The final implication is for workforces: in most states fewer workers will be supporting the young and old non-earners (Table 16.5); in some countries the reduction in working-age populations will provide even greater opportunities than at present for immigrant labour to fill the gaps. Currently Germany has over 1.5 million foreign workers, that is 47 per cent of the EC's 'guest workers', but its labour shortages may be eased with young workers from the eastern *lander*. For other states, Ireland with 5.08 workers for each retired person in 2025, Turkey with 7.58, and the former Soviet Union with 4.35 are likely to be major sources of labour. This will continue to be true for tourism, and perhaps also for sport and recreation with its labour-intensive market, especially for routine jobs. On the other hand, the state systems of Eastern Europe have had to shed sport's paid labour. Nine-tenths of the 10,000 former professional coaches in the former East Germany have lost their jobs in the unified system, and many have sought employment overseas.

Table 16.5 Retirement dependency: ratio of people aged 15–64 to those 65 and over

	1960	1980	2000	2025	reduction 2000–2025(%)
Europe (27 states)	6.62	4.95	4.46	3.15	29.3
Northern (6 states)	5.71	4.33	4.29	3.09	27.9
Western (7 states)	5.85	4.52	4.17	2.77	33.5
Southern (7 states)	7.75	5.59	4.41	3.26	26.0
Eastern (7 states)	7.75	5.46	5.18	3.65	29.5
EC (12 states)	6.45	5.01	4.49	3.14	30.0
USA	6.45	5.85	5.24	3.17	39.5
Japan	11.11	7.46	4.24	2.58	39.1

Source: United Nations, 1989

Table 16.6 Gross domestic product and leisure spending, 1988

	GNP at purchasing power standards ($US)	% household expenditure on leisure, entertainment, education and culture
Rich Europe Belgium, Denmark, Germany, France, Italy, Luxembourg, Netherlands, United Kingdom	12,867	7.9
EC Average	15,828	7.6
Poor Europe Greece, Spain, Ireland Portugal	9,825	7.2

Source: Eurostat, 1991

Table 16.7   Sports Expenditure in Germany, 1990

| | Annual Expenditure per head DM | |
	Western	Eastern
Average	601	352
Sports people	877	511
Non-sports people	154	207
People doing five sports	1,338	658
People doing only competitive sport	1,426	656

Rich Europe and poor Europe: unification or domination?

One of the purposes of the single market is to help under-developed states and regions, and there is still a gap between the richer eight and poorer four states in the EC in gross national product and leisure-related expenditure (Table 16.6). If the states of Eastern Europe join, the gap will become more marked. These differences are typified by sports expenditure in the old western and new eastern *lander* of Germany (Table 16.7). Reviews of the former East Germany sports system which is being absorbed show:

- an over-concentration on excellence and a lack of facilities, leaders and coaches for leisure-time sport for all;
- a reduction in club membership (by 5 per cent in two years in the former East Germany);
- little revenue to clubs other than from membership fees, for example from events, sponsorship.

So, there is a need for public investment in community and education facilities, the conversion of works-related clubs to voluntary ones, and training programmes for volunteers and paid leaders (Deutscher Sportbund, 1990, 1991).

Hungary (Nadori and Luchmayer, 1990) and Bulgaria face the same challenges but without the aid of cash transfers from Germany. Many sports people are seeking to move towards self-help with a degree of independence from state funds beyond what is common in the EC, though with little evidence as to where the money will come from while unemployment grows and disposable incomes decline in value as sheltered economies face open competition. This seems likely to confine opportunities to the better off.

The growth of multinational organizations

The bulk of sports enterprises—manufacturing, fishing tackle, sports shirts and emblems, repairing boats, running fitness centres, pony stables, boardsailing and gliding schools, providing ticketing systems and support services for events—are small enterprises, many new, many also failing, and little studied. Randolph and Collins (1992), for example, estimate that in Britain such firms numbered 46,000, employed 200,000 full-time and 123,000 part-time workers and turned over £6.4 billion.

But the news is made by multinational organizations and those who run them; the market for TV sports spectating has long transcended national boundaries, especially with the European Broadcasting Union arrangement which provides cheap coverage for many small national networks. Such multinational organizations include:

- *Sports good manufacturers*
  Of these Salomon and Rossignol for skiing and Adidas have the majority of the market for footwear and a substantial slice of that for clothing. Adidas's founder, Horst Dassler, diversified into sports promotion and sponsorship with companies whose coups were to get Coca Cola to sponsor the Federation of International Football Associations (FIFA) and a wide range of sponsors for the Olympics. Yet even Adidas is a commodity. Having built up a footwear company, Reebok, the Pentland group sold it at a profit of £400 million and then bought an outstanding 80 per cent interest in Adidas for £261 million in 1992.
- *Sponsorship agents*
  These are numerous, but the doyen is International Management Group founded by Mark McCormack, now employing 1,500 and turning over $1,070 million world-wide and its subsidiary Transworld International, which has a turnover of $160 million and handles the Winter Olympics.
- *Sports federations*
  These are nominally democratic, in that chairpersons and executive members are volunteers. International organizations connected with televised sport are no longer impecunious. The TV rights to the 1992 Barcelona Olympics were worth $633 million and attracted 2,100 million viewers; the Winter Olympics attracted $243 million in 1992 and $300 million in 1996; the new premier league football in the United Kingdom $565 million for 1992–6 (because of its Europe-wide transmission on TV satellite). So the reserves of the International Olympic Committee have grown from $214,000 in 1980 to $118 million in 1992; the International Amateur Athletic Federation had an income of $65 million for 1988–91 but for 1992–5 this will grow to $140 million.

These figures indicate not only economic power but also the ability of the leaders of these organizations to work globally. International law provides no real regulatory framework for them, even though their turnovers are more than the budgets of many small nations and they can wield substantial pressure on mayors and premiers of most cities or states. An enlarged EC would be the single greatest world consumer market and would need to tackle the legal and regulatory frameworks for such organizations.

Conclusions

In a review of sport in fifteen countries throughout the world, Roberts and Kamphorst (1989) identified eleven trends. How many of these can we identify in Europe, either in the EC or more widely defined?

- *Sport embraced by, incorporated in, fitness*: fitness has developed as a major interest mainly among the better off throughout Northern and Western Europe; as work-based physical activity continues to decline, the structure of sport will be increasingly valuable as a framework for freely chosen leisure-time exercise.
- *Walking, running, and swimming account for 50 per cent of activity*: this is substantially true throughout Europe.
- *The majority of sport is undertaken by a minority of participants*: this also is substantially true, though in many countries this 'core' market of organized users is growing (see Table 16.3).
- *Participation overall is declining*: Roberts and Kamphorst claim that this is happening because of ageing populations, stagnating economies, or the competition of other leisure diversions, but their claims would seem to be exaggerated. Total participation grows slowly in the 'rich' European states; gains in new indoor and outdoor adventure sports played individually are offset partly by declines in traditional team games. But the average frequency, and hence volume and associated consumption, has been increasing in most European states (see Table 16.3).
- *Separation of recreational, competitive and professional sport*: certainly the ethos and styles of taking part in these different ways are drawing apart. There is not yet strong evidence of institutional separation, though perhaps the separation of an English Sports Council from a United Kingdom Sports Commission in 1993 symbolizes such a move.
- *Disengagement by government, except from elite sport*: certainly sports budgets are being limited by economic stagnation in the West, but there is not yet evidence of mass disengagement: the pressures in the East are much greater and disengagement, especially from top sport, seems to be happening in the face of more basic priorities for survival.
- *Development of new sports for recreation*, for example frisbee, boardsailing: these certainly are spreading and have not yet attracted Eastern Europeans in large numbers.
- *Decentralization*: the bulk of public provision is delegated to local or regional governments and they have been particularly strong in claiming internal subsidiarity or devolution from the centre in federal states (Germany, Switzerland, Spain) and in France, but in the United Kingdom central control over local expenditure has grown strongly.
- *Individualization*: (of sporting choice both of activity and venue) has been increasing universally, and in most public services there have been moves to seek a greater element of payment by individual users, rather than by taxpayers collectively.
- *Professionalization/commercialization*: this process has been as strong in

Europe as in North America, though mitigated by a stronger state role. An enlarged market will reinforce its strength.

* *Spectatorization/mass media-ization*: live sports spectating is not growing rapidly in the rich countries and is unlikely to grow in the former Eastern bloc: it may still be growing in Southern Europe. Even with satellite and cable on a payment basis as options to networked programmes, it is difficult to see televized sport growing overall. Nevertheless, the widening of the single market and the continued development of 'niches' will extend sponsorship opportunities.

There are tensions that a growing European market will bring generally: between regulation and individual freedom, between the centre and traditions of the locality, the balance between self-generated state support and sponsorship, compounded by greater variety of cultures, national and regional. The alliance of sport with health may grow and provide more strength to the rationale for public support, which has weakened as politicians increasingly have seen sport as an enjoyable pastime to be chosen freely and paid for on an individual basis. None of these changes, however, will be likely to diminish the role of sport in European society. As Roberts and Kamphorst state (1989, p.400), 'sport is grounded in three fundamental human drives: namely to seek challenges, to compete and play'. The European stage is ever larger, the challenges and tensions greater.

References

Boulter, I., 1990, 'The commercial sector: views of an international producer', in M. F. Collins, ed: pp. 22–7.

Collins, M. F., (ed.), 1990, *Sport: an Economic Force in Europe*, Conference Proceedings, Lilleshall 1989 Sports Council, London.

Collins, M. F., (ed.), 1991a, *The Single European Market: the Facts and Challenges to the Leisure Industry*, Reading, Institute of Leisure and Amenity Management.

Collins, M. F., 1991b, 'Sport in the economy and the economics of sport', *Progress in Tourism Recreation and Hospitality Management*, 3: 184–214.

Commission of the European Communities, 1991, *The European Community and Sport*, SEC (91) 1438, Brussels, CEC.

Commission of the European Communities, 1992, *Panorama of EC Industries* 1991/92, Brussels, CEC.

Davies, I. G., 1991, 'Sport and physical recreation' in M. F. Collins, (ed.), pp. 48–57.

Deutscher Sportbund, 1990, 1991, *Sport fur Alle in Osten Deutschland*, Press Notice 19 and *Uke den Nacholbedarf in der neuen Bundeslandern*, Press notice 13.

Eurostat, 1991, *A social Portrait of Europe*, Luxembourg, Office of the Community.

Jones, H. G., 1989, *The Economic Impact and Importance of Sport: A European Study*, Strasbourg, Council of Europe.

Nadori, L and Luchmayer, L. T., 1990, 'Social changes and sports in Hungary' in *Planning the Future of Sport*, Seminar Proceedings, Pajulahati, Ministry of Education for the Council of Europe.

Randolph, L. and Collins, M. F., 1992, *Small Firms in Sport and Recreation*, Loughborough University.

Remans, A. and Deforge, M., 1987, *The Sports Structures in the Countries of the Council of Europe*, Brussels, The Sport for All Clearing House.

Riskjaer, S., 1990, 'The state and the voluntary sector' in M. F. Collins, (ed.), pp. 28–39.

Roberts, K. and Kamphorst, T., 1989, *Trends in Sports: a Multinational Perspective*, Amersfoort, Giordano Bruno.

Rodgers, H. B., 1977, *Rationalising Sports Policies*, Strasbourg, Council of Europe.

Sports Council, Health Education Authority, 1992, *Allied Dunbar National Fitness Survey*, London, SC/HEA.

United Nations, 1989, *World Population Prospects 1988*, New York, UN.

Wicklin, B., 1992, *Sports and Recreational Facilities in Sweden*, paper to Italian National Olympic Committee, Stockholm, Central Statistical Office.

Wilkinson, D. G., 1990, 'Sport and urban regeneration', in M. F. Collins (ed.), pp. 67–75.

17

TOURIST IMPLICATIONS OF NEW TRANSPORT OPPORTUNITIES: THE CHANNEL TUNNEL

ROGER. VICKERMAN

Introduction

The growth of tourism, especially car-based tourism, has been strongly related to the development of new transport infrastructure (Halsall, 1992). New infrastructure has opened up new opportunities at the same time as increasing incomes and a reduced working year have led to increasing demand for new destinations. This has often placed excessive pressure on land and other resources at those destinations, an issue which has featured strongly in Allan Patmore's work (Patmore, 1983).

Some twenty years ago, Allan Patmore and I discussed some of the possible impacts at local level which might be brought about by the completion of the Humber Bridge. In this chapter I examine the ways in which an even larger transport infrastructure project, the Channel Tunnel, is likely to influence tourism. There are two main dimensions. First is the pure transport effect—the potential which the tunnel has to divert existing tourist traffic from other routes and modes of transport. Second is the impact which this potential traffic could have on the development of the tourism sector in adjacent regions.

The Channel Tunnel

The significance of the Channel Tunnel is that it is an international infrastructure project creating a fixed link between the British Isles and continental Europe. The Tunnel has been financed entirely by the private sector, at a cost of over £8 billion, and is due to open in late 1993 after a construction period of some six years (Holliday *et al.*, 1991).

Although purely a rail tunnel, it will link both the road and rail systems of the United Kingdom and France (see Fig. 17.1). Eurotunnel, the Tunnel's developer, will operate its own shuttle trains carrying road vehicles between terminals in the United Kingdom and France. Through passenger and

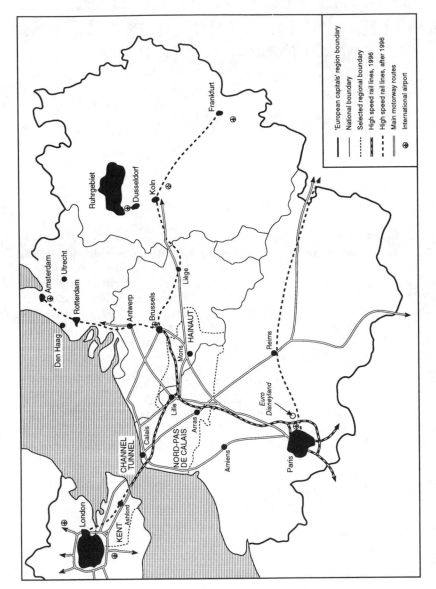

Figure 17.1 The Channel Tunnel in its European context

freight services will be provided by British Rail and SNCF, French Rail-ways, between points in the United Kingdom and on the continent. It is important to view the Tunnel in this way as part of the total networks and not just as an alternative to ferry transport across the Channel.

Considerable investment has gone into improving these overall networks. In France a major programme of road building will provide alternative routes to tourist destinations avoiding the Paris bottleneck and link Calais to the Belgian motorway system. The TGV-Nord high-speed railway line will link the tunnel at Calais to Lille and thence to Paris and the Belgian border from early 1994, with a high speed link to Brussels by 1996, and further extensions towards Amsterdam and Cologne planned for the late 1990s. This is the core of a northern European high-speed rail system linking all the major metropolitan centres in the so-called European Capitals Region (Commission of the European Communities, 1991). Developments in the United Kingdom, especially for rail, have lagged behind (House of Commons, 1992).

For road-based tourist traffic, the Tunnel offers a marginal saving in crossing time of about 30–45 minutes, a little more in total journey time. The actual savings will depend on the degree of congestion since Eurotunnel plan to offer a no-booking service which will inevitably lead to congestion at the busiest periods. The significance of this time-saving will vary considerably according to the total duration of a journey. Currently many tourists use the ferry crossing as a rest or meal break. Some of the associated road improve-ments, especially in France, will make total possible journey-time savings greater than this, but it is difficult to ascribe these directly to the Tunnel.

For rail-based tourist traffic, the time saving for through passengers from London to Paris or Brussels, even without a high-speed rail link in the United Kingdom, will be of the order of two and a half to three hours on the existing fastest journey (a saving of 50 per cent). The major saving will be in providing a through service, compared to the current situation where passen-gers have to change from train to ferry or jetfoil at one port and back at the other, handling their own baggage. Classic rail passengers are currently only a small proportion (around 5 per cent) of total cross-channel traffic for this reason of inconvenience. However, city-centre to city-centre journey times of three hours by rail, using the Tunnel, will be very competitive with air.

For longer-distance traffic by rail, although acceptable day-time journeys to destinations in the south and south west of France will be possible from London by changing in Lille, through sleeper services to a wider range of destinations will be more relevant. Sleeper services will not start until 1994–5 and currently look to be rather more limited than had originally been hoped (British Rail, 1989). Only two services are planned from beyond London, supplementing just five through daytime trains a day, from Edinburgh to each of Paris and Brussels, and from Manchester via Birmingham to Paris (possibly twice a day) and Brussels. These trains will need to serve a substantial number of intermediate points and consequently will only be appropriate for less time-sensitive trips (see discussion in House of Commons, 1992, paras 28–34; Appendix 10).

In discussing the impact of the Channel Tunnel on tourist travel, however, we must not forget that it will be an irrelevant competitor for many journeys. For many destinations, routes across the North Sea or Western Channel will still provide shorter journeys, or ones in which the ferry crossing can be used as an overnight rest. However, there may also be possible complementary uses of the Tunnel, for example in accessing major continental airports such as Charles de Gaulle, Paris. A major investment programme designed to increase its capacity to 100 million passengers a year may make this the major European hub for intercontinental flights. The airport is to be served by TGV services between Lille and other points in France, avoiding Paris by use of the Paris Interconnexion, which will also serve EuroDisneyland at Marne-la-Vallee (see Fig. 17.1).

Cross-Channel tourist markets

Although there has been large and sustained growth in tourist traffic across the Channel, there are problems in defining the precise market which is susceptible to competition from the Channel Tunnel. We would expect the diversion rate to the Tunnel to differ for different markets, defined geographically, by duration of visit and quality of product.

Table 17.1 The development of cross-channel tourist traffic

million passengers

Mode	1962	1971	1981	1990	1993	2003	2013
A. Base market[1]							
Car ⎱		3.5	6.8	11.2	12.6	18.2	23.5
⎰	1.4						
Coach ⎰		0.6	4.5	6.6	6.6	8.5	9.5
Rail	2.9	4.1	6.6	6.9	7.7	10.3	13.2
Air	5.3	11.8	20.7	40.1	46.5	75.8	103.2
Total	9.6	20.0	38.6	64.8	73.4	112.8	149.4
B. Eurotunnel Forecasts[2]							
Total Market					84.2	125.2	166.5
Shuttle Passengers					12.8	18.6	23.3
Rail Passengers					15.3	25.0	33.3

Notes:
1. Actual figures based on International Passenger Surveys, forecasts based on Eurotunnel's traffic and revenue consultants forecasts of growth in the market without the Tunnel.
2. Forecasts of traffic and Eurotunnel's share, total market based on 1990 figures, shuttle and rail forecasts based on 1991 updates which assumed a greater growth of rail traffic and a slower growth of shuttle traffic. 1993 figures assume a full year of operation by all services.

Source: Eurotunnel; Le Maire and Pevsner, 1992

Table 17.1 presents a picture of the historical growth of cross-Channel traffic and current forecasts, both for the base market and for the market including the Tunnel. An important factor to bear in mind is the two-way impact of the Tunnel on tourism as far as the United Kingdom is concerned. It may attract more continental European tourists into Britain, but it will also potentially increase the number of British tourists opting for continental destinations. This is particularly important since the United Kingdom is a net importer of tourism, that is expenditure by British residents outside the United Kingdom exceeds that by foreign residents in the United Kingdom.

We therefore need to know more detail than just aggregate flows across the Channel; in particular we need to include air arrivals. We start with the total picture of the tourist market for the United Kingdom (British Tourist Authority, 1991). Just under 50 per cent of tourist trips into the United Kingdom originate from other EC countries, with a further 10 per cent from non-EC western European countries. These European countries account for around 42 per cent of visitor spending, reflecting the shorter stays (average eight days) than from more distant origins. France and Germany dominate the EC market, though Italy and Spain show faster growth, reflecting their faster growth of real incomes. London dominates as a destination with 57 per cent of visits, 41 per cent of nights (reflecting the short-stay city tourism market) but 58 per cent of expenditure (reflecting both its cost and the dominance of markets seeking a higher-quality product). On average a rather higher proportion of European visitors were on business (30 per cent) than those from other origins; just under 40 per cent were on holiday, three-quarters on independent holidays. A further 20 per cent were visiting friends and relatives. Day excursionists represent 12 per cent of EC visitors, but this masks major variations from one per cent from Spain to 17 per cent from France and 26 per cent from Belgium.

Of tourism generated by United Kingdom residents, some 16.3 per cent of trips (21.5 million) were to non-United Kingdom destinations, but significantly 40 per cent of these were generated from London and the south east, the region with the easiest access to the Tunnel. Air travel dominates the market to European destinations with about two-thirds of all passengers. Package holiday destinations in Spain (with 28 per cent of air passenger journeys), France (15 per cent), Greece (8 per cent), and Italy (8 per cent) are the main focus, although, with the exception of France, these are declining at the expense of destinations such as Germany (13 per cent) and the Netherlands (8 per cent). Sea travel is more important for those going to closer destinations: excluding the 21.5 per cent of this traffic which is of day-trip excursionists, 50 per cent of sea passenger journeys made by United Kingdom residents were to France, followed by Belgium and the Netherlands (15 per cent), Germany (11.6 per cent), Spain and Portugal (8.5 per cent).

Among the main European markets it is only Germany where inward movements to the United Kingdom are substantially greater than the outflow, by about 21 per cent. In contrast, United Kingdom residents travelling to France are almost three times as numerous as the reverse flow. The most significant feature of the German market is the domination of the in-flow by car-sea passengers. There is approximate balance in air traffic, but German-based passengers account for over 60 per cent of the sea-travel market between the two countries. This is a major tourist market for the Channel Tunnel, for two reasons. One is the relative growth of the German market; the second is the response of German car-based tourism to easing the use of the car in travelling to the United Kingdom.

As one of the highest per capita income regions in Europe the German market generates high tourism expenditure. This has particularly resulted in an increase in the number of holidays taken, with particular growth in short breaks (Page and Sinclair, 1992). Notably some 68 per cent of holidays of more than five nights are taken outside Germany; 59 per cent use the tourist's own car, 63 per cent are organized individually and as many as 14 per cent make no advance booking. Research among German tourists suggests that the United Kingdom is perceived to be a difficult destination because the ferry crossing requires advance planning, involves separation from the car, and removes perceived control from the tourist. This may augur well for an increase in the tourist traffic from Germany if the Tunnel, with no advance booking and no need to leave the car, is perceived as fulfilling these characteristics.

This has important implications for marketing the United Kingdom as a destination, concentrating on the short-stay and speciality destination markets. These are markets for which time-savings will be critical, and despite the emphasis on car travel for the large German market, the growth of high-speed rail travel will be important for city tourism. The European Capitals region of the EC, including London, Paris, Brussels, Amsterdam, Cologne and Frankfurt, has 25 per cent of the total EC population and 30 per cent of its GDP. Within a decade of the Tunnel's opening, all of these centres will be within four and a half hours of London by high-speed train.

Forecasting future traffic through the Channel Tunnel needs to recognize both long-term trends in the development of the global market and specific opportunities in individual markets. Although existing forecasts are influenced by the commercial considerations of interested parties, the continuing strong growth of traffic through Dover during the current recession tends to confirm Eurotunnel's forecasts as of the right order of magnitude. Their forecasts have assumed a higher rate of economic growth but with a lower rate of growth of traffic. The effects of introducing a new form of transport are difficult to estimate *a priori*. Evidence from French experience (Plassard and Cointet-Pinell, 1986) suggests a greater diversion from air to high-speed rail than current forecasts for the Tunnel. This also suggests the importance of critical time thresholds as well as time savings. Up to a journey time of two hours there are strong generation effects, with high-speed rail creating new journeys. For journey times between two and three hours by rail, which is the target time for London–Paris and Brussels, there will be a major diversion of traffic from air to rail, affecting both business and short-stay traffic, but rather less new trip generation. Beyond three hours, both generation and diversion effects will be significantly less, but price and through service convenience may be critical in certain markets, for example for the young and the elderly and for longer stays.

Given this, Eurotunnel has started to move from relying on the more macro forecasts based on assessments of appropriate shares of a global market to forecasts based on stated preference analysis of individual segments of the market which can then be aggregated (Le Maire and Pevsner, 1992). Successful revenue generation will depend crucially on exploitation of the most captive markets (see also Kay *et al.*, 1990). To this end the traditional ferry-based holiday market may not be the key sector; rather it is Eurotunnel's advantage in developing growing tourist markets which will be critical. We may expect that the key factors will be new trip generation and destination switching, rather than mode switching. This leads conveniently to a discussion of the role of the Tunnel in promoting specific destinations.

The Channel Tunnel and tourist development

If a key impact of the Tunnel is to be the way it generates new tourist traffic, or diverts it to new destinations, this raises interesting questions about the role of transport infrastructure in the process of tourist-based regional development. This point has not been overlooked by the regions of Kent and Nord-Pas de Calais adjacent to the Tunnel, but there is also a wider context, especially the development of the EuroDisneyland theme park outside Paris (Page and Sinclair, 1992). EuroDisneyland could be seen to be the first major development influenced, if not by the Tunnel alone, at least by its associated infrastructure, the TGV-Nord high-speed rail line and the Paris Interconnexion.

The 1987 Kent Impact Study (Channel Tunnel Joint Consultative Committee, 1987) saw tourism as a major growth sector for Kent with the potential for creating 2,000–3,000 new jobs. This was a very optimistic scenario implying the creation of up to £90 million a year of extra tourist expenditure. A recent review of the study has suggested a more modest impact with perhaps a 5 per cent increase in tourist traffic, generating £15 million extra expenditure by 1996, implying 500 new jobs (PACEC, 1991).

There were some 3.8 million estimated tourist visitors to Kent in 1989, of whom just under 20 per cent were overseas visitors, generating £310 million expenditure. The sector had 12,300 full-time equivalent jobs in 1991; actual numbers employed, allowing for part-time working, could be 30 per cent above this. Overseas visitors were the largest number for any English county and, although about half were from Germany and France, over half had arrived in the United Kingdom by air. For the day-trip market, it is more difficult to estimate destinations accurately. However, it seems likely that a high proportion of such trips using sea had a destination in Kent, amounting to perhaps 225,000 visits in 1989 with a total additional expenditure of £5 million. Even more difficult is the presence of transit tourist traffic. Of the 15.7 million passengers using Kent ports in 1988, only 0.3 million had a destination in Kent. Of the remainder, 1.5 million used rail services passing through Kent, leaving 14 million in transit by road (60 per cent by car and 40 per cent by coach). A high proportion of the car travellers presumably made some stop, especially given the presence of important intervening tourist opportunities on the routes from the Channel ports. This is estimated to have involved a further £8.2 million expenditure in 1988.

The impact of the Tunnel will be in three areas: the attraction of more British tourists to Kent, using it as a base for short visits to continental destinations; the attraction of more continental visitors in a reciprocal way; the increase in transit traffic but offset by speeding up much of this (especially the diversion of much of the increase to rail). Much of the discussion about the extent to which nearby regions will benefit has been in terms of the relative expansion of the short-stay market, which is likely to benefit destinations near the major generators of traffic in Northern France, Belgium and the Netherlands and the Rhine-Ruhr area, all of which will be within four hours' drive of the Tunnel.

British tourists to Kent were estimated to increase at about 1.6 per cent per year over the 1990s; the Tunnel should increase this to just over 2 per cent, adding some 0.66 million extra visitors in total, or £35 million, of which just under one-quarter of the visitors and 20 per cent of the expenditure could be seen as directly Tunnel related. For overseas visitors the assumed base growth rate is higher, at about 3 per cent, a little below the figure for the United Kingdom as a whole. This would add an extra 240,000 visitors a year over the decade. The Tunnel is assumed to increase this by a further 30,000, increasing expenditure from £131.7 million to £178.45 million.

Adding in day-trip traffic and transit traffic the estimated increase in total annual tourist expenditure in Kent by 2001 is £112.7 million, to which a further £25.5 million of Tunnel-related expenditure should be added. This represents about 5 per cent of the estimated 1991 expenditure level and a 4 per cent increase on the estimated 2001 figure without the Tunnel. In employment terms this could mean between 600 and 650 extra full-time equivalent jobs supported by 2001 on top of the estimated growth of 2,600 to which the natural increase would lead.

Such estimates are based on a sober analysis of the growth in visitors and their associated expenditure patterns. They do not allow for the way in which growth may be affected by the provision of specific new developments. Such developments could both encourage a higher rate of generation of new tourist traffic to the United Kingdom and divert it from other areas. The earlier estimates were conditioned by the view that Kent may develop major new tourist attractions which would have this effect and to which we now turn. The tourist infrastructure of Kent (see Fig. 17.2) depends on major national attractions such as Canterbury Cathedral, Dover Castle and Leeds Castle, supplemented by a wide range of additional historical attractions of both primary and secondary significance. These are seen as of particular importance in establishing the type of tourism which is likely to grow, namely high-quality historical-educational short visits.

These established major tourist attractions have been supplemented by a deliberate policy to create a new set of staged attractions based on the region's heritage. These include both private-sector projects, such as The Canterbury Tales in Canterbury, and public–private sector partnerships, such as A Day at the Wells in Tunbridge Wells and the White Cliffs Experience in Dover. A further significant development has been the Eurotunnel

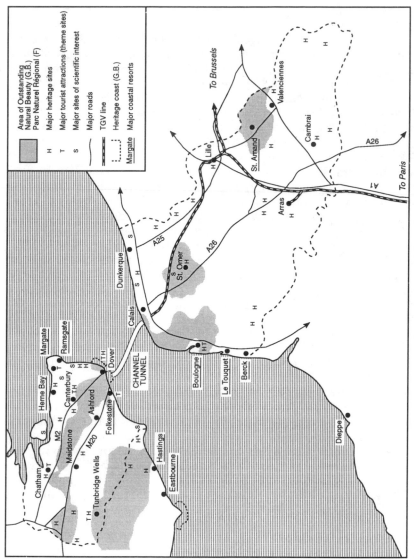

Figure 17.2 Major tourism attractions in Kent and Nord-Pas de Calais

Exhibition Centre at Folkestone which has rapidly become one of the leading tourist attractions in terms of numbers of visitors in south east England. Interestingly, a strong emphasis in this also has been the educational aspect. This suggests niche marketing of tourist facilities, avoiding the temptation to develop pure leisure theme parks, for which there are strong competitors in adjoining United Kingdom regions and which suffer from the relative nearness of EuroDisneyland.

The constraint in Kent is principally the lack of appropriate hotel accommodation to support the quality image. Much of the hotel capacity of Kent has been the traditional seaside variety which appeals neither to upmarket, high-spending visitors nor to the type of family accommodation expected by many European visitors. New hotel capacity has so far been concentrated around business developments, and along the major transit routes, away from main tourist sites. New developments have been difficult to justify on commercial grounds given their traditional dependence on day-visitor and transit traffic and also given the proximity to London which serves as a base for much tourist traffic.

A Tourism Development Action Programme was established to try and coordinate tourism developments across East Kent and principally to act as a way of bringing together public and private-sector interests and encouraging small enterprises in the sector. This had only a modest budget of £0.5 million over three years to 1992 which it is hoped will continue. The fear has been that without investment in tourist capacity the local economy will not benefit, and the costs of the increased tourism will be felt in the amount of transit traffic heading for other destinations (Vickerman, 1991). Moreover, much of the infrastructure investment has been in facilities for transit traffic along the main network; what local facilities need is improved connectivity to this network.

Space precludes analysis of the situation in Nord-Pas de Calais in as much detail (see Page and Sinclair, 1992; Essex and Gibbs, 1989 for more information). However, it is broadly similar, with a traditional seaside sector and historical sites (see Fig. 17.2), particularly those associated with the military history of the First World War, and a high proportion of transit traffic. The main difference has been the insertion of a substantial British property development interest, especially around Le Touquet, plus individual interest in buying up second homes in this and neighbouring regions. Such interest led to rapid increases in property values in Le Touquet, but the recession has caused this to stagnate more recently. There is also a much more substantial flow of cross-Channel day-trip traffic into France, conditioned mainly by duty-free sales.

A particular feature of interest is the singling out of tourism as a sector of special interest for joint development in the context of a Transfrontier Programme Initiative between Kent and Nord-Pas de Calais. Already visitors to Tourist Information Centres in either region can receive full information on attractions and activities in the other, and the intention is to develop tourism jointly in the hope of encouraging a wider range of tourist interest. This initiative is being extended to a Euroregion which also includes the whole of Belgium.

Infrastructure and tourism in regional development

We have reviewed above some of the *ex ante* expectations of the impact of the Channel Tunnel on both tourist flows to and from the United Kingdom and the specific impacts on the local region of Kent. Given the role of the existing ferry mode as a major carrier of tourist traffic, it is not surprising that the Tunnel is seen as having particular significance for the development of tourism. Although only time will tell how accurate forecasts are, it is interesting to note the way in which early views over the traffic impacts and optimism over locally induced developments have moderated.

The Tunnel's major role as a new traffic generator, and as a source of diversion from air, will be as a fast means of transport between the major conurbations for business and city tourism. For the United Kingdom, this is likely to benefit London in particular unless there is a wider development of through rail services to other destinations. There are certain markets, Germany in particular, where there could be an important generation of new car-based tourist traffic by easing the perceived difficulty of travelling to the United Kingdom, but the impact of the Tunnel will be mainly to provide additional capacity to handle a naturally growing market.

For the local economy, the main virtue of the Tunnel has been its use as a means of focusing development needs to capitalize on the inherent tourist advantages of a region which has not exploited them as fully as it could have done in the past. This now suggests a modest growth in tourist-related activity over the next decade, with perhaps 20 per cent of the increase in employment due to the Tunnel. To achieve this will require continued marketing intelligence and investment, however. The creation of cross-border links should be a major advantage here in ensuring that visitors to northern France are aware of the facilities available in Kent and vice versa. There are therefore many opportunities to create new tourist markets locally and further afield using the Tunnel; whether they will be fully realized depends on local investment and innovative marketing.

Acknowledgements

I am grateful to my colleagues Steven Page and Thea Sinclair for their comments and suggestions on an earlier draft; final responsibility, however, rests as always with the author.

References

British Rail, 1989, *International rail services for the United Kingdom*, London, British Railways Board.

British Tourist Authority, 1991, *1993 Cross-Channel Marketing Strategy*, London, British Tourist Authority.

Channel Tunnel Joint Consultative Committee, 1987, *Kent Impact Study—Overall Assessment* London, HMSO.

Commission of the European Communities, 1991, *Europe 2000: Outlook for the Development of the Community's territory*, Document COM(91)452, Luxembourg, Office for Official Publications.

Essex, S and Gibb, R., 1989, 'Tourism in the Anglo-French frontier zone', *Geography*, **74**: 222-31.

Halsall, D., 1992, 'Transport for tourism and recreation', in B. S. Hoyle and R. D. Knowles (eds), *Modern Transport Geography*, London, Belhaven Press.

Holliday, I. M., Marcou, G. and Vickerman, R. W., 1991, *The Channel Tunnel: Public Policy, Regional Development and European Integration*, London, Belhaven Press.

House of Commons, 1992, *Preparations for the Channel Tunnel*, 2nd Report from the Transport Committee, Session 1991-2, HC 12, London, HMSO.

Kay, J. A., Manning, A. and Szymanski, S., 1990, 'Pricing a new product: Eurotunnel', *Business Strategy Review*, **1**: 37-56.

Le Maire, D. and Pevsner, M., 1992, 'Eurotunnel: the development of traffic forecasts for a private sector project', in Bovy, P. H. L. and Smit, H. G. (eds) *Financing European Transport*, Proceedings of the European Transport Planning Colloquium 1992, European Transport Planning Colloquium Foundation, Delft, The Netherlands; 61-77.

PA Cambridge Economic Consultants *et al.*, 1991, *Kent Impact Study Review*, Report to Channel Tunnel Joint Consultative Committee, Maidstone, Kent County Council.

Page, S. and Sinclair, M. T., 1992, 'The Channel Tunnel and tourism markets in the 1990s', *Travel and Tourism Analyst*, No. 1, London, *Economist* Intelligence Unit.

Patmore, J. A., 1983, *Recreation and Resources*, Oxford, Blackwell.

Plassard, F. and Cointet-Pinell, O., 1986, *Les effets socio-economiques du TGV en Bourgogne et Rhone-Alpes*, Paris, DATAR, INRETS, OEST, SNCF.

Vickerman, R. W., 1991, 'Other regions' infrastructure in a region's development' in R. W. Vickerman (ed.), *Infrastructure and Regional Development* London, Pion.

PART VI
LEISURE IN SPECIAL ENVIRONMENTS: WILDERNESS AND NATIONAL PARKS

ACCESS, RECREATION AND TOURISM IN THE NATIONAL PARKS OF ENGLAND AND WALES: 'A THIRD LOOK AT THE SECOND PURPOSE'

ADRIAN PHILLIPS

There has been ambiguity towards public enjoyment of our finest scenery ever since people became conscious of the uplifting qualities of landscape. The issue is expressed in questions often put to national park planners like:

'What sort of recreation should we provide in our national parks?'
'For whom are the national parks created?'
'How can the public enjoy the parks without destroying the very qualities they seek?'

The first attempt to find answers came in the Dower Report (Dower, 1945) and the Hobhouse Report (National Parks Committee, 1947), and in the 1949 National Parks and Access to the Countryside Act. The second was that of the National Park Policies Review Committee—the Sandford Report (National Park Policies Review Committee, 1974). The most recent effort—the 'third look' of the chapter title—was the report of the National Parks Review Panel: the Edwards Report (National Parks Review Panel, 1991), of which Allan Patmore was a distinguished member.

This chapter traces changing attitudes towards the enjoyment of our national parks. It explains why the Edwards Panel called for another look at how to balance conservation and public enjoyment in the parks.

The first look

The British national parks movement has, from the outset, been driven by two distinct strands of thought: the safeguarding of our finest scenery and the rights of people to have access to open country. The former expressed the feelings of middle-class intellectuals, from the Romantic poets onwards, who derived artistic inspiration and personal fulfilment in being close to the beauties of nature. The latter was the voice of what Tom Stephenson—pioneer of the Pennine Way—called 'the humble and largely illiterate factory workers' who sought escape from their grim homes and workplaces on the nearby mountains and moors (Stephenson, 1989, p.57). Of course, Wordsworth and his ilk were great walkers, and of course, the early ramblers had a passion for the countryside. But it was only when these interest groups came together between the wars to argue for national parks that they had a political impact. Inspired also by the example of the great North American parks, they eventually persuaded the wartime government to commission John Dower to report on the case for national parks in England and Wales.

Dower recognized that there could be no question of establishing great wilderness national parks in the North American sense in the long-settled countryside of England and Wales. Rather our national parks were to be areas of relatively wild country but in which the normal economy of farming, forestry, village and indeed small-town life would continue. It follows that state ownership of land in national parks was never a serious possibility on a large scale and that the authorities to be set up to run the national parks would not have the sort of executive powers which national park bodies in other countries have.

But even if the countryside lacks the drama and wildness of scenery in many other parts of the world, the finest landscapes of England and Wales none the less play an inspirational role in national life, and it was Dower's genius to articulate this in words which were both expressive and influential. His report is rightly regarded as the foundation of all that has followed in the national park story. He articulated the basic concept of our national parks thus:

an extensive area of beautiful and relatively wild country in which, for the nation's benefit, and by appropriate national decisions and action,

(a) the characteristic landscape beauty is strictly preserved,
(b) access and facilities for public open-air enjoyment are amply provided,
(c) wildlife and buildings and places of architectural and historic interest are suitably protected, while
(d) established farming use is effectively maintained. [Dower, 1945, p.6]

Dower saw a close link between the public access and conservation purposes of national parks. He felt, indeed, that access was the justification for the conservation of landscape and wildlife. However, reading the words now, nearly half a century later, one is struck by the use of the words 'preserved' and 'protected', whereas we would now use 'conserved'. And also by the sequence, which places access and enjoyment between the protection of scenic quality and that of the wildlife and historic features of national parks, whereas we now see scenic, wildlife and heritage resources as making up a broader entity—the environment.

Sir Arthur Hobhouse's National Park Committee carried Dower's work forward. His report argued that recreation should be 'to the advantage of the whole nation' (National Parks Committee, 1947, p.39). Yet, in both reports, there are signs that the authors did not expect (and certainly did not wish) the national parks to be the destination for mass tourism. A qualitative judgement was made, implicitly at any rate, that access to and within the national parks was essentially for those who would appreciate the qualities of the area and whose recreational activities were of the 'outdoor' variety.

Moreover, in both reports there is recognition of the potential conflict between the pressures of recreation and the interest of local people. Hobhouse, for example, said that national parks should be managed so as to: 'ensure the peace and beauty of the countryside and the rightful interests of the resident population are not menaced by an excessive concentration of visitors, or disturbed by incongruous pursuits' (National Parks Committee, 1947, p.9).

The 1949 Act itself defined the purposes of national parks in a curiously roundabout way, by stating that the National Parks Commission, created by the same legislation, should designate those extensive tracts of countryside in England and Wales which appeared to it, by reason of (a) their natural beauty, and (b) the opportunities they afford for open-air recreation, having regard both to their character and to their position in relation to centres of population', to be especially suitable for the exercise of the powers conveyed by the legislation. (The tidy mind might have wished instead for a definition of a national park first; and then a statement of the purposes for which such areas were to be designated.)

In plainer words, the national parks were to be set up for two purposes:

1. to preserve and enhance their natural beauty, (that is the 'first' purpose);
2. to promote their public enjoyment, (that is the 'second' purpose).

In fulfilling their duties in these respects, the national park authorities and the Commission were to have due regard to the needs of agriculture and forestry.

The second look

In fact the powers conveyed to the national park authorities and the National Parks Commission by the 1949 Act were few and weak (moreover the 1949 Act did not cover Scotland, but that is another story). Although ten national parks came into being between 1951 and 1957, they received pitiful funding, and successive governments failed to protect them against threats of major and damaging development. Ministers fatally undermined the effectiveness of park administration by entrusting it to the care of the parent county councils in all but two cases (only the Peak District and Lake District were run by independent boards). Small wonder that Ann and Malcolm MacEwen should have summarized the first quarter century of the British national park experience in a chapter entitled: '1949–1974: downhill (nearly) all the way' (MacEwen and MacEwen, 1982, pp.21–9).

To address the administrative and financial shortcomings, the Countryside Commission and the then County Councils' Association agreed on a new deal for the national parks. Incorporated in the Local Government Act 1972, this came into effect in 1974. The funding of the parks was greatly increased and a much more robust framework created for their administration, planning and management, especially for the county-council-run parks.

But funding and administrative machinery were only some of the difficulties which the parks had encountered. There were major uncertainties on the policy side too, especially as the national parks found themselves faced with a very different set of issues than those which had concerned the founding fathers of the 1940s. To tackle this new agenda, the government set up the National Park Policies Review Committee under the chairmanship of a junior environment minister, Lord Sandford, in 1971. Foremost among the topics before the Sandford Committee was a fresh look at the second purpose of the national parks, their enjoyment by the public.

The committee was quick to recognize the new demands for recreational space in the parks, and the main reason for this:

When the parks were being set up, it was expected that most visitors to them would be of an active disposition and that their requirements would be access to open country, some improvements of footpaths, simple information about the features of the parks, accommodation of the youth hostel type to supplement that already available in hotels and farmhouses, and camping sites ... It was not long, however, before the motor car made its presence felt ... [As a result] the resources of park authorities, in money and skill, have from the early years of the parks been largely devoted to needs created by the motor-borne visitor. [National Park Policies Review Committee, 1974, pp.30–1]

When the first national parks were created in 1951, there were 2.4 million private cars. By the time that the Sandford Committee met twenty years later, the figure was 12.1 million. The impact on the national parks had been striking: congested country roads; poorly regulated parking; damage to vegetation, noise, fumes and the offending sight of steel and glass scattered across our wilder landscapes. In a largely vain attempt to deal with these pressures, most of the modest projects submitted for funding by the park authorities to the National Parks Commission were for car parks, lay-byes and loos. Indeed, it is an interesting comment on the priorities of the times that the first research publication of the Countryside Commission, set up in place of the National Parks Commission in 1968, was on techniques of charging for car parks.

But if the parks had wrestled to little effect with the problems of recreational traffic, they had achieved even less in those very areas of provision for outdoor recreation which had inspired the national parks movement. Thus, outside the Peak District, next to nothing had been done to extend the rights of public access on foot to open mountains and moors. However, the Sandford Committee found that there was much more *de facto* access to open country than was revealed by the statistics of land subject to formal access agreements or in the ownership of the National Trust. They recognized that there were problems of access for groups such as climbers and potholers, for whom the national parks contain many prime sites. And they acknowledged that the condition of many rights of way in the parks was deplorable.

In coming to solutions on the balance between the first and second purpose, the Sandford Committee adopted a more clear-cut philosophy than the ambiguities of Dower, Hobhouse and the 1949 Act. The cornerstone was what came to be known as The Sandford Principle: 'We have no doubt that where the conflict between the two purposes, which has always been inherent, becomes acute, the first one must prevail in order that the beauty and ecological qualities of the national parks must be maintained' (ibid., p.9).

The Sandford principle was reinforced by a proposal, borrowed from the United States' National Park legislation, that the statutory purposes of national parks should be amended to make clear that 'enjoyment by the public shall be in such a manner and by such means as will leave their beauty unimpaired for the enjoyment of this and future generations' (ibid., p.57).

All ten national parks set up in the 1950s were in the north and west of England or in Wales. The Committee recalled the wording of the 1949 Act and recommended that something be done to redress the uneven geographical distribution of the parks, none of which were close to the large populations of the south east (an omission partly remedied since by the setting up of the Broads as a national park in all but name and soon to be further redressed by giving the New Forest, too, a status equivalent to that of a national park).

The Committee called for more country parks, which had been introduced by the 1968 Countryside Act, to be set up nearer centres of population to help syphon some of the pressures off the national parks. They proposed a zoning approach to the planning and management of recreation pressures on the parks. They argued that caravan and camping provision should be made at the periphery of the parks. They suggested that more use could be made of traffic management schemes and public transport to diminish the destructive force of the car.

However, while proposing a more active role for the park authorities in rights of way, they focused on altering the network rather than opening it up. Their recommendations on access to open country were cautious. They had nothing to propose on tourism, apart from caravans and camping.

The government's response to the Sandford Report was less than full-blooded. No doubt the 'gruyère-like' way in which the report was riddled with notes of reservation by one member of the committee or another helped the bureaucrats to get away with a minimalist response. But the Sandford principle was endorsed and the new, better-resourced national park committees and boards enjoined to adopt it in all their planning and management functions and to incorporate it in the new national park plans.

The third look

Those most thoughtful of national park critics, the MacEwens, updated their pessimistic 1982 volume—*National Parks, Conservation or Cosmetics?*— with a more up-beat volume five years later, entitled *Greenprints for the Countryside? The Story of Britain's National Parks.* Even if the question mark remains, the contrast between the contents as well as the titles of the two volumes is revealing. Despite all the setbacks, the new deal for national parks brought about through the 1972 Act had given them more money, greater professionalism and a boost to self-confidence. Compared with the first twenty-five years, the past twenty years have been a success story.

So the case for a further review of national parks advanced by the Countryside Commission (and launched in 1989) did not rest so much on dissatisfaction with their recent record as with its concern about several emerging issues which it feared threatened the very survival of the parks. The first was the vulnerable state of hill farming: changes, such as those brought about by the Common Agricultural Policy of the European Community, threaten the survival of many small, family farms which form such a critical element in the traditional upland scene. The second issue involves a host of new pressures on the recreation, access and tourism fronts. The third concerned the sense that the long-term protection of the parks depended upon their being linked to national, European and international environmental policy.

The Edwards Panel, which had a broader remit than the Sandford Committee, was not chaired by a minister but by a tough academic with a good knowledge of how public-sector bodies work and much political 'savvy'. Ron Edwards admitted, however, that he knew little about national parks on taking up the post. But he gathered a good team around him and learnt fast. He set as a target the completion of the report within one year (not the three it had taken Sandford's Committee) and made it clear that he was looking for unanimity. After an intense period of consultation and debate, the report was duly delivered to the Commission, without any minority reports or notes of reservation, at the end of 1990.

The core of the Edwards Report was a call for new national parks legislation, containing an up-dated statement of national park purposes, a statutory duty on all branches of government to further those purposes, and independent authorities to run all the parks. There were, in addition, over 170 other recommendations.

In looking at the second purpose, the Panel found that the Sandford Committee had identified some of the required action but that the response since 1974 had been disappointing. Thus Edwards repeats almost word for word the Sandford call to park and highway authorities to be much bolder in using traffic management and public transport measures as a response to the demands of the car.

But many of the issues of the early 1990s were hardly evident twenty years before. They therefore call for a different policy response in respect of the second purpose. For example:

1. The great uncertainty over the future of hill farming, so vital to the economy and the landscapes of many parts of our national parks, raises an intriguing possibility. As incomes from sheep farming decline, national park farmers may look for more direct rewards from the public purse for what they can do for the visitor, especially the visitor on foot; that is payment for providing new public access. At the same time, upland farmers may come under pressure to provide more public access as a condition of their receiving support.

2. The greater public awareness of environmental concerns means there is growing impatience with forms of recreation which do violence to the qualities of the national parks, noisy sports, for example and those which disturb wildlife. And they strengthen the case for encouraging people to switch from private to public transport in getting to, and around, the parks.

3. New forms of recreation make novel demands on the countryside. Some, like holiday camps to carry out practical conservation work, actually help secure the first purpose of the parks. Some, like hang gliding, are wholly compatible (providing there is some control over the launching areas). Others, like mountain bikes, certainly have a place in the national parks but require active management. Others again, like off-road four-wheel driving, cannot easily be accommodated without conflict with other interests.

4. There has been an upsurge in the demands of the tourist industry. The enthusiasm for time-share may have peaked, but there have been other controversial applications, for example for conference facilities beside Lake Windermere and cable cars in the Mawddach Estuary. A policy framework for considering such applications is needed. Hence the interest in 'green' tourism in the national parks, that is small-scale tourism, which respects the environment and focuses on the special qualities of the area rather than on providing entertainment. A key criterion is that the tourist activity should not harm the environmental base upon which it depends.

5. In 1989, the Lake District National Park floated the idea of a tourist tax to levy funds to help meet the costs of managing recreation pressures on the park (the estimated cost of repairing the rights of way alone runs to £2 million annually). Though resolutely resisted by the tourist industry, which points out—reasonably enough—that overnight tourists cause only a small part of the problem, the initiative has opened a debate on the need to capture some of the tourists' expenditure to pay for the costs of managing visitor pressures.

6. In the countryside at large, there has been a new interest in the two oldest recreational assets. Common land, of which there is one-and-a-half million acres in England and Wales, is land over which grazing and other rights are held in common, and which therefore has not usually been improved for agriculture and retains its wildlife and scenic qualities. Rights of way, of which there are 140,000 miles in England and Wales, provide a legal right to pass over private land on foot, bicycle or horse. Yet, in the national parks, as elsewhere, the public has only limited rights of access to common land, and many miles of footpath and bridleway are still blocked or otherwise unusable.

7. Over a hundred years since the first, unsuccessful attempt to get right of access to open country through legislation, the debate has recently acquired a new urgency. But the arguments are complicated by evidence that unregulated access to all open country at all times of year can threaten wildlife, especially breeding birds.

8. There is concern that the wild areas of our countryside, and of our national parks in particular, have been greatly eroded over recent years;

and there are demands that this should stop and where possible be reversed. Proposals have been made to reduce road access to certain parts of the parks (to close the military road on Dartmoor, for example) and to create what Prince Charles has called 'the long walk in' to the remoter heartlands of the parks. This policy, coupled with the re-creation of semi-natural vegetation such as heather from areas recently 'improved' for agriculture, would make parts of our parks wilder and remoter places than they have been for many years.

These considerations led the Edwards Panel to reassess the place of recreation in the national parks. Since their ideas may appear more restrictive in some respects than past policy, one should note the Panel's reaffirmation that the enjoyment of the national parks 'for both physical and mental refreshment, and for physical challenge, [is] particularly precious in a crowded island such as ours' (National Parks Review Panel, 1991, p.36). They confirmed, too, that the public enjoyment of the parks is, and should be, derived from the special qualities of the parks. But this will not be achieved without new policies which respond to the expectations of a more environmentally aware society and reflect a new set of circumstances.

In proposing a definition of a national park in the following terms, the Panel consciously concluded that it was the resource qualities of the area which merit its designation rather than its proximity to centres of population: 'the essence of the concept of national parks lies in the striking quality and remoteness of much of the scenery, the harmony between man and nature it displays and the opportunities it offers for suitable forms of recreation' (ibid., p.5).

The definition still places recreation in a key position but includes the qualifying word 'suitable'. The meaning of this becomes clear in the statement of national park purposes proposed by Edwards for incorporation into primary legislation:

1. to protect, maintain and enhance the scenic beauty, natural systems and land forms, and the wildlife and cultural heritage of the area;
2. to promote the quiet enjoyment and understanding of the area, insofar as it is not in conflict with the primary purposes of conservation;
   In pursuance of these purposes, the national park authorities should support the appropriate agencies in fostering the social and economic well-being of the communities within the national park, in ways which are compatible with the purposes for which the national parks are designated. [ibid., p.11]

This proposed statutory definition of park purposes:

1. makes clear that 'quiet' recreation is what the national parks are there to provide; by implication, intrusive activities should be discouraged;
2. introduces the term 'understanding', which suggests a link to the educational role of national parks, and thus forms a bridge between the first and second purposes, and

3. spells out the relationship between the two purposes, thereby putting the Sandford principle into legislation to give it added force.

The Panel's detailed recommendations on the second purpose follow through the logic of this strategic analysis. Thus, there is much emphasis on providing new opportunities for quiet enjoyment of the countryside. The national parks are set a target of 1995 to get all their rights of way in shape and usable. The Panel calls for early legislation to implement the recommendations of the Common Land Forum (Common Land Forum, 1986) which would ensure the protection of the remaining commons, their effective management and a general right, subject to certain safeguards, of quiet access on foot to commons. While believing that the same set of principles should apply generally to open country in the park, the Panel perhaps shows the marks of uneasy compromise among its members in avoiding any specific call for national legislation to achieve its stated target of having all open land subject to management schemes by the end of the century.

The Panel called for a new agricultural support system for the Less Favoured Areas which would give incentives to farmers to protect and enhance the conservation values of the parks and to provide new access areas for the public. It also proposed setting up some experimental areas where all farming activity would cease and where natural progression would be allowed to proceed unhindered—a sort of 'wilderness by management' decision and suitable only for limited recreational access.

The Panel saw little place for noisy sports in national parks which caused annoyance or damage. But it readily acknowledged that the parks contained unique sites for such sports as climbing, canoeing and caving; and that more had to be done to safeguard such areas for sport, subject to the overriding needs of conservation.

The Panel recommended that the government endorse the *Principles for Tourism in National Parks* (already agreed between the Welsh and English Tourist Boards and the Countryside Commission) and require that these be carried through into development control policies. Under these principles, the form of tourism developed in the national parks should help to protect the distinctive environment of the parks, draw on their special character, serve the needs of the local community, respect the park environment, be sensitively designed and be marketed so as to deepen public understanding of national park aims and qualities (National Parks Review Committee, 1991, p.46).

The outlook

The Edwards Report was welcomed by the Countryside Commission and the newly formed Countryside Council for Wales (which came into being in 1991 in Wales, in place of the Countryside Commission and the Nature Conservancy Council). However, while both bodies were clear in their support for putting the Sandford principle into legislation, both were concerned that the wording proposed by Edwards for the statutory purposes had the effect of demoting recreation and access from a primary to a secondary purpose of national parks. They thought the word 'primary' in clause 2—see above—should be dropped (Countryside Commission, 1991, p.2; Countryside Council for Wales, 1991, p.3).

In its response, the government accepted the key recommendation that each park should in future be run by an independent authority. It has committed itself to introducing legislation at the earliest opportunity which will include a new statement of park purposes based upon the advice of the Panel as modified by the advisory agencies. And it has promised to give the New Forest a status equivalent to that of a national park.

So the short-term outlook is encouraging. Stronger national park authorities with a sharper sense of direction should provide a better framework for the pursuit of national aims. In particular, national parks should be clearer both about the kinds of recreation and tourism they wish to encourage and those which are out of place. But success will also depend on factors outside the control of the park authorities.

Managing recreation pressures costs money; park authorities will need to be better resourced than they have been in the past which means a further increase in the level of government funding. If they are to be more discriminating in the kinds of recreation and tourism provision they accept, their planning policies and development control decisions will need to be upheld by the Department of the Environment and the Welsh Office. If the parks are to be protected from intolerable recreation pressures, more needs to be done to meet those demands nearer the source, through support for the Countryside Commission's programme for community forests on the edge of cities, for example. If they are to make real progress on the open country issue, there must be a very strong lead—and in all probability legislation—from government (following the most recent general election, ministers have made it clear they have no intention of promoting such legislation and upsetting the grouse moor owners). All highway authorities will have to transfer rights-of-way responsibilities to the parks. Agricultural policy will have to recognize that the provision of more public access is a legitimate reason for supporting hill farming. And every government department and official body must be charged, as Edwards recommended, with the duty to further national park purposes where their activities impinge on the parks (the government's initial response to this key proposal was disappointingly cautious).

There needs, too, to be a new emphasis on cooperation between conservation and recreation interests. Creative thinking is needed on how visitors can make a larger contribution to the costs of running the parks. More work is required on codes of good environmental practice for the different sports which make use of the parks. The principles for tourism in national parks must now be turned into policies which stick. The park authorities need to improve their links with local, regional and national tourist and sports bodies. And the political will must be mustered to tackle the problems of the invasive motor car.

But, when the balance sheet is drawn up, the management of recreation in the national parks is not as daunting a challenge as faces the parks in the agricultural field, for example, or—over the longer term—against the prospect of climatic change. As this account of the pursuit of the second purpose shows, there has been a progressive clarification of ends, a flexible response to new demands and a fine-tuning of policy and practice. If this can continue, the national parks of England and Wales should still be able to make their very special contribution to human needs as places of mental and spiritual refreshment and of physical challenge.

References

Common Land Forum, 1986, *Common land: the Report of the Common Land Forum* Cheltenham, Countryside Commission.

Countryside Commission, 1991, *Fit for the Future: the Countryside Commission Response*, CCP 337 Cheltenham, Countryside Commission.

Countryside Council for Wales, 1991, *Fit for the Future: Response by the Countryside Council for Wales* Bangor, Countryside Council for Wales.

Dower, J., 1945, *National Parks in England and Wales*, Cmd.6628, Ministry of Town and Country Planning, London, HMSO.

MacEwen, A. and MacEwen, M. 1982, *National Parks: Conservation or Cosmetics?*, London, George Allen and Unwin.

MacEwen, A. and MacEwen, M., 1987, *Greenprints for the Countryside? The Story of Britain's National Parks* London, Allen and Unwin.

National Park Policies Review Committee, (the Sandford Committee), 1974, *Report of the National Park Policies Review Committee*, Department of the Environment London, HMSO.

National Parks Committee, (the Hobhouse Committee), 1947, *Report of the National Parks Committee (England and Wales)*, Cmd.7121, Ministry of Town and Country Planning London, HMSO.

National Parks Review Panel, (the Edwards Panel), 1991, *Fit for the Future* Cheltenham, Countryside Commission.

Stephenson, T., 1989, *Forbidden Land: the Struggle for Access to Mountain and Moorland* Manchester, Manchester University Press.

MANAGING THE WILDER COUNTRYSIDE

DEREK C. STATHAM

Ask average town dwellers what they think of as wilderness and they will suggest areas of uninhabited swamp, forests, deserts and arctic tundra. There is virtually no such land in Britain, certainly not in England. Instead, when we talk of the wilder areas, we really mean the mountains and moorlands of the north and west, though, on reflection, the more discerning student may include small fragments of lowland countryside such as the New Forest or the Norfolk Broads. Moreover, all these areas are managed in varying degrees by farmers, graziers and foresters.

That most cherished of British landscapes, the heather moorland (see Fig. 19.1), is very much a man-made, and managed, landscape. The main economic products from such land, sheep and grouse, are very different in kind and character but their requirements are broadly similar. They need fresh heather shoots for food and older heather for shelter and breeding. For optimum results, heather needs burning in rotation, although the best results for game populations are obtained from a longer rotation over smaller areas than is the case with sheep. The result of several hundred years of such management is bare landscape of grass and dwarf shrub communities, verging on a monoculture of the common ling, *Calluna vulgaris*, in the drier moors of eastern Scotland and England.

Competing uses of moorland

In addition to sheep grazing and grouse shooting, our northern hills and moors are used for grazing deer for sporting purposes and for a wide variety of recreational activities. These range from informal walking and sightseeing, for which the open moors are ideally suited, to car rallying and skiing in winter. Such activities frequently co-exist without significant impact on the primary grazing interests, but conflicts and problems do occur over the

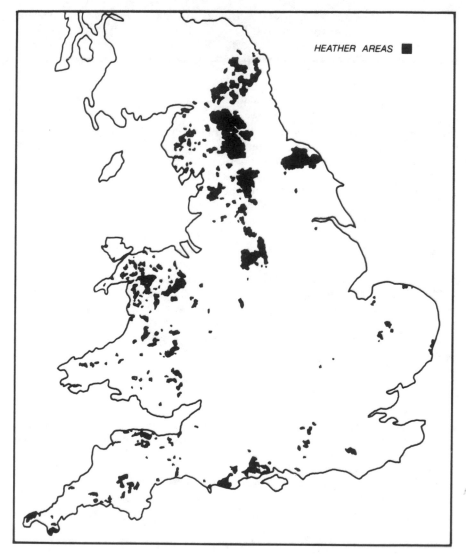

HEATHER AREAS ■

Figure 19.1 Moorland areas of heather, England and Wales
(*Source:* Institute of Terrestrial Ecology)

more heavily used moors, especially those near to urban areas in northern England.

These conflicts and interactions are summarized in Fig. 19.2. Hidden in this summary are more specific conflicts of a severe or controversial nature, including the impact of public access on moorland wildlife and the effects of certain types of specialist recreation, such as car rallies, or rambling and informal recreation. All of these interactions have been identified and studied for some time and are well known in principle, but whereas the relationships between grazing uses have been studied extensively, those involving recreation and grazing have been less well researched (see, for instance, Sidaway 1988; Thompson, *et al.* 1987).

Management issues

The managers of the wilder countryside are principally farmers, gamekeepers, landowners and their agents and tenants. They are guided in their decision-taking by several influences, including the policies of local and central government towards the countryside; grants and subsidies from public agencies; tradition; personal wishes; and the need, in many cases, to make a living from the land. Numerous public agencies have responsibilities in land management, and their involvement is seen at its sharpest in the designated areas, especially National Parks and SSSIs. Over the past two decades, certain issues have dominated the debate on the management of the wilder areas. It is instructive to examine how these have influenced the management of one particular area of land, the North York Moors National Park (see Fig. 19.3).

This Park is famous for its moors, though the moorland vegetation only covers about 35 per cent of the area of the Park, rather less than the area of enclosed farmland. Much of the remainder is woodland, of which recently planted Forestry Commission conifer plantations are the main component (see Fig. 19.3).

Moorland and bracken

Many of the moors are managed for grouse shooting, with sheep grazing as a subsidiary enterprise. They are dominated by the common ling, *Calluna vulgaris*, which forms dense patches and can best be described as upland heath. They are particularly vulnerable to summer fires, following a spate of which in the dry summer of 1976, the National Park Authority and the main landowners in the Park combined to set up a management programme for the moors. Initially concerned with the best ways of revegetating the burnt areas, it has developed into a long-term management programme for all the moorland with the objective of restoring and maintaining ecological health to the vegetation and wildlife. Numerous studies are in progress involving a wide range of scientists and practising land agents and owners as well as the National Park Authority and other public agencies (North York Moors National Park Committee, 1991).

A particular feature of the programme has been the control of bracken. This vigorous plant has spread in recent years from its traditional habitat on well-drained slopes to the plateau tops where it replaces heather. Although important for some wildlife, it is poisonous to stock, and carries a significant number of ticks which can cause disease in sheep and grouse and, more rarely, in humans. Numerous methods have been used to control it, including cutting, crushing by machines, and spraying. This last is now used on a large

(1)   Grouse management

(2)   Bracken control

(3)   Sheep grazing

(4)   Cattle grazing

(5)   Deer stalking

(6)   Informal recreation

(7)   Specialist recreation

(8)   Wildlife conservation

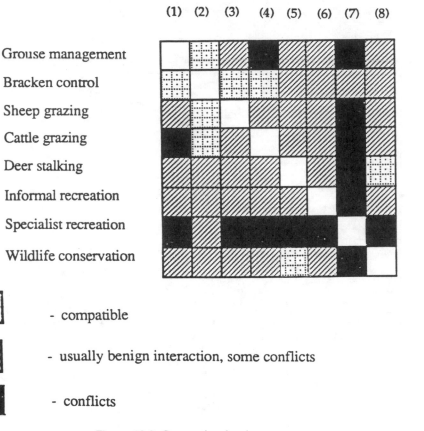

- compatible

- usually benign interaction, some conflicts

- conflicts

Figure 19.2 Competing land use

scale, grant-aided by the National Park Authority and the Ministry of Agriculture. A five-year eradication programme is being implemented for each estate, at an annual cost over the Park of some £100,000. By this means it is planned to reduce the bracken-dominated areas to their traditional habitat and to provide barriers to control further spreading. It is an expensive business with little obvious return, and will only succeed with follow-up every two to three years. Compromises will have to be struck involving an acceptance of the role of the species in the moorland habitat, rather than pursuing prohibitively expensive programmes to completely eradicate it from the Park.

Public access and wildlife

No issue generates more argument and controversy than the question of public access to open country. Indeed, this above all other issues focused the

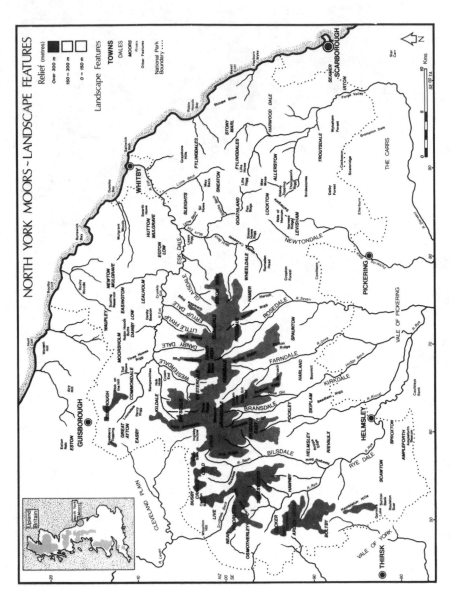

Figure 19.3 General map of North York Moors with location inset
(*Source:* North York Moors National Park Department)

argument for the creation of National Parks in Britain during the 1930s and 1940s. The stage has now been reached where in some areas the rambling interests are once again locked in battle with land owners. Since pre-war days, however, the basis of the argument has shifted. While the ideological differences remain, there is now a claim from landowning interests, backed by some ecologists, that walking over moorland, unless severely restricted in time and space, has a detrimental effect on wildlife in general and on upland breeding birds in particular (Moorland Association, 1987).

This is undoubtedly true if large numbers of people are involved over a long period. But what effect do small numbers have over short periods of time, which is the normal situation over most of the North York Moors? The evidence is scant. Some species, for example merlin, a small and rare bird of prey, are very shy and vulnerable to disturbance. Yet recent work in the National Park indicates little direct loss by disturbance, and stronger possibilities of decline by more pervasive environmental influences, possibly involving chemicals and pollution. Likewise, curlew and golden plover, two other species susceptible to disturbance at nesting time, show evidence of decline in areas popular with the visiting public in the Peak District but, again, little is known about the effect in less popular areas. The evidence for disturbance of the grouse population is also inconclusive, but it does not appear to be a major problem (Hudson, 1982).

Against this evidence, we have rather stronger indications that persecution of birds of prey by shooting interests is widespread and has affected the populations of hen harrier and peregrine falcon in some areas of northern England (RSPB and NCC, 1991). Independent studies of the results of disturbance are badly needed, but even these will only provide a guide, since each moor has a unique mix of variables acting on the relationship between access and wildlife.

Inheritance tax exemption

The tools available to the National Park Authority to influence management are a curious mixture of carrots and sticks. All forms of building development and most changes of land use are subject to control by the various Planning Acts, but these exclude most agricultural and forestry operations. Thus, the afforestation of moorland or agricultural land does not require consent, neither does the ploughing and reclamation of moorland to agriculture. Grants are available from the Park Authorities and other agencies to influence management, including such matters as tree planting, heather management, maintenance of stone walls and barns, and the conservation of important wildlife habitats.

There are compulsory powers to require public access and provide facilities but only voluntary mechanisms for conservation outside the SSSIs and National Nature Reserves. These latter usually take the form of management agreements between the National Park Authority and the landowning interests, normally involving annual payments to the landowner. Given the prominence of conservation in National Park purposes, it is clearly anomalous to have compulsory powers for recreation but not for conservation. The National Parks Review Panel which recently reviewed the management of the National Parks (Countryside Commission, 1991) recommended extending planning controls and introducing a last-resort power to protect specific landscape features and areas by means of Landscape Conservation Orders (LCOs). The government has made minor changes to planning control but has no plans to introduce powers to make LCOs or to bring major land use changes involving agriculture or forestry under planning control.

An increasingly popular, but little known, method of securing long-term management is by granting inheritance tax exemption in return for undertakings to manage land of high conservation value in accordance with an agreed management plan and to permit 'reasonable' public access. The undertakings are made with the tax authorities who do, however, take advice from the statutory countryside agencies. There is no requirement to consult the National Park Authority or to inform, let alone consult with, the general public for whose benefit the exemptions are supposedly granted. The Countryside Commission, or the Countryside Council for Wales, usually consults with the Park staff who are then faced with the invidious situation of giving policy advice on major management issues on a confidential basis.

The advantages to the National Park Authority can be very considerable, however. In return for professional advice and information, land can be protected at no direct cost to the Park budget with some, but unfortunately increasingly limited, public access. The sanction for breaking the agreement is, of course, the loss of tax exemption. A major shortcoming is the degree of public access that can be insisted upon, especially over open country. There is clearly scope for a wide degree of interpretation of what is 'reasonable' on different areas of land. The trend is for countryside agencies to require less, even less than that already enjoyed on a *de facto* basis. The value of such exemptions is quite clearly diminished if the public cannot even walk over the areas which they are, in effect, paying to protect.

At the time of writing, there is a Finance Bill before Parliament which, if enacted, will greatly extend the eligibility for exemption from inheritance tax without management conditions. This will considerably reduce the control over the management of scenic areas by the public.

Common land

About half of the moorland area in the North York Moors is registered common. This is land which is normally privately owned but over which other persons have rights to graze a specified number of animals and, sometimes, there are other rights such as the rights to collect firewood and cut peat turves for fuel. In three cases there are ancient Court Leets in existence to manage commons in accordance with traditional management practice. Court Leets are legal bodies established in medieval times to control the management of commons. They can levy fines for disturbing the surface of the common and settle disputes between commoners. There are few other formal commons management committees, and some commons are not subject to agreed management programmes. The standard of grazing and management varies considerably, therefore, ranging from overgrazing in some overstocked commons to neglect and undergrazing in others. Sometimes the lack of management of commons is not as serious as in other upland areas because the owner of the sporting rights is active in managing the common as a grouse moor.

The failure by government to implement the findings of the Common Land Forum to date has not posed serious problems in the North York Moors other than on the vexed question of public access. Urban commons, that is registered commons which were within the boundaries of former Urban District Councils and therefore enjoy a right of public access under the Law of Property Act, 1925, are few. Some commons are owned by benign landowners, for example, the National Park Authority, which permit open access, and most of the moors, whether common or not, still enjoy a considerable degree of *de facto* access. It is mainly because of this tradition that the North York Moors National Park Authority has not embarked on a programme of securing access agreements. Recent confrontations and a hardening of attitudes indicate that this period of *laissez-faire* is coming to an end, and a process of protracted bargaining could ensue unless the recommendations of the Common Land Forum are enacted. It is difficult to envisage a situation in which the public will tolerate exclusion from open land in a National Park without very convincing reasons, and landowners would appear to have much to gain by entering this debate with constructive proposals.

Introducing wildwood

Most of the woodland in the North York Moors consists of recently planted conifer plantations pioneered by the Forestry Commission. These contrast markedly, both visually and ecologically, with the older mixed and broadleaved woods found chiefly on dale slopes. However, some of the conifer plantations, mainly those planted between the wars, are now mature and are being felled and replanted. The replanting offers opportunities to create a more varied and ecologically richer woodland and to improve the potential for public recreational use.

The basic plan of the new plantations is to relate the species planted to soil and landscape conditions on a 'coupe' pattern. Each compartment is carefully analysed and surveyed and replanted with species that best suit individual sites or coupes. Streamsides and other features are left unplanted and a much greater proportion of broadleaved trees is introduced. The result is a diverse mosaic of mixed types with broadleaves becoming more dominant in the final crop as conifer nurse crops are thinned out.

In some areas there are deliberate attempts to create or extend wilderness habitats. Thus in the heart of the Dalby Forest, remnant heath pasture flora have been allowed to flourish by removing a large area of recently planted Sitka spruce. Elsewhere, wetland has been created by altering drainage patterns. Natural regeneration of both conifers and broadleaves is being encouraged on some sites, giving an untamed natural scene as opposed to a planted forest with trees of even age growing at regular intervals. The possible re-introduction of lost species such as black grouse and pine marten is being investigated by the Forestry Commission and the National Park Authority by creating optimum habitat conditions prior to release of imported stock. The recent spread of several rare species such as the nightjar gives an indication of the potential for enhancing wildlife conservation in these large areas of forests.

Alternative uses for farmland

Perhaps the most challenging problem is the use of moor edge land and farmland which is gradually becoming redundant as the EC food surpluses build up. Several potential alternative uses would contribute to National Park objectives. The first is to return recently ploughed out moorland back to heather and rough pasture. Experiments on the best ways of achieving this have already taken place on land owned by the National Park Authority at Nab Farm, Fylingdales. These proved the need to bury the top few inches of improved grassland and soil and to create the necessary acidic conditions for heather seedlings, introduced by spreading heather bales, to establish themselves in sufficient quantity to form tussocks of heather. A much larger area is now being treated on this basis and if it proves successful, other owners will be encouraged by grants and technical advice to extend their heather land. Such land is likely to have value not only for landscape, wildlife and public recreation but also for grouse management and sheep rearing.

On the wide belt of mixed pasture and arable land on the limestone in the south of the Park, there are possibilities for more radical landscape change. One such bold scheme at Murton Grange (Fig. 19.4) envisages the planting of former arable land to create a broadleaved, parkland landscape open for public access with areas of heath or common developed over the remainder. Obstacles to achieving such a transformation are not technical but financial as the present grant-aid schemes are not targeted at such land or such changes. And yet this is perhaps the best option for much redundant farmland in lowland areas as well as marginal upland. Other possibilities include natural regeneration, especially on farmland bordering existing woods, agro-forestry where a form of light grazing husbandry is combined with timber management, and energy cropping. This last is more suited to wet lowland rather than upland, but it may have possibilities on some sites. Likewise, there is scope for alternative crops, but clearly these will only be viable for short periods as production would soon outstrip demand. The overall aim with such changes should be to enhance the wildness of the Park, thus improving wildlife and the value of the Park as a natural resource and tourist facility.

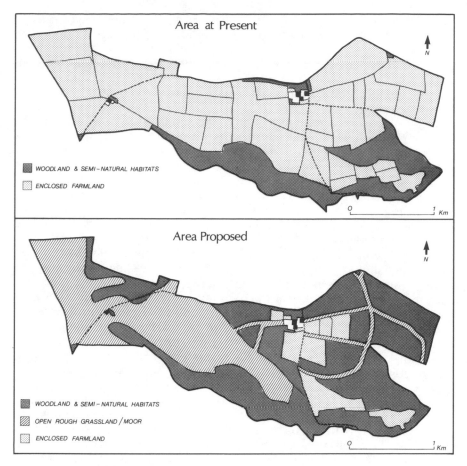

Figure 19.4 Murton Grange: new landscapes
(*Source*: North York Moors National Park Department)

Public recreation

Despite National Park status, the visitor can sometimes feel unwelcome in
the North York Moors. Access to moorland is unrestricted but increasingly
discouraged, while on farmland the public rights of way offer limited scope
to explore and recreate. In the Forestry Commission woodlands there is
greater freedom, but enjoyment is reduced by the dull blanket of even-aged
conifers in some areas. Some Forestry Commission land is being privatized,
and the rights of public access must be in doubt in future despite government
attempts to safeguard them.

One remedy in this situation is to invest in the promotion and management of routes for public use which give a variety of recreational experience
of the landscapes of the Park. The national trail, the Cleveland Way, is

being complemented by a network of well-marked and managed 'regional routes' which will provide a wide range of walking experiences. Lower down the scale is a large number of local 'waymark walks' of relatively short duration particularly suitable for families. In addition, there are several individually promoted competition walks, some of which conflict with wildlife interests and local communities. The classic route of the Lyke Wake Walk is one such example.

The prospects for informal recreation in the new landscapes with alternative uses are generally good. Indeed, there is no reason why public grant aid should not be conditional on the provision of suitable access. Without the economic pressures of crop production or game conservation, conflict with other uses is likely to be at a minimum in such areas.

The outlook for other forms of recreation is less certain or less encouraging. Horse riding is likely to be generally accepted and better catered for, but there are localized conflicts with other users, particularly ramblers. Mountain bikes create problems, but with the advent of a user organization and better visitor management by the National Park Authority the problems of erosion and conflict should not prove insurmountable. Increasing public concern and local hostility are manifest towards more specialized pursuits, especially motorized sports. In a National Park situation, they are generally viewed as out of place with the concept of 'quiet recreation'. Erosion problems are particularly severe and expensive to rectify. At Carlton Bank, the National Park Authority is currently resorting to compulsory purchase to secure the restoration of an area of moorland badly eroded by motor bike scrambling. The cost of restoration is likely to be measured in hundreds of thousands of pounds, all because of unauthorized use over the past decade.

A major deficiency is the lack of a regional approach towards the provision of suitable sites and facilities for motorized sports. Attempts to achieve this by Regional Sports Councils, National Park Authorities, local authorities and the user bodies have met with limited success. A possible way forward is to provide limited funding to Park Authorities to grant aid alternative sites outside the parks, thus expanding the very limited funds available from local authorities.

Future problems and opportunities

The problems referred to in Fig. 19.2 are easily defined; solutions are less easy to find in the absence of a clear consensus on behalf of those interests most involved, as the analysis of the management issues demonstrates.

One basic shortcoming is the lack of coherent national policy on the management of these areas. There are separate sectoral policies for landscape designations, wildlife protection, recreation and tourist use but no overview of national priorities. The manager at local level has to work with a mish-mash of sectoral policies, some of which can conflict and interact with others in odd ways. Moorlands can be, and frequently are, important for sheep grazing, grouse shooting, breeding sites for rare birds and attractive areas for informal recreation. Priorities are decided by a competitive process

Plate 19.1 Carlton Bank, North York Moors, erosion of moorland by motorbikes

Plate 19.2 Erosion on the Lyke Wake Walk, North York Moors

Plate 19.3 Cockshoot Broad, Norfolk, restoration of a traditional Broad to wetland wilderness

among owners, tenants, commoners, recreationists, local residents, visitors and a range of public authorities, with the owner frequently holding the whiphand, though often dependent on public authorities for protection. Conflicts can have a strong ideological component, especially those relating to public access and field sports.

There is little evidence on which to judge the effect of informal recreation in moorland areas on wildlife, for example. Yet proponents of the access lobby frequently deploy all the fervour of the religious fundamentalist if access is threatened, while landowners seem to travel backwards into feudal times in their attitudes or to concoct unholy alliances with wildlife conservationists to keep out the ramblers. The effect of the latter alliances can be quite persuasive, always providing that landowners can continue their sporting interests and that conservationists retain freedom to study their chosen species. One suspects that the wildlife, in this case chiefly the upland breeding birds, are far more adaptable than those engaged in this ideological struggle! Experience in the National Parks indicates that conflicts are mainly in the minds of those involved, rather than on the ground.

Successive governments have failed to protect valuable habitats. Despite the benefit of National Park status, some 25 per cent of the heather moors of the North York Moors have disappeared since the Park was designated in 1952 (Fig. 19.5). Similar loss has occurred in other National Parks, especially

Plate 19.4 Walkers on the Cleveland Way in the North York Moors

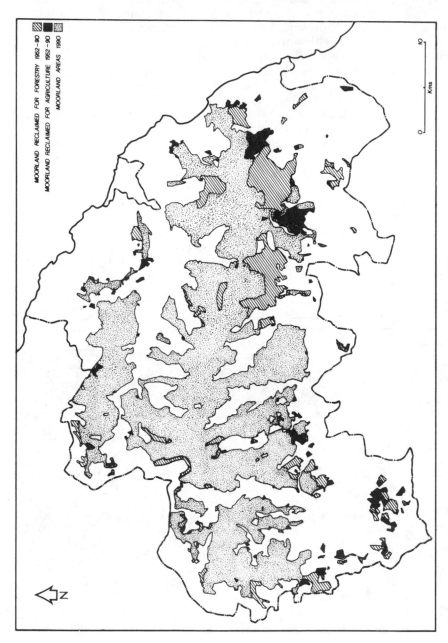

Figure 19.5 Loss of moorland. North York Moors. 1952–1990 (*Source*: North York Moors National Park Department)

Exmoor. In Exmoor in the 1970s, the opposition to the ploughing of moorland reached such a peak that the government was forced to hold an inquiry (Porchester, 1977). It found in favour of protecting the remaining moors, but in the early 1990s we still cannot protect moorland unless designated as an SSSI. The losers in moorland reclamation are not only the wildlife and the landscape but also tourists and recreationists. Conifer plantations and improved agricultural land offer few opportunities for recreation. Two important trends, however, are working in favour of the user and lover of the wilder areas. Firstly, environmental awareness has grown and continues to grow, rapidly. Values are now being placed on semi-natural habitats in legal and, increasingly, in financial terms. Public opposition to reclamation schemes is readily roused and increasingly influential. European Community policies and directives are also tending to become more environmentally orientated thus lending more support to conservation claims. Second, problems of over-production in the agricultural sector mean that pressures on farmers to intensify and reclaim are lessening. Indeed, the lack of management is already affecting some wildlife habitats. Herb-rich pasture and woodlands need positive management measures to optimize their wildlife diversity. Heather moorland also needs a degree of management to control bracken and to create a mosaic of heather communities. This necessitates labour, which has to be funded.

It is the abandonment of farmland, however, that presents the greatest challenge for the management of the wilder areas and offers an exciting opportunity for positive landscape enhancement as opposed to conservation of existing habitats. The scheme proposed at Murton Grange could set an important precedent for the future of large areas of farmland in the North York Moors.

In spite of all the problems, therefore, the future of our wilder areas seems full of opportunities. Boldness and imagination are required, coupled with strong government policies to protect valuable habitats and prevent exploitation. A sea-change of attitude is needed in the farming and landowning community towards the management of land which will take time. Pump-priming and experimentation by public agencies will be essential to start the processes of change. Although the most suitable agencies to stimulate this radical venture are perhaps the National Park Authorities, most of the Parks' landscapes are valuable in their existing state and it is in other upland and lowland countryside where the changes are needed. A rural equivalent of the Urban Development Corporation, an independent agency with specific objectives geared to land use change, and a budget to match, might be one way of concentrating skills and funding to get schemes off the ground in selected areas.

Disclaimer

The views expressed in this chapter are those of the author only and not necessarily those of the North York Moors National Park Authority.

References

Countryside Commission, 1991, *Fit for the Future*, Report of the National Parks
    Review Panel Cheltenham, Countryside Commission.
Hudson, P. J., 1982, 'Red Grouse Production and Management in Relation to Tourism'
    in K. Hearn, (ed.), *Moorlands, Wildlife Conservation, Amenity and Recreation*,
    Recreation Ecology Research Group Symposium, 8, Wye College, Ashford, Kent.
Moorland Association, 1987, *Comments on the Government's Consultative Proposals for
    Further Legislation on Common Land*. Lancaster, Moorland Association.
North York Moors National Park Committee, 1991, *Moorland Management Programme*,
    Helmsley, York, North York Moors National Park.
Porchester, Lord, KBE, 1977, *A study of Exmoor*, HMSO, London.
Royal Society for the Protection of Birds, Nature Conservancy Council, 1991, *Death
    by Design. The Persecution of Birds of Prey and Owls in the U.K. 1979–1989*, Sandy,
    RSPB and NCC.
Sidaway, R. M., 1988, *Sport, Recreation and Nature Conservation: Conflict or Co-operation*
    London, Sports Council, Study 32.
Thompson, D. B. A., Galbraith, H. and Horsfield, D., 1987, 'Ecology and Resources
    of Britain's Mountain Plateaux: Land Use Conflicts and Impacts' in M. Bell and
    R. G. H. Bunce (eds), *Agriculture and Conservation in the Hills and Uplands*, Institute
    of Terrestrial Ecology Symposium No. 23, Grange-over-Sands, ITE: 22–31.

20

AN INSIDER'S VIEW OF MANAGING THE BROADS

TIMOTHY O'RIORDAN

Allan Patmore served for twelve years as a distinguished appointee to the North York Moors National Park Committee, as an academic and an independent, throughout that time applying his vast knowledge of recreation and leisure to the policy and practical needs of formulating and executing the National Park Plan. In so doing, he combined scholarly ability with the folk knowledge of a politician. His personal diplomacy was instrumental in his long and successful tenure on the Committee. Allan Patmore was always courteous, considerate, thoughtful and ready to see the merits of contrary argument. Should others follow his example, all National Park committees would undoubtedly be more cooperative and more effective.

It is in this spirit that I write this chapter. My aim is to share the joys and opportunities of being an independent and an academic member of a local authority national park organisation. I have been a Countryside Commission nominee to the Broads Authority since the creation of the original voluntaristic body in 1978, as well as its statutory successor in 1989. I have also been elected since 1979 to chair the Authority's Environment Committee. On the basis of this experience I convey what I have learnt about environmental politics in the context of managing the Broads.

Six principles are interwoven in the chapter:

1. **Be conscious of history**—of the appearance of landscapes of the past as well as of the present, of the interrelationships of pre-existing organisations which still condition the viewpoint of those who serve in their successors, and of achievements and failures and how these are judged by those who gained and lost as a result.
2. **Treat people and arguments with respect and sincerity**. This may appear platitudinous, but it is not meant to be so. In local government politics every viewpoint carries the weight of party or organisational commitment and a particular, often strongly held, perspective. To treat all argument as

a basis for creating mutually advantageous reanalysis of both a problem and a solution enables effective alliances to be forged.

3. **Know your administrative law** and especially the shifting emphasis on the so-called amenity clauses. These are the duties or responsibilities on all ministers and statutory bodies to have regard, or to balance, or to further natural beauty and the well being of peoples and their economies. Invariably in this more environmentally sensitive age, such duties are being taken seriously even when they are not formally defined as a legal requirement. To anticipate and shape an argument with a partner agency so that environmental and social justice are properly taken into account allows more scope for effective negotiation.

4. **Prepare your ground painstakingly, and step by step.** Be sure to visualise the ultimate objective before embarking on sequential negotiations. Seek to use wording that appears benign and flexible, but which actually commits all parties stage by stage to common goals and to shared outcomes that would never be accepted at the outset.

5. **Never lose sight of the client interests** that buttress the groups and organisations with whom you are dealing. Seek to open up channels of communication that reinforce personal contact and a sense of personal conviction at all levels. The use of mediating panels or discussion forums, where viewpoints are guaranteed to be heard by sympathetic ears, can be very therapeutic as well as overtly democratic.

6. **Try to be on sure scientific ground and, where not sure, utilise the principle of precaution.** Environmental science as an integrating device for interlinking natural and social processes to political judgements and interacting organisations provides the best basis for ensuring stable funding over long periods. Well judged research also provides a solid basis of political support, even among those who are concerned about any long term commitments to public spending. The principle of precaution, if suitably applied, allows suspicious parties to spend money and enter into experimental schemes without feeling bound to possibly serious errors of scientific analysis. Experimental schemes help to bring parties together in commitments that they would not contemplate if the temporary and exploratory attributes of experiment were to be removed. Luckily, too, the British appear to enjoy the surprisingly binding requirements of voluntarism. Voluntary agreements create moral and political expectations that lock participants in to mutual obligations as soon as they accept its beguiling containment. Subsequent thought and action are forever altered.

These threads will be developed in the chapter that follows. But first a few words about the Broads Authority, its statutory remit, its internal organisation and its *modus operandi*.

The Broads Authority

The Broads Authority is arguably the national park organisational arrangement of the late twentieth century. It is, or should be, the model upon which new national park administrations should be structured. A few amendments are still required to make the Broads Authority a truly effective agency; these are considered later. But compared to the national park, county-led committees, the Broads Authority is administratively lean, adaptable, responsive, visionary and cohesive. Even in the light of the national park planning boards set up for the Peak Park and the Lake District, both more independent of their county mentors than the subsequent crop of eight national park committees, the Broads Authority is much more flexible and unfettered from county political machinery.

The Authority consists of thirty-five formal members and a further two coopted from navigation interests. Of the thirty-five, eighteen are from local authorities (four from Norfolk, two from Suffolk, and the rest from the six district councils with responsibility for the executive area). The seventeen appointed members are drawn from conservation, boating, farming, fishing and recreation-tourism. Figure 20.1 summarises the administrative structure of the Authority.

Why is the Broads Authority so unusual? The original Authority was created as an amalgam of local government nominees and non local government appointees under the rather weak administrative provision of the Local Government Act 1972. That structure was extremely brittle, for the organisation relied on the goodwill of the member local governments, namely six district councils and two county councils, plus the shifting collection of the appointed members, none of whom held any particular allegiance or brief.

The points made about voluntarism within a management collectivity are very pertinent. No local authority would have dared break ranks or would have refused to pay its levy, even though none was legally bound to the early Authority. In a curious way, voluntarism exacts a moral obligation to play the game that is not so evident in formal legal organisations. Also the large representation of district councillors—twelve out of an original membership of twenty-four—created a much greater sense of community and more direct responsibility for day to day Broads management. Consequently the delivery of schemes for environmental enhancement was much more evenly spread, so every member felt that his or her council had a direct stake in the work of the Authority as a whole.

The changing administrative status of navigation

The major problem, however, was the separation of navigation powers and water management responsibilities. In the case of navigation, the pre 1989 arrangement vested navigation matters in a Victorian relic, namely the Great Yarmouth Port and Haven Commissioners. Their attitude to navigation was centred on the control of Norwich and Yarmouth as commercial ports, and the supremacy of navigation activities over all other interests. Interconnected functions such as river dredging, river bank piling and maintenance, speed limit bye laws, and boat numbers and movement—all

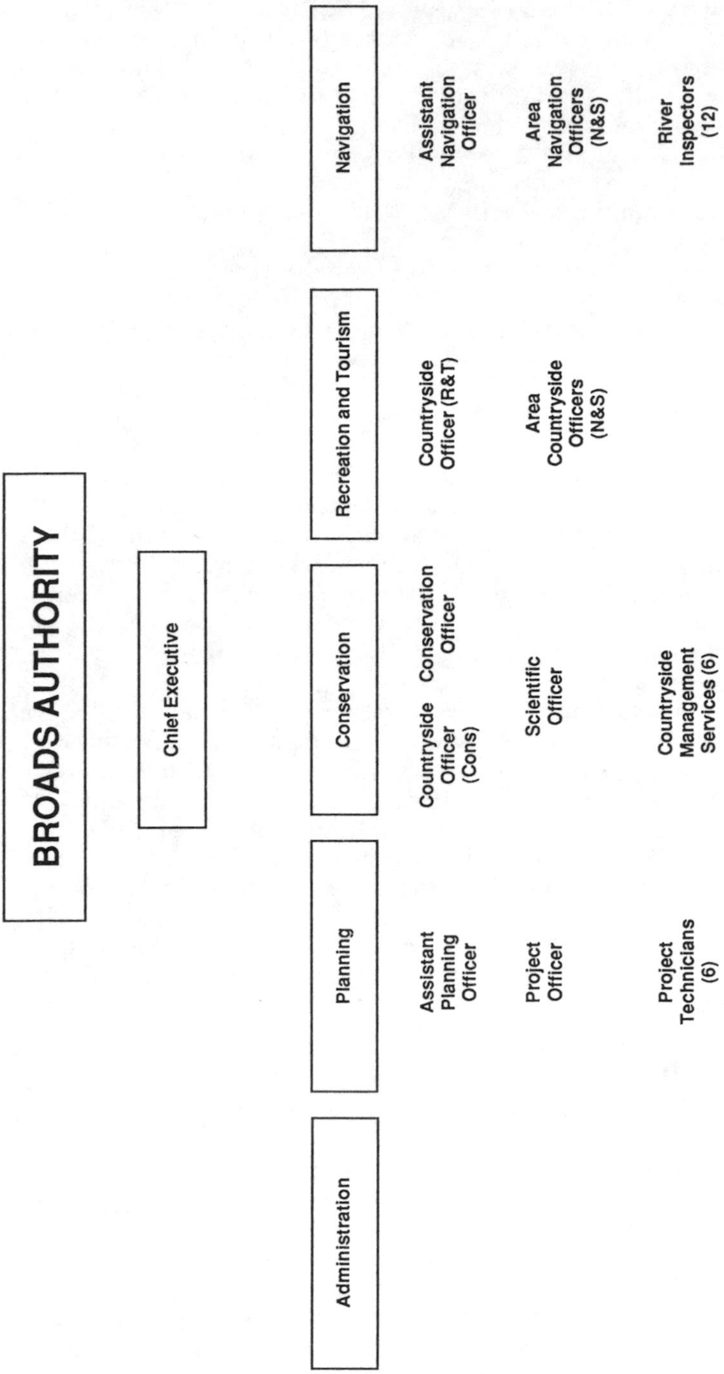

Figures 20.1 The administrative structure of the modern Broads Authority

central to the environmental well being of the area—were largely handled as if the Broads Authority did not exist.

This is why a sense of history and a knowledge of administrative law are so vital to sound national park management. The Port and Haven Commissioners were frankly too inflexible in their attitudes and perspectives—for good reason if one recognises both their remit and the client biases of the Commissioners—to be capable of adapting to the growing clamour for a more integrated approach to comprehensive river and land management in the Broads. The law played into the hands of the Commissioners, who had authority over the rivers and over all aspects of boat design and movement. Yet study after study showed that both hull shape and boat speed had noticeable effects on bank erosion and bank-side sedimentation.

Here is where both scientific research and the application of the precautionary principle became significant. The Broads Authority persuaded the Commissioners jointly to fund research into the effects of hull design and boat speed on bank erosion. The research was supervised by an independent engineer with extensive knowledge of wash characteristics and reviewed by three naval architects. This independent review allowed both sides to judge the merits of the research, and to accept an element of precaution—namely to accept reduction in boat speed even though cause and effect could not conclusively be proved—had to prevail via experimental schemes of low wash zoning.

This voluntaristic and adventurous arrangement, given the deep suspicion between the two organisations, was not sufficient to clinch a deal on completely renegotiated speed limits. So the navigation function had to be incorporated in the new Authority. The old Authority had legitimated the transfer through the experiment, and the Commissioners have contributed to their demise by failing to exploit a voluntaristic deal. Arguably the Commissioners probably would never have retained the navigation function. But at least they might have won more friends in the decline of their political fortunes and legal status.

Shifting perceptions in all-round water management

Similarly, prior to the 1989 Water Act, which created private sector water and sewage utilities with a major regionalised national agency, the National Rivers Authority, responsible for the river environment and flood defence, the control of both water supply and quality for recreation and amenity lay in the hands of the Anglia Water Authority. This body, based in Peterborough, was too far removed geographically and ideologically from the Broads to consider formal integration of powers and responsibilities around the complete water cycle, even though it had committed itself to a series of collaborative projects on broads restoration and more naturalistic bank protection. The difficulty was that the divisional organisation of the AWA was sympathetic to the management issues of the Broads, while the regional headquarters had other priorities.

The 'new look' Broads Authority

So the creation of the 1989 'new look' Broads Authority came at a time when it was opportune to wrest both navigation and water management powers away from agencies which, for a variety of internal organisational and administrative reasons, simply would not cooperate over the totality of environmental commitment.

The modern Authority took over the navigation powers in their entirety, with the Port and Haven Commissioners being confined essentially to the Port of Yarmouth and with nominal responsibility for sea-going vessels particularly upstream of the Port Haven. This removal of an historic power was not won easily. To mollify the navigation interests, who remain deeply suspicious to this day of the conservationist motives of the Broads Authority, three legal safeguards were imposed in the founding legislation:

(i)   There was to be a separate navigation account, fuelled by the licences of the boats using the Broads and rivers, and earmarked for navigation purposes only
(ii) There was to be a separate, executive, navigation commission with a bias of membership favouring navigation interests.
(iii) Any alteration of rights of navigation, whether permanent or temporary, had to be subject to formal inquiry and justification by those proposing the changes, with a right of appeal.

Tensions between navigation and conservation interests

As a consequence, there has always been an internal tension between the navigation and environment committees. For the most part this has been resolved on the basis of the analyses presented to members, based on good scientific evidence, on the advice of the Broads Authority's Research Advisory Panel, and as a result of the recognition that the over-riding objective is to ensure an ecologically viable wetland in the region. After all, there is no point in promoting a navigation where there is manifest danger to the very amenities the navigation user seeks to enjoy.

In the run up to the amended Broads Plan, published in 1993, the navigation interests sought to extend navigation rights over previously navigable but presently closed and private broads, and to open up new waterways in disused parts of the rivers. The legal position on navigation rights is very vague, being dependent on tidal action and historic and uninterrupted usage. To get round the possible conflict of an attempt to open up broads subject to restoration and/or located in an important nature reserve, the draft Broads plan created a policy whereby all initiatives had to be subject to the best management to retain and enhance the ecological integrity of the Broads. This was accepted by navigation interests, though it can be used to safeguard key habitats.

So on the big issues of cooperation over the restoration of the Broads, the management of the fen and the protection of vulnerable river margins there is no fundamental disagreement. On the more subtle questions of boat hull design, pricing to encourage more environmentally friendly boat shapes, and quasi-legal controls over the numbers of boats at boat-yards, there is no agreement. Attempts to establish an environmentally damaging charging regime for boats via hull design and location of boatyard have foundered before they even became serious policy proposals. Agreement is possible on the main principles of maintaining ecological integrity, for here there is a common aim. But for proposals to implement this in the context of the so-called 'ecological economics' of the modern age, there is fierce resistance, a resistance not confined to the navigation committee. The moral for academics interested in the political acceptability of novel resource management techniques, is that there is no unanimity over the principle or effectiveness of inventiveness in the application of economic incentives, or even for regulatory imagination, unless there is an unequivocal linkage to a broader resource sustaining objective and there is palpably no easier or apparently fairer means of arriving at that objective by measures which are already familiar even if they are inefficient and inequitable in economic terms.

The use of ecological economics becomes more attractive when there are no conventional ways to attract political attention to the additional cash requirements for resource management. So the NRA embarked on a study of the economic valuation of freshwater river flow acymentation to see the likely effects on fluvial habitat and nature conservation interests. It is possible that this interdisciplinary research co-sponsored by the Broads Authority, will be put to good use in future experimental schemes, also utilising the precautionary principle, for river augmentation to restrict saline intrusion in modest tides during drought periods of very low freshwater flows. This pioneering research will be completed about a year before a policy shift will be required to promote low flow manipulation. Without that proactive work, it would have been almost impossible to engineer that policy shift, a prospective innovation that will require cooperation by the Ministry of Agriculture and the Department of the Environment, because of both the flood control and river management implications.

Cooperation over water resources and flood alleviation

The creation of the NRA provided a golden opportunity to exploit the amenity clause of section 8 of the 1989 Act. This lays a duty on the NRA to further the interests of natural beauty in the pursuit of its activities. Even now the NRA is taking legal advice on the scope of this clause. But it is clear that on the key points of setting statutory water quality objectives, i.e. the basis of determining all future discharge consents, for ensuring adequate river flows in drought-prone regions, and for guaranteeing an element of enhancement of wildlife and science interest in the pursuit of flood defence, the NRA is now committed to courses of action that take environmental well being very seriously indeed.

Unlike the pre 1989 era when there was a division of interest between the regional and divisional headquarters of the AWA, the NRA eastern region is much more cohesive at regional and divisional level. Indeed, after a number of lengthy meetings, the NRA and the Broads Authority have combined to create a joint policy position on all matters of mutual interest. In essence, the two authorities are now acting as a single entity. The crucial point here is not just joint policy, but joint financing. On all aspects of river management and flood defence the two bodies are contributing cash for research, experimental schemes and long term restoration projects. These include

(i)   the naturalistic restoration of river banks and floodwalls using geotextiles, reed regeneration and coppiced alderpole piling, plus dredging that re-creates natural riverbed profiles.

(ii)   sharing the costs of a river-tidal regime hydrological model for flood defence and the water conditions of the upper Thurne catchment. In the case of the sea defence model, the calculations have been instrumental in establishing a flood alleviation scheme that will contain saltwater intrusion even on low tides, not just on North Sea surge tides. The environmentally rich north eastern region of the Broads is enormously sensitive to saltwater intrusion from groundwater caused in part by greater seawater penetration and by abstraction for irrigation. This area contains some of the most important fen in the whole Broads area, so the exclusion of saltwater is a vital objective.

(iii)   Cooperation on scientific research to restore the nutrient rich Broads to a low nutrient regime by techniques such as iron salt dosing of the surface sediment to precipitate the phosphate rich detritus of decaying algae, and bio-manipulation, namely the alteration of broads ecology by techniques such as fish removal and water plant replacement in order to create the maximal conditions for ecological reversal.

(iv)   Agreement in principle on both statutory water quality objectives and the consent limits for phosphate in the discharge of treated sewage and the wastes from the food processing industry, together with a joint plan of action to control seepage from septic tanks and other quasi point sources close to the sensitive areas of river and broads. This joint commitment also extends to the limitation of agricultural wastes.

The application of the principle of ecological engineering in the control of high tidal saltwater incursions into the Yare and Waveney rivers via the operation of washlands on Haddiscoe Island—the strip of land between Breydon Water and the confluence of the Yare and Waveney. This should result in the recreation of a salt-brackish water habitat plus wetlands that should add to the biological diversity of the area. Without the use of both environmental economics valuation techniques to justify the social welfare gains of this enhancement, plus the interest in promoting biodiversity as part of the post Rio commitment to the Biodiversity Convention, the tidal washland scheme would have been impossible to justify on a conventional cost benefit analysis. How times are changing.

In the context of seawater exclusion and agricultural pollution control, the Broads Authority is collaborating with the Ministry of Agriculture, Fisheries and Food on joint experiments and policy initiatives. Again this process utilises the modern 'environment friendly' images of those government agencies which seek to gain wider support by being, or appearing to be, green. In addition, the fen management programme, also based on solid scientific research, is co-financed between the Broads Authority and English Nature over a three year span.

The advantages and disadvantages of partnership

The buzz word in national park politics is partnership. This is a term of art for compromise via cooperation by a structure that is politically fragmented, financially weak, and legally fettered. National park authorities do not have the powers they ideally would like to put their purpose into action. As is well known, most of the land and water is owned by private individuals or companies, yet almost all land and water management policies, including most of the money available for environmental support, are the responsibility of various government departments, statutory agencies and voluntary organisations.

So a national park body can only go so far. It has to proceed via collaboration and mutual obligation. This requires some form of consensual arrangement that brings together all the interested parties in a voluntaristic forum. Few park committees have achieved this, for the simple reason that such a mechanism is administratively cumbersome and extremely inefficient if policy and finances have to be coordinated.

Figure 20.2 gives some idea of the problems, displaying all the partner links between the Broads Authority and various agencies responsible for conservation and resource management in the area. There is no mechanism for bringing them all under one collective entity. The Authority prefers to separate out its outreach links to various key interests via a series of advisory panels, as indicated in Figure 20.3. These panels are vital in acting as a conduit for informed opinion into the Authority's policy formulating machinery, and usually help to mediate conflict, especially when awkward cases have to be resolved involving individual landowners or special interests. Each Panel reports to a main committee, one for agriculture, (environment committee) one for recreation, (navigation committee), one for scientific advice (environment committee), and one for wide ranging policy review (the Authority as a whole).

Because the panels are small but reasonably representative, and because they feed in directly to the committee structure and their Chairmen, so they are effective to an unusual degree. They are also pro-active, warning the Authority of possible trouble if a particular policy option is pursued in a certain way. For example the Broads flood alleviation strategy, which involves a proposal for a combination of a tide-excluding barrier on the River Bure and washlands on Haddiscoe Island near the confluence of the Rivers Yare and Waveney, required the views of farmers on the marshes and the recreational navigation interests. In the former case, the washland proposition was welcomed so long as adequate compensation would be paid. But the navigation-recreation panel was not so enamoured of the Bure barrier, with its possible restrictions on navigation, so the calculations of possible closure involving further calibration of the tidal hydrological model had to be reproduced in a variety of ways in order to assuage the sceptics. The fact that such panels and ad-hoc consultative arrangements can be brought into play, where respect is given for a variety of viewpoints and where new scientific information can be incorporated on a sequential and consultative basis, is a key component in this form of partnership.

So partnership, which is essentially a reflection on the limitation of freedom of action of national park committees, can be converted into a strength if handled with care. There is no easy solution here. So much depends on goodwill, on trusting relationships between key players, and upon shifting government and European Community policies and favourable cross-over budgets. But the six principles listed at the outset all help to create both an atmosphere and a mechanism through which purposeful mediation can take place without excessive threat or diminution of respect to any party involved.

The New National Parks Committees

The Edwards report on the future of national parks argued persuasively for new, administratively independent, national park authorities. This is a long overdue requirement. The Broads Authority has many of the administrative arrangements sought by the Edwards Committee, yet even that body is by no means free to act with independence. So if the new-look authorities are to operate successfully, the following points should be part of a complete package.

(i)   **Financing and budget approval.** Right now, the Broads Authority can only obtain its budget via the approval of a majority of local authority members. In practice this means nine votes, because there are eighteen local authority representatives and the Chairman would normally cast a vote in favour of the proposed budget in the event of a tie.

The problem here is familiar to students of local government finance. To raise its element of the Broads Authority's budget, each local authority must levy its council tax payers. If any of these authorities is tax capped, due to over commitment elsewhere, or because of the distortions inherent in the calculation of the local authority support payments from the Treasury via the Department of the Environment, then it is quite likely that the authority in question will instruct its members to vote against the levy. Thus for no reason due to the Broads Authority's programme or performance, a budget request can be cut. For each pound of local authority refund, three pounds of government money is lost because of the 25/75 per cent financing formula for national parks.

In any forthcoming legislation on national park administration, it is almost certain that the Treasury will wish to continue to retain for mischievous purposes the local authority financial stranglehold. The effect on well-meaning and financially rigorous national park authorities can be very serious as the Broads Authority knows to its cost. The solution lies in a straight majority vote on the budget, subject to approval by local authorities of the merits of the performance and objectives for each park authority in the immediate past and for its following year allocation. In short, budgets should be approved on merit, not the quirks of Department of the Environment allocation and standard spending assessments which so hopelessly distort local authority judgements.

(ii) **Collaborative policy and financial partnerships.** The Broads Authority has worked hard to obtain the deals that it has with various statutory and voluntary parties. This is challenging and rewarding, but it is unnecessarily grinding. There should be a positive duty on the part of all statutory agencies and private resource managing bodies to cooperate with the new national park agencies via a general 'furthering' clause of amenity provision and protection. This need not be so strongly worded as to be politically unacceptable. Exhortatory words that lead to cooperation, along the lines of section 8 of the 1986 Water Act, should suffice. But meaningful partnership via genuine policy and programme interpretation is possible given the right legal environment and supportive co-financing arrangements. At present there is insufficient potential to exploit.

(iii) **Enterprise and job creation.** In an area where tens of thousands of talented people are unemployed in national park areas, the time has come to bind the skills and budgets of the employment promotion agencies with the conservation and resource management bodies. At present there is too little liaison between the private sector generally, the Training and Enterprise Councils and the various environmentally minded private sector companies to create jobs in the name of environmental improvement. There was a brief patch of support for this via the manpower service schemes of the early 1980s. Welcome as these were, they provided no continuity for considerably skilled people. The new national park agencies need to take a lead in collaborative ventures for employment creation, skill training in environmental management, and the promotion of jobs that link public and private money to public interest activities. In the Broads case there is a modest investment in a wherry wright, a millwright and in fen management and rights of way maintenance. This could be expanded to a variety of rural skills including thatching, biomass conversion, farm conservation planning, fen management and environmental education training. Other national parks in the uplands would doubtless have other priorities.

For this kind of development to occur there would need to be an injection of cash via employment creation programmes coupled to even wider partnership schemes as outlined in Figure 20.2 but obviously including even more interests. One needs to start slowly, for there could easily be created a bureaucratic nightmare. But the ingredients are in place for such an initiative. It is vital that the new look national park bodies are not too narrowly conceived for a period so very different from the post war context in which they were born.

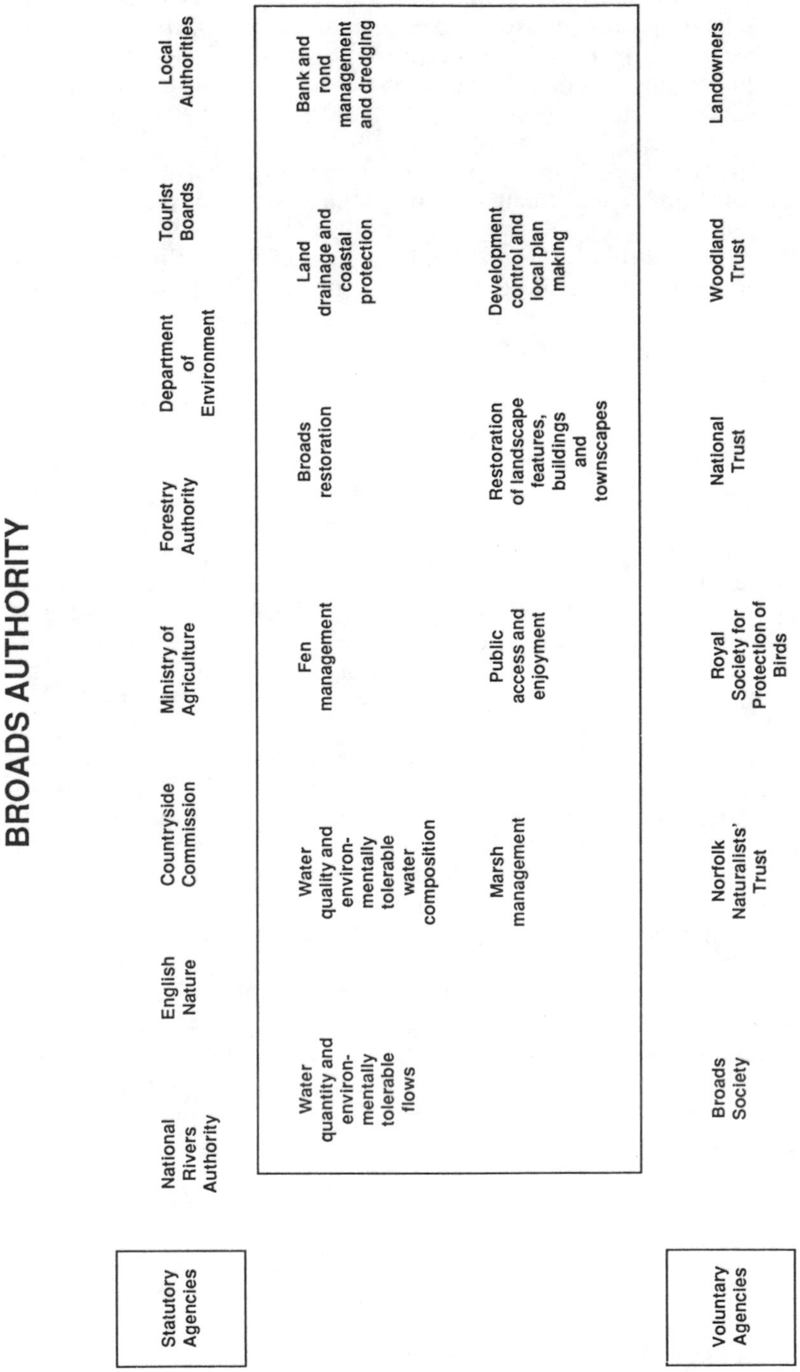

BROADS AUTHORITY

Statutory Agencies	National Rivers Authority	English Nature	Countryside Commission	Ministry of Agriculture	Forestry Authority	Department of Environment	Tourist Boards	Local Authorities
	Water quantity and environmentally tolerable flows		Water quality and environmentally tolerable water composition	Fen management		Broads restoration	Land drainage and coastal protection	Bank and rond management and dredging
			Marsh management	Public access and enjoyment		Restoration of landscape features, buildings and townscapes	Development control and local plan making	

Voluntary Agencies	Broads Society		Norfolk Naturalists' Trust	Royal Society for Protection of Birds	National Trust		Woodland Trust	Landowners

Figure 20.2 Partnership arrangements in the management of the Broads

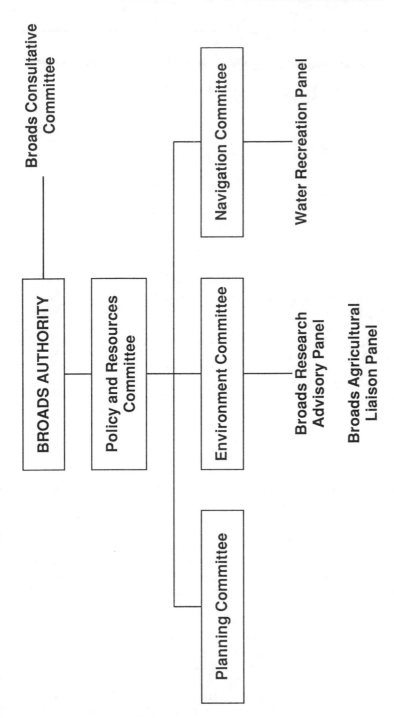

Figure 20.3 Advisory panels and pathways of guidance to the Broads Authority

21

WILDERNESS AND LANDSCAPE IN THE UNITED STATES

MARK BLACKSELL

Wilderness has long been a North American obsession, an integral part of the cultural identity of both the United States and Canada, and a concept that has been exported across the world in the course of the twentieth century. It is, therefore, not surprising to find that strenuous efforts have been made, particularly in the United States, to identify areas of wilderness and to take steps to ensure that they are permanently protected. This chapter seeks to address five issues. What exactly does the term 'wilderness' mean in the context of the United States? Why was there such eagerness to protect it? When was protection instituted? How has the wilderness been managed? What is the future for wilderness in the United States?

Wilderness in the United States

Wilderness is formally recognized in the United States as an official landscape protection category by the 1964 Wilderness Act, and the National Wilderness Preservation System covers some 30,000 square miles spread among more than 300 separate Wilderness Areas in the coterminous United States (see Figure 21.1). The Act defines the concept as follows: 'A wilderness, in contrast with those areas where man and his own works dominate the landscape, is hereby recognized as an area where the earth and its community of life are untrammeled by man, where man himself is a visitor who does not remain' (US Congress, 1964).

In practice the defintion is somewhat idealistic, since even the remotest corners of the American environment have been irrevocably altered by human activity, but it does encapsulate a commitment to setting aside selected tracts of land from the predations of human settlement and economic exploitation so that as far as possible natural processes may prevail.

The designated areas vary enormously in size, from the 520,000 hectares in the middle of the Everglades National Park in Florida to the 2.5 hectares

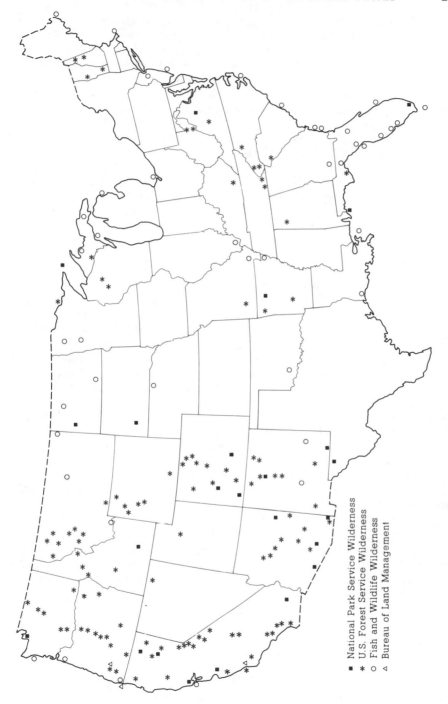

Figure 21.1 National Wilderness Preservation System (*Source*: The Wilderness Society. 1990)

■ National Park Service Wilderness
∗ U.S. Forest Service Wilderness
○ Fish and Wildlife Wilderness
△ Bureau of Land Management

of Pelican Island off the Florida coast. All are on Federally owned public land: 80 per cent of it administered by the Department of Agriculture through the US Forest Service, the rest by the Department of the Interior through the National Parks Service (16 per cent), the Fish and Wildlife Service (4 per cent), and the Bureau of Land Management (0.06 per cent). No attempt has been made formally to extend the concept to private or state-owned land, even though there are many areas of wild land protected by individual states which could qualify for Wilderness Area status. Restricting designations to land owned by such a small number of Federal agencies does have the effect of skewing the national distribution of Wilderness Areas very markedly. Federally owned land is overwhelmingly in the west of the United States (see Fig. 21.2) and, as a result, it is in the west that the bulk of Wilderness Areas are to be found. Nevertheless, the system is a formidable national achievement, covering nearly 1 per cent of the national land area, and its existence is a tribute to the public commitment to the wilderness concept in the United States.

Why was the wilderness protected?

Americans have a long-established fascination with natural scenery on the grand scale. In the nineteenth century, as the scenic wonders of their newly acquired, continental-sized nation were discovered and gradually revealed to the majority of the population living on or near the eastern seaboard, the Western wilderness—the Rockies and the other mountains of the Cordillera—became a symbol of a distinctively American landscape (Nash, 1982). There was deep resentment in the United States at the way the country was routinely dismissed as a second-class Europe, and the monumental landscapes of the West, largely unchanged by agriculture and very sparsely settled by an almost entirely non-European population, were viewed as a ringing riposte. The wilderness was the heart of America.

This was the fundamental reason for the public pressure to protect land-scape, but there were others, which also differentiated Americans from Europeans. The United States was an urban society without any of the deep, feudal, rural roots of Europe. Indeed most of the settlers who flocked in waves across the Atlantic in the course of the nineteenth century were con-sciously escaping from those European traditions. They viewed the land beyond the cities with totally different eyes and the distinctiveness of their visions was compounded by the fact that for the vast majority living in ugly cities on the eastern seaboard or the Mid-West, the land beyond the urban milieu was a remote and romanticized vision, rather than something of which they had first-hand experience. As Lowenthal so perceptively noted: 'Perception of *scenery* is open only to those who have no real part to play in the landscape'. (Lowenthal, 1968, p.72), a judgement that fitted perfectly the reality of the American population at that time.

Specific concern for the future of wilderness grew out of a deep-seated dis-agreement about how best to manage the vast and largely unsettled Federal lands, especially those in the West. The debate crystallized in the middle of

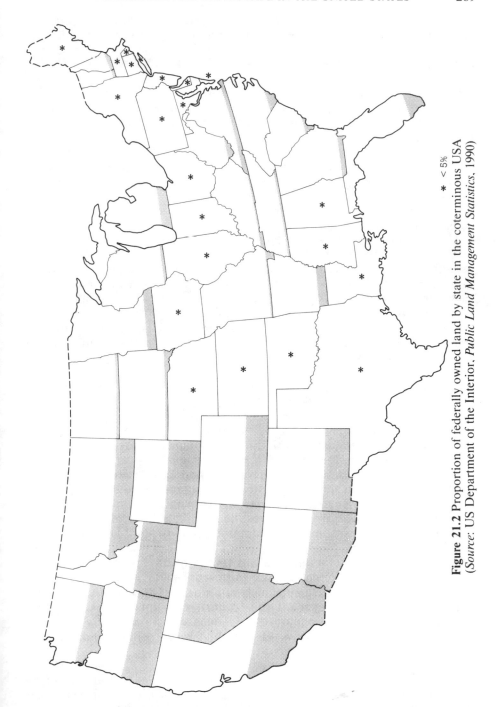

Figure 21.2 Proportion of federally owned land by state in the coterminous USA (*Source*: US Department of the Interior, *Public Land Management Statistics*, 1990)

* < 5%

the nineteenth century around the general consensus about the intrinsic value of the American landscape and the national duty to protect it (Runte, 1979). For the majority the lands of the West were a vast national resource, to be exploited wisely for the benefit of the people of the emergent United States. For them conservation meant sustainable exploitation, or, as Gifford Pinchot, the first Director of the US Forest Service, so memorably and contradictorily put it, 'Resources [land] should be managed for the greatest good of the greatest number for the greatest possible length of time' (quoted in Burton and Kates, 1965).

It did not imply, of course, that there should be no protected areas. National Parks, beginning with Yellowstone in 1872, began to be designated, but the bulk of the Federal lands, especially the huge tracts of the National Forests, were seen primarily as an economic resource. As Leighly observed 'The doctrine of subordination of nature to man has been central to our official conservational policies' (Leighly, 1958, p.317).

The counter-argument was that nature should allowed to dominate on the publicly owned Federal lands because nature was always right and people usually wrong about the impact of their works on the landscape. It was a radical minority view, championed initially by a few dedicated individuals such as John Muir. After the First World War it became more institutionalized, especially in California, with the establishment of societies, such as the Sierra Club and the Save the Redwoods League, dedicated to preserving the wilderness and holding back the tide of human development, no matter how benign and beneficial its proponents might claim it to be.

The debate was further polarized by the way in which the National Parks Service developed after 1916 under the directorship of Stephen Mather. In order to gain political acceptance and resources from the government, he pursued a policy of opening up the National Parks for public recreation, emphasizing their immediate value to the population as a whole, rather than their role in the long-term protection of the landscape. Even if this stance was primarily a front to try and gain political support for National Parks, it also raised worries about the ultimate survival of the wilderness.

A powerful movement began to emerge from within the US Forest Service for the designation of Wilderness Areas as such. It was led initially by Aldo Leopold, who was instrumental in organizing the first wilderness preserve in the Datil (now Gila) National Forest in 1924. He was a remarkable man with a very clear vision of what he was trying to achieve: 'By wilderness I mean a continuous stretch of country preserved in its natural state, open to lawful hunting and fishing, big enough to absorb two weeks' pack trip, and kept devoid of roads, certified trails, cottages or other works of man' (Leopold, 1921, p.719).

In a later paper he further developed the concept, claiming that it was built around two core ideas:

The first idea is that wilderness is a resource, not only in the physical sense of the raw materials it contains, but also in the sense of a distinctive environment which may, if rightly used, yield certain social values. Such a conception ought not to be difficult because we have lately learned to think of other forms of land use in the same way. We no longer think of municipal golf links for instance merely as soil and grass.

The second idea is that the wilderness varies enormously with location. As with other resources, it is impossible to dissociate value from location. There are wilderness areas in Siberia which are probably very similar in character to parts of our Lake states, but their value to us is negligible compared with what the value of a similar area in the Lake states would be, just as the value of a golf links would be negligible if located so as to be out of reach of golfers. [Leopold, 1925, p.398]

The combined effect of these two ideas was to establish clearly that, as far as Leopold was concerned, wilderness was not an absolute concept but one that was dependent on the relationship between the land and people. Wilderness was to be valued not for itself but for the contribution it could make to human society.

This conception of wilderness found a ready audience in the United States, foremost amongst its devotees being Robert Marshall, also a Director of the US Forest Service. He developed further Leopold's ideas, emphasizing the psychological necessity for wilderness in any civilized society. He espoused the prevailing inter-war view that a repressive civilization was responsible for much of the tension and unhappiness so pervasive in modern society. Wilderness offered a sanctuary; its solitude and silence eased the strains and encouraged contemplation. The basic idea was old, but the addition of modern psychology and the deeper understanding generally of the roots of mental health gave it a greater significance (Moore, 1965).

Marshall made two lasting contributions to the cause of preserving the wilderness. In 1935 he was instrumental in founding the Wilderness Society, a national pressure group that has since campaigned tirelessly for the designation and protection of Wilderness Areas. He was also, from his position in the Forest Service, responsible for the second wave of formal wilderness designations.

More than half a century later the argument has moved on and is now not about whether wilderness ought to exist, but what it should exist for (Hendee, et al., 1990). Should wilderness management (arguably itself a contradiction in terms) be basically anthropocentric, remaining true to the ideals of people like Leopold and Marshall, or should it be primarily biocentric and attempt, as far as possible, to exclude all human influence? The argument for the latter course is that unless areas are set aside where nature may evolve unfettered by human interference, then any insurance against the dangers of environmental destruction will be lost. It is a view that has steadily gained favour in the past fifty years, resulting in ever more positive action to define and preserve wilderness in the United States.

When was protection instituted?

Comprehensive, rather than *ad hoc*, protection for wilderness was first introduced by the Forest Service by the L-20 Regulation in 1929. It enabled the definition of so-called 'primitive areas', where development and all economic exploitation would be kept to an absolute minimum so that they would be permanently available for public education and recreation. The areas, a minimum size of 10,000 hectares, were chosen from the results of a 1926 survey by the Forest Service of roadless lands in its holding. Of the seventy-six designated, the largest covered 26,000 square kilometres, more than a number of east-coast states. Experience showed that the L-20 Regulation was insufficiently discriminating and in 1939, under the direction of Robert Marshall, it began to be replaced by the U-1, U-2 and U-3 regulations. U-1 was reserved for wilderness areas, tracts of land covering not less than 2,400 square kilometres; U-2 for wild areas, tracts between 125 and 2,400 square kilometres; and U-3 for roadless areas, which were not subject to any size limitation but were to be managed principally for recreation though maintained as far as possible in their natural state. The new scheme was complicated, costly and cumbersome to implement. Progress was painfully slow and virtually ground to a halt after the United States became embroiled in the Second World War in 1942.

After the war the priorities for wilderness began to change decisively in favour of legal, rather than administrative, protection. The regulations had demonstrated the Forest Service's total control over the designations it chose. They could be changed at will and this was felt to be an insufficient safeguard for such important and fragile habitats. Pressure mounted for a Federal act and, after protracted negotiation over more than a decade, the Wilderness Act went on to the statute book in 1964.

The Act allowed for the possibility of Wilderness Areas being designated on specified Federal land west of the 100°W meridian, which runs roughly from North Dakota south to Texas across the Great Plains. All the lands in the National Forest System, the National Wildlife Refuge and Game Range System, and the National Park System were to be systematically surveyed in order to identify potential Wilderness Areas. Originally it had been intended that the lands managed by the Bureau of Indian Affairs would also be included, but this proposal was abandoned because Congress felt that it might unduly restrict the scope for economic enterprise on the reservations. As a first step in the process, all the fifty-seven areas previously designated by the Forest Service as wilderness, wild or roadless areas were immediately reclassified as Wilderness Areas, and all the other designations were to be reviewed for possible inclusion within ten years. Every roadless area over 125 square kilometres in the National Park System and the National Wildlife Refuge and Game Range System was also to be assessed for possible classification as a Wilderness Areas within ten years, as was every roadless island administered by the Fish and Wildlife Service, no matter what its size.

Classifying Wilderness Areas from such a wide range of different Federal land holdings raised an immediate difficulty, which had to be addressed in the Act itself. Many of the potential locations were already partially settled, or being exploited by mining, grazing or forestry interests. Provision was therefore made for existing uses to continue indefinitely. Indeed, even where mineral prospecting licences had been granted these were not rescinded but allowed to run their full course, or continue until the end of 1983, whichever was the earlier. The compromise illustrates graphically the confusion surrounding the whole concept of wilderness. Substantial areas untouched by human activity simply did not exist in the United States in the second half of the twentieth century; the wilderness everywhere had to be coaxed back to a semblance of its primeval state. That this was recognized so unequivocally is a tribute to the essential pragmatism that accompanied the idealism of those fighting to establish Wilderness Areas in the United States.

There have been two important legislative developments since the 1964 Act came into force. From the outset, there had been widespread disappointment that lands east of the 100°W meridian could not even be considered for classification as Wilderness Areas. However, the argument that they should automatically be excluded, because the landscape of the whole of the eastern United States had been irrevocably altered by man, seemed feeble in view of the way in which the issue of conflicting uses in the west had had to be faced in the Act. Pressure steadily mounted for a change, and in 1975 the Eastern Wilderness Act was passed, enabling Wilderness Areas to be designated in the Appalachians and other parts of the eastern United States. They could still only be on land administered by the three chosen Federal agencies, but it was further recognition that Wilderness Areas are in reality reconstituted landscapes and not an ultimate form of protection for the last vestiges of the primeval. It should also be remembered that because of the very small amounts of Federal public land in the east the number and extent of Wilderness Areas will inevitably be small in comparison with the west. The second important development occurred in 1976 when the Federal Land Policy and Management Act extended the scope to designate Wilderness Areas to land administered by the Bureau of Land Management. The amount of territory in its care is greater than that of any of the three original chosen agencies, but much of it is not of great landscape value, and few Wilderness Areas have been established on Bureau of Land Management land.

How has the wilderness been managed?

In some respects the management of wilderness is a contradiction in terms, but no land exists in isolation and, if wilderness and Wilderness Areas are to be created and survive, then strategies have to be devised and implemented to ensure that the desire for protection is translated into practice. The problems and techniques of Wilderness Area management have received minute and exhaustive study over the years, and it is unnecessary to repeat all those findings here, even if there were space to do so. There are, however, fundamental issues that underpin the practical detail which do merit discussion.

All those involved with Wilderness Area management are constantly faced with the dilemma of how best to sustain the myth of wilderness. Despite the brave words and the sentimentalizing of the American landscape, the concept of pure wilderness has always been an illusion. The environment everywhere is subject to constant natural change; there is not and never has been an equilibrium, so that decisions have always to be made about how to cope with it. Furthermore, there is no way that Wilderness Areas can be isolated from the human world of which they are a part. Air pollution is an example of an intrusive by-product of human society affecting life within Wilderness Areas which it is impossible to exclude. Equally, the processes of change within cannot always be allowed a completely free rein. Vegetation development in much of the western United States is dependent on naturally occurring fire, but fires cannot always be allowed to burn themselves out in Wilderness Areas, not least because it would not be possible to contain them in all circumstances. They have to be controlled, but control can mean that vital regeneration processes are held in check and, therefore, managed fires sometimes have to be started deliberately by those responsible for maintaining the wilderness landscape. Similar arguments also apply to some pests and diseases, which may be natural but the effects of which are too devastating in the long term to be contemplated. Management decisions of this kind are a fact of life and they expose the anthropocentric-biocentric dichotomy, referred to above, for the falsehood that it is. Isolation from human society is never an option; controlled management within its framework is the only way forward.

The symbiosis between recreation and wilderness in the United States is complex. Quite understandably, a growing and uniquely mobile society is curious to find out about the Wilderness Areas that have been established on public land on their behalf. Indeed, as we have seen, those who dreamt up the very concept did so for the benefit of people and their needs, believing that access to wilderness would have a beneficial effect on their psyche. However, as those seeking to satisfy their appetites for recreation have flocked to Wilderness Areas in ever larger numbers, it has become imperative that formal management strategies be devised and implemented. In many cases, access is now restricted through a system of permits and visitor facilities, such as footpaths, campgrounds and information centres, have been constructed. Inevitably, such infrastructure requires staff to run and police it, so that the most popular Wilderness Areas now have their own rangers from the Forest Service or the National Parks Service as the case may be. In practice such developments have much to recommend them in addition to the immediate management of visitors. It is well known that people on holiday are easily influenced by the information and facilities provided for them, and this is true in Wilderness Areas just as much as anywhere else. If campgrounds, car parks, footpaths and the like are available, most people will use them, avoiding areas where there are no facilities. On public land, therefore, where the authorities have absolute discretion over land use, the recreation infrastructure becomes a potent tool for land management in its own right. Visitors can be guided away from areas by the simple expedient of not providing facilities and information; equally, areas in danger of over-use can be given respite by limiting access and removing facilities and information.

Finally, those with responsibility for Wilderness Areas are faced with a chronic dilemma. Superficially, the wilderness ideal is clear and unequivocal, rooted in a belief that in these areas natural processes should be allowed to take their course and nature should reign supreme. As we have seen, the whole concept is fundamentally flawed, but in addition it has been necessary to make accommodations with other land uses in many Wilderness Areas to allow them to be set up in the first place. Indeed, their continuation is enshrined in the 1964 Wilderness Act itself. The aim, of course, is to try and ensure that mining, grazing, forestry, and the like are gradually run-down and eliminated, but in the meantime Wilderness Areas have had to be developed with such non-conforming uses an integral part of their fabric and landscape.

The future for wilderness in the United States

No nation has made a greater public commitment to wilderness than the United States. The concept is firmly rooted in its cultural heritage and, through the National Wilderness Preservation System, it has been translated into a tangible reality across the continent: 'Wilderness has become a symbol imbedded in our national consciousness—a nostalgia for lost opportunity' (McCloskey, 1966, p.293).

Yet the wilderness is under threat and not only from those casting greedy eyes on its economic potential. The twentieth century has seen more and more citizens in the United States alienated from such romantic and fundamentally elitist views of the value of the natural world, and their opposition could undermine the apparently secure position of wilderness and Wilderness Areas. The counter-argument has been forcefully expressed by Peter Marcuse:

The conservation movement is in danger of becoming a politically and socially reactionary movement, anti-urban in its general orientation, anti-black, anti-minority, and anti-poor in its actual practice. It is dedicated to a mystic philosophy which has the net effect of trying to preserve a corner of the world for the exclusive preserve of a white upper-middle class for their play and recreation, insulated from the pressures and needs of the majority of people of the real world, all with just enough attention paid to the more vulgar recreation needs of the lower-middle class and skilled working class to avoid their opposition to the programme, and perhaps even enlist their support for it. [Marcuse, 1971, p.20]

Such a polemical judgement may overstate the threat of a widespread withdrawal of public support for preserving the American wilderness, but it does graphically describe why such a withdrawal of support might occur. Just as the idea of the wilderness itself as an eternal, unchanging verity is ultimately an ecological nonsense, so support for the preservation of wilderness must never be taken for granted. The wilderness must continually be reinterpreted and restated by each generation in its own terms if it is to survive.

References

Burton, I., Kates, R. W., 1965, *Readings in Resource Management*, Chicago, University of Chicago Press.

Hendee, J., Stankey, G. H. and Lucas, R. C., 1990, *Wilderness Management*, 2nd ed., Boulder, Colorado, Fulcrum.

Leighley, J., 1958, 'John Muir's image of the West', *Annals of the Association of American Geographers*, **48**: 309–18.

Leopold, A., 1921, 'The Wilderness and its place for forest recreational policies', *Journal of Forestry*, XIX: 718–21.

Leopold, A., 1925, 'Wilderness as a form of land use', *Journal of Land and Public Utility Economics*, **1**: 398–404.

Lowenthal, D., 1968, 'The American scene', *Geographical Review*, **58**: 61–88.

Marcuse, P., 1971, 'Is the National Parks movement anti-urban?' *Parks and Recreation*, **6**: 17–49.

McCloskey, M., 1966, 'The Wilderness Act of 1964: its background and meaning', *Oregon Law Review*, **45**: 288–321.

Moore, C., 1965, *The Wilderness Preservation Movement 1920 to 1964*, MA thesis, Frenso State College.

Nash, R., 1982, *Wilderness and the American Mind* New Haven, Yale University Press.

Runte, A., 1979, *National Parks: the American Experience* Lincoln, Nebraska, University of Nebraska Press.

US Congress, 1964, *An Act to Establish a Wilderness Preservation System*, Public Law 577, 88th Congress, 2nd session.

PART VII
LEISURE AND THE GLOBAL ENVIRONMENT

22

ADVENTURE TOURISM IN REMOTE PLACES

JEAN TALLANTIRE

To travel hopefully is a better thing than to arrive, and the true success is to labour

The line from Robert Louis Stevenson's 'El Dorado' gives expression to the spirit of adventure activities in remote places of the world. Remote places, in the context of this chapter, refer to wilderness areas where the lack of arable land discourages development and the inhospitable terrain sustains only a sparse population. They are typified in mountain, jungle, tundra and desert regions and have, until recent years, remained relatively isolated. Modern technology now provides greater ease of travel which, coupled with increasingly sophisticated equipment and clothing, facilitates access more rapidly and in comparative comfort where it was previously denied. These factors, together with the challenge and appeal of remote and relatively untouched places, have encouraged an escalation of interest in adventure tourism from the early 1970s onwards. Adventure tourism is symbolic of holidays with a difference. A sense of pioneering and physical effort is required to experience new environments through the challenge of activities like mountaineering, trekking, canoeing or rafting, usually living in tents or basic accommodation for most of the stay.

This chapter explores the background to this growth through the development of tourism generally and its relationship to the emergence of mass adventure tourism. Impacts on the environment, people and economy of remote areas are examined through three case studies in the Himalaya. The lessons from the case studies are used to suggest measures by which future impact on remote areas throughout the world might be minimized.

The growth of tourism

The idea of travel is far from new. Journeys have always been an essential part of life. The reasons are almost as varied as the individuals who undertake them and the motives for travel have become more sophisticated with the passage of time. In the earliest days, journeys were made of necessity and the traveller was inevitably confronted by challenge in the quest for food, shelter and protection and later for trade, exploration and discovery. In modern times, with the advent of tourism, journeys are frequently taken for pleasure and perceived as an adventure where challenge is sought as an essential element of the experience.

The metamorphosis from travel to mass tourism is a relatively recent phenomenon. The process began in the mid-nineteenth century, when Thomas Cook conceived the idea of acting as an agent in the organization of excursions for large groups of people at an affordable price, with arrangements for details such as tickets and accommodation being undertaken on their behalf. His first railway excursion in 1841 for 570 passengers from Leicester to a temperance demonstration at Loughborough is now legendary. With his first tour to the Continent in 1856, international tourism, as we understand it today, was born.

The next significant development occurred between the two World Wars when holidays with pay extended the availability of tourism in developed countries beyond the privileged few to all those with the disposable income to afford it. Annual bookings for holidays abroad, through the Workers' Travel Association in Britain, grew from 700 in 1922 to nearly 24,000 in 1937, with the 'all in' tour and conducted party travel being the most popular (Lickorish and Kershaw, 1975, p.24). Although the First and Second World Wars punctuated the development of the industry, the post-war years saw a rapid revival, with recovery to pre-war rates of growth being achieved in no longer than five years in each case. Since that time, international tourism has steadily increased.

Research into the factors affecting tourism growth is still developing, but, apart from fluctuations caused by conflicts and disasters, pervasive influences include income levels and education, together with distances between the permanent base and the trip destination. However, the single most important influence has undoubtedly been the jet aircraft, which combines shorter journey times with greatly increased carrying capacity.

The definition of a tourist used here is that of the World Tourism Organization which holds that a tourist is a temporary visitor, staying in a country for at least twenty-four hours for one of a range of reasons listed as leisure (recreation, holiday, health, study, religion, sport), business, family, conference or mission.

International tourism has grown remarkably since the early 1950s, with the most rapid expansion in the mid-1960s, averaging 8.7 per cent for the decade (see Table 22.1), followed by a slower 6 per cent for the 1970s. Growth rates suffered in the early 1980s because of economic recession, with a sharp recovery in 1984, only to fall again following the Libyan bombing incident and the nuclear disaster in Chernobyl. The end of the decade saw a revival followed by a further downturn as a result of the Gulf War. In spite of this rollercoaster effect, the growth rate for the decade achieved an average of 4.6 per cent, with almost 450 million tourists on the move world-wide during 1990 (Cooper and Latham, 1992, p.38). In 1991 the World Travel and Tourism Council stated that travel and tourism is the world's largest industry

Table 22.1   Growth trends in international tourism by arrivals world-wide. 1950–90

	Arrivals ('000s)	Average annual change (%)
1950–60	25,282	+10.6
1960–70	69,296	+ 8.7
1970–80	159,690	+ 6.0
1980–90	284,841	+ 4.6
1981	288,848	+ 1.4
1982	286,780	− 0.7
1983	284,173	− 0.9
1984	312,434	+ 9.9
1985	321,240	+ 2.8
1986	330,746	+ 2.9
1987	356,640	+ 7.8
1988	381,824	+ 7.0
1989	415,376	+ 8.8
1990	443,477	+ 6.8
1991	450,000 (E)	+ 1.5 (E)

Notes: (E) Estimate
The average % increase is calculated as the constant annual % increase which would result in the overall change over the specified period

Source: World Tourism Organization. *Travel and Tourism Barometer*. December 1991

and the major contributor to global economic development. One in fifteen employees—112 million people worldwide—is involved in this sector.

The growth of adventure tourism

Separate figures on the growth of adventure tourism have not been recorded, but opportunities have been available in Britain since the mid-1930s, although these were usually at domestic locations and for single activities. The mass market for international adventure tours from Britain began to flourish in the early 1970s with the emergence of specialist tour operators. The percentage market share of world tourism taken up by adventure-related trips today is difficult to assess. However, informal enquiries with a selection of the longer-established adventure tour operators suggest that an estimate of 2 per cent, or approximately eight million people annually, is not unreasonable.

In the absence of records relating specifically to the adventure tourism market, this subjective assessment can only serve as a general indication of the rapid growth of this sector. A recent issue of one outdoor magazine alone revealed no fewer than thirty-five firms specializing in adventure trips, advertising tours to remote areas of the world including the Himalaya, the Polar regions, the African interior and the jungles of South America. Although independent travel is increasingly popular, most people begin foreign holiday excursions from the security of professionally arranged packages. Many adventure tourists also follow this pattern. If we accept the link between tourism growth and ease of opportunity the trends for international tourism given in Table 22.1 serve as a broad indicator of expansion in the adventure sector, as a percentage of the general market, especially for the future.

Economic and environmental impact

Of all the factors influencing tourism growth, income level is the strongest. The richer countries generate the greatest foreign-travel expenditure. Adventure tourism is often directed towards remote areas of the world and frequently to Third World countries where economic and environmental impacts can be substantial. Paradoxically, resources to develop the infrastructure to sustain the influx of tourists from developed countries to the Third World are often inadequate, although the financial benefit which increased tourism brings to weak economies is considerable and usually energetically courted for that reason.

Balancing economic and ecological needs, so that the benefits from tourism can be translated into a sound basis for growth, is a slow and complex affair. Yet, it is interesting to note that both 'economic' and 'ecological' are derived from the Greek 'oikos' meaning house. It is the balance between economics, or the management of the house, and ecology, or the management of the life forms within it, which must be accurately struck if both are to remain healthy and survive. If tourism is allowed to develop too rapidly, with inadequate or ineffective planning and management, the consequences for fragile ecosystems in wilderness areas, hardly visited just twenty-five years ago, are likely to be serious.

Cultural impact

The erstwhile isolation of remote areas protected them from external influence and allowed the gradual evolution of ancient cultures from time immemorial. These cultures are often little understood by outsiders, and the effect of growing numbers of tourists on sparse populations of mainly illiterate subsistence farmers can be devastating.

Remote communities depend on each other for survival, requiring mutual support and trust. Unfortunately, in numerous instances this has been exploited by visitors from developed countries, and indigenous culture and mores have suffered as a result: for example from the theft of religious and cultural objects as souvenirs from monasteries and temples, from lack of recognition that payment of inflated rates for food and accommodation unbalances local economies and encourages greed. Misplaced generosity in bestowing gifts of money, sweets and pens on children has encouraged begging and unwittingly undermined the natural dignity of indigenous people.

There is also a lack of recognition by some that scant attire, which might be acceptable in a Western environment, can be shocking and often insulting in other cultures.

Virtually the only impression of Western culture which remote communities have is that given by visitors. Books, television and other means of communication and awareness, so familiar in the West, are not available. Good host/tourist relationships are important for economic, social and cultural reasons and are enhanced through mutual respect based on understanding and appropriate behaviour.

The Himalaya

The Himalayan region has been subjected to rapidly increasing numbers of visitors, particularly over the last two decades, from both domestic and foreign markets. The effect which this can have on the economy, the environment and the people of remote areas is shown through three selected case studies.

The great wall of the Himalaya straddles six countries from Afghanistan in the north west, through Pakistan, India, China and Nepal to Bhutan and Assam in the south east for a distance of 1,700 miles (2,800 kilometres). The collective title of the Himalaya consists of three major ranges—the bleak Hindu Kush in the far west beyond the reach of the monsoon, the Karakoram Range in northern Kashmir, and the vast extent of the eastern Himalaya which includes the lofty peaks of Everest and Kanchenjunga (see Fig. 22.1), both over 28,000 feet (8,500 metres). The Himalayan chain is approximately 155 miles (250 kilometres) to 250 miles (400 kilometres) wide, and roughly five vertical miles high (eight kilometres). The mountain ranges are interspersed with deep ravines and beautiful valleys cut by fast-flowing rivers carrying snow melt to the plains. They feature a range of climatic belts from the deserts of the north west to the tropical rain forests in Assam in the east and from the high Asian plateau to the low-lying Indian plains. They are rich in wildlife, with a wide variety of rare species of animals, birds and plants, including snow leopard, blue sheep, Ladakhi lynx, lammergeyer and Himalayan blue poppy.

Their geological history is relatively recent, as the Himalayan region rose from the sea bed only sixty-five million years ago. They are, therefore, the youngest mountains in the world as well as the highest. By definition, they are one of the world's wild places, lacking the comforts and conveniences of Western civilization. They offer some of the most varied and dramatic scenery in the world, with considerable challenge for a range of adventurous activities, especially mountaineering. In the Himalaya generally, however, trekking is the most popular tourist activity of all. In 1966, 11,361 visitors were recorded at the police check posts. In 1978, the number had increased to 26,089 and by 1985 the registers showed 180,989 (Shresthra, 1987, p.44). The increasing popularity of the most favoured tourist areas, together with the region's rapid population growth, is posing a real threat to the very qualities for which it is valued.

Such has been the concern that special projects have been undertaken in

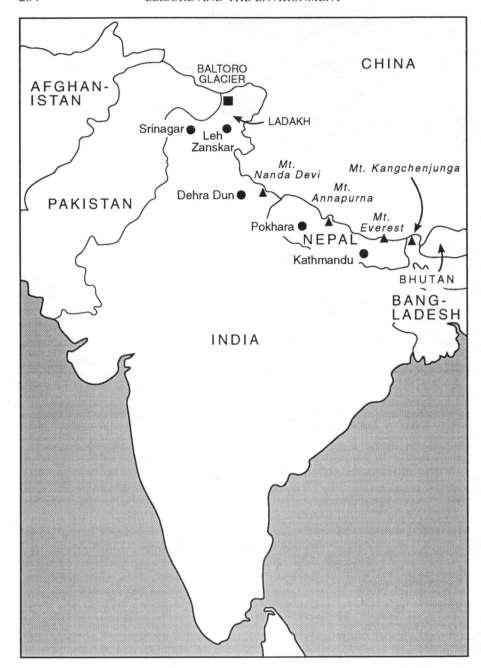

Figure 22.1 The Himalayan Region

some Himalayan regions to combat the destructive elements of adventure tourism and to redress the balance between the economic needs of the communities and the ecological and environmental quality of the areas visited. This is illustrated through two case studies of Nanda Devi National Park in northern India and the Annapurna region in Nepal (See Figure 22.1).

The ancient kingdoms of Ladakh and Zanskar (Figure 22.1) in the northern-most Indian state of Jammu and Kashmir provide a contrast. They have been selected as the third case study as they have not yet suffered a tourist invasion to the same extent, although their popularity is increasing. The vol-atile political situation has so far kept numbers of visitors in check and little has changed in this respect since the author visited the region in 1988.

Nanda Devi National Park

The Nanda Devi area is 330 miles (530 kilometres) north east of the Indian capital of Delhi. It is also evocatively called the 'Valley of the Lost Horizon' and is rich in animal, bird and plant life. As with many Himalayan regions, it is only accessible for four months of the year, July to October. The rest of the time it remains snowbound. The main peak of Nanda Devi is 25,645 feet (7,817 metres) high and regarded by many as the pearl of the Himalaya. When Bill Tilman and N.E. Odell completed the first successful ascent in 1936, Tilman expressed a feeling of remorse at the fall of a giant. His senti-ments were to prove prophetic.

Nanda Devi opened to tourist traffic in 1974. Over the next twelve years the numbers of mountaineers, trekkers, naturalists, ornithologists, botanists, geologists and researchers visiting the area increased a thousandfold, in spite of the fact that it takes at least ten days on foot to reach the base camp at the inner sanctuary from the last villages of Rini and Lata which connect it with the outside world. Between 1934, when Bill Tilman and Eric Shipton first visited the area, and 1982, thirty-one expeditions from all over the world have been to climb the Nanda Devi east and west peaks alone. Many more have climbed several of the seventy-odd other peaks, all approximately 20,000 feet (6,000 metres) or more which surround the Nanda Devi valley. G. Kumar, a research associate at the Wadia Institute of Himalayan Geology in Dehra Dun, reported that during a single year in 1982, twenty-two expeditions involving more than 209 mountaineers, 1,050 porters and 2,500 goats and sheep to carry baggage visited the area. Of these expeditions, two were Australian, one Indo-Australian and nineteen Indian. Such groups normally stay in the area between twenty and sixty days (Kumar, 1987, pp. 122-3).

The route to the base camp in the inner sanctuary of Nanda Devi is con-sidered one of the most fascinating treks in the world, and trekking expedi-tions, also accompanied by the required porters, sheep and goats, were a fur-ther threat to the natural environment. The results of this massive intrusion are manifold; only those of greatest impact can be mentioned here.

The first is overgrazing by the large number of pack animals supporting expeditions, resulting in replacement of the more fragile native vegetation by robust varieties palatable neither to the pack animals nor the indigenous wildlife, thereby reducing the territory for native wild animals. Second, porters accompanying expeditions to Nanda Devi were often not supplied with fuel for cooking or tents for shelter, resulting in large-scale felling of trees for the purpose alongside trek routes and at campsites. Even when fuel was provided, it was alien to traditional methods of cooking, and so the porters built wood fires anyway. Forest thinning eroded the top soil, disturbing plant life and creating unstable conditions. Third, accumulation of litter and garbage became a major problem, exacerbated by huge amounts of unused equipment and goods dumped by departing mountaineering expeditions. Medicines left behind entered the water system, polluting rivers at source and harming wild animals.

In India, one of the measures introduced to combat the detrimental effects of large invasions of visitors into sensitive locations is to create protected areas, which include 450 national parks. Although most national parks are aggressively promoted, admittance to others and the activities permitted in them are strictly controlled. In 1983, the Nanda Devi sanctuary closed for five years to allow time for recovery. It has been declared a protected area, with a number of measures advocated to prevent a return to the earlier degradation, including educational programmes, environmental awareness training and regular scientific monitoring together with guidelines for, and stricter controls on, the activities and behaviour of visitors.

In 1992, however, Nanda Devi remains closed, although the reasons are not entirely clear. The region has been recommended for consideration as one of twelve biosphere reserves being proposed for India. It is not clear what the significance of this will be for future access, but it seems likely that, even if complete prohibition does not continue, any measures which might be introduced to control numbers of visitors will be even more strictly enforced. The natural terrain is one of steep, broken boulder and scree, very susceptible to avalanche. The question must be asked whether, in areas subject to such high levels of natural erosion, access for any more than a limited number of groups each year can, or should, ever be sustained.

The Annapurna Conservation Area Project

Nepal was opened to Westerners in 1950. It is famed as the birthplace of Gautama Buddha and provides the main point of access to Mt. Everest, the world's highest peak, at 29,028 feet (8,848 metres). It is the world's fourth poorest country, covering an area of 56,140 square miles (145,391 square kilometres) and housing a population of 16.1 million, mainly subsistence farmers. Chandra Gurung, Director of the Annapurna Conservation Area Project, in an address to a conference organized by the British group Tourism Concern in January 1991, reported that tourism was the only hard currency earner in Nepal and was vigorously promoted for that reason, resulting in a rate of increase of more than 17 per cent per annum. Numbers are expected to double in the next decade to almost half a million visitors per annum. While tourism brings welcome income into the country, 93 per cent of it goes on imported goods and services, either from the tourists' home countries or to benefit large towns like Kathmandu and Pokhara (see Figure 22.1). Only 7 per cent goes to the villages through which the mountaineering and trekking expeditions pass and upon which they have so marked on impact.

Annapurna is one of the world's largest mountain massifs, with a main peak of 26,503 feet (8,078 metres). In 1990, more than 36,000 tourists visited the region, mainly bringing porters from outside the area and thereby bringing little benefit to local people. In total 72,000 extra people had to be fed, heated and housed in a desperately poor region accustomed to supporting only half that number.

Predictably, the problems of erosion, forest clearance, denudation of natural vegetation, river pollution and mounting litter seen in the Nanda Devi area in India were repeated here. Traditionally, 93 per cent of Nepal's energy comes from wood and, with the growth of tourism, 15 per cent of the forests disappeared in only five years. Clearance continues at a rate of 3 per cent, or an estimated 988,386 acres (400,000 hectares) per annum, mainly to provide fuel to cook food and heat water for tourists. Each acre cleared loses 30–75 tons of soil annually, resulting in huge landslides and flooding which devastate the land and rob local communities of their means of livelihood.

Nepal, as well as India, has adopted the western concept of designation as a means of protecting areas of landscape value. Eleven national parks are already in place. However, they are controlled by a central administration, which imposes on the local communities regulations favouring ecological protection which are not predisposed towards the needs of indigenous people. As a result the parks have become virtually inaccessible to them as they are prevented from either gathering wood or using the area for livestock fodder and thus, their traditional means of support has been removed, creating resentment.

Local Nepalese experts have rejected this approach in the Annapurna region in favour of holistic development. In 1986, they set up a non-governmental organization, the Annapurna Conservation Area Project, supported by the King Mahendra Trust for Nature Conservation. The main aims are sustainability, education and participation. Tourism and economic stability for local communities are seen as integral parts of the project, and local inhabitants are involved throughout. Since its inception, every tourist entering the Annapurna region has paid the equivalent of US$7 which, multiplied by more than 36,000 tourists visiting each year, is now providing a healthy endowment fund, the investment income from which is used to set up other projects.

There are now forest management committees, and tree nurseries have been developed on slopes cleared by earlier felling. The project's conservation education programme ensures that education and advice are given to local communities through school and literacy programmes, study tours, training programmes and campaigns on matters such as the use of alternative energy sources. Advice is available on agro-forestry, health and the maintenance of clean water supplies. There are community development projects for bridge and trail repair and courses in lodge management.

Villagers are helped to understand the need for alternative sources of energy to traditional wood burning as a means of conserving the forest and protecting their future. Financial help is given towards equipment such as kerosene stoves, solar cookers and ducted water heating linked to cooking fires. However, a proportion of the cost must be paid by the villagers themselves who must also accept responsibility for maintenance. The British based charity, Intermediate Technology Development Group, established by the economist and author of *Small is Beautiful*, E.F. Schumacher, responded to an approach for advice on the installation of the first microhydro system to generate electricity for several small communities and a tourist lodge. These small systems can function in severe temperatures, with fewer siltation problems than conventional schemes. They greatly reduce the need for tree felling and more schemes are planned.

In addition to helping local communities, there is also a wealth of advice and information available for tourists and tour operators. The scheme is progressing well and won the British 1991 'Tourism for Tomorrow' Award sponsored through the Thames Television holiday programme 'Wish you Were Here'. The principles are capable of replication elsewhere in the world. The key to success is through better education for, and involvement of, local people, so that they understand the issues, see themselves as architects of their own future and feel motivated to take control of it. The project requires considerable cooperation from all concerned to succeed well. Motivating distant bureaucrats in central government to understand and react appropriately to local problems is the greatest difficulty.

Ladakh and Zanskar

The high desert plateaux of Ladakh and Zanskar in the northernmost state of Jammu and Kashmir in India have been open to travellers since 1974. The area covers just under 38,600 square miles (100,000 square kilometres) and accommodates a population of 100,000 people, about 55 per cent of whom are Buddhists, made up of sedentary subsistence farmers and nomadic shepherds. The population has been stable for centuries due to the altitude, which ranges from 10,000 to 16,500 feet (3,000–5,000 metres), with the highest peaks rising over 23,100 feet (7,000 metres). The high passes which enclose the region put it beyond the reach of the monsoon, and the climate is very dry, with extremes of temperature ranging from −30 C in winter to +33 C in summer. The area is isolated from the outside world for nine months of the year, when snow blocks the high passes. Vegetation is sparse and, in the short summer months, communities grow only enough produce for their needs, close to watercourses and oases fed from the glacial waters above.

The traverse of Ladakh and Zanskar from the roadhead at Darcha to the famous monastery of Lamayuru on the Leh–Srinagar military road is considered one of the great long-distance treks of the world. The environmental fragility of this high, remote region and its primitive communities has been protected in the past by the physical difficulties of access. The political sensitivity of the area, bordering Pakistan and China, has also served to inhibit the growth of tourism to some extent, although tourism along the trekking routes was increasing in the mid-1980s until tempered by the most recent disturbances throughout Jammu and Kashmir. These constraints have provided some protection from the effects of tourism, except in the more accessible areas such as the Markha Valley, and created the opportunity to evaluate the economic and ecological future, using experiences from elsewhere.

When the author undertook the journey from Darcha to Lamayuru in 1988, the early signs of some of the adverse effects of tourism were observed. The semi-desert and alpine steppe vegetation, which is extremely vulnerable to overgrazing, provides fodder for the caravans of horses and mules which accompany the trekking groups. Opposition from local communities to grazing by pack animals was growing, and permission occasionally refused, because of the threat to their own slender survival. The loss of natural dignity by women and children begging for sugar and sweets was sad testimony to the misplaced generosity of earlier expeditions. Although there was some evidence of litter and garbage left by careless and inconsiderate travellers, it had not reached significant proportions on that route. However, in such a desert region this particular tourist phenomenon is a greater problem than at lower altitudes in moister conditions, as the high, dry atmosphere preserves material considerably longer than elsewhere, and the capacity for environmental degradation is thereby increased.

The need to establish controlled development based on the involvement and education of local communities was recognized at an early stage. A special project has been established, founded by a Swedish linguist, Helena Norberg-Hodge, a Scholar-in-Residence in the inaugural year of Schumacher College in Devon, England, who first visited Ladakh in 1975, just after the region had been opened up to tourism. The Ladakh Project is based in the capital of Leh (see Figure 22.1) and has two main aims. The first is to enable Ladakhi people to view Western values more realistically and to see their own culture in a more positive light. The second is to provide support for ecologically sustainable development within Ladakh itself. The project provides funding, advice and information. It is complemented by an indigenous organization, the Ecological Development Group, which works alongside it on day-to-day implementation of its principles. The extent and nature of the impact which tourism has on local ecosystems is studied, together with methods by which it might be sustained. The Group's work is now widely recognized, having won the prestigious Right Livelihood Award in 1986 (an Award established in Sweden in 1980 to promote the work of small grass roots agencies concerned with the environment, human rights and applied research), and the Danish Award for Sustainable and Participatory Development in 1989.

The regional boundaries with Pakistan and China are the subject of continuing territorial dispute. Recent troubles in Ladakh which, unlike other areas of Jammu and Kashmir, is seeking independence from Srinagar and union status with Delhi (Osmaston, 1990, pp.16–21), will continue to constrain tourism development for some time. Although trekkers continue to visit the area, numbers remain stable for the time being. There are similarities between the objectives and methods of the Ladakh and the Annapurna Conservation Area Projects. It is encouraging to note that the Ladakh Group has already undertaken programmes in Bhutan and other parts of India. Ladakh and Zanskar still have time on their side, and it is important for the long-term welfare of this remote and high-mountain desert and its communities that the lessons of less fortunate areas are turned to good effect here.

The future

Remote regions today, like Ladakh and Zanskar and many others worldwide, will no longer be remote tomorrow. The world's wild places are a source of pleasure, discovery and learning and, with proper planning and management, there is no reason why they should not continue to be so. Any development should be pitched at achieving a sensitive balance between the needs of the environment and the needs of the communities who live there. Clear lessons may be drawn from the experience of Nanda Devi, Annapurna and similar areas which are set out below and which should be considered in other remote places.

Research to gain more knowledge about the impact of tourism on different types of wilderness and their indigenous communities should be encouraged and findings widely disseminated. The knowledge thus gained would provide a sound basis for balancing tourist demand with the environmental and cultural ability of an area to sustain it. This would appropriately influence plans for development and the management structures to uphold them.

Planning to conserve the ecosystem is essential from the beginning, and the full involvement of local communities is crucial to its success. A development plan would assist coordination and the establishment of an adequate infrastructure to accommodate, feed and control large numbers of visitors with minimal threat to the natural environment. However, developments should put the needs of the local communities first and form part of an integrated plan within the context of the surrounding environment and neighbouring communities. If new roads are needed, the terrain should be surveyed by people knowledgeable about the geology of the area. Inaccurate and uninformed surveys have often resulted in new roads causing serious landslides.

Management structures to control and monitor visitor pressure at the earliest stage would help to avoid critical situations. Regular and systematic monitoring for changes in the ecosystem should be built in. Such measures may involve the sale of permits to control the number of visitors to an over-popular area, as is already the case for climbing Himalayan mountains above 18,000 feet (5,500 metres) and on some trekking routes. Entry charges may have to be levied to provide support for development and maintenance of the infrastructure, alongside education and management training for local people. Small countries can strictly control the number of visitors entering annually. The Himalayan kingdom of Bhutan was opened to tourists in 1974, the same year as Nanda Devi, but has a very different story to tell. Only 2,000 visitors per year have been admitted, although in late 1991 the Bhutan National Tourist Corporation was considering plans to increase this gradually to 6,000. All visitors are subject to a strict code of conduct.

Tipping and the distribution of sweets and pens to children are prohibited. Monasteries are closed to foreigners as past visitors refused to accede to requests not to take photographs. The policy is successful in pursuing Bhutan's aim, expressed by the King, of pursuing Gross National Happiness rather than Gross National Product (Elkington and Hailes, 1992, pp. 212–13).

Education, information and awareness for local people, visitors and tour operators is vital if the social structure and culture of host countries and communities are to be respected and maintained alongside the quality of experience for the visitor. Recognition of the importance of this, alongside measures to implement effective procedures to bring it about, will achieve a great deal. Excellent codes of practice already exist such as the Himalayan Tourist Code, produced by the voluntary British group, Tourism Concern, and the Minimum Impact Code, a series of conservation tips for trekkers to the Annapurna region. Widespread cooperation in disseminating these and other guidance, for example in travel brochures, would do much to educate and inform on a broad front.

International cooperation is the key to the effective control and management of the environmental and cultural impact of adventure tourism. Important conferences are taking place at international level in an attempt to illuminate the way forward, and the number of voluntary organizations which deal exclusively with the subject is growing throughout the world.

There are other unusual but effective ideas such as litter collection holidays to the Everest region and ecological survey holidays organized by groups like Earthwatch. Growing awareness among visitors is being turned to good effect in other ways too. For example, in 1992 a group of mountaineers from Britain, on an expedition to the Baltoro Glacier (Fig. 22.1) in the Karakoram Range, one of the longest glaciers in the world outside the Polar regions, took with them a micro-hydro system on behalf of sponsors to provide electricity for the local community.

All these ideas are encouraging and will help to cushion the impact of adventure tourism in remote places and enrich international understanding. The real need now is for a world-wide exchange of ideas at all major gatherings like the 1992 UN Conference on Environment and Development in Rio de Janeiro. Then might follow recognition of common problems, greater international cooperation and more effective planning and management. The developed countries, which generate the demand for adventure tourism, need to provide tangible support to those best able to implement it but at present unable to provide it for themselves. Only then will there be a chance for the healthy survival of the world's wild places which are so attractive for the adventure tourist. These unique environments must not be placed under threat from increasing ease of access and the natural appeal and challenge which they hold as adventurous leisure resources.

References

Cooper, C. and Latham, J., 1992, 'The tourism decade: a comment on global trends in tourism in the 80s', *Leisure Management*, February: 38–40.

Elkington, J., and Hailes, J., 1992, *Holidays that Don't Cost the Earth*, London, Victor Gollancz Ltd.

Kumar, G., 1987, *A Case Study of Nanda Devi National Park*, selected paper from international seminar on impact of tourism on mountain environment, Uttar Pradesh, India, Research India Publications.

Lickorish, J.L. and Kershaw, A.G., 1975, 'Tourism between 1840–1940', in A.J. Burkart and S. Medlik (eds), The Management of Tourism, London, Heinemann.

Osmaston, H., 1990, 'The Kashmir problem', *Geographical Magazine*, June: 16–21.

Shresthra, T.K., 1987, *Impact of tourism on the Himalayan ecosystem of Nepal*, selected paper from international seminar on impact of tourism on mountain environment: Uttar Pradesh, India, Research India Publications.

23

TOURISM IN A WARMER WORLD

GEOFFREY WALL

This chapter is concerned with the influence of climate upon tourism, in particular the possible implications of global climate change. It will be suggested that changes in global climate may have far-reaching consequences for many current tourist destinations and for places contemplating involvement in tourism. However, the topic has received little attention from researchers or representatives of the tourism industry.

Following a brief review of the greenhouse effect and the science of global climate change, the status of research on climate change and tourism is established through an international survey of climate and tourism organizations. Possible implications of climate change for global patterns of tourism are assessed and selected case studies presented.

The greenhouse effect

Increasing concentrations of carbon dioxide and other gases, commonly known as the greenhouse effect, are likely to have profound implications for world climate and, by extension, for international and domestic tourism. The major greenhouse gases are carbon dioxide, which is particularly associated with fossil fuel combustion and deforestation; methane, which is probably derived from agriculture, especially rice cultivation and animal husbandry; nitrous oxide from the use of fertilizers, land clearing, biomass burning and fossil fuel combustion; and halocarbons, particularly chlorofluorocarbons, which were introduced into the atmosphere for the first time this century. Concentrations of each of these gases continue to rise with far-reaching consequences for global climate.

Given existing trends, increases in greenhouse gases equivalent to a doubling of carbon dioxide since pre-industrial times are likely to occur by the middle of the twenty-first century. Such a doubling may induce average global surface temperature increases of between 1.5 and 4.5 degrees C. The magnitude of this warming is expected to be greatest in high latitudes, particularly in autumn and winter. Equatorial regions will experience a lesser but still substantial warming. Much less confidence can be placed in assessments of the implications for rainfall and the hydrological cycle. However, there may be reduced moisture availability, particularly in middle latitudes, because of increased evapotranspiration coupled with an increased demand for water. Sea-level is likely to rise chiefly because of the thermal expansion of ocean waters (and only secondarily because of glacial melting). These projections are based upon direct measurement of temperature and atmospheric concentrations of greenhouse gases, on estimates of future energy use and technological change, and on elaborate modelling of both the economic and ocean–atmosphere systems.

The eminent climatologist Kenneth Hare (1989) suggests that this would be a revolutionary change in world climate on a scale which is unprecedented in the history of civilization. He points out that not since the the end of glacial climates a little over 10,000 years ago have temperatures changed so much or so rapidly. He concludes that, 'I have no doubt that we are discussing the central environmental problem of our times' (p.63). Such changes in climate would have major consequences for tourism. However, it appears by the dearth of publications on the topic that little thought has been given to the matter.

The climate change–tourism survey

In order to assess the state of knowledge and concern with respect to relationships between tourism and climate change, an international survey was undertaken of governmental agencies responsible for either tourism or climate. This is now discussed.

The sample

Since agencies individually responsible for climate and for tourism might be expected to have an interest in the juxtaposition between the two topics, the relevant national climate and tourism agencies were identified as potential contacts. The addresses of the tourism organizations were obtained from *Annex 1* in the *Methodological Supplement to World Travel and Tourism Statistics*, 1985 edition, published by the World Tourism Organization. The addresses of meteorological organizations were obtained from the World Meteorological Organization's *Handbook* which lists all member organizations. Not all countries were covered by these two lists, the most notable exceptions being China, the former Soviet Union, and Canada. However, most countries were included on one or both lists, constituting a sampling of all geographical regions. In total, 192 addresses were obtained for national meteorological and tourism organizations around the world, 103 for tourism organizations and 89 for meteorological organizations.

The research instrument

In July 1989 a letter, in English, was sent to these organizations to gather as much information as possible concerning the climate–tourism interface. Four specific questions were asked:

1. Are climate and weather major determinants of tourism and recreation in your country at present?
2. Has global climate change been the subject of any research or discussion in your country, particularly in the context of tourism and recreation?
3. Are relationships between climate change and tourism likely to be significant issues in your country?
4. Are publications or reports available concerning the relationship between climate–weather and tourism–recreation in your country?

The first question was intended to determine the current level of influence that climate and weather have on tourism, in order to place the effects of climate change in context. The second question was meant to establish the current level of research into the relationship between climate change and tourism. The third question attempted to determine the attitudes of government agencies towards climate change and whether climate change is likely to be a consideration when policy decisions are made. The last question was designed to bring to light relevant research throughout the world and to open new avenues of investigation by revealing new contacts.

Responses

The letter elicited sixty-six replies, constituting a 33 per cent return rate. This was considered to be an excellent return rate for a 'cold call' particularly as the letters were sent to organizations rather than individuals and, in a large proportion of cases, were in a foreign language. Of the responses, six were referrals to other departments.

Each response was categorized based on the answers to the first three questions. The three questions were open-ended, and the classification of the answers was somewhat subjective since not all questions were answered in the same manner.

Since the importance of tourism to any particular country's economy reflects many factors, including tourist attractions and economic structure, the responses to the letter of enquiry were also categorized in different ways. First, they were sorted by answer without consideration of other factors. This provided a general overview of the attitudes of respondents towards climate change and tourism. Next, the responses were classified by type of organization, for although it is likely that both tourism and climate organizations in a given country might be concerned with the potential impact of climate on tourism, either organization might be in a better position to carry out research and influence government policy. Finally, returns were classified by factors that might influence responses to climate change and tourism, such as importance of tourism to the economy, number of tourist arrivals, GNP, and GNP per person. Space does not permit a complete reporting of results. Rather, selected findings are presented, together with extracts from survey responses.

Findings

GLOBAL RESPONSES

Figure 23.1 demonstrates that most respondents felt that climate is important to their country's tourism industry; very few were aware of climate change research specifically related to tourism; almost half felt that climate change is or could become a significant issue in their country; and almost no climate-change publications with direct bearing on tourism were available.

The majority (81 per cent) answering question one felt that climate and weather were major tourism determinants. This implies that any change in climate could have an impact on the tourism industry world-wide. This observation is further substantiated by the response to question three: more than 75 per cent of those answering felt that climate change could become a significant issue for their country. However, 50 per cent of respondents did not answer this question.

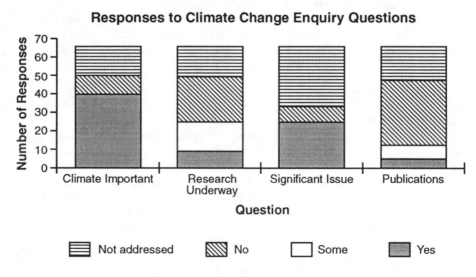

Figure 23.1 Responses to climate change enquiry questions

Even though many accept that climate change is a problem, research on tourism and recreation is lacking. Fewer than 20 per cent of respondents who addressed question two reported that research into the possible effects of climate change on tourism and recreation was in progress.

The response from the meteorological service in Jamaica was typical. Each question was answered with thoughtfulness, and additional concerns were mentioned:

Climate and weather are major determinants of tourism and recreation in our country at present. Further, . . . research on this topic is limited and is confined mainly to work at the University of the West Indies in its Geology and Geography departments in relation to changes in ecosystems. Given the expected rise in sea level and the possible change in coastal ecosystems, we have no doubt that the relationships between climate change and tourism are likely to become significant issues in the near future. However, publications and reports are currently unavailable in our library . . . Along with tourism and recreation, other areas which could be of interest would be possible impacts on food production and implications for pests and diseases affecting animals and humans [Survey response, 1989]

Many respondents provided information on present climate and its influences on their countries, although only a few included information on the possible effects of climate change on tourism and recreation, again reflecting the lack of research.

ORGANIZATIONAL COMPARISONS

It might be expected that, because of differing backgrounds and responsibilities, respondents from climate organizations might exhibit different responses to those from tourism organizations. Slightly more tourism organizations were consulted than meteorological organizations (103 to 89), but virtually equal numbers of each responded (32 and 31 respectively). The difference in response rate is not statistically significant.

Respondents from climate organizations were more likely to have opinions about the significance of climate change for tourism than those from tourism organizations: only twenty-six per cent of the former did not answer question three while 70 per cent of the latter chose not to comment on this question. The majority of the respondents that did answer this question, from both tourism organizations (80 per cent) and climate organizations (74 per cent), believed that climate change may be a significant issue for tourism in their country. Almost three times the proportion of respondents from climate organizations (16 per cent to 6 per cent) indicated that research was being conducted on climate change with specific reference to tourism. Thus, the climate respondents may have a stronger scientific basis for forming opinions about the significance of climate change since they are more likely to be aware of ongoing research than those from tourism organizations. However, even those from organizations which are conducting research, such as India's Meteorological Department, qualify their answers to the third question by reiterating the uncertainties associated with global climate change: 'No clear picture has yet emerged on the extent of climate change due to global warming . . . it is therefore still the subject of investigation as to how significant these issues are with respect to our country (Survey response, 1989). Thus, overall, climate organizations were currently conducting most of the research into climate change and the relationship between such change and tourism.

SOME EXAMPLES

Several respondents elaborated on the implications of climate change research for tourism and recreation. They can be grouped into three categories: those concerned with impacts on winter tourism, those concerned with impact on summer activities, and those concerned with both.

Not unexpectedly, respondents from countries that rely on sun–sand–sea tourism, such as Tonga and the Bahamas, expressed concern over the possible rise in sea level, while those from mountainous countries, such as Chile, New Zealand, and Switzerland, showed more concern over temperature rise and shifting precipitation patterns, which could affect winter skiing. Other countries, like Turkey and the former Czechoslovakia, were concerned with possible effects on both winter and summer tourism.

Impacts on summer tourism

The respondent from the Bahamas indicated the country's vulnerability to sea-level rise since it consists of many low-lying islands. Potential effects include inundation of the islands, and contamination of freshwater aquifers, which could lead to water shortages. The implications of such effects reach far beyond tourism to encompass agriculture, health and other concerns which, in turn, have implications for tourism. It was suggested that possible loss of beaches is, perhaps, a less devastating effect since it could be compensated for by diversification and development of other tourist attractions, or by human intervention to preserve and maintain beaches. The loss of fresh water, however, could be debilitating to the tourism industry. A reduced supply of fresh water could result in the introduction of restrictions on types of tourism practices and limits on the number of tourists permitted on the islands.

The Tongan respondent was more concerned with the possibility of increased frequency and magnitude of storms and cyclones as well as the increased frequency of droughts. Whereas an increase in the storm season could negatively affect the tourism industry, it was suggested that longer periods of rainless weather (or drought) could affect tourism positively and could be promoted as one of the benefits of vacationing in Tonga. Unfortunately, drought conditions would have a negative effect on other aspects of life in Tonga, such as agriculture, which, in turn, could have an indirect negative effect on tourism.

Impacts on winter tourism

Chile's studies indicate that the ski industry will be affected because of the expected higher temperatures and shifting precipitation patterns. There is concern that, due to higher temperatures, precipitation might fall as rain in seasons and in areas where it had previously fallen as snow. This could push the snowline higher, increasing the risk of poor snow cover at lower elevation ski areas and decreasing the length of the ski season in all areas. Hill operators at lower elevations might be forced to close, and even those areas operating at high altitude might be in danger of losing their investments because of the shortened season.

The same concerns were expressed from New Zealand—that the snowline could recede by about 400 metres, and that the ski season could be greatly shortened. This would make ski-area operations at low-altitude ski fields uneconomical. Nevertheless, there is a possibility that climate change may positively affect the skiing industry in New Zealand because skiing in Australia, which takes place at lower elevations than in New Zealand, could be eliminated:

We are looking at the snowline rising by about 400 m; this will significantly impact on some of the ski fields at lower elevations. What this might mean to the ski industry is that some ski fields may become uneconomic to operate and therefore commercial ventures may well have to look at relocation at higher altitudes . . . Evidence from Australia clearly indicates that any warming there may make all of their ski fields uneconomic; if we extend this further this may have a positive impact on the ski industry in New Zealand. [Survey response, 1989]

A respondent from Switzerland expressed less concern about the receding snowline than about a possible shift in weather patterns, which could preclude skiing during the most lucrative period for Northern Hemisphere ski hill operators: the Christmas holiday period. Switzerland would be more adversely affected by changes in the timing of snowfall than New Zealand or Australia because Christmas falls at the beginning of its ski season, while in the Southern Hemisphere, Christmas falls during the summer. Research from Switzerland suggests that climate change might reduce the amount of water available during the winter months while, at the same time, more demands might be placed on the water supply for artificial snowmaking. Climate change might also alter the size and distribution of glaciers. If there is less snowfall, the glaciers could shrink, threatening the summer glacier-skiing industry. The Swiss respondent felt that the loss of ski tourism (both winter and summer skiing) could not be compensated for by other summer activities.

Impacts on winter and summer tourism

Czech research indicates that winters in the former Czechoslovakia will generally become more oceanic in nature, especially in the lowlands, with higher temperatures and greater precipitation. The higher temperatures will force the snowline to retreat to above 1,200 metres and cause the snow conditions to deteriorate which, in turn, could shorten the winter recreation season. Summers will be longer, warmer, and sunnier. The water temperature is expected to rise between one and three degrees C, but lake and sea levels are predicted to drop because of a diminished moisture-storage capacity (as snow) in the mountains and because of a higher evaporation rate. This will affect sailing routes and could make forest fires more frequent and difficult to combat. The quality of summer recreational activities, such as hiking and camping, might decline because coniferous trees will gradually be replaced by less aromatic deciduous trees, and insects are likely to become more numerous.

The outlook for Turkey, according to another respondent, is that losses in one area of the country will be offset by gains elsewhere. Possible losses in coastal tourism on the Mediterranean and the southern Aegean could be counterbalanced by more favourable conditions for tourism in the northern Aegean and the Black Sea. Summer tourism would not be eliminated, but significant costs would be incurred in relocating tourism infrastructure from one area to the other. The loss may be partially compensated by habitat shifts which may make lakeside and nature tourism more feasible. Although the ski season in western Anatolia may be shortened, other ski areas in eastern Anatolia may benefit.

While each statement is specific to a particular country, together they reveal many of the effects which climate change may have on tourism and recreation. The examples are drawn from a diversity of climatological situations, ranging from tropical to temperate, and each country will have to adapt to its own climatic shifts and variations. Tourism also is a broad phenomenon, encompassing a wide variety of activities, on which the examples have only touched. Great climatological diversity, coupled with the variety of types of tourism, as well as each country's ability to respond to changing conditions, make generalization difficult. Each country will have to assess its own needs and opportunities based on changing supply and demand relationships, its present tourism infrastructure, the changes that may affect that infrastructure, and its goals for its tourism industry in the future. While climate is only one among many factors with implications for tourism, sufficient evidence has been provided to indicate that climate change merits attention in deliberations on the future of tourism. However, the survey results indicate that, to date, the possibility of climate change and its consequences for tourism have not received the consideration they deserve.

Implications of climate change for global patterns of tourism

Little research has been undertaken on climate change and tourism, and that which exists is more likely to have been undertaken by climatologists than by tourism experts. Nevertheless, it is possible to draw attention to some of the factors which will influence the vulnerability of tourist destinations to climate change.

Other things being equal, countries whose economies are currently highly dependent upon tourism would appear to be at the greatest risk. Patterns of international tourism, whether indicated by arrivals or receipts, are currently dominated by Europe and, secondarily, by North America. Countries in these locations, along with many small countries whose economies are dominated by tourism, have the greatest at stake. However, many Third World countries have turned to tourism in recent years, and the rates of growth in such areas have been greater proportionately than in Europe or North America. According to the World Tourism Organization, absolute numbers of annual international tourist arrivals grew from 214.4 million in 1975 to 443.9 million in 1990 so that even relatively small proportionate increases constitute large increases in absolute numbers. It may be unfortunate that many Third World destinations, with restricted alternative economic opportunities and limited economic buffers, have turned to tourism at a time when the natural resource base for tourism may be changing.

International tourism is only the tip of the tourist iceberg, for perhaps four out of five tourist trips do not cross international borders. The distribution of domestic travel is highly correlated on a global scale with discretionary income, and this is concentrated in the developed nations of the Western world. Domestic travel patterns are likely to be more stable than international travel in the face of global climate change. This is because the former often take place in relatively short periods of free time which place constraints on the destination choices of travellers. On the other hand, outside Europe where there are many relatively small countries in close juxtaposition, a larger proportion of international travel is long-haul, and potential travellers have a multitude of destinations to choose from. Should locations become less inviting, the international traveller may be able to switch destinations more readily than the domestic traveller. Many Third World destinations depend upon long-haul travellers and lack the security of a large domestic market. Thus, from this perspective also, many Third World destinations face greater uncertainty than their counterparts in the Western world.

Tourists travel for diverse motivations and not all are drawn solely by the attributes of the natural environment of the destination area. For example, many travel to visit friends and relatives, and the distribution of these travellers may remain largely unchanged unless modifications of global climate induce large, permanent migrations. Similarly, the distribution of major cities and historic sites is likely to remain much as it is today, at least in the short term. On the other hand, destinations which rely primarily upon their natural resource base to attract tourists may be more at risk.

Mountains and coasts are examples of such environments. Mountain ranges are extremely complex environments climatically with major differences in climate and weather occurring over short distances. The level of resolution of the currently available general circulation models used for projecting global climates does not permit us to make statements about future climates of mountainous areas with confidence. The sea–sun–sand attractions of coastal areas, and some historic resources, such as Venice and the shoreline temples of Bali and Tamil Nadu, India appear to be threatened by rising sea levels and associated increases in flooding and erosion. Although such destinations are found in both temperate and tropical areas, there are many developing countries, including those of the Caribbean and elsewhere in the 'south', whose tourist industries depend upon warm climates and attractive beaches. Such countries may lack the resources to combat rising sea levels and may be short of alternative attractions of sufficient allure to capture international markets. Furthermore, many such destinations have been developed with the assistance multinational corporations which may respond to changing circumstances by seeking new opportunities elsewhere.

Temperatures are expected to increase more markedly in high than in low latitudes. This may extend the lengths of summer seasons in middle latitudes and, coupled with milder winters, reduce the attraction of tropical climates. High-latitude destinations may become more attractive, and high-altitude hill stations may prosper. In addition, if the tropics become even warmer, demands on energy for air conditioning and water consumption may increase in areas where they are in short supply, for tourists are voracious consumers of these services.

This section has provided some very general observations concerning climatic factors which are likely to influence global patterns of tourism. The remainder of the chapter describes a case study from Canada which evaluates the implications of climate change in a specific situation and illustrates the kind of research which can be undertaken given the current availability of information.

Downhill skiing in Ontario

As in much research assessing the socio-economic implications of climate change, two scenarios for climate change associated with a doubling in atmospheric concentrations of carbon dioxide were employed and their implications assessed. Scenario A was based upon a model developed by the Geophysical Fluid Dynamics Laboratory at Princeton, whereas Scenario B used output from a similar analysis undertaken by the Goddard Institute for Space Studies. Such models and the challenge of using their output in impact analyses are discussed by Cohen (1990). While these and similar models constitute the most sophisticated attempts to project carbon dioxide-induced climatic change, their limitations should be considered.

First and foremost, it should be recognized that the projections are uncertain and cannot be verified. Second, the models employ coarse and different grids so that they are not completely comparable, and extrapolations have to be used to obtain information for specific locations.

Given these and other related problems, the scenarios are best regarded as possible futures rather than predictions of the future. Nevertheless, in spite of their limitations, such scenarios constitute the best estimates of future climate, and they are the sources of data on future climate employed in the case studies.

Even if the scenarios evolve as projected, it is improbable that they will be experienced in a world which has not changed in other ways. It is an impossible task (certainly beyond the scope of this contribution!) to predict what the world will be like in fifty years. Thus, in order to proceed, the assumption was made that, except for the changes in climate, all other things will remain as they are. No allowances were made for technological changes or policy initiatives which might modify climate change. Furthermore, it was assumed that future tourists will respond to the new climates in a similar

fashion to which they respond to weather and climate at present. It was further
assumed that variability about future climatic norms will be similar to that
which is currently experienced. Tourism was examined in isolation: little
attempt was made to investigate the implications of change in tourism for
other activities or economic sectors or, conversely, to assess the impacts of
change in those activities or society as a whole for tourism. Certainly, it may be
misleading to consider climate and tourism out of context, but it is necessary
to do this when that context cannot be established.

Detailed investigations were undertaken of the implications of climate
change in Ontario for skiing (a winter activity) and camping (a summer
activity). The interested reader can gain further information from Wall *et al.*
(1986), and McBoyle and Wall (1986). The following section presents brief
highlights of the investigation of downhill skiing.

Two areas of Ontario were selected for the study, the South Georgian Bay
area as a southern ski area and the Lakehead, near Thunder Bay, in northern
Ontario. These are the major downhill ski areas in the province.

The following procedures were undertaken:

(i)   snow-cover periods suitable for skiing were determined for present-day
      conditions as well as for conditions suggested by the scenarios using
      criteria suggested by Crowe, *et al.* (1978);
(ii) data on current skier visits and expenditures were used in conjunction
      with estimated season lengths to calculate changes in the number of
      skier visits and the economic consequences of the climate scenarios;
(iii) sensitivity analyses were conducted to determine the likely impacts of
      various small changes in temperature and precipitation combinations.

The ski season was divided into two major categories: the 'reliable season'
in which there is a 75 per cent or greater probability of there being suitable
snow cover for skiing; and the 'marginally reliable season' in which there is
a probability of between 50 and 75 per cent of there being suitable snow
cover.

For the Lakehead under scenario A, the present marginally reliable or
better season will be reduced from 131 days to 91 days, a reduction of 30.5
per cent (Figure 23.2). Further reductions in both the reliable and
marginally reliable seasons occur under scenario B. Although the reductions in the ski seasons are large, the key Christmas break when 20 per cent
of the year's business is done and the university/college mid-February break
still fall within the reliable ski season. The elimination of skiing in March,
when 20 per cent of skier visits currently occur, is the major loss and, under
scenario A, this will result in a reduction of annual skier expenditures at the
resorts of $1.9 million in 1985 Canadian dollars. However, it may not be nec-
essary to endure all of this reduced business because of the possibility of an
enhanced ability to draw upon the southern Ontario market.

The South Georgian Bay region, which is climatically marginal for skiing
at present, does not fare as well as the Lakehead. The present day
marginally reliable ski season of 70 days will be reduced to 40 days under
scenario A and will disappear altogether under scenario B. There will be no

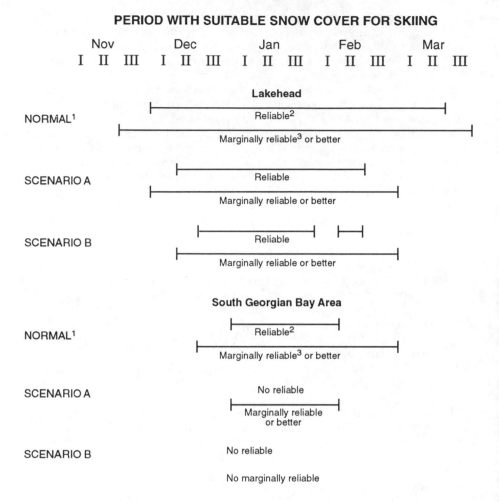

Figure 23.2 Periods with suitable snow cover for skiing

reliable ski season under scenario A or B. The calculations associated with both scenarios suggest the virtual elimination of the ski industry in the South Georgian Bay area with a loss to resorts in 1985 Canadian dollars of $36.5 million per annum in skier spending and a reduction of $412.8 million per annum in the retail trade of Collingwood, the major service centre. This is in addition to the millions of dollars invested in infrastructure by the ski industry.

These conclusions, particularly with respect to the South Georgian Bay area, may appear to be extreme. However, an analysis of climatic variability indicates that this is not the case and average conditions as indicated by the scenarios are experienced occasionally under the present climatic regime. Furthermore, it is not necessary for climatic change to be as great as that suggested in the scenarios for there to be a marked decrease in the length of the ski season in the South Georgian Bay area.

Tourists are extremely mobile and they may be able to divert their patronage from one destination to another with relative ease. It follows that the evaluation of specific sites, in the absence of a consideration of broader opportunities, may produce misleading results. Detailed results have been presented above for two areas in Ontario, but results of analyses of other areas are beginning to emerge. For example, research on the Laurentians in Quebec indicates that skiing may also be curtailed there (McBoyle and Wall, 1987; Lamothe and Periard, 1988). Unpublished results for Michigan suggest similar conclusions as for Ontario, that is that the downhill ski resorts in the south of the state will struggle, but resorts in the north may continue to operate successfully but with slightly diminished operating seasons. Diversification of activities, such as the addition of golf courses or water slides, is suggested as a management response, for the summer season may be lengthened and, in such ways, it may be possible to defray winter losses through summer gains.

Conclusions

In conclusion, although there is general international awareness and agreement that climate change may have repercussions for the tourism industry, more research and policy analyses are necessary to reduce uncertainties, further understanding, assess implications and enable the industry to adapt to changing circumstances. Global climate change will present both problems and opportunities for destinations. The climate changes discussed are projected to occur within the lifetimes of many current investment projects and within the lifetimes of many of the earth's present residents. Although the implications for tourism are likely to be profound, very few tourism researchers have begun to formulate relevant questions, let alone develop methodologies which will further understanding of the nature and magnitude of the challenges which lie ahead.

Acknowledgement

Catherine Badke acted as a research assistant for the survey of meteorological and tourism organizations and her contribution is gratefully acknowledged.

References

Cohen, S.J., 1990, 'Bringing the global warming issue closer to home: the challenge of regional impact studies', *Bulletin of the American Meteorological Society*, **71**, 4: 520–6.

Crowe, R.B., McKay, G.A. and Baker, W.M., 1978, *The Tourist and Recreation Climate of Ontario*, Downsview, Atmospheric Environment Services.

Hare, F.K., 1989, 'The global greenhouse effect', in World Meteorological Organization, *The Changing Atmosphere: Conference Proceedings*, Geneva: 59–69.

Lamothe and Periard Consultants, 1988, 'Implications of climate change for downhill skiing in Quebec', *Climate Change Digest*: 88–93.

McBoyle, G. and Wall, G., 1986, 'Recreation and climatic change: a Canadian case study', *Ontario Geography*, **28**: 51–68.

McBoyle, G. and Wall, G., 1987, 'The impact of CO2-induced warming on downhill skiing in the Laurentians', *Cahiers de Geographie de Quebec*, **31**: 39–50.

Wall, G., Harrison, R., Kinnaird, V., McBoyle, G. and Quinlan, C., 1986, 'The implications of climatic change for camping in Ontario', *Recreation Research Review*, **13**, 1: 50–60.

World Tourism Organization, 1985, *Methodological Supplement to World Travel and Tourism Statistics*, Madrid, WTO.

World Tourism Organization, 1992, *Yearbook of Tourism Statistics*, 44th edition, Madrid, WTO.

INDEX

WITHDRA

Child in Sport and Physical Activity

International Series on Sport Sciences

Series Editors: **Richard C. Nelson and Chauncey A. Morehouse**

The principal focus of this series is on reference works primarily from international congress and symposium proceedings. These should be of particular interest to researchers, clinicians, students, physical educators, and coaches involved in the growing field of sport sciences. The Series Editors are Professors Richard C. Nelson and Chauncey A. Morehouse of the Pennsylvania State University.

Since the series includes the eight major divisions of sport science, a Board of Associate Editors comprised of internationally recognized authors acts in an advisory capacity to the Series Editors. The Associate Editors with their institutional affiliations and designated areas of responsibility are as follows:

Biomechanics	Dr. Mitsumasa Miyashita	University of Tokyo (Japan)
History	Dr. John A. Lucas	The Pennsylvania State University (USA)
Medicine	Dr. Hans Howald	Sporthochshule, Maglingen (Switzerland)
Pedagogy	Dr. Herbert Haag	University of Kiel (West Germany)
Philosophy	Dr. Robert G. Osterhoudt	University of Minnesota (USA)
Physiology	Dr. James S. Skinner	University of Montreal (Canada)
Psychology	Dr. John E. Kane	Loughborough College of Education (England)
Sociology	Dr. Kalevi Heinilä	University of Jyväskylä (Finland)

Each volume in the series is published in English but is written by authors of several countries. The series, therefore, is truly international in scope and because many of the authors normally publish their work in languages other than English, the series volumes are a resource for information often difficult if not impossible to obtain elsewhere. Organizers of international congresses in The Sport Sciences desiring detailed information concerning the use of this series for publication and distribution of official proceedings are requested to contact either the Series Editors or the appropriate Associate Editor. Manuscripts prepared by several authors from various countries consisting of information of international interest will also be considered for publication.

The *International Series on Sport Sciences* serves not only as a valuable source of authoritative up-to-date information but also helps to foster better understanding among sports scientists on an international level. It provides an effective medium through which researchers, teachers, and coaches may develop better communications with individuals in countries throughout the world who have similar professional interests.

Volume 1
Nelson and Morehouse. **BIOMECHANICS IV** (Fourth International Seminar on Biomechanics)
Volume 2
Lewillie and Clarys. **SWIMMING II** (Second International Seminar on Biomechanics of Swimming)
Volume 3
Albinson and Andrew. **CHILD IN SPORT AND PHYSICAL ACTIVITY** (First International Symposium on the Participation of Children in Sport)
In Preparation:
Haag. **SPORT PEDAGOGY** (First International Symposium on Sport Pedagogy).

International Series
on Sport Sciences, Volume 3

CHILD IN SPORT AND PHYSICAL ACTIVITY

Selected Papers presented at the National Conference
Workshop "The Child in Sport and Physical Activity",
Queen's University, Kingston, Ontario, Canada.

Edited by: **J. G. Albinson, Ph.D.**
and
G. M. Andrew, Ph.D.
School of Physical and Health
Education,
Queen's University.

University Park Press
Baltimore·London·Tokyo

University Park Press

International Publishers in Science and Medicine
Chamber of Commerce Building
Baltimore, Maryland 21202

Library of Congress Cataloging in Publication Data

Conference on the Child in Sport and Physical Activity,
    Queen's University, 1973.
    Child in Sport and Physical Activity

    (International series on sport sciences; v. 3)
    Includes index.
    1. Child development—Congresses. 2. Sports for children—Congresses. I. Albinson, J. G. II. Andrew, G. M. III. Kingston, Ont. Queen's University. IV. Title. V. Series. [DNLM: 1. Physical education and training—Congresses. 2. Sport medicine—In infancy and Childhood—Congresses. QT255 N2754p 1973]
RJ131.C59 1973   612'.76   76-1953
ISBN 0-8391-0892-3

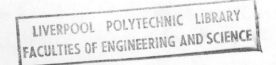

THE CHILD IN SPORT AND PHYSICAL ACTIVITY

PHYSIOLOGY

by   Per-Olof Åstrand,
       Department of Physiology,
       Gymnastik - och Idrottshögskolan,
       S - 114 33 Stockholm, Sweden.

I am supposed to give a general survey of the physical development of the child from the age of 5 up to post-puberty. There are only a few physiological studies to base such a summary on (most extensive are Robinson, 1938; Åstrand, 1952). For natural reasons I will start with figures from my own thesis. The data is old, but has the advantage of including both girls and boys from young age as subjects. The absolute figures do not represent a cross section of the Swedish population; they are high, for the subjects were not selected at random - many of them volunteered because they were particularly interested in sports. However, the study comprises a homogeneous group of subjects, a necessity when comparing girls and boys of different ages.

Maximal Oxygen Uptake and Age

Figure 1 presents data on maximal oxygen uptake measured on 141 subjects 4 to 18 years of age running on a treadmill (horizontal). There is a smooth, gradual increase in oxygen uptake with age, with the boys increasing their maximal aerobic power at a higher rate than the girls from the age of 13. It should be emphasized that the figure also includes data on subjects above the age of 20 (86 altogether). They were students in physical education, and therefore a very selected group. The difference between girls and boys in this aerobic power is more evident when taking the body weight into account.

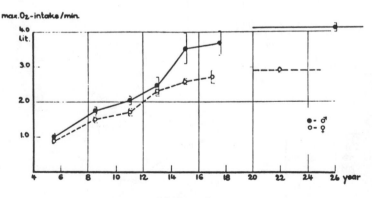

Figure 1

Average values for maximal oxygen in relation to age. Altogether 227 subjects are included. (Vertical lines denote ± 2 x SEM) (Åstrand, 1952).

This is evident from Figure 2 in which the maximal oxygen is related to the body weight. With a weight higher than 40 kg most girls attain a lower maximal $\dot{V}_{O2}$ x kg^{-1} x minimum^{-1} compared with the boys. The mean values for the maximal aerobic power expressed in this way was similar for girls and boys before the age of 10, but from then on significantly different (Figure 3). A peak in maximal $\dot{V}_{O2}$ x kg^{-1} x minimum^{-1} was attained as early as at the age of about 10 for the girls, but for the boys an almost constant level was noticed from the age of 9.

It should be pointed out that in nonobese children the body weight gives a rough estimate of the individual's maximal oxygen uptake (Figure 2); the improvement with age is to a great extent a consequence in increased body size. This size is reflecting the muscle mass. For the girls there is an increase of body fat at the beginning of puberty.

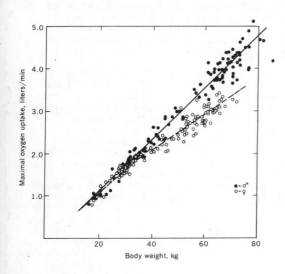

Figure 2

Maximal oxygen uptake during bicycling or running in relation to body weight. Same subjects as in Figure 1 (For male subjects y =0.108 + 0.070 x; r = 0.980 ± 0.004; deviation from regression line = 7.5 percent.)

Figure 3

Average values of maximal oxygen intake per kg body weight for different age groups. (The vertical lines denote ± 2 SEM.) Same subjects as in Figure 1.

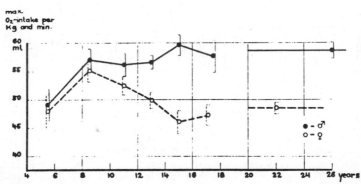

CONTENTS

Part VI (continued)

Preface

When a child engages in a physical activity, be it playing tag, a game of soccer or simply climbing a tree, he does so as a single entity. Likewise, the adult working with a child deals with a single entity. In contrast, when the research worker studies the interaction of the child in sport and physical activity, he may be concerned only with a particular component of a biological system, a specific learning process or a defined set of attitudes; in other words, seldom does a researcher deal with an integrated total human being. Similarly, when this topic "Physical Activity, Sport and the Child" is considered from the viewpoint of the numerous related disciplinary aspects (i.e. psychological, sociological, physiological, medical, growth and developmental, and motor learning aspects) one gets the impression that the child can be regarded as a linking of numerous unrelated segments. This is made further apparent when one examines the related literature. One concern that is inherent in this fragmented approach is at what stage and by what process does the accumulated knowledge get pieced together and integrated? Although there have been numerous symposia and indeed major research writings which have pertained to certain aspects of the present topic, there has not been a recent composite of writings in which the child was considered from a multi-disciplinary perspective. This was one of the considerations which gave rise to the Conference on "The Child in Sport and Physical Activity".

Aside from this purely academic consideration, there existed a myriad of other reasons why it seemed propitious to organize and host a major conference in which the child, rather than the discipline served as the focus for input and discussion. One concern of long standing to the organizers was the wide communication gap that exists between the academic - researcher - theoretician on the one hand and the practitioner on the other. The lack of a concerted thrust toward a comprehensive and integrated assessment of this topic has not been confined to the theoretician and practitioner. Indeed, one can cite many problems which prevail in respect to the topic at hand.

In the North American context at least, there prevails a rather fragmentary approach by society to the problems of the child, and especially in respect to the aspects related to play, sport and physical activity programs. From the viewpoint of facilities development, communities are planned for parents, with facilities such as play areas for the child left as an afterthought by the planners; indeed, all too often, such facilities are included only because of legislation rather than from natural desire or concern. Likewise, a similar low priority within school systems is given to physical activities. This is especially true of elementary school programs where leadership often is the responsibility of the classroom teacher who in many school jurisdictions lacks any interest, knowledge or professional training in physical education; accordingly, "gym" is commonly relegated to a level of minor priority in the educational system. As a consequence, it is often the case that when children have reached high school, (ironically where the best facilities and professional leadership usually exist) the child has developed negative attitudes toward sport and physical activity. Furthermore, sports and physical activity programs often operate on the principle

of exclusion rather than inclusion; that is to say, team selection
and even school physical education programs espouse the principle of
elitism which serves to enhance the motivation of the skilled
performer only. If sport and physical activity play roles of value
to society in general, and the child in particular, it is important
for concerned people to examine the past progress, current status,
present trends and future directions desirable. This was a major
objective of the Conference.

Representatives of the various practitioner -leader groups
directly involved with the child in the areas of sport and play and
some of the renowned academic writers and research workers in the
related disciplines whose concerns relate more closely to the
scientific and theoretical aspects of this topic were invited to
attend this Conference.

The Conference was planned so that the theoretician-researcher
presented a review of the current state of the knowledge in his or
her discipline area. What appears in this book is that input. The
editors have made no attempt to integrate this material. The
integration and intercommunication between groups and disciplines
occurred during the week long Workshops held concurrently with the
Conference; these proceedings are published elsewhere (1).

(1) Proceedings "The Child in Sport and Physical Activity",
     available through the Canadian Council on Children and
     Youth, 1407 Yonge St., Toronto, Ontario, Canada.

JGA
GMA

FOREWORD

This volume represents a departure from the normal publication procedures used for volumes within the *International Series on Sport Sciences*. The content includes aspects of sport science and focuses on a specific age group. This type of approach provides for a more thorough integration of current information that should be particularly relevant to researchers and teachers who are primarily concerned with the effects of physical activity on children.

The physical appearance of the text differs from that of previous volumes since photographic offset methods were used in its preparation. The original plan for publication of *Child in Sport* did not materialize after the manuscript had been edited and prepared for photographic reproduction. Some time later it was accepted as Volume 3 in the *International Series on Sport Sciences*. This is contrary to normal procedures in which arrangements for publication are made in advance. Under the circumstances, the Series and Volume Editors and University Park Press deemed it essential to publish these proceedings as quickly as possible. Therefore, photographic processing was utilized instead of the usual type set methods. This decision made the material available much sooner despite the fact that it departed from the normal format of the Series.

Richard C. Nelson
Chauncey A. Morehouse

Contributors

Per-Olof Åstrand (19)

D. A. Bailey (81)

Gordon R. Cumming (67)

Willi Daume (3)

M. J. Ellis (139)

Bengt O. Eriksson (43)

L. N. Guppy (161)

J. P. McKay (161)

B. D. McPherson (161)

G. Lawrence Rarick (203)

Gillian D. Rattray (97)

Thomas J. Ryan (133)

John H. Salmela (219)

Roy J. Shephard (35)

Carolyn W. Sherif (97)

The number in parentheses is the page upon which the contributor's article can be found.

Keynote
address

THE MAIN FEATURES OF PRESENT-DAY SOCIETY

by   Willi Daume,
      Vice President,
      International Olympic Committee.

Before addressing myself to the theme of this Conference "The Child in Sport and Physical Activity", I would like to digress to consider first some pertinent aspects of social conditions of the present. I do this on the assumption that the social conditions in Canada are essentially the same as those in my country.

In the Federal Republic of Germany the social conditions are determined principally by the Constitution, and specifically those clauses which pertain to human rights. Because of what I have to say later on the social importance of sport, and on the extent to which sport can contribute to man's achieving his rights, I wish to cite a few of the relevant clauses. Specifically, that each person is assured:

- the inviolable freedom to develop one's personality;

- equality among all human beings (including the equality of man and woman and the assurance that no person be either favoured or discriminated against because of birth, origin or social standing);

- the right to live, to achieve and maintain physical health.

However, these rights are not the only factors governing our life. Rather, they are ideals competing, as it were, with certain social structures and patterns of action imposed more from outside and their true value is measured by the way in which they stand up to these structures and patterns. In this regard, I am thinking specifically of the following features of an industrial society:

Firstly, this society is governed by the principle of efficiency both with regard to the economy and work. Efficiency is measured by visible results; for example, the volume of production or the amount of income. The principle of efficiency is often transferred to other spheres of life;

Secondly, the drive for efficiency is generally connected with a constant state of rivalry. People compete against each other both at their jobs and in the consumption of goods in order to attain as high a social status as possible;

Thirdly, and in contrast, many people follow exclusively their own economic interests, isolate themselves and withdraw from the community in which they were once fully integrated (i.e. the family, group, clan, etc.);

Finally, the effort to improve one's own standard of living is accompanied by growing automation involving increased application of technology.

4

Social Structure and its Consequences

One cannot deny, however, that this social situation has a number of positive corollaries: take the equal opportunity every person has to achieve something, the willingness of society to recognize individual achievements or the tremendous amount of leisure time gained by the rationalization of work to the point where a thirty-hour week is no longer a Utopian dream.

And yet we must realize that our existence is endangered if the principles and characteristics of an industrial society are so strongly emphasized that man's fundamental rights are curtailed as a result. We are already obliged to live with some such shifts of stress today.

The predominance of the principle of efficiency frequently leads to the sole recognition of expedient actions and to a loss of significance of activities unrelated to efficiency. Social standing depends entirely on achievement, thereby making the position in life and society precarious. Less efficient individuals, such as the aged or handicapped, and social groups which consciously reject the principle of efficiency, such as hippies, are neglected and form fringe groups of society.

If the principle of competition prevails at work and in man's private life, envy, ill-will and frustration occur. If this is met with at work, then this contained aggressiveness is transferred to other spheres of life and often directed against a person's own family. Moreover, such items as apartments, cars, furniture, drink and other goods are no longer bought just to satisfy real needs; rather such consumption is abused as a symbol of higher social status.

It is not uncommon that an individual's economic interests force him to seek as remunerative a job as possible and consequently to travel long distances from his home to his place of work. The gulf between his public and private life widens continuously. Frequently he lives his private life only in the close circle of the family or even quite alone; isolation increases and community security is lost. The fulfilment of collective needs (for example, establishing kindergartens, hospitals, old people's homes) recedes with the individual's attempts to achieve recognition and a high standard of living.

The automation of work and the general mechanization and motorization of life give rise to an increasing lack of movement and physical activity. Economic progress seems more important than personal well-being. Many of man's organs start functioning less efficiently and their structure degenerates affecting his health and well-being. The drive for economic progress makes it necessary to constantly build more roads, more houses, more factories, more machines, more cars. Since the population is also increasing, the natural living space is continuously reduced and the areas with clean air, unpolluted water and no noise are constantly becoming smaller. In the Federal Republic of Germany 175 acres are built up daily, or about 100 square miles a year, an area as big as Munich

with all its suburbs. The population of the Federal Republic of
Germany will reach 65 million in 1980 and of these, 35 million will
be living in urban conglomerates. This trend is common throughout
the world. Even apartments are no longer refuges of silence, since
they are usually far too small and not soundproof. Foodstuffs are
treated with harmful chemicals and packed in airtight containers
so that they look nicer and keep longer. There is only one way of
disposing of noncombustible packaging and containers after use—and
that is the rubbish-heap, which spoils the landscape and pollutes the
air.   Indeed, the increased leisure time gained through industrialization and mechanization is to a large extent spent without exercise,
for example with the ubiquitous television or in continuing to work
at home. Hence, in an industrial society man lives on a whole
within individual and social confines which make it difficult for
for him to develop freely, to pursue his interests and to commit
himself emotionally within a community.

Sport as a Field of Experience for Individuals and Groups

Sport presents numerous opportunities for relieving man of his
existential problems such as the pressures relating to the future
and of making decisions under which he is constantly placed.   In
games and athletic competition the seriousness of life recedes
temporarily into the background.   It provides man with carefree
moments in his meeting with his partner or group or in the encounter
with his opponent. The rules of the games, which are freely
accepted and recognized, help to break through the alienation
created by work mainly as a result of isolation at work and the vast
complexity of the production process.

At the same time, sport is a field of study for forms of
social behaviour. The individual can demonstrate his strength and
ability here. He can test his adaptation or resistance to a social
situation in sport without having to fear a loss of prestige in case
of failure. Sport presents a comprehensible field of action in which
a person can participate according to his interests. A striving for
and comparison of achievement also exist in sport. However, these
aspects only act as casual principles and are not dominant. Personal
achievements are recognized. Hence there is room in sport for the
less successful as well.   Both sport and its organization are a
cooperative undertaking. The aims of an athletic group are identical
with the personal interests of its members. This opens up a new
field of encounter, and independent sphere of life, for the individual
and the over-worked family.

Because they attached such great social importance to sport,
the German sports organizations in 1972 initiated a major movement
the theme of which was "Sports for Everybody". Needless to say, we
are far from achieving this goal. Perhaps in the process we have
learned a few truths, but a few truths do not add up to "the truth".
Sport exists for man. But "sport for everybody"? How does that
sound to some ears, particularly to those that would like above all
to hear discord in our country? We have no lack of critics. And
are we not being after all presumptuous in setting ourselves this
goal? The world is poor and we want the whole world to play! Do
we have the right to want this? We speak of "sport for everybody"

in a century in which we have not been able to obtain peace for everybody, guarantee everybody their daily bread or open the way to school for everybody. If we claim sport to be one of those things man cannot do without if he is to enjoy a full life, then we assume a great responsibility.

Dangers for Sport

If sport merely represents an escape from the reality of hunger, war and illiteracy and used only to surround us in a more easily manageable world of games, then we must not make it a way out for everybody. For in fact sport does not leave reality entirely behind. It is linked to the individual's personal and social problems as well as to the social conditions. Consequently it is possible for sport to become dependent on aims totally divorced from itself. Sport is in danger if it becomes an absolute aim in itself or if it is used as a vehicle for external interests. One can suggest numerous examples to illustrate potential dangers: if sport is not related to other spheres of life; if sport prevents social commitment; if victory and records are sought in competitive sport without regard for the full development of the athlete's personality; if athletic victories are intended to act as proof of the value of a given political system; if the quality of a game is compromised by economic manipulation; if the sports offered are determined by commercial interests; if physical education is used as a means of discipline and uncritical adaptation to the existing social and athletic order; if sport is only offered in order to increase working power.

Challenge for the Future - "Sport for Everybody"

However, if sport is to help in its own way to make life more livable and to develop vital forces, without which technical progress has no value, then all roads must be opened for it. Sport for everybody, therefore, means one more opportunity for everybody to live a better life. And this requirement must apply throughout the world. It must also apply to the young nations, who bear a far heavier burden of development. It must not be allowed to apply solely to the industrial nations, which have become prosperous enough to be able to afford the luxury of greater leisure time. Therefore, if sport is to help make the future more livable, then the right to play and do sports must become a fundamental human right. In the future sport must be organized in a way that will enable everybody, regardless of age, sex, position, ability or interest, to take part. The claim for "sport for everybody" means that room must be made for everybody to do sport as they want and with as little outside interference as possible.

"Sport for Everybody" involves:

- encouraging young people to doing sport out of school (at home, in kindergarten, preparatory school, school and college);

- offering an interesting program to all those who seek health and enjoyment in sport (recreational sport);

- providing sport for the handicapped, neglected, lonely and forgotten (social sport);

-    promoting the talented and those freely striving for top
     performance and championship (competition sport).

The demand of "sport for everybody" also includes the broadest
possible organization of sport, if democratization is to be achieved.
In organization "sport for everybody" means participation and codetermination (equal chances) for all groups concerned (for example, for
women and active athletes).

The demand of "sport for everybody" forms a part of social
reform; that is, sport must advocate an improvement of social
conditions (equal social opportunities, new curricula, codetermination
ecology, town planning, etc.) and at the same time react to changes
in society. "Sport for everybody" is a joint undertaking which can
only be completed in conjunction with the continuous changes in
society and which must itself encourage such changes.

Concern for Minorities and the Underprivileged

The fundamental right to sport and equal chances in sport are
far from being achieved. The democratization of sport has become
stuck half way. I do not mean the forms and rules of sport, but the
chance to take part.

In our country sport has become quantitatively speaking an
immeasurable social phenomenon. The Deutsche Sportbund (German Sports
Association), the body coordinating the sport in Germany, had 11
million members in more than 40,000 clubs in 1972, and in 1980 it will
probably have 18 million members. And this does not even include the
numerous anonymous participants who do not belong to a club: the
many people doing aquatic sports, the hikers and climbers, skiers,
cyclists, badminton players, volleyball players and bowlers. There is
also a vast number of people interested in watching sport. Apparently
one thousand million people throughout the world followed the Munich
Olympic Games through the mass media.

And yet the problem of the minority groups and underprivileged
in sport demonstrates how incomplete the democratization of this
otherwise so modern sphere of life still is. Whom do I mean? I
consider underprivileged those who are prevented from taking part in
sports because of lack of facilities, of insufficient training or of
financial opportunities. I consider minority groups those people who
are less talented in sport, former athletes who have given up
competition sport, women and girls, families, older people and, of
course, the so-called fringe groups of society, such as the physically
handicapped, mentally retarded, foreign workers, addicts and
prisoners. One of the largest minority groups is the child, both
those in school as well as those of pre-school age. In this
presentation, my remarks will be restricted to consideration of
children's sport and physical education for ages 3 - 12 years; that
is, to those in kindergarten, preparatory and primary school.

The Child's Position in Society

The twentieth century has been designated "the century of the
child". But this refers more to the willingness of some professional

educationalists and parents to pay more attention to children's
demands and interests than before and perhaps also to children's
natural desire to express their needs and wishes more energetically.
However, these attempts do not reflect the entire picture of
industrial society. In actual fact children suffer most from the
unfavourable social situation previously mentioned. This is all
the more harmful, since the damage and the wrong attitude it
engenders can last for the rest of their life. Thus, for example,
the parents' materially-oriented interest frequently leaves them too
little time for their children, because to an increasing extent both
parents are out making money; not surprisingly, these values and
attitudes in respect to property and prestige acquisitions are often
transferred to their children. The children accept their parents'
attitude to themselves and become restricted in their ability to
act. Above all they have less contact with other children and
experience a social learning deficit as a result.

The second decisive disadvantage of the common striving for
material property is a lack of playing room, from which children
suffer more than anyone else. Complete mobility and the ability to
get from one place to another is clearly more important for this type
of society than more freedom for individual movement; hence this is
increasingly restricted. The official building requirements demand
more room for a garage than for playing - only half a square meter is
prescribed per child. Undeveloped property is primarily used for
improving communications and for economic expansion, not for playgrounds. Environment-determined restriction is also found in the
home and the apartment. Socially underprivileged children, who often
do not even have their own room, have above all little opportunity
to grasp their environment through movement, action and curiosity.
The check on the spontaneous need for movement leads to 30-35% of
school-age children having poor posture or posture defects.

Physical passivity coincides with a tendency to mental and
psychic passivity. This is caused largely by constantly changing
excitements: the volume, speed and noise of traffic, the flood of
pictures on the television, the irritation of their overworked
parents and the reactions of the neighbours who want to rest.

This disturbance of the child's development cannot be made
good by education since there is simply a shortage of qualified
personnel in this field. In the Federal Republic of Germany kindergartens for three to five-year-olds are not integrated into the
general educational system, even though some very nice plans for it
do exist. They are either privately run or administered by churches
or communities; this variation prevents any clear definition of aims.
In addition, only half of the kindergarten staff is trained. In
1970, only 20% of all three and four-year-olds could be placed in a
kindergarten owing to a shortage of places. You will, therefore,
not be surprised to hear that it is above all the kindergartens
that lack of space for playing and doing sports.

Our schools are likewise overcrowded; above all the primary
schools for the six to ten-year-olds. The teacher to pupil ratio is

quite often 1:40, which primarily affects the less gifted children. Such facts only serve to illustrate the low status of the child's position in society today.

Child Development Characteristics

How can sport then help to improve the generally unsatisfactory social situation of the child? In order to determine this, a short survey of what children are capable of at a given age with regard to development and what their needs are for developing their personality as well as comprehending and mastering their environment is necessary before trying to change them.

It is fully realized that care must be taken when relating development characteristics to age groups, since learning, skills and ability are on the whole determined as much by objects and the environment and its problems as by the child's age or sex. Likewise, "talent" is not so much an irrevocable gift from birth as the result of learning processes, so that it would be more correct to speak of "standard of achievement". Nevertheless, there are certain features shared by a given age group, although these are more a result of cultural factors than ability. One must recognize that there are considerable differences between children of different social origins for example. No two five-year-olds are alike.

Pre-school age children (i.e. three to six years old) orient themselves much more by actions than by concepts. Movement plays a vital role in their behaviour and in managing their life. The simple actions of everyday life involve only a few movement series with which the child finds a specific approach to his environment in play. By experiencing fundamental insights he becomes acquainted with his own individuality and social ties. As an individual, he learns spontaneity, creativity, independence and self-reliance, as well as flexibility and patience in disappointment. As a social being he learns how to feel his way into a role, helpfulness, verbal communication, the control and exchange of ideas and feelings, joint action directed towards a given goal, the ability to criticize and how to manage social conflicts. Furthermore, what is particularly important, he experiences frustration, contradiction and the opposition of his own individual needs to social necessities: ability and inability, winning and losing, vigour and exhaustion, joy and discontent, play and conflict, partnership and rivalry, egoism and helpfulness, self-control and lack of control.

Playing becomes more differentiated and conscious among the six to ten-year-olds. It follows set rules and lets the roles of the participants and social positions appear more clearly. The children pay more attention to their individual achievements and want to compare themselves with others.

Sport - An Ideal Field of Action for Children

What other field of activity provides a better opportunity to gain this experience or fulfils these desires better than the action-oriented field of sport? It offers playing room, a greater degree of behavioural freedom, which provides the opportunity to come to

terms with practical problems, provokes conflicts, challenges
children to take risks. In short, it is a land of adventure
containing all the scenes they will encounter later in life. And
at the same time sport also improves the child's health and vitality.

Sport is impossible without movement. Therefore, there is no
comparable medium for pre-school age children for learning the basic
ability to move either outdoors or indoors, with or without apparatus:
running, jumping, rolling, swinging, balancing, climbing, swimming,
skiing, playing ball, cycling, roller-skating and sledding. Furthermore, all kinds of sports and games are highly suitable for relating
acquired abilities to the environment and to playmates.

This teaches the coordination of movements, agility in water,
training of the sense of balance, the anticipation of events, and a
sense of direction. Thus, the child practises free action in sport.
He learns how to handle signs, things and the actions of his partner,
to recognize the relationship between things, solve problems, achieve
given aims and finally to find his way in his environment.

At primary school level sport provides the opportunity to
differentiate movement abilities and possibly also to direct them
towards certain sports according to the child's inclinations. The
more highly developed powers of perception of this age group enables
their senses to be developed through sport and games and opens up an
entirely new field of sensory experiences; for example, a feeling of
location and place in a given area and a feeling for the correct use
and distribution of strength. A matching of achievements, rivalry and
competition, as well as the assumption of certain duties in the group
and an understanding of rules also play an important part. In this
case, sport becomes a vehicle for social abilities.

In short, one can say that sport is extremely well suited,
owing to its "sensitivity", distinctness and comprehensibility, for
preparing a child for social reality and further development and for
rousing and developing his abilities. In summary, it is concluded
that sport: helps maintain health, compensates deficiencies
(specially among physically handicapped children) and increases
ability; increases well-being and promotes emotional balance; permits
purpose-free and undirected action; provides important and inalien-
able fundamental experiences for living in our mechanized world;
provides an important field of communication through social experiences and insights; reveals behavioural manners and the necessary
techniques for using leisure time sensibly after classes and
following finishing school.

The Present Situation in Children's Sports

Unfortunately the present situation in children's sport and
physical education is far from doing justice to the educational value
of sport, particularly in our country. There is not enough time for
sport, too few sports teachers, and sports facilities and the sports
offered on the curriculum are also not very attractive not only for
children of the three to ten-year-old group but for the older child
as well.

It is regrettable that these short-comings should be greatest precisely at the pre-school and primary school level; that is, at an age in which the child is particularly receptive and eager to learn and in which the skills he will need later in life are developed. Omissions made at this point can hardly be amended later.

It is also bad that these short-comings are basically not due to a lack of financial means. The insufficient means available are only a symptom of more fundamental problems. Education in our schools is still far too one-sided, aimed at training the intellectual faculties. Sport is still only considered one subject among many others, and then not one of the most highly regarded. If lessons have to be cancelled then sport is usually one of the first to go. Teachers who have qualifications in sport and a so-called "scholarly" subject are usually if not always assigned classes only in the latter, since that is supposedly the more important subject. The real reason therefore for these short-comings is the fact that the principles of development and teaching theory as well as pedagogical knowledge about sport have not yet been introduced into the school system.

I have already mentioned the situation in my country in respect to the pre-school programs for sport and physical activity. To reiterate, there is a lack of playing areas both indoors and outdoors; there are too few qualified teachers; indeed, there is not even a clear teaching plan nor adequate teaching and resource material to guide the kindergarten teachers. Recognizing these problems, it is significant that sports organizations and clubs, which are not at all responsible for education, should try to fill in the gap. Thus, the Deutsche Sportjugend (German Youth Sports Organization) recently submitted a program for "Sports Education at Primary Level". For the last few years clubs have been giving more attention to children under six, particularly as part of its "Mother and Child" program. The number of children in this age group belonging to clubs increased from 24,000 in 1959 to 220,000 in 1972. But this is still only 4% of all the children in this age group!

A ministerial decree has set a minimum of three hours of physical education a week in primary schools. However, for the reasons already stated, only 1.6 hours are given a week on an average, or in other words only half the amount. In Nordrhein-Westfalen, the largest Federal Land, only 8% of the school children received the prescribed three hours a week, 22% receive only one hour and 12% get no physical education at all. Only 33% of the teachers taking physical education classes have been trained exclusively for this purpose, 49% have received no training at all! Twenty-nine percent of the primary schools in the region do not have their own gymnasium, 53% do not offer swimming.

In this sphere the activities of the sports clubs serve openly as an excuse for the neglect of sport in schools. Their membership includes 22% (900,000) of all girls and 30% (1.3 million) of all boys in the age group 6 - 14 years.

Aspects for a Gradual Improvement

To be fair I must acknowledge that the situation is slowly improving. Colleges, the Deutsche Sportbund, the federal government and a number of Ministers for Culture of Federal Lands are attempting to work out a new sports curriculum, prepare advanced programs for training sports instructors and build suitable sports facilities.

In general terms the following demands can be made for sport and the physical education of children in the future:

- The child must have more purpose-free playing room in kindergarten and at school. Non-professional interests and abilities, which can be used during leisure time after finishing school, can be developed. This is the only way to discover, develop and enjoy one's body.

- This means that physical education will have to be built up more on voluntary participation. It will have to be "de-schooled", as the educationalist Hartmut von HENTIG suggested, and divested of its subject, utility and compulsory character.

- Consequently, sport must lose its compensational character with regard to other subjects. In fact it is even conceivable that sport may be introduced into other subjects as an educational principle. Is there any better way of getting to know the structure of a tree than by climbing it or to recognize musical rhythm than by dancing to it? Thus, sport will change from being an artificial product to becoming a natural manner of behaviour.

- Voluntary participation presupposes a wider range of sports offered. It must not be limited to just a few sports, otherwise the child will again merely be integrated into the already existing system and the result would simply be club and competition sports. The curricula should be checked for this.

- The child must be able to find his own way and goals in sport. The teacher must recede further into the background in favour of free choice on the part of the pupil and the class. He must be able to back his instructions, activate the children and encourage them with praise rather than check them with reproof.

- The child should be encouraged to consider his own athletic activity and the sports instruction critically.

- The need to develop all the child's talents and to correct shortcomings demands that the instruction be differentiated; that is, that both the more talented, but also the less talented, be particularly encouraged, for example, by forming groups of different standards. Handicapped children require special compensatopma; omstrictopm/

- Children should learn "social sensibility" at an early stage. Sports instruction, therefore, must direct them to social action and give them the opportunity to join in and to cooperate, to have a say and to share responsibility.

- Sports instruction should help to break down the fixed roles set for the male and the female. Why shouldn't girls play football if they want to?

These demands are related to important general principles which must be respected throughout the whole of sport, both in school and outside. However, these principles must definitely form the basis of children's sport and physical education as well if sport is later to play a role in the leisure time behaviour and social life of young people and adults.

Some Features of Physical Education for Children

I should now like to add some concrete essentials for the physical education of children.

At the pre-school level provisions must first be made for all children to be able to attend a full-time kindergarten or similar establishment and for sports instruction to have a set place on their curriculum. The sports offered must be based on the children's needs and their mental, emotional and social level of development. They must encourage interaction and communication and give more freedom for action than the cognitive fields of learning in order to offer free movement tasks and awaken an interest in experimenting and taking risks.

All basic forms of movement (using small apparatus and obstacles) and small games which encourage assigning roles and discussing the rules, such as running games, ball games and play acting, are recommended. The surroundings should change as much as possible, from gymnasium, to playground, swimming pool and open areas (with depressions, slopes, ditches, hillocks, woods, fields and sand).

Sport for the six to ten-year-olds must be organized in such a way that it leads to a higher level of action: from dexterity to ability, technique to tactics, practice situation to a matching of ability and competition. Children at this age are already able to check the effectiveness of their own movements and recognize and influence connections between actions. Particularly suitable are methodical series of exercises and games which take them from the known to the unknown, from easy things to difficult and from simple situations to complex ones. This enables them to broaden their range of abilities.

The lesson must also give them an opportunity to notice and attend to the weaker members and to help them. Here is the aim of individualizing sports instruction, namely to meet the inclination and abilities of the individual. In organizational terms this can be achieved by setting up partner exercises and interest and ability groups, which can easily extend beyond the classroom.

At this stage sports instruction can also draw attention to sports terminology and teach the names of movements, disciplines, techniques, methods, equipment and facilities. This is an important prerequisite for considering their own athletic activity and for critically appraising sports events.

The Solution - Suggestions

Children's sport seen in these terms cannot be realized without sufficient suitable playing area. We, therefore, need:

- playgrounds in towns - two to three times as many as we have at present;

- recreation and common rooms, games and sports equipment, outdoor playing areas and areas in the kindergartens;

- children's playing rooms and swimming pools in apartment houses;

- sufficient sports facilities in each school.

There is no need for separate facilities for the different age groups, since the needs overlap and, furthermore, expenses have to be kept down. However, the facilities should be able to be altered by moveable walls and should not be too standardized to restrict the desire for movement. The ideal to my mind would be combined recreational and sports centres where both adults and children could do sports together.

A more modern form of sport, which is better adapted to development, more attractive, more oriented towards leisure time, and available for all children can only be realized if all the bodies responsible, parents, kindergartens, schools, political parties, governments, welfare organizations, religious bodies, sports federations and sports clubs, contribute toward its achievement. Cooperation at many levels is essential.

Parental involvement is the first stage. If they could be made aware of the great importance sport has for their children they would form by sheer number a powerful pressure group for getting the authorities concerned moving. In addition, their children's life at home would also become more sports oriented.

The political parties above all could contribute to forming an awareness of the situation. They would be able to impress on governments that the expansion of the external signs of well-being should not be achieved at the expense of the natural playing room. The same applies to the sciences. Their contributions on children's sport and games are necessary to win over parliaments, governments, schools and public opinion.

The sports clubs, however, still have a large role to play in this sphere. Apart from their normal sports activities, which are primarily devoted to competitions, they must create better models for recreational sport for children, such as small groups of children to intensify athletic activity, family groups including parents and children, setting up clubs for pre-school and school children, training specialized instructors who can also help with the other facilities and so on.

Ladies and gentlemen, we face an overwhelming task if we wish to achieve all this, particularly since we have many other branches of sport, and not only sport, to attend to. But I think that it is worthwhile. For, in the last analysis, what we are doing is opening up more room for man to live a happy life in a world which is becoming constantly more crowded.

Physiological aspects

Other studies have in principle given similar results, but the absolute values have been on various levels (9, 17, 18, 19, 21, 22, 23). I particularly want to mention recent data by Hermansen who studied 308 Norwegian girls and boys 11 to 16 years of age. (Slides will be shown). His data for maximal oxygen uptake are at approximately the same level as in our 1952 study; his subjects included all pupils in a class or were chosen in alphabetical order from a class. It is an open question why the Scandinavian data on maximal $\dot{V}_{O_2}$ is so much higher than those reported from Canada, Japan, U.S.A., (9, 18, 23).

The sex difference in body maturity, including the oxygen transporting system, has definite application in both the physical education in school and in the competitive sports.

Body Dimensions and Performance

For a discussion of the development of the human "combustion engine" during growth I shall try to analyse to what extent certain dimensions and functional capacities are determined by fundamental mechanical necessities (for details see Åstrand and Rodahl, 1970, Chapter 10).

If we take two geometrically similar cubes of different size, the relationship between the surface and the volume of the two cubes can easily be calculated if only the scale factor between the sides of the cubes is known. If this length scale is L:1, the surface ratio is L^2:1, and the volume ratio L^3:1.

If we consider two geometrically similar and qualitatively identical individuals, we may expect all linear dimensions (L) to be proportional. The length of the arms, the legs, the trachea, and the individual muscles will have a ratio L:1. If we compare two boys, one 120 cm high, and the other 180 cm high, the scale factor will be such that all length, levers, ranges of joint motions, and muscular contractions during a specific motion will be related as 120:180 or as 1:1.5 (Figure 4). Cross sections of, for instance, a muscle, the aorta, a bone, the trachea, the alveolar surface, or the surface of the body are then related as $120^2:180^2$, or $1^2:1.5^2$, i.e., 1:2.25. Volumes, such as lung volumes, blood volumes, or heart volumes should similarly be related as $120^3: 180^3$, or $1^3:1.5^3$, i.e., 1:3.375. The same applies to mass measured in units of weight, since the density of biological materials generally speaking is independent of size.

Let us see how from a theoretical point of view, individuals of different size ought to function and perform in some events. Work is determined by the developed force, and the distance the force is applied. Thus the work the larger boy in our example should be able to perform is 3.375 times larger than that which would be expected in the case of the smaller boy. In "Chin-ups", i.e., the ability to lift one's own body, the performance is proportional to L^{-1}, which means that the larger and stronger boy is actually handicapped by his greater body weight. Maximal running speed is for similar animals of different size, the same. Short limbs with short strides move more rapidly and can therefore cover as much ground as do longer ones moving more slowly. In jumping one should expect that small and large individuals being equally able to lift their center of gravity. In high jumping, in which the aim is to lift the body as high as possible, the larger animal has an advantage, however, since its center of gravity before the jump is already at a higher level, "... a fact to remember sympathetically in assessing the jumping performance of small boys" (Hill). Energy supply per unit of time, i.e., power, should be proportional to L^2. Maximal oxygen uptake, cardiac output, and pulmonary ventilation are volumes per unit of time and therefore also proportional to L^2 (or $M^{2/3}$; M = body mass).

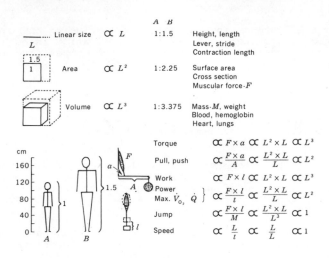

Figure 4

Schematic illustration of the influence of dimensions on some static and dynamic functions in geometrically similar individuals. A and B represent two persons with body height 120 and 180 cm respectively. (See text and Åstrand and Rodahl, 1970.)

Let us now see if children of different size behave according to this theoretical model. Figure 5 presents data on maximal speed in relation to body height for girls and boys of different age. From the age of about ten the body proportions are about the same. We may therefore consider the children represented in Figure 5 as geometrically similar. For 11- to 12-year-old boys there is no significant variation in speed with body size, which would not be expected from the discussion above. The somewhat better performance of the 12-year-olds to the 11-year-old boys may be due to maturity of the neuromuscular function, improving the coordination. Even better are 14-year-old boys, but one also found that the taller boys can run faster than the shorter ones. There is a further improvement in coordination with age, but this is also probably due to sexual maturity. Their male sex hormones may have influenced their muscular strength in a positive direction. The smaller 14-year-old boys may not have reached puberty, in contrast to the taller boys. In the 18-year-old-group there is

again hardly any variation in results in spite of a large difference
in body height. At this age all the boys have passed puberty and are
sexually mature.

In the girls there is an increase in maximal speed up to the
age of 14, but from then on there is no further improvement. The
results are not influenced by the size of the girls in any of the age
groups, which supports the assumption that the superiority of the
taller 14-year-old boys is due to the effect of male sex hormones.

Thus, the results obtained for boys of different size do not
strictly follow the results predicted from body dimensions. Apparently
biological factors may modify muscular dynamics. We have considered
an age factor as well as sexual maturity, which is particularly evident
for the boys' performance. For an analysis of the running performance
of children it is apparently helpful to have a theoretical model to
start with.

Similarly it can be concluded that the muscular strength and
ability to jump is not proportional to the dimensions, but subjected
to a biological quality modification. (The increase in strength from

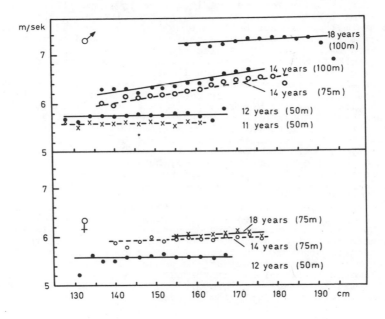

Figure 5

Maximal running speed in relation to body height for girls and boys
of different age; almost 100,000 subjects are included in the
statistics. (From Asmussen and Christensen.)

the 8-year to the 16-year-old boys is proportional to $L^{2.89}$, not to L^2 as expected from dimensions.) Thus, at least three factors affect muscle strength in ageing children: (i) increased size of the anatomical dimensions (See Figure 4); (ii) the results of ageing itself (one extra year of age increases the strength by 5 to 10% of the average strength of the same height group, and this gain may be attributed to the maturation of the central nervous system); (iii) the development of the sexual maturity of the child (probably the male sexual hormones are of special importance for this effect. As a matter of fact, between the ages of six and twenty, about one-third of the increase in body height occurs, but during the same period of time, four-fifths of the development of strength takes place (reference see Åstrand and Rodahl, 1970, pp. 93-96).

Is the Maximal Oxygen Uptake in Children Low or High?

I will now turn back to Figures 1-3 and discuss whether the observed maximal oxygen uptakes in children of different ages are proportional to their dimensions (to L^2 or $M^{2/3}$). For 16-to 18-year-old boys the maximum was 3.68 liters/minute, or 57.6 ml x kg^{-1} x $minutes^{-1}$. If we calculate the maximal oxygen uptake in the children aged 7 to 9, assuming that dimensions were the deciding factor, we find that they should attain 2.2 liters/minute or 70 ml x kg^{-1} x $minutes^{-1}$. The actually measured maximal were lower, or 1.75 liters/minute and 57 ml x kg^{-1} x $minutes^{-1}$. We may conclude that the children's maximal oxygen uptake is not as high as expected for their size and that they do not have the aerobic power to handle their weight compared to adults. It is also significant that the 8-year-old child could increase his basal metabolic rate only 9.4 times during maximal running for 5 minutes, but the 17-year-old boy could attain an aerobic power which was 13.5 times the basal power. Therefore the child has less in the way of a power reserve than adults. It should also be emphasized that the young subjects had a significantly higher oxygen uptake per kilogram of body weight than the older boys and adults when running at a given speed on a treadmill (P.-O. Åstrand, 1952). These two factors together may explain the fact that children have difficulty in following their parents' speed, even if maximal oxygen uptake per kilogram body weight may be the same. The children's lower efficiency can partly be explained by their high stride frequency which is an expensive utilization of energy per unit of time.

Since the oxygen is transported by the hemoglobin, it is of interest to compare the children's total amount of hemoglobin (Hb_T) with their body size and maximal oxygen uptake (Figure 6). In most of the subjects just discussed, the total hemoglobin was determined. In similar animals of different size Hb_T should be proportional to M. However, per kilogram of body weight the younger boys had only 78 percent of the amount of hemoglobin of the older boys. Thus the amount of hemoglobin was definitely not proportional to body size. The Hb-concentration is also relatively low in young children compared with adults.

The sample of subjects selected for these analyses is limited to 21 individuals, but it is a homogeneous group. They were nonobese and in the same state of training. The results support the assumption

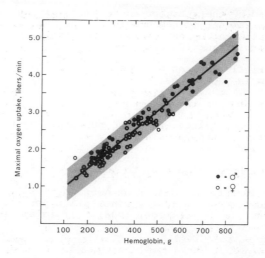

Figure 6

Maximal oxygen uptake for 94 of the subjects
included in Figure 1, age 7 to 30 years, in
relation to total amount of hemoglobin. In
the equation $\dot{V}_{O_2} = a \times Hb_T^b$ the exponent
b = 0.76. (Modified from Åstrand, 1952.)

that the maximal oxygen uptake in children and young adults is proportional to the muscular strength and to $Hb_T^{0.76}$, or roughly to $Hb_T^{2/3}$,
but not to $M^{2/3}$.

It may be concluded that children are definitely physically
handicapped compared to adults (and fully grown animals of similar
size). When related to the child's dimensions, its muscular strength
is low and so is its maximal oxygen uptake and other parameters of
importance for the oxygen transport. Furthermore the mechanical
efficiency of children is often inferior to that of the adults. The
introduction of dimensions in the discussion of children's performance
clearly indicates that they are not mature as working machines.

Maximal Aerobic Power in Women

For the female subjects 8-to 16-years of age, the maximal $\dot{V}_{O_2}$
is proportional to $L^{2.5}$. In light of the previous discussion the
noted discrepancy from the expected L^2 is not surprising. Women have
approximately the same maximal oxygen uptake per kilogram fat-free
body mass as men. However, it should be higher in women due to their
smaller size. The lower Hb-concentration in women may explain why
they cannot fully utilize their cardiac output for oxygen transport.
Figure 2 is stressing these points further. As pointed out, there is
a very high correlation between maximal oxygen uptake and body weight
for male, nonobese subjects. The lower maximal oxygen uptake for
female subjects above 40 kg of body weight (age about 14 years) is

largely explained by their higher content of adipose tissue. When one relates the total amount of hemoglobin to the maximal oxygen uptake, the difference between regression lines for the female and male subjects is insignificant (Figure 6).

I will briefly comment on some of the links in the oxygen transport system in young ages.

Lung Function

There are no evidences that the pulmonary ventilation or diffusing capacity of the lungs normally limits the aerobic power in adults nor in children. The lung volumes in young subjects were related to body size and varied approximately as the cube of a linear dimension such as body height, up to the age of 25. In other words, these volumes in children are of a size that could be expected from theoretical considerations (data from Åstrand, 1952). The younger the child, the higher is the pulmonary ventilation per liter oxygen uptake, Figure 7 (Åstrand, 1952; Robinson, 1938). It is apparently a true

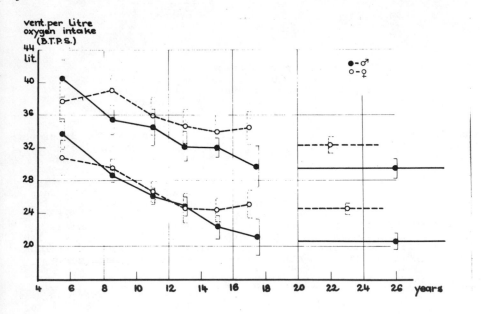

Figure 7

Average values for pulmonary ventilation per liter oxygen uptake in relation to age. The upper curves show maximal values (running); and the lower ones submaximal values (running or cycling), with an oxygen uptake which was 60 to 70% of the subject's maximal aerobic power. Same subjects as in Figure 1. (Vertical lines denote ± 2 SEM.) (From Åstrand, 1952.)

hyperventilation giving a relatively low alveolar CO_2 and higher O_2 tension. I cannot present any good explanation for this ventilatory response. During exercise up to about 50% of the vital capacity is utilized as tidal volume, irrespective of sex and age.

Cardiac Output

At submaximal oxygen uptakes children from the age of 10 have been studied with regard to their cardiac output (Andrew et al., 1972; Bar-Or et al., 1971; Eriksson, 1972). The cardiac output was lower in children than in adults, and with necessity the $a-\bar{v} O_2$ difference larger. In Bar-Or et al. (1971) studies on girls 10 to 13 years of age had a higher cardiac output than boys of the same age. A similar sex difference has been noted in adults (Åstrand et al., 1963), but for that group the women's lower hemoglobin concentration in the blood could explain this finding. The girls and boys had, however, identical Hb-concentration so a similar explanation for the noticed different cardiac outputs in the Canadian study is not at hand. The younger the person, the higher is the heart rate at a given oxygen uptake (Figure 8), partly compensating for the children's small stroke volume compared with adults. When taking differences in body size into account, the

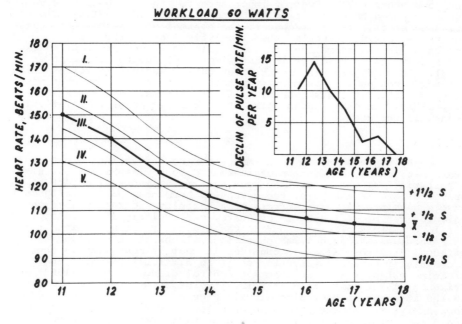

WORKLOAD 60 WATTS

Figure 8

Developmental physiogram of heart rate per minute at steady state in 52 boys followed during the years. The rate of decline of average heart rate is given in one-year intervals. Group 1 was least physically active, Group V the most active one. (From Ulbrich, 1971.)

young individual seems to have a stroke volume proportional to his height cubed (L3), i.e., it is "normal". The maximal heart rate is in average well above 200 in youngsters but declines with age. This is actually what we should expect, that the larger animal should have a lower heart rate than the smaller one. From a theoretical consideration, with maximal heart rate proportional to L-1, the difference between a 10-year-old child and an adult should be some 40 beats/minute, not only 10 beats as noticed. Again, there is some sort of an additional biological adaptation.

Skeletal Muscles

Most of the oxygen molecules transported during exercise are consumed by the muscles' mitochondria. The number of muscle cells in a muscle group is probably finally established after the embryo has reached the age of 4 to 5 months. The proportion between fast twitch fibers (also named white) and slow twitch fibers (red) is also a question of endowment not possible to modify by training, (discussion see Åstrand and Rodahl, 1970; Edström and Ekblom, 1972; Eriksson 1972; Gollnick et al., 1972).

Boys have the same concentration of ATP, creatine phosphate and some other key enzymes of importance for the metabolism as adults (those studied have been from 11 up to 15 years of age (Eriksson, 1972; Eriksson et al., 1971). However, the content of phosphofructokinase, the rate-limiting enzyme of the glycolytic energy-yielding system resulting in the formation of lactic acid as an end product, is strikingly low in children in comparison with adults (Eriksson et al., 1973). This may explain why children during maximal exercise attain a lower blood as well as muscle lactate concentration compared with 25-year-old individuals (Robinson, 1938; Åstrand, 1952; Eriksson et al., 1971). In other words, also the anaerobic power is relatively "weak" in children.

Training

The improvement in performance during the child's growth is, as mentioned, partly a question of increased body dimensions, but also a "maturity" of the central nervous system, an eventual effect of practice; and in the boys, the effect of hormones, particularly on the muscle development. The effects of a training program applied on children can be difficult to evaluate, particularly if it is applied for long periods of time. During the training, ageing in itself will to a large extent accomplish physiological changes simulating training effects. Another factor to consider is that in most schools there is a compulsory physical education so it is difficult to match the training subjects with an inactive control group. Ekblom (1969) and Eriksson (1972) have tried to relate the effects noted during training to the increase in body dimensions. Figure 9 gives an example of such analyses. Fourteen boys were followed over a period of 32 months and 6 to 7 of them participated in a special training. The expected change in various parameters, due to increased dimensions, was evaluated on a theoretical basis (the same principles as presented in Figure 4).

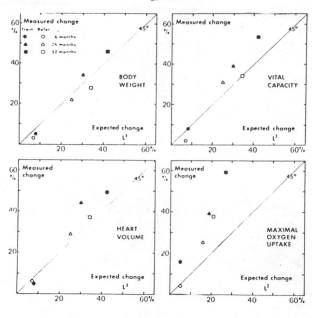

Figure 9

Group means of measured changes in body weight, vital capacity, heart volume, and maximal oxygen uptake after 6, 26, and 32 months' observation compared with corresponding expected changes, as predicted from the relation body height after to height before raised to 2.0 (L^2) and 3.0 (L^3). Altogether 14 boys, initially 11 years of age are participated, training or as controls. (From Ekblom, 1969.)

Various longitudinal studies have shown that children react to training by an improved performance as do adults. Compared with untrained individuals of equal height, weight, and age, the physically well-trained persons at any age have in average a higher density (lean body mass), maximal oxygen uptake and maximal cardiac output (reference see Parisková, 1968; Ekblom, 1969; Eriksson, 1972). The heart rate decreases at a standard oxygen uptake.

There are hypotheses that a rational training during adolescent growth would yield relatively better results than later on in life, particularly on same static dimensions like lung volumes, heart volume, body height (Åstrand et al., 1963; Ekblom, 1969; Andrew et al., 1972; Eriksson, 1972). Well-trained girl swimmers have actually a very large heart volume (Figure 10) and lung volumes, but they comprise a very selected group of individuals. Dr. Bengt Eriksson will devote some time to discuss this group of swimmers, which has been subjected to a longitudinal study. During the after physical activity there is an increase in the growth hormone concentration in the blood, and during maximal exercise also in androgens (reference see Sutton et al., 1973). A raised level of androgen during exercise may act in

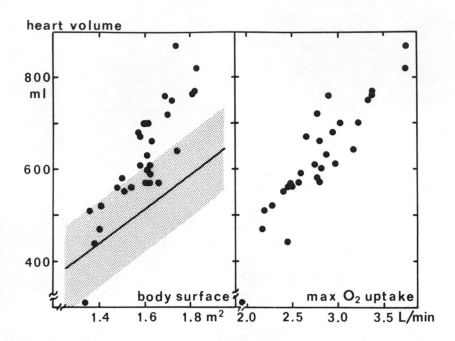

Figure 10

Relationship between heart volume and (a) calculated body surface area
and (b) maximal oxygen uptake in 30 young well-trained girl swimmers.
Shadowed area gives the 95% range for "normal" girls. (Modified from
Åstrand et al., 1963.)

association with growth hormone to increase the pubertal growth
velocity. The last word is not said in this discussion. Pariskova
(1968) did not in her longitudinal study on 96 boys, followed from 11
to 15 years of age, notice any difference in height, weight, and
several other anthropometric measurements between the boys divided
into four groups according to intensity of habitual physical activity.
Ulbrich (1971), who followed about 130 boys over 7 years (example on
data, see Figure 8), points out that constitutional factors were most
decisive for the child's interest for physical training. Those most
interested were fit above average. In their heart rate response to
a standard load on the bicycle ergometer, the boys followed a curve
parallel to the average response (following example line 1 or IV etc.
in Figure 8), with periodic exceptions depending particularly on the
time for puberty. He emphasized that a test result on a child of the
age of 11 can predict his cardiorespiratory fitness some 7 years later
(this is not the case in adults, Åstrand et al., 1973).

Eriksson (1972) points out that ".... a certain degree of physical exercise is necessary for functionally harmonious somatic development and that the boys studied had a level of physical activity before training which was less than the minimum level required."

Regular Physical Activity in Youth

For further discussions I now want to make a few specific comments. In my opinion these are important aims for the physical activity in the schools:

1. Train the oxygen-transporting system (respiration and circulation).

2. Generally train the locomotive organs (especially the muscles of the back and abdomen).

3. Give instruction on how to lie, sit, stand, walk, lift, carry, etc. (ergonomics).

4. Give instruction in technique, tactics, rules, etc. in games and sports in order to reduce or eliminate accidents (the events are eventually practiced in the students' leisure time).

5. Provide physical and psychological recreation and variety.

6. Aroused interest in regular physical activity after schooling has been finished.
   (These goals are based only on physiological-medical consider-ations.)

Some arguments have been given above. Particularly many girls have an intake of some vitamins and iron below the recommended amount. Being physically active, they can eat more without being obese, and will get more of essential nutrients.

In the activities sponsored by the school there should be less emphasis on competition and more on recreational activities which are suitable for future use.

It is most unfortunate that the real pleasure of exercise which effectively trains the cardiorespiratory functions comes after the exercise and that one so easily forgets this pleasure when facing a new training period. One must "indoctrinate" the youngsters in the biological, psychological "know-how" of training and teach preventive health care. Considering that we have so many millions of habitually inactive adults, smokers, people with poor dieting habits, etc., the school has in these respects, so far, been something of a failure. Is it time to change the school curriculum in biology and physical education? (Åstrand, 1972)

References

1. Andrew, G.M., M.R. Becklake, J.S. Guleria, and D.V. Bates. Heart and lung functions in swimmers and nonathletes during growth. J. Appl. Physiol. 32:245-251, 1972.

2. Åstrand, P.-O. Experimental studies of physical working capacity in relation to sex and age. Copenhagen: Munksgaard, 1952.

3. Åstrand, P.-O. Health and fitness. Stockholm: Skandia and the Swedish Information Service, 1972.

4. Åstrand, I., P.-O. Åstrand, I. Hallbäck, and Å. Kilbom. Longitudinal variations in maximal oxygen uptake with age. Submitted for publication in J. Appl. Physiol. 1973.

5. Åstrand, P.-O., T.E. Cuddy, B. Saltin, and J. Stenberg. Cardiac output during submaximal and maximal work. J. Appl. Physiol. 19:268-274, 1964.

6. Åstrand, P.-O., L. Engström, B.O. Eriksson, P. Karlberg, I. Nylander, B. Saltin, and C. Thoren. Girls Swimmers. Acta Physiol. Scand. Suppl. 147:3-75, 1963.

7. Åstrand, P.-O. and K. Rodahl. Textbook of work physiology. New York: McGraw-Hill, 1970.

8. Bar-Or, O., R.J. Shephard, and C.L. Allen. Cardiac output of 10- to 13-year-old boys and girls during submaximal exercise. J. Appl. Physiol. 30:219-223, 1971.

9. Cumming, R.G. Current levels of physical fitness. Canad. Med. Ass. J. 96:868-877, 1967.

10. Edström, L. and B. Ekblom. Differences in sizes of red and white muscle fibres in vastus lateralis of the muscular quadriceps femoris of normal individuals and athletes. Relation to physical performance. Scand. J. clin. Lab. Invest. 30:175-181, 1972.

11. Ekblom, B. Effect of physical training on oxygen transport system in man. Acta Physiol. Scand., Suppl. 348, 1969.

12. Eriksson, B.O. Physical training, oxygen supply and muscle metabolism in 11 - 13-year-old boys. Acta Physiol. Scand. Suppl. 384, 1972.

13. Eriksson, B.O., P.D. Gollnick, and B. Saltin. Muscle metabolism and enzyme activities after training in boys 11 - 13 years old. Acta Physiol. Scand. In Press 1973.

14. Eriksson, B.O., J. Karlsson, and B. Saltin. Muscle metabolites during exercise in pubertal boys. Acta paediat. Scand. Suppl. 217:57-63, 1971.

15. Gollnick, P.D., R.B. Armstrong, C.W. Saubert IV, K. Piehl, and B. Saltin. Enzyme activity and fiber composition in skeletal muscle of untrained and trained men.
J. Appl. Physiol. 33:312-319, 1972.

16. Hermansen, L. Oxygen transport during exercise in human subjects. Thesis from the Institute of Work Physiology, Oslo, Norway, 1973.

17. Hollman, W. Höchst- und Dauerleistungsfähigkeit des Sportlers. Munich: Johann Ambrosius Barth, 1963.

18. Ikai, M., M. Shindo, and M. Miyamura. Aerobic work capacity of Japanese people.
Res. J. Phys. Ed. 14:137-142, 1970.

19. König, K., H. Reindell, J. Keul, and H. Roskamm. Untersuchungen über das Verhalten von Atmung und Kreislauf im Belastungsversuch bei Kindern und Jugendlichen im Alter von 10 - 19 Jahren.
Int. Z. angew. Physiol. einschl. Arbeitsphysiol. 18:393-434, 1961.

20. Pařisková, J. Physical activity and body composition. In J. Brozék (Ed.)
Human body composition Oxford: Pergamon Press, 1965, pp. 161 - 176.

21. Pařisková, J. Longitudinal study of development of body composition and body build in boys of various physical activity.
Human Biol., 40: 212-225, 1968.

22. Robinson, S. Experimental studies of physical fitness in relation to age.
Arbeitsphysiologie. 10:251-323, 1938.

23. Rodahl, K., P.-O. Åstrand, N.C. Birkhead, T. Hettinger, B. Issekutz, Jr., D.M. Jones, and R. Weaver. Physical work capacity: A study of some children and young adults in the United States.
Arch. Environ. Health. 2:499-510, 1961.

24. Sutton, J.R., M.J. Coleman, J. Casey, and L. Lazarus. Androgen responses during physical exercise.
Brit. Med. J. 13:520-522, 1973.

25. Ulbrich, J. Individual variants of physical fitness in boys from the age of 11 up to maturity and their selection for sports activities.
Medicina dello Sport. 24:118-136, 1971.

THE CHILD IN SPORT AND PHYSICAL ACTIVITY

Physiology - Comment

by   Roy J. Shephard, M.D., Ph.D.
Department of Environmental Health,
School of Hygiene,
University of Toronto.

I much appreciate the invitation of Professor Åstrand to comment on his very interesting paper and amplify his remarks by reference to the experience of our own and other Canadian laboratories.

Experimental design. One very practical application of physiological data is to assess the normality of the developing child before and/or after institution of a program of sport or physical activity. However, in order to do this, we must understand something of experimental design with regard to both the sampling of population and the type of survey that has been instituted.

(a)   Sampling. Professor Åstrand rightly drew attention to the possibility of bias in his material; certainly, we still do not know if the Swedish schoolchild is unusually fit, but the values of aerobic power reported from Stockholm are 10-15% higher than those seen in almost every other urban area of the world (Shephard, 1972). In a small community, the ideal approach is to test everyone. We were able to approach this objective in our Eskimo study (Rode & Shephard, 1971), where about 70% of the villagers agreed to be examined. A second valuable alternative is to use a random sample of the population; the study of working capacity in Canadian schoolchildren (Howell & MacNab, 1968) with the detailed physiological examination of one sub-sample (Shephard et al., 1969) provides a unique example of this methodology. If the sample is nonrandom, then it becomes necessary to seek for possible biasses and if possible to make appropriate allowances.

(b)   Type of survey. The growth and development of physiological variables has traditionally been studied by cross-sectional surveys. The theses of Robinson (1939) and Åstrand (1952), and the C.A.H.P.E.R. study of the Canadian schoolchild (Howell & MacNab, 1968) are all excellent examples of such methodology, cohorts of data being collected on children of all ages from perhaps 6 or 7 to 17 years. More recently, longitudinal surveys have gained popularity; currently two groups of Canadian children are being followed annually throughout childhood (Bailey, this conference, pp. 87; Lavallée, Brisson, Larivière and Shephard - in preparation).

The longitudinal study is naturally much more costly than the cross-sectional approach but it has certain advantages when seeking to interpret the influence of sport and physical activity upon function. It is not sufficient to know the average development of a child at a given age -- the precise timing of spurts in muscle strength, aerobic

36

power and the like must be identified with respect to
maturation, for activity may be influencing the onset
of maturation rather than enhancing the ultimate
development of the child. Unfortunately, there are
wide variations in the age of maturation, and it is
almost impossible to derive the necessary information
from cross-sectional data; peaks of development are
both blurred and displaced by the averaging process.

A further complicating factor is cultural change.
Robinson's measurements were made in 1938, Åstrand's
in 1950. Much change can occur even over the period
when a child is growing from six to seventeen years
of age. We have encountered the problem rather acutely
in our studies of the Eskimo, who is rapidly adopting
a white pattern of civilization (Rode & Shephard, 1972,
1973a), and in the rural areas of Quebec, where the
"quiet revolution" progresses apace (Lavallée et. al.,
in preparation). But even in apparently stable urban
areas, habitual activity is still diminishing (Shephard,
1973) and cigarette smoking and other forms of drug usage
are affecting ever younger children. Cultural changes
bias cross-sectional and longitudinal growth curves in
opposite directions, and if change is rapid, the most
accurate information on child development is probably
derived from a semi-longitudinal study, where cohorts
of children from 6 to 17 years of age are reexamined after
the elapse of twelve months. This is the method we have
used in our studies of the Eskimo child (Rode & Shephard,
1972, 1973a).

(c) Dimensional analysis. The dimensional type of analysis
used by Professors Eriksson and Åstrand is intriguing,
although it would be wrong to be bound too slavishly by
it. If function fails to develop in the manner predicted
by hypothesis, the problem may be with the hypothesis
rather than the child! While discrepancies between
hypothesis and child are of limited significance,
differences in the height exponent between populations are
of more interest.

Let us take as an example vital capacity; in Åstrand's
children this varied as the third power of standing height.
But as with aerobic power, his group seems atypical. There
are now many large studies of vital capacity in "white"
children, and all show exponents of less than three, with
some as low as 2.5 (de Muth et al., 1965). On the other
hand, in Eskimo children, vital capacity varies almost
exactly as the third power of standing height (Rode & Shephard,
1973b). One may suspect that because of a low level of
habitual activity, the potential development of vital
capacity is not fully realized in the "white" child.

A further complication arises from differences of body build.
Many "primitive" peoples have traditionally had a short leg
length. The older Eskimos show this trait, and at all ages
the Eskimo schoolchild is still shorter than his "white"
contemporary, although he is catching up fast, and within

one or two decades will probably be as tall as the child
from a more southerly community (Rode & Shephard, 1973a).
During early adolescence, girls are normally taller than
boys for a few months; in the Eskimo girls, the advantage
is greater, and persists for about three years -- perhaps
one more example of a realization of growth potential
through greater habitual activity.

Ethnic groups. The distinct geographical regions of Canada have
preserved many relatively pure "genetically isolated" populations,
thus giving opportunity to explore not only the development of the
average child, but differences between races and between cultures.

Interesting differences are emerging between French and English-
speaking Canadian children (Demirjian et al., 1971; Lavallée,
Brisson, Larivière and Shephard - in preparation), with further differences between urban and rural areas; in general, the francophones
are smaller, stronger, and have a larger aerobic power than the anglo-
phones.

Our data on the traditional Eskimo child provides information
on the growth of a population that is highly active from an early age.
The boys maintain this activity through to manhood, but in later
adolescence some of the girls begin to copy the inactive habits of
"white" children. Implications for height and vital capacity have
already been noted. The growth of muscle strength of the Eskimo girls
does not taper off at about twelve years, as would be anticipated in
a "white" girl (Howell et al., 1964); indeed, it exceeds that of the
boys until about fourteen years of age. Again, if maximum oxygen
intake is expressed per kg of body weight, both boys and girls of 9 -
10 have much higher readings than those found in Toronto (Shephard et
al., 1969) and other parts of Canada (Howell & MacNab, 1968; Cumming
& Cumming, 1963), matching the unusual figures that Åstrand found in
Stockholm. The Eskimo boys retain an aerobic power of around 60 ml./
kg. minute throughout the period of growth, but in the girls there is
a progressive decrease, not all of which can be attributed to an
increase of body fat. You will note the use of a weight rather than a
height standard for aerobic power (ml./kg. minute). The reason for
this is that the cost of body movement is roughly proportional to
body weight, and it is thus appropriate to scale the driving power of
the oxygen transport system in a similar manner.

Cardiac output. Professor Åstrand referred to the low cardiac outputs
that seem a feature of the child during exercise. We have now
documented this phenomenon as occurring not only in Toronto schoolchildren, but also in the francophones of Quebec and in the Eskimos.
Among possible explanations, we suspect (Shephard, Rode & Bar-Or,
1972):

(i) greater tissue extraction of oxygen in the child due to more
active enzyme systems,

(ii) lesser oxygen demand by visceral tissues (because these are
smaller than in the adult), and

(iii) more ready elimination of body heat and thus a lesser need for
blood flow to the skin.

Needs of Canadian schools. Our needs are essentially as seen by
Professor Åstrand. In particular, we need to answer the challenge
that existing physical education programs are insufficient to improve
the physiological variables associated with fitness (Cumming et al.,
1969), and fail to develop patterns of habitual activity that will
persist into adult life.

References

Åstrand, P-O. Experimental studies of physical working capacity in relation to sex and age.
  Copenhagen, Denmark: Munksgaard, 1952.

Cumming, G.R., Goulding, D., & Baggley, G. Failure of school physical education to improve cardiorespiratory fitness.
  Canad. Med. Ass. J. 101, 69 - 73, 1969.

Cumming, G.R., & Cumming, P.M. Working capacity of normal children tested on a bicycle ergometer.
  Canad. Med. Ass. J. 88, 351 - 355, 1963.

Demirjian, A., Dubuc, M.B., & Jenicek, M. Etude comparative de la croissance de l'enfant canadien d'origine française à Montréal.
  Canad. J. Publ. Health 62, 111 - 119, 1971.

de Muth, G.R., Howatt, W.F., & Hill, B.M. The growth of lung function.
  Pediatrics 35, Supp. 1965.

Howell, M.L., Loiselle, D.S., & Lucas, W.G. Strength of Edmonton schoolchildren.
  Unpublished report, Fitness Unit, University of Alberta, Edmonton, 1964.

Howell, M.L., & MacNab, R.B.J. The physical work capacity of Canadian children aged 7 to 17.
  Toronto, Ont.: Canadian Association for Health, Physical Education and Recreation, 1968.

Robinson, S. Experimental studies of fitness in relation to age.
  Arbeitsphysiol. 10, 251 - 323, 1939.

Rode, A., & Shephard, R.J. The cardiorespiratory fitness of an Arctic community.
  J. appl. Physiol. 31, 519 - 526, 1971.

Rode, A., & Shephard, R.J. Growth and Development in the Eskimo.
  Proc. 2nd Canadian Workshop on Child Growth and Development, Saskatoon, Nov. 1972.

Rode, A., & Shephard, R.J. Growth, development, and fitness of the Canadian Eskimo. Med. & Sci. in Sports.
  In press, 1973a.

Rode, A., & Shephard, R.J. Pulmonary function of Canadian Eskimos.
  Scand. J. Resp. Dis. In press, 1973b.

Shephard, R.J., Allen, C., Bar-Or, O., Davies, C.T.M., Degré, S., Hedman, R., Ishii, K., Kaneko, M., LaCour, J.R., DiPrampero, P.E., & Seliger, V. The working capacity of Toronto schoolchildren.
  Canad. Med. Ass. J. 100, 560 - 566, 705 - 714, 1969.

Shephard, R.J. The working capacity of schoolchildren. pp. 319 - 344.
  Frontiers of Fitness, Ed: R.J. Shephard. Springfield, Illinois: C.C. Thomas, 1971.

Shephard, R.J., Rode, A., & Bar-Or, O. Cardiac output and oxygen
conductance. A comparison of the Canadian Eskimo and the city dweller.
   In: Proceedings of 4th International Symposium on Pediatric Work
   Physiology. Wingate Institute, Israel, 1972.

Shephard, R.J. Alive, Man! The physiology of physical activity.
   Springfield, Illinois, C.C. Thomas, 1973.

Medical
aspects

THE CHILD IN SPORT AND PHYSICAL ACTIVITY - MEDICAL ASPECTS

by Bengt O. Eriksson,
      Department of Pediatrics,
      University of Gothenburg,
      Östra Sjukhuset, S-416 85 Göteborg, Sweden.

This presentation will deal basically with the medical effects of physical training in both healthy and handicapped children. Due to the necessity of limitation, it is impossible to consider all aspects of this issue.

Human beings are created with a natural urge for physical activity. Even in the newborn infant there is a need for activity - to kick about. With increasing age the child shows a more developed type of activity with an increased demand on the oxygen transport system. However, the technical progress in our modern society has facilitated the child's existence and reduced the amount of physical activity which was associated with a more primitive way of life. The question then is: to what extent has this development influenced the child's physical working capacity and the organs involved in oxygen transport and metabolism? In a recently published study[10] this question has been investigated. It was found that the living conditions of the normal 11-year old Swedish boys included in the study were abnormal with respect to physical activity. The change in body composition and physical performance capacity obtained after a four-month period of physical training resulted in enhancement of the oxygen transport system to approach normal values. Therefore, it can be stated that a certain amount of physical activity is necessary for the harmonious development of a child.[12]

On the other hand, does very hard physical training have any deleterious effects on the growing child? This is an important question, especially as in many sports hard physical training is engaged in by children to an ever-increasing extent. This is particularly pronounced in competitive swimming, where hard physical training is started before the age of ten. In a detailed study of 30 top girl swimmers in Sweden these girls, 12 to 16 years old, had been training extensively for some years. Some of them trained 28 hours a week and covered in that time a distance of 65,000 metres (Figure 1). This hard training had improved the girls' maximal oxygen uptake (Figure 2) but also increased the dimensions of some components of the oxygen transporting system (Figures 3-5). Taking these dimensions individually, and without considering the increased maximal oxygen uptake, one might conclude that these girls were damaged by the hard physical training; this does really happen sometimes, especially when a physician sees only the x-ray of the heart. On the other hand, the increased dimensions correlated very well with each other (Figure 6) as well as with maximal oxygen uptake (Figure 7). Thus it may be stated that the hard physical training had given these girls the increased size of the organs involved in the oxygen transport system, thereby enabling an increase of the maximal oxygen uptake. From these data, there was no indication that the hard physical training had caused any damage to these girls at that time.

---

*The author deeply thanks associate professors Kristina Berg, Göteborg and Claes Thorén, Stockholm for their kind permission to use their data and figures.

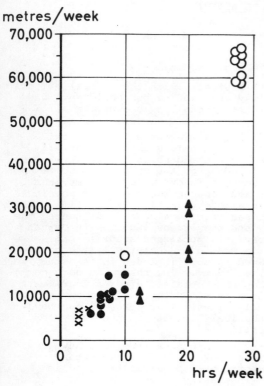

Figure 1

Average training volume
in 30 girl swimmers from
4 different clubs
(= different symbols),
expressed as hours/week
and meters/week. Data
from (1).

Figure 2

Oxygen uptake during
maximal exercise on a
bicycle ergometer in
relation to body
weight in the 30 girl
swimmers. Broken
line: normal regres-
sion line with 95%
confidence interval.
For symbols, see
Figure 1. Data from
(1).

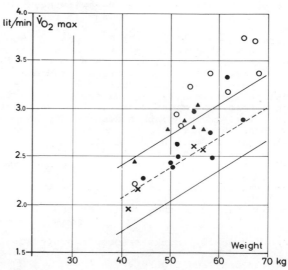

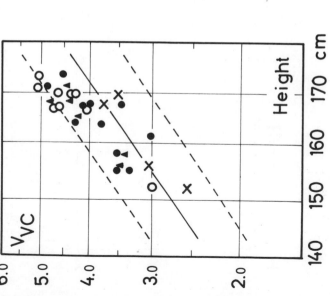

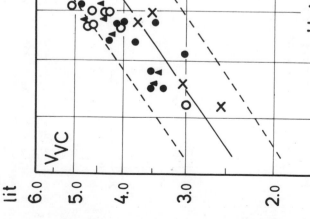

Figure 4

Total haemoglobin in relation to body
weight. Broken line: normal regression
line with 95% confidence interval.
For symbols, see Figure 1. Data from
(1).

Figure 3

Vital capacity (Vvc) in relation to
height: double logarithmic scale.
Unbroken lines: normal regression line
with 95% confidence interval. For
symbols, see Figure 1. Data from (1).

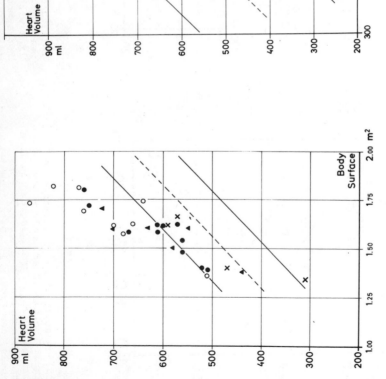

Figure 5

Heart volume in relation to body
surface. Broken line: normal
regression line with 95% confidence
interval. For symbols, see Figure 1.
Data from (1).

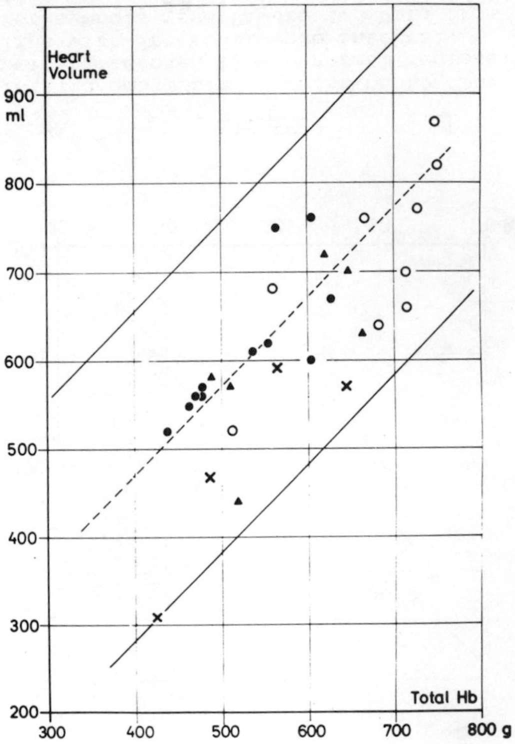

Figure 6

Heart volume in relation to total
haemoglobin. Broken line: normal
regression line with 95% confidence
interval. For symbols, see Figure 1.
Data from (1).

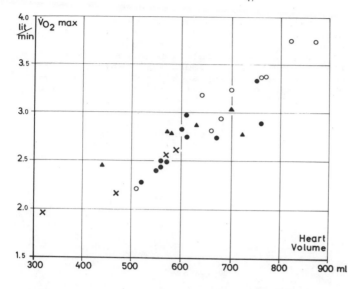

Figure 7

Maximal oxygen uptake in relation to heart volume. For symbols, see Figure 1. Data from (1).

Another important question to be answered is whether this hard physical training might have harmful effects which become manifest later on in life. To study this problem, these girls have been followed for ten years after the first examination. During this time all girls had stopped their regular training and most did not engage in any specific physical activity in their spare time. Their daily lives were filled with studies, working in their professions, domestic work, working with their children and so on. Due to the very low grade of physical activity, the girls showed a pronounced decrease in their aerobic power (Figure 8).

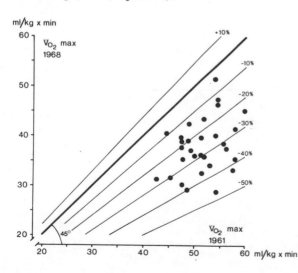

Figure 8

Individual values of maximal oxygen uptake per kg body weight in 1968/69 as compared to 1961 of former girl swimmers. The heavy line denotes 45° identification line and the thinner lines denote the deviation in per cent from the identification line. Data from (13).

Mean value for the girls' maximal oxygen uptake had decreased 29%, from 52 to 37 ml/kg x min. On the other hand, the dimensions of the lungs and hearts were relatively unchanged (Figures 9-10); as a consequence, there was a change in the correlation between these dimensions and the maximal oxygen uptake (Figure 11). What this means is still unknown. As heart volume has been supposed to be an indirect measure of stroke volume[3] these results could indicate a remaining large stroke volume. However, this was not the case. Thus it is still an unsolved problem what constitutes these big hearts, and whether it has any deleterious effects later on in life. However, when examining post-active top athletes in endurance sports, an increased heart volume has also been found[16, 27] without causing any evident medical problems. Further studies of these girls are necessary.

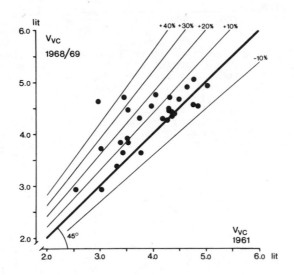

Figure 9

Individual values of vital capacity in
former girl swimmers in 1968/69 as
compared to 1961. For explanation of
the lines, see Figure 8. Data from (13).

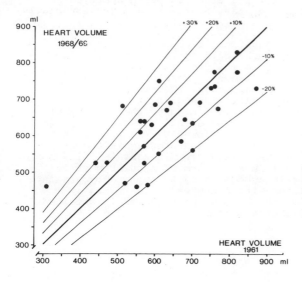

Figure 10

Individual values of
heart volume in supine
position in former girl
swimmers in 1968/69 as
compared to 1961. For
explanation of the lines,
see Figure 8. Data from
(13).

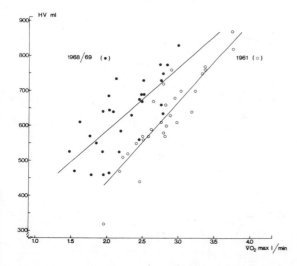

Figure 11

Individual values of
heart volume and maximal
oxygen uptake 1961
(unfilled symbols) and
1968/69 (filled symbols).
Regression equations;
1961: $y = -13.46 + 227.21x$; 1968/69:
$y = 230.8 + 178.35x$. Data
from (1 and 13).

Thus it can be stated that hard physical training influences the normal development of the child. At present no deleterious effects have been demonstrated. Furthermore, the top athletes who continue with regular physical training after stopping sport competition have a lower incidence of coronary heart disease and especially death in cardiac diseases.[29]

The second part of my presentation is concerned with the medical aspects of the handicapped child in sport and physical activity. Important groups of handicapped children include those with bronchial asthma, congenital heart disease, obesity, diabetes, neurological diseases and mental retardation. These children are often restricted in their physical activity due to their disease. However, an important restriction is caused also by the anxiety of physicians, nurses and parents. Thus, as recently as ten years ago in Sweden, children with diabetes were not allowed by the school physicians to participate in the physical education program in the schools.[19] In my opinion there are very few diseases in childhood which should prohibit the child from some form of regular physical activity. Indeed, physical training does play an important part in the medical treatment of children with diabetes.[18, 30] This is suggested by the improvement of the aerobic power which is obtained when training children with diabetes (Figure 12).

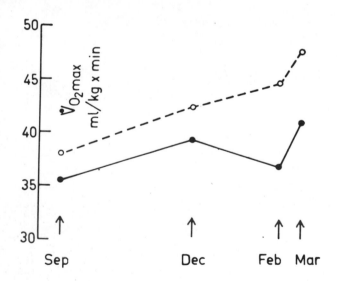

Figure 12

Increase during training in max. $\dot{V}_{O2}$. Unbroken line denotes diabetics, broken line nondiabetics. Data from (18).

The obese child is restricted because of his being overweight, one cause of which is his lack of physical activity. Thus, physical inactivity leads to obesity, and obesity leads to physical inactivity, creating a dangerous circle. The psychological problems related to obesity and physical activity are also of great importance. The Swedish school authorities have therefore decided to offer these children extra and special physical training in small groups in addition to their regular school program. One important step has been to group children with the same problem together, making them more willing to take part in physical training (Figure 13). The effect of physical training on obesity has been the issue for many studies (8, 25, 31, 32). One such study (32) which the author has had the opportunity to follow rather closely was done on 15 boys, 11-12 years old. They participated in a physical activity program twice a week in addition to their regular physical training classes in school. The boys decreased their degree of overweight significantly (Figure 14) and at the same time their physical work capacity increased (Figure 15). This approach in treating obesity seems to be a more economical way than ordinary medical and dietary regimes. However, the best results are achieved when combining all methods.

Figure 13

Overweight Boys in physical training. Data from (31).

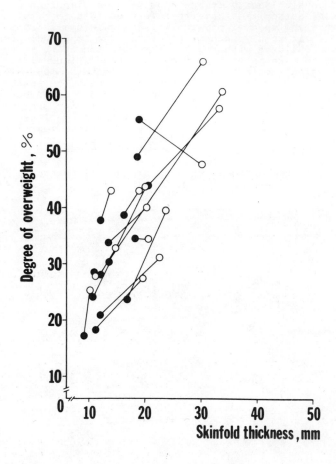

Figure 14

Effect of physical training on degree
(S.D.) of overweight in 16 preadolescent
boys. Open circles represent pre-
training, solid post-training values.
Data from (31 and 33).

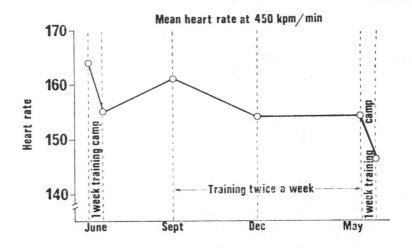

Figure 15

Changes in mean heart rate at unchanged submaximal
work load during one year with different degrees
of training in obese prepubertal boys. Data from
(31 and 33).

Bronchial asthma is the most frequent chronic disease in childhood. The morbidity in Sweden is about 1.5%. Children with bronchial
asthma are often regularly excluded from physical training. The
reason for this may be that physical exercise often induces asthma-
like attacks(9, 17, 26) and also that parents and teachers restrict
the physical activity of the children because of an overprotective
attitude. Another reason may be that these children may be fearful of
inducing breathing disturbances when exercising.

The question then arises of how the combination of inactivity
and the disease influences the child's physical working capacity and
the dimensions of the oxygen transporting organs. In a study of 20
Swedish boys, 8-13 years of age(4) with mild (3 boys), moderate (7
boys) and severe asthma (10 boys), values of maximal oxygen uptake
fell within the limits which are accepted as normal in Swedish boys
today. These results contrast with the results of Vavra et al.(35)
who found 20 to 30% lower values in asthmatic than in normal children.
A good correlation was found between heart volume and maximal oxygen
uptake (Figure 16). However, in the children with the more severe
asthma the lactate concentration in blood was higher in both submaximal and maximal exercise (Figure 17). The underlying reason for
the larger anaerobic component in children with severe asthma is
unknown, but factors such as arterial oxygen desaturation and increased
work of breathing may be responsible.

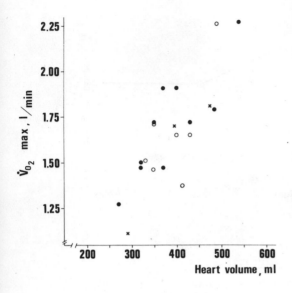

Figure 16

Heart volume in relation
to maximal oxygen uptake
in 20 boys with bronchial
asthma. Crosses indicate
mild, unfilled circles
moderate and filled
squares severe asthma.
Data from (4).

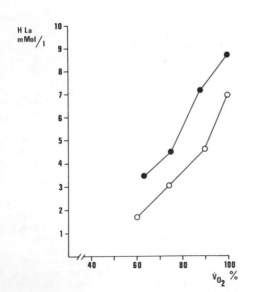

Figure 17

Blood lactate concen-
tration as a function of
the oxygen uptake during
work expressed as
percentage of maximal
oxygen uptake ($\dot{V}_{O_2}$%).
Unfilled circles denote
boys with mild and
moderate asthma and
filled circles boys with
severe asthma. Data
from (4).

Investigations on the effects of physical training in children with bronchial asthma speak in favour of clinical improvement (17, 22, 35). However, workers are not in unanimous agreement on the specific effects of training on the asthmatic child. In particular, some studies have failed to observe an increase in maximal oxygen uptake as found by others (15, 24, 34). In our own recent study(6) on Swedish boys with asthma we observed an increased maximal oxygen uptake. It is clear that further study of this question is required. However, it is evident from these studies that it is possible to carry out a maximal exercise test in spite of asthmatic problems. In the aforementioned Swedish study(4) around 50% of the boys got asthma-like symptoms when exercising (Figure 18). In another Swedish study, when determination of cardiac output and intrapulmonary gas exchange was performed, a dramatic drop in arterial oxygen pressure was found in a boy who got rather severe asthmatic attacks during exercise.(5) Without medical treatment he recovered within 10 to 20 minutes with normalization of the arterial oxygen tension. Cardiac output at sub-maximal and maximal exercise, as well as the intra-arterial blood pressures, were normal in children with bronchial asthma.(5)

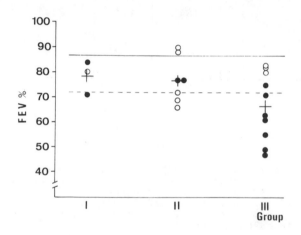

Figure 18

FEV % in relation to clinical severity of bronchial asthma in 20 boys. Group I indicates boys with mild, group II boys with moderate and group III boys with severe asthma. Crosses denote average values for the groups and filled circles denote boys who got asthma-like attacks during exertion. Solid line denotes normal value and dotted line -25%. Data from (4).

Children with congenital heart disease may have quite normal physical working capacity. This concerns especially the more "benign" types of heart malformations. However, even children with cardiac malformation who require surgery may have a normal maximal oxygen uptake. Cyanotic children, on the other hand, have a markedly reduced maximal oxygen uptake (Figure 19) and decreased maximal heart rate.

MAXIMAL WORK

	n	Load kpm/min	HR slag/min	$\dot{V}_{O2}$ l/min	$\dot{V}_{O2}$ ml/kg x min	Blodlaktat mM
♀	8	431	165	0,85	14,6	5,4
♂	7	579	161	1,11	21,1	5,4
Total	15	493	163	0,97	17,7	5,4

Figure 19

Work load, heart rate and blood lactate concentration at maximal exercise compared to maximal oxygen uptake per kg body weight in 8 female and 7 male subjects with cyanotic heart malformation, Fallot's tetralogy. Data from (7).

One limiting factor is the decrease in arterial oxygen saturation during exercise,[7] another is the severe acidosis which is due only in part to lactate accumulation (Figure 20). After "successful" surgery, maximal oxygen uptake is still lower than normal, partly due to lower maximal heart rate and partly due to decreased stroke volume.[7] Whether a postoperative training program would improve the situation is still unclear.

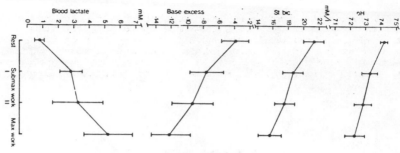

Figure 20

Arterial blood gases and blood lactate
concentration in subjects with tetralogy
of Fallot at rest, at sub-maximal and
maximal exercise. Data from (7).

Children with cerebral palsy have a reduced physical working
capacity (2, 11, 20, 21). This is due primarily to inactivity but also
to an inappropriate diet. One result of this is a changed body
composition (Figure 21). It is possible for these children to partake
in physical training, but account must be taken of their neurological
disturbances (Figures 22-24).

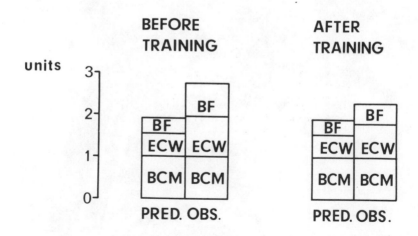

Figure 21

Body fat (BF), extracellular water (ECW) and body
cellmass (BCM) compared to predicted values in a boy
with cerebral palsy before and after physical training.
Data from (2).

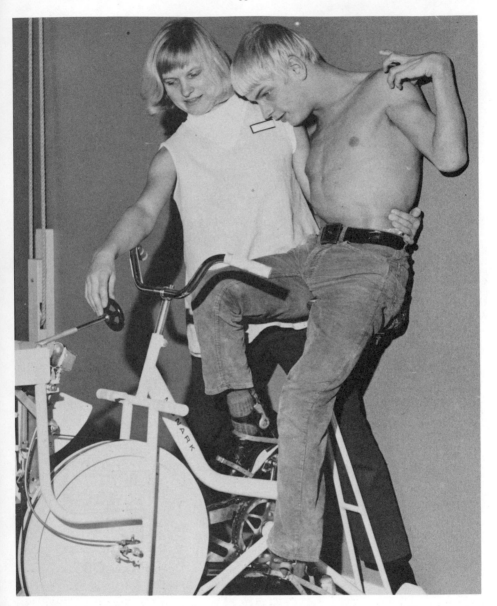

<u>Figure 22</u>

Training of a severely handicapped boy on a bicycle ergometer.
Figure from (2).

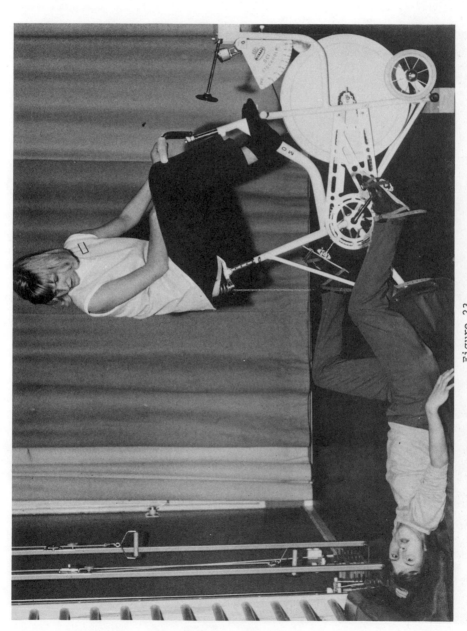

Figure 23

Training of a severely handicapped subject on the floor behind the bicycle ergometer. Figure from (2).

<u>Figure 24</u>

Training of a child with spastic diplegia on "saucer".
Figure from (2).

With physical training an improvement of the maximal oxygen uptake from 10 to 100% (Figure 25) was achieved[2] and also a normalization of the body composition (Figure 21). As a consequence of these findings by Berg,[2] children with cerebral palsy presently are prescribed regular physical training accompanied by an appropriate diet.

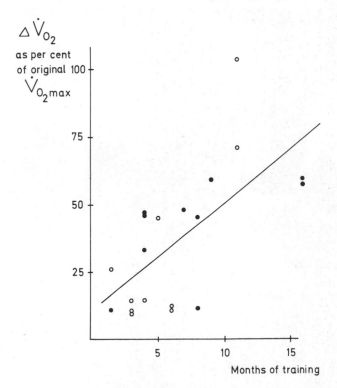

Figure 25

Relationship between effect of physical training and duration of training in children with cerebral palsy. The solid line indicates regression line (correlation coefficient 0.68). Data from (2).

The last group of handicapped children I would like to mention is the mentally retarded. Many times these children are admitted to special schools or nursing homes for years without any contact with their biological parents. In these institutions there is always a great risk of physical inactivity. One of the most important results is that it is possible both to get mentally retarded children to exercise up to maximal level[32, 33] and to test their maximal oxygen uptake (Figure 26). Physical training twice a week during 4 months resulted in an improvement in the physical working capacity of 30%, from 35 to 48 ml/kg x min. However, this increase showed a wide individual variation from almost 0 to nearly 100%.

Physical activity and physical training are important for children. In our modern industrialized society the growing individuals must be given a sufficient amount of physical training both during school hours and during spare time. This is especially the case for handicapped children. It is important for the community to allocate resources for this purpose.[12]

<u>Figure 26</u>

Determination of oxygen uptake in a mentally retarded girl.
Figure from (32).

References

1. Åstrand, P.-O., L. Engström, B.O. Eriksson, P. Karlberg,
   I. Nylander, B. Saltin and C. Thorén. Girl swimmers.
   Acta Paediat. Scand. 1963. Suppl. 147.

2. Berg, K. Adaptation in cerebral palsy of body composition,
   nutrition and physical working capacity at school age. Effects
   of physical training and improved nutrition.
   Acta Paediat. Scand. 1970. Suppl. 204.

3. Bevegård, S. Studies on the regulation of the circulation in
   man. With special reference to the stroke volume and the
   effect of muscular work, body position and artificially induced
   variations of the heart rate.
   Acta Physiol. Scand. 1962. 52. Suppl. 200.

4. Bevegård, S., B.O. Eriksson, V. Graff-Lonnevig, S. Kraepelien
   and B. Saltin. Circulatory and respiratory dimensions and
   functional capacity in boys aged 8-13 years with bronchial
   asthma.
   Acta Paediat. Scand. 1971. Suppl. 217. 86.

5. Bevegård, S., B.O. Eriksson, V. Graff-Lonnevig, S. Kraepelien
   and B. Saltin. Cardiac output, systemic arterial pressure and
   pulmonary gas exchange at rest and during maximal exercise in
   a group of boys with bronchial asthma.
   Abstract. 4th International symposium on paediatric work
   physiology. Wingate Institute, Israel 1972.

6. Bevegård, S., B.O. Eriksson, V. Graff-Lonnevig, S. Kraepelien
   and B. Saltin. Effect of physical training on boys with
   bronchial asthma.
   To be published.

7. Bjarke, B., B.O. Eriksson and C. Thorén.
   Personal communication.

8. Blomqvist, B., M. Börjesson, Y. Larsson, B. Persson and
   G. Sterky. The effect of physical activity on the body
   measurements and work capacity in overweight boys.
   Acta Paediat. Scand. 1965. 54. 566.

9. Crompton, G.K. An unusual example of exercise induced asthma.
   Thorax 1968. 23. 165.

10. Von Döbeln, W. and B.O. Eriksson. Physical training, maximal
    oxygen uptake and dimensions of the oxygen transporting and
    metabolizing organs in boys 11-13 years of age.
    Acta Paediat. Scand. 1972. 61. 653.

11. Ekblom, B. and Å. Lundberg. Effect of physical training on
    adolescents with severe motor handicaps.
    Acta Paediat. Scand. 1968. 57. 17.

12. Eriksson, B.O. Physical training, oxygen supply and muscle
    metabolism in 11-13 year old boys.
    Acta Physiol. Scand. 1972. Suppl. 384.

13. Eriksson, B.O., I. Engström, P. Karlberg, B. Saltin and
C. Thorén. A physiological analysis of former girl swimmers.
Acta Paediat. Scand. 1971. Suppl. 217. 68.

14. Eriksson, B.O., A. Lundin and B. Saltin. Physical training
of post-active girl swimmers. In: O. Bar-Or, ed.: Paediatric
Work Physiology. Proceedings of the fourth international
symposium, Wingate Institute, Israel 1973. 217.

15. Geubelle, F., C. Ernould and M. Jovanovic. Working capacity
and physical training in asthmatic children at 1800 m altitude.
Acta Paediat. Scand. 1971. Suppl. 217. 93.

16. Holmgren, A. and T. Strandell. The relationship between heart
volume, total hemoglobin and physical working capacity in
former athletes.
Acta Med. Scand. 1959. 149. 163.

17. Jones, E.S., M.H. Burton and M.J. Wharton. The effect of
exercise on ventilatory function in the child with asthma.
Brit. J. Dis. Chest. 1962. 56. 78.

18. Larsson, Y., B. Persson, G. Sterky and C. Thorén. Functional
adaptation to rigorous training and exercise in diabetic and
non-diabetic adolescents.
J. Appl. Physiol. 1964. 19. 629.

19. Larsson, Y., G. Sterky, K. Ekengren and T. Möller. Physical
fitness and the influence of training in diabetic adolescent
girls.
Diabetes 1962. 11. 109.

20. Lundberg, Å., C.-O. Ovenfors and B. Saltin. Effect of
physical training on school-children with cerebral palsy.
Acta Paediat. Scand. 1967. 56. 182.

21. Lundberg, Å. and B. Pernow. The effect of physical training
on blood flow through exercising muscle in adolescents with
motor handicaps.
Scand. J. Clin. Lab. Invest. 1970. 26. 89.

22. McElhenney, T.R. and K.H. Peterson. Physical fitness for
asthmatic boys. A cooperative pilot study.
Am. Med. Ass. 1963. 168. 178.

23. Milman, M., W.G. Grundon, F. Kasch, B. Wilkersson and
J. Headley. Controlled exercise in asthmatic children.
Ann. Allergy. 1965. 23. 220.

24. Mrzena, B., M. Máček, J. Vávra and V. Spičák. Effect on the
long-term training of children with bronchial asthma.
In press.

25. Pařízková, J., M. Vaněčková, S. Šprynarová and M. Vamberová.
Body composition and fitness in obese children before and
after special treatment.
Acta Paediat. Scand. 1971. Suppl. 217. 80.

26. Rebuck, A.S. and J. Read.   Exercise-induced asthma.
    Lancet 1968. 429.

27. Saltin, B. and G. Grimby.   Physiological analysis of middle-
    aged and former athletes.   Comparison with still active
    athletes of the same age.
    Circulation 1968. 38. 1104.

28. Scherr, M.S. and L. Frankell.   Physical conditioning program
    for asthmatic children.
    Am. Med. Ass. 1958. 168. 1996.

29. Schnorr, P. Longevity and causes of death in male athletic
    champions.
    Lancet 1971. 7738. 1364.

30. Sterky, G. Physical work capacity in diabetic schoolchildren.
    Acta Paediat. Scand. 1963. 52. 1.

31. Sterky, G.   Clinical and metabolic aspects on obesity in
    childhood.   In: B. Pernow and B. Saltin, eds.:   Muscle
    metabolism during exercise.   New York: Plenum Press, 1971.

32. Thorén, C. Physical training of handicapped school-
    children.
    Scand. J. Rehab. Med. 1971. 3. 26.

33. Thorén, C., V. Seliger, M. Máček, J. Vávra and J. Rutenfranz.
    The influence of training on physical fitness in healthy
    children and children with chronic diseases.   In: F. Linneweh,
    ed: Current aspects of perinatalogy and physiology of
    children.
    Springer Verlag.   Berlin-Heidelberg-New York. 1973. 83.

34. Vávra, J., M. Máček, B. Mrzena and V. Spičák.   Intensive
    physical training in children with bronchial asthma.
    Acta Paediat. Scand. 1971.   Suppl. 217. 90.

35. Vávra, J., M. Máček and V. Spičák.   La capacité de travail
    chez les enfants asthmatiques .
    Rev. Pédiat. 1969. 5. 3.

Specific comments to Dr. Eriksson's paper.

I am concerned about the overall impression that might be created by Dr. Eriksson's comments on asthma. I agree with all that he has said, but do not want the audience to be left with the idea that asthma is not a serious and sometimes disabling disease, and that all that is necessary is for the wheezing child to push on. The maximum studies carried out by Eriksson and his colleagues were done on children that were not in the middle of a severe asthmatic episode. The asthmatic child may be badly abused in sports by his coach and colleagues because he or she may be a large, healthy, child whose appearance suggests complete normalcy and a large exercise capacity. When exercise precipitates an attack with an increase in airway resistance to over thirty times normal, and a drop in blood oxygen saturation to 50% of normal, it is obviously not prudent for the child to force himself and continue exercise. When the asthmatic child is free of major symptoms, he can exercise maximally, but an asthmatic attack may be precipitated but is usually mild and goes away twenty to thirty minutes after the exercise is stopped. The kind of exercise is of some importance, running which demands a lot more ventilation than bicycle riding brings an attack on more than bicycle riding, and horizontal exercise like swimming seems to be the least likely to bring on an attack. Maximal exercise of short duration is better tolerated than longer exercise. I don't think asthma can be minimized as a disease, it may be fatal. There are more fatalities every year in asthmatics in Canada and other countries, and this is now being related to some forms of treatment that are available. The asthmatic child who is laboring under extreme difficulty should certainly be allowed to stop and not be encouraged to work to exhaustion. There are several reports in the literature where training results in programs, changes in lung volumes and gains in aerobic power have been negligible. The major accomplishment of training programs in asthmatics is to give them confidence about exercise, and this in itself may reduce the frequency of attacks.

Gordon R. Cumming, M. D.

THE CHILD IN SPORT AND PHYSICAL ACTIVITY

MEDICAL COMMENT

by Gordon R. Cumming, M. D.,
    Cardiologist,
    The Children's Hospital of Winnipeg.

Childhood training for specific motor skills and overdevelopment of certain body systems may be required to achieve success in many sports in the modern world. A minimum of physical activity is likely necessary for optimal growth or development of children, but this minimum will likely never be known with certainty, just as the minimal activity patterns for the health of adults are likely to remain unknown. We cannot even define optimal growth and development, either in generalities or in specifics such as height, or heart volume, or maximal oxygen uptake. There are, however, definite medical reasons that support the need for physical activity programs in children, and these can be summarized as follows:

1. Physical exercise is important during childhood for the proper development of the functional capacity of the heart, the lungs and the strength of bones and muscles. If undeveloped during the growing years, the opportunity for optimal development of these organ systems has likely been lost.

2. Continued physical exercise is important in later life for the prevention of premature heart disease. Population surveys suggest that coronary mortality in the physically active worker is half that of the physically inactive worker. (1) In this regard, children should be taught the importance of lifetime physical activity and be fully exposed to the many choices of leisure activities to develop skills and attitudes. Regular physical exercise in adult life might reduce the number of heart attacks by as much as 30% in men under the age of sixty-five years in a country such as Canada where the frequency of coronary events is amongst the highest in the world, and most of the population is sedentary.

3. Physical exercise has a contribution to make towards mental health in the relief of mental tension throughout life.

4. Physical exercise is important in childhood as well as in adult years for weight control. It allows a satisfying food intake and an adequate supply of protein, minerals and vitamins, while the extra calories that accompany these necessities are burnt up by the added physical exercise.

5. Physical conditioning likely has a role in the prevention of other medical diseases. Physical fitness increases the body's resistance against general stress and illness throughout life. Continued physical activity may protect that 20% of the population who are at risk for diabetes mellitus, by preventing overweight and by assisting glucose metabolism. Strong back muscles may prevent back problems.

Many of these reasons are based on the premise that good activity habits are easier to develop in children, and that children are more easily influenced, and that if "properly" influenced, attitudes and activity patterns developed in childhood will last a lifetime. Leventhal[2] has indicated that there is no evidence that children are more likely than adults to learn, believe in, or act on health information. Because of the rapidity of the maturation processes in childhood, teaching of habits and attitudes to children has special problems. What parents have proof that their way has been the best way to rear their children?

Teenage smoking is an easily investigated health habit, and investigations suggest that the peer group has the most influence on the habits of the maturing child.[3] Ninety percent of children will try a few smokes, whether they continue or not likely depends on availability, and the chance feelings of their peer group, including their need to put on a front of sophistication and sexual maturity. Any habits developed in children need continuous reinforcement in adult life. Children and youth like to emulate adults who are successful, are in a position of power, and are doing the IN thing, and the example of this portion of society, and not necessarily parental influence, becomes their model.

The potential for growth, physical and mental development, is an obvious difference between the child and an adult. Much more is known about the effects of complete inactivity on growth and skeletal changes than about intense physical training. The post polio leg is shorter, the bones are demineralized, radiologic milestones are delayed in appearance. Even a few weeks in a cast leads to demineralization which may be more related to lack of normal weight bearing than to actual lack of physical movement. Striking examples of demineralization can be shown radiologically in various pathological situations, but these demonstrations do not tell us whether intense programed physical activity has any postiive or negative effects on bone and muscle development of children compared to natural play activities, and a total lack of programed physical activity. These pathological examples have no bearing on whether a normal child should receive one hour or five hours of physical activity each week. Nor can the radiologist tell us whether the athletically active child has any skeletal advantages over the relatively inactive child in later years.

A few animal experiments suggest that animals put through forced exercise when young will be more active when given freedom of choice after maturity. When intense physical exercise is carried out by growing rats, they end up with more muscle, less fat, and bigger hearts, kidneys, lungs, adrenals, and, incidentally, gonads. There is no genetic transmission of these effects, and overall length is not altered.[4] Rats initially restricted in activity cannot achieve these gains with exercise after maturity.[5] In younger rats, the heart hypertrophies in response to exercise; in the older rat slight atrophy occurs.[6] Already active boys aged ten to eleven, placed in an intensive exercise program, may make slight gains in aerobic power and heart size; they may even show slight growth acceleration, but their final height is likely not changed.[7] The only consistent positive finding in most training experiments is the reduction of fat mass and an increase in lean body mass (muscle).[8] Many of the gains seem to be quickly lost by return to normal activity.

In girls (except for the important swimmers' studies by Dr. Eriksson and his colleagues), little effort has been made to study growth and development in relation to sports activities. In a 1938 U.S.A. study, negro women who had strenuous manual labor as children, were taller, heavier, and had larger skeletal dimensions than a group who did not work as children.[9] In contrast, in Japan a group of children who worked hard tended to have reduced stature because of early epiphyseal closure.[10] The children's nutritional status in these studies was possibly suboptimal.

Extreme overuse of one part of the body leads to bony and muscular hypertrophy, examples being the baseball pitcher's arm, the tennis arm, and the shoulders and lung volumes in girl swimmers. These are overuse syndromes and are not necessarily desirable. Radiologic studies suggest that the dominant hand may be slightly larger (width not length),[11] and the dominant upper limb slightly longer.

Parizkova et al.,[8] concluded that increased physical activity in boys decreased their body fat, increased their lean body mass, and had no significant effect on skeletal dimensions. A widely quoted study by Ekblom[7] concluded that boys who had extra physical conditioning had increased height, $\dot{V}_{O2}$ maximal and heart volume compared to those without extra training - but the gains in vital capacity, $\dot{V}_{O2}$ maximal per kg body weight, and heart size were actually quite small and required special manipulations (i.e. relating functions to height[3]) to show any differences from control subjects. The final height at maturity was not known, and growth may have been accelerated temporarily only to later slow down sooner. Differences between children receiving 90 minutes of physical education weekly compared to five hours weekly in growth and organ development are likely to be negligible, particularly if the extra time is devoted largely to learning experiences and recreation and not to high intensity athletic conditioning. Growth should not be cited as a reason for promoting physical activities.

I feel that those who wish to have more physical education and recreation included in elementary school programs are on the wrong track if they primarily seek scientific physiologic and medical support for their beliefs. In a free society, absolute proof will likely never be available concerning the medical benefits of a little recreation and sport, or a lot. Do our school boards have proof that their current mathematics programs are the best available for the current goals of education? There are many cultural and philosophical reasons to support strong physical activity programs; any medical advantages should be looked upon as a bonus and not the raison d'être. This does not mean that we should not fully evaluate the physiological and other effects of exercise programs, it is very important that studies as described by Dr. Eriksson are continued.

If by chance this conference led to a major change in the priorities given to physical activity programs in schools, how would we evaluate whether any gains were made as a direct result of the change in the program. We could wait twenty years and see if the thirty-year-old was less inactive, healthier and more fit than the thirty-year-old of today, but relating this directly to the physical activity program given in grade 6 might be difficult. An obvious answer is to have a test battery and measure if we are doing any good or not, but this is not as simple as it seems.

The test battery would, of course, contain performance items such as in the CAHPER test, and we already know if a group of ten-year-olds practise the items in this test enough, under the motivating influence of a gold star, that large improvements in many of the performance items are possible. Such programs make a real and positive contribution to fitness in the young, although the carryover to adult years in terms of fitness and motivation is not known. We can look to specific test items such as heart, lung and strength tests. Lung function test results are unrelated to most performance items in children.[12] While detailed statistical studies can show 5-15% improvement in some measures of pulmonary function in children in various vigorous training programs (particularly swimming), the clinical significance of any improvement is dubious, and most children don't want to swim ten hours per week or to start training for the next marathon.

Because it is so easily measured, the capacity of the oxygen transfer system (aerobic power, maximal oxygen uptake, $\dot{V}_{O_2}$ maximal) has been the main measure of physical fitness in the past fifteen years. We know that there is a genetic factor explaining some of the differences in $\dot{V}_{O_2}$ maximal, and we know that body build strongly influences the $\dot{V}_{O_2}$ maximal result, particularly when expressed per kg body weight. In this context, $\dot{V}_{O_2}$ maximal can become a rather round-about way of measuring obesity. One can eliminate this problem by expressing $\dot{V}_{O_2}$ maximal in terms of height, or height[3]. The fact remains, however, that very few childhood sports or recreational activities are continuous, so that very few sports demand a high $\dot{V}_{O_2}$ maximal for high quality performance. We have found the correlation of various performance items in children to be poorly correlated with $\dot{V}_{O_2}$ maximal (13, 14). The majority of activities in children are skill oriented, if they are related to power in any way, it is likely to be anaerobic sources rather than aerobic, and satisfactory measures of the former are yet to be developed. On any team, the best hockey player or the most effective football player usually does not have the highest $\dot{V}_{O_2}$ maximal.

While I feel that too much emphasis has been placed on aerobic power as a measure of fitness, this is a reproducible index of the functional and anatomic capacity of the heart, lungs and large muscle groups. We have no idea as to optimal values, there is no proof that the protective effect of physical activity against coronary heart disease is in any way related to a higher aerobic power or fitness. If aerobic power is to be used as a guide to the effectiveness of acitvity programs, it seems reasonable to improve this value in the bottom third of the population; this is where gains are most easily achieved and is likely the group that will benefit most from "aerobic" programs.

Three groups of Manitoba children were followed for on year; no change in aerobic power (beyond that expected from growth) were observed.[15] No gains in aerobic power were expected in the group

with only 60 to 90 minutes physical education per week, but the lack
of any improvement in $\dot{V}_{O2}$ maximal in students with over five hours of
activities per week, or in students taking part in vigorous physical
work, plus canoeing and snowshoeing programs, was more difficult to
explain.

Finally, during the course of a sports season such as football[16] (Table I) or hockey (Table II), very little improvement may
occur in working capacity (an indirect measure of $\dot{V}_{O2}$ maximal) despite
considerable time devoted to training. This, in part, reflects the
type of training coaches have used for these sports programs. The
youth taking part in these sports were already moderately fit, they
devoted much more time in their sport and worked much harder at
training than could be expected from a nonathletic class in school
given one hour daily of physical activities ranging from learning
experiences to outdoor activities to actual running. The point is
that if the effectiveness of a physical activities program in already
active children is judged on whether or not it improves aerobic power,
it may well be labelled a failure.

TABLE I

PWC 170 kpm/min/kg HIGH SCHOOL FOOTBALL TEAMS

School	Pre season	Post season
1	14.4±1.8	14.4±1.3
2	14.5±2.1	14.6±1.8
3	15.3±2.9	17.3±3.2*

* Increase of 19% (p < .02) in school where team spent considerable
  time training on river bank with hill runs and other endurance
  runs. No improvement in other schools despite daily practises
  of two hours each (including running, calisthenics, and drills)
  for 2.5 months.

TABLE II

MEAN PWC 170 kpm/min/kg OF HOCKEY TEAMS

Age Class	November	March	Change	p Value
17	16.7	15.2	-1.5	>.1
15	16.4	16.9	+0.5	>.1
14	16.2	18.5	+2.3	<.001
13	15.1	16.3	+1.2	<.01
12	15.5	16.0	+0.5	>.1
9	12.6	13.1	+0.5	>.1

17 and 15-year-olds practised 4 x weekly and had 2 games per week, yet no improvement.

12, 13-and 14-year-olds practised 3 x weekly and had 1 game per week. Considerable endurance type skating drills likely responsible for improvement in the 13-and 14-year olds.

9 year olds had 2 practises and 1 game weekly. They worked hard. Average 8-15-year-old population mean for PWC 170 is about 3 kpm/min/kg Mean values for 10-16 players.

In the hockey study in Table II, it is to be noted that the nine-year-old team had an average PWC 170 value, the other teams were all above average, but it was only when specific emphasis was placed on aerobic training that the athletic season led to a further improvement.

There are very few medical conditions where physical activities programs are totally contraindicated, and the majority of school children with diabetes, asthma, rheumatic and congenital heart defects, and mild orthopedic problems can take part in regular physical education classes with their classmates. Severely handicapped children require special programs, but this presents several logistic problems because in many school systems these children are integrated into the general school system and only a handful of children in any one school may require special classes.

There are many professional groups who would like to take part in providing exercise programs for the handicapped, but the dispersion and the low frequency of disorders make effective programs difficult and expensive except in high density population areas or special schools. An idea of the frequency of the various defects is indicated from the handicap registry of the City of Winnipeg (Table III). Special activity classes are not needed by many of the children; over 80% of the subjects with reported heart lesions, the diabetics and asthmatics are taking part in regular classes. Of interest is that asthma was the most in the registry.

In one study (17), 30% of visually handicapped children had
working capacities below the 15 percentile level, an indication of
the difficulties these children have in obtaining a normal amount of
exercise. These problems are easily overcome in special schools, but
what of the school where there are only two or three such children?
Of special interest is that deaf children are usually above average
in fitness (they do not sit around talking or listening to records
or TV), and retarded children have average fitness levels (17).

Sports performance in childhood is closely related to maturity.
In one study, performance in most track and field events correlated
more closely with bone age than height, weight or chronologic age
(18). Height and weight are much better than age to create a
classification system for competitive sports, and are practical
indices of maturity. More exact measures of maturity, such as bone
age from wrist X-rays, dental mapping, testicular size in boys, are
not practical. As participation, fair competition, and prevention of
injuries should be the general goals of most sports programs for
children, equalization of the maturity factor is a worthwhile goal
when this is feasible.

TABLE III

CITY OF WINNIPEG SCHOOL HANDICAP REGISTRY 1972-1973

Condition	Number per 1000 children	Condition	Number per 1000 children
Congenital heart	1.4	Cystic fibrosis	0.7
Rheumatic fever (heart)	0.8	Kidney disorders	.40
Rheumatic fever (no heart)	1.0	Rheumatoid arthritis	.19
Visual impairment	1.8	Growth failure	.07
Visual impairment (special class)	0.4	Obesity	.62
Asthma	4.1	Hemophilia	.17
Cerebral palsy CP	1.4	Muscular dystrophy	.21
Neuromuscular excluding CP	1.7	Perthe's disease	.10
Trainable mentally handicapped	4.2	Spina bifida	.21
Diabetes mellitus	0.9	Convulsive disorder	2.7

Figures supplied by Dr. Harry Medovy, Consultant, Child Health Services

Summary

1. We do not know the "optimal" amount of physical activity for childhood, and likely never will.

2. There are many potential health benefits of physical activity programs in children, but perhaps these should be regarded as fringe benefits rather than the reasons for such programs.

3. Once reasonable fitness is achieved (i.e. $\dot{V}_{02}$ max about 50 ml/kg/M^2 for boys), further gains require considerable effort - likely more than is desirable for a general activities program. Measuring the success of such programs by improvements in various fitness measurements presents many difficulties.

4. The incidence of significant medical handicaps in Canadian children is low. Most of these children can take part in regular physical activities programs. Provision of special activity programs for the small number of handicapped requiring them is difficult when the children are totally integrated into neighborhood schools, yet the advantages of this policy may outweigh the disadvantages.

References

1. Fox, S.M. III, Naughton, J.P. and Heskell, W.L. Physical activity and the prevention of coronary heart disease. Annals of Clin Res 3:404-432, 1971.

2. Leventhal, H. Changing attitudes and habits to reduce risk factors in chronic disease. Amer J Cardiol 31:571-580, 1973.

3. Salber, E.J., Reed, R.B., Harrison, S.V. et al. Smoking behaviour, recreational activities and attitudes toward smoking among Newton secondary school children. Pediatrics 30:911-918, 1963.

4. Donaldson, H.H. and Meeser, R.E. On the effects of exercise carried through seven generations on the weight of musculature and on the composition and weight of several organs in the albino rat. Amer J Anat 50:359, 1932.

5. Montoye, H.J., Nelson, R., Johnson, P. and MacNab, R. Effects of exercise in swimming endurance and organ weight in mature rats.
   Res Quart 31:474, 1968.

6. Leon, A.S., Bloom, C.M. Exercise effects on the heart at different ages.
   Circulation 41:50, 1970.

7. Ekblom, B. Effect of physical training in adolescent boys. J Appl Physiol 27:350-355, 1969.

8. Parizkova, J. Longitudinal study of the development of body composition and body build in boys of various physical activity. Human Biol 40:212, 1968.

9. Adams, E.H. A comparative anthropometric study of hard labor during youth as a stimulator of physical growth of young colored women.
   Res Quart 9:102, 1938.

10. Kato, S. and Ishiko, T. Obstructed growth of children's bones due to excessive labor in remote corners, in, Proceedings of International Congress of Sports Sciences, 1964. K. Kato, ed. Tokyo. Japanese Union of Sports Sciences 1966, page 479.

11. Greulich, W.W. and Pyle, S.I. Radiographic atlas of skeletal development of the hand and wrist. 2nd Ed. Stanford University Press, 1959.

12. Cumming, G.R. Correlation of athletic performance with pulmonary function in 13 to 17-year-old boys and girls. Medicine & Science in Sports 1:140-143, 1969.

13. Cumming, G.R. and Keynes, R. A fitness performance test for school children and its correlation with physical working capacity and maximal oxygen uptake. Canad Med Assoc J 96:1262-1269, 1967.

14. Cumming, G.R. Correlation of athletic performance and aerobic power in 12 to 17-year-old children with bone age, calf muscle, total body potassium, heart volume and two indices of anaerobic power.
Pediatric Work Physiology - Proceedings of the Fourth International Symposium, O. Bar-Or (ed). Wingate Institute, Israel, April 1972.

15. Cumming, G.R., Goulding, D. and Baggley, G. Failure of school physical education to improve cardiorespiratory fitness.
Canad Med Assoc J 101:69-73, 1969.

16. Cumming, G.R. and Goulding, D. Aerobic power and working capacity changes in high school football players (Unpublished data).

17. Cumming, G.R., Goulding, D. and Baggley, G. Working capacity of deaf, and visually and mentally handicapped children.
Arch Dis Child 46:490-494, 1971.

18. Cumming, G.R., Garand, T. and Borysyk, L. Correlation of performance in track and field events with bone age.
J of Pediatrics 80:970-973, 1972.

Growth and development aspects

THE GROWING CHILD AND THE NEED FOR PHYSICAL ACTIVITY

by   Dr. D.A. Bailey
       Professor, College of Physical Education
       University of Saskatchewan,
       Saskatoon, Canada

A.   INTRODUCTION

This paper will attempt to provide some substantiation for the belief that in our sedentary post industrial society of today, growing children must be provided with wider opportunities to participate in vigorous programs of physical activity. Canadian children today are entering a society characterized by sedentary living patterns, emotional stress, poor dietary habits and lack of physical activity. And yet, many of the programs of physical activity being offered currently both in and out of school, tend to deprive a great many youngsters of their normal childhood instincts for play, and in fact discourage those very children who need activity the most.

B.   WHY PHYSICAL ACTIVITY FOR CHILDREN?

On the basis of research findings to date we can say:

1)   Physical activity is necessary to support normal growth in children.

2)   Inactivity as a youngster can have a bearing on mature functional capacity and consequently may be directly related to a number of adult health problems.

3)   The basic orientation toward experience is established early in life. If we want adult participation in physical activity it should be remembered that motivation towards activity is probably laid down at a very early age. "As the twig is bent, so grows the tree."

4)   Learning inside the classroom may be enhanced and supported by activity outside the classroom. "All work and no play makes Jack a dull boy."

There are probably a number of other reasons for physical activity for the child which can be scientifically supported. In particular, in the psychological area, there is evidence that a positive enjoyable exposure to physical activity during the formative years has a great deal to do with self concept, confidence, and adult adaptability. This, however, is best left for others who are more expert in the psychological area to deal with. The present paper will limit itself to a discussion of the four listed reasons for activity.

1.   PHYSICAL ACTIVITY TO SUPPORT NORMAL STRUCTURAL GROWTH

Reviews on the effect of exercise on structural growth have recently appeared in the literature (1, 2) which update earlier reviews published in 1960 (3, 4). Rarick (5) has recently edited a book entitled "Physical Activity - Human Growth and Development"

which delves deeply into the subject. These reviews all reach
the general conclusion that a certain amount of physical activity
is necessary to support normal structural growth.

Exercise is known to increase bone width and mineralization
while inactivity decreases mineralization. Inactivity as a
result of prolonged periods of recumbency, periods of
immobilization in casts, and more recently prolonged space
flights, leads to decalcification of bones. Resumption of normal
activity corrects the imbalance, although sometimes it takes
several years to restore loss of calcium due to immobilization
(6). Demineralized bones, of course, are weaker and more brittle.
Athletes in good condition tend to have stronger bones and
muscles and as a consequence their bones are less easily broken.

In this context, a statement by Dr. C. Stuart Houston, Professor
of Diagnostic Radiology, University of Saskatchewan, Saskatoon,
is worth quoting.

*"Bones are not solid unchanging structures as people once thought.
Instead, a bone like any other organ in the human body, is a dynamic
structure. New cells are laid down and old cells are taken away.
New calcium ions enter the scaffolding as old calcium ions return
to the blood. The body has a very precise balancing mechanism to
maintain normal levels of calcium and phosphate in our blood. For
this reason it takes extreme deficiency of calcium or vitamin D in
our diet, or a marked abnormality of the parathyroid glands to cause
demineralization of bone. Yet only one week of inactivity often
causes noticeable demineralization - loss of half the calcium from
a bone. So the amount of activity we get is much more important
than the amount of milk we drink. If we are active, our bones will
be well mineralized and both bones and muscles will be strong. This
is true in children, true in adult life and true in old age. As a
radiologist, I see almost every day, dramatic changes appearing in
bones and muscles from disuse. It seems obvious that continued
exercise is necessary for the maintenance of normal bone and
muscle strength - and normal health. This is not new or original
but it is important. Inactivity is very harmful."*

Applying the research in this area to the growing child, it can
be accepted that weight bearing and physical activity are not
only important but necessary in terms of healthy growth.

PHYSICAL ACTIVITY, FUNCTIONAL GROWTH, AND ADULT CAPACITY

The question of what, if any, are the effects of exercise on the
functional growth of children, and on functional capacity when
maturity is reached, has increasing relevance today. We live in
a country where cardiovascular diseases are the cause of every
second death. Recently, as interest has been focused on the possible role of inactivity as a factor in the increasing incidence
of cardiovascular disease, we are finding more and more adults
becoming interested in exercise. This is good, but exercising
throughout life particularly during the growing years may be of
primary importance. Just as many cases of adult obesity, have
been linked to childhood nutrition, so adult health problems

related to inactivity may possibly be linked to sedentary childhood activity patterns. As Åstrand has said speaking about physical activity, "Anything neglected during adolescence can in many cases not be made up later on" (7).

The importance of looking at the child when trying to identify basic causes of degenerative cardiovascular disease in adults can best be emphasized by looking at a paper by Dr. Kenneth Rose, University of Nebraska (8). Rose documents the developmental history of arteriosclerotic disease in man. The first signs appear around age 2 and the disease process is reversible until the age of 19. At about 19 the process of the disease is essentially irreversible, and from then on it inexorably progresses until it becomes clinically manifest usually in the 40's.

Dr. John Kimball, noted University of Colorado cardiologist has stated that, "Evidence is growing stronger that the earliest bodily changes leading to heart disease begins early in life." He notes that more and more autopsy reports on children show that their blood vessels have already begun to clog with fatty deposits that can eventually lead to heart attack. Clearly, the importance of proper diet and adequate exercise during the growing years cannot be overemphasized.

Dr. Nathan Smith, talking about the increasing incidence of obesity in children has stated,

"If infants and children are not to be obese, there must be family activity and home activity patterns developed from infancy that will effectively increase energy expenditure. Restricted play pens can contribute as much to obesity as a high calorie, unsupervised diet. Mothers and families need our guidance from the birth of their infant in developing activity lifestyles that are going to provide a healthy energy expenditure." (9)

Biochemical studies on exercise and functional growth: A recent approach that has been taken in studying the effect of exercise on functional growth is biochemical in nature. Researchers have been investigating growth at the cellular level using biochemical techniques which are based upon the recognition that for most tissues the amount of DNA per cell nucleus is constant. This provides a chemical unit which can be applied in studying the growth phenomenon, whereby DNA per gram of tissue can be used as an index of cell number and the protein to DNA ratio can be used as an estimate of cell size.

These studies (10, 11, 12, 13) have shown that the rate of cell division and the ultimate number of cells that comprise a particular tissue or organ are determined not only by instrinsic (genetic) factors but also may be influenced by extrinsic (environmental) factors. The state of nutrition, prenatally and neonatally, either undernutrition or supernutrition, has been shown to be one such factor.

The question arises, are there other extrinsic factors that may influence cellular growth? What about a factor like exercise, particularly if it is introduced during a period of active growth?

Skeletal muscle tissue would appear to be a tissue of particular interest in this respect because it has been shown to be in an active state during adolescence. As Cheek has said,

"The usual growth pattern for most organs is that the period of hyperplasia or cell division eventually stops and does not begin again. However, skeletal muscle is a striking exception. Most muscle hyperplasia occurs in fetal life and early postnatal life, but during adolescence, presumably under the influence of androgens, hyperplasia of muscle cells undergoes marked resurgence." (14)

A valid working hypothesis would seem to be that just as nutritional insults at a given time during growth have permanent repercussions throughout life, perhaps the lack of strenuous exercise or the excess of it during the growing years may affect the ultimate adult complement of cells and hence the functional capacity to perform as an adult.

Studies by Buchanan and Pritchard (15), Cheek (16), and an investigation conducted in our own laboratory, Bailey and Bell (17) on the effect of exercise on skeletal muscle tissue in growing rats would seem to provide some backing for this hypothesis. Obviously work of this type must be continued, but if these studies can be substantiated by further animal work, and verified in man, the impact will be profound. What it will mean is that adult capacity may be a function of activity during the growing years in addition to genetic determinants.

Some knowledgeable people closely related to sports have been speculating along these lines for a number of years. Dr. Roger Bannister, the first man to break the four minute mile, has said,

"Recently, as the average age of record breakers has fallen, I have realized that another factor is at work. If "interval" training is started when the athlete is young enough, his body can be "stretched" physiologically and anatomically to a degree that is impossible if the training starts after maturity when growth has ceased." (18)

Physiological studies on exercise and functional growth: A more traditional approach that has been used to study the influence of exercise or physical activity on functional growth has been to compare athletes with nonathletes, or to compare subjects classified according to various levels of physical activity. In the Saskatchewan Child Growth and Development Study (19) children were followed on a longitudinal basis for 10 years from ages 7-16. A variety of measures were taken annually to try and find out if physical activity was related to growth in any way. Children were grouped into physical activity categories (very active, active, sedentary, etc.) on the basis of parental questionnaires and teacher interviews. On measures of strength, suppleness and stamina (aerobic power) very active boys were significantly superior to sedentary boys at all ages (20). These findings are in agreement with a similar longitudinal study on boys ages 11 to 18 reported by Parizkova (21) who reported body composition as well as functional differences between boys classified according to activity.

A study of the best young girl swimmers in Sweden who were extensively studied over a period of years starting at age 14, showed that large functional capacities in lung volume and heart size were maintained into adult years. In commenting on this study, Åstrand speculated,

"During adolescence there may be a second chance to improve those dimensions which are of importance for the oxygen-transport system. This is an interesting problem, especially with regard to physical education in school. It may not be possible to repair later in life what is neglected during the adolescent years." (22)

These and other studies confirm that physical activity and exercise are basically beneficial. But such comparisons do not establish what comes first. Are active children functionally superior because they are active, or are they active because they are functionally superior?

Ekblom (23) used a dimensional approach to try and answer this question. He noted that if physical training is started in a grown man there is an upper limit in functional capacity over which one cannot go, even if the physical training is very hard and extended over many years. He investigated the effect of physical training on boys during adolescence to try to answer the question - when in life is this upper limit set? Is it strictly genetic or can it be influenced by physical training before and during puberty? He followed a training group of boys and a control group for six months and concluded that heart volume and functional capacities like maximal oxygen uptake increased in the training group more than could be expected from normal growth. Apparently an extrinsic environmental factor like exercise was involved along with intrinsic genetic growth factors.

Bailey and Ross (24) applied a similar dimensional approach to 8 years of longitudinal growth data on boys ages 8 to 15. Expected and actual changes in aerobic power as a result of increasing linear dimensions were calculated. Presently data on very active boys and very sedentary boys are being compared to the expected base line and the results of this analysis should provide further information on the influence of physical activity on functional growth.

Do functional changes as a result of training during youth persist into adult years? A study by Saltin (25) provides evidence to support this contention. He compared the adjustability to effort of three groups of subjects in the age group 50-59 years. One group consisted of men who were former athletes who had given up all sports 20 years earlier, and followed a sedentary occupation. A second group comprised men who had achieved the same athletic performances in their youth as their former colleagues in cross-country running or long distance skiing, but had kept up regular training during the adult years. A third group consisted of men who were nonathletes during youth. The results confirm the hypothesis, maximal oxygen uptake was 30 ml/min/Kg body weight in the men who were nonathletes during youth, 38 ml. for the former youthful athletes who followed sedentary adult living patterns and

53 ml. for the former athletes who had kept up regular activity
in the adult years. Generally speaking, functional capacity as
an adult appeared to be partially a function of activity during
the growing years.

Obviously, many questions regarding exercise and functional growth
remain unanswered but as the above studies indicate, data is now
coming in and long overdue investigations are now being undertaken.
On the question of whether physical training as a youth can affect
mature functional capacity, the evidence while not yet clear cut
is suggestive and indicates that an increase in physical activity
for children is advisable not only for the immediate effect on the
child, but also over the long-term as it applies to adult health.

Before leaving this discussion of adult health, the study by
Leaf (26) on long-lived people is of interest. He evaluated the
living patterns and lifestyle, of very old people living in three
geographic locations in the world where longevity of the people
has been documented to be well above normal expectations. The
one common link between the old people of the three communities
was a high degree of physical activity.

*"The old people of all three cultures share a great deal of
physical activity. The traditional farming and household
practices demand heavy work, and male and female are involved
from early childhood to terminal days. Superimposed on the
usual labor involved in farming is the mountainous terrain.
Simply traversing the hills on foot during the day's activities
sustains a high degree of cardiovascular fitness."*

3. POSITIVE CHILDHOOD EXPERIENCE IS IMPORTANT

As adult health problems associated with sedentary living patterns
become more pronounced, the importance of physical activity not
only for children but for adults as well becomes increasingly
important. The human body is built for action, not for rest.
This used to be a historical necessity. The struggle for survival
demanded good physical condition. Optimal function of the human
body can only be achieved by regularly exposing the heart,
circulation, muscles, skeleton and nervous system to some loading,
that is to say, physical work. In earlier times the body got its
exercise both in work and in leisure. However, in our modern
society machines have taken over an ever increasing share of the
work which was formerly accomplished by muscle power alone. Too
often even our leisure time is spent watching rather than doing.
Our lifestyle has changed to such a degree that it seems now to be
dominated by lying, sitting and riding.

As a result of this situation we have recently seen a mounting
campaign on behalf of governments and other agencies to increase
public awareness concerning the need for increased physical
activity. Through the use of the mass media, advertising
campaigns of the type sponsored by Participaction have urged
Canadians to participate in more physical exercise in order to
attain a generally higher level of physical fitness.

The long-term success of approaches of this nature depend, at
least in part, on the motivation towards physical activity that is
established at an early age. One way of assuring adult
participaction in physical activity is to make sure that all young
children receive positive, enjoyable exposures to activity.

A study by Orlick (27) provides substantiation for this premise.
Extensive interviews were conducted with eight- and nine-year-old
organized sport participants and nonparticipants.   The findings
of this study showed that by 8 or 9 years of age many children had
already been either turned on to or turned off sports. Many non-
participant (and drop out) children in this study indicated that
they never (or never again) would go out for a sports team,
whereas, the vast majority of the participant children indicated
that they would always want to go out for a sports team. As
Orlick says, "If one is to seriously think about maximizing adult
participation in sports and physical recreation, it seems
imperative that all young children receive positive, enjoyable
exposures to physical activity".

This then is another reason why physical education in our schools
is so important. Along with parents, it is the school that must
play a decisive role in leading people to physical activity. It is
in the school where recreative skills should be taught and where
facts concerning the positive health benefits of physical activity
should be imparted. It is in the school where opportunities for
fun, self expression, discovery and the chance to succeed
physically should be provided for all children.

Unfortunately, many schools have failed the children in this
regard. School curricula tend to reduce the time available for
physical activity rather than increase it. In Canada at the
elementary level the time devoted to physical education as
compared to the time spent in intellectual pursuits during a
school week amounts to about 6 per cent of the total class time.
The time allocation for physical education in the school day in
Canada ranks among the lowest in the civilized world. Is there
any rationale for this situation?

The UNESCO Council concerned with setting guidelines for
education in emerging countries recommends the following.

*"An individual, whatever his ultimate role in society, needs in his
growing years a due balance of intellectual, physical, moral and
aesthetic development which must be reflected in the educational
curriculum and timetable . . Between 1/3 and 1/6 of the total timetable should be devoted to physical activity." (28)*

But, in Canada over the last quarter century we have seen the
steady erosion of the time available for organized physical
activity within the school setting. At the upper secondary level
the overemphasis upon academic education is so pronounced that in
some cases it becomes almost total. This situation has developed
because educational authorities have adopted the premise that
learning will progress as a direct function of the amount of time
spent behind a desk. Evidence in industry tells us this is not
the case. There comes a point of diminishing returns beyond which
productivity drops as working time increases.

Along these lines, there may be some lessons to be learned from
the "1/3 time" school experiments in Europe, which seem to
indicate that academic learning progresses better if
proportionately less time is spent behind the classroom desk.
The following material on the Vanves school in France has been
drawn from a paper by MacKenzie (29).

4. PHYSICAL ACTIVITY TO SUPPORT ACADEMIC LEARNING (1/3 TIME SCHOOLS)

Vanves is situated in the southern suburbs of Paris, France. The
Vanves Primary School has nine classes of children, ages 6 to 11
years. The staff now consists of nine classroom teachers, who
teach everything except swimming, dance and part of the games and
gymnastics; plus two part-time specialist physical education
teachers, plus the principal (directrice), Mme Boes. Since 1951,
this little school has been the focus of bold new education
practices that now, almost twenty years later, are about to sweep
across that nation's schools.

Both before and after World War II, many French doctors and
educators were concerned about the heavily overloaded intellectual
(i.e., academic) program in the schools. In the elementary
(primary) schools, only two hours per week were devoted to
physical education, plus three hours of recreation, compared with
23½ hours per week of academic work, with homework in addition.
Increasingly, medical and educational opinion indicated that such
an unbalanced program was not in harmony with what was known
about the nature and growth of children that it was not good for
their healthy development. Many French headmasters had drawn
attention to the inefficiency of afternoon intellectual work for
most of the children in elementary schools.

As a result of these evaluations from the medical and teaching
professions, several experiments were set up in Vanves (and later,
in other regions), beginning in 1951, by the Ministry of Education.
These were aimed at obtaining a better balance between the
pupils' physical and intellectual activities, thereby arriving at
a much more effective way of educating children. This was done by
selecting certain classes in the Vanves school, revising quite
significantly their daily program, and then comparing intellectual,
physical, cultural, social and other educational components with
those of carefully paired controlled classes which continued
under the normal school schedules. The whole series of
experiments took place over a ten-year period. Essentially, the
experimental classes did their academic work in the mornings, and
devoted the afternoons to physical education (daily), art, music
and supervised study. No written homework was assigned for the
evenings. The time spent on academic education was reduced to
about four hours per day, and that devoted to physical education
raised to 1 to 2 hours per day (7 to 8 hours per week).

By 1960, the results of the experiments more than confirmed the
basic hypothesis. Not only were the health, fitness, discipline
and enthusiasm superior in the experimental schools, but the
academic results surpassed those of the control classes. It
appeared that a better balance in educational activities resulted
in better performance all around. Similar experiments were then
repeated in Brussels and Japan, with similar results.

At the beginning of the Vanves experiments, the parents' concerns were mainly twofold:

1) That their children would fall behind academically.

2) That (with the outdoor emphasis upon physical education) pupils would catch colds, etc., and miss school.

Neither of these actually occurred; - in fact, the reverse.

The following chart indicates the 1969 weekly timetable used in Vanves (actually used since 1961).

	Monday	Tuesday	Wednesday	Thursday	Friday	Saturday
8:30						
	ACADEMIC				ACADEMIC	
9:30						
	10 MINUTE EXERCISE				BREAK	
10:30	ACADEMIC			N O	ACADEMIC	
11:30				S		
12:30	LUNCH			C H	LUNCH	
1:30	GAMES & GYMNAS-TICS	SWIMMING	GAMES & GYMNAS-TICS	O O L		N O
2:30					DANCE	S C H
3:30	FREE TIME - RECREATION				RECREATION	O O
4:00	SUPERVISED STUDY - ART - MUSIC				S.S. PROJECTS	L
5:00	CONTINUATION FOR				OLDER PUPILS	
5:30	NO WRITTEN HOMEWORK IN EVENINGS					

The results of extensive research in these schools - which have come to be known as "1/3 time" schools because nearly one-third of the daily or weekly timetable is devoted to physical education - are indicated in the following summary, as expressed in an interview in 1969 with Dr. H. Perie, Chief of the Medical Services in the Ministry of Youth and Sports in Paris.

1. Doctors and educators in France now think alike - physical education is an integral part of education, perhaps even the main part.

2. Scientific research into the effects of physical education establish that:

a) It promotes the growth of children.

b) Those taking physical education have better health and much less trouble.

c) Motor development is better, and is better balanced.

3.   Those taking 1/3 time physical education had better performances academically and less susceptibility to stress. Differences have shown up markedly in intellectual development.   We wouldn't conclude that those taking physical education are more intelligent, but the tools of intelligence are much keener.   As the physical education pupils have less problems, their minds are more open, and they will receive more from their teachers.   This is why school results are better.

4.   Study between the experimental and control groups showed:

a) The 1/3 time physical education pupils mature more quickly, and are more independent.

b) The physical education groups will accept the social way of life better. By playing with and against others in a good setting, children learn the "life game" better than those who don't.

c) Aggressions can be controlled better by physical education opportunities.

Mme Boes, the Principal of Vanves School, outlined the main benefits of 1/3 time physical education in her school as follows:

1.   Pupils can enter the secondary school at least as well as pupils from other schools.

2.   They are in better health, stronger, not so tired, keener.

3.   They are happier, have better attitudes and less stress.

4.   Discipline is better - very few problems.

5.   It is easy for them to change to other schools.

6.   The "esprit de corps" among the teachers is improved - things are better for all.

Despite this impressive research, the number of classes in France which adopted this Vanves way of education grew only slowly during the 1960's, perhaps to 1,500 classes. Many people hoped the Vanves example would become general in France, but many also felt that only if and when the Ministry made the plan general, would it in fact become so. Some of the reasons for the limited growth of the plan were attributed to tradition, inertia, increased costs, and a shortage of well-trained elementary physical education teachers - the "resources don't follow" (although the idea might be good).

However, a dramatic breakthrough came in October, 1969. As of that date, the Ministries of Education, and Youth and Sports have specified "1/3 time" physical education for elementary schools in France - that is, to Grade VI - amounting to about six hours per week. (At the same time, the Ministries have also inserted five hours of physical education per week in the French secondary schools, dependent upon personnel and equipment).

Two obvious questions face us here in Canada, in view of this research and development in Europe.

a) What are the implications for our schools?

b) What evidence do we have that our present distribution of educational experiences, and arrangement of the school day is the best we can provide for our children.

C. CONCLUSION

An attempt has been made to emphasize the importance of physical activity for all children. Physical activity is necessary to support normal growth in children, it is important for children to be active to ensure a healthy childhood. The importance of physical activity in terms of preventive medicine is also becoming clearer. Our present way of life can no longer spontaneously satisfy the biological need for physical activity, as in the past. Clearly, it is important to get people interested in regular physical activity at an early age. Anything that is neglected as a youth can in many cases not be made up later on. Positive early experience is essential for all children if we hope to change adult lifestyles.

Unfortunately, as this paper has shown, school curricula have tended to reduce rather than increase the available time for physical activity and recreation within the school day. This is regrettable since it is during the school years that young people acquire the motivation, understanding and skills necessary for effective adult living. Hopefully, as a result of this conference, changes will be made in a system of education that constrains our children during the vulnerable period of active growth to bend over books and desks five and one-half hours a day without providing them with the time and resources to discover and use their physical faculties.

References

1. Elliott, G.M.: "The effects of exercise on structural growth." J.Can. Assoc., HPER, 1970, 36: 21.

2. Malina, R.M.: "Exercise as an influence upon growth". Clin. Pediatr., 1969, 8: 16.

3. Rarick, G.L.: "Exercise and growth", in Science of Medicine of Exercise and Sports, Harpers, New York, 1960.

4. Espenchade, A.: "The contributions of physical activity to growth". Res. Quar., 1960, 31: 351.

5. Rarick, G.L. (ed): Physical Activity: Human Growth and Development, Academic Press, New York, 1973.

6. Kottke, F.J.: "The effects of limitation of activity upon the human body." J.A.M.A., 1966, 196: 825.

7. Åstrand, P.O.: Health and fitness, Scandia Insurance Co., Stockholm, 1972.

8. Rose, K.: "To keep the people in health". J.A.C.H.A., 1973, 22: 80.

9. Smith, N.: "The challenge of obesity". Maternal and Infant Nutrition Seminar, Atlanta, 1972.

10. Widdowson, E.M.: "Harmony of growth". Lancet, 1970, II: 901.

11. Winick, M.: "Cellular growth during early malnutrition." Pediatr., 1971, 47: 969.

12. Cheek, D.B.: "Cellular growth, nutrition and development". Pediatr., 1970, 45: 315.

13. Knittle, J.M., Hirsch, J.: "Infantile nutrition as a determinant of adult adipose tissue, metabolism and cellularity." Clin. Res., 1967, 15: 323.

14. Cheek, D.B.: in "Problems of nutrition in the perinatal period", Report of the Sixtieth Ross Conference on Pediatric Research, Owen G.M. (ed), Ross Laboratories, Columbus, 1969.

15. Buchanan, T., Pritchard, J.: "DNA content of tibialis anterior of male and female white rats measured from birth to 50 weeks." J. Anat., 1970, 107: 185.

16. Cheek, D.B., et al.: "Skeletal muscle cell mass and growth: The concept of the deoxyribonucleic acid unit". Pediatr. Res., 1971, 5: 312.

17. Bailey, D.A., Bell, R.D., Howarth, R.E.: "The effect of exercise on DNA and protein synthesis in skeletal muscle of growing rats". Growth, 1973, 37: 323.

18. Bannister, R.: "Limits of human performance". Documenta Geigy, Basle, 1968.

19. Bailey, D.A.: The Saskatchewan child growth and development study, University of Saskatchewan, Saskatoon, 1968.

20. Bailey, D.A.: "Exercise, fitness and physical education for the growing child - a concern", Can. J. Pub. Health, 1973, 64: 421.

21. Parizkova, J.: "Somatic development and body composition changes in adolescent boys differing in physical activity and fitness: a longitudinal study", Anthropologie, 1972, X/1.

22. Astrand, P.O.: "Commentary - Symposium on physical activity and cardiovascular health", Canad. Med. Ass. J., 1967, 96: 760.

23. Ekblom, B.: "Physical training in normal boys in adolescence". Acta Paediat. Scand. Suppl., 1970, 217: 60.

24. Bailey, D.A., Ross, W.D., Weese, C.H., Mirwald, R.L.: "Maximal oxygen intake (VO_2 max) and dimensional relationship in boys studied longitudinally from age 8 to 15". VI International Symposium on Pediatric Work Physiology, Prague, 1974.

25. Saltin, B., Grimby, G.: "Physiological analysis of middle aged and old former athletes, comparison with still active athletes of the same ages." Circulation, 1968, 38: 1104.

26. Leaf, A.: "Getting old". Scientific American, 1973, 229, 3: 45.

27. Orlick, T.D.: "Children's sports - a revolution is coming". J. Can. Assoc. HPER, 1970, 39: 12.

28. International Council of Sport and Physical Education: Declaration on sport, UNESCO, Place de Fontenoy, Paris, 1964.

29. MacKenzie, J.: "1/3 time physical education". Saskatchewan Movement and Leisure, 1974, 1: 6.

Psychological aspects

PSYCHOSOCIAL DEVELOPMENT AND ACTIVITY
IN MIDDLE CHILDHOOD (5 - 12 YEARS)

by   Carolyn W. Sherif and
       Gillian D. Rattray*

The purpose of this paper is to present major problems and research findings on psychosocial development as these bear on children's sports and activity between the ages of 5 to 12 years. That age period corresponds, roughly, to the years of elementary education. The somewhat arbitrary cutoff point at a dozen years of life was chosen because the years immediately following mark the most frequent age of pubescence, first for girls and then for boys. Aside from the important structural and physiological changes occurring, the psychosocial changes of early adolescence are sufficiently striking that they warrant another paper. Some of those changes will be indicated in summary form at the end of the paper, in the interests of continuity.

Several limitations hinder our purpose. The first set stems from limitations in the research literature available to the authors. Notably, the research surveyed was preponderantly done in the United States, despite watchfulness for cross-national and cross-cultural materials. Second, the great bulk of research on children during this period pertains most directly to academic performance, and was automatically eliminated by the criteria of the literature search. Third, on almost every topic of interest, the research literature is more abundant before the age of 5 years and after the age of 12 than in between. Finally, we noted with some distress that studies of boys outnumbered those concerning girls, and that sex comparisons were sparse.

The second set of limitations concerns the professional interests and biases of the senior author as a social psychologist. Perhaps unfortunately, these do not include concern about the shaping of the exceptionally skilled athlete. In any event, the little research bearing on the future champion that we encountered confirmed initial hunches. Those boys who make varsity or "first string" teams in competitive sports during this age period are chosen, by adults of course, from among boys most advanced in physical maturity--as measured by skeletal age and indicators of pubescence (Clarke and Peterson, 1961; Hale, 1956; Krogman, 1959). In a society where team competition is highly valued, what this means is that certain adults are selectively rewarding the faster maturing boy--and incidentally not the girl--because his development and performance more closely approximate adult standards. In other words, adults selectively choose and cultivate the skills of the earlier maturing boys, especially for those sports emphasizing speed, strength and endurance. The social psychology of this state of affairs should focus equally on the selecting adults and the developing athlete.

* The senior author is Professor of Psychology, The Pennsylvania State University, University Park, Pennsylvania, U.S.A. The junior author, currently a graduate student in physical education, provided invaluable assistance in surveying research literature and summarizing certain of the studies reported here. Opinions and evaluations are the responsibility of the senior author, who gratefully acknowledges the assistance.

Presumably, a similar selective interaction between adults and children occurs for other sports as well, no doubt emphasizing those bodily characteristics and skills prized in the sport in question.

Another bias, amply confirmed by the research survey, is that psychologists and social scientists in fact know comparatively little about children's physical activity and sports. Their research has concentrated heavily on problems relating to academic success or failure or on problems relating to particular theories of psychosocial development that may have little bearing on activity. Therefore, this paper will focus on trends and influences in psychosocial development that appear to us to have the greatest relevance on activity and sports, indicating where information is available and where it is lacking.

Physical Development

The period from 5 to 12 years is one of steady growth, but at a velocity markedly reduced from earlier childhood until about 11 years of age. Then girls, on the average, exhibit the beginning of a growth spurt that ordinarily levels off after pubescence. However, this prepubescent growth spurt also affects a minority of boys, approximately 17 percent of whom are pubescent or post-pubescent by age 12 (Horrocks, 1969). By 12, approximately 40 percent of girls have some breast development and pubic hair, the average age of menarche in the U.S. being during the thirteenth year. Thus boys and girls start the period about the same size, on the average, growing steadily at a level or slightly declining rate. Toward the end of the period, marked differences are evident between the physical status of girls and boys (with girls slightly taller and more mature, on the average). Furthermore, individual differences in the timing of the growth spurt yield 10 - 12-year-olds of strikingly different growth and maturity status within each sex.

Body Build, Physique and Cultural Stereotypes

Cultural norms for body build are translated into fairly definite individual preferences for society's favored body images by 5 years of age. Kindergarten children respond to drawings of various human physiques with fairly accurate identifications of their own physical type, with preferential choices of average body builds and dislike for fatness (Lerner and Schroeder, 1971). By about 7 years, definite stereotyping of persons with different body images is found for girls as well as boys, with unfavorable traits attributed to the tubby (endomorph) body and more favorable ones to the average (mesomorph) image. Girls of this age, however, also respond favorably to the longer lean lines of the ectomorph--a build typified in the culture by the ethereal fashion model and hardly the prototype of the athlete.

The early influence of cultural preferences for mesomorphs and the accompanying private "theories of personality" about individuals who deviate from that mode are significant on two counts. First, throughout this age period, low positive correlations are reported for males between mesomorphic physique and popularity with peers (Clarke and Greene, 1963), between popularity and athletic skills (Clarke and Clarke, 1961) and, more generally, between mesomorphy and athletic skills (Davidson, et al., 1957). It should be emphasized, however,

that although statistically significant, the level of these
correlations is far too low to account for much of the variance of
individuals in any of these respects (physique, popularity and
athletic skills). They do indicate, however, a generally positive
evaluation of mesomorphy and athletic skills among children, in line
with the adult culture, and a generally negative evaluation of
obesity.

Second, the early influence of the cultural norms concerning
body build is salient because, in effect, it exerts a conservative
influence on both peer and adult evaluations of the child's
capabilities and personality. In fact, physique does change during
growth, and established expectations about a child based on body
image at an earlier point in time may well hinder adaptation to later
alterations.

Solley (1959) studied 502 children aged 6 - 12 years over a
five-year period, reporting that variability in physique increased
with age, particularly among girls. Maturity status and speed of
growth were related to changes in physique, and the implication is
that individual differences increase accordingly. Such findings
suggest caution in the early assessment of body type and personality
as a mode of developing individualized programs for children. Such
programs may become obsolete before adults discard them. For
example, the suggestion by Davidson, et al. (1957) that adult
expectations be governed by measurements of body type and personality
traits at age seven goes far beyond their data obtained from 50 boys
and 50 girls of that age. The case for a reliable and substantial
relationship between body type and personality characteristics has
never been as strong as supporters of Sheldon's research would have
us believe. Measures of physique and personality are not very
reliable at age seven and scarcely predictive of later status in
either respect with sufficient accuracy to warrant a wager involving
any sizeable sum of money. Such advice runs the risk of elevating a
cultural preference for a body type into a "law of nature" by
reinforcing adult expectations before much stabilization has occurred.

A far stronger trend in the research literature shows the
social advantages of the faster and earlier maturing boy for physical
activity and for the peer popularity associated with that early
superiority as well as "male-ness", as culturally stereotyped
(Clarke and Peterson, 1961; Clarke and Wickens, 1962; Hartup, 1969).
The slower or late maturing boy suffers the slings of an outrageous
fortune created by an adult society rewarding physical maturity because
of its advantage in athletic and male competitions, which is also
mirrored in the status criteria of boys. By age 12, the slow or late
maturer begins to experience the blows to achievement efforts and self
esteem which may, indeed, transform him from a happy well-adjusted
child to an unhappy teen-age prepubescent. However, within fairly
short time, his growth status will catch up to peers.

One final word, lest those in physical education take too
seriously the low correlations between mesomorphy in childhood and
athletic skills, it should be added that mesomorphy is also correlated
with the incidence of behaviour labelled "juvenile delinquency"
(Horrocks, 1969). Educational plans had best be laid with the precept
that only the extremes in physique constitute genuine differences and
that the educational problem in physical activity is properly the

design of alternatives to accommodate individual differences in body type rather than to select body types conducive to championship performance. Even in the latter endeavor, with a range of physiques limited by the mechanics of the sport in question, the builder of champions plays better odds by concentrating on earlier maturing children. That such concentration does in fact occur speaks more to the personal ambitions of the adult than to concerns with education in any broad sense.

<u>Sex Differences</u>

The intertwining of developmental trends, of out-of-school experiences promoting physical activity and of quality of instruction is probably crucial for any assessment of skill differences between boys and girls, particularly later during the period. There is apparently a large body of contradictory findings to be reconciled with the everyday wisdom that boys are superior to girls in sports at all ages. Indeed, we find reports that boys exceed girls in working capacity, with the sex differences becoming greater from 6 to 14 (Adams, 1961). From ages 4 to 6, girls excel over boys in ball catching (Gutteridge, 1934) but boys of the same age profit more than girls from specific training (Dusenberry, 1952). Six- to nine-year-old girls, on the other hand, improve more than boys in training at hopping (Carpenter, 1940), but 8-year-old boys gain more from training in throwing and kicking than girls (Dohrman, 1964). Girls perform better than boys on a balance board up to about 8 years, but boys surpass them thereafter (Cron and Pronko, 1957). While boys improve from 10 to 17 years on the California Physical Performance tests, girls' performance decreases on some tests (e.g., situps and knee pushups) while increasing between 10 - 13 years of age on the dash, broad jump and in throwing ability. On the other hand, other studies report greater sex differences among younger children (7 - 8-year-olds) than older (up to 17) and equal performances by the sexes in some skills (e.g., vertical broad jump).

The upshot of the mass of confusing evidence is that there seems to be very little basis for assuming invariant, non-task specific sex differences, a lot of indicating male superiority in a variety of specific respects and females in a few, and almost no clue as to what is responsible for the sex differences that are reported, particularly where size alone is no issue. It seems at least possible that many of the differences are produced by the combined effects of differential treatments, social interests and social influences on the sexes that are consistent and pronounced during this period, particularly in promoting practice in a variety of physical skills by boys outside of school.

There is very, very good evidence that in the socialization of boys and girls lots of different things occur; but even the direction of the pressures is different. Little boys are made aware early in life that to be physically active, to excel in sports, is an important thing to do. It brings them the greatest rewards. They are also made aware, very early on, what little boys do and do not do. They do not cry, they do not play with dolls, and so on. Little girls of the same age (the 5 to 6-year-old group), really have a much wider range of opportunity in sports and activity, and in almost everything else. They can be tomboys if they want to. But during the period from 5 to 12, two different things happen to the sexes. The little boy, having

learned the reward system early, just continues to learn. The girl
finds a different thing happening. The nearer she gets to pubescence,
the more she becomes aware, not only from adults, but from her peers--
including boys, that if she is physically active (particularly in
some of the sports involving power, strength and speed) she is not
going to get any rewards from them. On the contrary, she may
actually be penalized. It is not, after all, very soft and feminine
to run around a track every day. This is the difficulty that girls
face; it could be largely responsible for the fact that, on the
average, there is an actual decline in girls' performance. There are
other physical and physiological changes involved, but the drama of
those changes is too great to attribute solely to hormonal influence.
The best way to show the effect of hormonal influences would be to
change the environment, and study the effects of this change.

Cross-cultural and cross-national studies may clarify some of
the confusing research literature. However, it is impossible to
attribute any specific portion of the sex differences reported to the
"natural development" of the two biological sexes. Some assiduous
investigators will have to elucidate how the confused research
findings now available indicate anything but that boys and girls
develop in different social contexts that differentially train, evaluate
and encourage the acquisition of physical skills from a very early age.

HOW CHILDREN SPEND THEIR TIME

Any educator, even the one-room school teacher, sees children
for only a fraction of their daily 24 hours and almost never on non-
school days. If we grant that the fruits of their efforts are
dependent upon the total context of a child's daily living--in
particular upon the relative significance of the educational program
relative to the child's other activities--then educators have a vested
interest in knowing how children spend their time out of the
educational situation.

In some parts of the world, perhaps the majority of children
begin during this age range to engage in productive work or family-
centered tasks like child care. Even in those countries where
universal education is required, there are striking differences in the
role played by physical activity and physical education in the child's
total day. Our remarks will concentrate on what can be gleaned from
research in the United States about how children spend their time, and
changes in this respect.

A word of caution is needed about social class differences.
Most of the available data concern middle-class white children. Yet,
to the extent that the impact of mass media of entertainment, education
and sports upon time consumption and interests is society-wide, none
of what we shall say is irrelevant to non-middle-class children. If
anything, available research suggests that lower-class children have
more free time than their middle-class counterparts who, at least in
the United States, are proportionally over-represented in all
organized community and youth programs.

Twenty years ago, Sullenger, et al. (1953) surveyed the
leisure time activities of children in the working class districts
of Omaha, Nebraska and found that only a fraction of the children

were playing in civic, community or church recreational facilities. Home and neighborhood were the recreation centers for half of the children. At that time, before the widespread availability of television, the first two preferences for leisure activities were radio and motion pictures, with twelve of the remaining 20 most frequently preferred activities involving physical activity but only three of these specifying organized sports (softball, baseball, football). A few years later McCullough (1957) reported that television was the favored recreation of 10 - 11-year-olds in low, middle and upper socioeconomic levels. Children of comparable age in Czechoslovokia most frequently chose sports (41 percent) as their free activity preference, followed by the arts (31 percent) (Muradbegovic and Sarajevo, 1970).

The relevance of these data is to a long-term pattern of change in children's use of leisure time. More recently, survey research in the United States indicates that 85 percent of children 6 - 11 years watch television during their "average day" and 98 percent in an average week (Cole, 1970). Weekly viewing time averages a little over 26 hours. Very likely a substantial portion of this viewing is on weekends, so let us make estimates of time based on 168 hour, 7-day week. Eliminating 8 - 12 sleeping hours per day and a minimum time for eating and other maintenance activities, we have an estimated remainder of about 60 - 65 hours per week, from which 5 - 6 hours must be deducted for each school day plus time going to and from school. The upshot is that the schoolchild has a remainder of, say, 20 - 30 hours a week in which to perform household chores, homework, attend movies, go to church or cultural events, take lessons of various kinds, engage in organized recreation and athletic programs, read or play informally with peers.

Our point is that American children are busy and that the long idyllic hours of free time glorified in childhood fiction are fast disappearing for middle-class children in direct proportion to the efforts adults make to involve them in organized activities.

Devereux (1972) has recently reported an observational study over several months in Ithaca, New York, in which he observed on warm, fairweather days during school lunch periods and after school around twelve different elementary schools and several neighborhoods. Although he saw over 3600 children departing from school, he reported a striking lack of self-generated spontaneous play activities involving traditional children's games. Devereux feels strongly that television combined with adult organized and supervised activities are programing out the spontaneous and informally organized play characteristic of earlier periods and still to be observed in other countries (Segoe, 1962, 1971; Eifermann, 1971). His observations are supported somewhat by earlier research (Sutton-Smith and Rosenberg, 1961) that reported a decline during the past half century in preference for spontaneously organized children's games along with less clear-cut differentiation of preferences of boys and girls.

If these selected observations are indeed representative of general trends, the implications for children psychosocial development are vast. In addition to George Herbert Mead and Piaget, numerous theorists of psychosocial development--notably Sutton-Smith--have analyzed children's spontaneously organized and traditional games as prototypes of the interpretation of culture and personality (cf.

Sutton-Smith, 1968; Roberts and Sutton-Smith, 1962; Roberts, Sutton-Smith and Kendon, 1963; Sutton-Smith and Rosenberg, 1961). To the extent that children are actually spending most of their time in other ways, such analogy is more appropriately a study of traditional culture patterns with little implication for contemporary psychosocial development. Clearly the issues are empirical and can be settled only through comparative and representative research. At least one earlier research report suggests that even 40 years ago, American boys spent less time in spontaneously organized play activities than myth would have it. Reeves (1931) reported observations of street play in 20 cities and reported that at least two thirds of the children observed were not playing games.

For those children, largely boys, who enter into an organized, adult sponsored program of competitive sports during these years, the opportunity for free play or spontaneous games are further limited by the demands of the competition. Skuberic (1955) reported that boys who had been chosen as players on Little League or Middle League baseball teams devoted from one-half to most of their leisure time to baseball throughout the year. In surveying the physical education and interscholastic sports in one entire state (Oklahoma) Dobson (1971) found that half of the elementary school districts had interscholastic sports and, when they did, allotted more time per week to these programs than to general physical education classes. Presumably here too boys who "made the team" spent a great deal of out-of-school time in practice.

Evidence from earlier (e.g., Volberding, 1948) and more recent research (Hartup, 1969) is fairly clear that children's preferences for use of free time continue to center upon interaction with peers, whether spontaneous forms of traditional games form the content or not. The importance of peer associations is sufficient to warrant a special section later in this paper.

PSYCHOSOCIAL DEVELOPMENT

By far the most numerous research on psychosocial development that bears on children's activity pertains to cooperation, competition, the setting of goals or standards for performance, and motivations for achievement. In order to deal with this research in coherent fashion and to speak of developmental trends, it is necessary to be very clear about what these concepts mean. Before defining the terms, emphasis must be placed on certain properties of the behaviors in question and their social context. These provide the keys to understanding developmental trends.

Cooperation, competition, setting goals or standards for performance and achievement are highly abstract labels for activity that is patterned and more or less consistently oriented with respect to other persons. In development, it is the patterned and consistent properties of behavior that distinguish the activities of the older from the younger child much more than other characteristics of the behavior, such as frequency, verbalization, or intensity of response. Consistent patterns of social activity by the child develop, and their development implies that the child is less bound by unique social situations he or she confronts from moment to moment and less dominated by the ups and downs of momentary needs, desires or bodily states. Concomitantly he or she is more and more attentive to the roles and actions of other persons in the situations, taking these into account in certain predictable ways.

Each of the social behaviors mentioned implies a particular structure in the social situation that must be understood in its own right if we are to grasp fully the import of the child's specific actions in the situation. For example, there are tasks or problems whose solution demands division of labor or coordination of activities, while there are others that require solitary or side-by-side individual performance. Some situations contain rewards only for coordinated group effort while others reward only individual effort and still others carry rewards for both. In some contexts, other people are present in significant relationship to the activity as onlookers or judges, and in others they are not. The development of social behavior and the child's mentality cannot be understood apart from such structural properties of the social context.

Contrary to folk wisdom and many schools of thought in psychology, we are not dealing with the development of an isolated child who has, acquires or forms personal qualities and motives that absolutely determine his or her behavior. We are dealing with a child whose social development is contingent upon the structure of social contexts at every step as well as those contexts experienced in the past. It is crude primitive psychologizing and poor science to treat psychosocial development as a process of shaping the child as an isolated being. The structure of social contexts--including those in games and sport--are human creations that do change, that can be changed and that have to be included in accounts of psychosocial development with an importance as great as any aspect of the human organism itself.

Having stated these critical conditions for understanding psychosocial development, we can clarify what is meant by some of the important topics that have been studied.

1. Cooperation refers to performing activity together, but in the literature on child development invariably implies more. Three-year-old children who individually dig a spadeful of sand and dump it into the sea are scarcely cooperating, though they are working side-by-side. Two children each carrying one end of a large board to place across a crevice are cooperating because the activity of each is essential to the common end. Thus cooperation refers to the structure of the activity quite as much as to the behaviors of the children. It refers to tasks and situations requiring division of activity and its coordination toward a common end. Cooperativeness is nothing more nor less than the consistent participation by the child in such tasks. The complexity of the cooperative tasks and their demands upon the child increase with age, as developing conceptual abilities increasingly enable the child to perceive the roles of others in the activity and to coordinate his or her actions with theirs.

No one can cooperate alone. Contrary to political or popular dogma, children's cooperation is not necessarily a polar opposite of competition even with regard to the individual's share of rewards. Especially in games and sports, children have to learn to cooperate in increasingly complex role structures in order to compete with others. Further, successful cooperation endeavors even include a great deal of individual and group competition directed toward the completion of the larger common task. Cooperation and competitive activities need not be bipolar opposites, but aspects of social processes that can become polarized when reward systems deprive or compensate individual or group effort for one at the expense of the other. The two become polarized when political ideologies favoring differing reward systems contend for primacy. Such contentions are important, of course, but it is sad indeed when they become bases for justifying practices in sports. In blatant extreme, such ideological bias amounts to justifying the use of sport for competitive economic gain or eliminating sports competition altogether.

2. Competition, in turn, consists of activities directed more or less consistently toward meeting a standard or achieving a goal in which performance by a person or by a group is compared and evaluated relative to that of selected other persons or groups. Note that, by definition, competition implies a social context involving certain other people. Not any old person will do, for there is invariably a selective process determining to whom one's performance is compared, what the standards or goals shall be, and who does the evaluating. Such social context is quite as essential for individual as for group or team competition (which is inevitably both cooperative and competitive in structure). In fact, the social context is absolutely essential for understanding the erection of standards and goals for one's own performance. We regard behavior as "self competitive" only when the definition of the standards to be attained is socially acceptable, as opposed to entirely unique or arbitrary individual definitions.

3. It follows, then, that the individual child's level of aspiration, expectations and standards for performance, including those defining excellence or achievement in some respect, are related to social standards held by some other persons--typically peers, parents or teachers and occasionally all three. The child's experiences of success or failure in various activities are relative to such standards and are, therefore, defined by the social context, even though the experiences are private affairs. As William Jones pointed out experiences of success or failure are invariably relative to one's pretensions. While personal pretensions are built slowly in the school of hard knocks relative to one's performances in actual situations, they are also colored by social expectations of those significant in one's eyes, hence are social as well as personal (Lewin, et al., 1944). Similarly, what is called achievement or excellence is much less strictly personal and much more a social definition, both of the value of the activity itself in the eyes of others and the levels of performance defined as superior. For example, Yoga exercises are not highly valued in the United States and no amount of excellence in that respect is defined as an achievement by the vast majority of its citizens.

With these terms in mind, we can summarize research on psychosocial development in these respects.

Developmental Trends

In the sense defined here, children as young as two or three do not cooperate, compete, or strive for excellence, or set consistent standards for their own performance in an activity (Greenberg, 1932; Leuba, 1933; Owens, 1970; McClintock and Nuttin, 1969). This fact has profound implications for understanding the social behavior of children early in the age range under review (5 - 6 years).

The initial appearance of consistently competitive or cooperative behaviors is ordinarily noted around 4 - 5 years, but is typically indicated by an increasing frequency of consistent responses and/or an increasing number of children who exhibit them at all. The implication is clear that cooperative and competitive processes can be engaged in only sporadically or by certain children of these ages. Setting goals or standards for one's own performance is ordinarily dated after six years of age (e.g., Gesell and Ilg, 1943; Goodenough, 1945), and almost all of the research literature on achievement motivation has studied elementary school or older children.

On the one hand, this developmental trend undoubtedly reflects changes in intellectual functioning as studied by Piaget and his co-workers (1959) from an initial sensorimotor stage tied closely to concrete activities and situations toward cognitive operations approaching the formal logic and level of abstraction that characterized adult cognition which, according to these researchers, is ordinarily achieved by the close of the age period (11 - 12 years). Children of 5 - 6 years are still in a stage of concrete operations in which, thinking is closely tied to the appearance of things and events. Certainly the developmental changes in intellectual functioning between 5 - 12 years are first-rate in importance for educators and adult workers with children. During this time, children's conceptions of rules, of causality and of the roles of self and others in competitive and cooperative situations are transformed (Piaget, 1932).

On the other hand, there is very considerable evidence that the child's experiences in interacting with others in the cultural milieu exert profound influence on the development of competitive and cooperative activities. Most of the pertinent research has utilized very simple game situations, such as dropping different colored marbles into appropriately colored holes or pulling on cords to move an object. Almost all of it has been done in laboratory-like atmospheres, which doubtless are interpreted differently by children from different backgrounds. Yet, if we may agree that behavior in such situations bears some relationship to behavior in active game and sport situations, there seems little doubt that cultural experiences encouraging and rewarding cooperation and competition leave their mark in the form of response tendencies.

For example, in the United States, middle-class children ages 2 - 8 years exhibit competitive responses earlier and more frequently than lower-class children (Owens, 1970). In the same experiment, girls competed more than boys, and once again it is necessary to emphasize that the task was dropping marbles into holes performed in a laboratory and school setting. Azrin and Lindsley (1956) showed that in a simple coordination game that required cooperation for successful execution, rewarding cooperation increased cooperative responses. These older children (7 - 12 years) responded to the task and reward by quickly developing leader-follower relations that enhanced their cooperation; therefore it seems an oversimplification to suggest that rewarding cooperative or competitive behavior is all that is necessary to increase the frequency of one or the other. The demands of the task and the rewards together induced the children to develop interpersonal roles suitable to the task.

This primacy of interpersonal relationships as the context of competitive or cooperative behavior has been demonstrated even for five-year-olds, among whom consistency is just beginning to be evidenced (Philip, 1940). Kindergarten children paired for a marble dropping game preferred to cooperate with another child they liked and their performance was noisy and excited while doing so. On the other hand, competition was preferred with a child not known previously, and the proceedings were marked by quiet pursuit of the task.

In a series of experiments, Madsen and his co-workers have used a variety of simple games designed to compare the frequencies of cooperative and competitive strategies chosen by 5 - 11-year-old children from different cultural backgrounds. Again it should be emphasized that the choice of activity by a researcher and the character of the research situation itself are always important influences on response in the research situation. Nevertheless it seems quite clear that the cultural experiences of children by the age of 5 years do affect their responses in such research situations.

For example, Israeli children ages 5 - 11 years who have grown up in a kibbutz cooperate more effectively in a game rewarding group performance than children growing up in urban settings (Shapiro and Madsen, 1969; Shapiro, 1971). When the rewards were shifted to individual rewards, fewer of the kibbutz children shifted to a competitive response which, in this game, was also maladaptive. If anything, the cultural differences were more pronounced at age 5 than for older children, perhaps because the older children's increasing cognitive development enhanced their ability to size up the games, the reward situations and the roles of others in order to select the winning strategy regardless of whether it was competitive or cooperative.

Children 7 - 9 years of age from different cultural backgrounds in the United States and Mexico also exhibit such differential tendencies to compete or cooperate (Madsen and Shapiro, 1970; Kagan and Madsen, 1971). Briefly, Anglo-American children compete more frequently than Afro-American children who, in turn, compete more than Mexican-American children. However, when village Mexican children were compared with Mexican American children, the village children in Mexico exhibited the greatest tendency to cooperate and lesser tendency to compete (Kagan and Madsen, 1971). Sex differences, when found, showed girls competing more frequently than boys. It should be noted that this finding is clear evidence against the general assumption that boys are more competitive than girls. On the other hand, in all such generalizations, it is even more important to emphasize that the particular activity chosen for study is bound to affect competitive proclivities. If the games had emphasized more active play, the boys might well have competed more frequently. There is a great deal of evidence that with age successful competition in physical activity increasingly ceases to be rewarded for girls, and may even be sanctioned as "unfeminine."

These important researches showing cultural differences in the development of tendencies to compete and cooperate must be interpreted with some caution. It cannot be concluded from them, for example, that U.S. children do not learn how to cooperate nor Mexican children how to compete. In each research, a game is presented that has been carefully designed to allow the child a choice of competitive or cooperative responses. Nevertheless, the definition of what is competitive or cooperative is closely tied to the structure of the game, and the winning strategy itself is often cooperative. The importance of these definitions is evident in a recent study (Kagan and Madsen, 1972) in which the structure of the games were varied to study rivalry in conditions ranging from the opportunity to gain the largest score by rivalry to conditions in which rivalry permitted one to best the opponent but not to accumulate the largest possible score for oneself. In the latter case, rivalry was sheerly keeping the opponent's score low at any cost to oneself. These varied conditions of the reward structure significantly affected the frequency of rivalrous choices by both Anglo-American and Mexican children (age 5-6 and 8-10 years). The tendency toward rivalrous choices was greatest when by rivalry one could both make absolute gains for oneself and best the opponent, and least when a rivalrous choice was made at the expense of one's own absolute gain. Nevertheless, the older children were more rivalrous than younger children, the Anglo-American children were more rivalrous than Mexican children, and the difference between them increased with age. The importance of this research is, we believe, in showing the development in the United States of a highly individualistic form of rivalry in which "if I can't win, no one can," or the "object of competition is to beat the rival, regardless of whether one's own performance reaches a level of excellence."

The age trend in rivalrous responses of the kind studied by Kagan and Madsen (1972) toward greater cultural differences with age is interpreted by these authors in terms of increasing sensitivity among Mexican, but not U.S. children to cultural norms valuing conflict-free interpersonal relations. It is exceedingly difficult to generalize in this respect until further research utilizing different task and reward structures is undertaken. However, it should be noted that in comparing U.S. and Belgian children ages 7-11 years, McClintock and Nuttin (1969) reported the opposite age trend. Early differences toward more frequent competitive choices by U.S. children were dissipated by age 11, when competitive responses were clearly dominant for children in both cultures in the game they played. In contrast to the games used to study rivalry among Mexican and U.S. children, however, the game they used unequivocally rewarded competitive behavior. It seems likely that older children were better able to figure this out and respond to it in that specific situation than younger children.

Finally, research by Sutton-Smith and Roberts (1964) may serve to caution us from drawing blanket conclusions about cooperative-competitive tendencies of children based on their behavior in only a few selected games. These authors correctly pointed out that even within a culture, the types of activities and the strategies

appropriate to competition in them strikingly affect the types and
frequency of specific competitive behaviors. Studying 9-12-year-old
children, they found that both peers and teachers have arrived at
fair consensus on the typical styles of children's competition, based
on the activities and strategies they were typically observed to
engage in. Using an adapted sociometric technique, they found
agreement in classifying children as primarily "soldiers of fortune"
who relied on luck, as competitors relying on physical skill and
power, as strategists who used their wits in primarily non-active
sports, and as "failures", who were of course scorned by these American
children. Such findings may well caution us from attributing
competitive tendencies only to those who participate effectively in
active sports, or to attributing to competitive tendencies the sole
responsibility for such successful sport activity.

In fact, research on developmental trends can be interpreted to
indicate that the development of abilities both to cooperate and to
compete is an interrelated process in which cultural experiences
emphasize one or the other in particular classes of concrete
situations. The young child who fails to compete in a given activity
may be responding specifically to that activity, while competing
actively in others, such as school, games of chance or strategy. In a
culture that prizes individual excellence, the total lack of competitive
tendencies is likely to be mirrored also in inability to cooperate
well with others. Conversely, in a society that prizes cooperative
activities, competition for a group purpose is likely to be prized,
but not tapped in the research of individualistic American researchers.
In such a setting the child who has difficulty in cooperating is
likely to be a poor competitor in the name of his group.

Such differential emphasis in societies on different kinds and
organizations for games and sports are translated to children in
concrete situations fairly early in childhood. For example, Dennis
(1957) asked U.S. Armenian, Jewish and Arab children ages 5 1/2 to
11 years in Lebanon to describe incidents in which their behavior had
been praised by adults. U.S. children reported praise for
participating in sports and games twice as often as Armenian children
and three times as frequently as Jewish or Arab children. Clearly,
the opportunity and the approval systems for physical activity are
largely in the hands of adults who, alone, are in a position to
organize these systems in ways calculated to benefit the health and
well-being of the largest possible number of children.

Several implications emerge from this account of the development
of competition and cooperation among children:

1. The capacity to direct behavior consistently toward abstract
standards or remote, uncertain goals in which one's behavior is
compared and evaluated relative to others develops with age. The
crucial evidence supporting this conclusion stems from a body of
research showing that not only consistently competitive behavior, but
also consistently cooperative behavior, consistent helping behavior,
consistent sympathetic actions at the distress of others and--most
unfortunately--consistency in prejudicial hostility toward groups
traditionally discriminated against in a society--all of these emerge
at about the same period in the child's development.

2. The process of development occurs in a social context in which parents, siblings and peers are very important in providing the medium for testing one's own performance and for learning the reciprocal nature of rules and standards. Recreation leaders and teachers are important--but all of these significant figures are surrounded, like it or not, by a cultural context that is at least equally significant for the child's development. How else are we to understand the earliest buds of competition in rivalry over who gets to be father or mother, in divisions into good guys and bad guys for bang-bang conflict when the good guys and bad guys are precisely those the children meet in story books and on television? If, as the evidence indicates, the social context for competition is crucial, it is utter nonsense to speak of "born winners and born losers." There are, and always will be, individual differences. But the "winners" and the "losers" are shaped in a variety of ways by their social context, at times obviously and at others more subtley. It is more accurate to state that winners are made and losers are made by their experiences in a social context of other people who, to a major degree, shape their selection of targets for their efforts and the structure of standards and goals related to those efforts.

3. The social context in which competitive behavior develops affects not only its rate of development but also the targets for competition, that is, what is important to the child and what can be left to the birds. In this country, at a very early age, boys learn that sports of various kinds are <u>the</u> avenue for recognition to a far greater extent than girls. As a result some boys are placed in untenable situations psychologically and many girls simply fail to persist in sufficient physical activity to develop a strong and healthy body.

It is commonplace to point out that societies differ enormously in the prizes they proffer for different activities, including sports and recreation. What is not so obvious is that societies that prize physical activity and health need not place the enormous value on competitive sports and <u>organized</u> competitive sports that is so striking in our own. In some societies, physical fitness is prized for everyone and may be encouraged through universal physical activity, including work as well as fun and games. In others, excellence in sports is prized but rewarded indirectly through extra time for practice, opportunity to instruct, while those most outstanding are expected to be self-effacing in directing their efforts to the general improvement of physical well-being rather than personal aggrandizement and public acclaim.

Setting and Attaining Standards for Aspiration

Competitive activities, as we said, refer to performance that is compared to standards set by other persons and is assessed by other persons. However, until the child is able to erect abstract standards and goals for his own performance, he or she is not able to compete consistently nor to cooperate in team play directed consistently toward attaining some standards. This capacity to erect and strive for one's own aspirations for an abstract level of performance, often in the absence of tangible concrete rewards, develops slowly during the age period 5-12 years and varies from child to child. Too often, adult workers with children of younger ages fail to recognize these facts, hence present games and tasks to younger children that they may be able to _perform_ but that require conceptual abilities in goal setting and self-regulation too advanced for their age.

Accumulated research on the setting of aspiration levels and on achievement striving by children is heavily weighted toward academic endeavors which are not necessarily correlated with behavior in physical activity. Therefore, it is both surprising and gratifying that available research on aspiration and achievement striving in physical activities is in striking agreement on certain important conclusions.

In a given activity, there is a strong tendency to maintain one's level of aspiration despite the fluctuations in actual performance, particularly if the activity is highly valued by the child. For example in dart throwing, both the child and an adult highly involved in the child's performance tend to maintain a fairly rigid level of aspiration for the child's performance, which is _not_ typical in appraising a performance of no personal consequence (Sherif, 1948).

The absolute level of the standard set by children for their own performance depends upon knowledge of their own performance, with the highest levels being set by the best performers (e.g., Clarke and Clarke, 1961). However, the crucial determinant of a child's experiences of success or failure is not how high or low the standard is set, but the _difference_ between their actual performance and the standard. In terms of this _difference_, the peculiar and unfortunate effect of the level of aspiration set by the child is to assure the better performer more frequent experiences of success than the child who may be trying just as hard, but performs less well. Specifically, performers in the higher ranks on a physical task tend to set their aspiration level near or below their performance level, thus assuring frequent success experiences (Clarke and Stratton, 1962; Hilgard et al, 1940; Anderson and Brandt, 1939). Children in the lower ranks of performance erect standards for performance lower than the superior performance but _higher_ than their own performance; thus they are almost bound to experience repeated failure. The larger the gap between expectations and aspiration and actual performance level, the less the satisfaction a child can gain by slow improvement in performance, for the gap remains large despite the child's efforts. Improvement in performance, therefore, has quite different meaning for the child who performs well and the one who is average or below. The latter is still failing in his own eyes because his aspiration level is still distant, while the successful child has set the aspiration level near enough to performance level that improvement spells increased experience of success.

Ultimately, these somewhat self-fulfilling differences between the high and average or low performer start to make sense when we find _where_ the child gets his notions of the standards or goals that are desirable for him or her. Early in the age period (5-7 years), children seem to be very responsive to adult definitions of standards (e.g., Child, 1946; Allen, 1966; Versteeg and Hall, 1971). For example, Anglo-American children of 5 years are more likely than Mexican-American children to set high standards even when these are very unrealistic, no doubt owing to adult emphasis on individual achievement. However, as performance occurs more and more in the context of peers, the standards tend to be set more and more in terms of the actual performance by peers, toward the levels that are average or above (Anderson and Brandt, 1939). The powerful effect of peers and the relationships between different groups of peers was shown by Yackley and Lambert (1971) in a study comparing English-Canadian and French-Canadian boys in a table hockey tournament. When competing, the boys set standards for performance that would result in victory for their own team, an effect often found in intergroup competition as we shall see. But the English Canadian boys had better assurance for feelings of success by keeping their aspiration levels near their own performance levels. The French Canadian boys, who had less favorable self concepts, were probably guaranteed a sense of failure by setting unrealistically high levels of aspiration.

These findings have obvious implications for adults working with children, which will become clearer if we borrow additional findings from research on adults that is no doubt applicable to children by ages 10-12 at least in terms of their cognitive capacities. These findings show that over time the effect of comparing a person's performance to that of a group whom he or she considers inferior in performance is to raise the person's own standard. But cumulatively, the effect of comparing performance to a superior group is to lower one's own standards. Persistent failure in the face of a high standard provided by a superior group produces lower and lower aspiration levels and, finally, lack of personal pretensions to perform well at any level. There can be little doubt that similar dynamics occur in relation to physical activity.

These findings mean that adults who would use the performance levels of other children in attempts to motivate performance have to be insightful and careful in choosing the standards they set up at any given time. The performance of high school students may motivate a few 9-10-year-olds to try harder, but for the great bulk of the children, such constant reminder of their own lower performance will simply lower their own aspirations.

The net result of success experiences over time relative to standards set and performance achieved is to increase persistence and effort in the activity. If this were not the case, the research would be of very little interest. In fact, research on physical activity using physical fitness tests shows its relevance to actual performance (Strong, 1963; Waterman et al, 1967). In studies of 9 and 11-12-year-olds, performance level was raised most when the child chose the level of performance he or she wanted to attain or when his or her team competed with another of comparable ability than when the child competed against his own past performance, with another individual of nearly equal or different ability, or competed to establish a class record.

In a 12-week study of 9-10-year-olds, Waterman et al. (1967) found that instead of directing such attempts toward the individual whose performance was compared to this or that standard, it was far more effective to have individuals set aspiration levels as a member of a group for increasing the group performance. The increased performance levels by individuals that were found as a result were not in the highest or lowest 25% of the performance scores, but in that

50% of intermediate performers who succeeded in raising performance
levels from low average to superior on the Washington State Physical
Fitness Test when aspiring for improvement as a group member.

Since most teachers and parents firmly believe that they are
largely responsible for the achievement striving of children, it
should be added here that, of course, family background is important
in shaping the level of a child's aspiration and the child's
persistence in pursuing achievement. Again, the great bulk of the
research concerns academic achievement. However, the study by Rosen
and D'Andrade (1959) used a variety of motor games to study the
parents as well as boys labelled high and low in achievement
motivation.

The parents of high achievers did, as we might expect, evidence
greater interest in their son's performance, set higher standards and
expected efforts to meet them. However, these parents did not
otherwise fit the stereotype of the enthusiastic "little league"
parent. Fathers tended to be competent men who, however, did not
push or dominate their son's efforts. Mothers of high achieving boys
were more likely to be more dominating than other mothers, to stress
achievement more than independence in their son and to both reward
achievement and reject deviation from performance standards more
frequently. This is hardly the picture of the dominant male parent
leading his son to success nor of the warm nurturant mother soothing
his wounds. Needless to say, the same pattern is not reported for
highly motivated girls (Stein and Bailey, 1973), but the research on
girls has so little bearing on physical activity that it scarcely
deserves mention in this context. In plain truth, few researchers
have been concerned at all about achievement by girls in physical
activity or conditions promoting it.

Peer Influences

The research on effects of observers or an audience on
children's performance is very clear in showing a change with age.
Younger children ages 4-6 years react to the presence or the
approval of others, but seldom if ever by improving their performance
(Crabbe, 1971; Missiuro, 1964; Hartup, 1964). In fact, the audience
proves distracting for most little children, and this seems to be
particularly the case if the onlookers are personally related to the
child as parent or friend (Stevenson et al, 1963; Hartup, 1964).

By about age 7, however, children do tend to respond
positively to onlookers by improving their performance, on the whole,
and they respond more positively to friends than to non-preferred
peers' evaluations (Patterson and Anderson, 1964). This heightened
responsiveness to peer influence is revealed in a variety of research,
including experimental studies of peer vs. non-peer influence on
perception and judgment of ambiguous stimuli (cf. Hartup, 1969 for a
thorough review of this literature). In fact, in general, children
during this period seem to perform better when their performance is
rewarded or criticized by someone than when no appraisal at all is
forthcoming (Allen, 1966; Harney and Parker, 1972). Apparently this
responsiveness to "feedback" (positive and negative) increases from
ages 7 to 10 years (Patterson and Anderson, 1964).

Nevertheless, children do respond differently to different adults (teachers, parent, or experimenter) depending upon their confidence or anxiety about their own performance. Studying Australian children, Cox (1966) reported that 7-year-old boys performed a repetitive motor task better with a parent or adult present unless they were anxious about test-taking. The latter boys did poorly with parents or teacher, actually performing better with a complete stranger. No doubt this finding is related to past experiences of failure. As Baldwin and Levin (1958) found, failure leads to more variable and less accurate performance when the child is tested.

Such findings indicating differential responsiveness to different adults by different children are not paralleled by research on responsiveness to different peers, but there is every reason to expect this to be the case. In reviewing the research literature on sociometric choices made by elementary school children, Hartup (1969) concluded that peer preferences are relatively stable over time, whether one looks at the particular choices made by a child as preferred associates or at a particular child's standing among his peers.

As we might except, stability of the child's status with peers is directly related to age of the children in the peer group (increasing with age), to the degree of acquaintanceship (how long the children are together) and is greater for those high and those low in acceptability than those in the middle ranks (a fact that also is true later in adolescence; Witryol and Thompson, 1953; Sherif and Sherif, 1964). Incidentally, social acceptance by peers at ages 4-5 is, according to research summarized by Hartup, much more stable than commonly supposed. He reported correlations of .68 for scores obtained at a five month interval among pre-schoolers (Hartup, Glazer and Charlesworth, 1967).

Similarly the stability of friendship choices by children increases with age, so that by the close of this period the same friends are chosen by children from 60-80% of the time (Horrocks and Thompson, 1946; Thompson and Horrocks, 1947). Incidentally, fluctuations in friendship choices during this age period are rather consistently greater for boys than for girls (cf. Speroff, 1955), a finding that should lay to rest the assumption that girls do not form peer groups as intensely as boys. The fact remains, however, that studies of peer groups themselves have been made almost exclusively on boys.

Now what does all of this indicate? The findings are strong support for according major weight to peer influence in this age period in setting standards and in assessing one's own performance relative to others. In his earlier work, Piaget (1932) attributed to peer interaction the source of the child's growing ability for reciprocity in play, for "taking the role of the other" and in genuine understanding of the rules of games, as opposed to sheer acceptance of rules imposed by adults. Age trends in these respects have been reported paralleling children's cognitive growth in the elementary grades (Rardin and Moan, 1971; Borshevskii, 1965); the size of groups and the length of time that a child interacts in them in games both increase with age (Eiferman, 1970).

It is frustrating, therefore, that studies of the relative influence of children with different status in their groups at different ages are so rare. What we do know is that children of these ages spend a great deal of time with peers and that those few studies we have of the relative influence of different children show very clearly that high status children do affect the behavior of those of lower status (Lippitt et al, 1952; Hunt and Solomon, 1942; Sherif and Sherif, 1953, 1969).

There is every reason to believe that in the later years of this age range children are perfectly capable of forming and do form their own groups with leader-follower relations and shared norms or rules for behavior that are every bit as binding as those that adults organize and sponsor.

Significance of Children's Groups

As mentioned earlier, Piaget (1932) regarded the peer group as a major medium for the child's psychosocial development toward self-regulation of behavior (as opposed to mere compliance to power of others) and understanding of genuine reciprocity in interpersonal relationships. While his hypotheses have borne fruit chiefly in the study of moral development (e.g. Kohlberg, 1964), there seems little doubt that similar studies specifically involving children's play and friendship groups would reveal significant relationships with other aspects in the development of the child's self system--such aspects as "what kind of boy or girl am I?" "How competent am I in such and such an activity?" "How do my actions affect others?"

There may justifiably be some doubt about the relative stability of children's associations at age 5, depending largely on opportunity to interact with fair regularity and some autonomy from adults. There need be no doubt at all that as the child grows from 5 through 12 years, small groups of peers increasingly become important anchors for his self-concept. The personal qualities and activities they value do count for the child's own self-evaluations and their evaluations frequently exceed in importance those of adults in certain spheres of living (cf. Sherif and Sherif, 1964).

It is perhaps not surprising that researchers in the United States and similar countries have attended so little to children's group formation for, in fact, they are accorded little attention by educational theory or practice and by adults working with children. The adult orientation is to assume that the organization of children's lives imposed by adult society in the form of schools, clubs, churches, etc. dominates their existence. In adult eyes, the classroom is the group, as is the adult sponsored team, scout troop or church class. As a consequence, teachers and other adult workers are prone to regard informal, but more psychologically significant social organization among peers as troublesome aberrations that they identify chiefly when there is "trouble."

One consequence of such an adult viewpoint is that peer associations do arise during these years and throughout adolescence which are to a surprising degree autonomous of adult sponsorship or regulation and, at times, even countervailing to adult precepts. Whether for good or evil in the eyes of the viewer, this network of

informal and significant peer associations contrasts with that found
in societies where peer groups are not only recognized as significant
but in addition fostered by adults as one principal medium of
socialization.

The contrast was clearly shown in a series of studies by
Bronfenbrenner and co-workers (1970) on moral judgment of school
children. Their focus was upon the child's evaluation of transgressions from societal norms (e.g., cheating) when the child believed
that his evaluation was private as compared to when peers or adults
would know about it. The striking finding was that children in the
United States and Germany, for example, changed their evaluations of
such transgressions in directions more acceptable by societal precepts
when they believed adults would know their responses, but not when the
information would be available to peers. Peers, they seemed to
believe, would share and understand their tacit approval of behaviors
violating or circumventing adult precepts. In the Soviet Union,
however, children were as likely to alter private approval of
transgressions when they believed peers would know of it. Such weight
of the peer group in supporting adult values is harmony with the
pedagogical theories in that country, for example the influential
writings of Makarenko (1951), which not only recognize the import of
peer associations but direct adult efforts toward fostering them in
directions concordant with major adult values.

One of the research findings with the greatest importance in
physical education, as well as all education, is that the social
structure among children is not necessarily equivalent to their
expressed or observed friendship choices. Popularity, in the sense
of being liked, is of course an important and readily observable
dimension of children's associations, even though teachers are
notoriously poor judges of it. Teachers are also prone to equate the
popular child with the most influential, yet the correlations between
popularity and power to influence others are at best modest (cf.
Hartup, 1969). Social influence or power among boys is typically more
closely correlated with athletic skills and/or competence in other
valued activities, but again the correlations are far from perfect.
For girls, status in the influence network of peers may be related to
physical competence in early childhood, although evidence is weak, but
it assuredly is not closely related by about age 12 years, a signal of
the decreasing or vanishing weight of physical activity as a
determinant of peer status as girls grow older.

The psychological significance of the informally generated and
maintained status systems among peers is perhaps shown most clearly by
a series of studies in which status was defined by a variety of methods
(including prolonged observation) as "effective initiative" that is
the child's relative ability to initiate, control and sanction
behaviors during interaction in peer groups. While status so defined
correlated with popularity, these correlations were far from perfect
nor were they identical with athletic competence. The boys studied
had interacted regularly for more than a week in summer camps.
Physical activities were introduced for experimental purposes, such as
throwing a ball at a target or maneuvering a canoe about a course. In
each case the outcome was made ambiguous in an important respect so
that sheer skill at the particular event could not dominate the boys'

expectations and judgments of each other's performance. (For example, the target for ball pitching was unmarked leaving no trace when the ball rebounded, or canoe races were measured by time when the boys had no watches.)

The significant finding in each study was high positive correlations between a boy's ranks in effective initiative in peer interaction, as previously observed, and the level of performance that other boys judged that he had attained (Sherif, White and Harvey, 1955; Koslin et al, 1968). Actual skill in the task was taken into account; therefore one may say that <u>regardless</u> of actual performance, the boys' expectations were higher for boys of high social power and lower for those low in the status scheme. The boys in these experiments were 10-12-years-old.

Surprisingly, such generalized expectations based on relative status in a group have also been reported for 6-year-olds who had been together for sometime and who judged each others' performance at tossing balls into a box hidden from their view (Pollis and Doyle, 1972).

In a prolonged study of eight groups of boys in a summer camp, the relative social standing of a group at the end of three weeks was found to correlate significantly with both individual judgments and group estimates made by the seven other groups of the score expected for that group in a game of orienteering (Sherif & Sherif, unpublished). This finding illustrates how quickly children in groups appraise the relative power and prestige of other groups of peers and how such appraisal affects their estimates of the competence of those groups in laudatory or derogatory fashion. In these particular experiments, actual performance in the task was not significantly correlated with the level of expectation held for a group by other groups. (Indeed, a novel task was chosen precisely to reduce the possibility that estimates would merely reflect actual competence.) Therefore, there is evidence that the expectations for a group by others reflect generalized low or high social standing or power more than specific group competencies. The same conclusion can be drawn about individual power within groups. The implications for discriminatory treatment of individuals or groups of low social status and for unwarranted privileges for those of high status should be readily apparent.

Group Norms or Values

If research on nursery school groups (e.g., Merei, 1949) and adolescent groups (e.g., Sherif and Sherif, 1964) is any guide, the prolonged associations of children ages 5-12 should also result in the mutual acceptance of standards, customs, traditions and values regulating aspiration levels and conduct in the eyes of group members.

In keeping with the cognitive development during this period, we would expect that the elaboration and complexity of such normative systems would increase with age. Experimental evidence indicates that, while such normative systems reflect values of the adult world, they also include standards for conduct distinctive to the peers or distinctively selected by them during their give and take with one another under particular circumstances (Sherif and Sherif, 1969, Chapter 11). For example, two groups that arose in a summer camp among previously unacquainted 12-year-olds during a week's interaction in separate circumstances developed quite different value emphases, even though the boys in each had specifically been selected from a homogeneous, middle-class population. Owing to their respective experiences in the camp, one emerged as self conscious extollers of virtue, sportsmanship and godliness, engaging in frequent discussions and prayers. The other group became rough tough he-men who ignored injuries and turned the air blue with their language. Clearly both models were available in the adult cultures. Yet the two groups selectively emphasized one or the other.

It must be admitted that we know very little about the formation or selection of normative guides by groups of peers in this age group, perhaps because children at these ages less frequently present severe social problems than older children. However, any school teacher with observational acumen can report instances of collective actions, typically in the form of "discipline problems" but at times no more notorious than fads in dress that exemplify such peer products. Unfortunately schools typically treat such incidents as though they were instigated solely by maladjusted or unruly individuals; therefore we seldom learn much about the group processes that undoubtedly underlie many of them. For example, such an approach was recently taken in public schools in Pennsylvania regarding junior high school students who persisted in wearing surplus army jackets to school and, in another case, the publication of an underground newspaper. Information available to us shows clearly that in both cases the actions were initiated and supported by peer interactions. Yet the reaction of authorities was to attempt to locate and deal with the "disruptive" individuals.

RESEARCH ON SEX DIFFERENCES

During the past year, the senior author has had occasion through graduate seminars, preparation of literature surveys, and benefit of the surveys of other authors to review and ponder research on sex differences in a wide variety of psychological and performance measures. This section represents her appraisal of the research literature most pertinent to children's activities during this age period.

1. Sex differences in the performance of specific skills recur throughout the literature, although they are by no means as consistently favorable to one sex or the other as one might expect. Whether boys or girls of younger ages perform better depends quite as much on what skills are selected for measurement and the ages of the children as upon their sex. It is no doubt possible to demonstrate that one or the other sex is superior by selecting activities and ages at which a particular sex will excel.

2. By the age of 12, superiority of boys on most skill measures is the more general rule, a fact that reflects the more frequent activity, psychological preoccupation and societal value accorded to sports for boys, regardless of whatever else it may show.

3. Research on toy, game and play preferences as well as studies on adult treatments of young boys and girls reveal trends quite different for the two sexes. On the one hand, younger girls

prefer and choose a wider range of activities at early ages than boys, including many traditionally labeled as "masculine" as well as those labeled "fenimine." They are typically neither discouraged nor punished by adults for doing so, even when they earn the label of "tomboy." Social pressures on a girl both from adults and from peers to restrict her preferences and choices toward those defined as "feminine" increase during this age period. Typically by age 12, if not before, the growing awareness of impending sexual maturation as well as social processes increasingly restrict both the preferences, choices and activities of girls to the "feminine," defined more and more in terms of sexual stereotypes and subordinate social status. On the other hand, boys receive more pressure early in life to behave "like a little man," to abjure feminine play or actions; they are punished for it (cf. Maccoby, 1966, 1972; Hartley and Hardesty, 1964). Their choices of toys, games and activities take on traditionally masculine character earlier in childhood. Status among peers hinges early on physical prowess, and this state of affairs has continuity through adolescence. Children themselves define active sports as more masculine than feminine, thereby mirroring adult stereotypes (Stein et al, 1971).

4. So far as the senior author is able to discover, organized sports and programs of physical education have taken existing sex differences and trends during development as completely "natural" and have, therefore, contributed to them. Only recently have efforts started in physical education circles to examine implicit assumptions about the sexes and physical activity, some of which hark back to the Victorian era (cf. Harris, 1973).

5. Psychological theorizing about competition and achievement motivation contains profound sex bias through its failure to recognize that what is worth competing for and what is worth achieving is socially defined very differently for the two sexes (Sherif, 1973; Stein and Bailey, 1973). By the age of 12, if not before, girls learn very well that physical activity, as well as assertive manipulative skills prized in the masculine market place are not matters worth achieving or competing for, in the sense that no one cares when they strive to do so, and there is a high probability that they will lose approval of peers and adults. When girls compete in groups in matters that are high in their now-personalized scheme, they compete as hard as males and react to possible loss in much the same fashion (Avigdor, 1952). When girls are aroused to meet or excel in activities that are rewarded for girls, they strive to achieve as mightily as boys (Stein and Bailey, 1973). It is sad but true that, except in academic tasks, the matters in which strivings by girls are rewarded are not regarded by society as areas for "achievement," and therefore are not important enough to be studied. In any event, there is little point in bemoaning the lack of motivation of girls in physical activities when in fact neither society nor their own peers recognize or reward their efforts they do make. If one regards physical activities as essential for health and welfare, one should instead bemoan the social arrangements that lead so many girls and women to be deficient in that essential.

WHEN GROUP COMPETITION BREEDS CONFLICT

An issue that persistently crops up in discussions of sports is their apparent fertility as a breeding ground for destructive social conflicts. There are those who would say that competitiveness and aggression by tooth or claw are native to the human animal, particularly the male and, having said so, enumerate the latest examples in sports -- starting with the recent Olympic incidents, through professional and college sports, right down to most recent brawls between rival children in the neighborhood school. Such prophets and vultures of doom are content, therefore, to let the world go to the dogs, since in their view it is in nature's scheme. Let there be no argument with such views, for their advocates are convinced, closed to evidence and contented with their pat explanation. Instead, let us look at evidence: When does competition in sports erupt into violence and destructive hatred and when does it not? For, indeed in the vast majority of instances, sports are conducted through cooperative inter-group arrangements regulated by rules of sportsmanship without unfortunate consequences and even with mutual benefit.

A series of experiments by Sherif and his co-workers (Sherif and Sherif, 1953; Sherif, _et al._, 1961; Sherif and Sherif, 1969, Chapter 11) with 11 - 12-year-old boys contain evidence of the primary importance of the structural arrangements for competition in modifying the behavior of participants either toward hostility and aggression or toward friendly interchange.

These experiments were conducted in summer camps specifically designed for research purposes to be as natural and spontaneous as possible. Experimental control was achieved by changing the conditions in which the boys met for the first time, then lived and played in two separated groups, competed in sports and came into intense conflict. Briefly, these conditions were, in order, as follows:

1. Highly attractive activities requiring cooperation within each group.

2. A series of intergroup competitions lasting several days for highly prized awards in which victory by one group in the series meant total loss of the series for the other group.

3. Contacts between the groups in which each group separately participated in noncompetitive activities highly attractive to each group.

4. Contact between the groups in a series of situations in which a goal urgently desired by each group could be attained _only_ if both groups utilized all of their efforts and resources jointly (_superordinate_ goals).

The boys were carefully selected from stable, middle-class families of the same ethnic and religious background (white, Protestant). Each was progressing normally in school, was accepted by peers, physically active, and normal by all standards. They were unacquainted at the outset; they were not aware that their behavior was being observed throughout the camp, although parents were informed of study purposes. They were eager to participate in camping and in sports.

1. For about a week, the 22 boys lived and camped separately in two groups that were matched in terms of the size, skills and interests of members. By the end of that time, as expected, two definite groups had formed with leader-follower relationships and a variety of local customs, prized places and procedures and other group norms. Members developed a high level of commitment to their own groups.

2. As though acceding to the boys' spontaneous requests for sport competition a tournament of games was arranged, with valuable and conspicuous awards for the tournament winners. Both groups plunged enthusiastically into the tournament -- confident of their group's eventual victory, evenly matched, and thoroughly committed to sportsmanlike conduct.

3. But what happened? Several trends became evident: As victory or defeat for each group came in its turn, the tournament began to absorb all of their preoccupations, plans, conversations, and activities, even at times of rest. Despite occasional defeats, each group responded to the competition by renewed solidarity and greater cohesiveness. The ups and downs in the fortunes of one's own group wore sportsmanlike rules thin. Surely, anyone could see the glorious and virtuous efforts of one's teammates, and surely anyone could see that the rivals were gaining their advantage by unfair means! The glowing solidarity within each group became a prism distorting the actions and intentions of the rivals into those of an enemy of ruthless methods, determined to gain the ultimate victory at all costs.

The result was open conflict, first sporadically, then at every opportunity, and finally stealthily planned and executed at night in the form of raids on the rivals' cabin. To any outside observer who walked into the camp at this time, the boys' behavior would have seemed bizarre, dreadful, perhaps pathological. Yet, these were "normal" boys, part of the "cream of the crop". Psychological assessments of their individual views confirmed observations that their views of their own group were loyal and laudable, but their views of the other group were categorically negative and hostile. In brief, when members of a group single-mindedly invest themselves in efforts to obtain exclusive victory at the expense of a rival, over time, conflict and hostility will develop.

So the tournament -- the arrangements made by the adults -- bore its fruit. A victor was proclaimed. The losers shared one sentiment with winners -- bitter dislike for each other and the urgent wish to have nothing further to do with each other.

Couldn't a bit of pleasant social contact change all of this? For 3 days, a series of events was arranged in which the groups were together doing things each group wanted to do, albeit separately. They ate delicious meals; and they threw leftovers, paper and tableware at each other. They attended the same movie, and never spoke. Each group enjoyed activities, and hurled insults at the others. The cessation of competition, the ample opportunity to release aggressive feelings served only to increase their occurrence and their intensity. No "catharsis" was to be seen.

4. A water shortage was impending, so it seemed (and had been arranged). It was hot. "Fill your canteens, for the trouble can't be located until tomorrow." The response was spontaneous: "We can look -- we can all look." The groups went their separate ways to search and, according to the researcher's plan, found the difficulty together. Rejoicing, they returned to camp -- and began to insult one another again. A series of such superordinate goal conditions occurred in the days that followed: Another movie would be shown only if both groups would chip in. A big truck going to get food when everyone was hungry at an isolated picnic area failed to start; it succumbed to the efforts of all boys pulling on a rope attached to the front bumper. The tent poles became hopelessly mixed up, and it took everyone to untangle the mess.

Over time, the groups learned to cooperate with each other as groups toward such superordinate goals. Imperceptibly at first, but in cumulative fashion, their views of each other changed. They started to invite each other as groups to do things together, even to compete in turn with entertainment around the campfire. One group entertained the other with refreshments. At last, they asked that they all go home on the same bus -- together.

So, we say to the cynic who sees aggression as rooted in human nature, to the skeptic who sees potential conflict in all sport or in any competition: the ways that human beings act and feel are responsive to the structure of their relationships with one another, to the arrangements of the goals toward which they strive, to the demands of activities that they urgently desire to participate in. Stop moaning about human nature or about competition, and look toward the ways human nature and competitive activities can be utilized in directions and combinations that are not conducive to destructive conflict. Can competition between groups be directed toward the attainment of more encompassing goals desired by both groups? Research bearing on such questions is lacking.

The attempts to study the structure of arrangements in which groups interact are in their infancy. We do know, in addition, that when groups of girls are placed in the same competitive conditions in activities that are equally important to girls (competing to put on plays to earn money for club jackets), girls also respond in comparable fashion to the boys in camps (Avigdor, 1952). Grown-up men and women respond similarly when competing in discussion groups on personally involving matters (Blake, Shepard and Mouton, 1964). Children who are discriminated against as a group by adults become aggressive toward the adults when conditions permit (Thibault, 1950). From the classic Lewin, Lippitt and White studies (1939), we also know that restrictive adult treatment may lead to aggression by boys against each other. Groups of children who have a disadvantage relative to peers but are placed in a competitive situation, tend to withdraw -- and to protect themselves from invidious comparison (Jamous and Lemaine, 1962).

But all of the questions that should be asked about the arrangement of activities and goals for competition between groups of children or relationships with adults should not be left to researchers. Those who are actually involved in arranging parts of children's lives or working day-to-day in those arrangements have more at stake and are in a better position to pose the questions. The broad areas of physical education should become the field for inquiry, for experiment and change. Educators who are genuinely interested in broad educational problems, not merely its technical issues, should begin to examine the effects of the arrangements for human activities and lives within which they conduct their work.

A Postscript on Changes with Pubescence

It is doubtless true that the groundwork for the love of physical activity, the prizing of competence, and the mastery of many skills are rooted in experiences of childhood before pubescence. It is also true that with the advent of the adolescent period (about $12\frac{1}{2}$ years for girls and $13\frac{1}{2}$ or so for boys) the child's world begins to change. Both the physiological changes and the social expectations of adults and peers alter the child's relationship to the social world, thus require with varying degrees of urgency, uncertainty or conflict that the childish self he altered or reformed anew.

In modern societies, the result is a turning toward peers with an intensity greater than in childhood, an absorption in peers and a caring about their evaluations that few adults appreciate. Adults forget their own adolescence and are not sensitized to the changes that are compelling to youth today. For the boy who is apt in sports, who matures early enough and whose peers value sports -- as they typically do -- adolescence is an age to ride high. Sports are a vehicle to attain approval of other males, of adults and of girls. They are also excellent preys for exploitive adults interested in using their abilities. When sports arrangements competitively reward individual achievement only at high levels, the majority of males will suffer through invidious comparison. At least, however, they can immerse themselves in a male world that offers a great variety of less prestigeful opportunities for physical activity and a world of vicarious participations for fans of school and professional teams.

The girl who retains strong interests in sports, particularly of a vigorous type, runs the opposite risk: the invidious distinction of not being as feminine nor as sexually alluring nor as submissive as her sisters, the vast majority of whom retain only a token interest in sports. Tennis anyone? Yes, if a male might venture on the courts.

On the average, between the ages of 12 - 16, girls' physical performance in a variety of skills levels off or declines, while boys' are increasing (Horrocks, 1969, p. 445). Both achievement test scores and academic performance in school level off or decline while boys' are improving. This physical and intellectual settling, which sounds more like old age than becoming mature, is not inevitable, it is allowed, even encouraged to happen. It occurs in recognition, that for all adult society cares, this decline might as well occur, for sports and intellectual achievement are pursued by girls in adulthood at a price. The price is far greater than the reactions of other girls to the "sport nuts". It is at the risk of "femininity," which is ultimately sexual attractiveness. As long as society, including educational systems, offer no other key to girls for their future life, sexual attractiveness will continue to be the prize of girlhood, no matter what the Rationale or what bogus awards are promised for other attainments. This state of affairs can change only when society can find other reasons for being a girl in addition to her sex.

As you will also know, the world is changing; young women and men are changing. Some no longer want the world created by adults in high schools where the greatest heroes are athletic heroes and the greatest heroines the cheer-leading camp followers or the admiring marshmallow who sinks respondingly at every suggestion of a male. It behooves educators and administrators to reexamine the roots of their own assumptions and the practices they preach to see whether these traditions are truly in line with the aims of physical education. It behooves them to listen to the voices of the young and to look for signs of change to see if, indeed, their programs are helping adolescents to find paths that will serve to carry them to the world as it may be tomorrow -- or as they may change it when we are dead and gone.

125

References

Adams, et al. The working capacity of normal school children: I. California. Pediatrics, 1961, 28, 55.

Allen, S. The effects of verbal reinforcement on children's performance as a function of type of task. Journal of Experimental Child Psychology, 1966, 3, 57 - 73.

Anderson, H.H., and Brandt, H.F. Study of motivation involving self-announced goals of 5th grade children and the concept of level of aspiration. Journal of Social Psychology, 1939, 10, 209 - 232.

Asmussen, E., and Nielson, K.H. Physical performance and growth in children; influence of sex, age, and intelligence. Journal of Applied Physiology, 1956, 8, 371 - 380.

Avigdor, R. The development of stereotypes as a result of group interaction, Ph.D. dissertation, Graduate College of Arts and Sciences, New York University, 1952.

Azrin, N.H., and Lindsley, O.R. The reinforcement of cooperation between children. Journal of Abnormal and Social Psychology, 1956, 52, 100 - 102.

Bachman, J.C. Motor learning and performance as related to age and sex in two measures of balance and coordination. Research Quarterly, 1961, 32, 2, 123 - 137.

Baldwin, A.L., and Levin, H. Effects of public and private success and failure in children's repetitive motor behavior. Child Development, 1958, 29, 363 - 372.

Blake, R.R., Shepard, H., and Mouton, J.S. Managing Intergroup Tensions in Industry. Houston, Texas: Gulf Publishing Co., 1964.

Borshevskii, M.I. The child's attitude toward rules of the game. Voprosy Psikhologii, 1965, 4, 44 - 54. Abstracted in Psychological Abstracts, 1965. 9, 14632.

Bronfenbrenner, U. Two Worlds of Childhood. New York: Russell Sage Foundation, 1970.

Child, I.L. Children's preferences for goals easy or difficult to obtain. Psychological Monographs, 1946, 60, 280.

Clarke, H.H., and Clarke, D.H. Relationship between levels of aspiration and selected physical factors of boys aged nine years. Research Quarterly, 1961, 32:1, 12 - 19.

Clarke, H.H., and Clarke, D.H.   Social status and mental health of boys as related to their maturity, structural, and strength characteristics.
  Research Quarterly of the American Association of Health, Physical Education and Recreation, 1961, 32, 326 - 334.

Clarke, H.H., and Peterson, K.H.   Contrast of maturational, structural, and strength characteristics of athletes and nonathletes ten to fifteen years of age.
  Research Quarterly, 1961, 32, 163 - 176.

Clarke, H.H., and Stratton, S.T.   A level of aspiration test based on the grip strength efforts of nine-year-old boys.
  Child Development, 1962, 33, 897 - 905.

Clarke, H.H., and Wickens, J.S.   Maturity, structural, strength, and motor ability growth curves of boys nine to fifteen years of age.
  Research Quarterly, 1962, 33, 1, 26 - 39.

Carpenter, A.   Tests of motor educability for the first three grades.
  Child Development, 1941, 11, 293 - 399.

Cole, B.G. (Ed.).   Television.
  New York: Free Press, 1970.

Cox, F.N.   Some effects of test anxiety and the presence or absence of other persons on boys' performance on a repetitive motor task.
  Journal of Experimental Child Psychology, 1966, 3, 100 - 112.

Crabbe, J.M.   Social facilitation effects on children during early stages of motor learning.
  Dissertation Abstracts International, 1971, 32, 2463A.

Cron, G.W., and Pronko, N.H.   Development of a sense of balance in school children.
  Journal of Educational Research, 1957, 51, 33 - 37.

Davidson, M., McInnes, J., and Parnell, R.   The distribution of personality traits in seven-year-old children.
  British Journal of Educational Psychology, 1957, 27, 48 - 61.

Dennis, W.   A cross-cultural study of the reinforcement of children's behavior.
  Child Development, 1957, 28, 431 - 438.

Devereux, E.C.   Some observations on sports, play and games in childhood.   A paper given at a conference on the physiology and psychology of sport.
  EAPEWC.   October, 1972.

Dobson, M.L.   An investigation of the status of physical education and interscholastic sports in the State of Oklahoma.
  Dissertation Abstracts International, 1971, 31, 6382A.

Dohrman, P.   Throwing and kicking ability of eight-year-old boys and girls.
  Research Quarterly, 1964, 35, 4, 464 - 471.

Dusenberry, L. A study of the effects of training in ball throwing by children.
Research Quarterly, 1952, 23, 9 - 14.

Eiferman, R.R. Levels of children's play as expressed in group size (6 - 14 years of age).
British Journal of Educational Psychology, 1970, 2, 161 - 170.

Eiferman, R.R. Social play in childhood. In R.E. Herron and B. Sutton-Smith (Eds.), Child's Play.
New York: John Wiley and Sons, 1971, 270 - 279.

Espenschade, A.S. Most appropriate basis for grouping students and for the establishment of norms.
Research Quarterly, 1963, 34, 2, 144 - 153.

Gesell, A., and Ilg, F. The Infant and Child in the Culture of Today.
New York: Harper, 1943.

Greenberg, P.J. Competition in children: An experimental study.
American Journal of Psychology, 1932, 44, 221 - 248.

Goodenough, F.L. Developmental Psychology.
New York: Appleton-Century-Crofts, 1945.

Gutteridge, M.V. A study of motor achievements of young children.
Archives of Psychology, 1934, 244.

Hale, C.J. Physiological maturity of Little League Baseball players.
Research Quarterly, 1956, 27, 3, 276 - 284.

Harney, D.M., and Parker, R. Effects of social reinforcement, subject of sex, and experimenter sex on children's motor performance.
Research Quarterly, 1972, 43, 2, 187 - 196.

Hartup, W.W. Friendship status and the effectiveness of peers as reinforcing agents.
Journal of Experimental Psychology, 1964, 1. 154 - 162.

Hartup, W.W. Peer interaction and social organization. In P. Mussen (Ed.), Manual of Child Psychology.
New York: John Wiley, 1969.

Hartup, W.W., Glazer, J.A., and Charlesworth, R. Peer reinforcement and sociometric status.
Child Development, 1967, 38, 1017 - 1024.

Harris, D.V. (Ed.), Women and Sport: A National Research Conference. The Pennsylvania State University, College of Health, Physical Education and Recreation.
Penn State HPER Series No. 2, 1973.

Hartley, R.E., and Hardesty, F.P. Children's perceptions of sex roles in childhood.
Journal of Genetic Psychology, 1964, 105, 43 - 51.

Hilgard, E.R., Sait, E.M., and Margaret, G.A. Level of aspiration as affected by relative standing in an experienced social group. Journal of Experimental Psychology, 1940, 27, 411 - 421.

Horrocks, J. The Psychology of Adolescence. Boston: Houghton Mifflin, 1969.

Horrocks, J., and Thompson, G.G. A study of the friendship fluctuations of rural boys and girls. Journal of Genetic Psychology, 1946, 69, 189 - 198.

Hunt, J.M., and Solomon, R.L. The stability and some correlates of group status in a summer camp group of young boys. American Journal of Psychology, 1942, 55, 37 - 45.

Johnson, R.D. Measurements of achievement in fundamental skills of elementary school children. Research Quarterly, 1962, 33, 94 - 103.

Kagan, S., and Madsen, M.C. Cooperation and competition of Mexican, Mexican-American, and Anglo-American children of two ages under four instructional sets. Developmental Psychology, 1971, 5(1), 32 - 39.

Kagan, S., and Madsen, M.C. Rivalry in Anglo-American and Mexican children of two ages. Journal of Personality and Social Psychology, 1972, 24, 214 - 220.

Kohlberg, L. Development of moral character and moral ideology. In M.L. Hoffmann and L.W. Hoffmann (Eds.), Review of Child Development Research. New York: Russell Sage Foundation, 1964, I, 383 - 431.

Koslin, B.L., Haarlow, R.N., Karlins, M., and Pargament, R. Predicting group status from member's cognitions. Sociometry, 1968, 31, 64 - 75.

Krogman, W.M. Maturation age of 55 boys in the Little League World Series, 1957. Research Quarterly, 1959, 30, 1, 54 - 56.

Lerner, R.M., and Schroeder, C. Physique identification, preference, and aversion in kindergarten children. Developmental Psychology, 1971, 5(3), 538.

Leuba, C.J. An experimental study of rivalry in young children. Journal of Comparative Psychology, 1933, 16, 367 - 378.

Lewin, K., Dembo, T., Festinger, L., and Sears, P.S. Level of aspiration. In J. McV. Hunt (Ed.), Personality and Behavior Disorders. New York: Ronald Press, 1944.

Lewin, K., Lippitt, R., and White, R.K. Patterns of aggressive behavior in experimentally created "social climates". Journal of Social Psychology, 1939, 10, 271 - 299.

Lippitt, R., Polansky, N., Redl, F., and Rosen, S. The dynamics of power.
  Human Relations, 1952, 5, 37 - 64.

Madsen, M.C., and Shapiro, A. Cooperative and competitive behavior of urban Afro-American, Anglo-American, Mexican-American and Mexican village children.
  Developmental Psychology, 1970, 3(1), 16 - 20.

Maccoby, E. Sex Differences. Stanford, Calif.:
  Stanford University Press, 1966.

Maccoby, E. Paper to annual meetings, American Association for the Advancement of Science, Washington, D.C., December, 1972.

McClintock, C.R., and Nuttin, J.M., Jr. Development of competitive game behavior in children across two cultures.
  Journal of Social Psychology, 1969, 5, 203 - 213.

McCullough, C.M. A log of children's out-of-school activities.
  Elementary School Journal, 1957, 58, 157 - 165.

Makarenko, A.S. The Road to Life: An Epic of Education. 3 vols.
  Moscow: Foreign Languages Publishing House, 1951.

Merei, F. Group leadership and institutionalization.
  Human Relations, 1949, 2, 23 - 39.

Missiuro, W. The development of reflex action in children. In E. Jokl (Ed.), International Research in Sport and Physical Education.
  Springfield, Illinois: Chas. C. Thomas, 1964, 372 - 383.

Muradbegovic, M., and Sarajevo, I.D. The free activity preferences of elementary school pupils.
  Society and Leisure, 1970, 77 - 86.

Nelson, G.A., and Henry, F.M. Age differences and interrelationships between skill and learning in gross motor performance of ten-and fifteen-year-old boys.
  Research Quarterly, 1956, 27, 162 - 175.

Owens, K.L. Competition in children as a function of age, sex, and socioeconomic status.
  Dissertation Abstracts International, 1970, 30(8-B), 3873.

Patterson, G.R., and Anderson, D. Peers as social reinforcers.
  Child Development, 1964, 35(3), 951 - 960.

Philip, A.J. Strangers and friends as competitors and cooperators.
  Journal of Genetic Psychology, 1940, 57, 247 - 258.

Piaget, J. The Moral Judgment of the Child.
  London: Routledge, 1932.

Piaget, J. The Psychology of Intelligence.
  New York: Harcourt Brace, 1950.

Pollis, N.P., and Doyle, D.C. Sex role, status and perceived competence among first graders.
Perceptual and Motor Skills, 1972, 34, 235 - 238.

Rardin, D.R., and Moan, C.E. Peer interaction and cognitive development.
Child Development, 1971, 42(6), 1685 - 1699.

Reeves, W. Report of committee on street play.
Journal of Educational Sociology, 1931, 4, 607 - 618.

Roberts, J.M., and Sutton-Smith, B. Child training and game involvement.
Ethnology, 1962, 1, 166 - 185.

Roberts, J.M., Sutton-Smith, B., and Kendon, A. A strategy in games and folk tales.
Journal of Social Psychology, 1963, 61, 185 - 199.

Rosen, B.D., and D'Andrade, R. The psychological origins of achievement motivation.
Sociometry, 1959, 22, 185 - 218.

Seagoe, M.V. Children's play as an indicator of cross-cultural and intra-cultural differences.
Journal of Educational Psychology, 1962, 35, 278 - 283.

Seagoe, M.V. A comparison of children's play in six modern cultures.
Journal of School Psychology, 1971, 9(1), 61 - 72.

Seils, L.G. The relationship between measures of physical growth and gross motor performance of primary grade children.
Research Quarterly, 1951, 22, 244 - 260.

Shapiro, A. Competition, cooperation and conformity among city and kibbutz children in Israel.
Dissertation Abstracts International, 1971, 31, 3641.

Shapiro, A., and Madsen, M.C. Cooperative and competitive behavior of kibbutz and urban children in Israel.
Child Development, 1969, 40(2), 609 - 617.

Sherif, C.W. Variations in judgement as a function of ego-involvement.
In M. Sherif (Ed.), An Outline of Social Psychology.
New York: Harper, 1948.

Sherif, C.W. Females in the competitive process.
In D. Harris (Ed.), op. cit. 1973, 115 - 140.

Sherif, M., Harvey, O.J., White, B.J., Hood, W.R., and Sherif, C.W.,
Intergroup Conflict and Cooperation. The Robbers Cave Experiment.
Norman: University of Oklahoma, 1961.

Sherif, M., and Sherif, C. Groups in Harmony and Tension.
New York: Harper, 1953.

Sherif, M., and Sherif, C. Reference Groups: Conformity and Deviation of Adolescents.
  New York: Harper and Row, 1964.

Sherif, M., and Sherif, C. Social Psychology.
  New York: Harper and Row, 1969, Chapter 11.

Sherif, M., and Sherif, C.
  Unpublished Research Study, 1973.

Sherif, M., White, B.J., and Harvey, O.J. Status in experimentally created groups.
  American Journal of Sociology, 1955, 60, 370 - 379.

Singer, R.N. Physical characteristics, perceptual-motor, and intelligence differences between third and sixth grade children.
  Research Quarterly, 1969, 40, 803 - 811.

Skuberic, E. Emotional responses of boys to Little League and Middle League competitive baseball.
  Research Quarterly, 1955, 26, 342 - 352.

Solkoff, N., et al. Effects of frustration on perceptual motor performance.
  Child Development, 1964, 35, 569 - 575.

Solley, W.H. Status of physique, change in physique, and speed, in the growth patterns of school children grades one to eight.
  Research Quarterly, 1959, 30(4), 465 - 478.

Speroff, B.J. The stability of sociometric choice among kindergarten children.
  Sociometry, 1955, 18, 129 - 131.

Stein, A.H., and Bailey, M. The socialization of achievement motivation in females.
  Psychological Bulletin, 1973 (in press)

Stein, A.H., Pohly, S., and Mueller, E. The influence of masculine, feminine and neutral tasks on children's achievement behavior, expectancies of success, and attainment values.
  Child Development, 1971, 42, 195 - 208.

Stevenson, H.W., Kleen, R., and Knights, R.M. Parents and strangers as reinforcing agents for children's performance.
  Journal of Abnormal and Social Psychology, 1963, 67, 183 - 186.

Strong, C.H. Motivation related to performance of physical fitness tests.
  Research Quarterly, 1963, 34(4), 497 - 507.

Sullenger, T.E., Parke, L.H., and Wallin, W.K. The leisure time activities of elementary school children.
  Journal of Educational Research, 1953, 46, 551 - 554.

Sutton-Smith, B. Play preference and play behavior: A validity study.
  Psychological Reports, 1965, 65, 16, 65 - 66.

Sutton-Smith, B.   Games -- play -- daydreams.
  Quest X, 1968, 47 - 48.

Sutton-Smith, B., and Roberts, J.M.   Rubrics of competitive behavior.
  Journal of Genetic Psychology, 1964, 105, 13 - 37.

Sutton-Smith, B., and Rosenberg, B.G.   Manifest anxieties and game
preferences in children.
  Child Development, 1960, 31, 307 - 311.

Sutton-Smith, B., and Rosenberg, B.G.   Sixty years of historical
change in the game preference of American children.
  Journal of American Folklore, 1961, 74, 17 - 46.

Thompson, G.G., and Horrocks, J.   A study of the friendship
fluctuations of urban boys and girls.
  Journal of Genetic Psychology, 1947, 70, 53 - 63.

Versteeg, A., and Hall, R.   Levels of aspiration, achievement and
socio-cultural differences in preschool children.
  Journal of Genetic Psychology, 1971, 119, 137 - 142.

Volberding, E.   Out-of-school behavior of 11-year-olds.
  Elementary School Journal, 1948, 48, 432 - 441.

Waterman, A.D., Northrop, G.W., and Olsen, L.D.   Motivation and
achievement in the elementary school.
  Elementary School Journal, 1967, 67, 375 - 380.

Witryol, S.L., and Thompson, G.G.   A critical review of social
acceptability scores obtained with the partial rank order and paired
comparison scales.
  Genetic Psychology Monographs, 1953, 48, 221 - 260.

Whittle, D.H.   Effects of elementary school physical education upon
aspects of physical, motor, and personality development.
  Research Quarterly, 1961, 32, 249 - 260.

Yackley, A., and Lambert, W.E.   Inter-ethnic group competition and
levels of aspiration.
  Canadian Journal of Behavioral Sciences, 1971, 3(2), 135 - 147.

PSYCHOSOCIAL DEVELOPMENT AND ACTIVITY IN MIDDLE CHILDHOOD -- COMMENTS AND EXTENSIONS

by   Thomas J. Ryan,
       Carleton University.

This excellent paper (Sherif and Rattray, 1973) has been highly successful in presenting the problems and research findings regarding the psychosocial development of the elementary school child and implications for the child in sport and physical activity. To comment on all aspects of the presentation would require a manuscript of undue length. Consequently, the following is intended to represent the biases and special interests of the writer.

I.   Research Limitations

The paucity of relevant research is lamentable. Specifically, Canadian research in physical activity and sport with the 5-to 12-year-old, with females as well as males, and covering all social classes is indeed rare. Even more serious is the dearth of research with native Canadian people.[1]

Hopefully, one result of this conference will have been the stimulation of research interests amongst the social scientists in the area of physical activity and sport. In addition, the educators and parents who would have to collaborate both in supplying information and in making children available for research and the appropriate granting agencies should similarly have been moved. The recent influx of psychologists, sociologists, physiologists and medically trained individuals in faculties of physical education in Canadian universities promises hope for the future.

II. Leisure Time

(a) Television

Much concern is evident over the fact that children spend a large portion of their leisure time watching television. In fact, the current average of four hours per day will likely increase to six in the near future. Furthermore, average viewing time is likely even higher amongst children living in low socioeconomic conditions. This would be especially true for young children who are confined to their quarters in high-rise rent-to-income apartment dwellings since television viewing provides a more attractive alternative to standing in the hallway.

---

(1) By the way, how come I did not encounter any native people at this "National" conference?

One obvious reaction to this state of affairs comes from those who are concerned with the consequent physical inactivity associated with television viewing is to conceive of ways of changing this behavior pattern. Such a change would require the development of an alternative lifestyle for many people and although this may be an admirable goal it is not easily obtainable. A more fruitful approach may stem from the physical educator to make use of the fact that television commands a good deal of time from children.

Without jumping on the bandwagon for Sesame Street because its benefits have yet to be proven (Sprigle, 1971), it may be stated that we have a prototype available which may be followed. A few years ago early childhood educators attempted to make use of television as a means through which children's cognitive development could be promoted. Where were the physical educators when Sesame Street came along? Television offers an ideal opportunity for imaginative early morning and after-four programing to stimulate the interests of children in physical activity and sport. Furthermore, if school curricula were revised, as is needed, to include a greater amount of time for physical activities, television could be used as a means through which the program could be extended. It goes without saying that the researcher should tie in at the beginning of such programing in order to assess its effectiveness.

(b) Spontaneous play

Much concern has also been expressed over the fact that there has been a decline in self-generated spontaneous play activities during the last several decades. Reasons for this state of affairs include (i) the amount of time taken up by television viewing, (ii) the extreme amount of adult organization imposed upon the leisure time of children, and (iii) the fact that children model their behavior after their relatively immobile parents.

Although certain theorists view spontaneous play activities as prototypes of the interpretation of culture, no one has ever shown any relationship between the presence or absence of spontaneous play and various aspects of psychosocial development. As Sherif has indicated, comparative and representative research is needed to settle this empirical issue. What has been shown is that children prefer to spend their leisure time with peers. The question of whether play should be spontaneous or organized may be of lesser importance than the issue of whom the child is playing with. Furthermore, there is every reason to believe that research will eventually show that there are certain children, e.g., those with extremely high amounts of television viewing time or other idle activity, for whom we must organize free time, while for others the opposite would be true.

In the meantime, caution must be exerted in interpreting the trends regarding the change in children's use of leisure time. The change may reflect a healthy response to our rapidly changing culture rather than a matter for concern.

III. Social Context

One of the most important points made in Sherif's presentation was the notion that children do not develop with a set of traits which can be measured so that we can accurately predict how they will behave. The social context within which behavior occurs is as important a determinant of behavior as are the characteristics of the child. A few examples adequately illustrate the point.

It is a well known finding that anxiety results in interference with certain learning, problem-solving and test-taking activities. A former student of mine was both a teacher and a coach. He hypothesized that the children whom he coached would have lower anxiety scores than the other children in his class presumably because of the greater rapport he had developed with them. The opposite turned out to be true. Our analysis of the situation revealed that he actually acted as a threatening (e.g., "If you don't do well in class you can't be on the team") and stress-producing figure for the coached children, whereas this was not the case for the noncoached children. An alteration of this particular social context was clearly indicated. A clear implication is that coaches and physical educators be trained to be aware of the psychosocial consequences of their actions.

Another example is portrayed in a film "We Can Ski" which shows how a specific training program for institutionalized retarded children resulted in these children learning how to ski. In this case, the changed social context involved (a) a change in the expectancies of the teaching and care-taking personnel and (b) the introduction of a specifically tailored training program. The result was the development of a skill which is enjoyed by so many "nonhandicapped" members of society and which can provide a source of pleasure throughout one's lifetime.

IV. Aspiration

Sherif has noted a peculiar and unfortunate effect pertain to the setting of one's level of aspiration in the performance of certain physical tasks. On the one hand, high performers tend to set their aspiration level near or below their performance level and thus assure frequent success experiences. On the other hand, poor performers tend to set their aspiration level lower than that for superior performers but higher than they can actually attain and repeated failure is guaranteed.

I would like to add here that the infrequently occurring failure trials for high performers probably play a very important role in maintaining performance not only at a

high level, but even at a higher level than would have
been maintained had the child's expected level of performance
always been reached. In a series of studies (Ryan and
Watson, 1968), it has been clearly shown that children who
are successful (i.e., 100% reward) on every trial of a
lever-pulling task actually perform at a lower level than
children who do not obtain the expected reward on each
trial. Presumably, the occasional occurrence of nonreward
leads to a mild frustration-produced arousal level which
maintains performance at a relatively high level. Of course,
if no reward is received on any trial, the performance in
question will deteriorate. However, it is perhaps more
important to emphasize the fact that to reward a child on
every trial, that is, to meet his expectancy, is as inefficient a procedure insofar as maintaining a high performance
level as never giving any rewards at all.

V. Females

Sherif has bemoaned the social system which has resulted in
a less-than-adequate level of physical activity for females.
Amidst a confusing assortment of research findings, one is
able to discern that even from very young ages, sometimes
males and sometimes females are superior in the performance
of a specific physical activity. However, by adolescence
male superiority becomes the rule as society-forced inactivity allows the females to grow into a "senescent" decline.

This nonbiological, societal value system is now showing
signs of breaking and females are beginning to participate
across a broad range of physical activities. Some noticeable
forces behind this changing value system have been the
following: (a) the broad movement for liberating females
across all aspects of society, (b) the rapidly increasing
popularity of individually-performed physical activities,
and (c) especially in Canada, prominence in world competition
has been demonstrated mainly by females rather than males.
We must do everything possible to encourage this trend to
continue.

VI. Peer Influences

It is now well known that by middle childhood, children
show a heightened responsiveness to peer influences.
Although there are still many gaps in our knowledge per-
taining to the development and maintenance of peer influences,
there are implications in the available data which may be
put to use by a coach and assessed by the researcher. In
recent years, we have seen a marked increase in peer teaching
even at the elementary school levels. (Of course, Maria
Montessori used this techinque very early in the twentieth
century).

The question of interest is the extent to which the coach or physical educator in Canada has made use of children's peers in the setting of goals and standards as well as in assessing the performance level of children. The possible effect of this type of approach upon individual and group accomplishments, whether these be winning and/or personal satisfaction, remains an empirical question.

References

Ryan, T.J., & Watson, P.   Frustrative nonreward theory applied to children's behavior.
  Psychological Bulletin, 1968, 69, 111 - 125.

Sprigle, H.A.   Who wants to live on Sesame Street?
  Young Children, 1971, 26, 202 - 217.

Sherif, C.W., & Rattray, G.D.   Psychosocial development and activity in middle childhood (5 - 12 years).   Presented at the National Conference and Workshop on The Child in Sport and Physical Activity.
  Kingston, Ontario, May 13 - 18, 1973.

REWARDING CHILDREN AT WORK AND PLAY[1,2]

by M. J. Ellis[2],
   Dean, School of Physical and
     Health Education,
   Dalhousie University.

> *". . . it is a confusion of means and ends when we make*
> *children physically fit by means that will prevent them*
> *from wanting to be physically fit as a permanent life*
> *style" (Locke, 1969, p. 13).*

> *"Social psychology seems to have been passing through a*
> *disorderly phase in its life cycle . . . Discovery*
> *appears to have outdistanced map-making; we have examined*
> *so many trees and things that we are no longer sure where*
> *we stand in the forest" (Steiner, 1973, 14 - 16).*

This paper deals with the rewards that affect children's participation in play, games, and sport. The topic is so large that no
one person can be an authority on all of its aspects; however, we must
attempt to draw some sort of a "motivational map", which will place
the findings of various scientific specialties within a larger and
more inclusive whole. We need to integrate our explanations because
those who care for children must care for them as whole people. This
is in contrast to science which in dealing with the fundamental
questions of "How and Why Children Act?" must separate and isolate
their behaviors in order to be able to answer. If a map can be drawn
then all of us - practitioners, teachers, recreation workers or medics
- will be able to find some implications from science for our
practices.

This chapter builds the map by integrating many findings from
different branches of psychology. The findings to be incorporated all
deal with those events in the world that change a child's behavior.
In common terms, rewards and their opposite punishments.

Much has been discovered about rewards, sufficient for us to
see relationships between the different types, and to draw implications.

---

[1] This work was supported by a research grant to the Motor
Performance and Play Research Laboratory via the Adler
Center by the Department of Mental Health of the State of
Illinois and by the Canadian National Conference on "The
Child in Sport and Physical Activity."

[2] I acknowledge the help of Rainer Martens, my colleague in the
Motor Performance and Play Research Laboratory, who gave me the
opportunity to preview his book and permitted me to use the
structure of his discussions of social influences here. I am
also grateful for his counsel and thinking, but recognize that
the responsibility for this paper remains mine.

The chapter begins by dealing with rewards that are rooted in our biology. These rewards seem to control our efforts to survive and that are shared by all animals. Then the chapter goes on to deal with the rewards for play, something shared with us by the higher mammals. Then it moves to the rewards that stem from the common experiences of people.

Having organized and integrated the findings in the first part, the integration is summarized both in words and in a diagram that draws attention to the relations between the different kinds of rewards. With the map drawn the chapter proceeds to give some of its implications for practice. (Figure 5, page 156).

The Map

First, let us separate the motives of the practitioner managing some portion of children's informal behavior from those of the children. Children do not play because an adult wants them to, just as adults do not work because someone decides that work will improve the world. They work or play because of the consequences these activities have for themselves. The consequences of a child's work or play, the rewards or punishments, may be controlled by an adult in the service of an adult conception of what is good, but the control must be expressed in terms of what the child considers to be consequential.

For example, Linford and Duthie (1970) wanted to control the exertion levels of two young mongoloids, Geoff and Kathie. Using standard teaching procedures, they taught the children a simple but energetic circuit-training routine. Geoff was burly and overweight, but Kathie was slim, and circuit training came easily to her. Both would perform at a level which regularly raised their heart rates to 180 plus, but only when rewarded; and the reward had to suit the children's requirements. Kathie would work for smiles, but Geoff made it quite clear that he worked for mayonnaise sandwiches. No mayonnaise sandwiches in sight meant no circuit training.

The point is clear and general. We are all concerned with children, with developing them according to some image of what is good, and with providing services for them. Adults can control the behavior of children, but only by using the children's own motivations. This is why we need "a motivational map", which will give us a clearer view of the motives which urge children to participate in play, games and sports.

Extrinsic Rewards: Homeostasis

Some of a child's behavior results from his need to remain intact. The processes of metabolism place limits on our actions. Intolerable deviations in physiological processes are prevented by feedback loops that work directly e.g., blood pressure, or indirectly, by signalling to the central nervous system that some local condition is unbearable. These signals are unpleasant, and the return to the tolerable range, like moving away from a hot stove, is relatively pleasant or rewarding. This is called the Law of Effect, which states that those responses which are accompanied by a reduction in the level of intense stimulation are more likely to be tried again under

similar circumstances. This mechanism ensures that organisms learn
to respond to circumstances in a way likely to keep them intact.

Feedback mechanisms which involve events outside the central
nervous system (CNS) constitute well-known homeostatic mechanisms:
hunger, thirst, cold, local muscular fatigue, etc. These are primary
mechanisms that come "wired into" the organism, and since the events
that trigger the reinforcement lie outside the CNS, these mechanisms
for processes are referred to as <u>primary extrinsic motives</u>.

The behavior controlled by this set of motives reduces the
level of stimulation experienced. When an animal is not being driven
by hunger, thirst, it is satisfied and quiescent. This is a drive
reductionist view of behavior.

<u>Figure 1</u>

Primary Mechanisms of Reinforcement Rooted in Biology

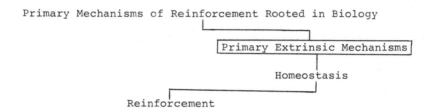

Primary Extrinsic Mechanisms

Homeostasis

Reinforcement

Intrinsic Rewards

A <u>primary intrinsic motive</u> for behavior is an inborn mechanism
that reinforces events that take place within the CNS. There is no
necessity for an exchange of energy or material with the environment
like in eating. What is consumed seems to be information. Such an
internal process maintains a given form of behavior in the absence of
external reinforcers. This view contradicts the opinion that all
behavior is controlled by extrinsic reinforcers, whose goal is to
reduce the level of stimulation coming in from the periphery. Intrinsically motivated behavior, however, does not lead to a state of
quiescence, but to behavior designed to increase the number of information carrying stimuli. Often when people are comfortable they get
bored after a while and they then do things to overcome their boredom.
The questions then become, "What kind of things do they do?" and
"Why?" Primary extrinsic mechanisms do not provide the answer.

When our primary needs are satisfied, then we often seem to
seek out activities or aspects of our environment that increase stimulation. We, like the other mammals, cannot tolerate bland familiarity
and we are rewarded by the opportunity to attend to interesting
happenings and the thinking that results. We all often behave in a
way that produces information flow through our CNS. The view that
some behavior is a form of stimulation seeking has a long academic
history. That history contains a major contribution from Hebb at
McGill and Berlyne, now at Toronto.

Sensoristasis

Much research on many different mammals has demonstrated that the opportunity to explore and to manipulate things around them is rewarding. At first this was explained by claiming there was an instinct to do so. Since then research on human machine operators and the aversive effects of isolation from stimuli have coalesced into one area of research concerning the phenomena of attention and arousal. A new drive has been postulated and linked, like others, to the Law of Effect. <u>Viz</u>:

> The organism tends to acquire those reactions which, when overall stimulation is low, are accompanied by increasing stimulation; and when overall stimulation is high, those which are accompanied by decreasing stimulation (Leuba, 1955, p. 29).

Stimulus-seeking behavior can be reconciled to the drive-reductionist theory of behavior by postulating a need to optimize the rate at which information flows through the CNS. A bored animal tries to reduce the discomfort by seeking excitement, for the same reason a thirsty animal drinks. The process whereby the correct level of information flow through the CNS is produced has been called "sensoristasis".

> Sensoristasis can be defined as a drive state of critical arousal which impels the organism (in a waking state) to strive to maintain an optimal level of sensory variation. There is, in other words, a drive to maintain a constant range of varied sensory input in order to maintain cortical arousal at an optimum level (Schultz, 1965, p. 30).

Figure 2

Primary Mechanisms of Reinforcement Rooted in Biology

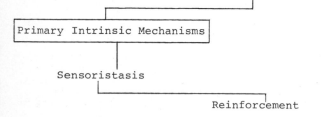

Primary Intrinsic Mechanisms

Sensoristasis

Reinforcement

The effect of a particular stimulus on an animal depends on its previous experience. A novel, complex, or dissonant stimulus contains information because it hasn't been experienced before. After repeated presentations, the stimulus becomes familiar, simple, and expected. It loses its information content and, with that, its power to hold the animal's attention and elevate its level of arousal. Fiske and Maddi (1961) have referred to this as "<u>impact</u>". Impact is the capacity of the stimulus to arouse an organism and is determined by the CNS, not by the effect a stimulus may have on the body. The need for continual exposure to stimuli with the right level of impact provides the <u>primary</u>

<u>intrinsic motive</u>. Thus animals even when not under the control of the powerful primary motives do not sink into quiescence. They continue to interact with those items in their surroundings that are new or changing or unexpected.

This sensoristatic mechanism is important to those animals that, like man, live in changing circumstances. Whenever they are free to do so they are driven to deal with those stimuli in their world that are changing and changeable. If and when one of those changes become critical for survival there is an increased chance that the animal that has explored and investigated and manipulated it beforehand will survive. The mechanism, and the play behavior it produces has been stabilized in the mammals over the aeons of their evolution because it has conveyed an advantage to the playful in the struggle for survival. Berlyne (1960), Fiske and Maddi (1961), Schultz (1965), Jones (1969) and Ellis (1973) give a fuller treatment of the stimulus-seeking mechanisms as they relate to play.

In man, the problem of arousal is complicated, because man is a thinking animal. For a short time, at least, he can reach optimum arousal by thinking novel, complex, and dissonant thoughts. This is an addition to the mammals playful behavior, of exploration, investigation, and manipulation. As we become more experienced, it is easier to think such thoughts without the need for overt exploration. We can play inside our CNS. Berlyne (1960, 1966) called this "epistemic," OR "knowledge-seeking," behavior. The change may explain the reduction in overt play with age: not that we play less, but that we play more often inside.

This concept, that the individual changes as he accumulates experience, is remarkably similar to that of Piaget and other developmentalists. Clearly, if the animal is to seek new experiences, it must have some reward, either in the search or in the experience. The notion that organisms grow more complex as they gather information from their environment was neatly expounded by Dember and Earl (1951) and Sackett (1965).

Clearly then the content of the interactions with the environment cannot remain static. If the animal is to maintain an information flow it must ever contain new elements of increasing complexity.

What is new or arousing can only be defined in terms of the preceding experiences of the individual organism. So the level of complexity of the organism and what is arousing are dependent on the phenotype. Today's arousing interactions are part of the stream of interactions between inheritance and experience (Ellis, 1973, pp. 95 - 96).

A primary intrinsic motive reinforces the search for information. This arousal-seeking mechanism causes the animal to learn the responses that will lead to its optimum level of arousal. However, it is not enough merely to learn a set of responses, because the animal soon finds them familiar. The animal learns that exploration, investigation and manipulation lead to reinforcement by producing something interesting and arousing to attend to. The animal learns to play.

The process is dynamic. The organism learns also that to maintain an optimum level of arousal, it must continue to play and learn. Consequently, it continues to explore, investigate, manipulate, and think -- and so to advance.

Secondary Rewards

The behavior of humans is exceptionally complex and much behavior seems to fall under the control of yet another mechanism - secondary reinforcement. The concept is simple: stimuli that are regularly associated with a primary reinforcement may eventually acquire reinforcing properties of their own. For example, a newborn baby comes with a built-in need for milk. It either has or rapidly acquires the necessary responses to suckle. Since suckling reduces the need for milk, it is reinforcing. Learning to nurse is thus mediated by a primary extrinsic motive. However, suckling usually takes place in the presence of the mother, who comes to be associated with the primary reinforcement. Eventually, the sight and touch of the mother become reinforcing in themselves. When the child is old enough to discriminate between facial expressions, he associates some with feeding. These expressions such as smiling, also acquire their own value.

Figure 3

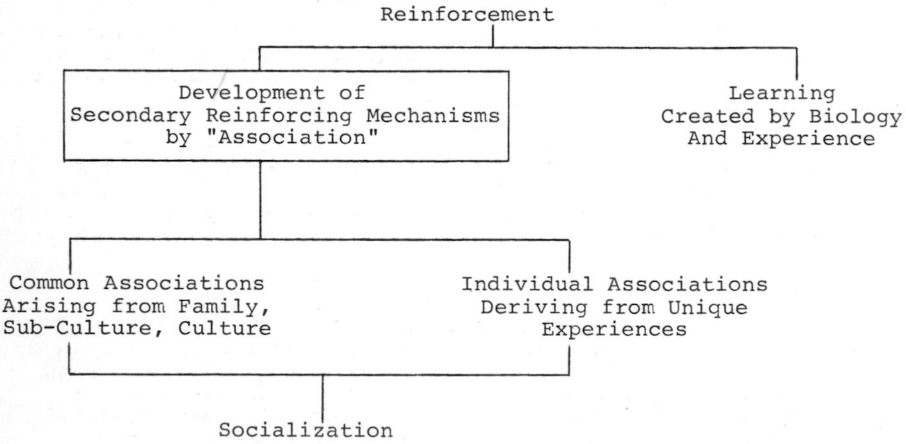

Reinforcement

| Development of Secondary Reinforcing Mechanisms by "Association" | Learning Created by Biology And Experience |

| Common Associations Arising from Family, Sub-Culture, Culture | Individual Associations Deriving from Unique Experiences |

Socialization

Some of these secondary reinforcers are highly individual; others, however, may be common to whole cultures, and a few to all mankind. A major class of secondary reinforcers are these stimuli involved in the interactions of people. Acquiring social competence consists of learning to manage a complex array of these incentives and to be responsive to them. Similarly, "socialization" means acquiring the social competence appropriate to a given society, culture, or sub-culture. It implies consistent behavior and predictable relationships with other members of the society, and it requires correct use and interpretation of commonly used signals. In our society, these

signals include smiles, nods, and praise statements, or frowns, withdrawal of attention, and shakes of the head -- all of which can be used to
manage behavior (see Morris, 1971, for a popular, or Birdwhistell,
1970, for a more scholarly treatment). These reinforcers
are inexpensive (how much does a smile or a wink cost?), easy to
dispense and powerful. They should be clearly understood by leaders
trying to manage the behavior of people.

Social psychology concerns itself with the orderly patterns in
the interactions of people, and has described reliable, common or
predictable patterns of secondary reinforcement that are useful to
those dealing with sport and play. These orderly patterns of behavior
in people stem from their long continued histories of rewards and
punishments, the rewards currently embedded in their surroundings,
and the responses that are possible. These ingredients all interact,
but, for the moment they will be dealt with separately.

All three are collections of constraints on the responses made
by people. Each individual's long history of reinforcements, both
primary and secondary, has developed within them, expectancies about
outcomes that produce "sets" toward external stimuli. The individual
has acquired dispositions to interpret stimuli in a given way. For
each person not all interpretations are equally probable and so there
are limiting regularities in the way in which the person perceives and
reacts to settings. In other words people are often predictable.

These regular sets toward stimuli can be used to separate
people into classes or personality types. Personality variables can
often be traced back to common rearing patterns that are created by
common cultural, religious, and socioeconomic influences surrounding
their rearing.

The setting defines the expected role for people who have
learned what to do during their socialization. The situation may
allow a wide variation in role behavior or allow the individual to
express deep rooted personality dispositions. Sometimes the situation
may so constrain behavior that they allow little expression of individual behavior.

What remains are the responses available in the setting.
This is clearly intimately related to the setting and the skill of
the client. If the situation has someone in a gymnasium many classes
of responses are excluded. In the same way the learning history of
the individual will also constrain the responses emissable in the
setting. If the gymnasium is set up for basketball, the basketball
player is going to react differently than if it were set up for
tumbling.

The surroundings, including other people, may allow individuals to express their own tendencies or personalities. Frequently,
however, the situation may contain such strong rewards for a given
activity that different individuals respond similarly. Finally, whole
sets of responses are prevented by the responses that are possible.
Here the limits are set by the physical nature of the setting and the
current capacity of the people involved.

Figure 4

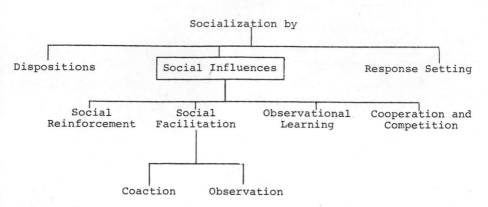

Dispositions

Experiences shared among members of a culture interact with the individual's genotype during rearing to produce particular dispositions and predictable actions. Some of these acquired dispositions, usually referred to as personality factors, have been shown to influence physical activity, for example, dispositions like achievement motivation or need achievement (Atkinson, 1957), need for affiliation (Schachter, 1959), anxiety (Spielberger, Gorsuch and Lushene, 1970), and internal/external control (Rotter, 1954).

However, these dispositions do not act so that an individual is always governed by a disposition like competitiveness or achievement orientation, because they are modified by the social influences and by the kinds of responses available. Bishop and Witt (1970) have given us evidence upon which to reject the simple view that an individual always manifests certain dispositions. They showed that the quantity of factors that can be explained in a setting is increased if both personality and the nature of the setting are combined. They also argued that if these two factors are combined in a complex interaction with the responses available, still more behavior would be explained. However, dispositions are complex and the study of their interaction with social influences is not well advanced. Furthermore, activity professionals have very little control over the personality of their clients although they used the social competency necessary to recognize and make allowances for them.

Social Influences

Martens (1974) has identified four social influences relevant to our concern, namely social facilitation, observational learning, social reinforcement, and cooperation/competition. An overview of the most salient points follows.

Social Facilitation

"Social facilitation" is now used to define the effect on behavior that results from the mere presence of other persons. Early workers used the word to describe <u>improvements</u> in performance, but the concept now includes inhibition of performance also. The presence of others, either as an audience or as coactors independently performing the same task simultaneously, affects the actor, presumably because they perceive that others may be evaluating them. Concern for the evaluation suggests that a host of other factors will also interact, e.g., the subject's need for achievement, the presumed importance of the evaluator, the subject's skill, and the kind of task.

The actor estimates the importance of the evaluation and visualizes rewards or punishments contingent on performance. The apprehension, or arousal that results from the situation, interacts with the task difficulty. The disposition to react to evaluation e.g., by anxiety, need achievement, need affiliation alters their level of arousal, and this influences their ability to perform. When the task is simple or well-learned, such arousal facilitates performance; but, when the task is being learned or is difficult, arousal reduces performance. The point at which these effects change over, i.e., how well learned or how difficult, reflects the interaction of disposition, setting, and task. In general, then, tasks difficult for an individual should be taught privately by someone who does not threaten with evaluation. This means ensuring privacy for the learner in the class or gymnasium -- publicity or humiliation clearly will be counterproductive. However, those who have mastered the skill will perform better when it is possible for an audience to evaluate them. Often the others in a class who are asked to express some opinion can provide just such an evaluative audience.

Observational Learning

In our society much behavior changes after observing the consequences that stem from another individual's responses. Through observational learnings we learn which models and which performances are desirable or undesirable. The motivation to imitate some other behavior is modified by personality dispositions and by other social learnings.

Not all behaviors can be learned through observation or modeling; some require trial-and-error processes. From observation we can learn, discrete elements of a task <u>plus</u> the procedural or symbolic components. The assembly of parts and the formulation of corrective loops can only be learned by actually trying to mix the ingredients of skills into an effective performance. Modeling, then, is the process whereby initial symbolic information about the desired response is communicated. The information may be provided learners verbally or by demonstration and when done effectively it narrows down dramatically the learner's hypotheses concerning the kinds of response necessary. The learner can more rapidly get to the point where he is testing responses that have a high probability of being correct.

Clearly the information necessary for the above must be communicated. The model must contain the relevant information, and the learner must attend to and retain it long enough to make a test response. The kind of information the learner needs is clear. The correct response should be modeled. Observing, the interplay between an incorrect response and the consequences does not teach us as much as observing the correct response (Zentall and Levine, 1972; Martens et al., 1973). Theoretically there are an infinite number of wrong responses, and we learn most by imitating the one effective response.

The teacher can often control the information contained in the model but the learner must have confidence in the model and desire to receive that information and act upon it. The former concern is one for educational technology -- the quality, quantity, and type of information. The latter depends on social influences working on the learner.

Social Reinforcement

Social reinforcement is "feedback" provided by some other person, which is contingent on some attribute of the performance viz, a smile, praise, a verbal report on the performance, a hostile gesture and so on. Reinforcement conveys information and influences the motivation and affect of the performer. Incentive describes the expectation that reinforcement will follow which has been acquired through previous responses or through observing the responses of others. (The development of a map of likelihoods of reinforcement is extremely important in our society). Consistent reinforcement leads to people mapping out the consequences of responses, and leads them to select his responses. If knowledge of the incentives, predictions concerning payoffs, did not exist, rapid learning would be impossible. As a society we would produce myriads of wrong responses on the way to a gradual strengthening of the desired responses by trial and error.

The potency of smiles and reproofs is obvious, but many dispositions and situations modify their effectiveness. The sex of respondent and reinforcer interact. Opposite sex reinforcement is more potent, except for children under five years of age. More intelligent and younger children are more powerfully influenced, and social reinforcement by an unfamiliar person is more effective than by a familiar one. Lower-class children are more influenced by praise than those of the middle-class, and praise from a disliked peer works wonders.

The individual's past history of reinforcement influences the present reinforcement. Deprivation of social reinforcement increases its potency afterwards, as if a child develops expectations concerning the amount of social reinforcement appropriate to his performance. Deviations from that level reduce its effectiveness. Absence of social reinforcement after what is perceived to be an appropriate response, or the receipt of a reinforcement after a poor response, weakens the effect of social reinforcement on learning. The incentive structure - "the expectancy map," is weakened and the children have to fall back and rediscover the limits of the contingencies. To do this, they often produce a deliberately poor or inappropriate response to see what the consequences are.

Different dispositions interact also. People differ in their perceptions of which or whether any events are under their control. Some people perceive that they are influencing the events in their world. When this control seems to be within them, they are said to possess an "internal locus," and when they perceive the control to lie outside themselves they possess an "external locus" of control. Social reinforcement is less effective in those with an external locus. They do not see that the reward was delivered as a result of their own selection of a specific response.

Punishment - negative social reinforcement can be effective if it informs the subject that he selected or executed a response incorrectly. It works in the short run, but if the child gets no positive reinforcement he has no incentive to continue to try to select the right response. In other words when the punishment contains significant information about the selection of a response, it is effective. When the skill to be learned is complex, the choice should be tipped in favor of consistent positive reinforcement of the right, or improved, performance.

Martens and others have pointed out that social reinforcement may have little effect on the learning of motor skills if the subject can get performance feedback in other ways. Usually the response produces an effect that is perceived, for example, a target is hit, and as long as the subject knows what is good, this feedback is often enough to allow the person to make progress. The internal dispositions may maintain the incentive to struggle to select the appropriate response.

To study the effect of social reinforcement on skill, the experimenter has to go to heroic lengths to prevent the information controlling the modification of the responses from reaching the subject by means other than social reinforcement. Why then, in practice, is social reinforcement so highly thought of and so earnestly provided?

First, social reinforcement may provide the child with a general incentive to continue to try to identify and learn "appropriate responses". For example, it might have the same status as the direct reinforcement of creative responses. This has been done with dolphins (Pryor, Haag and O'Reilly, 1969) and has currently been undertaken with children in our lab using social reinforcement (Reynolds, 1973). Here the subject comes to expect that a new response will be reinforced. However, the response itself is not reinforced but the struggle for a set of responses that are, perhaps, graceful, creative, novel, appropriate, precise, is rewarded by a generalized positive social reinforcement. In this case consistent reinforcement gives the child an incentive to make one of a set of responses.

Secondly, social reinforcement may maintain the processes whereby well-learned skills, those that are highly redundant and therefore less interesting intrinsically, are maintained by attaching other external positive reinforcers to it. For example, a diver must continue to practice dives learned and mastered long ago. The dives themselves are not very rewarding and the diver is usually successful. In this case continuing to struggle to maintain high standards is rewarded by the encouraging smiles, etc. from peers and teachers.

Competition and Cooperation

Cooperation and competition, which are obviously social and are obviously influential, are inextricably linked. The competitors have to cooperate in order to compete. Competition, in simple terms, involves individual participants who perceive the activity as a competition and who cooperate within a set of guidelines to permit a decisive outcome. On one end of the competitive continuum lies war with its codes of conduct, and at the other end lie the very simple rules of the central person games of "tag" and "king of the mountain". In all cases with which we are concerned there is a mutual agreement as to the goal and the boundaries of the activity.

Competition as a process involves four elements that find their link in the individual (Martens, 1971). In the objective competitive situation (the real world setting) performances must be compared and one other person must be present who is aware of and can make the comparison. The criterion against which the performance is judged can be another's performance, the other team's performance, a tape measure, or a past or ideal performance.

The subjective setting is the individual's view of the real world setting which the subjects have to accept. They have to agree to cooperate. This individual acceptance of the setting is clearly modulated by the individual's competitiveness. Competitiveness - this disposition to agree to compete or to actively seek objective competition situations is presumably generated by the potential competitor's history of socializing experiences. Some people are more predisposed to be more competitive than others. However, the individual's capacity to produce the responses required by the objective situation, their ability to perform the criterion behaviors, and the consequences of the outcome all interact to determine whether a competition will take place. Thus it is possible for some to agree to compete for formal outcomes that are impossible at the objective level. This is done by defining, at the subjective level, intermediate outcomes that reflect the competitor's own ability, providing that the consequences are not seriously detrimental. Thus, in handball, the competitive goal may be merely to take two points per game from a superior opponent. Onlookers may not know about this agreement, but the competitors are satisfied.

Performances evaluated by the individual performer; say a person practicing on his own and "competing" against former performances fall on the boundaries of competition. Since others are not present, there is no social interaction, but in a sense the person is activated by social evaluations, that have either already been made or are about to.

Competitiveness is characteristic of some cultures and not others. Martens has reviewed some of the work dealing with the propensity for competitiveness and for demonstrating achievement that is common in Northern European nations and the cultures influenced by them. For example, why are urban Anglo-North American children more competitive than other North American children (Nelson and Kagan,

1972)? It seems that they are responding to the need to achieve and hence seek out the comparisons inherent in competition. Those interested should read Maloney and Petrie's (1972) article showing that Canadian children are more competitive than United States children.

To summarize, competition affects performance. The evaluation inherent in competition facilitates social responses, and the facilitating effects are generated by the evaluation of others. In general, performance of well-learned skills improves in competition while that of poorly mastered skills or skills being learned deteriorates. If the outcome is important, competition is stressful because of the consequences of evaluation. Anxiety increases as the subject anticipates the consequences of losing and often performance is diminshed.

AN INTEGRATION AND SUMMARY

When the figures that have been used as illustrations throughout the text are combined they provide the "map," that serves to summarize the message to this point (see Figure 5). At the top are the two primary reinforcing mechanisms. Homeostatic drives are satisfied by the exchange of energy or the rectification of material imbalance. The situation homeostasis is rewarding. The sensoristatic mechanism produced a continual need to process information. The reward lies in the attributes of the stimuli, not their quantity. Stimulus events generated outside or inside the body must contain information. The information is consumed in the process and the organism is driven to seek for new uncertainties. Of the two mechanisms, the homeostatic drives seem prepotent, but when they are satisfied the organism does not sink into quiescence. Control of behavior is then assumed by the sensoristatic mechanism that ensures an ongoing active engagement with a changing environment. Further, the sensoristatic processes also reinforce novel variations on old behaviors. This mechanism confers a selective advantage on the higher mammals who occupy environments characterized by change. Homeostatic and sensoristatic mechanisms lead the individual to learn responses that satisfy them.

A further mechanism derived from homeostasis and sensoristasis involves the acquisition of secondary reinforcing capability by stimuli that are regularly associated with primary reinforcement. These kinds of stimuli are rooted in an individual's experiences, but, to the extent that individuals share common experiences, they develop classes of common secondary mechanisms like the smile mentioned before turning away from someone acting inappropriately, touching in reassurance, or stamping the foot. The meaning of these secondary reinforcing stimuli were learned during social interactions and their regularities allow people to modify each other's behavior.

The accretions of secondary mechanisms are vast and complex, but those that are predictable are amenable to study. Those regularities that seem relevant have been included in this treatment, so that dispositions and social influences appear at the bottom of the chart. These are linked because they interact to influence behavior, and both are the products of the individual's primary and secondary reinforcement. Disposition implies that an individual has predictable

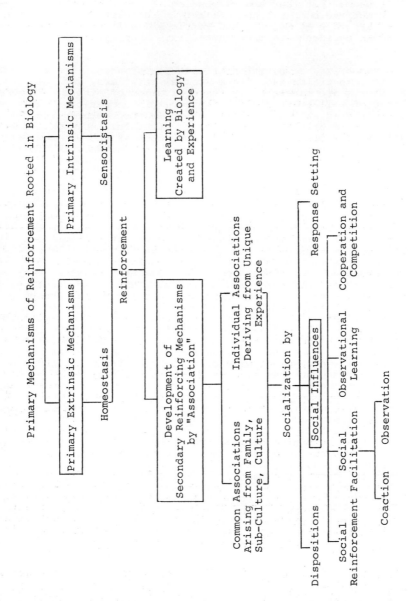

Figure 5

Primary Mechanisms of Reinforcement Rooted in Biology

tendencies to react in certain ways to stimuli in the setting. The social influences recognize the common effects which social stimuli in the setting have on people and the way these stimuli interact with dispositions.

Implications for Practice

Of what use is the map. First, it enables one to think about the kinds of reinforcement mechanisms that exist and the way one can control them. The primary extrinsic mechanisms are of little real use to us because their use threatens life. A child starved to 80% of his normal weight like rats in the traditional annual learning experiment will learn arithmetic readily if his correct responses bring small food pellets, but the user of such a teaching method would be punished. We have to rely on more subtle management.

Sensoristatic mechanisms make the organism responsive to novel, complex, and dissonant stimuli. Knowing this, we can arrange settings so that they sustain the kind of information-seeking behavior that is intrinsically rewarding. Children learn which kinds of activities expose them to stimuli with impact; stimuli worth attending to. If these activities are to remain intrinsically motivating, they must always be sufficiently complex to provide uncertainty and permit its resolution. Only if an outcome contains some information will it sustain interest. A lopsided competition in which the outcome is completely predictable will be boring. Unless trapped by other consequences, the participant will withdraw. Luckily for many teachers who do not understand this principle, the law requires the child to stay in their classes despite the boredom generated there. This concept is highly individual. What interests one person may bore another.

Further, what is interesting today will be boring tomorrow. Each individual needs a constant and upwardly spiraling complexity to remain optimally aroused - a concept that is clearly understood by the entertainment industry. They organize TV offerings, plays, music, novels, even our newspapers, to provide information and capture our attention (Stephenson, 1967). Novel, complex, and dissonant stimuli are offered in profusion, with careful attention given to common patterns of preferences, and to their generation.

Recently developments have increased the importance of the individual. Comparisons between the learning that takes place in response to intrinsic motives, and that which follows the application of external sanctions and social pressures has brought experiments in open schools and individualized instruction. The sophistication to which some activities, hobbies, and sports are practised by children intrinsically interested in them often compares odiously with those we press them into.

Play is not just play but the expression of the individual's mental engagement with their own settings. Play is learning. In the areas of physical education and recreation, this principle is not clearly understood. Recreators profess to respect individual motivations and responses, but often trample individuality in the rush to deliver services to the many. In PE, the recent interest in modern dance and educational gymnastics, the "movement movement," has been misunderstood. Relatively few have seen it as a practicable procedure whereby individuals can solve their own problems in the motor domain. An understanding of the power of intrinsically reinforcing events to motivate is crucially important to those programming the experiences of others.

Finally, the ability to think about secondary mechanisms, in particular those that are common to many individuals, permits better management of activity services. This is especially true when the interactive nature of dispositions and social influences is recognized and the knowledge about the social influences is used.

The map also provides an insight into the procedures used when the leader seeks specific responses or new responses. Education and recreation may often have similar content, but they have different intent. Education is preparatory. Recreation concerns itself with the demands of the present and is, therefore, simpler to operate. Recreation services are justified if the client enjoys them and returns for more.

Education is concerned with predicting what kinds of responses the student will need in future. Since our society changes only slowly, we can predict that certain classes of responses will be necessary. The decisions as to what is necessary depend on local philosophies, but no matter what philosophy is used, school will have done a poor job if it only prepares a student for what was predictable. How do we prepare others for a life characterized by changes that we cannot predict?

Nature of course has already answered. The sensoristatic mechanism is preparatory. Ashby, in his book Design for a Brain (1960), raised the same issue. A species has to deal with specific problems. The responses effective in dealing with these problems can be handed on via the germ plasm. The animal inherits the homeostatic mechanisms and reflexes. The existence of the problems and the responses that deal with them are predictable. For example, the need for food, the avoidance of injury, the need to cough, and clear the windpipe when it's blocked are constant across generations. The situation demands only that the individual recognize the problem when it occurs and take action. Ashby points out, however, that more highly developed animals can deal with problems that have not occurred before. This class of problems consists of those disturbances that, although not constant over a span of many generations (and thus not adaptable to by the gene-pattern, for the change is too rapid) are none the less constant over a span of a single generation. When disturbances of this class are frequent, there is an advantage in the development of an adapting mechanism that is (1) controlled in its outlines by the gene-pattern (for the same outlines are wanted over many generations), and (2) controlled in detail by the adaptations applicable to that particular generation.

This is the learning mechanism. Its peculiarity is that the gene-pattern delegates part of its control over the organism to the environment. Thus, it does not specify in detail how a kitten shall catch a mouse, but provides a learning mechanism and a tendency to . . . play (underline added) so that it is the mouse which teaches the kitten

the finer points of how to catch mice. This is regulation, or adaptation, by the indirect method. The gene-pattern does not, as it were,
dictate, but puts the kitten into the way of being able to form its
own adaptation, guided in detail by the environment"(Ashby, 1960,
p. 234).

Ashby's ideas can be extended by asking what inheritable
mechanism would enable a species to adapt directly to conditions that
require it to be flexible? You already know of such a mechanism,
namely sensoristasis.

Playful behavior consists of the responses made when the child
or animal is under the control of sensoristatic mechanisms. The
subsequent processing of information generates new interactions with
the environment and/or new combinations of symbolic representation of
past experiences -- the thinking of new thoughts. From the thinker's
point of view (observable play seems to be merely the overt responses
necessary for the covert thinking processes of the moment) all that
is necessary is that it continue to generate novelty, complexity or
dissonance. During play, then, the right thoughts are those bearing
information.

Education seems to have a dual preparatory role. It has to
hand on the direct defenses to the given problems in a situation. It
acts as a kind of germ-plasm of experience. This aspect of education
resembles the teaching of specific responses. Education also must
prepare the child for the unpredictable, and must encourage the
acquisition and expression of playful responses.

Teachers should be able to recognize which of these two broad
functions they are trying to foster at any particular time. If they
are trying to generate a specific response, a direct defense, then
they should set out to use all the rewards available to them. The
society's motives acting via the teacher may preempt those of the
child since the responses are critical and must be acquired. This is
legitimate. The attachment of positive consequences to the right
response, and negative to the wrong, is appropriate and effective.
However, if that is all the teacher does, children as individuals have
no time to practice the intrinsically rewarding processes of
generating and solving problems -- playing.

Play has such an important by-product, the improved capacity
to deal with change, that it must be protected. Play is the
expression of the organism's propensity to increase its individuality,
increase its repertoire of responses, and to acquire sets toward new
responses and changing settings. Variety is as critical to our
survival as a species as the behavioral flexibility engendered by
play is to the survival of the individual.

Neumann, 1971, dealt explicitly with the process of different-
iating between play and work. This differentiation is important to
all of us, because the behavior that is rewarded is quite different.
During work, specific responses are rewarded. The problem is to
eliminate other possibilities and select the right response. During
play, new or varying (creative) responses are intrinsically rewarding
but are fragile and can easily be preempted by a teacher who, forget-
ful of the need for play, punishes or fails to support playful

behavior. The setting must be arranged so that intrinsically rewarding responses become available. As a class, the responses are new,
creative, divergent, humorous (dissonant). If they are to be
rewarded, the rewards must be attached to these attributes rather than
to specific responses. For example, teachers often reward the right
way of performing an expressive movement or use of a piece of
apparatus. This is acceptable if a specific stunt is being learned,
but if children have been invited to explore themselves and their
relationship to the world, there is no right way.

Neumann set down some simple criteria to guide the practitioner
in deciding whether a response is play or work. These criteria when
reversed become principles of practice necessary to engender play.
They take the form of the following simple questions:

Does the locus of control of the behavior rest with the
individual?

Are the rewards inherent in the process rather than the
product?

Are some of the constraints of reality relaxed?

The questions are all interrelated and are different ways of
asking whether the person's behavior is intrinsically motivated.
They cannot, of course, be answered. They are intended only as guides
to a practitioner faced with making snap decisions in the situation as
to preserve the essential attributes of play or nonplay. A more
extensive treatment of this topic can be found in Ellis (1973), but
this provides framework within which this issue of work or play can
be discussed.

Finally, since this is an interdisciplinary meeting, the map
should enable us to determine where our collective research efforts
should now be directed. We need research on the processes of reward
that fall under our control -- that are useful. We need to dramatically emphasize the need for research on the social and psychological
implications of our interactions with children's physical activity.
We know so much about the adaptations of homeostatic mechanisms to
activity and so little about the social and psychological mechanisms
that sustain the activities that create those adaptations.

References

Ashby, W.R. "Design for a brain: The origin of adaptive behavior" (2nd ed.) New York: John Wiley & Sons, 1960.

Atkinson, J. W. "Motivational determinants of risk-taking behavior" Psychological Review, 1957, 64, 359-372.

Berlyne, D. E. "Curiosity and exploration" Science, 1966, 153 25 - 33.

Berlyne, D. E. "Conflict, arousal and curiosity" New York: McGraw-Hill, 1960.

Birdwhistell, R. L. "Kinesics and context" Philadelphia: University of Pennsylvania Press, 1970.

Bishop, D. W., & Witt, P.A. "Sources of behavioral variance during leisure time". Journal of Personality and Social Psychology, 1970, 16, 352-360.

Dember, W. N., & Earl, R. W. "Analysis of exploratory, manipulatory and curiosity behaviors". Psychological Review, 1957, 64, 91-96.

Ellis, M. J. "Why people play". Englewood Cliffs, New Jersey: Prentice-Hall, 1973.

Fiske, D. W., & Maddi, S. "A conceptual framework". In D. W. Fiske & S. Maddi (Eds.), Functions of varied experience. Homewood, Illinois: Dorsey Press, 1961.

Jones A. "Stimulus seeking behavior". In J.P. Zubek (Ed.), Sensory deprivation: Fifteen years of research. New York: Appleton-Century-Crofts, 1969.

Leuba, C. "Toward some integration of learning theories." Psychological Reports, 1955, 1, 27-33.

Linford, A. G., & Duthie, J.H. "The use of operant technology to induce sustained exertion in young trainable Down's Syndrom children". In G.S. Kenyon (Ed.), Contemporary psychology of sport. Chicago: The Athletic Institute, 1970. Pp. 515-521.

Locke, L. "Research in physical education: A critical view". New York: Teachers College Press, 1969.

Maloney, T.L., & Petrie, B. M. "Professionalization of attitude toward play among Canadian school pupils as a function of sex, grade and athletic participation." Journal of Leisure Research, 1972, 4, 184-195.

Martens, R. "Social psychology of physical activity". New York: Harper & Row, in press.

Martens, R. "Competition: In need of a theory". Paper presented at the Conference on Sport and Social Deviancy, State University of New York College at Brockport. December, 1971.

Martens, R., Zuckerman, J., & Burwitz, L. "Model's behavior as a determinant of motor skill acquisition through observation". Unpublished report, 1973.

Morris, D. "Intimate behavior". New York: Random House, 1971.

Nelson, L. L., & Kagan, S. "Competition: The star spangled scramble". Psychology Today, 1972, 5, 53-56, 90-91.

Neumann, E. A. "The elements of play". Doctoral dissertation, University of Illinois, 1971.

Pryor, K. W., Haag, R., & O'Reilly, J. "The creative porpoise: Training for novel behavior". Journal of the Experimental Analysis of Behavior, 1969, 12, 653-661.

Reynolds, R. P. "The operant conditioning of creativity in children". Unpublished doctoral dissertation proposal, University of Illinois, 1973.

Rotter, J. B. "Generalized expectancies for internal versus external control of reinforcement". Psychological Monographs, 1966, 80 (Whole No. 609).

Runkel, P. J., & McGrath, J.E. "Research on human behavior. A systematic guide to method". New York: Hold, Rinehart & Winston, 1972.

Sackett, G. P. "Effects of rearing conditions upon the behavior of rhesus monkeys (Macaca mulatta)". Child Development, 1965 36, 855-866.

Schachter, S. "The psychology of affiliation". Stanford, California: Stanford University Press, 1959.

Schultz, D.D. "Sensory restriction: Effects on behavior". New York: Academic Press, 1965.

Spielberger, C.D., Gorsuch, R.L., & Lushene, R. E. "The state-trait anxiety inventory". Palo Alto: Consulting Psychology, 1973, 27, 14-15.

Steiner, I.D. "Let there by order please". Contemporary Psychology, 1973, 27, 14-15.

Stephenson, W. "The play theory of mass communication". Chicago: University of Chicago Press, 1967.

Zentall, T. R., & Levine, J. M. "Observation learning and social facilitation in the rat". Science, 1972, 178, 1220-1221.

Sociological aspects

THE SOCIAL STRUCTURE OF THE GAME AND SPORT MILIEU

by B.D. McPherson, L.N. Guppy and J.P. McKay,
Department of Kinesiology,
University of Waterloo,
January, 1974.

Human behavior, whether at work or play, is greatly influenced by both the social environment the individual is in at a specific point in time, and by the environments they have been exposed to in the past. Therefore, any consideration of the involvement of children in sport and physical activity must examine the social milieu in which this behavior occurs. Thus, in this paper we are primarily interested in gaming and sporting behavior which occurs within social systems. A social system is comprised of a set of individuals who interact on the basis of shared patterns of expectations as to how they should and should not behave while in that system. For example, children interact verbally, physically or symbolically with others in a variety of social systems such as, the family, the peer group, the school, the church, and minor sport organizations. Within each of these systems, values and norms dictate the type of behavior that should be exhibited, positive sanctions reward individuals for engaging in normative behavior, while negative sanctions punish them for engaging in deviant behavior. Furthermore, the social structure within each system facilitates interaction among individuals holding specific social positions (eg., father-son, coach-athlete, peer-peer) which vary in prestige (social status). More specifically, within a given social structure, individuals occupy social roles[1] which define the duties and responsibilities of a specific social position.

In summary, a child learns to interact within a number of social systems, each of which has values and norms which dictate what roles he will play, who he will interact with, and how he will interact. Thus, however talented individuals may be in the motor domain, unless they are exposed to social systems wherein sport and games are valued, wherein they are given an opportunity to engage in this form of behavior and wherein positive sanctions are provided, it is unlikely that games and sport will become a salient aspect of their lifestyle. Figure 1 illustrates the social systems to which a child is exposed. In each of these systems the child is exposed to a set of values and norms held by significant others who occupy positions which vary in prestige. Finally it must be noted that within each of these social systems, the values, norms and levels of expectation are frequently established by adults, including those related to games and sports (Devereux, 1971; Sherif, 1971; Vaz, 1972). Thus, although the behavior may be child-centered, the values and norms are often externally-induced, and since they may be unrealistic in view of the child's level of physical and social maturation, are often not in the best interests of the child.

---

(1) Basically there are two types of roles, ascribed, which are present at birth; and, achieved, which are learned at some stage in the life cycle.

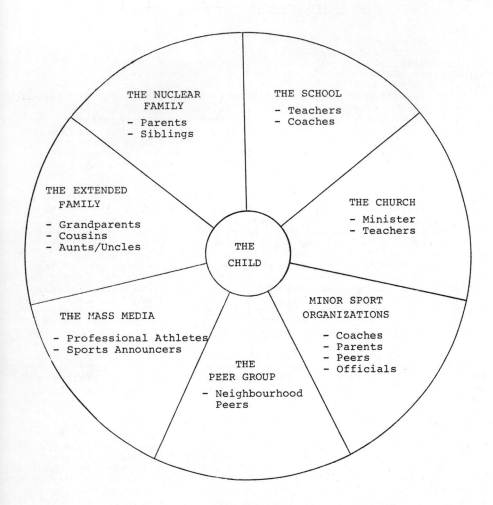

Figure 1

SIGNIFICANT OTHERS IN THE SOCIAL SYSTEMS
IN WHICH A CHILD MAY INTERACT.

SOCIALIZATION INTO GAMES AND SPORT: BECOMING INVOLVED IN THE LUDIC MILIEU(2)

Since sport roles are achieved, rather than ascribed, they must be learned through the process of socialization wherein individuals acquire the motor and social skills, the knowledge, and the attitudes that make them functioning members of a sport milieu. In this section we briefly outline the process of socialization, present some evidence which suggests how elite athletes are socialized into the role, and indicate some social correlates which influence whether children will become involved in sport or not.

The Process of Socialization

Although several theoretical orientations (Zigler and Child, 1969) have been utilized to study the process of socialization, the most fruitful in terms of theory and empirical findings are the social learning orientations (Bandura and Walters, 1963; Brim and Wheeler, 1966; Clausen, 1968). In this approach it is argued that social learning occurs via imitation and modelling of significant others who are found within one or more social systems to which the individual is exposed throughout the life cycle. While it is generally agreed that most learning occurs very early in life, in recent years some efforts have been directed toward studying the process of socialization throughout the life cycle (Brim and Wheeler, 1966). However, when one considers the learning of sport roles, it is quite likely that most of this process occurs during childhood and adolescence. In summary, the socialization process whereby sport roles are learned involves <u>significant</u> <u>others</u> (socializing agents) who exert influence <u>within</u> <u>social</u> <u>systems</u> upon role learners who are characterized by a wide variety of relevant <u>personal</u> <u>attributes</u> (Figure 2). More specifically, social systems such as the family, the school, the church and the peer group are most important for sport role learning (Kenyon and McPherson, 1973).

Socialization Into Sport Roles

Until recently, little was known about the process whereby sport roles are learned. Since it is possible to be involved in sport as an athlete, a consumer, and a producer (Kenyon, 1969), the following section outlines some of the findings which are available to date. Although these studies are mainly concerned with elite athletes who have attained a high level of success, the retrospective approach does have some implications for childhood socialization into games or sport. For example, it will become apparent that the earlier the age at which an individual becomes involved in sport, the greater the level of success attained.

---

(2) The ludic milieu as used in this paper refers to any social situation in which play, games or sport occur.

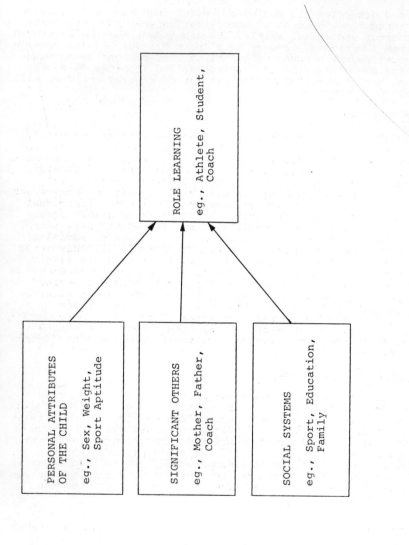

Figure 2

THE THREE ELEMENTS OF THE SOCIALIZATION PROCESS

Socialization into the Role of Athlete

In one of the earliest studies (Kenyon and McPherson, 1973), the factors which influence an individual to achieve the role of Olympic track and field athlete were studied. Although all subjects (N = 113) had a high level of sport aptitude, the learning of the specific role of track athlete was situationally influenced by significant others who taught and reinforced specific role behaviors within specific social settings. For example, over seventy-five percent of the respondents indicated that their interest in the activity was first aroused at school. In addition, they reported that they attended a school where a high percentage (over 80%) of the students and teachers considered track and field to be an important extracurricular activity for students. Thus, a social situation which highly values a pattern of behavior, and provides opportunities for the learning of the behavior, influences which roles will be learned and enacted.

In addition to the social situation, significant others with whom the respondents interact also contribute to the socialization process. For example, the peer group and school personnel (teachers and coaches) were reported as the agents who were most responsible for arousing an initial interest in track and field, and also for reinforcing the enactment of the role via appropriate sanctions. In general, it appears that the elite athlete receives encouragement and reinforcement from many sources, several of which act simultaneously.

In a similar study, Roethlisberger (1970) investigated the factors accounting for socialization into the role of Olympic gymnast. He found that elite gymnasts had a high level of general sport aptitude, having participated in several individual sports before they specialized in gymnastics. An analysis of the early socialization setting indicated that the educational system was primarily responsible for socializing an individual into the elite gymnast role, and that fathers and coaches were the most influential significant others.

In a related study, McPherson (1968) examined the factors influencing tennis and hockey players on Canadian university teams to become involved in sport. He found that interest in sport was initially aroused within the family, mainly by the father. In many cases the parents were still actively involved in sport as a participant, and thus served as active role models. However, during the high school years familial influence decreased and any interest in a new activity was aroused mainly by peers, coaches and physical education teachers. Thus, there appears to be a temporal factor involved, although sanctions for participating were received from parents and peers at all stages in their career. It was interesting to note that approximately seventy-five percent of the respondents reported that they consumed sport via television, radio and newspaper prior to their initial participation in sport. In summary, it appears that successful university athletes receive the stimulus to compete from involved peers and from a home environment which considers sport to be an important facet of life. This latter finding was supported by Pudelkiewicz (1970:93) who noted that a positive evaluation of sport by parents gives rise to sport interests among their children (see also Orlick, 1972; Sofranko and Nolan, 1972; Kelly, 1973; and Snyder and Spreitzer, 1973).

Vaz (1972), in a study of the culture of young hockey players, found that certain criteria were essential for initiation into the role of professional hockey player. For example, he reported that aggressive fighting behavior is normative, institutionalized conduct, and as such, is an integral facet in socializing future professional hockey players. This behavior, because it is institutionalized, becomes an integral part of the role obligation of young hockey players and is learned by subsequent novices via formal and informal socialization in the hockey milieu.

Malumphy (1970), in a study concerned with the role of female college athlete, reported that family influence was a major factor in college women competing in sport. She reported that the typical female athlete receives family approval for participation and competition, and is encouraged by at least fifty percent of her "significant others".

In summary, it appears that college athletes and Olympic aspirants become interested and involved in sport by age eight or nine; that they participate, usually with a great deal of success, in a number of sports before they begin to specialize in one sport; and that they receive positive sanctions to become involved and to compete from a number of significant others, of which the family, peer group and coaches appear to be the most influential. More specifically, if a child is to become interested in participating in sport then they must receive encouragement and reinforcement from significant others found in various social systems. Furthermore, the degree to which an individual gets involved in a specific sport is often determined by the specific social systems to which they are exposed. Finally, recent studies by Sofranko and Nolan (1972) and Yoesting and Burkhead (1973) have suggested that the activity level of a child has a direct effect upon their level of activity in later adult years. Similarly they found that inactivity in youth resulted in inactivity in adulthood. Furthermore, Yoesting and Burkhead (1973) suggested that it was more probable that an individual would continue an activity started in childhood, rather than switch to a new activity later in life.

Socialization Into the Role of Sport Consumer

In addition to the role of athlete, recent studies have also been interested in the problem of how sport consumers are socialized. These are described in the following section. In the earliest attempt to study socialization into sport, Stone (1957) found that the formation of loyalty to a team occurs prior to the formation of a loyalty to a specific player. He also noted that men form these loyalties at an earlier age than women, and that there are class differences as to when these loyalties are initiated. In a paper primarily designed to introduce and test the utility of path analysis for sport sociologists, Kenyon (1970a) investigated the causal factors influencing college students to consume major league baseball and the 1964 Summer Olympic Games. Although most of the variance in the two models remained unexplained, this initial attempt indicated that the most influential factors leading to baseball consumption were, in order of importance: sport aptitude (motor ability), general sport interest in high school, involvement by same-sex peers in sport consumption, and a high level of consumption of baseball during high school. The most important factors accounting for the consumption of the Mexico Olympic Games included: consumption of the previous Olympic Games (Tokyo), and familiarity with the athletes who participated in the Tokyo Olympics.

Kelly (1970), in a secondary analysis of some factors hypothesized to be important in the sport socialization of male adolescents in Canada, the United States and England, found that frequency of attendance at sport events was directly related to family size and indirectly related to age. He also noted that frequency of attendance at winter sport events was positively associated with social class background in Canada and the United States and negatively associated in England.

In a study of the sport consumer, Toyama (1971) investigated the influence of the mass media on the learning of sport language -- specifically, football terminology. She found that sixty-five percent of her sample spent more than three hours per week consuming televised sport, and, of these, thirty-six percent spent five hours or more. It was not surprising then to find that sixty-five percent of the sample reported that they learned football terms by watching television. In addition, another sixteen percent learned the terms while actually playing the game. Thus, it appears that the mass media, especially television is an important agent in teaching knowledge about sport and game phenomena.

The most recent study (McPherson, 1972) in this area examined the process whereby urban Canadian adolescents learned the role of sport consumer during childhood and early adolescence. It was found that for males, in order of importance, the peer group, the family and the school were the influential social systems, while for females the family, the peer group and the community were most influential. Thus, the findings suggest that the process differs by sex and that social systems vary in their degree of supportive influence.

In summary, the process of becoming a sport consumer varies by sex; begins early in life; is reinforced by significant others in the family and peer groups; and, is increasingly dependent on the mass media for providing knowledge and an opportunity to play the role.

Social Attributes Influencing Involvement In Sport

Social Class

The social class into which a child is born and raised is a reflection of varying combinations of the parents' education, occupation, income, prestige and power in the community. As will be shown in the following section, a number of studies have suggested that sport and game involvement is related to the social class in which one is raised[3], since this in turn influences the opportunities that are available to a child in terms of facilities, equipment, coaching, and reinforcement from significant others. Again, while many of these studies are concerned with the class background of successful athletes, it does suggest that involvement in sport as a child is influenced by the social class of the parents. That is, each child does not have an equal opportunity to become acquainted with or develop his ability in a specific sport.

Historical data suggests that involvement in sport has been associated with the class structure of society since earliest times. For example, in ancient Greece the athlete held a prestigious position in society, while in the declining years of the Roman Empire the professional athlete was utilized by the ruling class to provide entertainment for the masses. In the middle ages, sport was the exclusive right of kings and nobles who either participated in or consumed certain sports. Thus, throughout history different social classes have been involved in sport depending on the place of sport in the value structure of a particular society. More specifically, at a given point in time, either the upper class participated in sport while the lower class consumed sport, or vice-versa.

A number of studies have been concerned with the class-based involvement in sport of young males and females. Hollingshead (1949) reported that bowling was a popular indoor sport in the higher classes while roller skating was popular in the lower classes. Lynd and Lynd (1956:285), in their study of Middletown, reported that although both boys and girls participated in various sports during their elementary and high school years, there were no class differences in either the type or amount of participation. Luschen (1969), in a cross-national survey of young members of sport clubs, found that sport participation was greatest in the middle class and upper-lower class. Eggleston (1965) found that the athletic letters awarded at Oxford and Cambridge Universities in soccer, rugby and cricket were related to the class background of the recipient. More specifically, boys from private secondary schools were more likely to earn letters in cricket or rugby whereas the boys from the nonprivate schools were more likely to earn a letter in the less-prestigious sport of soccer. He concluded that different social experiences in high school rather than differences in athletic ability accounted for these findings. Similar findings with an American sample of athletes at Harvard and Yale were presented by Berryman and Loy (1971).

Kenyon (1966) investigated participation in, and consumption of, sport among young adolescents. He concluded that involvement by boys in the United States tended to be greatest in those whose head of the household had received the greatest amount of education; while among English children, the involvement in specific sports was a function of social class background. MacDonald, McGuire and Havighurst (1949) argued that differences in lifestyles are learned

---

[3]   For example, at the conference in Kingston, informal conversations with representatives from the Y's in Canada suggested that membership in this organization is predominately middle class or above. Therefore, access is limited, resulting in an opportunity set for a limited number of Canadian children.

via rewards and punishments received from parents, other adults and peers. They found that there was a relationship between the social class background of a child and his selection of leisure activities.

In addition to the studies of child involvement in sport, a number of studies have been concerned with adult involvement. These are reported here since the relationship between social class and adult involvement has a direct influence on the subsequent leisure pursuits of children. First, in an investigation of the use of leisure in relation to levels of occupational prestige, Clarke (1956) found significant differences between occupational prestige and the use of leisure time. He reported that the degree of involvement in golf increased directly with the prestige of the job until the middle status was reached; and then the frequency of participation began to decline at the higher occupational levels. Clarke also investigated the patterns of sport consumption and found that the majority of respondents at all occupational levels devoted most of their time to nonspectator activities. In addition, he noted that football spectators were most likely to at level 2 (managers, officials) on the occupational prestige scale, while baseball spectators were most likely to be at prestige level 5 (service workers, semi-skilled workers, unskilled workers).

In order to examine the effect of membership in a particular occupation upon nonoccupational behavior, Gerstl (1961) held social class and prestige level constant. He compared dentists, advertising executives and college professors and found that while forty percent of the professors did not participate in any sport activity, advertising executives and dentists participated to a great extent, especially the former, in golf. He concluded that:

> comparisons between occupations in a similar social stratum indicate that the crucial explanatory factor is that of the occupational milieu consisting of the setting of the work situation, the nature of the work performed, and the norms derived from occupational reference groups (Gerstl, 1961:68).

In a similar study, Jordan (1963) compared the sport involvement of sociologists, attorneys, and physicists. He found that the attorneys were more active as participants than the sociologists and physicists. Kenyon (1966), in an investigation of the significance of physical activity and sport for adults as a function of education and social economic status, found that active participation, and to a lesser extent sport consumption, tended to vary directly with the level of educational attainment. Sutton-Smith et al., (1963), in an attempt to replicate earlier findings with children, and findings in other cultures, studied the involvement of adults in games. They reported that (1) games of strategy were preferred by higher status groups, and by women compared with men; (2) that games of chance were preferred by members of the lower status groups, and by women as compared to men; and, (3) that games of physical skill were preferred by the upper class, and by men as compared with women. This finding is supported by Loy (1969) who stated that members of the middle and upper-middle class are likely to engage in competitive games while those from the lower class are more likely to engage in games of chance or mimicry.

In recent years a number of sport sociologists have examined the relationship between class background and present participation in sport by a variety of elite athletes. For example, Weinberg and Arond (1952) found that boxers were recruited from the lower social economic stratum. Similarly, Stone (1957) reported that members of upper class preferred hockey, golf, and tennis; the middle class preferred football, basketball and bowling; while the lower class preferred combative sports such as boxing and wrestling.

More recently, studies have examined the class background of college athletes. In all studies it was found that athletes participating in different sports tend to come from different class backgrounds. For example, whereas tennis players who were attending Ontario universities came from upper-middle and upper-class families, hockey players came from a middle or lower-middle class background (McPherson, 1968). Similarly, Vaz (1972) in his investigation of all-star minor hockey in an Ontario community, found that most of the players were from a working or lower-class background. He observed that boys from a higher socioeconomic status level dropped out as they grew older. Finally, in one of the most comprehensive studies of Canadian athletes to date, Gruneau (1972) examined the class backgrounds of 509 male athletes and 368 female athletes who participated in the 1971 Canada Winter Games. He found that elite athletes were generally over-represented in the upper-middle and upper socioeconomic status levels. Furthermore those who participated in individual sports tended to come from either the extreme upper end or the extreme lower end of the social scale, depending on the sport.

In summary, involvement in sport appears to be influenced by the social class in which one is raised. That is, a child's opportunity to get involved in a specific sport, and to ultimately attain success in this sport, is greatly influenced by the opportunity set he experiences as a child.

Birth Order

In recent years, sociologists have suggested that the order of birth within a family may have an impact on such behavioral factors as, educational attainment, educational aspirations, juvenile delinquency, motivation, mental illness, anxiety, conformity, authoritarianism, initiative and various aspects of parent-child relationships. [4] As a result of this interest in the phenomenon, sport sociologists have examined the relationship between ordinal position and sibling's sex and sport participation. For example, although Landers (1970) hypothesized that females with an older brother would participate more in sport than first-born females, this was not supported. In a similar study, he (Landers, 1972) found that males with an older sister participated in more high school sports than first born males or than males with an older brother. Levanthal's (1968) explanation

---

[4] For an extensive review, see Adams (1972).

for this finding was that an older female sibling serves as a negative
model and thereby motivates the younger male to adopt a behavioral
pattern opposite that of his sister. This interpretation also
supports Rosenberg and Sutton-Smith (1964) who found that preadolescent
boys with two sisters express more psychological masculinity than a
boy with one sister.

Schachter's (1959) observation that first-borns are more
fearful than later-borns stimulated an extension of this hypothesis
into the sport domain. Nisbett (1968) and Gould and Landers (1972)
both found that first-borns are less involved in dangerous sports
(those involving body contact and high physical risk), and that they
also have less desire to participate in dangerous sports than later-
borns (Gould and Landers, 1972).

In summary, the ordinal position of a child may affect both
the type and degree of involvement in sport. Therefore, the influence
of siblings is an important family structural variable since siblings
close in age interact in play and games throughout the early socialization years. That is, sibling sex and ordinal position influence
the type of environment and the kinds of experiences to which the
child is exposed.

Geographic Location

The opportunity to engage in a variety of sports varies according
to such geographical factors as climate, city size, topography, and
urban or rural residence. For example, Northern Alberta is more
conducive to hockey than Southern British Columbia because of the
climate, while Southern Ontario is more conducive for golf than
Northern Ontario because of the topography. In recent years, again
using college or professional athletes, Greendorfer (1970); Rooney
(1971); and Lea (1973) studied the birthplace of baseball, football,
basketball, and hockey players. In all studies there was considerable
geographical variability in the production of athletes within each
sport. For example, the majority of the baseball players came from
the Pacific states; the football players from Ohio, Pennsylvania and
Texas; the basketball players from Illinois, Indiana and Kentucky;
and hockey players from the Prairie Provinces, Ontario and Quebec.

While the above findings relate to the effects of geographical
location on the propensity of an individual to become an elite
athlete, they do not offer any direct indication of the effects of
place of residence on the sport involvement of average participants.
However, data presented by Knopp (1972) and Sofranko and Nolan (1972)
suggests that for the average participant, the opportunity set
provided by an individual's place of residence does have an impact
upon their sport involvement.

In summary, geographical location would seem to be an important
factor not only in ititiating sport involvement, but also in providing
a social milieu wherein reinforcement and facilities are present to
encourage a high level of involvement or success in sport. Furthermore, children, because they are born in a specific geographical
region, regardless of the natural talent they have for a specific
sport, may never get involved, or if involved, may never interact
within a social milieu which fosters maximum development of their ability.

SOCIALIZATION VIA SPORT: OUTCOMES OF INVOLVEMENT IN THE LUDIC MILIEU

Socialization is the process of inculcating in individuals the "knowledge, skills, traits, dispositions and value attitudes associated
with the performance of present or anticipated roles" (Aberle and
Naegele 1966).   Since play, games, and sport involve roleplaying, they
are frequently considered to be basic contributors to the socialization
process.   For example, since the attitudes and beliefs of individuals
have their origins in primary social interaction, games and sport
provide a milieu for this interaction so that the child can internalize
the complexities of the adult world.   In this section we review the
literature relating to socialization via sport and indicate a number
of specific behavioral and attitudinal patterns learned via involvement
in a game or sport milieu.

Anthropologists have recently suggested that play and game
experiences are structurally isomorphic to expereinces in the larger
society.   In fact, in many societies it is largely through imitative
play that individuals learn the culture of their society.   This is in
contrast to the formal educational system found in Western societies
where, as children develop, play behavior becomes more highly
structured and may, by varying the complexity, take the form of games.
These games then become an integral part, not only of play, but also
of the dynamics of socialization and child-rearing.   For example,
Roberts and Sutton-Smith (1962), in a cross-cultural study of 56
societies, related prevalent game forms to cultural configurations.
They reported that games of strategy are more likely to be found in
structurally-complex societies and are linked directly with obedience
training; that games of chance are found where a culture's religious
beliefs emphasize the benevolence of coerciveness of supernatural
beings and are linked with training for responsibility; and that games
of physical skill are salient whenever the culture places a value on
the mastery of the environment on personal achievement.

In their development of the conflict-enculturation hypothesis
of game involvement, Roberts and Sutton-Smith (1962) suggested that
conflicts induced by child-training processes and subsequent learning
lead to involvement in games, which in turn provide buffered learning
or enculturation important both to the players and to their societies.
Since all games model a competitive situation, it was suggested that
the three classes of games represent different competitive or success
styles.   Such observations certainly emphasize the interrelatedness
of game behavior, variations in child-training practices, and general
cultural demands.   Of particular concern in this regard is the highly
competitive nature of our success-oriented culture wherein boys, 8 to
12 years of age are able to distinguish various success styles, that
is, success through strategy, power, or a combination of the two.

Sociologists and psychologists have also examined the importance
of play and games in the socialization process.   Levy (1952) stated
that childhood participation in competitive sports is one of the most
important educational elements in society, and although they may not
be of the real world, they have essential functions for socialization,
integration and as a general reinforcement of the social structure.

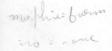

Ritchie and Koller (1964) reported that sport is functional in the socialization process in that the play orientation and play experience gained in childhood is carried over into adulthood. Specifically they noted that play and games involve attitudes, values, norms, roles and skills that are similar to those found in adult work activities. Lindesmith and Strauss (1964:206 - 209) noted that participation in play and game activities enables the child to gain the repertoire of social skills necessary for participation in the adult world. Helanko (1957) stated that sport and games provide the medium for socializing individuals into the values of society.

Kenyon (1968) challenged this belief when he suggested that there was little if any evidence to indicate that experiences in such diffuse roles as "democratic citizen" or "responsible individual" are provided through sport or physical education programs. He suggested that through physical education an individual may be socialized into specific roles such as athlete, spectator or official. More recently, Snyder (1970:1 - 7) concluded, without presenting data, that some physical activity results in the development of role-specific characteristics, while other activity contributes to the learning of diffuse roles. Despite the suggestions of Kenyon and Snyder, people still attempt to justify sport by proselytizing its value as a socializing medium. The claim that sport introduces a child to valuable knowledge, skills, traits, dispositions and value attitudes, which are not readily acquired in other social systems, has not been substantiated by empirical evidence to date. Physical educators and sport administrators, however, continue to legitimate sport involvement by referring to its socialization potential, rather than justifying it as an expressive activity (Ingham and Loy, 1973).

The variety of socialization outcomes that have been predicted to result from game activities can be classified into three types:

1. the development of individual traits and skills;

2. learning about the environment; and,

3. learning to interact with the environment.

Although it is beyond the scope of this paper to review the literature in each of these areas, a summary of a review by Inbar and Stoll (1968) follows.

It has been claimed that participation in games: promotes personality integration; develops creativity, need-achievement, independence, mental reactions, emotional dispositions and stability; and, facilitates modes of social expression. Thus, at various times, it has been suggested that play is critical for virtually every facet of personality development. Mead (1934) stated that in play the child first develops a sense of the role of other. Next, he internalizes the rules which form an organized set of responses applicable to all players. As a result of this process the child eventually generalizes the activity of the others and the rules into a unity, the "generalized other". It is at this stage that the child has learned to go beyond taking the role of the other and has generalized attitudes from individuals to the social group itself. Mead observed that play functions to help a child learn basic roles, whereas games, which are learned later in childhood, instill knowledge in more complex roles.

He concluded that, as a lifelong process, socialization through gaming behavior teaches us that man never outgrows his need for play and games. Similarly, Piaget (1965) noted that games give children practice with societal rules.

While many have considered games to be functional, Spencer (1896) believed that games and sports were essentially useless for society. Soule (1966) noted that many consider the frivolity of games to be damaging since adult life requires the performance of many serious and unpleasant duties, whereas play and games overemphasize pleasure-seeking pursuits. Similarly, Aries (1962) stated that tennis, bowling and the like are essentially quasi-criminal activities no less serious in their deleterious social effects than drunkenness or prostitution. Finally, in a recent paper, Bend (1971) identified a number of dysfunctional effects of sport. These included: the intrusion of adult expectations on the play of children; an over-involvement in one activity rather than involvement in a number of leisure pursuits; pressures from parents to participate and achieve; and, the emergence of deviant normative patterns such as the "win at all costs" philosophy and unethical practices by coaches and athletes.

In summary, parents and children must realize that while in-volvement in sport and games does enhance the social learning process, deviant normative behavior may also be learned in the ludic milieu.

Outcomes of the Socialization Process Inherent In Games and Sport

In this section, the impact of participation in games and sport on sex-role identification, the development of self-esteem and the acquisition of achievement values is discussed.

Sex-Role Identification

The ludic environment provides us with some of the best illus-trations of how the socialization process influences human behavior. Studies of play and game preferences of children have suggested that there are significant differences between male and female roles. Rosenberg and Sutton-Smith (1959), for example, reported that boys' games involved forceful physical contact, dramatization of conflict between males, propulsion of objects in space, and complex team organization. In a similar vein, Eiferman's (1968) research based upon observations of play among Arab and Israeli children presented detailed descriptions of variations in game contact by sex. For example, boys' games were characterized by far greater interdependence of roles, high division of labour, zero-sum competition, physical contact and quarreling. In comparison, girls' games displayed low division of labour, less group activity and the absence of end-game characteristics. Thus, these studies suggest that games provide preparation for different social roles. Tiger (1971) argued that such differences reflect underlying biological variations between the sexes which cause males to be more aggressive and competitive than females.

Despite the existence of genetic variations it would appear that cultural influences are more important in shaping sexual differ-ences in behavior. Since Mead's (1935) classic cultural anthropolog-ical treatise, most social scientists have recognized that each society has definite conceptions of what constitutes femininity and masculinity and explicitly and implicitly prescribes the appropriate type of behavior for each sex.

In North American society females have been culturally expected to perform an expressive or secondary role in society (cf. Lopata, 1966). Traditionally males have been expected to be aggressive, independent and competitive while females are expected to behave in a passive, dependent and supportive manner. These expectations are particularly evident in the social world of play, games and sport. Brown (1965:161), for example, commented that "a real boy climbs trees, disdains girls, dirties his knees, plays with soldiers and takes blue as his favourite colour (whereas) a real girl dresses dolls, plays house and takes pink for her favourite colour". As in society at large then, stereotyped assumptions are made regarding how males and females should conduct themselves in various social systems. In our culture it is common knowledge that games and sport have traditionally been masculine domains (cf. Stone, 1955; 1969). Participation in sport has therefore been positively associated with the male sex role and negatively associated with the female sex role.

Recent research by Lewis (1972a, 1972b) indicates that social influences may affect a child's play activities before he or she is one year old. Lewis studied the play activities of babies and found that parents varied their behavior qualitatively and measurably according to the child's sex. For example, parents allowed boys freedom to explore the play environment, to display aggressive be- havior and to engage in vigorous activities with toys. Thus, it would appear that parents are influential in maintaining cultural expect- ations with respect to how children should play.

In the game stage these expectations are reinforced when parents assign toys and clothing to their children on the basis of sex differences. In this way children engage in what Stone (1962: 102) termed "anticipatory socialization" whereby the child plays roles which he or she is likely to enact later in life. Parents and peers also make sure that children know the differences between boys' and girls' games during the game stage. The use of epithets such as "sissy" or "tomboy" is one way of sanctioning "deviants" who parti- cipate in an opposite-sex sport. As Beisser (1967:214 - 225), Hart (1971) and Hoffman (1971) have indicated, the tomboy is not a real problem because it is expected that "she will grow out of it". The feminized male, however, is different, since participation in feminine games by males has homosexual overtones -- a source of grave concern for most parents. Nevertheless, the girl who wishes to participate in organized sport is usually discouraged from doing so by parents and peers. A multitude of conventional wisdoms are presented to convince the aspiring female athlete that sport parti- cipation is unladylike, masculine and physiologically harmful. As Hart noted:

> Conditioning begins early - in elementary
> school a girl feels pressure to select some
> games and avoid others if she is to be a
> 'real' girl. If she is told often enough
> that sports are not ladylike, she may at
> that point make a choice between being a

lady and being an athlete. This forced choice
may create deep conflict that persists into
womanhood. Sport is male territory; therefore
the participation of female intruders is a
peripheral, noncentral aspect of sport. (Hart,
1971:64).

The girl who decides to play the athletic role finds that she
experiences role conflict. For example, Harris (1971:2) stated that
the female athlete is caught in a "double bind" -- in achievement-
oriented situations such as competitive athletics she has to worry
not only about failure but also about success. It is not surprising
then that many young girls select expressive sport roles or completely
withdraw from participation. Metheny (1965) contends that masculine-
feminine roles are a dominant force in controlling women's sport
experiences as there exists a "socially sanctioned image" of the female
sport participant which specifies the suitable sports for women.

Several authors have noted that physical educators, minor sport
league officials, athletic directors and parents maintain a hypocritical
position regarding female participation in games and sport (cf. Hart,
1971; Ingham et al., 1972:264 - 66; Edwards, 1972; Gilbert and
Williamson, 1973a, 1973b, 1973c; Ulrich, 1973). On the one hand it is
claimed that participation in physical activity is of positive socio-
emotional benefit to those involved but on the other, females, who
represent one-half of our population, are denied access to these
advantages.(5) Despite the fact that recent research has failed to
support most of the psychological, sociological and physiological
myths surrounding sport participation for females (Higdon and Higdon,
1967; Hart, 1971; Angeloni, 1973; Gilbert and Williamson, 1973b;
Rarick, 1973; Ulrich, 1973), institutional and legal barriers must
still be overcome in order to achieve egalitarianism in sport
(Edwards, 1972; Gilbert and Williamson, 1973a, 1973c; Talamini,
1973). Until these obstacles are removed or become less formidable,
the role of female athlete is likely to persist in the manner
described by Clarenbach:

> The overemphasis on protecting girls from strain
> or injury, and underemphasis on developing skills
> and experiencing teamwork, fits neatly into the
> pattern of the second sex. They organize the
> pep clubs, sell pompoms, make cute, abbreviated
> costumes, strut a bit between halves and idolize
> the current football hero. This is perfect
> preparation for the adult role of women -- to
> stand decoratively on the sidelines of history
> and cheer on the men who make decisions.
> (Gilbert and Williamson, 1973c:73)

---

(5)   It is worthwhile pointing out that black women athletes accrue
      considerable prestige from their community (Hart, 1971). Also,
      in the Soviet Union and in many European nations sport partici-
      pation by females is actively encouraged.

In summary, this section has outlined how socialization via play, games and sport contributes to the formation of sex-role identification. More specifically, children are prepared for the roles which society expects them to enact in later life by being involved in a ludic milieu where cultural values and norms indicate the type of behavior appropriate for each sex.

Development of Self-Esteem

Self-esteem is defined as the degree to which an individual holds a favourable perception of himself. Coopersmith (1967:4), for example, defined self-esteem as an attitude of approval or disapproval which an individual makes and customarily maintains regarding the extent to which he considers himself to be "capable, significant, successful and worthy". An important correlate of self-esteem is the influence of certain parental socialization practices. Studies completed by Rosenberg (1965), Coopersmith (1967), Bachman (1970), Gecas, et al., (1970), Sears (1970), and Gecas (1971) indicate that a child who receives support and praise from his parents is more likely to develop favourable perceptions about himself than a child who does not accrue this attention. It seems apparent that the ramifications of the evaluative interaction between a child and significant others in his social environment has consequences for the development of his level of self-esteem.

Although self-esteem has usually been conceptualized as a "global" or "trait" phenomenon, it would appear that one's level of self-evaluation fluctuates in various social situations (Wylie, 1961, 1968). For instance, if a person's athletic ability is important to him, then his self-appraisal on this dimension will greatly influence his overall self-esteem (Rosenberg, 1968:389; Shaver, 1972:48; Hellison, 1973: 8-10). Essentially then, evaluative interaction occurs in a variety of social settings with different significant others and the importance which an individual attaches to this evaluative interaction will influence his level of self-esteem. In the present discussion the term "ludic self-esteem" is employed to refer to the degree to which individuals hold favourable evaluations of themselves with respect to their involvement in the world of play, games and sport.

Physical educators and coaches, among others, have claimed that involvement in physical activity enhances the psychosocial development of participants. However, as Kenyon (1968) has stated, the idea that the relationship between athletic success and certain psychosocial characteristics is one of cause and effect is a tenuous assumption. Kenyon further suggests that high levels of performance may be a function of certain social and psychological characteristics already inherent in the performer. Similarly, in her recent review of the literature, Allen (1972) concluded there was no evidence to support the belief that performance in physical activities influenced self-concept or that self-concept affected motor performance.

Unfortunately nobody has attempted to accurately investigate the correlates of ludic self-esteem by constructing scales which are pertinent to the sport milieu. In light of the research findings

discussed above we might infer that the greater the praise, encouragement and warmth a child receives from significant others with respect
to his conduct in the sport milieu, then the greater his ludic self-
esteem.

Loy and Ingham (1973) recently completed an extensive review
of how play, games and sport act as agents of socialization. They
also discussed how involvement in the ludic world contributes to the
development of the self, since a child's impressions about the self
are influenced to a great extent by his interaction with significant
others in play, games and sport situations. A synopsis follows.

Play. The child who is constantly berated by his parents because he
plays too "noisily" or because his toys or games are always "in the
way" is unlikely to develop a favourable self-attitude regarding his
ludic ability. Children who are over-protected and not permitted to
engage in "rough" sports may develop a similar attitude.

Games. As the child gradually moves out of the play stage and into
the institutionalized game context it is obvious that in addition to
his parents, significant others such as teammates influence his ludic
self-evaluation. Helanko (1957:242-3), for instance, noted the
importance of the peer group in the same context by stating that "for
the first time in his life, the boy is called upon to create a social
position for himself among his equals". A more specific example of
how one's ludic self-esteem may be affected by evaluative interaction
with one's peers is the case of the individual who is constantly
selected last when teams are chosen, or the one who is always relegated to a specific position (e.g., goaltender) on the basis of
inferior ability. These individuals are likely to have a different
level of self-esteem than the player who is repeatedly elected captain
or leader by his peers.

Sport. Even though coaches are significant others for children
engaged in organized minor league sports, many researchers have pointed
out that their importance as socializing agents has been overlooked
(Bend, 1971; Hendry, 1972; Singer, 1972; Frost, 1973; Snyder, 1973).
As Snyder (1973) suggested, some coaches may simultaneously act as a
normative guide, a role model and an audience for the athlete. His
comment would seem to be important in light of Kemper's (1968) statement that socialization is most effective when all three types of
reference groups coincide. Although positive evaluation by coaches in
the sport milieu would seem to facilitate a high level of ludic self-
esteem, it is worth considering the dysfunctional aspects of what Bend
(1971:7) has termed an "overinflated self-esteem" possessed by those
athletes who are groomed and feted, given special attention and
treated as "community heroes". Bend implied that some athletes may
develop a dependency on their athletic evaluations but are unable to
match this image in nonathletic endeavours. Thus, he argued that
there must be some mechanism through which one's awareness that "I am
a good football player" is generalized to support the overall image
that "I am a worthy person".

Given the amount of attention which parental intrusion in minor
league sports has received in the media, it seems appropriate to
discuss how involvement in highly structured athletic competition may

influence the development of self-esteem. It seems quite obvious that some minor league athletes may develop negative self-evaluation if parents indicate that they have not lived up to their "expectations". As Bend noted:

> Induced competition ... is based on adult standards and the youngster who can't manage these standards is assigned adult levels of disparagement. If he can't sustain his level of utmost effort until the "final out", he is labelled as the "quitter". How many young athletes conceal injuries during a game to avoid evaluation by self and others as a 'quitter'? If the young athlete is somehow responsible for his team's defeat, he is singled out as the 'goat'. How many poor players who regularly jeopardize the team's victory over-react to defeats they have brought about? (Bend, 1971:6 - 7).

In summary, this section has indicated that an individual's self-evaluation in the ludic environment is influenced by the appraisals he receives from significant others, such as parents, peers, coaches and teammates. However, it must be emphasized that this evaluation can have functional and dysfunctional consequences for the development of one's ludic self-esteem.

The Acquisition of Achievement Values

Success is of great importance in contemporary North American society. In fact, we are continually reminded of what represents victory and what constitutes failure, and our life patterns revolve around attempts to achieve the former and avoid the latter. Success-striving and achievement-oriented behavior are therefore important components of contemporary lifestyles.

The importance of achievement in the social system of games and sport has been frequently discussed (Lenk, 1971; Schafer, 1971; Hoch, 1972; Keating, 1972; Kenyon, 1972; Scott, 1973). Moreover, empirical investigations by Roberts and Sutton-Smith (1962), Webb, (1969); Vaz, (1972); Albinson, (1973); and Vaz and Thomas, (1973), have generated evidence to support this idea. Since individuals initially entering a social system must learn the appropriate attitudes they are expected to display, children who wish to remain involved in highly organized competitive games and sport must acquire achievement values if they are to successfully perform their roles.

Not only do adults who dominate the children's world of games and sport expect these values to be displayed (Vaz and Thomas, 1973), but these values are also seen as being functional later in life in the educational and economic sphere (Rehberg and Schafer, 1968; Loy, 1969; Webb, 1969). As Sadler (1973:128) noted, "Sports contribute to the development of a lifestyle which is competitive in its total orientation ....". Whether these values are functional or dysfunctional for the child is beyond the scope of the present analysis. However, questions which concern the process by which these achievement values are acquired are of concern. For example, how does a participant come to acquire the achievement values which are manifest in the sport system? Are these values learned prior to one's entry into games and sports, or are they developed while one is involved within the sport system? These two questions will guide our analysis of achievement values in games and sport.

First, Webb (1969) presented data from 1,274 males and females (grades 3 through 12) which supported his basic proposition that as age increased there was a gradual rise in the level of achievement values in both sexes. Similar results were found by Maloney and Petrie (1972) using a sample of 659 Canadian students (grades 8 through 12). Furthermore, both studies reported that generally males possessed higher achievement values than females. One may argue that such results support the idea that achievement values are either acquired or strengthened within the sport system. To the extent that Webb's (1969) "Play Scale" is a valid measure of achievement values, the argument may be supported. However, alternative interpretations may explain these results. For example, it may be that such values are developed in other contexts such as, the academic sphere, and these "academic values" may then influence both educational achievement and sport achievement. If this latter suggestion is a realistic explanation of the above findings, then one would have to reassess the work of both Webb, and Maloney and Petrie.

One might also suggest that students in grade six in a given year may be exposed to different child-rearing practices than students in grade ten in the same year. This exposure to differential socialization experiences by the two different cohorts may influence the respondents' acquisition of achievement values. Similarly, differential socialization experiences may explain the variation in achievement values of males and females. As noted in an earlier section, Roberts and Sutton-Smith (1962) argued that boys are involved in games of physical skill (in which achievement is stressed) and girls are more involved in games of strategy and chance (in which obedience and responsibility are stressed). If males are exposed to more achievement training than females, and if males acquire achievement values as a result of such training, then they should possess higher achievement orientations than females. In general, data presented by Webb (1969) and Maloney and Petrie (1972) support this proposition. However, data reported for male and female Catholic preadolescents suggest that this proposition does not always hold. Both Webb (1969) and Guppy (1973) found that in the lower grades, Catholic females had a more professionalized attitude toward play than did males. Webb's results showed Catholic females had higher achievement values than their male counterparts in both grade three and grade six, while Guppy's data showed a similar pattern for Canadian Catholics in grades four and six.

These results would support the arguments of both Sherif (1972) and Zoble (1972) who imply that feminine achievement may exist in the early years of a girl's involvement in the sport system, but that gradually girls are discouraged from engaging in the competitive processes of games and sport. Support for this assertion is also offered by Birch and Veroff (1966:59) who noted that goals may be

perceived differently by males and females since "girls are taught to
do well in competition with boys during their formative years in
school .... Later, because of impending adulthood, girls are discouraged from achievement".

The data collected by both Webb and Guppy showed that for male
and female Catholic students a decrease in achievement values occurred
between grades three or four, and grade six. Guppy (1973) attempted
to explain this by suggesting that the impact of intramural and
interschool sport in the Catholic school may have been responsible
for the apparent decreased emphasis upon achievement.

Research by Mantel and Vander Velden (1971) revealed that
preadolescent males involved in organized sport possess higher
achievement values than a similar cohort of males not involved in
organized sport. Maloney and Petrie (1972) and Guppy (1973) added
further information by showing differences between levels of organized
sport. Their data suggested that individuals with high achievement
values are usually found in interscholastic and community sport, while
individuals who possess low achievement values are generally found in
intramural sports. Two basic explanations may be offered for these
results. First, if socialization were to occur within the sport
system, then differences in socialization could be expected between
various levels of competition. That is, one might expect interscholastic and community sport to be dominated by coaches, teachers,
or parents who stress a "win-at-all-costs" ethic. Conversely,
intramural sport might exhibit components of fairness and equity, and
less emphasis upon competition as an end in itself. That these
various levels of competition do exist, and that they do manifest
differential value orientations seems plausible. Thus, individuals
participating in intramural sport may not be exposed to high achievement stresses and therefore they may not acquire high achievement
values. However, a second explanation is also possible. This
argument would suggest that individuals with high achievement values
are attracted to inter-scholastic and community sport because of the
competitive processes these activities provide. That is, individuals
are "selected into" different competitive levels of sport because of
unique achievement emphases at each level.

If one does assume that some socialization is occurring in the
sport system, then the significant others which one encounters in
this domain may have an effect upon an individual's acquisition of
sport achievement values. Heinila (1970), Albinson (1973), and Vaz
and Thomas (1973) have all shown that coaches in minor league sport
programs are very concerned with skill and victory, often to the
neglect of fairness. Similarly, it may be argued that friends,
teachers, teammates, parents, sisters and brothers may also influence
an individual's acquisition of achievement values. If parents, peers,
teachers, and coaches are influential in the process of socialization,
it is important to specify the practices by which this process
operates. That is, what are the training practices which are
responsible for a child's development of sport achievement values?
McClelland (1961) suggested that socialization practices which stress
doing things well and doing things alone may be important in one's
development of achievement values. That is, individuals who are
exposed to socialization agents who stress these two practices will
possess higher achievement values than individuals who are not exposed

to either of these stresses. At present little is known about how these two training practices operate in the sport system. Data collected by Guppy (1973) offered only moderate support for the proposition that parental stresses upon achievement training practices influence an individual's sport achievement values.

The degree to which these achievement training practices are stressed by significant others may also vary according to the religious affiliation and the social status of the significant others. That is, the family socialization practices of the middle and lower classes may be different due to the various educational or occupational experiences of the parents. For example, Webb (1969) found that the higher the social status, the greater the child's level of sport achievement. Since parental social status partially determines the significant others an individual will encounter (Campbell, 1969), then this relationship between social status and achievement values may generalize to other "significant others" as well.

With respect to parental religious affiliation it can be argued that Protestants will employ different socialization techniques than Catholics. Webb (1969) found that from grade eight to grade twelve both Catholic males and females had higher achievement values than did their Protestant counterparts. This finding is contrary to what one would expect from Weber's proposition concerning the Protestant Ethic, but it is consistent with studies in other contexts which have explored the relationship between church affiliation and achievement values (see Bouma, 1973). Thus, both religion and parental social status may influence the types of socialization practices to which a child is exposed. In turn this differential socialization may result in various degrees of sport achievement.

To summarize, this section has attempted to provide an overview of the research concerned with achievement values in games and sport. It has been suggested that two competing explanations may be offered to account for the differences in achievement values at distinct levels of sport competition. First, individuals may be socialized while participating (or even aspiring to participate) within a certain competitive level of sport, and second, individuals may be selected into different levels because of the correspondence between an individual's personal values and the values manifest in sport. Furthermore, it has been suggested that more emphasis must be placed upon describing the specific socialization practices of significant others which may lead to the acquisition of sport achievement values on the part of the child.

SOCIAL PROBLEMS IN THE CHILD'S SPORT MILIEU

Introduction

Although social problems which involve children, such as delinquency, poverty and drug addiction have been identified and studied, it is only in recent years that conditions or situations inherent in the sport milieu have been judged by a significant number of persons to be intolerable. As a result of this increased awareness, the situations presented in this section have been studied in an attempt to provide constructive reform. As the reader will note, most of these problems lack solutions at the present time.

Aggressiveness

For many years, instinct theorists (Ardrey, 1961; Lorenz, 1966) have argued on the basis of psychoanalytic cases and observation of animals that man is inherently aggressive. However, more recent evidence suggests that the frustration-aggression theory (Dollard et al., 1939; Miller, 1941; Berkowitz, 1962; Bandura and Walters, 1963) is a more likely explanation of aggressive behavior, in both sport and other facets of life. According to this theory, aggression is usually caused by frustration, but, frustration may not always lead to aggression. The occurrence of aggression, then, appears to be socially-induced and therefore learned via the socialization process. Thus, through exposure to significant others (role models) and reference groups, an individual observes aggressive behavior or is explicitly taught to be aggressive in certain situations. For example, Smith suggests that within some sporting social systems there are:

> values which legitimize aggression, norms which
> provide rules for the conduct of aggression,
> and mechanisms by which individuals are mobilized
> into aggressive roles. The techniques of violence
> may be socially learned, legitimized, and rein-
> forced by various types of reference groups.
> (Smith, 1971:25).

Vaz (1972) also suggests that physically aggressive behavior is normative, institutionalized behavior that is learned during the formal and informal socialization process of young hockey players. In a participant observation study of boys eight to twenty engaged in minor league hockey, Vaz found that many of the attitudes and values common to minor league hockey fit into the general value system of the lower socioeconomic strata. Thus, he reported that the occupation of hockey player is more highly valued by members of the lower class. Furthermore, he noted that physical aggression, especially fighting, is normative, institutionalized behavior learned via social-ization, and is part of the role expectations of the player. As a result, under certain conditions a failure to fight is negatively sanctioned by coaches, players and spectators (parents). In fact, Vaz observed that:

> illegal tactics and tricks of the game are both
> encouraged and taught; rough play and physically

aggressive performance are strongly encouraged,
and sometimes players are taught the techniques
of fighting (Vaz, 1972:230).

Faulkner (1971) and Smith (1972) also studied aggression in hockey.
Faulkner, in a case study of a minor league professional team, found
that players consider violent behavior (eg., fighting) to be a
personal and occupational resource to be used in achieving and
maintaining mastery over opponents, and for attaining positive evaluations from their work peers. These are the role models which
children often emulate! Smith (1972), in a study of 83 high school
hockey players in Metropolitan Toronto, found that for all reference
groups there was:

> general approval of "hard, but legal bodychecking"
> and of "fighting, but because the other guy
> started it". Conversely, "rough play like
> boarding or crosschecking which results in
> penalties" and "starting a fistfight" tended to
> be - nonplaying peers excepted - negatively
> sanctioned (Smith, 1972:7).

The nonplaying peers were perceived by the players as eager to observe
violence, regardless of the motive or type.

In summary, aggressive behavior in sport appears to be socially
acquired normative behavior, and in fact, may be a product of a
culture or subculture of violence. Given this situation, how can
aggressive behavior in sport be eliminated, or at least controlled?
First, if role models exhibiting aggressive forms of behavior are no
longer available, then children will have fewer opportunities to
imitate, and will be less likely to learn such deviant patterns as
fighting. This, of course, requires legislation in the form of
negative sanctions. In many minor sport leagues, fighting results in
a one or two-game suspension. Furthermore, when the National Hockey
League initiated progressive legislation whereby they introduced the
"third man into the fight" rule, role models were eliminated and the
number of mass fights in recent years has been substantially reduced.
Other ways to reduce aggressive behavior include changing the
behavioral norms which coaches require their players to meet, and
understanding players so that when signs of frustration appear, the
player can be removed from a potentially aggressive situation.

Adult Domination

A second major problem is the increasing tendency for adults
to enter and dominate children's sport. In some cases this intrusion
is caused by parents and coaches who wish to interact with highly
skilled individuals (Sherif and Rattray, 1973), perhaps to vicariously
experience success that is lacking or unavailable in their adult world;
by adults who invest emotion in the athlete and expect to receive
gratification (Bend, 1971) in this domain (the quest for excitement
in an unexciting lifestyle); by adult significant others who seek
prestige and status in the community through organized competition
for children (cf. Havemann, 1973); and by parents who establish early
career aspirations in the world of professional sport for their son
or daughter. As a consequence of this interference in the world of

children's games and sport, adults now dominate the social organization and social interactions within this milieu. Both Bend (1971)
and Sherif and Rattray (1973) have stated that because adult expectations are imposed, the levels of aspiration held by the child are
externally-induced and often lead to unrealistic norms, regardless of
age, within the particular sport system (eg., win at all costs, play
with pain, only a winner can be proud, etc.). For example, a recent
study of minor league baseball (Brower, 1973) concluded that the
league's organization and games are really for the pleasure and
benefit of adults. The boys are like pawns in a chess game. The
adults call the shots, the kids get in line and do what they are told.

Furthermore, Devereux (1971 suggested that highly organized
little league sport may extinguish the spontaneous culture of free
plan and games which, in the past, was a characteristic artifact of most
societies, including our own. As a result, children are having less
fun and are being deprived of some of their most valuable learning
experiences. Based on an observational study of the behavior of
3,600 children as they left elementary school in a variety of neighbourhoods, he found little evidence of spontaneous play, especially
that involving traditional games. This is in marked contrast to
previous generations who had knowledge of games, the motivation to
play, and the ability to organize and pace their own activities,
without adult instigation or supervision. Thus, it appears that
there should be a greater tendency to let the group select and
establish their own levels of aspiration and the mechanism of attaining the desired end.

In order to reattain this state, Devereux (1971) argued that
we must reduce the amount of television consumption by children,
especially sporting events where the value of success in sport is
clearly displayed and promulgated. In addition, he proposed an
alternative to little league sport, namely backyard sport, as a result
of a concern for "what the ball is doing to the boy, rather than what
the boy is doing to the ball" (Devereux, 1971:11). More specifically,
his description of backyard baseball included the following characteristics: fun; small in scale; minimal risks; freedom; spontaneity;
agent responsive; self-pacing; continual and relevant feedback;
recognition of individual differences in physical and social skills;
minimal evaluation; the ability to handle "poor sports", "cry babies",
little kids, and girls; a winner is not always determined; and, the
game can begin and end at any time. In short, the spontaneous
participation and self-induced control found in the play of previous
generations has been replaced by highly organized participation and
externally-induced control of children's game and sport behavior.

In summary, the almost total adult intrusion into children's
sport has resulted in loss of spontaneity and control by the children.
In the most extreme case of adult interference, adult sports are now
legitimated as children's sport for "mini-men" and "mini-women" in
such activities as, motorcycle racing (Havemann, 1973). If the trend
continues, will roller derby, professional wrestling, horse racing,
motorboat racing, parachute jumping and stock car racing become the
"in" activities for children in the near future?

Declining Involvement In Sport

In recent years, there has been an increasing tendency for children to "drop out" of organized sport programs, or not to become involved at all. For example, a 1973 report by the U.S. Department of Labor indicated that of the two million Little League Baseball players who compete at a given point in time, 400,000 will play high school baseball, about 25,000 will go on to college baseball, approximately 1,200 will be drafted by professional teams, of which about 100 will be invited to the major leagues for even a brief attempt to make a team. A similar drop-out rate exists in Canadian hockey.

While many of these boys are forced to drop out of organized sport when they are "cut" from a team by the coach, an increasing number are removing themselves from organized sport. For example, in a study completed in a western Canadian city, Orlick (1973) interviewed 16 eight-and nine-year-olds who were participating in sport, and 16 who were not. Although one should not generalize from such a limited sample, some interesting trends were found. First, many of the nonparticipants had never tried out for a team because they believed they were not good enough to make the team. That is, fear of failure led to lack of participation. Among those who dropped out, the most common reason given was that "they never let me play" (Orlick, 1973:12). He also reported that many children would like sport to be scaled down to their level with respect to the size of the playing areas, the length of games, the amount of physical contact, and a greater opportunity for playing as opposed to sitting and standing. He concluded that many children have been "turned off" by sport at eight or nine years of age and that if participation is to be maximized, then the experience must be fun, positive, and rewarding, with less emphasis on winning. Perhaps, as Sherif (1971) suggests, there should be a shift to an emphasis on degree of success, rather than on the dichotomous "win" or "lose" situation that presently exists. Similarly, Loy (1973) speaks of a shift from a success orientation (winning for winning's sake) to a satisfaction orientation (sport for sport's sake).

More recently, Guppy (1974) found that by grade seven, only three percent of the males and four percent of the females who had participated in sport at one time had stopped. However, there were a considerable number who stopped participating in a specific type of organized sport. For example, 39 percent of the males and 30 percent of the females ceased participation in inter-school sport. Of these, 75 percent of the males and 50 percent of the females continued to be involved in organized sport in the community. Furthermore, all but ten percent of the inter-school competitive dropouts continued to play intramural sport. The corresponding drop-out rates in community sport were 13 percent for males and 14 percent for females. Most of these individuals continued to participate at either the inter-school or intramural level. Thus, although there appears to be a high drop-out rate, it may reflect a shift of involvement from one level of organized sport to another, rather than a complete withdrawal from the role of athlete. Therefore parents and coaches should be aware that a child may drop out at one level for a variety of reasons, but he may continue to be involved at another level.

Three additional reasons for declining involvement may be:
(1) the verbal attack on organized sport by sport anti-heroes (eg.,
Meggyesy, Sauer) who have retired from professional sport because of
the dehumanizing aspects; (2) a changing status system wherein the
role of athlete may not be the way, or the only way, to attain status
or prestige in the peer group; and, (3) the increasing emphasis on
all-star teams in urban centres wherein teams are not neighbourhood-
based but community-based. In this latter situation, the individual
establishes only a few close relationships with individuals on the
team as they meet only in the sport milieu and then each returns to
his neighbourhood gang. While there is no empirical data to support
these claims, observation of the minor league scene suggests that
these may be contributing factors, especially in large urban centres.

Sport and Social Criticism

One of the most conspicuous features of the past decade has
been the amount of criticism directed toward the "establishment" in
contemporary society. Critics, usually subsumed under the heading of
the New Left, radicals or the counter-culture, have called for an
examination and revision of the prevailing societal norms and values
(cf. Bookchin, 1971; Reich, 1971; Neville, 1972; Roszak, 1972). Until
recently sport has enjoyed a semi-religious stature in society. At
one time or another it has been depicted as an agent of democratization (sport as the great leveller), a vehicle for upward social
mobility (as exemplified by Jackie Robinson and Mickey Mantle), as
a medium for character building and as an arena which is functional
for the cathartic release of hostility and aggression. In light of
the problems discussed in the preceding section it is not surprising
that sport has also come under the scrutiny of social critics.
Contemporary "jock-rakers" have therefore examined the values and
norms which have legitimized sport in the past (cf. Edwards, 1969;
Schecter, 1970; Barnes, 1971; Meggyesy, 1971; Scott, 1971; Hoch, 1972;
Kidd and Macfarlane, 1972; Shaw, 1972).

These critics claim that many of the alleged benefits of participation in sport are nothing more than myths which have been
employed to justify the existence of organized competitive sport.
They contend that there is as much sexism (Hart, 1971; Edwards, 1972;
Ulrich, 1973) and racism (Edwards, 1969, 1973) in sport as in other
social institutions. They also suggest that coaches may remove (i.e.,
"cut") undesirable or deviant athletes from the system. This implies
that the "survivors" already possess specific personality traits in
spite of, rather than because of sport involvement (Ogilvie and Tutko,
1971).

Sport critics have also strongly argued that the intrinsic
rewards of sport participation have been eradicated. As Stone (1972:
2) stated, play has become work since the masses view athletes (both
young and old, amateur and professional) as commodities who are
expected to give expert performances. Similarly, Ingham and Loy
(1973), contend that, as a social institution, sport has become
increasingly rationalized and bureaucratized to the point where
instrumental and utilitarian values have superseded expressive values.

Recently, Scott (1973) synthesized the various "sport ethics" which have arisen in recent years. The Lombardian ethic (typified by the "win-at-all-costs" syndrome) has been challenged by the counter-culture ethic. The stance of the latter is opposed to what it feels are the authoritarian, professionalized, élitist aspects of the former and favours the substitution of cooperation for competition in sport. But as Scott notes, the counter-culture philosophy completely misinterprets the dynamics of contemporary competitive sport when it eschews the importance of victory - "It is just as wrong to say winning isn't anything as it is to say winning is the only thing" (Scott, 1973:74). Scott further argues that the "radical ethic" presents a more humanistic perspective of sport. This orientation attempts to synthesize the other two approaches while simultaneously eliminating their abuses and excesses. In short, the "radical ethic" adheres to the principle of victory through athletic excellence but shuns all dehumanizing techniques which are employed to attain it.

While most people associated with physical activity would certainly agree with Scott's point of view, concerned individuals must ask how realistic they may be with respect to the probability of sport becoming "radical". Scott himself, for instance, contended that sport is a mere reflection of dominant cultural values and if the prevailing societal values are dehumanizing then the values of institutions within that society will be also dehumanizing. As implied throughout this paper, the values and norms which a child encounters in the ludic world are isomorphic to those in society at large. To quote Kenyon (1972:41), "Thus sport can hardly be claimed as a shaper of society. Ignoring this fact is failing to recognize that: as society goes, so goes sport".

In summary, there exist in sport, opportunities to eliminate sexual inequality and aggression but unless these phenomena are alleviated at the macro level, it is unlikely that a "greening" of sport will occur since historically, sport has not been an innovative, progressive agent. As Hoch noted:

> There is, of course, no such thing as jock
> liberation, apart from the more general
> cultural revolution in society as a whole,
> apart from black liberation, women's liberation,
> the students' and workers' control movement.
> The cultural revolution in sports is nothing
> more nor less than the reflection of those
> larger movements in society as a whole. It
> can be no more successful than their combined
> effectiveness (Hoch, 1972:211).

SUMMARY AND CONCLUSIONS

In summary, this paper outlines the social structure in which the games and sport of children occur; describes the process whereby children become involved in sport, including the social attributes which influence this process; discusses the social outcomes of involvement in the ludic milieu; and, describes current social problems inherent in the child's sport and game milieu.

Based on the review, the following conclusions concerning children's involvement in sport appear warrented. First, the social influences to which the child is exposed early in life determine the type of sport they get involved in, the type of experiences which they encounter while involved, the degree to which they adopt sport as part of their lifestyle in later years, and the ultimate level of success they may attain in a given sport. More specifically, interaction with social systems such as the family, peer group, school and the mass media early in life facilitate the learning of sport roles which may be enacted to varying degrees throughout life. Furthermore, the learning of sport roles is greatly influenced by ascribed social attributes such as the social class of the parents which influences the child's opportunity set for participation and consumption, the ordinal position of a particular individual, and the geographical locale in which they spend their childhood years.

A second major conclusion is that game and sport involvement during childhood is important for learning social skills in general, but more specifically for sex-role identification, for developing self-esteem, and for acquiring achievement values. Each of these is influenced by the religion, socioeconomic status and socialization practices of the parents.

In spite of the many beneficial outcomes of involvement in games and sport, deviant or nonnormative behavior may also be learned in the child's ludic milieu. As a result, it can be concluded that: first, overt aggression is often present in organized sport and that this aggressive behavior is socially-induced. Second, there is an increasing tendency for children's sport to be dominated by adults who impose their goals and norms on the child's system; and third, there is a trend toward declining involvement in some forms of organized sport by children, perhaps because of the emphasis on success rather than satisfaction in performance. In short, there are both social benefits and social problems inherent in the world of children's sport.

References*

Aberle, D.F. and K.D. Naegele. 1966 "Raising Middle-Class Sons."
Pp. 97 - 107 in A. Inkeles (ed.), Readings in Modern Sociology.
  Englewood Cliffs, New Jersey: Prentice-Hall Inc.

Adams, B. 1972 "Birth Order: A Critical Review."
  Sociometry. 35: 411 - 439.

Albinson, J.G. 1973 "Professionalized Attitudes of Volunteer Coaches
Toward Playing a Game."
  International Review of Sport Sociology. (2) 9: 77 - 88.

Allen, D. 1972 "Self-Concept and The Female Participant." Pp. 35 - 54
in D. Harris (ed.), Women and Sport: A National Research Conference.
  Penn State HPER Series No. 2. The Pennsylvania State University.

Angeloni, R. 1973 "Does Sport Make Men Out of Women?"
  Sport and Fitness Instructor. 2 (December): 11.

Ardrey, R. 1961
  African Genesis. New York: Dell Publishing.

Aries, P. 1962 Centuries of Childhood.
  New York: Vintage Books.

Bachman, J. 1970 Youth in Transition, Vol. 2: The Impact of Family
Background and Intelligence on Tenth-Grade Boys.
  Ann Arbor, Michigan: Braun-Brumfield, Inc.

Bandura, A. and R. Walters. 1963 Social Learning and Personality
Development.
  New York: Holt, Rinehart, and Winston.

Barnes, L. 1971 The Plastic Orgasm.
  Toronto: McClelland and Stewart Ltd.

Beisser, A. 1967 The Madness in Sport.
  New York: Appleton-Century-Crofts.

Bend, E. 1971 "Some Potential Dysfunctional Effects of Sports Upon
Socialization." A paper presented at the Third International Symposium on the Sociology of Sport, Waterloo, Ontario.

Berkowitz, L. 1962 Aggression: A Social Psychological Analysis.
  New York: McGraw-Hill Book Company.

Berryman, J. and J. Loy. 1971 "Democratization of Intercollegiate
Sports In the Ivy League."
  A paper presented at the Third International Symposium on the
  Sociology of Sport, Waterloo, Ontario.

---

* The unpublished material listed in this section is available in
   SSIRS, an information retrieval system for the Sociology of Sport.
   Interested readers should write to SSIRS, Faculty of Human Kinetics
   and Leisure Studies, University of Waterloo, Waterloo, Ontario.

Birch, D. and J. Veroff. 1966 Motivation: A Study of Action.
  Belmont, California: Brooks/Cole Publishing Company.

Bookchin, M. 1971 Post-Scarcity Anarchism.
  Berkeley: Ramparts.

Brim, O.G. and S. Wheeler. 1966 Socialization After Childhood.
  New York: John Wiley and Sons, Inc.

Brower, J. 1973 "Little Leagues Mostly For Parents."
  Unpublished study, Department of Sociology, California State
  University at Fullerton.

Brown, R. 1965 Social Psychology.
  London: The Free Press.

Campbell, E.Q. 1969 "Adolescent Socialization." Pp. 821 - 60 in D.A.
  Goslin (ed.), Handbook of Socialization Theory and Research
  Chicago: Rand McNally and Company.

Clarke, A.C. 1956 "The Use of Leisure and Its Relation to Levels of
  Occupational Prestige."
  American Sociological Review. 301 - 7.

Clausen, J.A. 1968 Socialization and Society.
  Boston: Little, Brown and Co.

Coopersmith, S. 1967 The Antecedents of Self-Esteem.
  San Francisco: Freeman.

Devereux, E.C. 1971 "Backyard versus Little League Baseball: Some
  Observations On the Impoverishment of Children's Games in Contemporary
  America."
  A paper presented at the conference on Sport and Social Deviancy,
  Brockport, New York.

Dollard, J., L.W. Doob, N.E. Miller, O.H. Mowrer, and R.R. Sears.
  1939 Frustration and Aggression.
  New Haven, Connecticut: Yale University Press.

Edwards, H. 1969 The Revolt of the Black Athlete.
  New York: The Free Press.

Edwards, H. 1972 "Desegregating Sexist Sport."
  Intellectual Digest. (November): 82 - 3.

Edwards, H. 1973 Sociology of Sport.
  Georgetown, Ontario: Dorsey Press.

Eggleston, J. 1965 "Secondary Schools and Oxbridge Blues."
  British Journal of Sociology. 16: 232 - 42.

Faulkner, R.R. 1971 "Violence, Cameraderie, and Occupational
  Character in Hockey."
  A paper presented at the Conference on Sport and Social Deviancy,
  Brockport, New York.

Frost, R. 1973 "Motivation and Arousal."
A Paper presented at the North-East Section of AAHPER Conference, Buffalo, New York.

Gecas, V. 1971 "Parental Behavior and Dimensions of Adolescent Self-Evaluation."
Sociometry. 34: 466 - 82

Gecas, V., D. Thomas and A. Weigert. 1970 "Perceived Parent-Child Interaction and Boys' Self-Esteem in Two Cultural Contexts."
International Journal of Comparative Sociology. 77: 317 - 24.

Gergen, K. 1971 The Concept of Self.
New York: Holt, Rinehart, and Winston.

Gerstl, J. 1961 "Leisure, Taste, and Occupational Milieu."
Social Problems. 9 (Summer): 54 - 68.

Gilbertson, B. and N. Williamson. 1973a "Sport is Unfair to Women."
(Part 1: Women in Sport.)
Sports Illustrated. 38 (May 28): 88 - 98.

Gilbertson, B. and N. Williamson. 1973b "Are You Being Two-Faced?"
(Part 2: Women In sport.)
Sports Illustrated. 38 (June 4): 44 - 54.

Gilbertson, B. and N. Williamson. 1973c "Programmed to be Losers."
(Part 3: Women in Sport.)
Sports Illustrated. 38 (June 11): 60 - 73.

Gould, D.R. and D.M. Landers. 1971 "Dangerous Sport Participation: A Replication of Nisbett's Birth Order Findings."
A paper presented at the North American Society For the Psychology of Sport and Physical Activity, Houston, Texas.

Greendorfer, S. 1970 "Birthplace of Baseball Players: City Size, State and Region."
Unpublished paper, University of Wisconsin.

Gruneau, R. 1972 "An Analysis of the Socioeconomic Characteristics of The Athletes Who Competed in the 1971 Canada Winter Games."
Unpublished Masters Thesis, University of Calgary.

Guppy, N. 1973 "The Development of Sport Achievement Orientations In Preadolescent Males and Females as a Function of Age, Religiosity, Sport Involvement, and Parental Socialization Practices."
(Mimeographed), University of Waterloo.

Guppy, N. 1974 "The Effect of Selected Socialization Practices On the Sport Achievement Orientations of Male and Female Adolescents."
Unpublished Masters Thesis, University of Waterloo.

Harris, D. 1971 "The Social Self and Competitive Self of the Female Athlete."
A paper presented at the Third International Symposium on the Sociology of Sport, University of Waterloo, Ontario.

Hart, M. 1971 "Sport: Women Sit in the Back of the Bus."
Psychology Today. (October): 64 - 66.

Havemann, E. 1973 "Down Will Come Baby, Cycle and All."
Sports Illustrated. 39 (August 13): 42 - 9.

Heinila, K. 1970 "Survey of the Value Orientation of Finnish Sport
Leaders."
A Paper presented at the Seventh World Congress of Sociology, Varna,
Bulgaria.

Helanko, R. 1957 "Sports and Socialization."
Acta Sociolpgica. 2: 229 - 40.

Hellison, D. 1973 Humanistic Physical Education.
Englewood Cliffs: Prentice-Hall.

Hendry, L. 1972 "Coaches Personality and Social Orientation."
Pp. 438 - 65 In I. Williams and L. Wankel (eds.), Proceedings of the
Fourth Canadian Psycho-Motor Learning and Sports Psychology
Conference.
Ottawa: Fitness and Amateur Sport Directorate, Department of
National Health and Welfare.

Higdon, R. and H. Higdon. 1967 "What Sports for Girls?"
Today's Health. 45: 21 - 3, 74.

Hoch, R. 1972 Rip-Off The Big Game.
Garden City, New York: Doubleday and Company.

Hoffman, A. 1971 "Super-Jock in Decline: Liberating Sport from the
Sexist Stereotypes."
Canadian Dimension. 8: 41 - 42.

Hollingshead, A.B. 1949 Elmtown's Youth.
New York: John Wiley and Sons.

Inbar, M. and C. Stoll. 1968 "Autoletic Behaviour In Socialization."
Report Number 29.
Baltimore: Center for the Study of Social Organization of Schools,
The John Hopkins University.

Ingham, A., J. Loy, and J. Berryman. 1972 "Sport, Socialization and
Dialectics." Pp. 235 - 277 In D. Harris (ed.), Women and Sport:
A National Research Conference.
Penn State HPER Series No. 2. The Pennsylvania State University.

Ingham, A. and J. Loy 1973 "The Social System of Sport: A Humanistic
Perspective."
Quest. 14: 3 - 23.

Jordan, M.L. 1963 "Leisure Time Activities of Sociologists, Attorneys,
Physicists and People at Large From Greater Cleveland."
Sociology and Social Research. 47 (April): 290 - 297.

Keating, J.W. 1972 "Paradoxes in American Athletics." Pp. 17 - 31 in A. Flath (ed.), Athletics in America.
  Corvallis, Oregon: Oregon State University Press.

Kelly, C. 1970 "Socialization Into Sport Among Male Adolescents From Canada, England, and the United States."
  Unpublished Master of Science Thesis, University of Wisconsin.

Kelly, J.R. 1973 "Socialization Toward Leisure: A Developmental Approach."
  A paper presented at the Midwest Sociological Society Meetings, Milwaukee, Wisconsin.

Kemper, T. 1968 "Reference Groups, Socialization and Achievement." American Sociological Review. 33: 31 - 45.

Kenyon, G.S. 1966 "The Significance of Physical Activity As A Function of Age, Sex, Education and Socio-Economic Status of Northern United States Adults."
  International Review of Sport Sociology. 1: 41 - 57.

Kenyon, G.S. 1968 "Sociological Considerations."
  Journal of Health, Physical Education and Recreation. 39 (November - December): 31 - 33.

Kenyon, G.S. 1969 "Sport Involvement: A Conceptual Go and Some Consequences Thereof." Pp. 77 - 84 in G.S. Kenyon (ed.), Aspects of Contemporary Sport Sociology.
  Chicago: The Athletic Institute.

Kenyon, G.S. 1970 "The Use of Path Analysis in Sport Sociology with Special Reference to Involvement Socialization."
  International Review of Sport Sociology. 5: 191 - 203.

Kenyon, G.S. 1972 "Sport and Society: At Odds or in Concert?" Pp. 33 - 44 in A. Flath (ed.), Athletics in America.
  Corvallis, Oregon: Oregon State University Press.

Kenyon, G.S. and B.D. McPherson. 1973 "Becoming Involved in Physical Activity and Sport: A Process of Socialization." Pp. 301 - 332 in G.L. Rarick (ed.), Physical Activity: Human Growth and Development.
  New York: Academic Press.

Kidd, B. and J. Macfarlane. 1972 The Death of Hockey.
  Toronto: New Press.

Knopp, T.B. 1972 "Environmental Determinants of Recreation Behaviour." Journal of Leisure Research. 4 (Spring): 129 - 138.

Landers, D. 1970 "Sibling-Sex Status and Ordinal Position Effects on Females' Sport Participation and Interests."
  Journal of Social Psychology. 80: 247 - 248.

Landers, D. 1972 "The Effects of Ordinal Position and Sibling's Sex on Male's Sport Participation." Pp. 235 - 241, in A.W. Taylor (ed.), Training: Scientific Basis and Application.
  Springfield, Illinois: Charles C. Thomas.

Lea, S. 1973 "Factors Related to the Regional Variability In The Development of Professional Hockey Talent In Canada." Unpublished paper, Department of Kinesiology, University of Waterloo, Waterloo, Ontario.

Lenk, H. 1971 "Sport, Achievement, and the New Left Criticism." A paper presented at the Third International Symposium on the Sociology of Sport, Waterloo, Ontario.

Leventhal, G.S. 1968 "Some Effects of Having a Brother or Sister." A paper presented at the American Psychological Association Meetings, San Francisco.

Levy, M.J. 1952 The Structure of Society. Princeton: Princeton University Press.

Lewis, M. 1972a "Culture and Gender Roles: There's No Unisex in the Nursery." Psychology Today. 5: 54 - 57

Lewis, M. 1972b "Sex Differences in Play Behavior of the Very Young." Journal of Health, Physical Education, and Recreation. 43: 38 - 39.

Lindesmith, P.R. and A.L. Strauss. 1964 "The Social Self." Pp. 206 - 209 in R.W. O'Brien et. al., (eds.), Readings in General Sociology. Boston: Houghton-Mifflin Co.

Lopata, H. 1966 "The Life Cycle of the Social Role of Housewife." Sociology and Social Research. 51: 5 - 22

Lorenz, K. 1966 On Aggression. London: Methuen and Company.

Loy, J.W. 1969 "The Study of Sport and Social Mobility." Pp. 101 - 119 in G.S. Kenyon, (ed.), Aspects of Contemporary Sport Sociology. Chicago: The Athletic Institute.

Loy, J.W. 1973 "Sport For Adults - Athletics For Children: Satisfaction or Success." A paper presented at the Conference on Sport or Athletics: A North American Dilemma, University of Windsor, Windsor, Ontario.

Loy, J. and A. Ingham. 1973 "Play, Games and Sport in the Psychosociological Development of Children and Youth." Pp. 257 - 302 in L. Rarick (ed.), Physical Activity: Human Growth and Development. New York: Academic Press.

Luschen, G. 1969 "Social Stratification and Social Mobility Among Young Sportsmen." Pp. 258 - 276 in J.W. Loy and G.S. Kenyon (eds.), Sport, Culture, and Society. London: Collier-Macmillan.

Lynd, R. and H. Lynd. 1956 Middletown; A Study in American Culture. New York: Harcourt, Brace.

MacDonald, M., G. McGuire, and R. Havinghurst. 1949 "Leisure Activities and the Socio-Economic Status of Children." American Journal of Sociology. 54: 505 - 519

Maloney, T.R. and B. Petrie. 1972 "Professionalization of Attitude
Toward Play Among Canadian School Pupils as a Function of Sex, Grade
and Athletic Participation."
Journal of Leisure Research. 4 (Summer): 184 - 195.

Malumphy, T.M. 1970 "The College Woman Athlete -- Questions and
Tentative Answers."
Quest. 14: 18 - 27.

Mantel, R.C. and L. Vander Velden. 1971 "The Relationship Between
the Professionalization of Attitude Toward Play of Preadolescent Boys
and Participation in Organized Sport."
A paper presented at the Third International Symposium on the
Sociology of Sport, Waterloo, Ontario.

McClelland, D.C. 1961 The Achieving Society.
Princeton: D. Van Nostrand Co., Inc.

McMurtry, J. 1973 "A Case for Killing the Olympics."
Maclean's. 86 (January): 34 - 35, 57 - 58, 60.

McPherson, B.D. 1968 "Psychosocial Factors Accounting for Learning
the Role of Tennis and Hockey Player."
Unpublished Study, University of Wisconsin.

McPherson, B.D. 1972 "Socialization Into the Role of Sport Consumer:
The Construction and Testing of a Theory and Causal Model."
Ph.D. Dissertation, University of Wisconsin.

Mead, G.H. 1934 Mind, Self, and Society.
Chicago: The University of Chicago Press.

Mead, M. 1935 Sex and Temperament in Three Primitive Societies.
New York: Dell.

Meggyesy, D. 1971 Out of Their League.
New York: Paperback Library.

Metheny, E. 1965 "Symbolic Forms of Movement: The Feminine Image in
Sports." Pp. 43 - 56 in Connotations of Movement in Sport and Dance.
Dubuque, Iowa: Wm.C. Brown.

Miller, N.E. 1941 "The Frustration-aggression Hypothesis."
Psychological Review. 48: 337 - 342.

Neville, R. 1972 Play Power.
London: Paladin.

Nisbett, R.E. 1968 "Birth Order and Participation In Dangerous
Sports."
Journal of Personality and Social Psychology. 8: 351 - 353.

Ogilvie, B. and T. Tutko. 1971 "Sport: If You Want to Build
Character Try Something Else."
Psychology Today. (October): 61 - 63.

Orlick, T.D. 1972 "Family Sports Environment and Early Sport
Participation."
  A paper presented at the Fourth Canadian Symposium on Psycho-Motor
  Learning and Sports Psychology, Waterloo.

Orlick, T.D. 1973 "Children's Sports - A Revolution Is Coming."
  C.A.H.P.E.R. 39 (January-February): 12 - 14.

Piaget, J. 1965 The Moral Judgement of the Child.
  New York: The Free Press.

Pudelkiewicz, E. 1970 "Sociological Problems of Sports in Housing
Estates."
  International Review of Sport Sociology. 5: 73 - 103.

Rarick, L. 1973 "Competitive Sports in Childhood and Early
Adolescence." Pp. 364 - 386 in L. Rarick (ed.), Physical Activity:
Human Growth and Development.
  New York: Academic Press.

Rehberg, R. and W. Schafer. 1968 "Participation in Interscholastic
Athletics and College Expectations."
  American Journal of Sociology. 73 (May): 732 - 740.

Reich, C. 1971, The Greening of America.
  New York: Bantam Books,

Ritchie, O. W. and M. Koller. 1964 Sociology of Childhood.
  New York: Appleton-Century-Crofts.

Roberts, J.M. and B. Sutton-Smith 1962 "Childhood Training and Game
Involvement."
  Ethnology. 1: 166 - 185.

Roethlisberger, F.A. 1970 "Socialization of the Elite Gymnast."
  Unpublished Master of Science Thesis, University of Wisconsin.

Rooney, G.F. 1971 "Participation in High School Athletics and Success
at the College and Professional Level."
  A paper presented at the Third International Symposium on the
  Sociology of Sport, Waterloo.

Rosenberg, B.G. and B. Sutton-Smith 1964 "Ordinal Position and Sex
Role Identification."
  Genetic Psychology Monographs. 70: 297 - 328.

Rosenberg, M. 1965 Society and the Adolescent Self-Image.
  Princeton: Princeton University Press.

Rosenberg, M. 1968 "Psychological Selectivity in Self-Esteem
Formation." Pp. 339 - 346 in C. Gordon and K. Gergen (eds.), The Self
in Social Interaction.
  New York: Wiley.

Roszak, T. 1972 Where the Wasteland Ends: Politics and Transcendence
in Post Industrial Society.
  New York: Doubleday.

Sadler, W.A. 1973 "Competition Out of Bounds: Sport in American Life."
  Quest. 19 (January): 124 - 132.

Schachter, S. 1959 The Psychology of Affiliation.
  Stanford: Stanford University Press.

Schafer, W. 1971 "Sport and Youth Counterculture: Contrasting Socialization Themes."
  A paper presented at the Conference on Sport and Social Deviancy, Brockport, New York.

Schecter, L. 1970 The Jocks.
  New York: Paperback Library.

Scott, J. 1971 The Athletic Revolution.
  New York: The Free Press.

Scott, J. 1971 "Sport and the Radical Ethic."
  Quest. 19: 71 - 76.

Sears, R. 1970 "Relations of Early Socialization Experiences to Self-Concept and Gender Role in Middle Childhood."
  Child Development. 41: 267 - 289.

Shaver, P. 1972 "Measurement of Self-Esteem and Related Constructs."
  Pp. 45 - 160 in J. Robinson and P. Shaver (eds.), Measures of Social Psychological Attitudes (Appendix B to Measures of Political Attitudes).
  Ann Arbor, Michigan: Institute for Social Research.

Shaw, G. 1972 Meat on the Hoof.
  New York: Dell.

Sherif, C.W. 1971 "The Social Context of Competition."
  A paper presented at the Conference on Sport and Social Deviancy, Brockport, New York.

Sherif, C.W. 1972 "Females in the Competitive Process."
  A paper presented at the Women and Sport Conference, University Park, Pennsylvania.

Sherif, C.W. and G. Rattray. 1973 "Psychosocial Development and Activity in Middle Childhood (5 - 12 years)."
  A paper presented at the National Conference and Workshop on the Child in Sport and Physical Activity, Queen's University, Kingston, Ontario.

Singer, R. 1972 Coaching Athletics and Psychology.
  New York: McGraw-Hill.

Smith, M.D. 1971 "Aggression In Sport: Toward a Role Approach."
  C.A.H.P.E.R. 37 (January-February): 22 - 25.

Smith, M.D. 1972 "Parents', Peers' and Coach's Sanctions for Assaultive Behaviour in Hockey."
  A paper presented at the Congress: Sport in the Modern World, Munich, Germany.

Snyder, E. 1970 "Aspects of Socialization in Sports and Physical Education."
  Quest. 14 (June): 1 - 7.

Snyder, E. 1973 "High School Athletes and Their Coaches: Education Plans and Advice."
  Sociology of Education. 45: 313 - 325.

Snyder, E. and E. Spreitzer. 1973 "Correlates of Behavioral, Affective, and Cognitive Involvement in Sports."
  A paper presented at the Midwest Sociological Society Meetings, Milwaukee, Wisconsin.

Sofranko, A.J. and M.F. Nolan 1972 "Early-Life Experiences and Adult Sports Participation."
  Journal of Leisure Research. 4 (Winter): 6 - 18.

Soule, G.H. 1966 Time For Living.
  New York: Viking Press.

Spencer, H. 1896 The Principles of Psychology.
  New York: Appleton.

Stone, G. 1955 "American Sports: Play and Dis-play."
  Chicago Review. 9: 83 - 100.

Stone, G. 1957 "Some Meanings of American Sport."
  Proceedings of the College Physical Education Association. Pp. 6 - 29.

Stone, G. 1962 "Appearance and the Self." Pp. 86 - 118 in A. Rose (ed.), Human Behavior and Social Process.
  Boston: Houghton-Mifflin.

Stone, G. 1969 "Some Meanings of American Sport: An Extended View." Pp. 5 - 16 in G.S. Kenyon (ed.), Aspects of Contemporary Sport Sociology.
  Chicago: The Athletic Institute.

Stone, G. 1972 Games, Sport and Power.
  New Brunswick, New Jersey: Transaction Books.

Sutton-Smith, B., J.M. Roberts, and R.M. Kozela. 1963 "Game Involvement in Adults."
  The Journal of Social Psychology. 60: 15 - 30.

Talamini, J. 1973 "School Athletics: Public Policy versus Practice." Pp. 163 - 182 in J. Talamini and C. Page (eds.), Sport and Society: An Anthology.
  Toronto: Little, Brown, and Company.

Tiger, L. 1971 Men in Groups.
  London: Panther.

Toyama, J.S. 1971 "The Language of Sport: A Study of the Knowledge of Sport Terminology As a Function of Exposure To the Mass Media."
  Unpublished Master of Science Thesis, University of Wisconsin.

Ulrich, C.   1973 "She Can Play as Good as Any Boy."
  Phi Delta Kappan. (October):   113 - 117.

Vaz, E.   1972 "The Culture of Young Hockey Players: Some Initial
Observations."   Pp. 222 - 234 in A.W. Taylor (ed.), Training:
Scientific Basis and Application.
  Springfield, Illinois: Charles C Thomas.

Vaz, E. and D. Thomas.   1973 "What Price Victory: An Analysis of
Minor Hockey League Players' Attitudes Towards Winning."
  Unpublished paper, Department of Sociology, University of Waterloo,
  Waterloo, Ontario.

Webb, H.   1969 "Professionalization of Attitudes Toward Play Among
Adolescents."   Pp. 161 - 178 in G.S. Kenyon (ed.), Aspects of
Contemporary Sport Sociology.
  Chicago: The Athletic Institute.

Weber, M.   1930 The Protestant Ethic and the Spirit of Capitalism.
  London: George Allen and Unwin.

Weinberg, S.K. and H. Arond.   1952 "The Occupational Culture of the
Boxer."
  American Journal of Sociology. 57: 460 - 469.

Wylie, R.   1961 The Self-Concept: A Critical Survey of Pertinent
Research.
  Lincoln: University of Nebraska Press.

Wylie, R.   1968 "The Present Status of Self-Theory."   Pp. 728-787 in
E. Borgatta and W. Lambert (eds.), Handbook of Personality Theory and
Research.
  Chicago: Rand-McNally.

Yoesting, D.R. and D.L. Burkhead.   1973 "Significance of Childhood
Recreation Experience on Adult Leisure Behaviour: An Exploratory
Analysis."
  Journal of Leisure Research. 5 (Winter):   25 - 36.

Zigler, E. and I. Child.   1969 "Socialization."   Pp. 450 - 589 in
G. Lindzey and E. Aronson (eds.), The Handbook of Social Psychology,
Volume 3.   Reading, Massachusetts: Addison Wesley.

Zoble, J.   1972 "Femininity and Achievement in Sports."
  Paper presented at the Conference on Women and Sport, University
  Park, Pennsylvania.

Motor learning aspects

CONCEPTS OF MOTOR LEARNING: IMPLICATIONS FOR SKILL DEVELOPMENT IN CHILDREN

by G. Lawrence Rarick,
University of California, Berkeley.

Man reacts to environmental stimuli through his neuromuscular system. Some neuromuscular responses are reflex in nature, but the vast majority are learned. Some become completely automated early in life, others become partially automated, while some require varying degrees of attentive direction throughout life.

The early years of life, particularly the periods of infancy and early childhood, are devoted largely to developing movement patterns which might be categorized as self-sufficiency skills, such as walking, eating and dressing, while others fall into the category of skills used in the child's world of play. Few of these could by any stretch of the imagination be called sports skills, although some entail movement patterns that are strikingly similar to those used in certain sports. Thus, the foundation for many of the fine and gross motor skills that the individual acquires during the school years is developed early in life. In our society the organization of these relatively crude movement responses into coordinated movement patterns constitutes a part of the early formal education of the child. The range and diversity of such responses in the young child are astonishing, amounting within a 24-hour period, according to Barker and Wright (1958), to as many as 2,200 distinct transactions using over 660 behavior objects.

Products versus Processes

Learning may be defined as a change in behavior or improvement in performance coming directly as a result of practice in which there is the intent to learn. Learning is usually measured by the results the performer achieves, i.e., the product of his efforts, rather than by an assessment of how he executed the skill. The reason for this is obvious --- the ultimate payoff is the end product, a performance score, or a performance rating. This is usually a relatively simple measurement to obtain. On the other hand, for the learner and for those concerned with helping him achieve his learning goals, the processes involved in the skill assume major importance. Many motor skills involve complicated movements of lever systems through the coordinated action of many muscle groups. The strategy the learner utilizes and the steps he goes through in acquiring the most appropriate form for yielding consistently good performance is of great significance in all skill learning. Unfortunately assessments of these dimensions of motor learning have received only limited attention. Within limits we know what is involved in skilled performance, but we are not so sure of the behavioral adaptations the individual goes through in improving his performance.

In order to appreciate the complex nature of motor learning, it should be recognized that a motor response is never conducted twice under exactly the same conditions nor is it performed twice in exactly the same way. Sensory input varies with different movements, as do physiological conditions, stress, and fatigue. Even so, a particular motor skill has a characteristic style or movement pattern that makes it relatively easy to identify. What the individual is attempting to establish is some constancy and predictability of response under conditions that are never quite the same. Clearly, with each attempt, the performer is bringing to bear his earlier experiences in his effort to meet the demands of the situation. This is accomplished, according to Smith and Smith (1966) by a performer's cybernetic control system which supports all motor learning.

Cybernetic theory holds that motor learning never starts at behavior zero. It starts with organized patterns of behavior, feedback regulated responses which can be modified with practice. Smith and Smith (1966) considers motor learning to be the process of reorganizing feedback regulated neuromotor patterns in response to new environmental settings. Such a system can (1) generate movement toward a defined goal; (2) detect errors; and (3) utilize the error to redirect the system. In addition, other feedback mechanisms such as those from vision and the organs of balance provide essential information for motor learning. Experiments with delayed visual and auditory feedback and the disturbing role such delays play in motor behavior and in motor learning provide testimony of the importance of feedback in motor learning (Smith and Smith, 1962).

For the young child it is clear that a wide range of sensory motor experience is needed if he is to have a repertoire of movement patterns upon which to draw. It is not reasonable to think that previous experience means nothing to the child as he attempts to learn a new skill. He brings to the new learning situation a vast array of motor experiences and feeling states, all of which bear upon the learning situation. The broader the range of these experiences under conditions that have been satisfying the better the chances for learning.

Age, Maturity, and Motor Learning

It is well known that motor skills improve with age in the young child, but it is equally clear that the learning of skills in the very young is not independent of maturational level. The emergence of basic movement patterns in both animals and humans in the early period of development follows a well defined and orderly sequence (Coghill, 1929; Gesell and Ames, 1940; Shirley, 1931). Efforts to speed up the appearance or the functioning of these phylogenetic traits through special training has met with little success (McGraw, 1935). Similarly, research on skill learning of humans in later infancy and early childhood clearly demonstrated the futility of attempting to bring about skill learnings prior to the establishment of maturational readiness (Gesell and Thompson, 1929; Hicks, 1931; and Hilgard, 1932).

The above supports the belief that there are "critical periods" in the development of the preschool child when a particular neuro-muscular skill is most susceptible to modification. Unfortunately the influence of maturation on motor skill acquisition during the school years is less clear. With increasing age performance scores improve, but how much of this is the result of growth and general use and how much is the result of planned experiences is not at this point known. Isolated bits of data provide only limited information on the most opportune time to introduce skills into the program.

The evidence now indicates that mature patterns of throwing behavior can be attained by the time the child is 6-1/2 years old (Wild, 1938) and that improvements in performance resulting from instruction may occur as early as 5 to 6 years. Dusenberry (1952) in studying the effects of specific training in ball throwing of young boys and girls reported that three weeks of practice (two sessions weekly) elicited little if any improvement in 3-and 4-year-old boys and girls, but did result in performance gains in the 5-and 6-year-old children, the gains of the boys being substantially greater than that of the girls.

Interpretations of the literature on generalized learning and learning rates as a function of age differ markedly. McGeoch and Irion (1952) conclude that the rate of learning increases with age until approximately age 20, whereas Munn (1954) in his interpretation of the research holds that learning is not a function of age. Only limited research has been published on age as a factor in the learning of gross motor skills and the research that has been published has for the most part not employed sports skills. This is not surprising since those who are scientifically studying learning logically select tasks with which the learner is unfamiliar, and also tasks upon which learning can be expected to occur within a few trials or within a limited period of time. Evidence in support of age independence in motor learning is provided by Henry and Nelson (1956) who demonstrated that there was no significant age difference in the rate of learning rapid arm movement tasks in boys, ages 10 and 15 years. Similarly, Bachman (1961) reported that the rate of learning two novel gross motor skills (the stabilometer and the ladder climb) was independent of age and sex in the age range 6 to 26 years. Alderman (1968) using a speed of arm movement task (Rho task) with 10-and 14-year-olds found that while boys performed the task faster than girls, the amount of learning showed no age or sex differences.

It should be kept in mind that the above investigations involve skills that are not strictly sport-type skills and the experiments were limited to a single learning session. In a six-week experiment in which daily instruction was given in jumping and throwing skills the percentage gains achieved by fifth grade children on measures of these skills were significantly greater than those made by second graders (Taylor, 1953). At the present time we simply do not have sufficient evidence to pinpoint the role that maturation plays in learning of sport-type skills.

In view of the complex movement patterns involved in certain sports and the strength and power requirements in others it would seem self-evident that young school age children are not yet sufficiently mature to undertake these skills. The consideration is in part one of economy of learning. By waiting a year or two to involve the child, the added maturity may result in much more rapid learning and likewise lessen the danger of loss of interest in the activity.

As children get older they become stronger, but the gains in strength (maximum volitional strength) are proportionately greater than the gains in muscle cross section. There is evidence to indicate that this disproportionate gain in strength is not solely a function of qualitative changes in muscle, but may, in fact, be due to learning.

In other words, the changes observed in muscular strength coming from training can in part be attributed to learning (Hilsop, 1963; Asmussen and Heebøll-Nielson, 1955). If indeed, this is true, then the general superiority in strength of boys as compared to girls is not necessarily attributable solely to quantitative and qualitative differences in muscle tissue. The difference may, of course, be due to differences in motivation at the time of testing. It is widely recognized that strength may increase without proportional muscular hypertrophy (McMorris and Elkins, 1954), thus indicating that central as well as peripheral factors are significant in bringing about increases in strength from training.

Basic Abilities and Motor Learning

Children like adolescents and adults enter new learning situations with many specific motor skills and a group of more generalized abilities. The learner's previous experience and his background of more generalized motor abilities significantly influence learning and learning rates. Fleishman (1966) distinguishes between "ability" and "skill". He refers to an ability as a more general trait which is itself the product of learning. Skill he considers to be more limited, namely task oriented. The learner, he holds, utilizes these more generalized traits or abilities in acquiring specific skills. Thus, knowledge about the basic components of gross motor behavior that are relevant to learning a particular sport skill should be helpful in predicting the rate of learning and the ultimate level of proficiency in this skill. Reynolds (1952) has hypothesized that the learner's performance during the early stages of learning is to a great extent dependent on previous experiences, thus reflecting many abilities. As learning takes place, the learner's performance depends more and more upon his experience with the task at hand. In the later stages of learning the responses become highly task specific.

Fleishman (1954) has shown through factor analytic techniques that the quantitative pattern of abilities that differentiate individual levels of performance during learning changes with practice. This indicates that individual differences on a task following specified amounts of practice are likely to depend more on some abilities and less on others than was the case initially. As the task becomes learned a factor specific to the task emerges.

In one of the few studies which has focused attention on the learning of sports skills with children Brace (1946) provided evidence to indicate that motor learning of a sport type skill is dependent more on certain basic athletic abilities of speed, power, and strength than on the ability to learn stunt-type skills. The evidence to date, while not conclusive, would support the general observation that individual differences in learning ability depend to no small degree upon the fundamental abilities the learner brings to the task. Exactly what basic abilities are needed to support learning of particular tasks would, it would seem obvious, be dependent on the task. Our own research (Rarick and Dobbins, 1972) indicates there is a well defined structure of some 10 basic motor abilities that in young children accounts for approximately 75 percent of the variance in the performance of a broad range of fine and gross motor tasks.

Length and Distribution of Practice Sessions.

Research has generally shown that distributed practice produces better results than massed practice. Massing practice during the initial stages of learning with increasingly longer intervals between practice has proved to be effective (Harmon and Miller, 1950). Frequent and relatively brief practice sessions have been shown to result in more rapid learning of motor skills than longer working periods at less frequent intervals (Knapp, Dixon, and Lazier, 1958; Knapp and Dixon, 1950; and Franklin and Brozek, 1947). Singer (1965), however, found that massed and relatively massed practice resulted in better performance of a novel basketball skill than distributed practice.

The decline in performance with the massing of trials is according to Hull (1951) due to the fatigue coming from the practice itself. This performance decrement he calls reactive inhibition. Hull holds that reactive inhibition is a function of the amount of work done. Upon cessation of practice its effects are gradually dissipated. It should be pointed out, however, that recent studies (Alderman, 1965; Schmidt, 1969) indicate that while the interpolation of fatiguing tasks during learning impairs performance, it does not seem to adversely affect learning itself. Studies of this kind have not, however, been conducted over sufficiently long periods of time to assess the effects on motor learning where the fatiguing practices are continued day after day.

Retention of Motor Skills

It is widely recognized that motor skills that are overlearned are retained longer than verbal skills. The skills we repeat many times each day over periods of months and years are over-learned and are retained for long periods without practice. Sports skills, however, are usually seasonal. Yet, experience has taught us that performance may be remarkably good the first day of the new season, not infrequently better than at the close of the preceding season. This improvement in performance which comes after a period of no overt practice has been termed "reminiscence" (Hovland, 1938). It may occur after a short period of rest, but in sport skills its effects are most dramatic after long periods without practice.

The results of research are not in complete agreement regarding the degree of skill retention following extended periods without practice. Retention of as much as 94 percent of the best performance on five gross motor skills after intervals without practice of 9 to 15 months was observed by Purdy and Lockhart (1962). Reminiscence of significance in one or more of the five tasks was noted in almost 90 percent of the cases. It should be pointed out that the retention estimate was based on several minutes of relearning and hence would be an overestimate of net retention.

Data on retention of skill on balance type tasks are contro-versial. Ryan (1965) reported rather large losses in stabilometer performance in adult males (22 - 37 years of age) 3 months, 6 months, and 12 months after initial learning. The group tested 3 months after cessation of practice showed 50% retention, whereas the group without practice for 12 months retained only 19%. "Good performers" and "poor performers" had approximately the same retention. However, the 12-month group took longer to relearn the skill than the 3-month group. In an earlier study Ryan (1962) found that shorter periods without practice (3, 5, 7, and 21 days) showed greater retention on the stabilometer. The retention was high and approximately the same for the four spaced groups. Retention on the pursuit rotor for the same periods without practice was higher than that on the stabilometer, possibly due, according to the investigator, to a different distribution of practice on the two tasks ... a greater massing of practice on the pursuit rotor. Meyers (1967) using senior high school girls found almost complete retention of partial learning (50% of the potential performance level) of the Bachman ladder climb after 13 weeks of no practice.

Of general interest is the question of retention of skill as a function of initial performance level. Carron and Marteniuk (1970) reported that skill retention on the stabilometer was not different after layoffs of 1 to 7 days for groups that varied in ititial ability. After 14 days of no practice, however, the retention of those with initially superior ability was the greater.

In sports and striking types of skills the research (Fox and Lamb, 1962; Fox and Young, 1962; Rivenes and Mawhinney, 1968) is not in complete accord, the results ranging from slight to almost complete retention. There would seem to be no question, but that skill retention does occur after long periods without practice, but the research suggests the extent of it varies with the time without practice and with the skill. One might ask if it varies with the skill or with the extent of mastery of the skill prior to the period of no practice. On the basis of what we now know, probably the latter.

Transfer of Training

Transfer of training has generally been held to be a function of the extent to which elements are common to the initial learning task and to the task to be learned. The ease of learning a new motor skill should therefore depend upon how easily the learner can adapt previously learned movement patterns to the new situation. Negative as well as positive transfer can occur depending on the stimulus similarity and the response similarity in the tasks. One would logically expect there to be positive transfer from learning to roller skate to learning to ice skate. On the other hand, a change from driving a car with automatic shift to one with a standard gear shift usually results in interference, or negative transfer. In the latter case, we are dealing with a sub-habit on the transfer task which is materially different than the sub-habit on the initial task, the remainder of the response patterns being highly similar.

While a considerable body of research has been done on transfer of conceptual and manipulative abilities only limited research has been done on transfer of gross motor skills and none with children. There is some evidence to indicate that students exposed to a basic skills program exhibit greater success in later sports activities than a control group (Broer, 1955). In general, the published research indicates that for the most part motor learning tends to be highly specific and the extent of positive transfer is limited. One would hypothesize that those sports in which similar movement patterns are used should show transfer. Published data on this are not available. In fact the evidence we now have suggests that activities involving similar elements (tennis and badminton) should not be learned concurrently and the best procedure for learning skills with similar elements is to focus learning on one exclusively and practice the other at a later time (Nelson, 1957).

The question of whether the learner should practice a precision skill slowly in the initial period of learning and gradually work for speed is a matter of concern to those interested in skill development. The evidence is reasonably clear that there are rather fundamental differences between slow and fast movements (Stetson, 1923; Peters and Wenborne, 1936). The research generally indicates that if the ultimate goal is speed with accuracy, speed should be emphasized in the early stages of learning (Fulton, 1942; Solley, 1952). A compromise suggested by Ragsdale (1950) is speed with control.

Specificity of Learning

Are individuals who show proficiency in learning one type of motor task likely to be proficient in learning other types of skills? Over the years physical educators have had rather strong convictions that there is an underlying "motor talent" that some possess that is missing in others. There is little evidence to support this point of view for the research strongly indicates that performance capabilities and motor learning abilities are task specific. For example, Bachman (1961) using two novel tasks, the stabilometer and the free-standing vertical ladder found that motor learning on these two tasks was highly specific. Among the subjects the greatest amount of communality in learning the two tasks was among males 6 to 11 years of age ... representing less than 3% of generality. Relationships between static strength and speed of movement of an unloaded segment are also low (Henry, 1960) as are the relationships between reaction time, movement time and speed of movement (Lotter, 1961; Mendryk, 1960). On the other hand, there is research (Rarick and Dobbins, 1972) which indicates that there is greater generality than indicated above among gross motor tasks having elements of similarity such as jumping and running performance. For example, correlations between a short dash and jumping performance (broad jump or vertical jump) in young boys and young girls, ages 6 to 9 year ranges between .74 and .80. Correlations between performance on these skills in adolescents is on the average only slightly lower.

There is some evidence to indicate that task specificity becomes more clearly defined with advancing age. Using a peg shift task and the Rho task Todor (1972) reported that six, eleven, and eighteen-year-old subjects exhibited 23%, 6%, and 10% common variance, respectively, on the two tasks prior to practice. The effect of practice on the two tasks was quite dramatic in the six-year-olds, reducing the common variance to 5%. Thus, Todor concluded that task generality was markedly reduced as a result of practice in the younger group. In the older group on the other hand, the common variance on the two tasks increased to 28% and 25%, respectively, indicating that once the underlying abilities reached a state of relative invariance, practice did not decrease the percentage of generality.

Individual Differences in Motor Learning

Practice ordinarily results in performance changes. The fact that learners bring to the learning situation a vast array of individual differences in abilities that have an effect on learning would indicate that individuals would differ substantially in their learning characteristics. This has been demonstrated repeatedly on a wide variety of motor learning tasks. Since learning is accomplished through a series of trials one has only to correlate the first trial with each succeeding trial to learn that the correlation coefficients systematically drop with succeeding trials. In other words, as practice continues the performance levels of the learners are changing at different rates.

In most instances variance, or individual differences in performance increase with practice (Woodrow, 1938). Clearly, some profit more from practice than others. Under conditions where reasonably skilled performers are practicing, some may be approximating a ceiling performance level making gains for them more difficult than for those performing at a lower level. In such instances variance may decrease with practice. The increase in variance that accompanies learning clearly makes the teacher's task more difficult.

Knowledge of Results

A variety of terms have been used interchangeably with knowledge of results, namely information feedback, reinforcing feedback, reinforcement, and reward. Most studies on knowledge of results, as in the case of most motor learning studies, have been done with tracking, manipulation, and positioning studies. Few have used the skills or abilities common to our profession.

In all motor learning tasks information feedback is the source of error detection and provides the cues for error correction. How effectively one uses information feedback is obviously all important in motor learning. Current thinking likens the central nervous system to an electronic computer, in that it has the capabilities of rapidly sorting and channeling input in a way to guarantee correct output. A big difference is in the programming, which is essentially learning. While learning is a type of programming it is not very efficient. In motor learning the learner seeks through his own conscious efforts to make his movements fit the requirements of the task. This requires continuous adjustments and readjustments of the timing and magnitude of muscular force. Many of his generalized movements (already computerized) the learner will want to utilize, modifying them to meet the demands of the new task. Information feedback will provide him with the necessary cues from the external environment and the proprioceptive cues from the muscles, tendons, and joints. The fewer the details that have to be attended to the more rapid will be the learning. Ultimately the skill will become almost completely automatic. Attention can then be directed to the task and not to details.

Adams (1971) has proposed a closed-loop theory of motor learning which is error-centered, with a reference mechanism against which response feedback may be compared for error detection and correction. He hypothesizes that the central nervous system establishes a "neural model" or an "image" with which the response is matched. The model is a result of trials and reinforcements and its formation occurs as learning takes place. When the feedback from the response matches the model, there has been a successful behavioral sequence, and the learner knows that a successful performance has resulted. Bernstein (1967) proposed a similar concept in which the feedback from a response enters a comparator in the motor command center of the brain where it can be tested against the ideal response.

Support for the closed-loop theory is provided by the research of Laszo and Bairstow (1971) who cut off tactile and kinesthetic sensations (by nerve compression block) under conditions in which subjects were asked to reproduce designated letters of the alphabet with the index finger. The evidence clearly indicated that in the absence of sensory information improvement in performance did not occur.

The importance of withholding speed and accuracy feedback on the overarm throwing behavior of boys ages 14 to 16 is illustrated by the research of Malina (1969). While both speed and accuracy were both affected negatively as a result of withholding information feedback during the 12 practice sessions, the effect was greater on accuracy than on speed. The group receiving both speed and accuracy information improved in both parameters of performance. The latter experienced difficulty in simultaneously improving both speed and accuracy during the early practice sessions, with speed improving and accuracy remaining fairly stable. As practice continued accuracy improved while speed remained moderately stable. The adverse effect of delayed information feedback on a tossing skill is illustrated by the work of Lavery (1964).

Gentile (1972) building on Poulton's (1957) concept of "open" and "closed" skills stresses the importance of structuring the environment during the initial stages of learning to maximize closed skills learning. This means enhancement of constant regulatory conditions so that the learner will not be distracted by stimuli unrelated to the task, nor will be placed in a situation that may require a choice of responses (open skills). It means that the goal is clear to the learner and that the requirements of the learning task can be easily comprehended.

Using video-taped feedback with young women performing a modification of the classical fencing lunge for accuracy under closed and open environment conditions, Del Rey (1971) found that those exposed to the closed skill approximated closely the imposed form and had higher accuracy scores after 54 trials spread over 3 days than those exposed to the open skill.

Knowledge of results provides the learner with concrete evidence of the progress he is making toward his learning goal. In this sense it is a powerful motivating force in learning. It may also be the means whereby the individual reassesses his goals in a realistic and meaningful way.

Concluding Comments

The volume of literature in the area of motor learning is extensive and the research cited here is only one person's point of view as to what is relevant to the theme of this conference. It is evident that only a small segment of the research on motor learning has focused attention on the skills and abilities involved in sports and physical activity programs as we know them. This is not surprising since until recently only a few physical educators have been seriously involved in research on motor learning.

Much of the research of our own people has followed the pattern of psychologists, utilizing skills that are far removed from those employed in sports. This is understandable in view of the controls needed in learning experiments, but the question remains regarding the extent to which the findings from such experiments can be applied to our field! One of the greatest research needs is for exploration of the motor learning abilities of the child in the age range 5 to 15 years. Very little research of consequence has been done here. Experience continues to be our guide. I believe that you would agree that this is not enough.

References

1. Adams, J.A. "A Closed Loop Theory of Motor Learning,"
   J. of Motor Behavior, 3:111 – 150, 1971.

2. Alderman, Richard B. "Age and Sex Differences in Learning and
   Performance of an Arm Speed Motor Task,"
   Res. Quart., 39:428 – 431, 1968.

3. Alderman, Richard B. "Influence of Local Fatigue on Speed and
   Accuracy in Motor Learning,"
   Res. Quart., 36:131 – 140, 1965

4. Asmussen, E. and Kr. Heebøll-Nielson. "A Dimensional Analysis
   of Physical Performance and Growth of Boys,"
   J. Appl. Physiol., 7:593 – 603, 1955.

5. Bachman, J.C. "Motor Learning and Performance as Related to
   Age and Sex in Two Measures of Balance Coordination,"
   Res. Quart., 32:123 – 137, 1961.

6. Barker, R.G. and H.F. Wright.
   Midwest and Its Children, Evanston, Illinois: Row Peterson
   and Co., 1955.

7. Bernstein, N.
   The Coordination and Regulation of Movement, New York:
   Pergamon, 1967.

8. Brace, D.K. "Studies in Motor Learning of Gross Bodily Motor
   Skills,"
   Res. Quart., 17:242 – 253, 1946.

9. Broer, Marion R. "Evaluation of a Basic Skills Curriculum for
   Women Students of Low Motor Ability at the University of
   Washington,"
   Res. Quart., 26:15 – 27, 1955.

10. Carron, A.V. and R.G. Marteniuk. "Retention of a Balance Skill
    as a Function of Initial Ability Level,"
    Res. Quart., 41:478 – 483, 1970.

11. Coghill, C.E.
    Anatomy and the Problem of Behavior, Cambridge: University
    Press, 1929.

12. Del Rey, P. "The Effects of Video-Taped Feedback on Form,
    Accuracy, and Latency in an Open and Closed Environment,"
    J. Motor Behavior, 3:281 – 287, 1971.

13. Dusenberry, Lois. "A Study of the Effects of Training in Ball
    Throwing by Children Ages Three to Seven,"
    Res. Quart., 23:9 – 14, 1952.

14. Fleishman, E.A. and W.E. Hempel. "Changes in Factor Structure of
    a Complex Psychomotor Test as a Function of Practice,"
    Psychometrica, 19:239 – 252, 1954.

15. Fleishman, E.A. "Comments on Human Abilities," In _Acquisition of Skill_ edited by E.A. Bilodeau. New York: Academic Press, 1966.

16. Fox, M.G. and E. Lamb. "Improvement During a Nonpractice Period in a Selected Physical Education Activity," _Res_. _Quart_., 33:381 – 385, 1962.

17. Fox, M.G. and V.P. Young. "Effect of Reminiscence in Learning Selected Badminton Skills," _Res_. _Quart_., 33:386 – 94, 1962.

18. Franklin, C.C. and Josef Brozek. "The Relation Between Distribution of Practice and Learning Efficiency in Psychomotor Performance," _J_. _of Experimental Psych_., 37:16 – 24, 1947.

19. Fulton, R.E. "Speed and Accuracy in Learning a Ballistic Movement," _Res_. _Quart_., 13:30 – 36, 1942.

20. Gentile, A.M. "A Working Model of Skill Acquisition With Application to Teaching," _Quest_, XVII:3 – 23, 1972.

21. Gesell, A. and L.B. Ames. "The Ontogenetic Organization of Prone Behavior in Human Infancy," _J_. _Genet_. _Psychol_., 56:247 – 263, 1940.

22. Gesell, A. and H. Thompson, "Learning and Growth in Identical Infant Twins: An Experimental Study of the Method of Co-Twin Control," _Genet_. _Psychol_. _Monogr_., 6:1 – 124, 1929.

23. Harmon, J.M. and A.G. Miller. "Time Patterns in Motor Learning," _Res_. _Quart_., 21:182 – 187, 1950.

24. Henry, F.M. "Specificity vs. Generality in Learning Motor Skills," _College Physical Educ_. _Assoc_. _Proceed_., Washington, D.C.: The Association, 1958.

25. Henry, F.M. and G.A. Nelson. "Age Differences and Inter-relationships Between Skill and Learning in Gross Motor Performance of Ten-and Fifteen-Year-Old Boys," _Res_. _Quart_., 27:162 – 175, 1956.

26. Henry, F.M. "Factorial Structure of Speed and Static Strength in a Lateral Arm Movement," _Res_. _Quart_., 31:440 – 447, 1960.

27. Hicks, J.A. "The Acquisition of Motor Skills in Young Children. 1. A Study of the Effects of Practice in Tracing the Porteus Diamond Maze," _Child_. _Develop_., 2:156 – 158, 1931.

28. Hilgard, J.R. "Learning and Maturation in Preschool Children,"
    J. Genet. Psychol., 41:31 - 56, 1932.

29. Hilsop, H. "Quantitative Changes in Human Muscular Strength
    During Isometric Exercise,"
    J. Am. Phys. Ther. Ass., 43:21 - 38, 1963.

30. Hovland, C.I. "Experimental Studies in Rate-Learning Theory.
    III. Distribution of Practice With Varying Speeds of Syllable
    Presentation,"
    J. Exp. Psychol., 23:172 - 190, 1938.

31. Hull, C.L. Essentials of Behavior,
    New Haven: Yale University Press, 1951.

32. Knapp, C.G. and W.R. Dixon. "Learning to Juggle: I. A Study
    to Determine the Effect of Two Different Distributions of
    Practice on Learning Efficiency,"
    Res. Quart., 21:331 - 36, 1950.

33. Knapp, C.G., W.R. Dixon, and M. Lazier. "Learning to Juggle:
    III. A Study of Performance by Two Different Age Groups,"
    Res. Quart. 29:32 - 36, 1958.

34. Laszo, J.I. and P.J. Bairstow. "Accuracy of Movement, Peripheral
    Feedback and Reference Copy,"
    J. Motor Behavior, 3:241 - 252, 1971.

35. Lavery, J.J. "The Effects of One-Trial Delay in Knowledge of
    Results on the Acquisition and Retention of a Tossing Skill,"
    Amer. J. Psychol., 77:437 - 43, 1964.

36. Lotter, W.S. "Intercorrelations Among Reaction Times and Speed
    of Movement in Different Limbs,"
    Res. Quart., 32:55 - 62, 1961.

37. Malina, R.M. "Effects of Varied Information Feedback Practice
    Conditions On Throwing Speed and Accuracy,"
    Res. Quart., 40:134 - 145, 1969.

38. McGeoch, J.A. and A.L. Irion. The Psychology of Human Learning,
    New York: Longmans, Green and Co., 1952.

39. McGraw, M.B. Growth: A Study of Johnny and Jimmy,
    New York: Appleton Century, 1935.

40. McMorris, R.O. and E.C. Elkins, "A Study of Production and
    Evaluation of Muscular Hypertrophy,"
    Arch. Phys. Med. Rehabil., 35:420, 1954.

41. Mendryk, S. "Reaction Time, Movement Time and Task Specificity
    at Ages 12, 22, and 48 years,"
    Res. Quart., 31:156 - 162, 1960.

42. Meyers, J.L. "Retention of Balance Coordination Learning as
    Influenced by Extended Lay-offs,"
    Res. Quart., 38:72 - 78, 1967.

43. Munn, N.L. "Learning in Children,"
    in Manual of Child Psychology by L. Carmichael, New York:
    Wiley, 1954.

44. Nelson, D.O. "Studies of Transfer of Learning in Gross Motor
    Skills,"
    Res. Quart., 28:364 - 373, 1957.

45. Peters, W. and A.A. Wenborne. "The Time Pattern of Voluntary
    Movements,"
    Brit. J. of Psych., Part I, 26:388 - 406, 1936; Part II, 27:
    60 - 73, 1936.

46. Poulton, E.C. "On the Prediction in Skilled Movements,"
    Psychol. Bull., 54:467 - 478, 1957.

47. Purdy, B.J. and A. Lockhart. "Retention and Relearning of Gross
    Motor Skills After Long Periods of No Practice,"
    Res. Quart., 33:265 - 272, 1962.

48. Ragsdale, E. "How Children Learn the Motor Types of Activities,"
    in Learning and Instruction.
    Part I. Forty-Ninth Yearbook, Nat. Soc. for the Study of
    Educ., Chicago: University of Chicago Press, pp 69 - 91, 1950.

49. Rarick, G.L. and D.A. Dobbins. Basic Components in the Motor
    Performance of Educable Mentally Retarded Children: Implications
    for Curriculum Construction, Final Report, Project No. 142714,
    Grant No. OEG-0-70-2568 (610), Bureau of Education for the
    Handicapped, USOE, Department of Health, Education and Welfare,
    1972.

50. Reynolds, B. "The Effect of Learning on the Predictability of
    Psychomotor Performance,"
    J. Exp. Psychol., 44:189 - 198, 1956.

51. Rivenes, R.S. and M.M. Mawhinney. "Retention of Perceptual
    Skill: An Analysis of New Methods,"
    Res. Quart., 39:684 - 689, 1968.

52. Ryan, E.D. "Retention of Stabilometer and Pursuit Rotor Skills,"
    Res. Quart., 33:593 - 598, 1962.

53. Ryan, E.D. "Retention of Stabilometer Performance Over Extended
    Periods of Time,"
    Res. Quart., 36:46 - 51, 1965.

54. Schmidt, R.A. "Performance and Learning a Gross Motor Skill Under
    Conditions of Artificially-Induced Fatigue,"
    Res. Quart., 40:185 - 190, 1969.

55. Shirley, M.M. The First Two Years: A Study of Twenty-five
    Babies.
    Vol. I. Postural and Locomotor Development, Minneapolis:
    University of Minnesota Press, 1931.

56. Singer, R.N. "Masses and Distributed Practice Effects on the Acquisition and Retention of a Novel Basketball Skill," Res. Quart., 36:68 - 77, 1965.

57. Smith, K.U. and W.M. Smith. Perception and Motion: An Analysis of Space-Structure Behavior, Philadelphia: W.B. Saunders Co., 1962.

58. Smith, K.U. and M. F. Smith. Cybernetic Principles of Learning and Educational Design, New York: Holt, Rinehart and Winston, 1966.

59. Solley, W.H. "The Effects of Verbal Instruction of Speed and Accuracy Upon the Learning of a Motor Skill," Res. Quart., 23:231 - 240, 1952.

60. Stetson, R.H. "Mechanism of the Different Types of Movement," Psychol. Monogr., 32:18 - 40, 1923.

61. Taylor, E.G. A Study to Determine the Influence of Training on Selected Second and Fifth Grade Children in the Throw for Distance and the Standing Broad Jump, unpublished Master's Problem, Madison: University of Wisconsin, 1953.

62. Todor, J.I. Age Differences in the Generality and Specificity of Motor Learning and Performance, Ph. D. Dissertation, University of California, Berkeley, 1972, 88p.

63. Wild, M.R. "The Behavior Pattern of Throwing and Some Observations Concerning Its Course of Development in Children," Res. Quart., 9:20 - 24, 1938.

64. Woodrow, H. "The Effect of Practice on Groups of Different Initial Ability: J. Educ. Psychol., 29:268 - 278, 1938.

A HUMAN INFORMATION PROCESSING APPROACH
OF THE CHILD AND SKILL

by   John H. Salmela, Ph.D.,
       Département d'Education Physique,
       Université Laval,
       Québec, Québec, Canada.
       G1K 7P4

A.   THE INFORMATION PROCESSING MODEL:

It can be simplistically stated that the development of a science requires first the accurate description of the events or objects to be studied, followed by the integrating of these described events with theoretical laws so that future performance may be predicted. In exercise physiology, for example, only a few years ago the parameters of maximum oxygen uptake were first measured with normative data. Today athletic performance in certain endurance events can be quite nicely predicted using some of the performance models designed and these performance constructs are being further supported by biochemical findings. A glance over the years at the subject areas found in Research Quarterly would also indicate that the researchers in the traditional area of motor learning have also amassed quite a large body of descriptive literature in whole-part learning, generality-specificity, massed-distributed practice, etc., but have mainly done so without a common theoretical base. Often the coach having found success without the aid of the jargoned research journals, has tended to dismiss them as being dissociated from reality. The phenomena of the local shoe salesman's team beating the degree-carrying high school coach, is too prevalent to discard the lack of impact of our learned "facts" in regards to motor skills. It becomes evident that rather than discarding the last half century of Research Quarterly, it would seem worth the effort of integrating this information within the context of an existing theoretical model.

One such model that has been used extensively to integrate the diverse areas of medicine, education, engineering, perception, neuro-biology and human motor performance has been the information processing model of man. This model holds that man can be considered as a processor of information with a limited capacity -- i.e., comparable to the simple receiver, conveyor and sender of information as exemplified by a telephone system. This is best demonstrated by the diagram (figure 1), as a system that takes in information from the environment (input), processes this information within a central system of limited capacity (the "little black box"), and then elicits a response (output). While the importance of both internal and external feedback is acknowledged, both of these loops of the model will not be emphasized in detail to aid the clarity of presentation of the lesser known aspects. Though this model seems at first to be

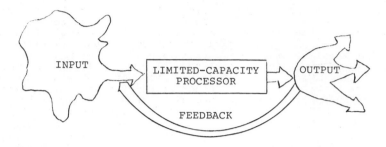

Figure 1.

The Simplified Information-Processing Model

quite simple, one soon finds that this simplicity must not be
confounded with naivety.[1] The very fact of stating that a
particular task may make different demands on one of these
components in sports skills (Higgins, 1972), or that a "learning
problem" may result from deficiencies at one of these three cites
(Morris and Whiting, 1971) provides useful information to the
analysis of both practical and theoretical problems.

While the detailed functions of what occurs where, in this model
can be obtained from comprehensive texts (Fitts and Posner,
(1967); Whiting) (1969), it might be useful to briefly indicate
the types of phenomena that must be considered at the above -
mentioned locations.

Input problems: Detection of the appropriate stimulus in the
environment is an important limitation to the efficient performance of skills in an unstable environment. The facility for this
type of detection is based upon a variable threshold that changes
according to the performer's level of activation; motivation,
payoffs and the intensity of the environmental signals in relation
to the background (signal-noise ratio). Also important at the
input or sensorial end of the system is the performer's ability
to compare the stimulus to another physical standard, as in
aiming or pointing, (or what are called comparative judgements)
and his ability to compare or, more properly, recognize the
stimulus in comparison to an internalized standard (or what are
called absolute judgements). While the performer is often very
accurate at the former, his capacity for performing the latter is
somewhat limited (Fitts and Posner, 1967).

Processing problems: Problems that occur within the processing
system, within or "the little black box", are somewhat more

---

(1) The various aspects of the power and complexity of this approach
can be quickly obtained by glancing at Fitts and Posner's
Human Performance (1967) or Lindsay and Norman's Human Information Processing (1972).

difficult to handle as we can only infer what happens within, as a result of what type of output we measured for a given input. This becomes increasingly difficult with retarded children when introspection or questioning fails - and we must ask before proceeding, "Is the information getting in?". General research topics that deal with the central processor include selective attention, or the direction and utilization of the important aspects of the input to the exclusion of the irrelevant information; the short-term memory system that must hold information from the input in temporary store while other information is being acted upon; and the general decision processes in either simple or more complex tasks, as usually measured by reaction times of a simple or complex nature.

Output problems: Aside from limitations that might be considered in the physiological domain, such as strength and power, the independent and coordinated study of both the speed and the precision of different motor acts usually fall within this realm of research topics. Methods of shaping responses, ranging from very simple to complex are also of major concern. While output problems account for much of the variance in many physical skills, the point must be emphasized that motor skills have also sensory and processing, or intellectual components as well. This is often forgotten by these who generally classify physical skills as "non-intellectual".

B. MODIFICATIONS OF THE MODEL'S COMPONENTS FROM CHILDHOOD TO ADULTHOOD:

The limited literature search involved in this paper has indicated that there certainly is a large quantity of descriptive long-itudinal and cross-sectional data that can be readily attached to the figurative handholds provided by the above-mentioned inform-ation processing model. In that the author's area of expertise does not run across the child-adult dimension, but rather rests in that of adult performance, the following guidelines will be presented and then the reader must integrate, where he will, his appropriate experiences or data.

Input Modifications with Development

Visual Information: a) One structural limitation that seems to be "wired-in" the system is the gradual development of the spheroidal shape of the child's eyeball up to the age of 6 or 7 years of age. This tells us that before we interpret something as an input problem of a more serious nature, we must first ensure the stimulus to be perceived is far enough away to over-come this structural limitation in the young far-sighted child (Smith, 1970). b) Smith (1970) also indicates that there appears to be a differential preference for certain dimensions of the environment that evolve with age. That is, up to 3 - 4 years of age, the child will code the environment according to the shape of the objects. At five years of age, colour of objects becomes the dominant factor in interpreting sensory input. According to the visual search literature, adults continue to code most efficiently with the dimension of colour. c) Smith (1970) also contends that the child's ability to select from the environment

the appropriate signals for a given action is not completely
developed until the early teenage years. Whether this is purely
an experiential occurrence or has to do with developmental
differentiation of input is not alluded to, but a combination of
both factors seems most likely. d) Kiphard (1970) asserts that
catching skills in children may not be limited by lack of motor
control, though Kay (1969) does cite this as being a problem up
to five years of age, but rather by slow imprecise eye-movements
that fail to orientate to moving objects in the environment.

It appears that before attempts can be made to diagnose whether
there exists an "input problem" with a child learning skills,
there should be consideration taken of the above and other
developmental milestones before corrective therapy is undertaken.
Again the number of factors mentioned above is far from complete,
but the organizing structure provides some direction towards a
classification that is not altogether arbitrary.

Kinesthetic Information: The reception and integration of
kinesthetic information has been both considered as an input
function (Pepper and Herman, 1970) and more traditionally as a
function of a central processing system (Kephart, 1960). The
former point of view is based upon the point of view that kinesthetic input, by itself, can be used consciously, independent
of any visual or spatial coordinates. That is, the information
from movements is meaningful or codable at a cognitive level.
It is the author's opinion that for effective use of this information, in the absolute judgement sense, this information must be
integrated with visual or auditory information, and therefore
will be considered within the classification of a central
processing function. However, for completions sake, it will be
mentioned that Millar (1972) stated that the ability to
accurately use kinesthetic information improved up to about 11
years of age, and then began to plateau.

Central Processing Modifications with Development

Once the input from the environment has been received by the
system, there arise certain problems of recognizing or classifying
the stimulus in relation to others that might have occurred;
integrating this information with kinesthetic or somaesthetic
information on the present state of the system itself; and
selecting of an appropriate response if the environment is stable;
or in a changing environment, to predict upon the basis of present
information, the response that will be appropriate, given the
lags in the system and the environmental demands.

First of all, it becomes very apparent to the teacher of young
children who have their selective attention mechanisms set by
adults to the appropriate stimulus, that very quickly, their
attention is directed elsewhere. This has been termed the short
attention span phenomena (Elliot, 1970). However, more severe
limitations do arise.

Unidimensional Input: Fitts and Posner (1967) have shown that
man's capacity to recognize errorlessly, classifications of input
across a single dimension (i.e., a simple absolute judgement), is

relatively limited. However, this capacity increases in a non-multiplicative fashion by the increase of organizational dimensions. That is, one could not recognize twice the number of errorless categories by doubling the number of organizational dimensions, although the number would certainly increase. This additional utilization of organizational dimensions is a function of age and the intellectual processes. In a more practical view, Whiting states that the "progression hypothesis" (Fitts, Bahrick, Noble and Briggs, 1961) allows the individual with practice, to use increasingly higher derivatives of visual information, i.e., from position to velocity to acceleration to "jerk" information. This may explain why children, at certain stages, cannot visually track a ball in flight because they can only handle the lowest derivative, or the position information of the object, and not its changes in position. This same phenomena has been demonstrated for movement information using tracking tasks. This indicates that before looking at input or output problems of the young diagnostically, care must be taken not to overload the processing system with a task that has too many central demands.

Multidimensional Integration: The performing of physical skills as fine as handwriting, or as gross as catching a ball while both the individual and the ball are moving, requires an accurate integration of the motor act with the environmental input. Empirical studies in this domain have been carried out under the rubric of intersensory or cross-modality matching. Many of the "perceptual-motor" programs, as cited by Kephart and Frostig, can also be considered within this framework. Millar (1972) and Smothergill (1973) have indicated that there seems to be a problem for children to integrate information from different sensory modalities up to the age of 11 years, after which there seems to be a correspondence between all forms of visual, kinesthetic or haptic input. This ability to match external and internal information in coordinated activity with body centered and with decentered or variable environmental activities, seems to be compatible with the often discussed concepts of body image, laterality and directionality. Some developmental milestones for these concepts have been outlined by Long and Looft (1972) and are presented in Table 1.

One further indication of developmental trends within the central processing system was recently indicated by Surwillo (1972) who found that over an age span of 4 to 17 years, reaction times of children decreased three-fold. Deviations from the established norms have been taken to indicate abnormal processing of information on this simple motor task.

Output Modifications with Development

Kay (1969) has stated that up to the age of 5 - 6 years of age, input and output problems can be easily confounded, since the motor system has not been completely differentiated. This was demonstrated by the fact that with perfect stimulus-response tasks (a tracing task), children up to 5 years old were not capable of making the accurate responses necessary. Response differentiation has been shown to be a lengthy process as indicated by the EMG studies quoted by Spaeth (1972). This differentiation might be best called response efficiency.

TABLE 1

Age Norms For The Appearance Of Stages In The Development Toward Directionality

| Researcher(a) | Substages (in yr.) | | | |
| | Body image | Laterality | | Directionality(c) |
		Egocentric	Decentered	
Cratty (1969)(b)		6	8 – 9	
Piaget (1929)		5 – 8	8 – 11	11 – 12
Elkind (1961)		7 – 8	8 – 10	10 – 11
Swanson and Benton (1955)	6	9		
Belmont and Birch (1963)		7	11	
Wapner and Cirillo (1968)			12 – 14	

(a) These studies were selected for the purpose of illustration; by no means is this table
to represent an exhaustive list of relevant research endeavors.

(b) Cratty used mental age; other studies employed chronological age.

(c) Acquisition of initial aspects of complete directionality.

(Taken from Long and Looft, 1972)

Increases in stength and power with age, while not of direct
importance within the contents of this paper, must be considered
in any diagnostics of the output aspects of skill performance.
These changes with age are readily available in growth and
development textbooks.

C. THE MODEL'S COMPATIBILITY WITH THE REAL WORLD:

The strength of any theoretical model lies in its ability to
clearly define methods of attack and to predict performance under
a given set of conditions. The problem that therefore faces us
is to develop a form of task taxonomy, or classification of the
relative environmental demands of any given physical skill or
activity. Since the model attempts to compartmentalize the human
performer, whether child or adult, into an input component a
limited-channel central processor and an output system, then it
would be logical to attempt to classify the environmental demands
in a compatible manner, i.e., input, processing and output
demands. Just such a system of analysis has been investigated at
Université Laval across a wide range of sport activities. Again,
on a very simplified level, it can be demonstrated that this
approach provides innovative directions to be followed in the
studying of sports skills; maintains guidelines for the modifications of sport and play equipment for the maximization of
learning, and therefore the enjoyment, for children; and finally,
provides a fruitful, diagnostic tool for the study of the
"atypical" child. While conceptually simple, to be compatible
with the model, this classification allows profound analyses
when coupled with certain features of Information Theory.

An attempt is made, first of all at the intuitive level, to
determine what the relative environmental demands of a given
physical skill might be. The task of giving relative weightings
to a given activity (based on the assumption that the total
demands must equal 100%) is relatively easy, if the choice of
activities are extreme. For example, the vigilance of a radar
screen at the Dew Line could be considered to be an input-weighted
task as compared to the processing and output tasks of chess
and sprinting, respectively. These three tasks might be
represented by the graphs in Figure 2. A more sophisticated
approach for the calculation of these demands has been outlined by Salmela and Alain (1972) and Alain and Salmela (1973).

The above graphs have been estimated with the guidance of the
knowledge developed in the area of human performance theory,
that is, the information that describes man's capacities to
receive, to process and then to act upon environmental information (see Part A). But, as has been established in Part B,
these limiting conditions change from childhood to adulthood as a
result of developmental as well as experiential conditions. It
becomes the task of the innovative teacher or therapist to
discover where and when exactly, do these changes take place.
The aforementioned list is far from being complete, but using
its contents one can hypothesize how these relative environmental demands would change between adult and child on the three
activities mentioned in Figure 2. Performances would drastically
change because of limitations of eye movements, search problems,

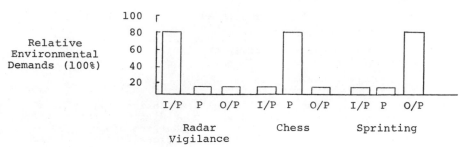

Figure 2.

Relative Environmental Demands of Three Physical Skills

attention span or any of the named and yet unnamed factors
discussed in Part B. A direction has been established by the use
of these very simple tools by which detailed analyses of complex
behavioral phenomena may be better understood.

D. NEW DIRECTIONS WITH OLD INFORMATION:

The primary concern when starting this deliberation on how we might
view the child and physical skills, was that the area of physical
skills per se, the child per se and both the child and physical skills
had been studied extensively in the past, yet little direction
or overlap in these varied approaches was evident. Rather than
playing one school of thought off against another, and therefore,
possibly rejecting "pieces" of valuable information, an attempt
was made to provide an organizational framework within which
most, if not all, of the fragmented data could be compartmental-
ized, without value judgement. The strength of this information
processing approach is the ubiquitous nature of the model, i.e.,
its usefulness for all classes of data. Yet, this broad general
model provides, unlike other non-nullifiable, or post-hoc
approaches e.g., Freudian psychology, testable hypotheses to be
pursued, knowing the limitations of the various components of
the system.

Adaption of this model's directions does not force one to reject
other approaches to skilled behavior, and it may, in fact,
provide new insights to these other methods.

However, an important consideration is that, within each individual who has a skill learning problem, the problem may lie at
either the input end, within the central processor or on the
output side, or at all three. By establishing test situations
that are loaded in favour of one of the three components, the
therapist, teacher or coach can more effectively diagnose the
location of the problem. It must be cautioned, however, that
not much work has been done using this approach in relation to
the child and the capacities of the various components have not

yet been integrated under a single rubric. Much data that lacks organization is available, only the integration, at this moment, is lacking, in regards to the child and skill.

Once the primary limiting factors on performance have been determined through this form of analysis, remedial steps can be taken so that performance could be maximized by reducing the weighting of the "problem" factor, by environmental manipulation. For example, what are the limiting factors that prevent an 8-year-old child from spiking a volleyball? Is it an input, processing or output problem? If it was an input problem the colour and size of the ball could be varied to increase the signal-noise ratio. If it were a processing problem, in that the child could not visually track and then time his response, the ball could be suspended motionless above the net. If it was an output problem, it could either be one of a lack of force to jump high enough or of the spiking response itself. To remedy the former case, the net would be lowered, for the latter shaping procedures of the action itself could be undertaken. Many of these diagnostic procedures provided by this approach, would not be any more difficult than conventional procedures used presently. However, the emphasis upon the maximization of the limiting factor in the performance, while being scientifically sound, is also intuitively sound as the child's frustration of failure is reduced proportionally to the approriateness of his treatment.

References

1. Alain, Claude and John H. Salmela, "Performance humaine, habiletés motrices et manipulation de l'information II: Application",
    Mouvement, 1973, (in press).

2. Elliot, R. "Physiological activity and performance in children and adults: A two-year follow-up"
    J. Exper. Child Psychol. 1966, 3, 58-80.

3. Fitts, P.M., H.P. Bahrick, M.E. Noble and A.E. Briggs, Skilled Performance.
    New York, Wiley and Co., 1961.

4. Fitts, P.M. and M.I. Posner, Human Performance, Brooks/Cole, Belmont, Calif., 1967.

5. Higgins, J.R. "Movements to match environmental demands."
    Research Quarterly, 1972, 43, 312-336.

6. Kay, Harry. In Principles of Skill Acquisition.
    (Bilodeau, E.A. and I.M. Bilodeau eds.), Academic Press, New York, 1969.

7. Kephart, N.C. The Slow Learner in the Classroom.
    Merrill, Ohio, 1960.

8. Kiphard, E.J. "Behavioral integration of problem children through remedial physical education".
    In Approaches to Perceptual-motor Experiences. JOHPER Reprints, 1970.

9. Lindsay, Peter H. and Donald A. Norman, Human Information Processing.
    Academic Press, New York, 1972.

10. Long, A.B. and W.R. Looft, "Development of directionality in children: Ages six through twelve",
    Developmental Psychology, 1972, 6, 375-380.

11. Millar, S. "The development of visual and kinesthetic judgements of distance",
    Brit. J. Psychol., 1972, 63, 271-282.

12. Morris, P.R. and H.T.A. Whiting, Motor Impairment and Compensatory Education.
    Lea and Febiger, Philadelphia, 1971.

13. Pepper, R.L. and L.M. Herman, "Decay and interference in the short-term retention of a discrete motor act."
    J. exp. Psychol. Monograph, 1970, 83.

14. Salmela, John H. and Claude Alain. "Performance humaine, habiletés motrices et manipulation de l'information: Vue d'ensemble",
    Mouvement, 1972, 7, 173-177.

15. Smith, H.M. "Implications for movement education experiences drawn from perceptual-motor research."
    In Approaches to Perceptual-motor Experiences. JOHPER Reprints, 1970.

16. Smothergill, W. Daniel, "Accuracy and variability in the localization of spatial targets at three age levels.
    Developmental Psychology, 1973, 8, 62-66.

17. Spaeth, K. Ree, "Maximizing goal attainment",
    Research Quarterly, 1972, 43, 337-361.

18. Surwillo, W.W. "Human reaction time and period of the EEG in relation to development."
    Psychophysiology, 1971, 8, 468-482.

19. Whiting, H.T.A., Acquiring Ball Skill, Lea and Febiger, Philadelphia, 1969.

NATIONAL STEERING COMMITTEE

MEMBERS

Members of the National Steering Committee and the organization or agency which they represent are as follows:

Dr. J. G. Albinson, Queen's University (Co-Chairman)

Dr. G. M. Andrew, Queen's University (Co-Chairman)

Dr. D. Bailey, Canadian Association of Health, Physical Education & Recreation

Prof. C. Bouchard, Canadian Association of Sport Sciences

Dr. G. Brisson, Health Science Research Centre, University of Quebec, Trois Rivieres

Dr. M. Grapko, Institute of Child Study, University of Toronto

Mrs. P. Hill, Consultant, Central Mortgage and Housing Corp.

Dr. M. King, Canadian Council for Children and Youth

Mr. A. Lundquist, Youth and Recreation Branch, Province of Ontario

Mr. J. Miller, Federal Dept. of Welfare

Mrs. J. Svendsen, Canadian Parks and Recreation Association

Dr. J. Weber, Canadian Medical Association, Canadian Pediatric Society

Mr. C. Westland, Recreation Canada, Dept. of Health and Welfare

Mr. S. Zacher, Youth and Recreation Branch, Province of Ontario

Sponsors

The National Steering Committee expresses its thanks and appreciation to the following without whose financial assistance the Conference would not have been possible:

Government:

 Recreation Canada
 Sports and Recreation Branch (Ontario)
 Secretary of State Federal Government
 Province of Nova Scotia
 Province of Quebec
 City of Kingston

Queen's University:

 Faculty of Arts and Science
 School of Physical and Health Education

Industry:

 Ford Motor Company of Canada
 Coca Cola Ltd.
 IBM Canada Limited
 Millhaven Fibres Limited
 Molson Breweries of Canada Limited
 The House of Seagram Ltd.
 John Labbatt Limited
 The Empire Life Insurance Company
 Gulf Oil Canada Limited
 The Manufacturers Life Insurance Company
 Mills Office Suppliers Ltd.

Other:

 Ontario Heart Foundation
 Dr. B. DePape

Acknowledgements

The co-chairmen of the Conference wish to acknowledge the contributions of the many people whose help and support were invaluable. In particular, we are grateful to Mr. Cor Westland, Director of Recreation Canada, for his interest and concern during the initial planning and for the substantial financial support of his Department; to Mr. Bob Secord, Director of the Youth and Recreation Branch of Ontario, for the leadership assistance of his staff and financial contribution of the branch.

Thanks are extended to members of the National Steering Committee who gave willingly and freely of their time and expertise in the planning of the Conference. We are indebted to our Faculty colleagues, and students as well, who shared the hosting responsibilities.

A special bouquet of appreciation is reserved for Mrs. Donna Ede who served unstintingly and with a deep sense of committment in her capacity as Conference secretary; the contribution of her assistant Miss Erlene Waghorn is also acknowledged. Finally we would be remiss if we failed to express the gratitude owed our wives whose sense of understanding and unfailing support helped sustain us through the endeavor.